20 YEARS & STILL KICKING!

GARFIELD'S

TWENTIETH ANNIVERSARY COLLECTION

BY JIM DAVIS

BALLANTINE BOOKS • NEW YORK

A Ballantine Book
Published by The Random House Publishing Group

Published in the United States by Ballantine Books, an imprint of The Random House Publishing Group, a division of Random House, Inc., New York, and simultaneously in Canada by Random House of Canada Limited, Toronto.

www.ballantinebooks.com

Library of Congress Catalog Card Number: 97-97062

ISBN: 0-345-42126-4

Manufactured in China

First Edition: March 1998
9

CONTENTS

You can't take it with you, so eat it now.

Garfield

ACKNOWLEDGMENTS

Garfield and I have always gotten by with a little help from our friends. And this book is no exception. A lot of talented people helped in the conceptualization and production of 20 Years & Still Kicking!: Betsy Knotts, art director/designer; Scott Nickel and Mark Acey, writers; Kenny Goetzinger and Tom Howard, designers/production artists; Brett Koth, cartoonist; Linda Duell, Lynette Nuding, Larry Fentz, Mike Fentz, Lori Barker, Jeff Wesley, James Davis, and Gary Barker, production artists; Jon Barnard, photographer; Sheila Bolduc, production manager; Kim Campbell, public relations director.

We've tried to approach this book the same way we approach the daily strip: to make it as entertaining as possible. But enough fanfare. It's time to make yourself a snack (preferably something deep-fried), sit back, and enjoy!

JIM DAVIS

FOREWORD

Imagine, if you will, an archaeological dig several thousand years hence.

Imagine that the excavation is proceeding on the site of a former Wal-Mart. Because of its shape and mass it might be perceived as some form of twentieth-century temple or place of worship. And what would the icon be in this temple? What would the image of the deity be? Why, of course, the image that adorns all manner of clothing and household goods and printed materials. As in the temples of ancient Egypt, the deity would be a cat. But not just any cat. The deity of the twentieth century would be an orange cat, a Garfield cat.

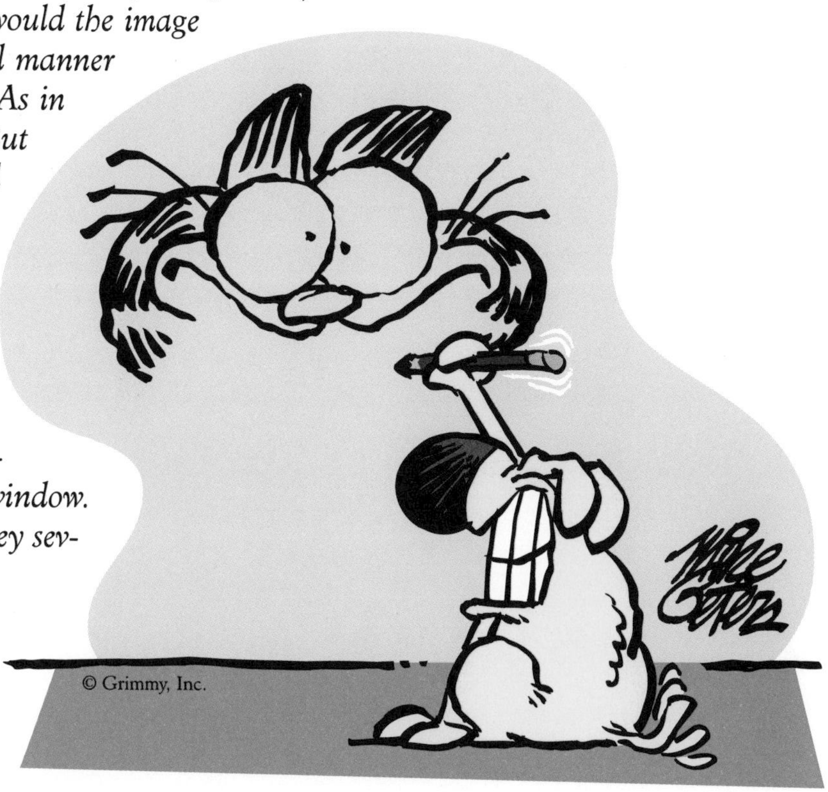

© Grimmy, Inc.

And yet it's been only twenty years since Garfield came on the scene. I knew him when he was a kitten! I guess we should have suspected something special was happening when the books began to sell in the millions. And now the great orange cat hovers over the Macy's parade. He soars through the heavens stuck on the shuttle window. He's even going to have his own theme park. It took Mickey seventy years to do this stuff!

Why all the fuss? That's easy! Garfield taps into everything that we humans believe we know about cats. There have been other cat strips and other cat characters over the years. But none has reflected the true essence of cat. Jim Davis had the courage to say out loud the well-known but unspoken secret about cats. Cats have never really been domesticated. Jim tapped into this dark side of cat nature. They don't care about people or need them. They tolerate us. And don't forget there are many more cat lovers than dog lovers.

Dogs, on the other hand, love people . . . and really need to be loved by people. I mean, can you imagine your cat dragging you from a burning building? Maybe, but only if the can opener is in your back pocket! Not only would Garfield not rescue Jon, he would light the fire just to hear the sirens.

Even so, we can always be thankful that Jim's first strip never made it. You can be sure that Jim would have worked just as hard if the strip were in 6 newspapers or 2,500 newspapers. Gnorm Gnat has gone down in cartoon folklore as a most fortunate failure. Can you imagine a bright orange gnat on every car window? A great, huge gnat for the Thanksgiving Day Parade. A big fat gnat saying "I hate Tuesdays."

For all these reasons we need Garfield. Most of all we need a laugh every day that makes us feel good about finishing the last of the pizza at 3:00 A.M.!

Mike Peters

A Boy Named Jim: PRE-GARFIELD

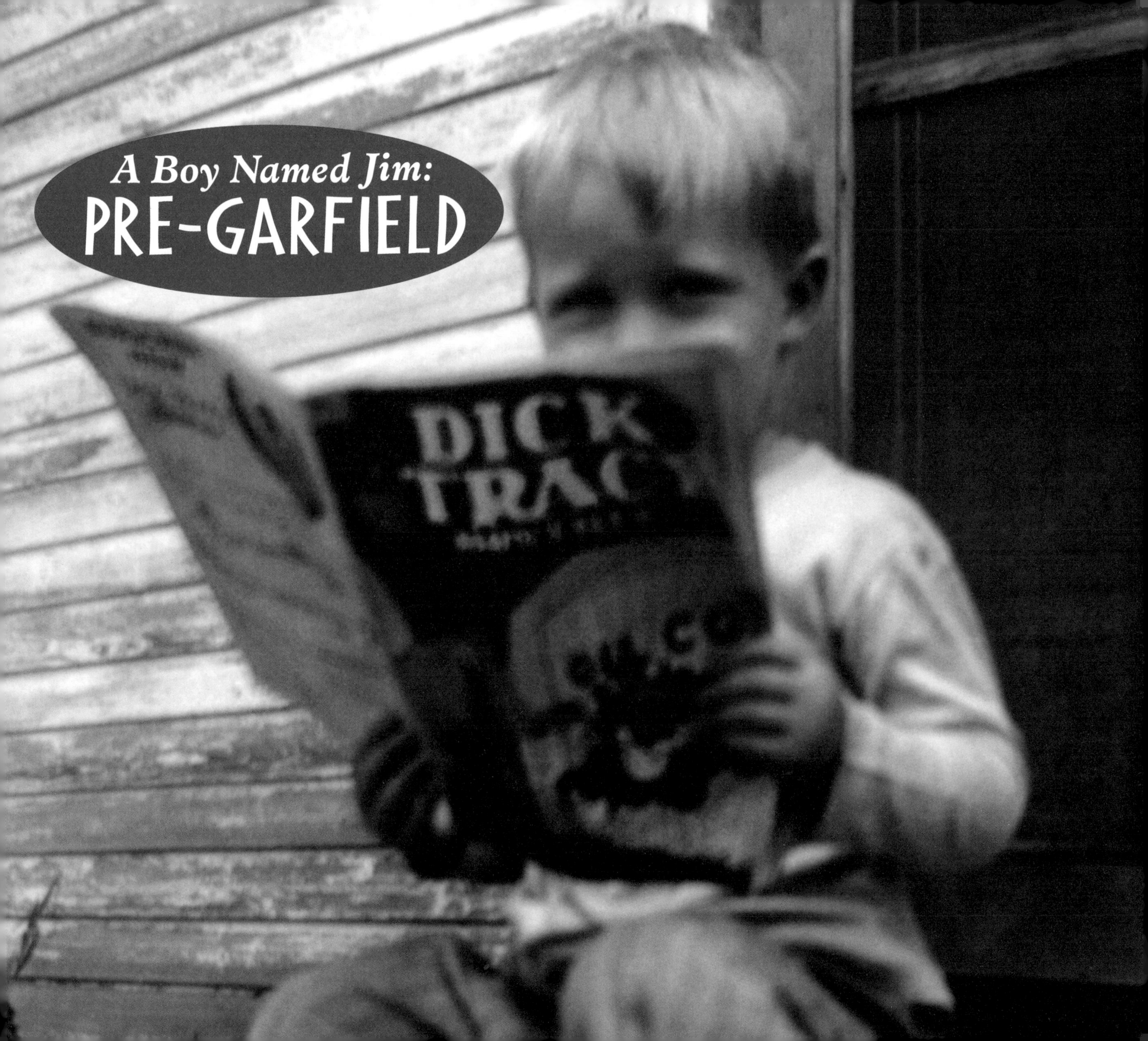

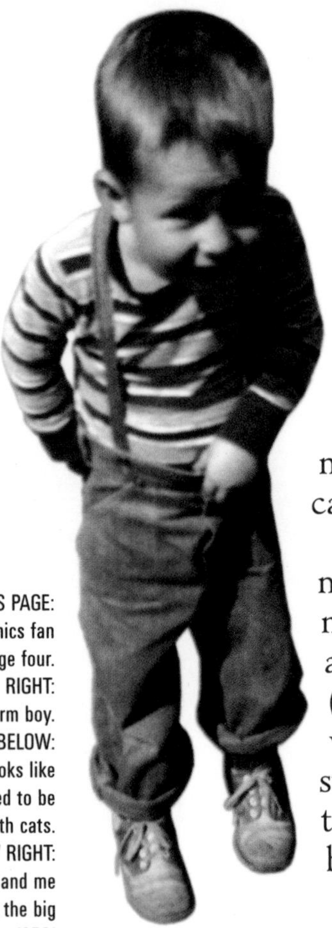

PREVIOUS PAGE:
A comics fan
at age four.
RIGHT:
Farm boy.
BELOW:
Age two; looks like
I was destined to be
involved with cats.
BELOW RIGHT:
Doc and me
catching the big
ones circa 1958!

I was born July 28, 1945, in Marion, Indiana, and was promptly dropped on my head — which explains my lifelong desire to become a cartoonist.

I grew up on a small farm near Fairmount, Indiana, with my dad, Jim, my mom, Betty, and my brother, Dave (nicknamed "Doc"). Later, when I started the *Garfield* strip, I used my family as characters. (Yes, Doc Boy really is my brother!)

Dad raised Black Angus cattle, and Mom took care of Doc and me and the twenty-five assorted cats that were always underfoot. Hanging around these furry felines gave me an appreciation for, and understanding of, cats that would later prove invaluable.

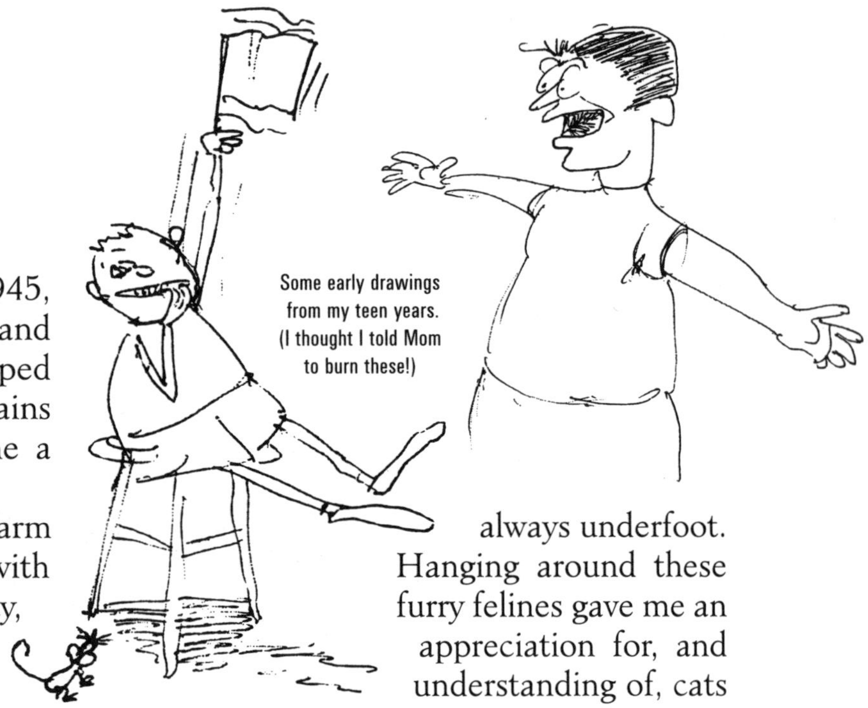

Some early drawings
from my teen years.
(I thought I told Mom
to burn these!)

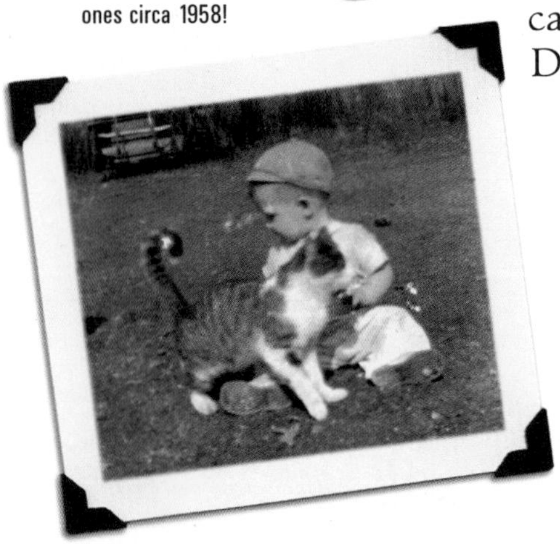

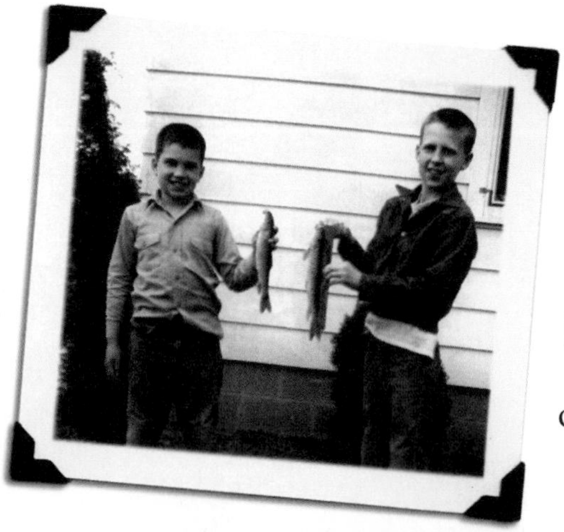

As a kid, I was asthmatic and was forced to stay in bed a lot, away from the farm chores. During those long bouts, Mom would shove a pencil and paper in my hands and urge me to entertain myself. My drawings were so bad at first that I had to label everything. But Mom, a talented artist in her own right, showed me how to draw realistically, using shading to give the pictures depth. I'd spend hours happily drawing and writing.

Asthma made it difficult for me to help with the hard work of running a farm, but my parents were very understanding (they just gave all the work to Doc!).

It was clear that my asthma was a serious problem that wasn't going to go away on

its own. Overcoming it was a long and difficult process, and Mom and I traveled fifty miles each week for my special cortisone treatments. With the treatments, over time my asthma attacks decreased. I was getting better.

When I was in grade school, I began having problems with stuttering. Fortunately, a wonderful and sympathetic teacher worked with me. She taught me to always think about what I wanted to say before saying it (something that would come in handy later during interviews). With her help, I stopped stuttering.

Growing up, I loved reading the newspaper comics, especially the Sunday funnies. Looking back, I can see how influential these comic strips were on my cartooning career. Charles "Sparky" Schulz's *Peanuts* showed the humor inherent in the gentle things of life; Milton Caniff's *Steve Canyon* whisked me away to exotic places I never dreamed existed; Mort Walker's *Beetle Bailey* made me laugh with its classic humor; Hal Foster and John Cullen Murphy's *Prince Valiant* set an artistic standard that remains unequaled; and Walt Kelly's *Pogo* carved a niche on the comics page for true creative genius. These people were my heroes, my mentors. Years

later, I would be fortunate enough to count many of them as my friends, too.

After graduating from Fairmount High School in 1963, I enrolled in Muncie, Indiana's Ball State University. College was great: the friends, the parties, the activities, the parties, the quest for knowledge, the parties. As an art and business major, I distinguished myself by earning one of the lowest cumulative grade point averages in the history of the university. (Incidentally, a fellow classmate named David Letterman earned the other.)

After college, I worked for a local advertising agency for two years doing layout and pasteup for

ABOVE:
1962: Go, Team! Wearing my letterman's jacket from Fairmount High.
ABOVE LEFT AND BELOW:
More doodles from my high school days.

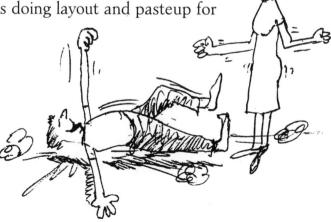

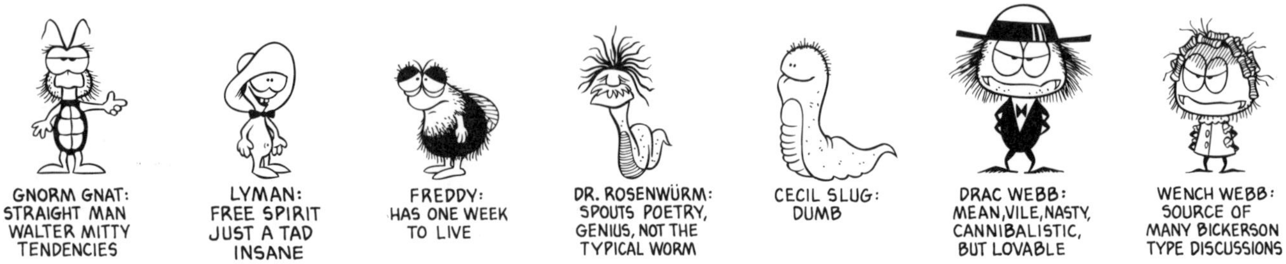
GNORM GNAT: STRAIGHT MAN WALTER MITTY TENDENCIES
LYMAN: FREE SPIRIT JUST A TAD INSANE
FREDDY: HAS ONE WEEK TO LIVE
DR. ROSENWÜRM: SPOUTS POETRY, GENIUS, NOT THE TYPICAL WORM
CECIL SLUG: DUMB
DRAC WEBB: MEAN, VILE, NASTY, CANNIBALISTIC, BUT LOVABLE
WENCH WEBB: SOURCE OF MANY BICKERSON TYPE DISCUSSIONS

brochures and catalogs. (Who says advertising isn't glamorous?)

In 1969, I got a lucky break. I became Tom Ryan's cartoon assistant on the comic strip *Tumbleweeds*. Tom was a fellow Hoosier and spotted my talent immediately. Plus, I worked cheap. As Tom's assistant I did backgrounds, lettering, and other assorted art tasks. The pay may not have been terrific, but it was great experience and taught me the discipline required for a daily strip as well as the business of syndication. To make ends meet, I moonlighted as a freelance commercial artist, copywriter, political promoter, and exotic dancer. (Just kidding. I was never a political promoter!)

ABOVE: Characters from my first strip, *Gnorm Gnat*. (Yes, that's where I got the name Lyman!) BELOW: Gnorm in *The Pendleton Times* circa 1975.

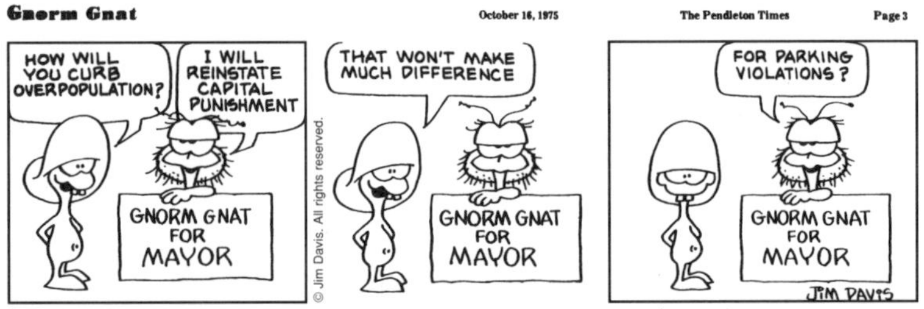
Gnorm Gnat
October 16, 1975
The Pendleton Times
Page 3
HOW WILL YOU CURB OVERPOPULATION?
I WILL REINSTATE CAPITAL PUNISHMENT
GNORM GNAT FOR MAYOR
THAT WON'T MAKE MUCH DIFFERENCE
GNORM GNAT FOR MAYOR
FOR PARKING VIOLATIONS?
GNORM GNAT FOR MAYOR
JIM DAVIS
© Jim Davis. All rights reserved.

During my stint with Tom, I worked at night and on weekends, developing my own comic strip. I thought I had the perfect idea: *Gnorm Gnat*.

My experience with comics convinced me that nonhuman characters could be placed in many more interesting situations with greater flexibility than human characters.

Gnorm ran weekly in an Indiana newspaper, *The Pendleton Times*, and over the next few years, I tried to sell the strip to the syndicates. Gnorm was met with overwhelming indifference. One editor, however, offered a little consolation. He said, "Your art is good, your gags are great, but bugs — nobody can identify with bugs!"

After five years of doing *Gnorm Gnat*, I drew a giant foot falling out of the sky, crushing little Gnorm in his last comic appearance.

But I wasn't through with comic strips. Not by a long shot. I just needed to find a character everyone could relate to.

TOP TEN COMIC STRIPS JIM DAVIS TRIED BEFORE GARFIELD

10. *Andy Amoeba*
9. *The Domestic Squabblers*
8. *Randy Rash*
7. *Crazy Crayfish*
6. *Sid the Sperm Whale*
5. *J.M. Keynes, Kid Economist*
4. *Billy the Bagman*
3. *Milt the Incontinent Hamster*
2. *Gnorm Gnat*
1. *Garfield the Toaster*

A STAR IS BORN

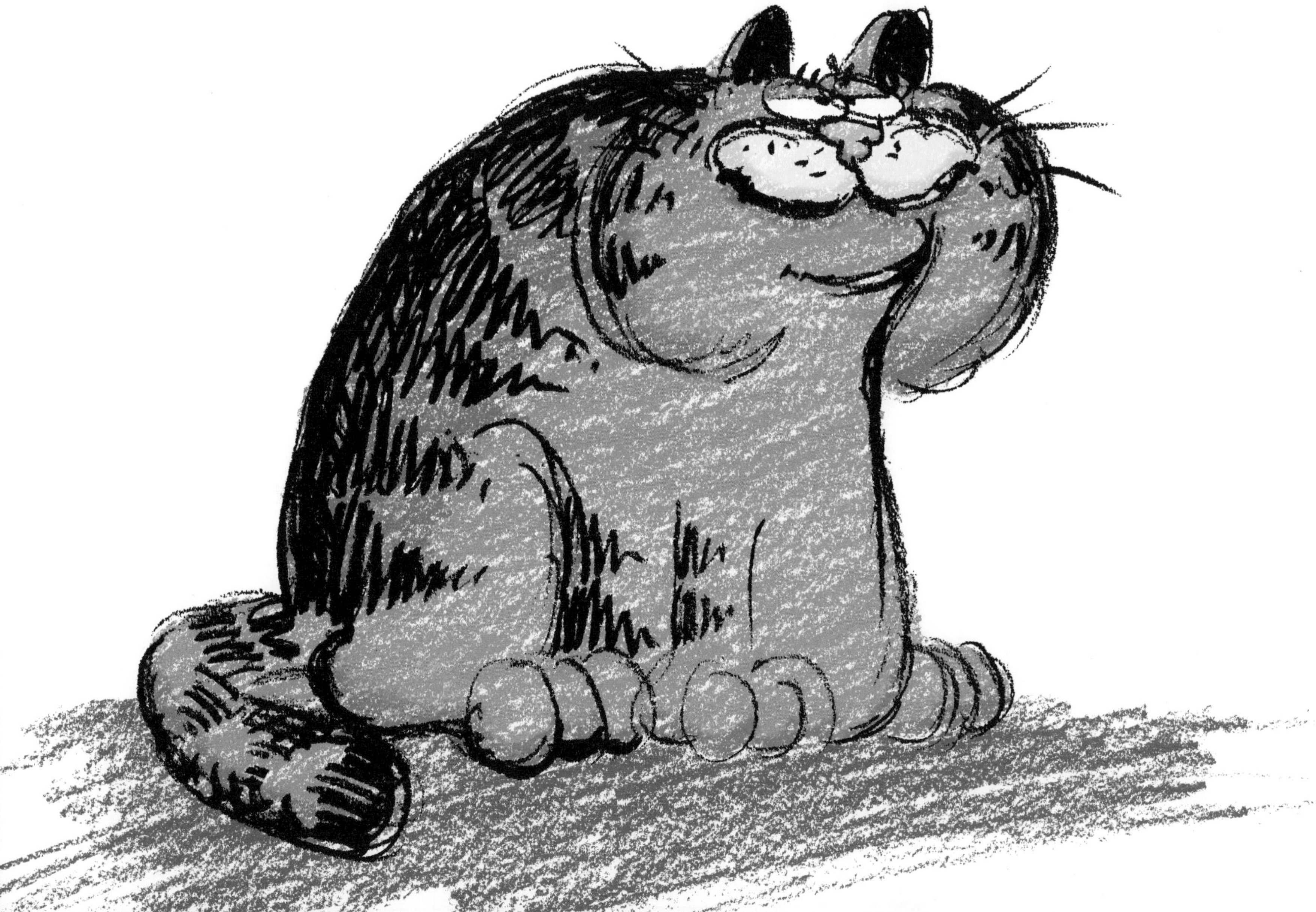

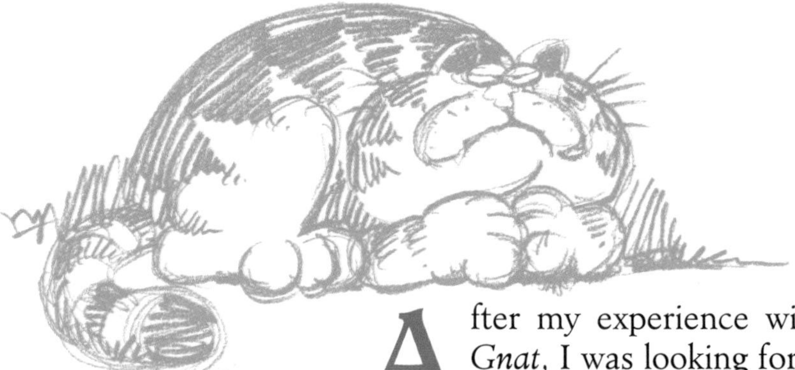

After my experience with *Gnorm Gnat*, I was looking for a character that would be funny and have broad appeal. I wanted to use an animal. Then it hit me. There were lots of dogs in the comics — Snoopy, Marmaduke, Fred Basset — but very few strips with a cat in the lead.

I started sketching and came up with a big, cantankerous, cynical orange cat. I needed a name and thought of my grandfather, James A. Garfield Davis, a big, cantankerous, cynical man. The name just seemed to fit the personality and shape of the character. And so Garfield the cat was born.

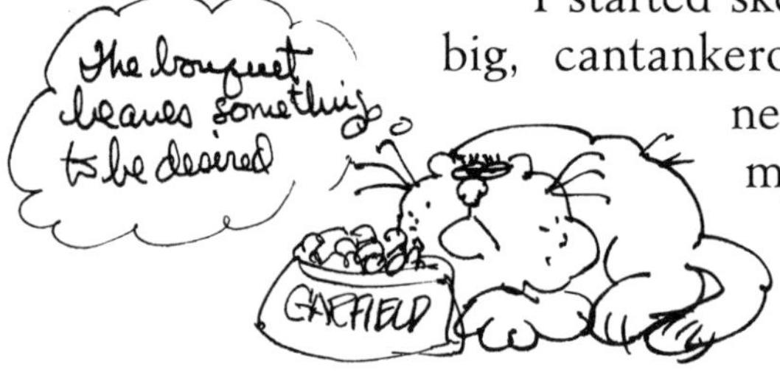
The bouquet leaves something to be desired
GARFIELD

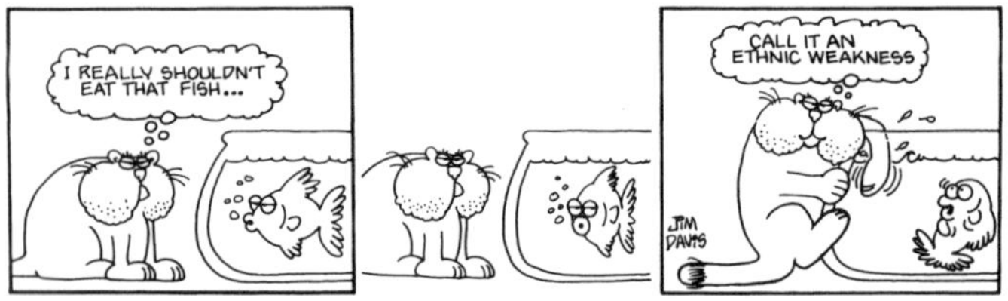
I REALLY SHOULDN'T EAT THAT FISH...
CALL IT AN ETHNIC WEAKNESS
JIM DAVIS

TOP LEFT:
A pencil sketch circa 1978.
TOP RIGHT:
A rough doodle for an early strip.
ABOVE:
Garfield went through a variety of looks in the early stages. (I tried everything, short of giving him dreadlocks!) One thing never changed: his feisty, funny attitude.

In these early drawings, Garfield didn't have any stripes (but he did have his rude 'tude!). I spent the next year and a half developing the comic strip, designing and redesigning the characters, and fine-tuning the humor. At last it was ready.

I packaged up a bunch of sample strips and sent them off to several syndicates, then crossed my fingers for luck.

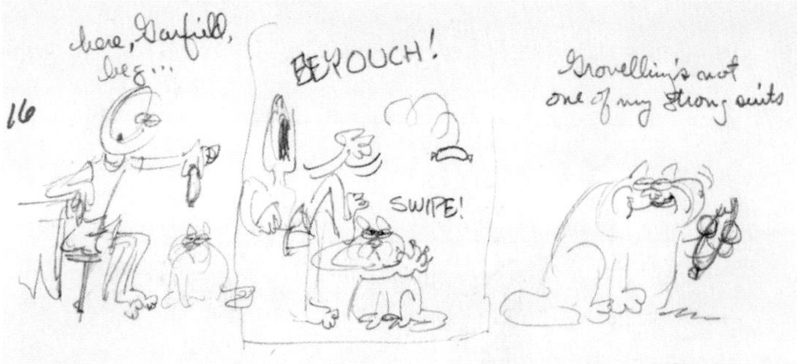
16
Here, Garfield, beg...
BEYOUCH!
SWIPE!
Grovelling's not one of my strong suits

King Features liked the strip but ultimately rejected it (I needed a unanimous vote and secured only three of the five editors), and the *Chicago Tribune–New York News* passed on the strip, too, as they had just chosen a cartoon feature called *Shoe*, written and drawn by Pulitzer Prize winner Jeff MacNelly.

But I wasn't discouraged. I knew I had a good idea, and I knew success was in sight. The next syndicate I contacted was United Feature. As it turned out, they had been approached by Bernard Kliban about a Sunday comic feature. Kliban was a talented cartoonist who had created a minor sensation with his cat characters. United wanted to do something with a cat, but — for whatever reason — passed on Kliban's material. It must have been fate. United held my initial submission and asked to see more strips. Encouraged, I rushed out another batch.

On January 24, 1978, I got the call. United had accepted *Garfield*! I was ready to celebrate, but I was snowed in during one of the worst blizzards Indiana had ever seen.

But, celebration or not, I was going to be

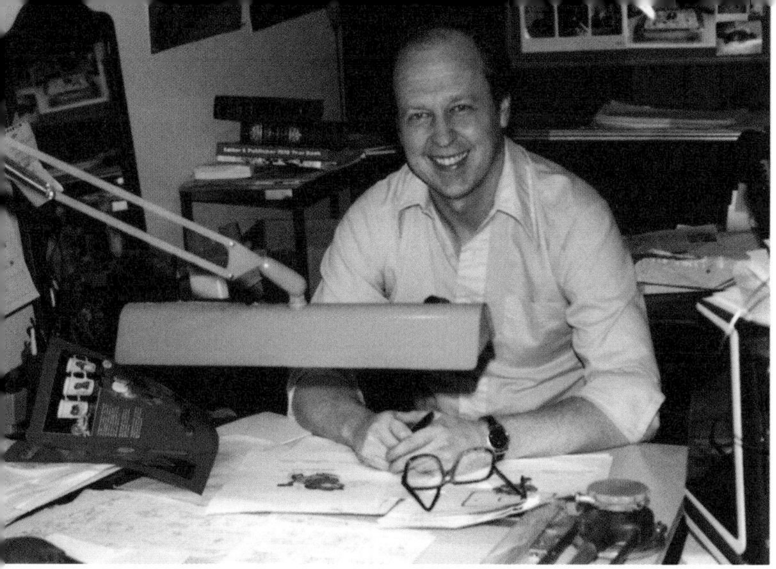

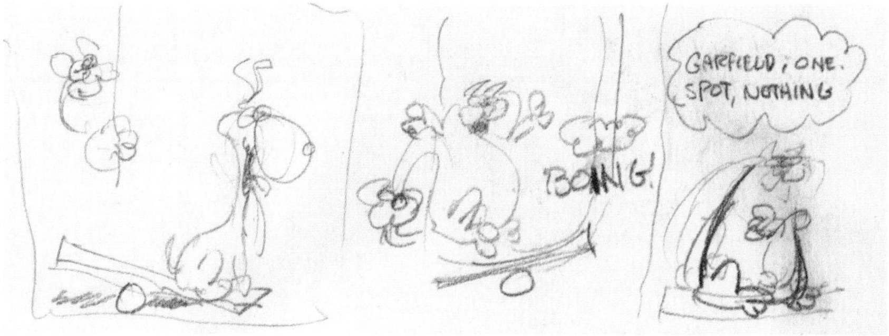
BOING!
GARFIELD, ONE.
SPOT, NOTHING

syndicated! There was just one minor catch. United wanted to move up the release date. Instead of six months, I had just two weeks to create the strips that would introduce *Garfield* to America. I ran to my drawing board, cranked out the first week's worth of strips, and popped them in the mail.

Garfield and I were off and running. We debuted June 19, 1978, in forty-one U.S. newspapers. We still celebrate Garfield's birthday every year.

Even though I was finally syndicated, I wasn't necessarily on easy street. After three months of test runs, *Garfield* was canceled by the *Chicago Sun-Times*. I knew it took from one to three years for a strip to attract and retain a loyal readership. I thought we were sunk.

Then something surprising happened. Apparently a legion of Garfield fans had arisen, and — bless their little cat-loving hearts — they were protesting the cancellation of the strip. Within a few days of pulling the comic, the *Sun-Times* had heard from 1,300 angry readers who insisted that *Garfield* be reinstated. The *Times* put the strip back in, and United was able to use the publicity to sell *Garfield* to other papers.

And the comic strip was working. I think part of Garfield's appeal was that he was such an accessible character. I made a conscious effort to include all readers. I kept the gags broad and the humor general and applicable to everyone. Most of the gags were about eating and sleeping. Plus, I avoided any social or political comments. My grasp of world affairs isn't that firm anyway. For years I thought OPEC was a denture adhesive.

People love Garfield because he says and does things they want to but can't. People relate to him. Garfield relieves our guilt, too. We live in a world where we're made to feel guilty for eating a potato chip. Garfield defends our right to eat not only a chip — but a whole bag! With dip! Sure he's a glutton, but someone has to stand up and defend gluttony! Garfield's out there making people feel less guilty. In a way, he's a public servant. Yeah, that's it.

TOP LEFT:
At work in my Muncie, Indiana, studio in the late 1970s.
TOP RIGHT:
Originally, the dog in the strip was going to be named Spot. I found out that name was taken and thus Odie was born.
BOTTOM:
An early character sketch.

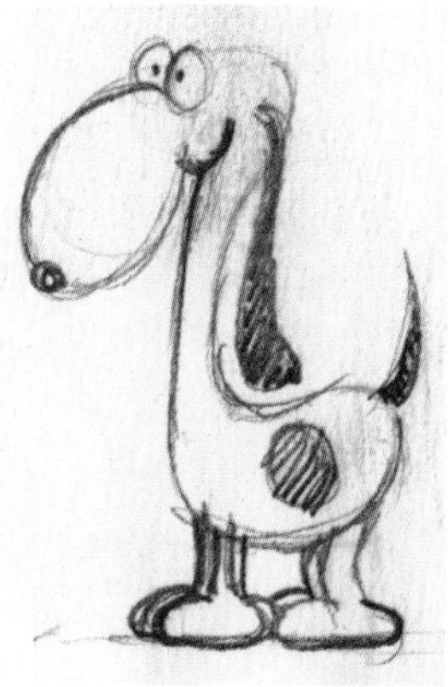

GARFIELD: THE FIRST WEEK

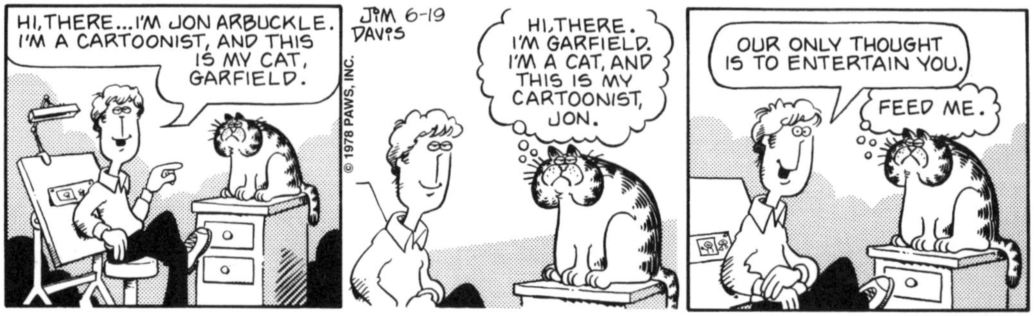
HI, THERE...I'M JON ARBUCKLE. I'M A CARTOONIST, AND THIS IS MY CAT, GARFIELD.
JIM DAVIS 6-19
© 1978 PAWS, INC.
HI, THERE. I'M GARFIELD. I'M A CAT, AND THIS IS MY CARTOONIST, JON.
OUR ONLY THOUGHT IS TO ENTERTAIN YOU.
FEED ME.

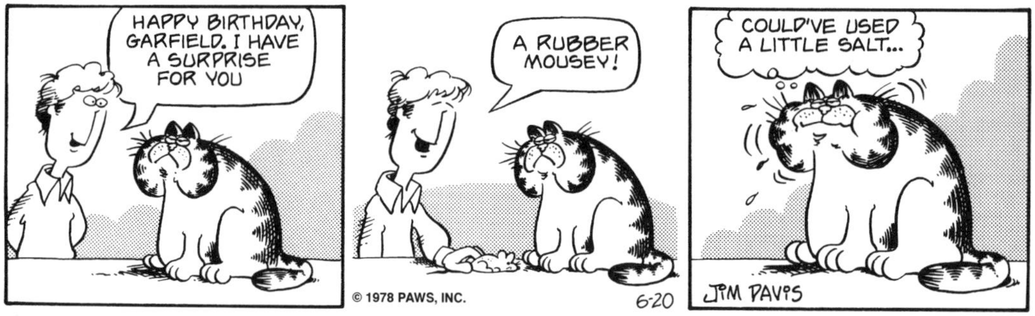
HAPPY BIRTHDAY, GARFIELD. I HAVE A SURPRISE FOR YOU
A RUBBER MOUSEY!
© 1978 PAWS, INC.
6-20
COULD'VE USED A LITTLE SALT...
JIM DAVIS

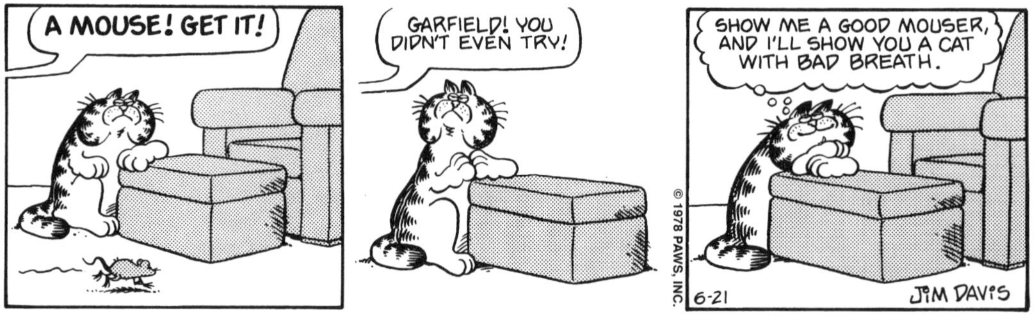
A MOUSE! GET IT!
GARFIELD! YOU DIDN'T EVEN TRY!
© 1978 PAWS, INC.
SHOW ME A GOOD MOUSER, AND I'LL SHOW YOU A CAT WITH BAD BREATH.
6-21
JIM DAVIS

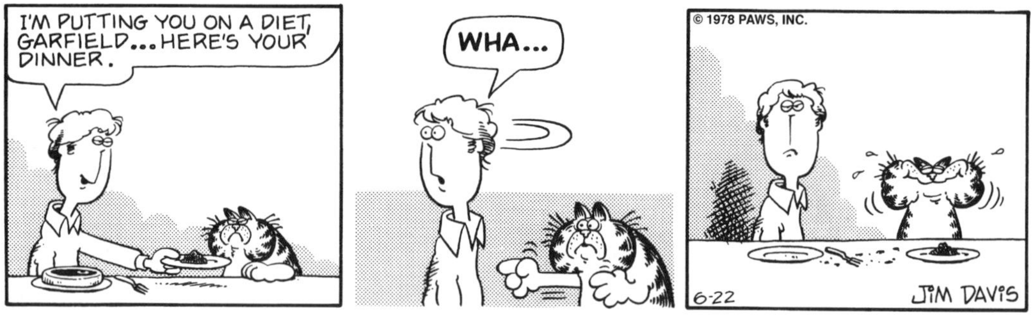
I'M PUTTING YOU ON A DIET, GARFIELD... HERE'S YOUR DINNER.
WHA...
© 1978 PAWS, INC.
6-22
JIM DAVIS

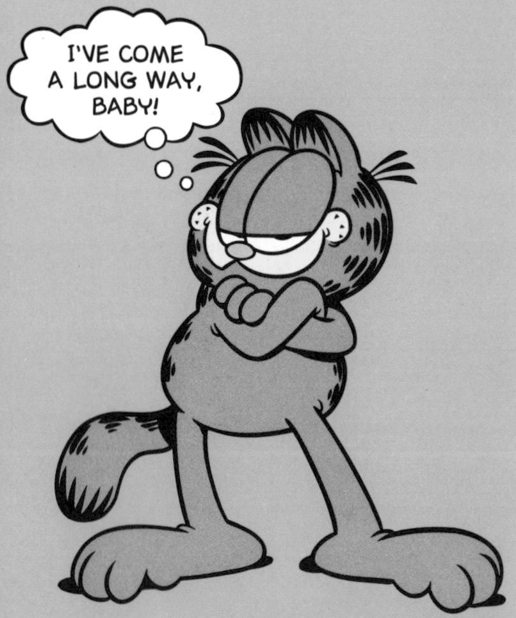
I'VE COME A LONG WAY, BABY!

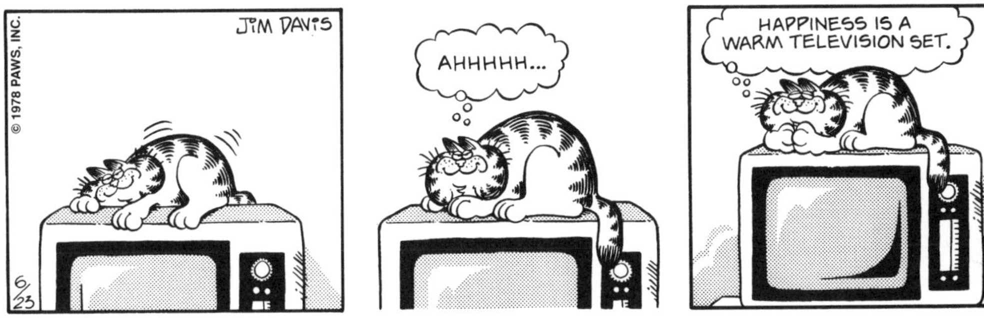
© 1978 PAWS, INC.
JIM DAVIS
6/23
AHHHHH...
HAPPINESS IS A WARM TELEVISION SET.

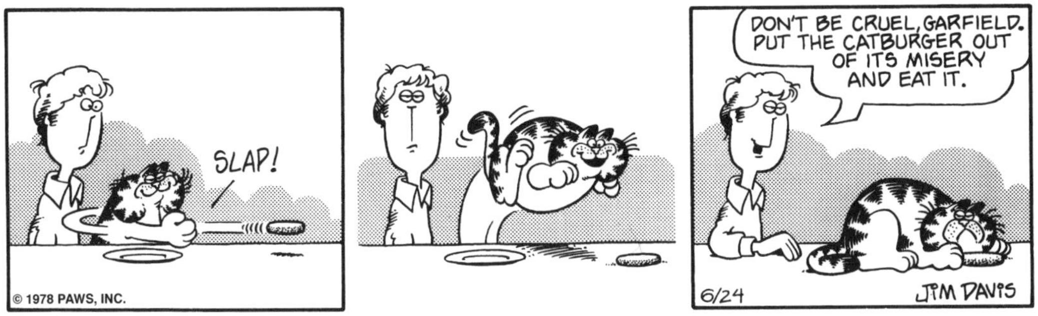
SLAP!
© 1978 PAWS, INC.
DON'T BE CRUEL, GARFIELD. PUT THE CATBURGER OUT OF ITS MISERY AND EAT IT.
6/24
JIM DAVIS

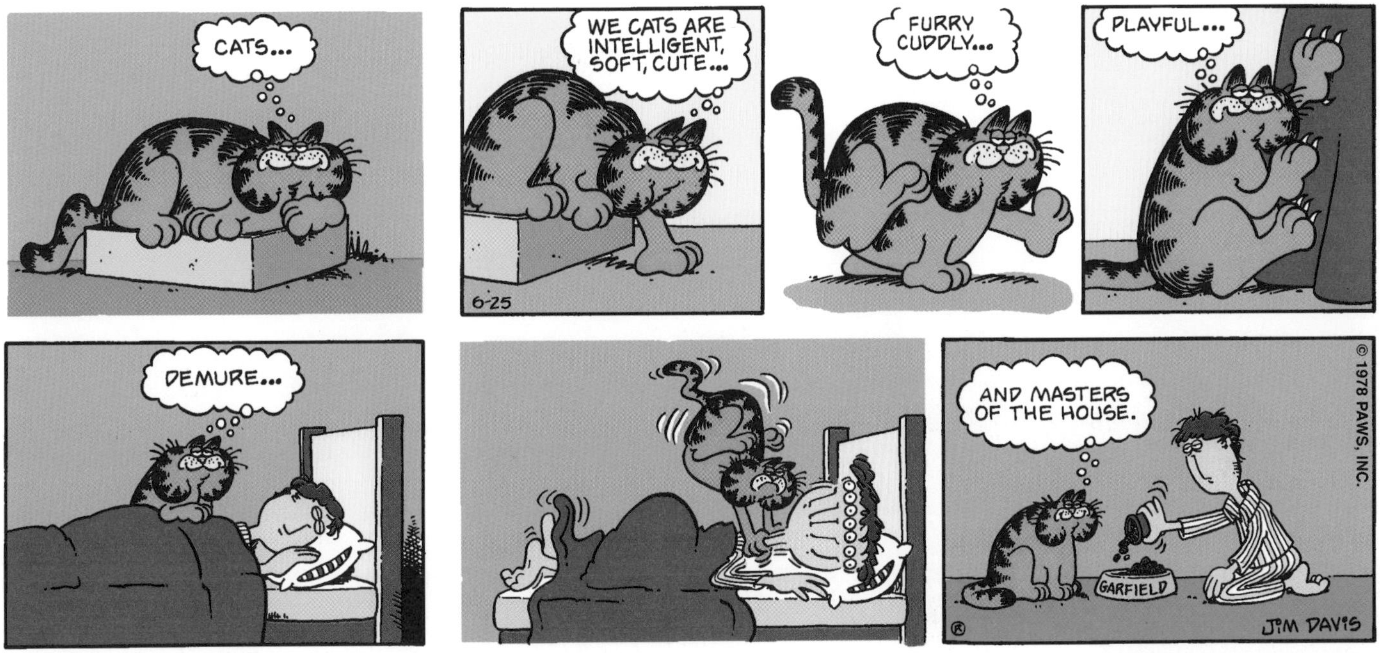
CATS...
WE CATS ARE INTELLIGENT, SOFT, CUTE...
6-25
FURRY CUDDLY...
PLAYFUL...
DEMURE...
AND MASTERS OF THE HOUSE.
GARFIELD
© 1978 PAWS, INC.
®
JIM DAVIS

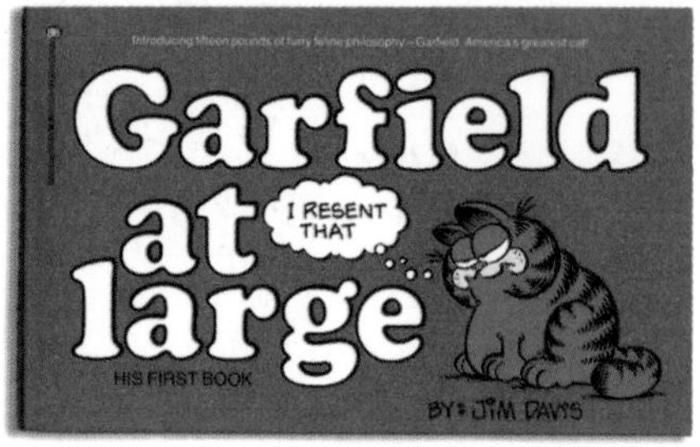
Garfield at large
I RESENT THAT
HIS FIRST BOOK
BY: JIM DAVIS

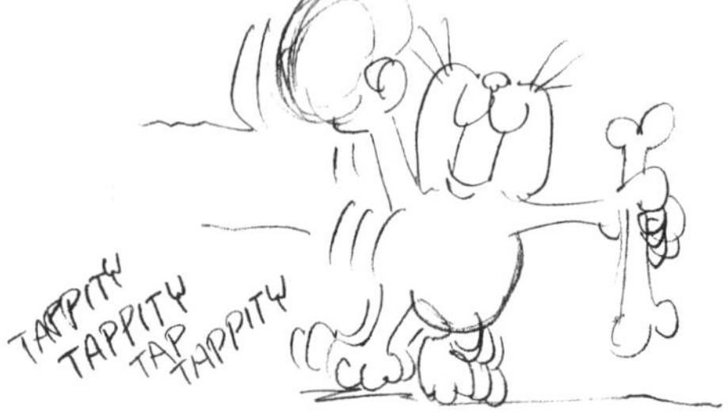
TAPPITY
TAPPITY
TAP
TAPPITY

GOTTA DANCE!

TOP:
I fought hard for this special format. Thankfully, I was proved right. The compilation books really jump-started Garfield's rise to fame.

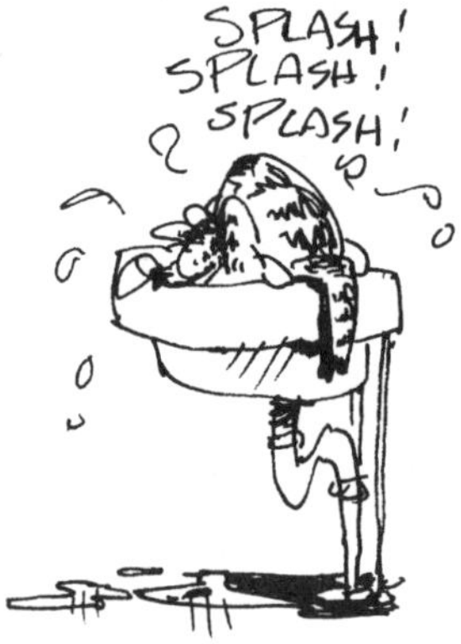
SPLASH!
SPLASH!
SPLASH!

Whatever the reasons, more and more newspaper readers were discovering the feisty fat cat. By 1980, we were in over one hundred papers. I met with the syndicate and discussed a compilation book, a collection of the daily and Sunday strips.

I'd always hated the standard mass-market-paperback comic strip books that stacked the strips vertically. The strip should be read across the page, just as it is in the newspaper.

I mocked up a book that displayed the strips in a horizontal format. Next, I put a number 1 on the cover. The strips would be run chronologically in numbered books. I thought this would promote collectibility. There was only one little problem. The book I had designed wouldn't fit in the standard bookstore racks. So I designed a special rack for the books. All of this activity was accomplished without the advice of printers, cutters, packagers, or rack jobbers who generally provide guidance on the feasibility of such projects. Looking back, I realize if I had talked to these experts, the entire idea would probably have been dropped.

With production and marketing concepts in hand, I presented the idea to the head honchos at United Feature. They were less than thrilled. I think the words *unrealistic* and *unworkable* were used. Disillusioned, I returned to my studio in Muncie on a Saturday. In the mail on Monday was a letter from Ballantine Books asking how they could obtain publishing rights to *Garfield*. I called a representative from United Feature, and then presented my idea to Ballantine. Ballantine loved the concept and even used the size issue to our advantage. Because the books wouldn't fit in the regular bookstore racks, they had to be displayed in their own area — like near the cash register (darn!).

Today in the publishing industry, a book shaped like the Garfield compilation book is called a "Garfield format" book. After the first book was published, I went on a twenty-city book tour. At the start of the tour, *Garfield* was being added to newspapers at the rate of about seven papers a month. Two months after the tour had begun, the strip was being added to newspapers at the rate of one a day. There's no question that the book accelerated Garfield's success.

And I felt very lucky. I'd spent over ten years struggling, trying to create a syndicated comic strip. Finally, I was doing what I loved, and I was successful, too. I owed it all to a fat orange cat.

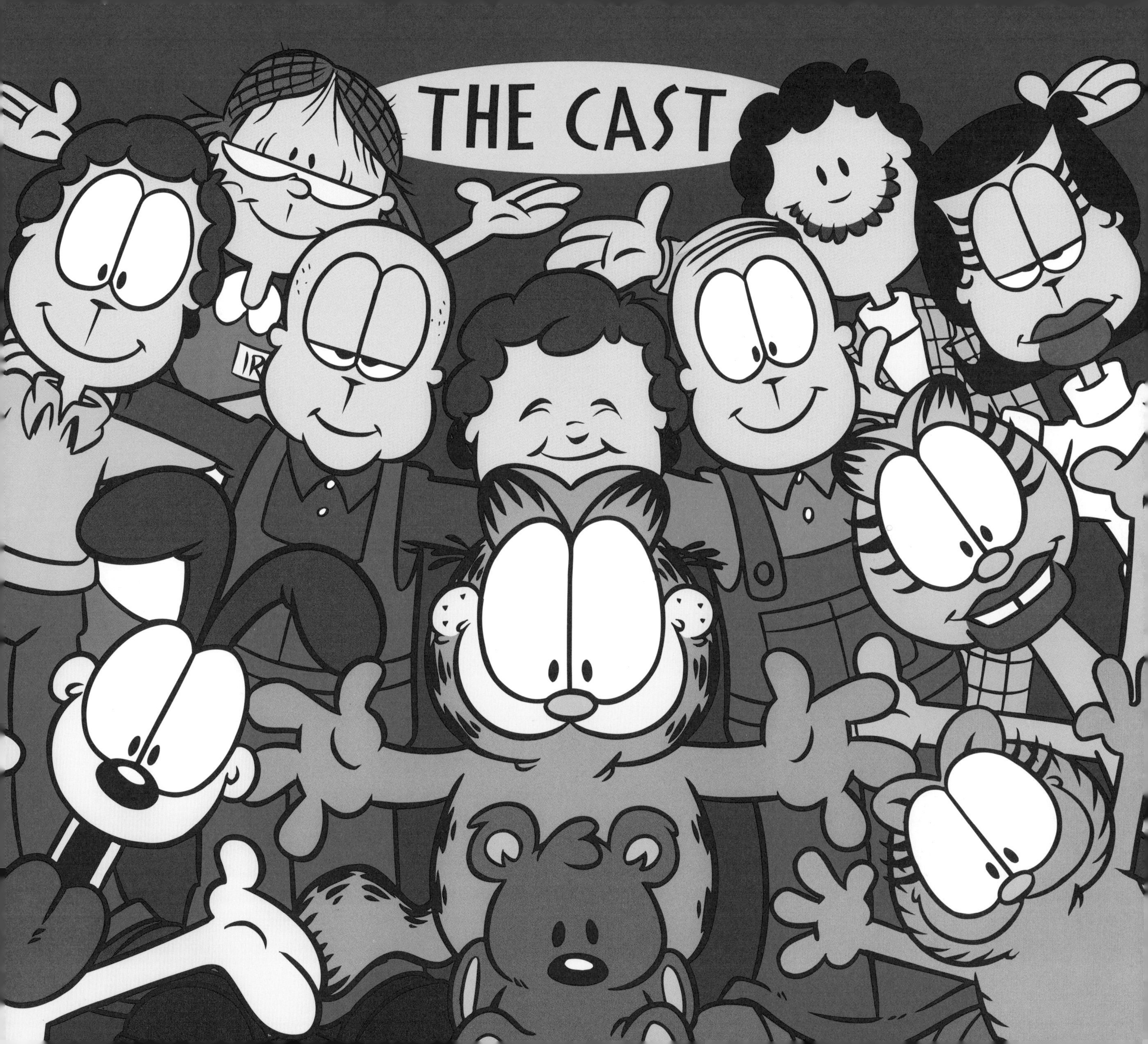
THE CAST

GARFIELD

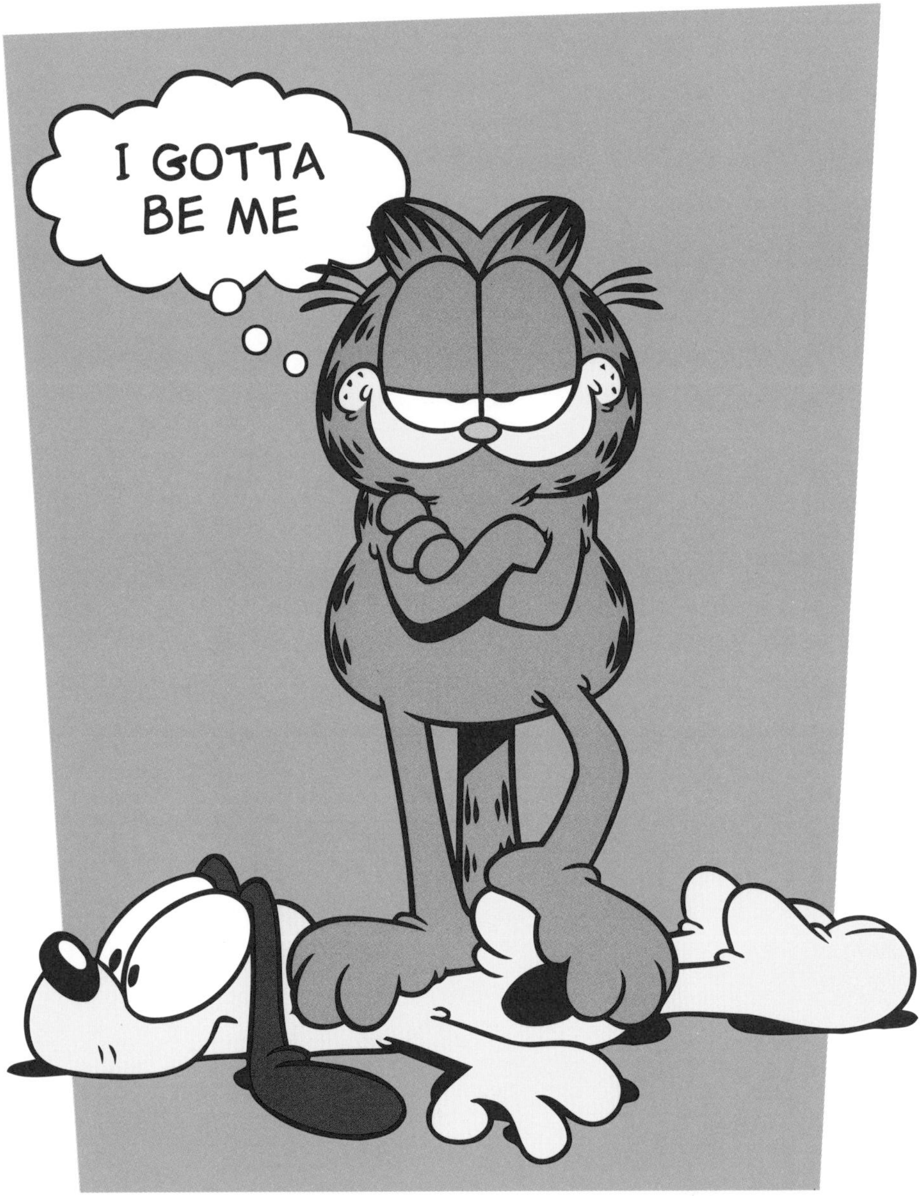
I GOTTA BE ME

He's a wisecracking, nap-taking, coffee-guzzling, lasagna-loving, Monday-hating, dog-punting, spider-whacking, mailman-mauling fat cat. He's Garfield . . . the world's feistiest (and funniest) feline!

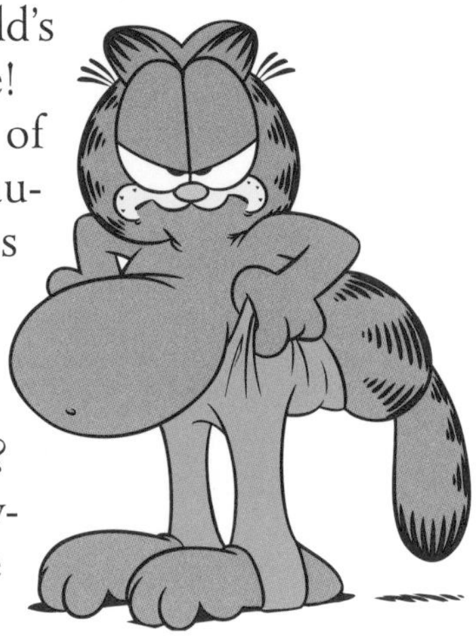

Born in the kitchen of Mamma Leoni's Italian restaurant in 1978, Garfield has been pigging out on pasta ever since. But what's so appealing about a tubby tabby with a rude attitude? What makes Garfield so lovable? It's simple . . . people relate to him because he *is* them. After all, he's really a human in a cat suit. Garfield loves TV and hates Mondays. He'd rather pig out than work out; in fact, his passion for food and sleep is matched only by his aversion to diet and exercise (he prefers lie-downs to sit-ups). He'd like mornings better if they started later. Coffee strong enough to sit up and bark is the only way to start the day. What could be more human?

But Garfield isn't all sass and sarcasm: he also has a soft side. He really loves his teddy bear, Pooky, and deep down, he loves his owner, Jon, and his dopey dog pal, Odie,

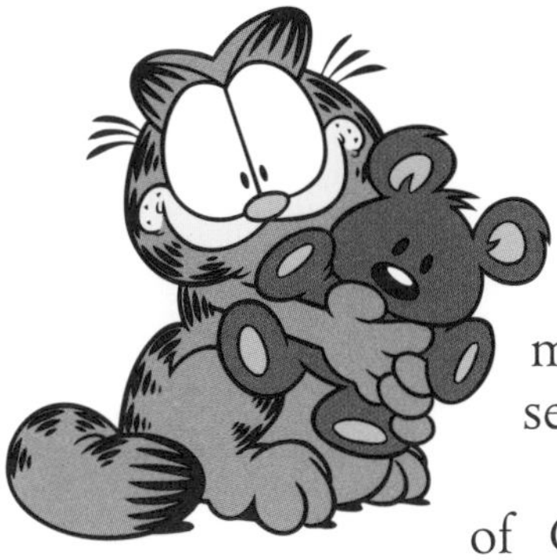

too (just not as much as he loves himself, of course).

Much has been made of Garfield's size. Sure, he's a little rotund. Sure, he's been mistaken for a small planet. Sure, he's so big he has his own zip code. But in Garfield's opinion, he's not overweight . . . he's undertall. He's not fat . . . he's experiencing a cell surplus.

And lazy? Garfield listens to his inner slug and always takes life one nap at a time. After all, there's one good thing about lethargy: you don't have to work at it.

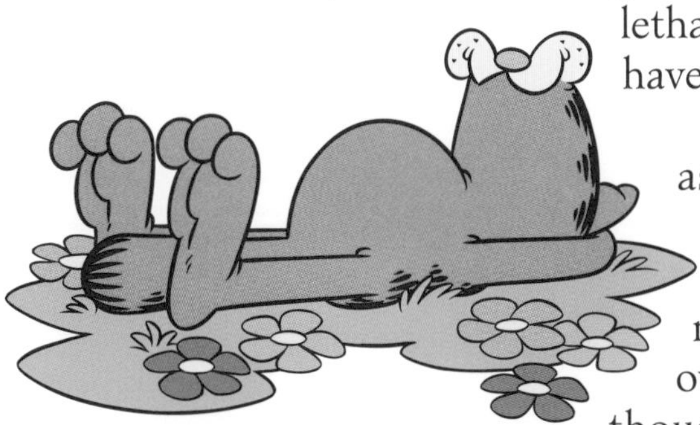

People often ask me if I'm like Garfield. Well, yes and no. I'm not overweight — though I am fat inside. I love food — and yes, lasagna! And I don't really care for exercise. I'm an ex-jogger. It's a pretty sweaty proposition.

Garfield's appearance has changed a lot since he first waddled onto the comics page. Here are a couple of views of the famous fat cat.

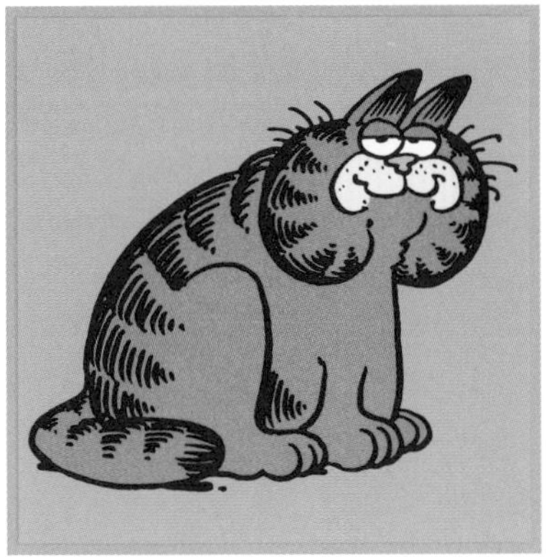

1978

This is the way Garfield appeared in his very first comic strip, June 19, 1978. His body was larger then, and his eyes were smaller. He had pointier ears, a T-shaped nose, and numerous dots on his upper lip and cheeks. More whiskers stuck out of his head. He even had more stripes. He also had a cynical, wisecracking personality and an enormous appetite. Some things haven't changed at all.

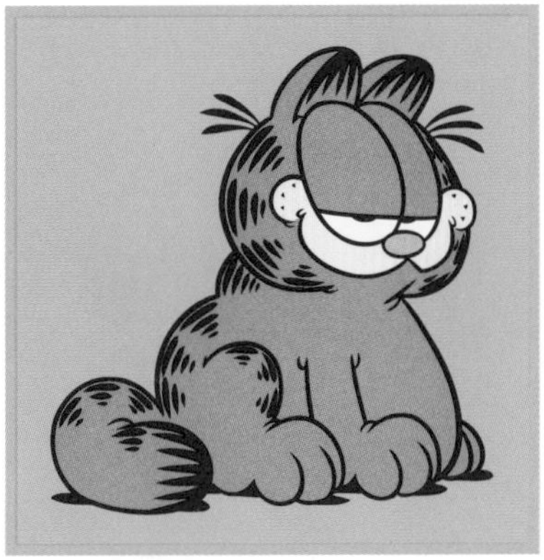

1998

This is Garfield today. The fat cat is a more well-rounded character now. His head is spherical and almost as large as his body. His eyes are also bigger, allowing him to express more emotion (and keep a closer watch on his food!). His nose is a simple oval, his whiskers have been reduced to three on each side of his head, and he has just three tick marks on each cheek. Since the mid '80s, Garfield has been walking upright. But don't worry, the flabby tabby still takes life lying down.

THE MANY MOODS OF GARFIELD

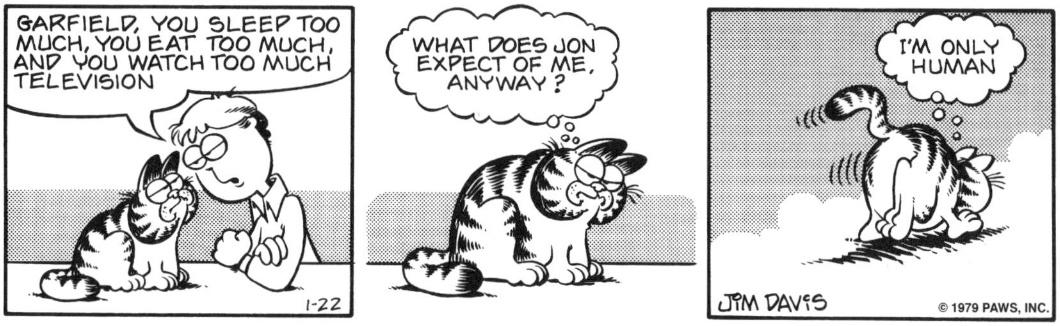
GARFIELD, YOU SLEEP TOO MUCH, YOU EAT TOO MUCH, AND YOU WATCH TOO MUCH TELEVISION
1-22
WHAT DOES JON EXPECT OF ME, ANYWAY?
I'M ONLY HUMAN
JIM DAVIS
© 1979 PAWS, INC.

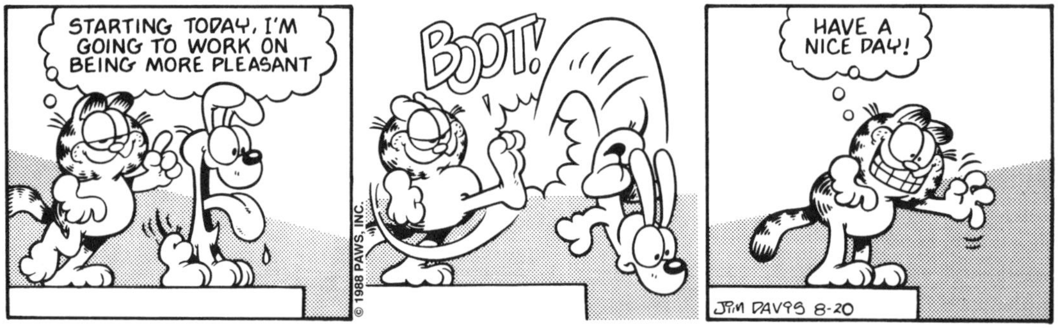
STARTING TODAY, I'M GOING TO WORK ON BEING MORE PLEASANT
BOOT!
© 1988 PAWS, INC.
HAVE A NICE DAY!
JIM DAVIS 8-20

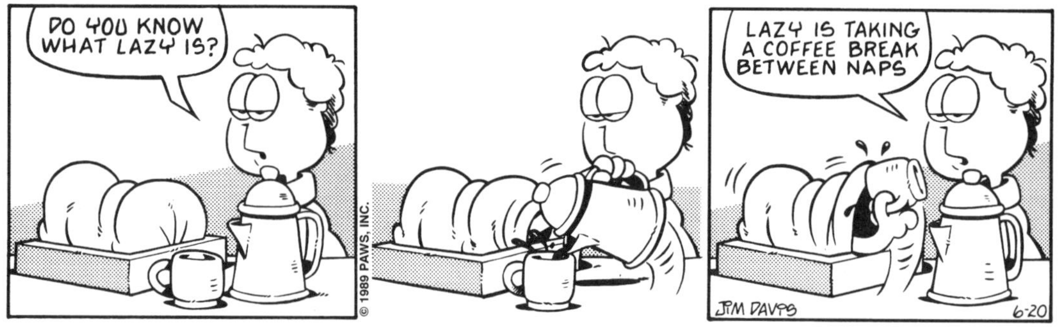
DO YOU KNOW WHAT LAZY IS?
© 1989 PAWS, INC.
LAZY IS TAKING A COFFEE BREAK BETWEEN NAPS
JIM DAVIS
6-20

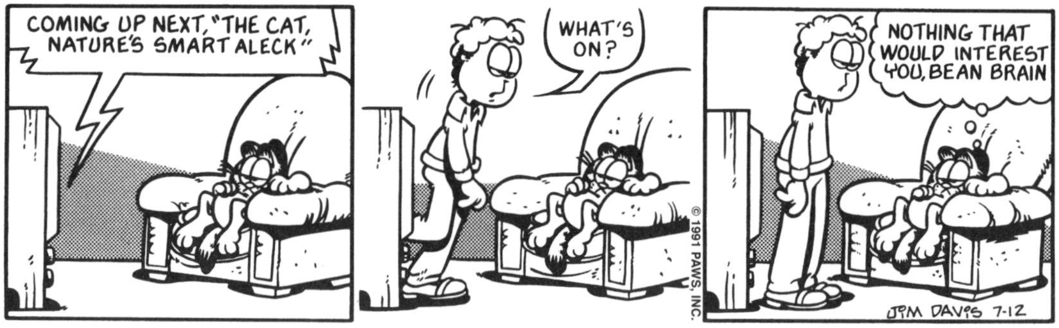
COMING UP NEXT, "THE CAT, NATURE'S SMART ALECK"
WHAT'S ON?
© 1991 PAWS, INC.
NOTHING THAT WOULD INTEREST YOU, BEAN BRAIN
JIM DAVIS 7-12

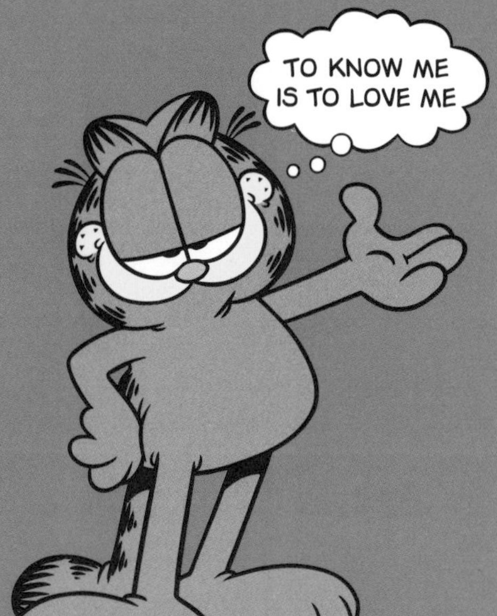
TO KNOW ME IS TO LOVE ME

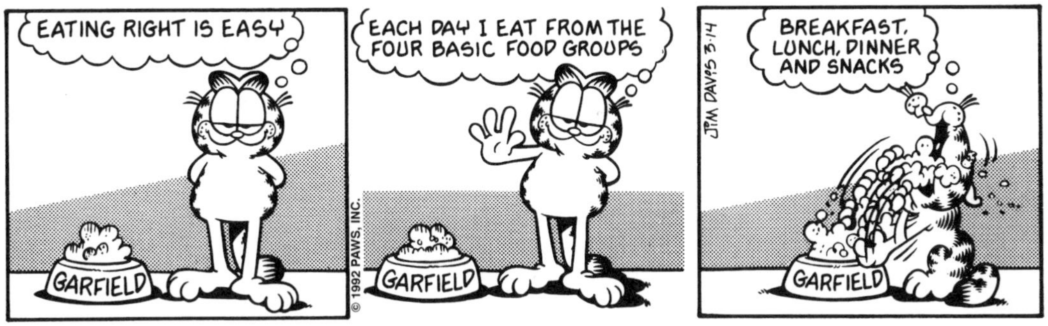
EATING RIGHT IS EASY
EACH DAY I EAT FROM THE FOUR BASIC FOOD GROUPS
BREAKFAST, LUNCH, DINNER AND SNACKS
GARFIELD
© 1992 PAWS, INC.

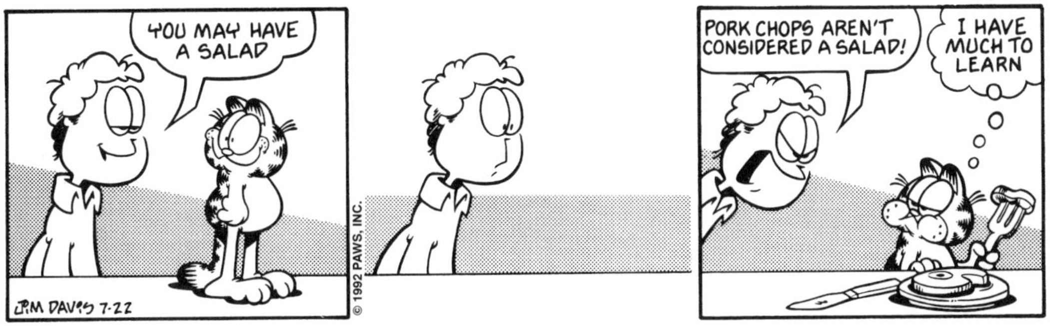
YOU MAY HAVE A SALAD
PORK CHOPS AREN'T CONSIDERED A SALAD!
I HAVE MUCH TO LEARN
© 1992 PAWS, INC.

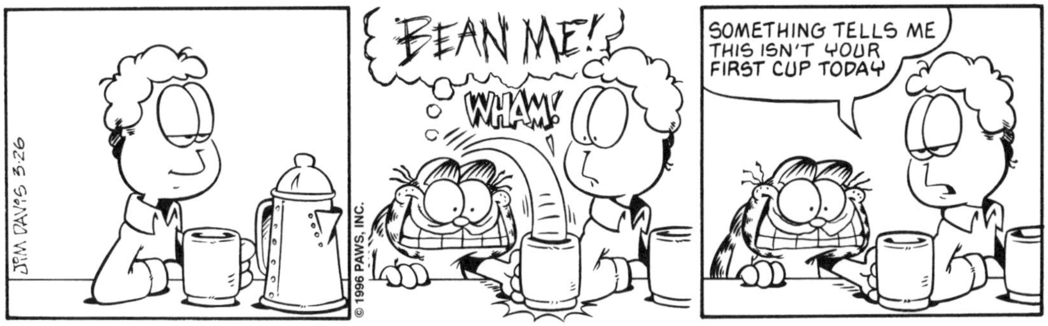
BEAN ME!
WHAM!
SOMETHING TELLS ME THIS ISN'T YOUR FIRST CUP TODAY
© 1996 PAWS, INC.

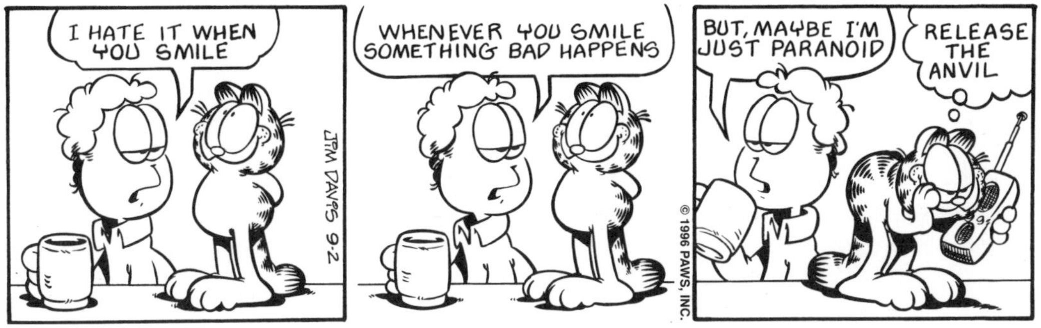
I HATE IT WHEN YOU SMILE
WHENEVER YOU SMILE SOMETHING BAD HAPPENS
BUT, MAYBE I'M JUST PARANOID
RELEASE THE ANVIL
© 1996 PAWS, INC.

TOP TEN MISCONCEPTIONS ABOUT GARFIELD

10. *He was once banned from the comics page for betting on a* Peanuts *baseball game*

9. *He can cure scurvy with the touch of his paw*

8. *He's really an Ewok in a cat suit*

7. *If you read his strip backward, it says, "Elvis, your pork rinds are here"*

6. *He graduated from Harvard Medical School*

5. *He and Bill Clinton once came to blows over a cheeseburger*

4. *He won a Tony for Cats*

3. *He was Shirley MacLaine in a previous life*

2. *He already knows the winners of the next eight Super Bowls*

1. *He's stuck to the windows of every single car in America*

JON

WILL WORK FOR DATE

Jon Arbuckle is Garfield and Odie's hapless owner. Decent but dull, with a fatally flawed fashion sense, Jon is a geek with a heart of gold.

The name Jon Arbuckle came from an old coffee commercial I remembered hearing. I'd also used the name as an "expert source" to add "credibility" to my speeches during debates in my college days. When I was creating the comic strip, the name Jon Arbuckle just seemed to fit the kind of poor sap who would get stuck with a cranky cat with an overactive appetite.

Originally Jon was a cartoonist, but eventually I dropped that from the strip. These days Jon seems to have his hands full playing straight man to Garfield (not to mention being the butt of all of the fat cat's practical jokes).

And poor Jon doesn't fare any better when it comes to romance, either. With his wardrobe straight out of Geeks "R" Us and his pathetic pickup lines straight out of the '70s, the hopelessly unhip Jon is always courting disaster.

Here's a look at Jon over the years.

1978

When Jon first appeared, his eyes were smaller and his hair was a little longer, but not much else has changed. In fact, I think he's still wearing that very same shirt from 1978.

1998

Jon as he appears today. His eyes are rounder now, too, but he's still the same bumbling, boring nerd who provides love, food, and shelter while his playful pets provide the laughs.

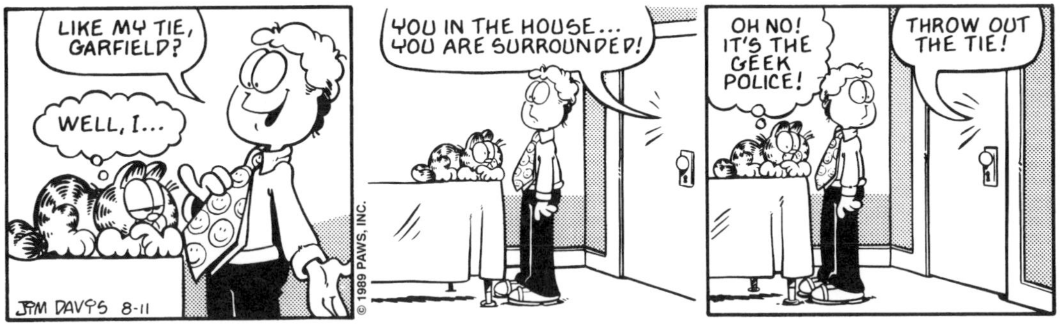
LIKE MY TIE, GARFIELD?
WELL, I...
JIM DAVIS 8-11
© 1989 PAWS, INC.
YOU IN THE HOUSE... YOU ARE SURROUNDED!
OH NO! IT'S THE GEEK POLICE!
THROW OUT THE TIE!

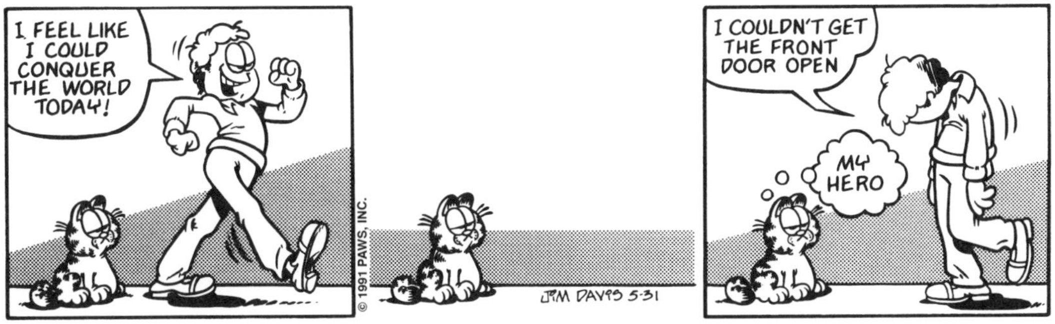
I FEEL LIKE I COULD CONQUER THE WORLD TODAY!
© 1991 PAWS, INC.
JIM DAVIS 5-31
I COULDN'T GET THE FRONT DOOR OPEN
MY HERO

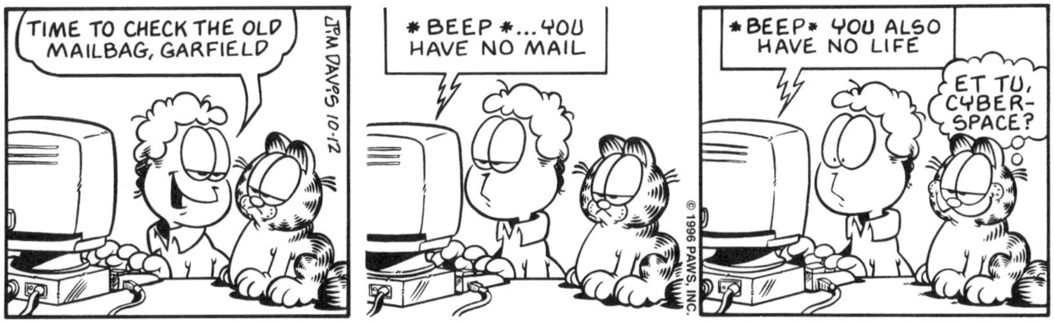
TIME TO CHECK THE OLD MAILBAG, GARFIELD
JIM DAVIS 10-12
BEEP...YOU HAVE NO MAIL
© 1996 PAWS, INC.
BEEP YOU ALSO HAVE NO LIFE
ET TU, CYBER-SPACE?

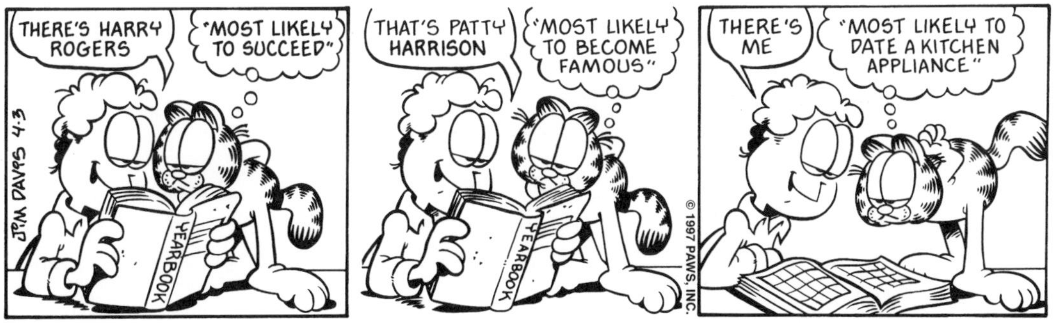
THERE'S HARRY ROGERS
"MOST LIKELY TO SUCCEED"
JIM DAVIS 4-3
YEARBOOK
THAT'S PATTY HARRISON
"MOST LIKELY TO BECOME FAMOUS"
YEARBOOK
© 1997 PAWS, INC.
THERE'S ME
"MOST LIKELY TO DATE A KITCHEN APPLIANCE"

TOP TEN MOST LIKELY MEANINGS FOR THE NAME ARBUCKLE

10. *wiener-chested*

9. *rash giver*

8. *pudding-brained*

7. *man of socks*

6. *dances with cows*

5. *he who giggles in battle*

4. *uh-oh, here he comes*

3. *royal bore*

2. *village dweeb*

1. *cat-whipped*

ODIE

Lovable, playful, and brainless as a brick . . . that's Odie, Garfield's faithful friend and whipping dog. Odie never thinks, sometimes barks, and always drools. In fact, he drools so much his fleas have flood insurance!

And dumb? It took Odie three years just to learn how to breathe. His IQ is so low, you can't test it; you have to dig for it. Of course, he was bred to be a working dog — specifically, a paperweight or a doorstop.

The name Odie is really an inside joke. I chose the name because it connoted stupidity, at least to me. In the early 1970s, I wrote a radio commercial for a local car dealership. The spot featured Odie, the village idiot. I liked the name, so I used it again. Hey, why reinvent the fool?

Odie was originally owned by Jon Arbuckle's roommate, Lyman. Lyman left the Garfield comic strip, but Odie remained — much to Garfield's chagrin.

Here's Odie then and now.

1978

Like Garfield, Odie has evolved over the years (Garfield would say Odie evolved from a rock). Back then Odie was skinnier (weren't we all?), and his ears were black. But in the summer of 1979, I was told by the president of United Feature to change the color because another dog — with more bite — had black ears. (Hint: The pooch works for "peanuts," but he doesn't work cheap.) So, like the autumn leaves, Odie's ears turned brown in October 1979, in that month's first Sunday strip.

1998

By this time, Odie's legs and eyes have gotten bigger — but not his brain, of course. Odie still can't walk and drool at the same time. But he's my kind of dog. The world can always use a good Odie.

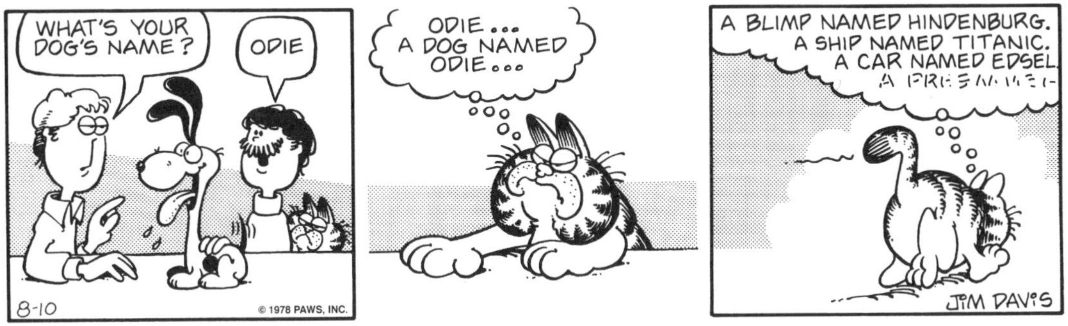
WHAT'S YOUR DOG'S NAME?
ODIE
ODIE... A DOG NAMED ODIE...
A BLIMP NAMED HINDENBURG. A SHIP NAMED TITANIC. A CAR NAMED EDSEL.
8-10
© 1978 PAWS, INC.
JIM DAVIS

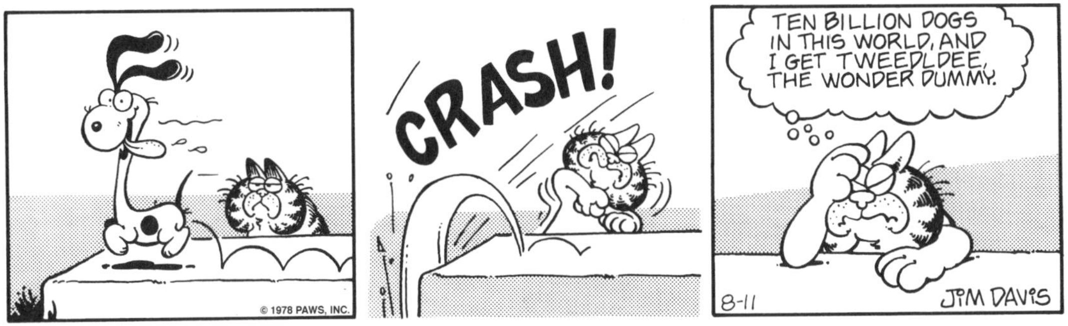
© 1978 PAWS, INC.
CRASH!
TEN BILLION DOGS IN THIS WORLD, AND I GET TWEEDLDEE, THE WONDER DUMMY.
8-11
JIM DAVIS

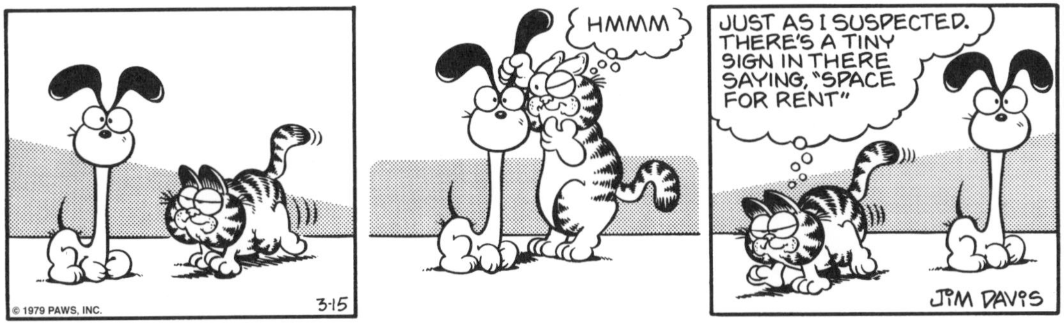
© 1979 PAWS, INC.
3-15
HMMM
JUST AS I SUSPECTED. THERE'S A TINY SIGN IN THERE SAYING, "SPACE FOR RENT"
JIM DAVIS

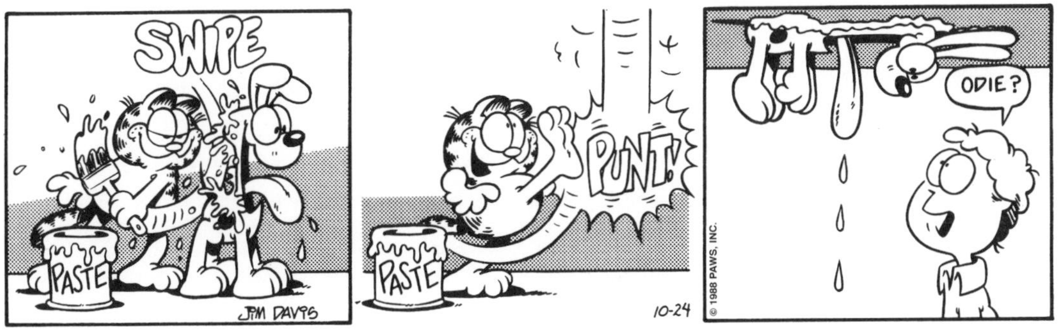
SWIPE
PASTE
JIM DAVIS
PASTE
PUNT!
10-24
© 1988 PAWS, INC.
ODIE?

TOP TEN ADVANTAGES TO BEING ODIE

10. *Never has to read* Paradise Lost

9. *Plenty of saliva for throwing spitballs*

8. *Isn't embarrassed if he forgets to give "Jeopardy" answer in the form of a question*

7. *Relief always as close as the nearest tree*

6. *Tongue can reach those "hard-to-lick" places*

5. *Teenage girls think stupidity is cute*

4. *Can buy and sell Marmaduke*

3. *Okay to scratch himself in public*

2. *Lack of brains means big-time bliss*

1. *All the toilet water he can drink*

POOKY

HELLO, WHAT'S THIS?
A TEDDY BEAR. A DUMB, STUPID, SILLY-LOOKING OLD TEDDY BEAR
I THINK I'LL CALL HIM "POOKY"
JIM DAVIS
© 1978 PAWS, INC.
10-23

Pooky allows Garfield to show his softer side. He's a teddy bear extraordinaire: cuddly, understanding, and always there when Garfield needs him. Plus he never tries to hog Garfield's blanket or food. Garfield likes that.

NERMAL

GUESS WHAT, GARFIELD? WHILE MOM AND DAD'RE ON A WEEK'S VACATION, WE'RE GOING TO BABY-SIT FOR THEIR KITTEN
9-3
MEET NERMAL
WAKE ME IN A WEEK
© 1979 PAWS, INC.
JIM DAVIS

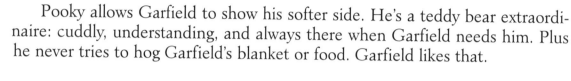

Nermal calls himself "The World's Cutest Kitten." He often ridicules Garfield's looks and age, but Garfield gets in his licks. He once mailed Nermal to Abu Dhabi. Nermal was introduced as a kitten belonging to Jon's parents, but that connection was quickly dropped. Now he simply wanders into Garfield's house to annoy the crabby tabby.

ARLENE

IT'S TIME I MET A CAT OF THE FEMALE PERSUASION
JIM DAVIS
12-17
WHAT TOOK YOU SO LONG?
© 1980 PAWS, INC.

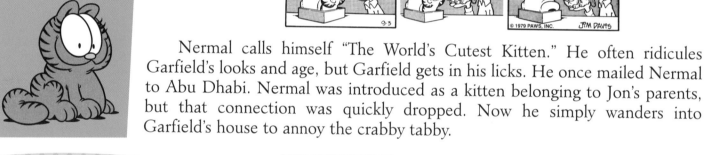

Arlene is the female cat most likely to share dinner and insults with Garfield. They have a love-hate relationship: Garfield loves himself and Arlene hates that. Garfield's gap-toothed gal pal was introduced to add a little romance to the strip. But don't look for anything serious to develop. Garfield's still looking for a mate who will accept him for what he is . . . perfect in every way.

MOM

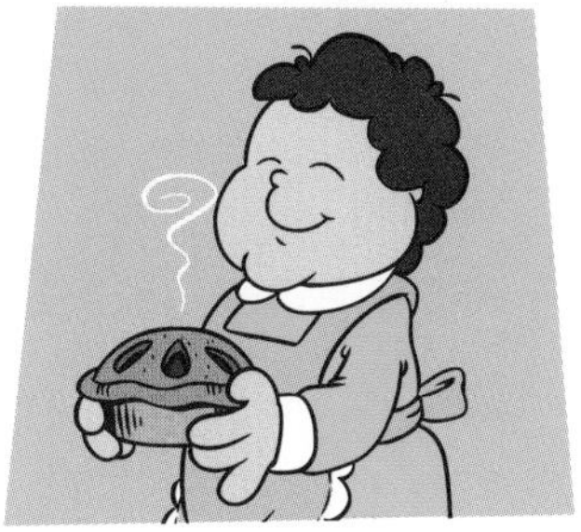

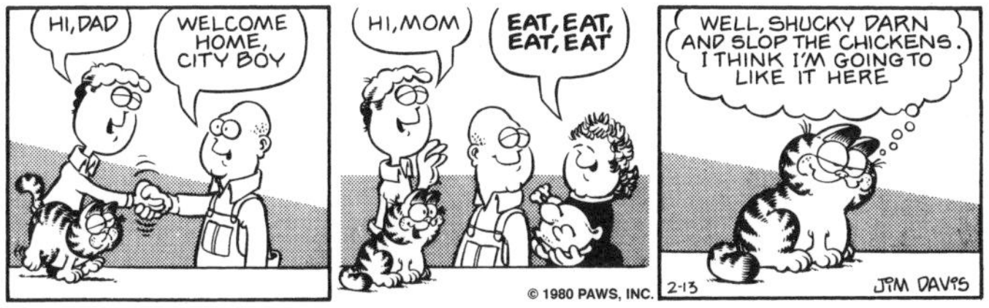
HI, DAD
WELCOME HOME, CITY BOY
HI, MOM
EAT, EAT, EAT, EAT
© 1980 PAWS, INC.
WELL, SHUCKY DARN AND SLOP THE CHICKENS. I THINK I'M GOING TO LIKE IT HERE
2-13
JIM DAVIS

Jon's mom is a loving, hardworking farm wife who's very proud of her husband and sons. Much like my own mother (on whom she's based!), Jon's mom is a wonderful cook who believes strongly in quality and quantity. As she sees it, the two most important food groups are potatoes and pies.

DAD

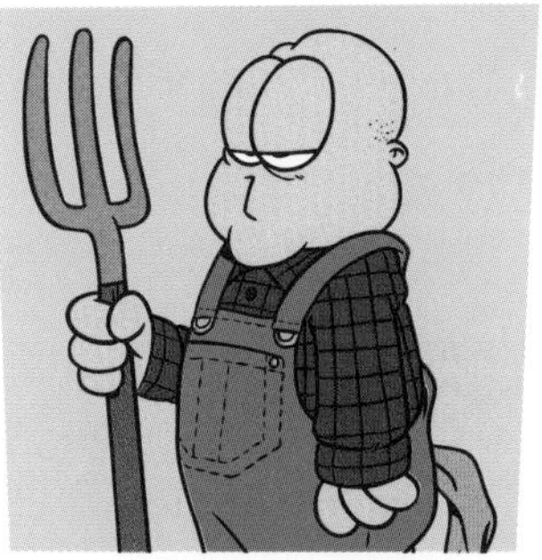

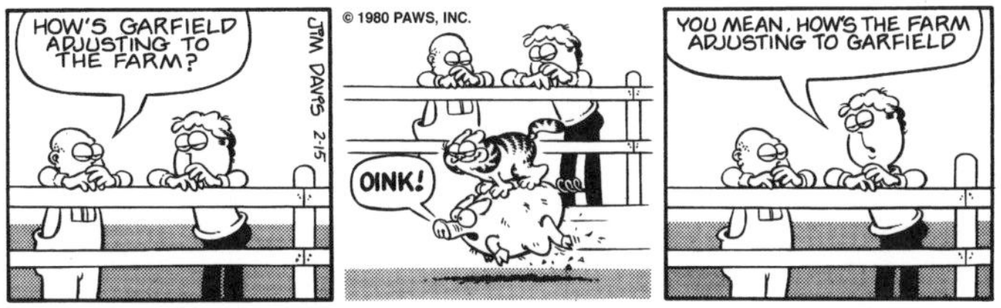
HOW'S GARFIELD ADJUSTING TO THE FARM?
JIM DAVIS 2-15
© 1980 PAWS, INC.
OINK!
YOU MEAN, HOW'S THE FARM ADJUSTING TO GARFIELD

As a farmer, Jon's dad is outstanding in his field. Patterned after my own father, he's a down-to-earth guy (literally) in charge of the Arbuckle farm. Jon visits his folks regularly. This annoys Garfield, whose favorite farm activities are eating and leaving.

DOC BOY

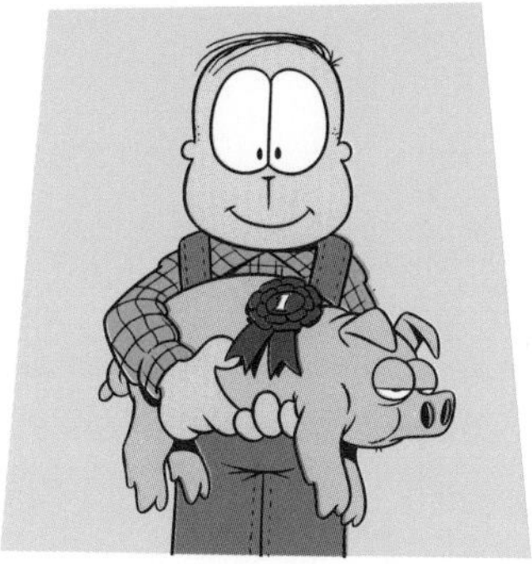

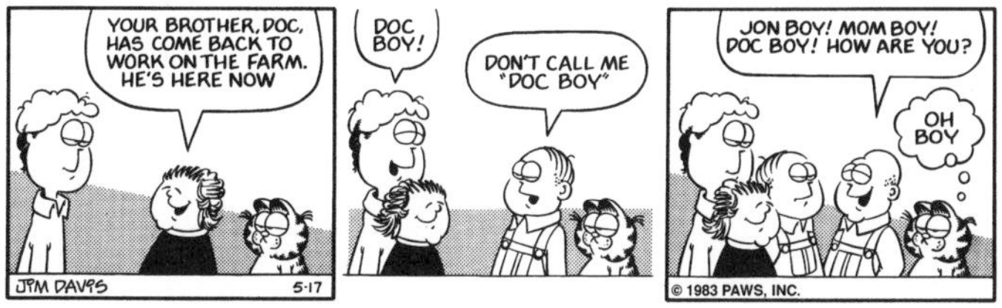
YOUR BROTHER, DOC, HAS COME BACK TO WORK ON THE FARM. HE'S HERE NOW
JIM DAVIS
5-17
DOC BOY!
DON'T CALL ME "DOC BOY"
JON BOY! MOM BOY! DOC BOY! HOW ARE YOU?
OH BOY
© 1983 PAWS, INC.

Jon's only sibling, Doc Boy, lives on the Arbuckle farm with his parents. Like his city-slicker brother, Doc Boy leads a pretty boring life. But at least he only has to feed the hogs. Jon has to feed Garfield. Doc Boy was named after my own brother, Dave "Doc" Davis. Doc isn't nearly as goofy as his cartoon namesake; he's goofier.

LIZ

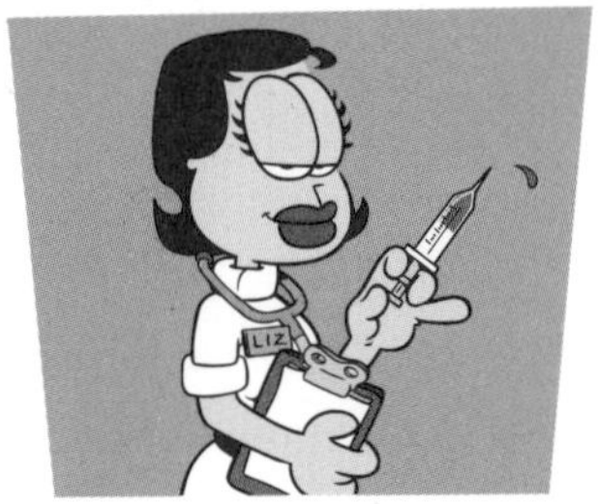
LIZ

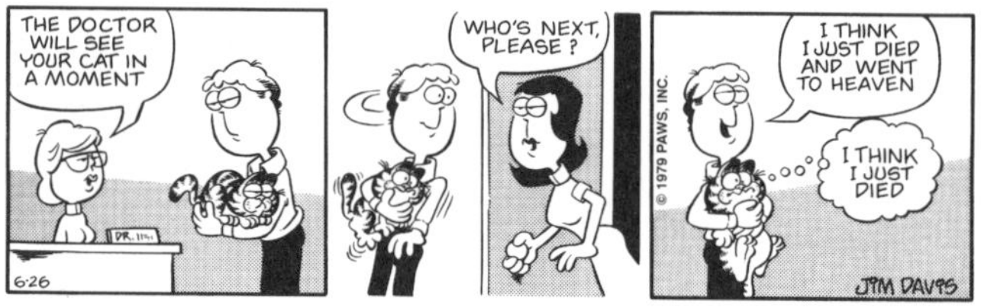
THE DOCTOR WILL SEE YOUR CAT IN A MOMENT
6-26
WHO'S NEXT, PLEASE ?
© 1979 PAWS, INC.
I THINK I JUST DIED AND WENT TO HEAVEN
I THINK I JUST DIED
JIM DAVIS

Dr. Liz Wilson is Garfield's veterinarian. She treats Garfield like a patient and Jon like the plague. Liz does occasionally date Jon, but the romance hasn't clicked, primarily because Jon is afflicted with terminal geekitis.

IRMA

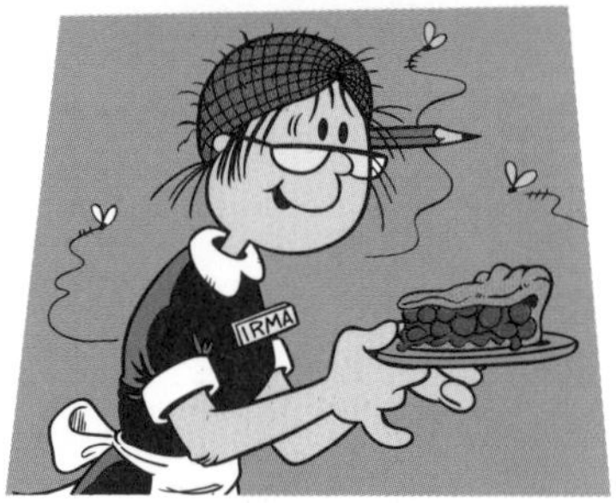
IRMA

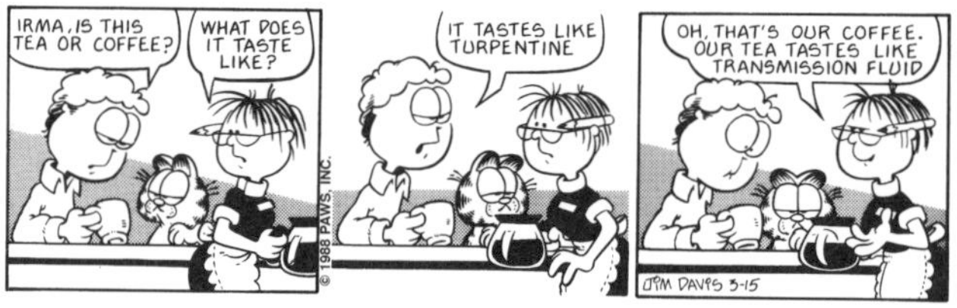
IRMA, IS THIS TEA OR COFFEE?
WHAT DOES IT TASTE LIKE?
© 1988 PAWS, INC.
IT TASTES LIKE TURPENTINE
OH, THAT'S OUR COFFEE. OUR TEA TASTES LIKE TRANSMISSION FLUID
JIM DAVIS 3-15

Irma is the waitress at the diner occasionally patronized by Jon and Garfield. Irma is a model waitress, when she isn't abusing her customers or shaving her legs at the counter. But then the food isn't much, either.

BONUS CHARACTER!

LYMAN

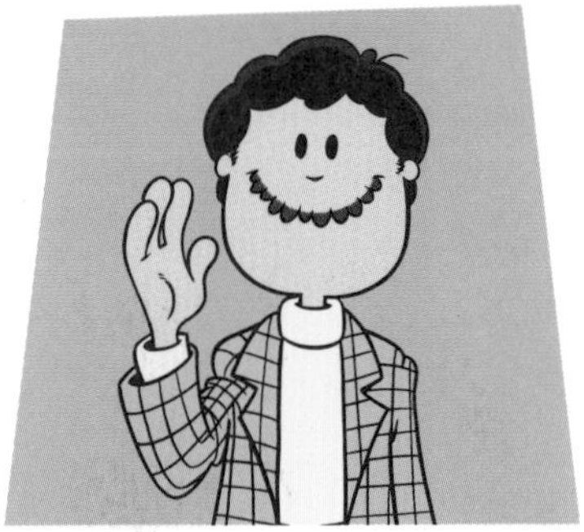

Lyman entered the strip as Jon's roommate and Odie's owner. Lyman's primary function was to give Jon someone to talk to, a role that was gradually assumed by Garfield. Though he reappeared briefly for Garfield's tenth anniversary strip, Lyman's last regular appearance was in 1983. Poor Lyman. Life can be tough for an out-of-work supporting cartoon character. Whatever happened to Lyman? Funny you should ask . . .

TOP TEN EXPLANATIONS FOR LYMAN'S DISAPPEARANCE

10. *Left strip to pursue dream of Olympic figure-skating gold*
9. *Joined CIA, working undercover in Russian comics*
8. *Had lunch with Jimmy Hoffa, and then . . .*
7. *Took role of Elaine on "Taxi"*
6. *Hit on Blondie and Cathy; editors complained; Davis fired him*
5. *Disfigured in drawing accident*
4. *Moved to San Francisco*
3. *Opted for career in hotel/motel management*
2. *Ballooned to 270 pounds; wouldn't fit in cartoon panels*
1. *Don't look in Jon's basement!*

CREATING THE STRIP

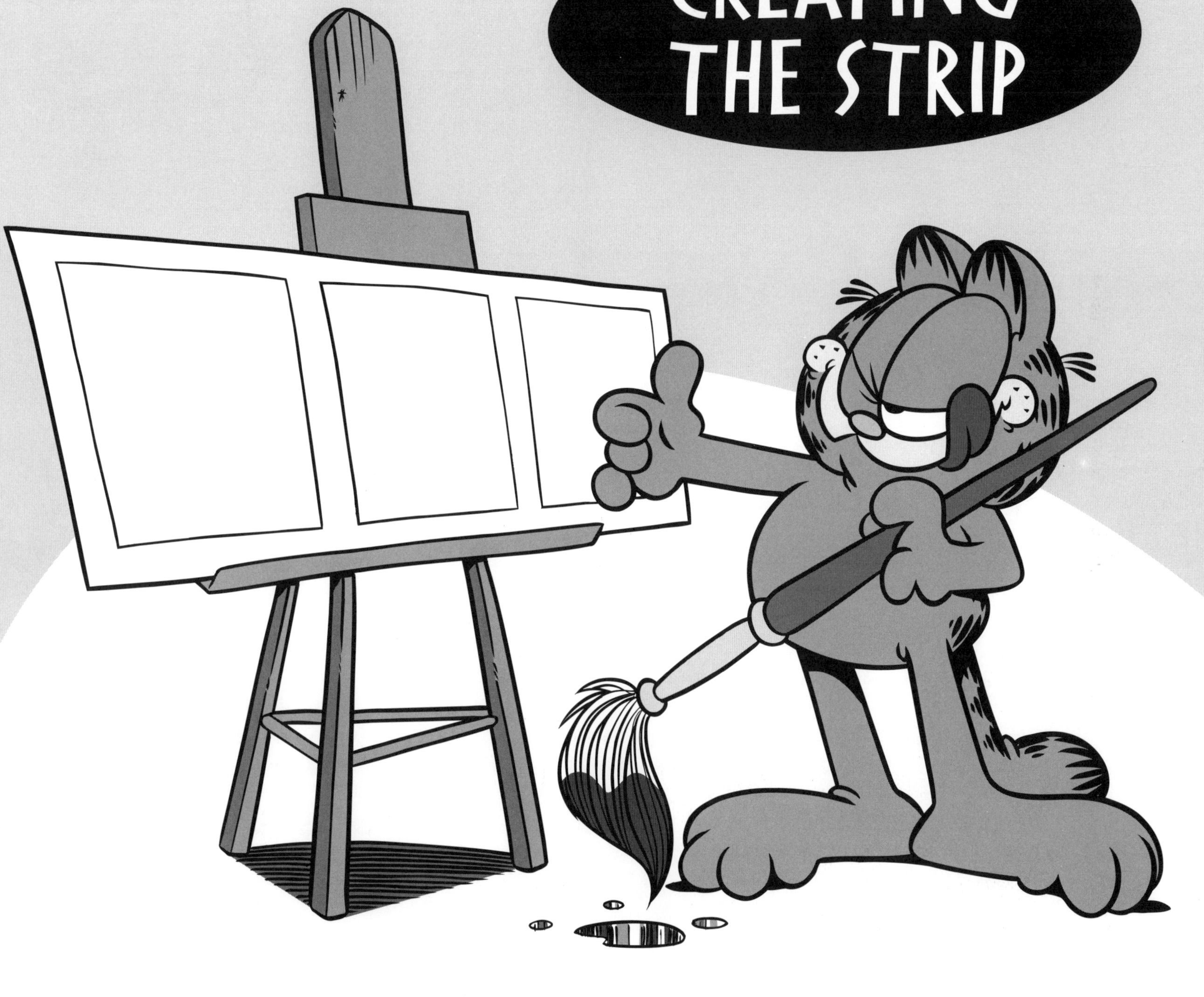

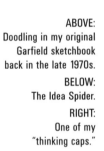

ABOVE:
Doodling in my original Garfield sketchbook back in the late 1970s.
BELOW:
The Idea Spider.
RIGHT:
One of my "thinking caps."

Cartoonists are often asked where they get their ideas. Personally, I buy mine in bulk at the grocery warehouse. Seriously, though, coming up with gags is work. It may be enjoyable work, but it's still work. Of all the many interesting and significant aspects of my job, creating the strip is still the most important.

With all the licensing work, my schedule is pretty busy, but I set aside three consecutive days each month to work on the writing of the *Garfield* strip.

The process begins by reviewing gags with my assistant Brett Koth, a crack (or is that cracked?) Florida cartoonist who flies into Muncie for the monthly idea sessions. We select material from a pile of ideas, and then polish and add to it. As we review gags, Brett and I often use the Idea Spider — a big rubber squeak toy we whack when one of us comes up with a gag.

Sometimes we build a week of strips around a theme, such as sleep, spiders, or diet. Garfield fans like to see Garfield doing Garfield things. If I didn't put him on a diet every now and then, readers would write and complain!

Creating the strip requires a lot of energy and concentration. I tend to pace the floor and drink lots of coffee. I sweat. My pulse races. It's great!

Coming up with gags is like watching a film of Garfield in my head. I visualize Garfield in a given situation. Then I ask myself "Where would he go? What would he say? What would he do?" I watch the story unfold until it ends with something funny, then I back up three frames and cut it off.

During the sessions, we try to stay in a relaxed mood. If you work too hard, the humor will be strained. I try to write only on days when I feel funny. But if we run into a block, we pull out our bag of tricks. Sometimes Brett and I will wear funny hats or play with sound-effect toys. Sometimes I just need a walk in the woods to clear my head.

34

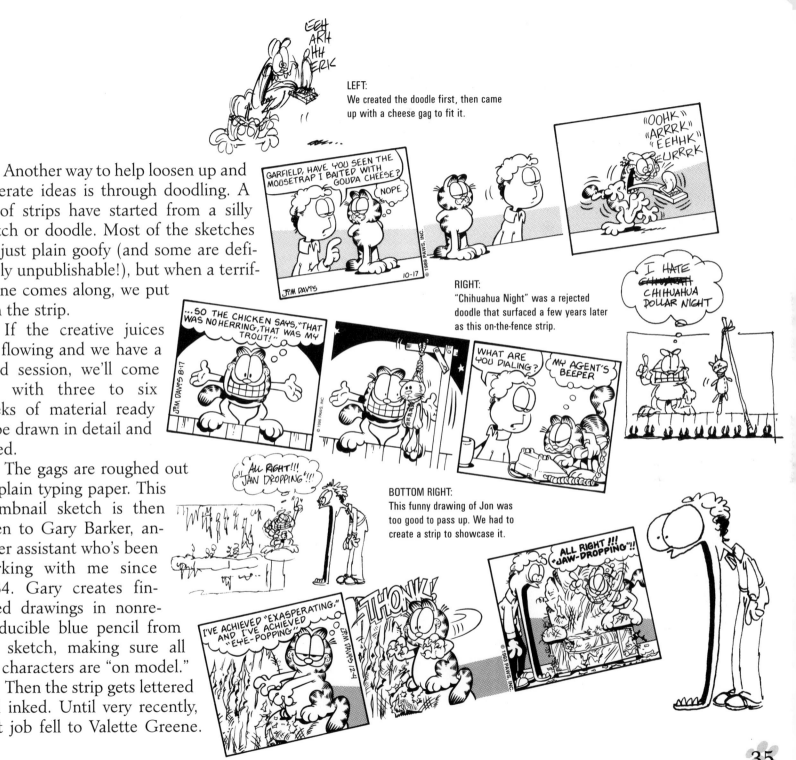

Another way to help loosen up and generate ideas is through doodling. A lot of strips have started from a silly sketch or doodle. Most of the sketches are just plain goofy (and some are definitely unpublishable!), but when a terrific one comes along, we put it in the strip.

If the creative juices are flowing and we have a good session, we'll come out with three to six weeks of material ready to be drawn in detail and inked.

The gags are roughed out on plain typing paper. This thumbnail sketch is then given to Gary Barker, another assistant who's been working with me since 1984. Gary creates finished drawings in nonreproducible blue pencil from the sketch, making sure all the characters are "on model."

Then the strip gets lettered and inked. Until very recently, that job fell to Valette Greene.

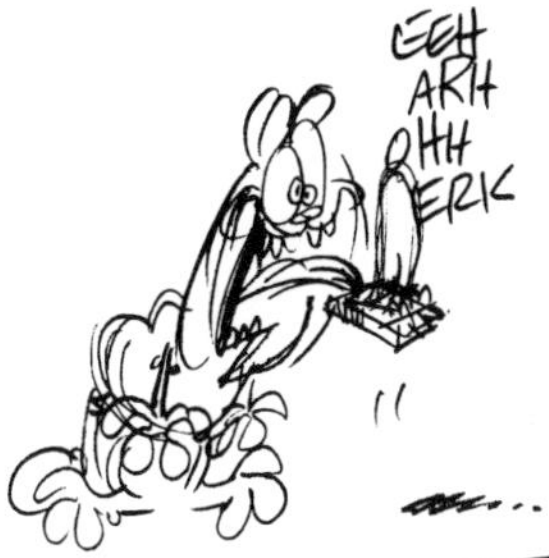
EEH
ARH
OHH
ERK

LEFT:
We created the doodle first, then came up with a cheese gag to fit it.

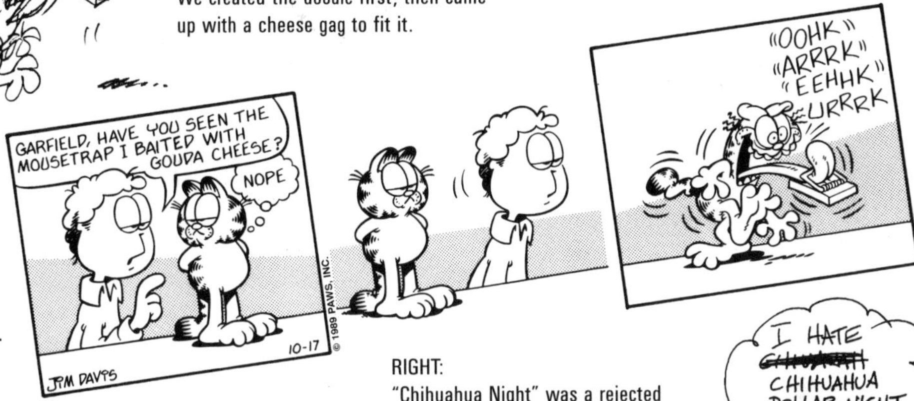
GARFIELD, HAVE YOU SEEN THE MOUSETRAP I BAITED WITH GOUDA CHEESE?
NOPE
"OOHK"
"ARRRK"
"EEHHK"
URRRK
JPM DAVPS 10-17
© 1989 PAWS, INC.

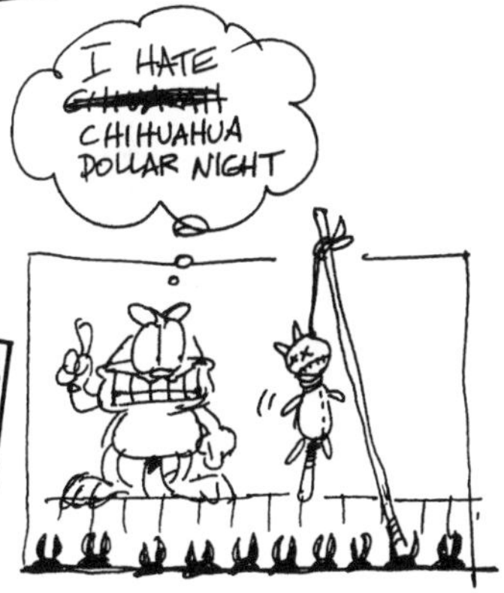
I HATE CHIHUAHUA DOLLAR NIGHT

RIGHT:
"Chihuahua Night" was a rejected doodle that surfaced a few years later as this on-the-fence strip.

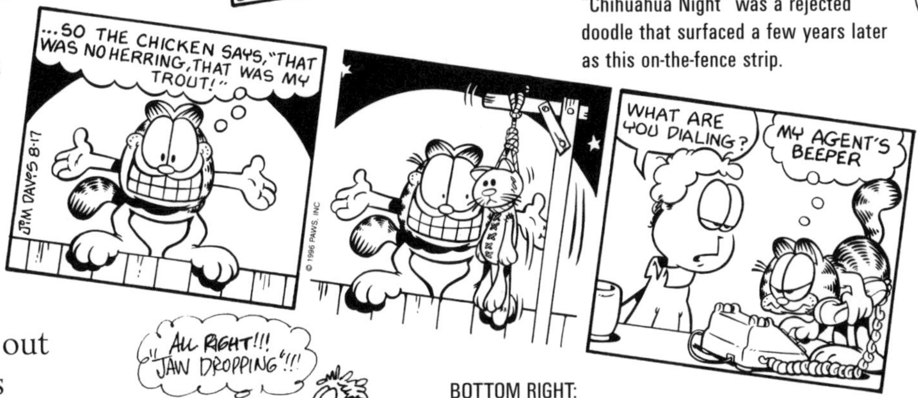
...SO THE CHICKEN SAYS, "THAT WAS NO HERRING, THAT WAS MY TROUT!"
JPM DAVPS 8-17
© 1996 PAWS, INC.
WHAT ARE YOU DIALING?
MY AGENT'S BEEPER

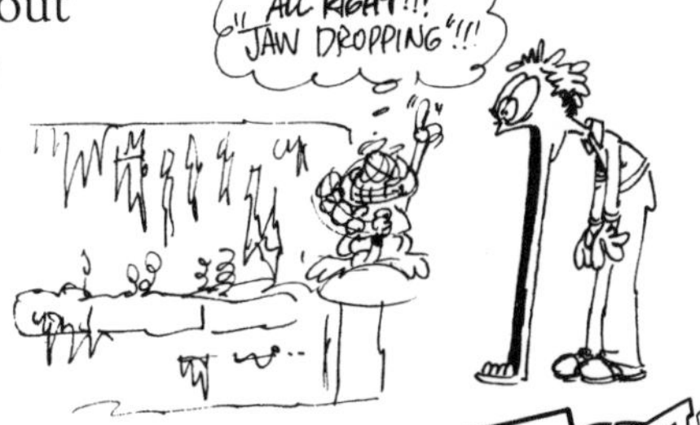
"ALL RIGHT!!! JAW DROPPING"!!!

BOTTOM RIGHT:
This funny drawing of Jon was too good to pass up. We had to create a strip to showcase it.

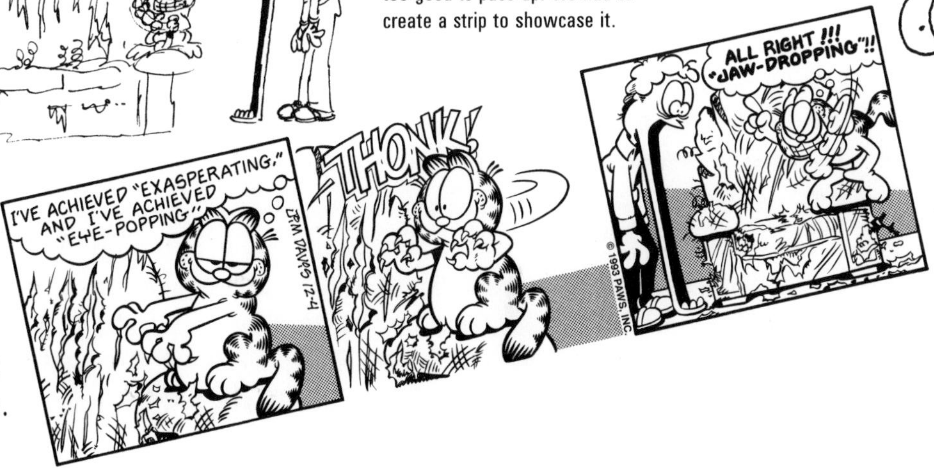
I'VE ACHIEVED "EXASPERATING," AND I'VE ACHIEVED "EYE-POPPING"
JPM DAVPS 12-4
THONK!
ALL RIGHT!!! "JAW-DROPPING"!!
© 1993 PAWS, INC.

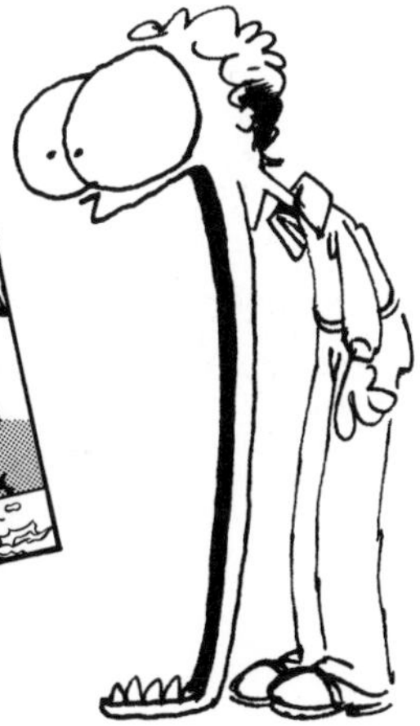

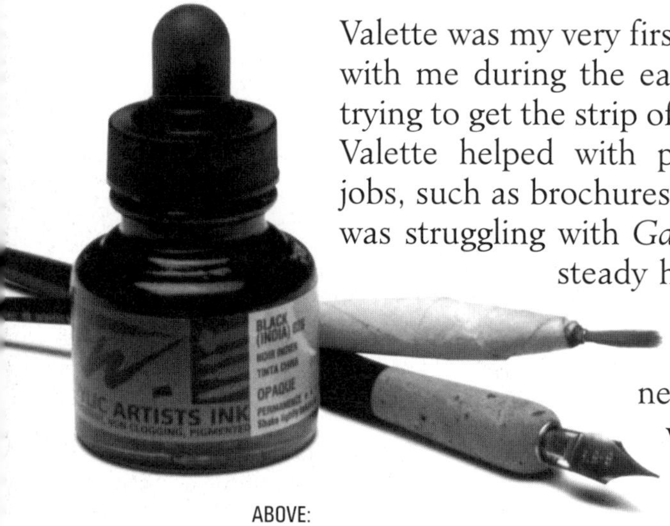
ARTISTS INK
BLACK (INDIA)
OPAQUE

Valette was my very first assistant — she was with me during the early days, when I was trying to get the strip off the ground. Initially Valette helped with pasteup on freelance jobs, such as brochures and catalogs, when I was struggling with *Garfield*. Eventually her steady hand won her the job of inker and letterer for *Garfield*. For nearly twenty years, she was the only artist besides me to ink and letter the strip. In 1997, Valette decided to hang up her sable brush, and she retired. Now inking chores are divided between Lori Barker and Larry Fentz. Lettering and coloring are handled by Eric Reaves (who also assists in bluelining the strip). As you can see, it takes more than one hand to help our flabby tabby into the funny papers.

ABOVE: Tools of the trade; we wrap masking tape around the barrel of the brush for a better grip.
RIGHT: Hot off the presses!

Once the strip is inked and completed, I check it over one final time, then sign and date it.

We work several months ahead, so that the newspapers can meet their deadlines. A typical daily strip is finished eight weeks before it appears in the paper; a Sunday strip must be done at least twelve weeks in ad-

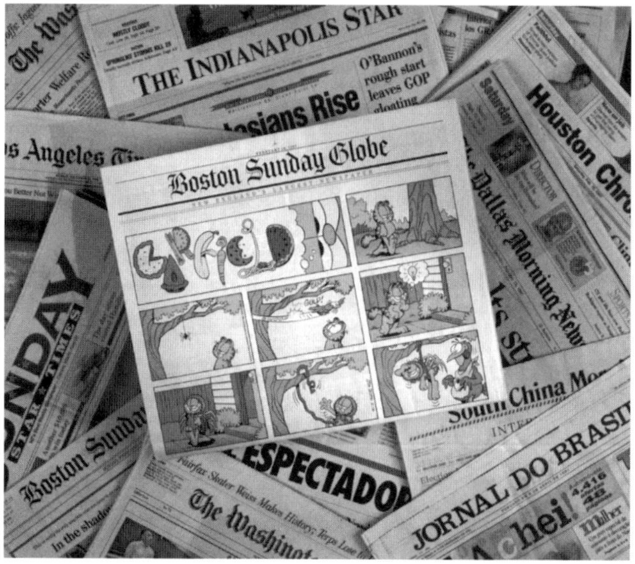
THE INDIANAPOLIS
Boston Sunday Globe
GARFIELD

vance. That means a strip about Christmas must be drawn in September! (It's a good thing Garfield is always in the mood for presents!)

Today, *Garfield* appears in over 2,500 newspapers (quite a difference from 41 papers in 1978!) in 87 countries, and I'm very much aware of the millions of fat cat fans who don't speak English. I'm careful to avoid puns, plays on words, and colloquialisms that are often impossible to translate from one language to another. Fortunately, cats are the same everywhere. So in any language, "Garfield" means "fat" — I mean, "fun."

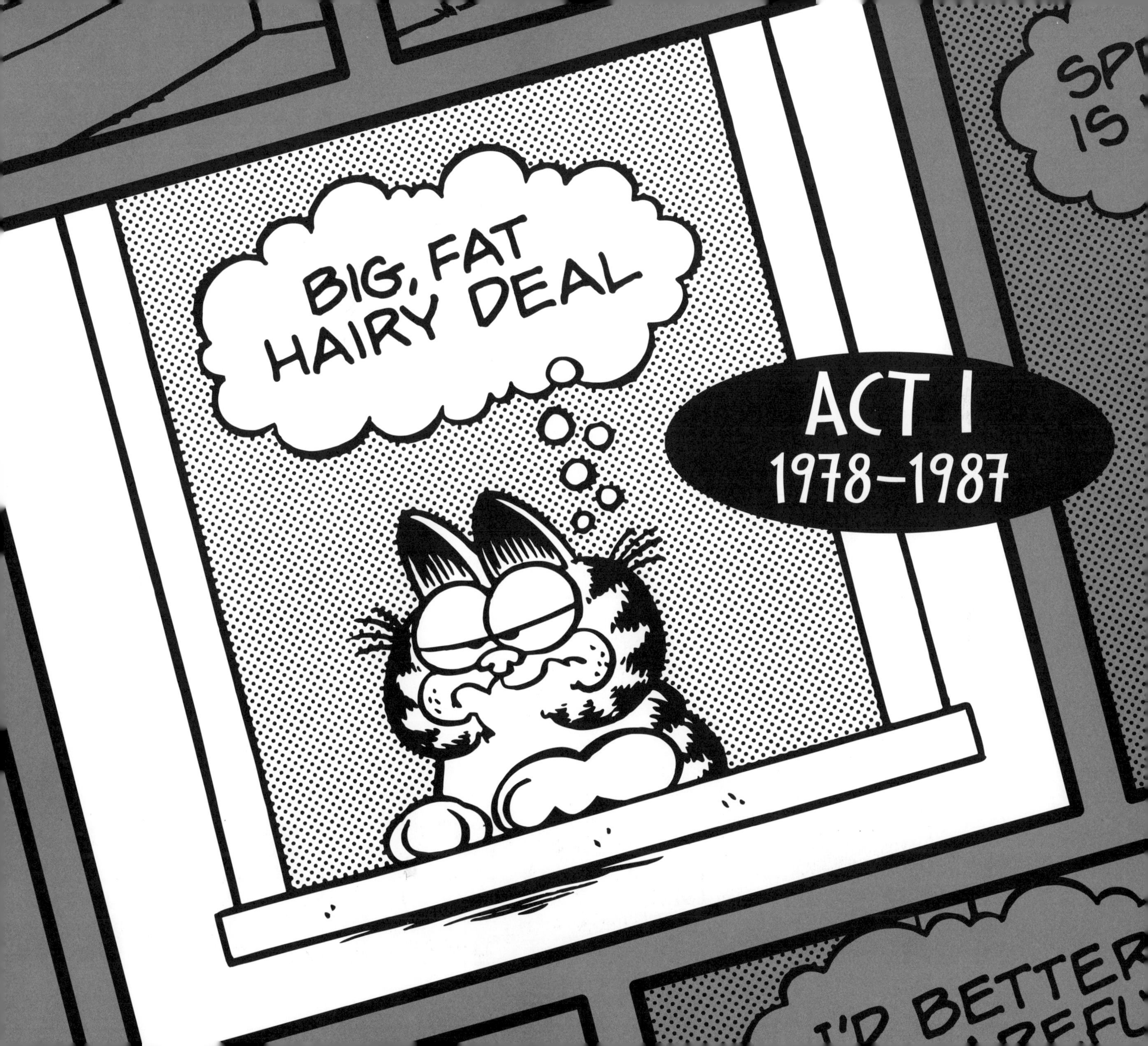
BIG, FAT HAIRY DEAL
ACT I
1978–1987

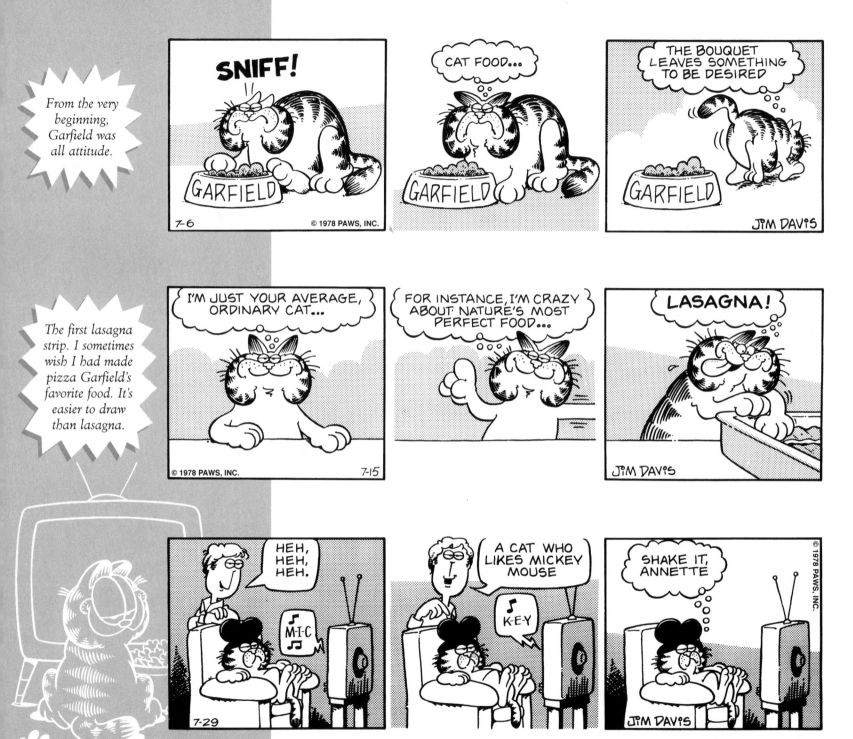

From the very beginning, Garfield was all attitude.

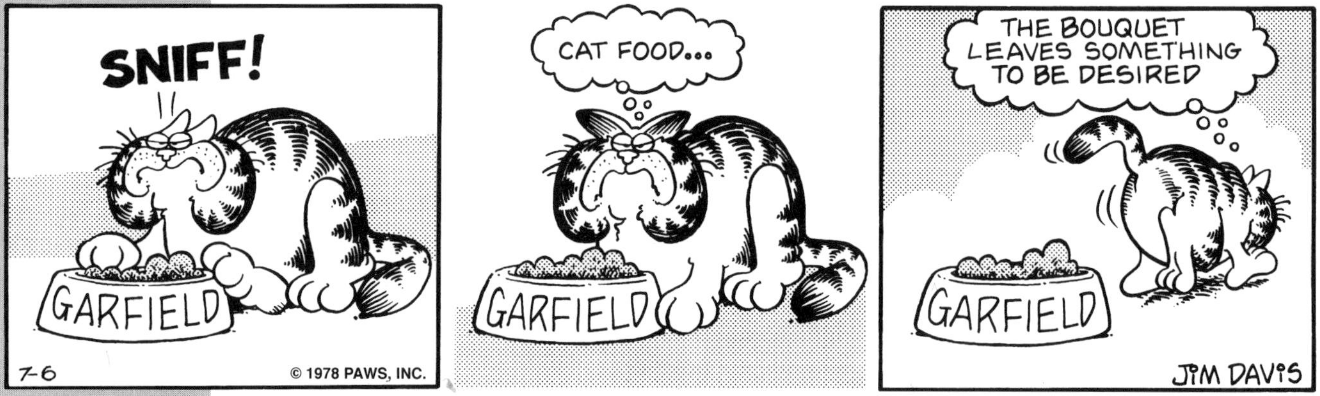
SNIFF!
GARFIELD
7-6
© 1978 PAWS, INC.
CAT FOOD...
GARFIELD
THE BOUQUET LEAVES SOMETHING TO BE DESIRED
GARFIELD
JIM DAVIS

The first lasagna strip. I sometimes wish I had made pizza Garfield's favorite food. It's easier to draw than lasagna.

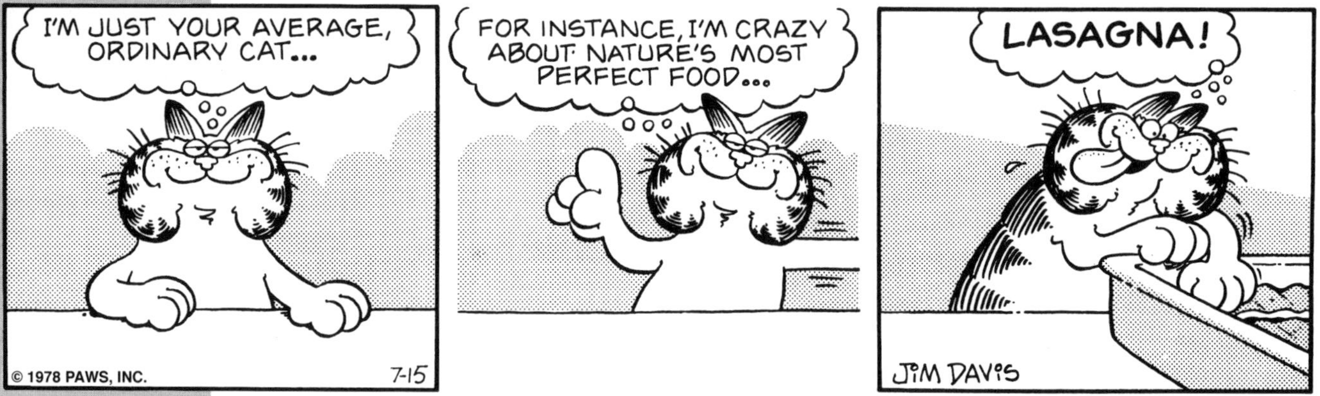
I'M JUST YOUR AVERAGE, ORDINARY CAT...
© 1978 PAWS, INC.
7-15
FOR INSTANCE, I'M CRAZY ABOUT NATURE'S MOST PERFECT FOOD...
LASAGNA!
JIM DAVIS

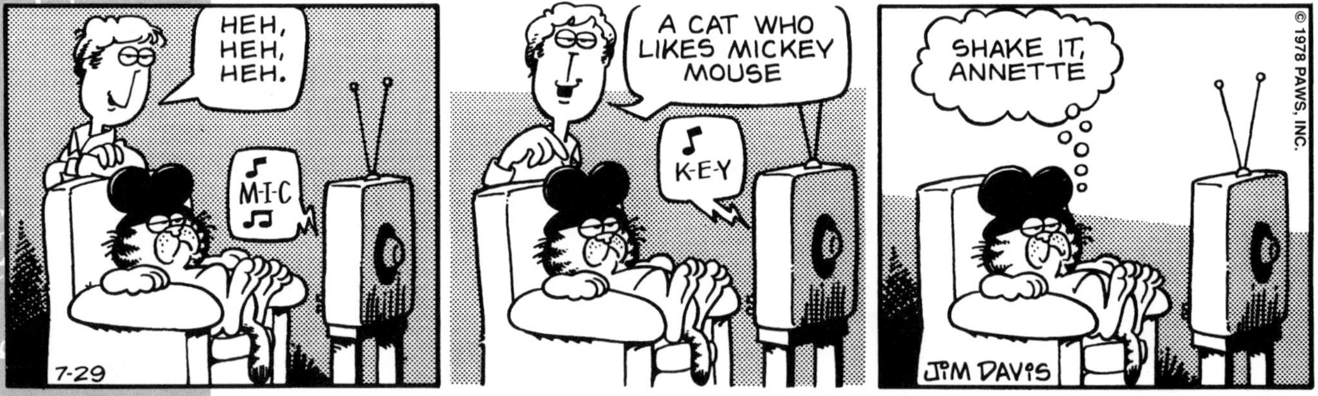
HEH, HEH, HEH.
M-I-C
7-29
A CAT WHO LIKES MICKEY MOUSE
K-E-Y
SHAKE IT, ANNETTE
JIM DAVIS
© 1978 PAWS, INC.

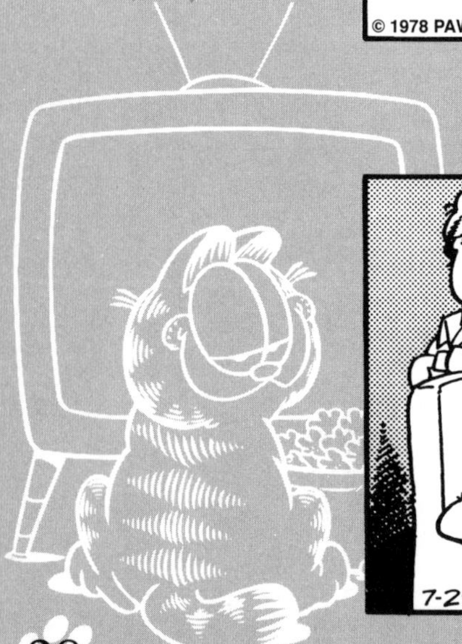

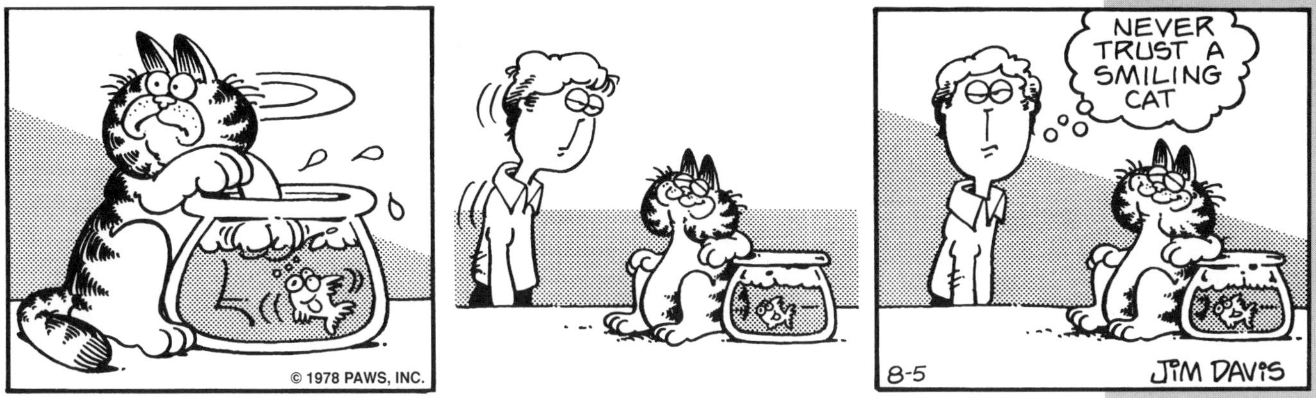

© 1978 PAWS, INC.
NEVER TRUST A SMILING CAT
8-5
JIM DAVIS

FAT CAT FACTOID

~1978~

Morris the cat passes away at the age of 17.

Garfield makes his debut on June 19 in 41 U.S. newspapers!

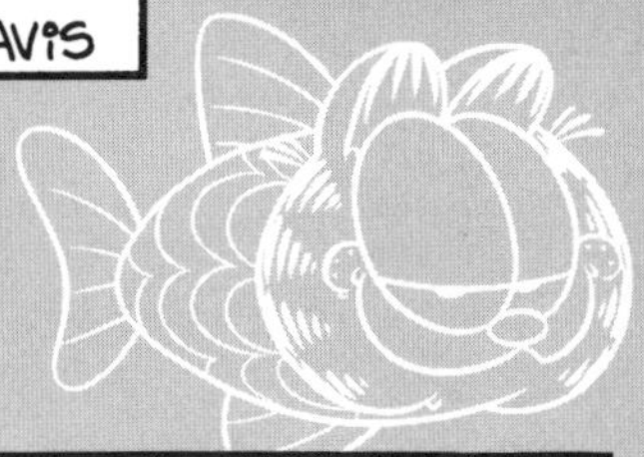

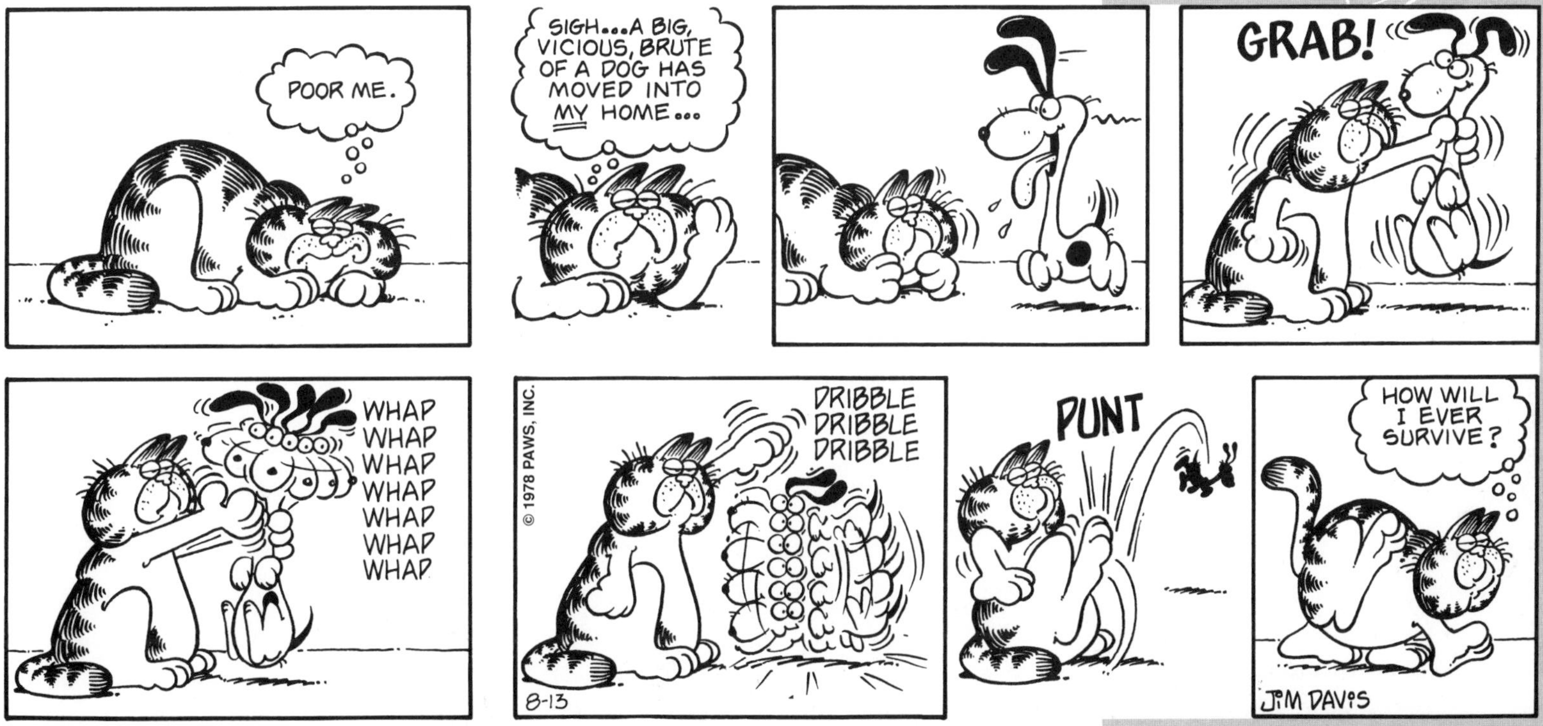

POOR ME.
SIGH...A BIG, VICIOUS, BRUTE OF A DOG HAS MOVED INTO MY HOME...
GRAB!
WHAP WHAP WHAP WHAP WHAP WHAP WHAP
© 1978 PAWS, INC.
DRIBBLE DRIBBLE DRIBBLE
PUNT
HOW WILL I EVER SURVIVE?
8-13
JIM DAVIS

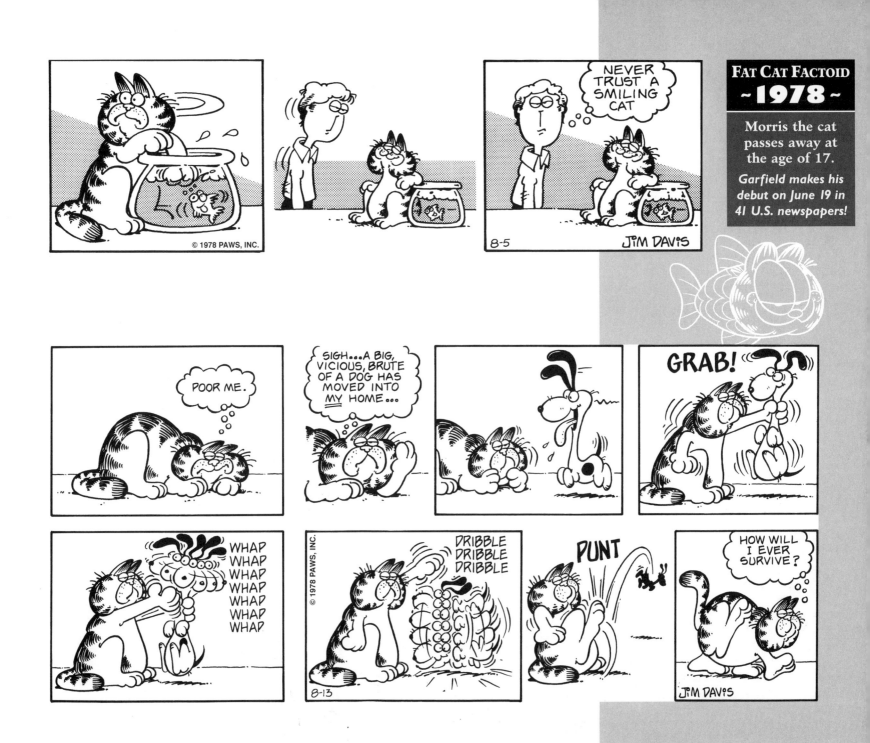

FIRST DIET STRIP!

SO I'M ON A DIET... BIG DEAL
© 1978 PAWS, INC.
8-30
YOU KNOW WHAT A "DIET" IS, DON'T YOU?
IT'S "DIE" WITH A "T," THAT'S WHAT IT IS!
JIM DAVIS

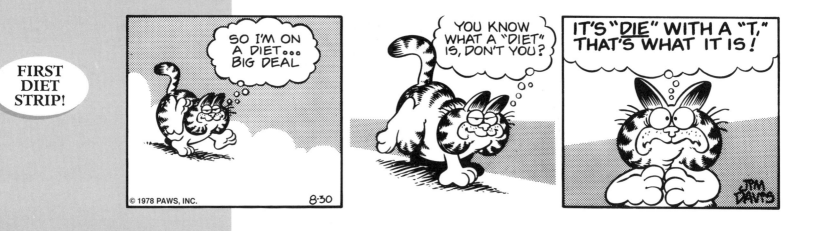

GARFIELD ON MORNINGS

Here's what Garfield has to say about mornings . . .

I'd like mornings better if they started later.

I'll rise, but I won't shine.

The early bird is insane.

Start each day with a smile and get it over with.

Waking up is hard to do.

"Good morning" is a contradiction in terms.

MORNINGS SURE ARE PEACEFUL
JIM DAVIS 9-16
© 1991 PAWS, INC.
CLANG
SPLOT!
RIGHT UP TO ABOUT THIS TIME EVERY DAY

I HATE MORNINGS. THEY START TOO EARLY IN THE DAY
I HEREBY DECLARE THAT MORNINGS SHALL NOT START UNTIL NOON
SCRATCH SCRATCH
© 1993 PAWS, INC.
LUNCH TIME
TAKE THAT AWAY AND BRING ME BREAKFAST
JIM DAVIS 4-12

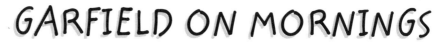

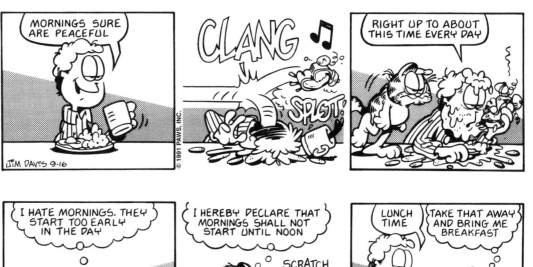

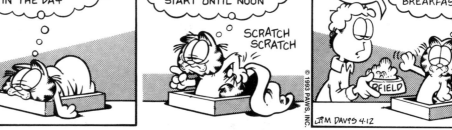

FIRST MONDAY STRIP!

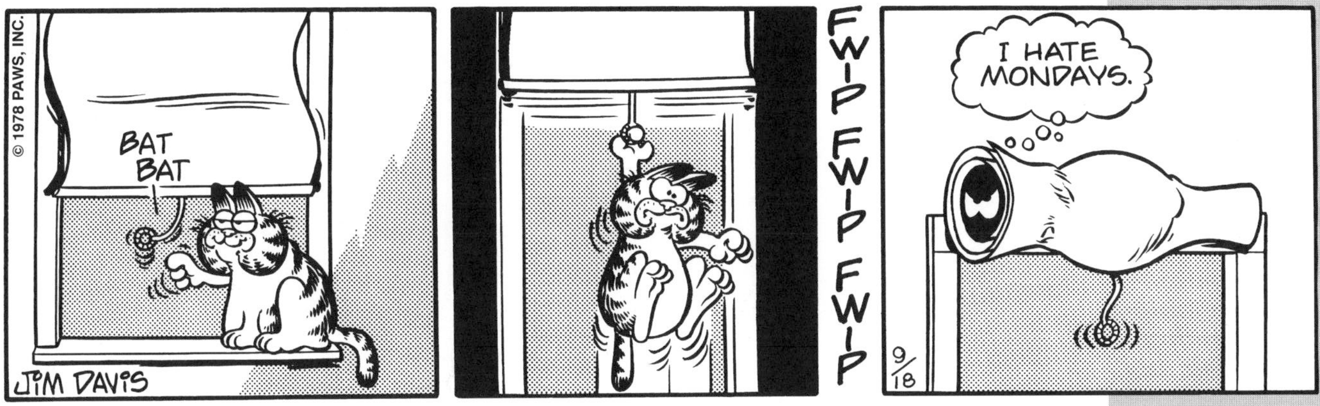
© 1978 PAWS, INC.
BAT BAT
JIM DAVIS
FWIP FWIP FWIP FWIP
I HATE MONDAYS.
9/18

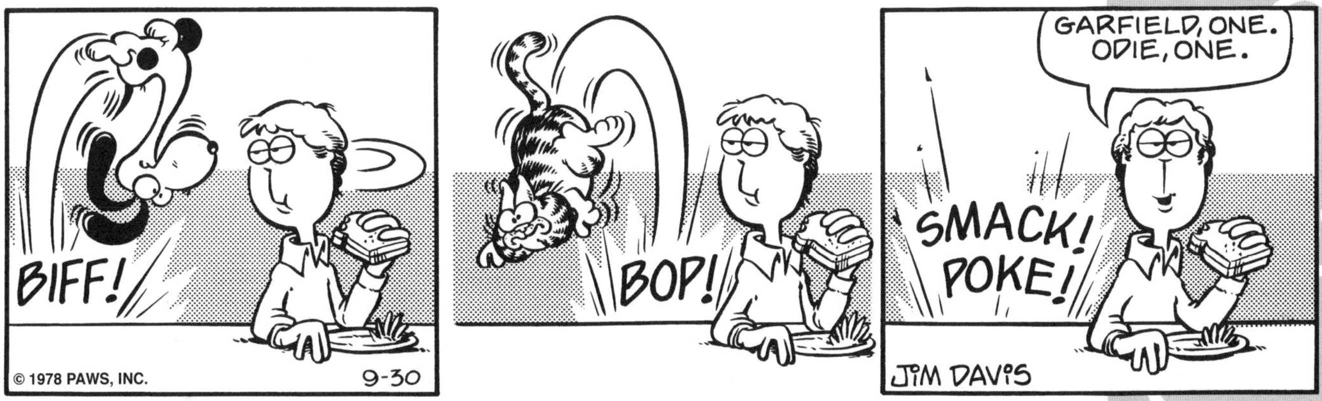
BIFF!
© 1978 PAWS, INC.
9-30
BOP!
GARFIELD, ONE. ODIE, ONE.
SMACK! POKE!
JIM DAVIS

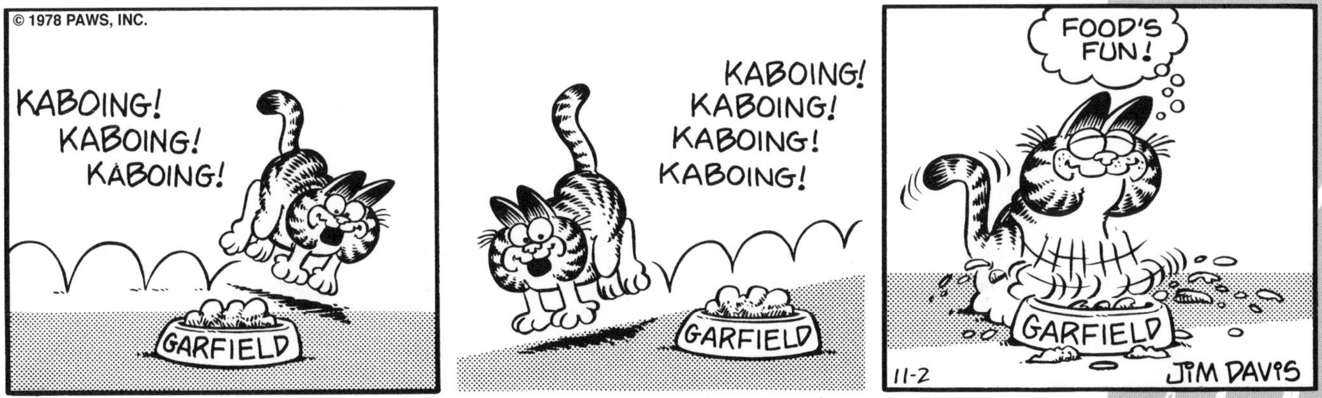
© 1978 PAWS, INC.
KABOING! KABOING! KABOING!
GARFIELD
KABOING! KABOING! KABOING! KABOING!
GARFIELD
FOOD'S FUN!
GARFIELD
11-2
JIM DAVIS

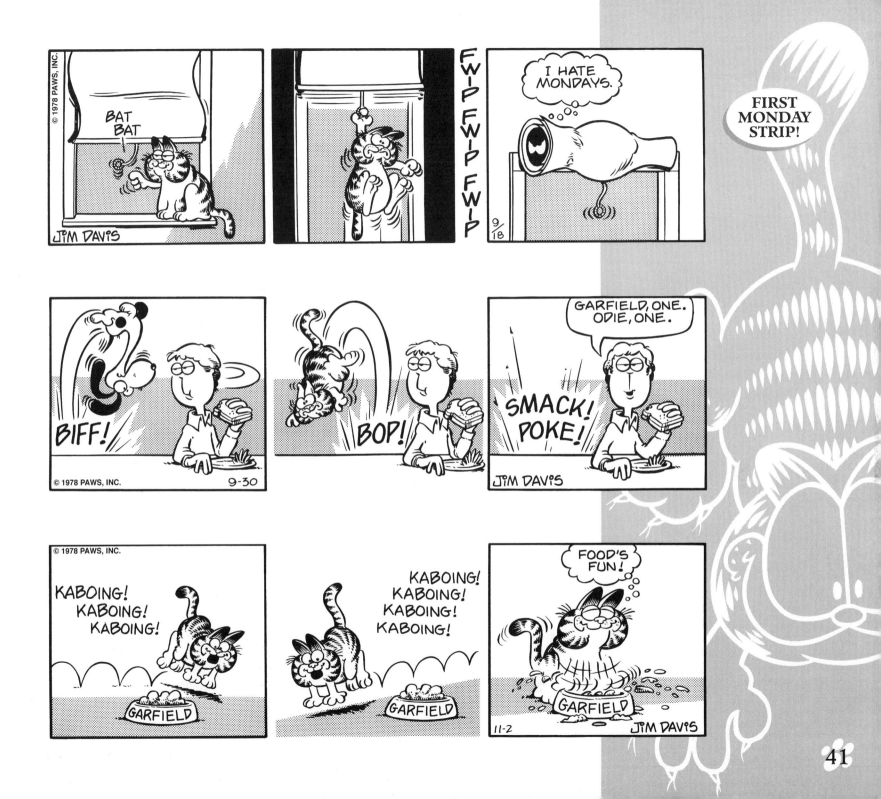

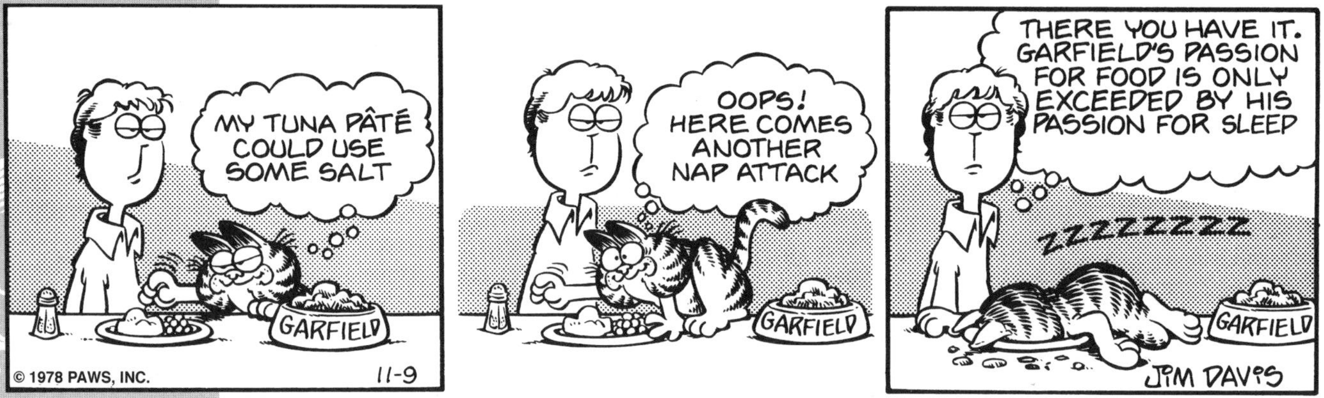
MY TUNA PÂTÉ COULD USE SOME SALT
GARFIELD
© 1978 PAWS, INC.
11-9
OOPS! HERE COMES ANOTHER NAP ATTACK
GARFIELD
THERE YOU HAVE IT. GARFIELD'S PASSION FOR FOOD IS ONLY EXCEEDED BY HIS PASSION FOR SLEEP
ZZZZZZZZ
GARFIELD
JIM DAVIS

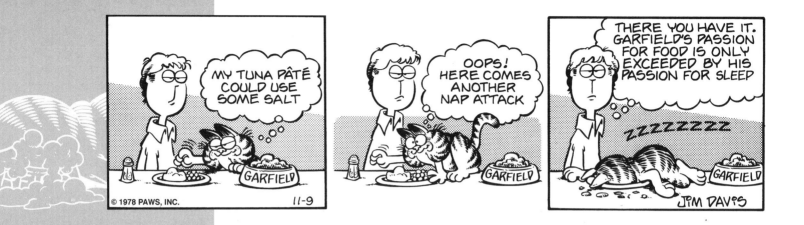

GARFIELD WEIGHS IN

Garfield's idea of a "weight problem" is having a fork that's so full he can't lift it. Still, every now and then Garfield has to face the fat facts, usually put to him in the unkindest way by his talking bathroom scale. This electronic nemesis has launched numerous jabs at Garfield's flab over the years. But no matter how witty the scale is, it can't win; it still winds up with a fat cat standing on its face.

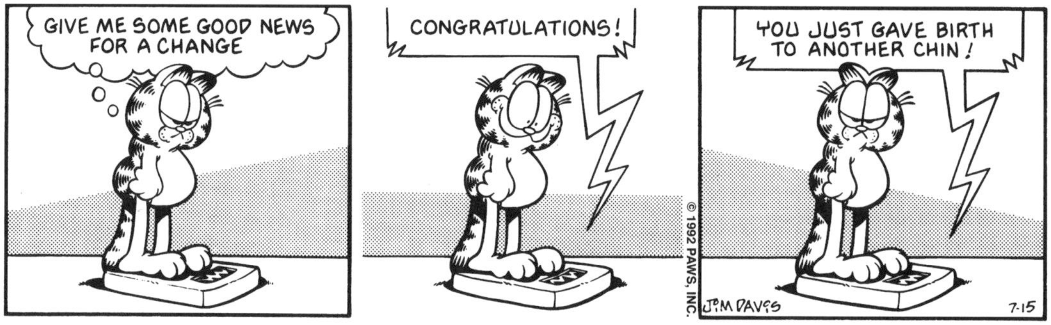
GIVE ME SOME GOOD NEWS FOR A CHANGE
CONGRATULATIONS!
© 1992 PAWS, INC.
YOU JUST GAVE BIRTH TO ANOTHER CHIN!
JIM DAVIS
7-15

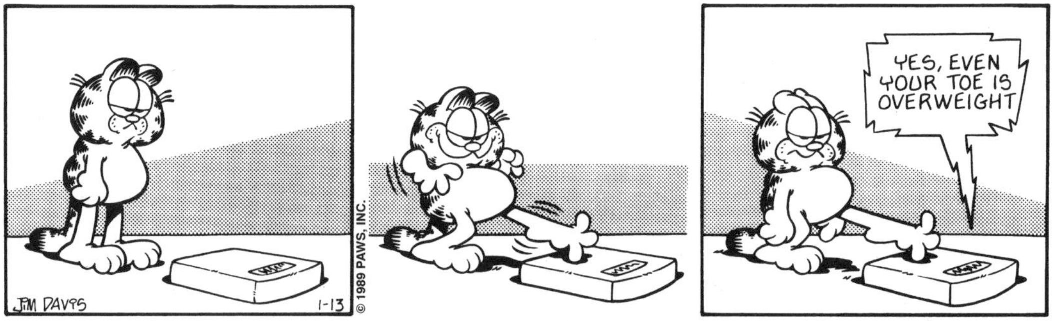
JIM DAVIS
1-13
© 1989 PAWS, INC.
YES, EVEN YOUR TOE IS OVERWEIGHT

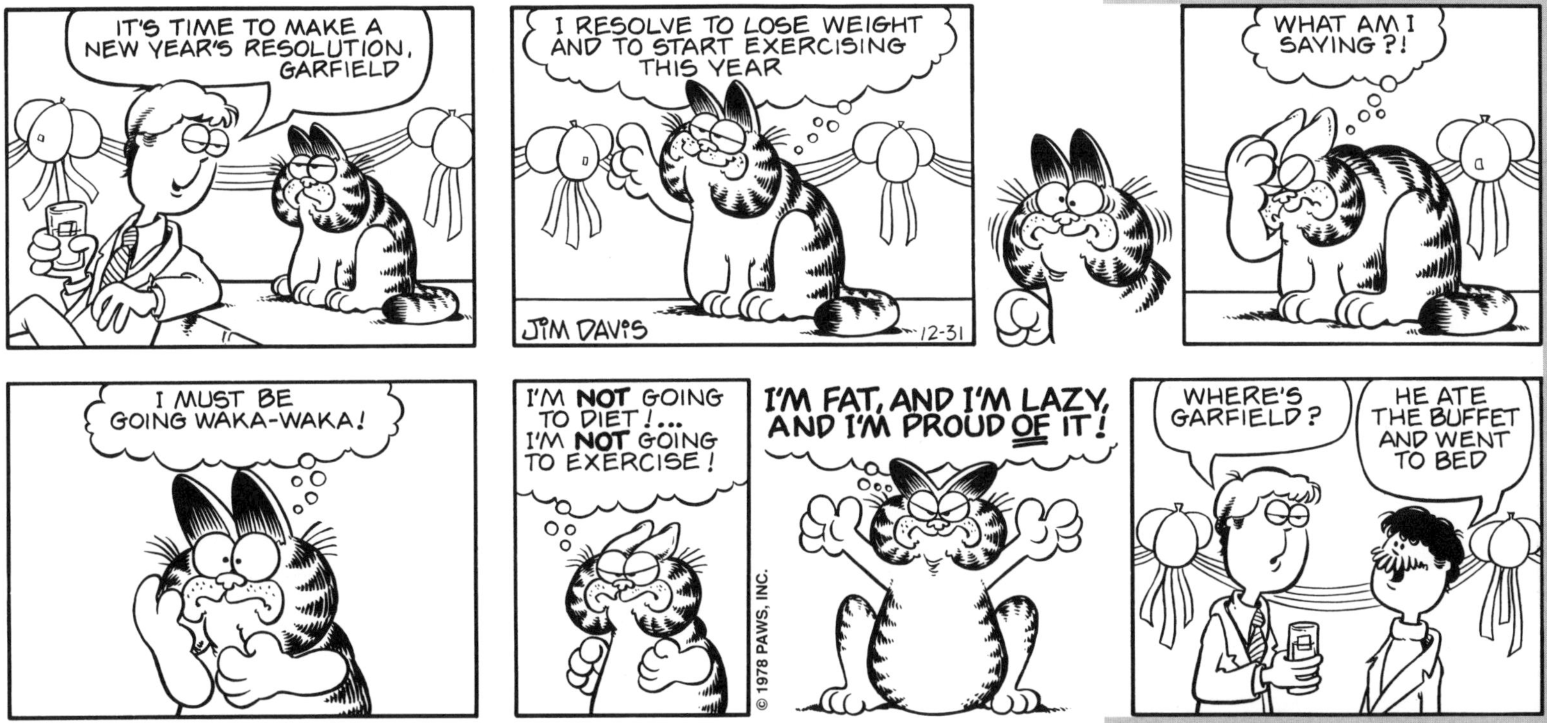
IT'S TIME TO MAKE A NEW YEAR'S RESOLUTION, GARFIELD
I RESOLVE TO LOSE WEIGHT AND TO START EXERCISING THIS YEAR
JIM DAVIS
12-31
WHAT AM I SAYING ?!
I MUST BE GOING WAKA-WAKA!
I'M **NOT** GOING TO DIET!... I'M **NOT** GOING TO EXERCISE!
© 1978 PAWS, INC.
I'M FAT, AND I'M LAZY, AND I'M PROUD OF IT!
WHERE'S GARFIELD?
HE ATE THE BUFFET AND WENT TO BED

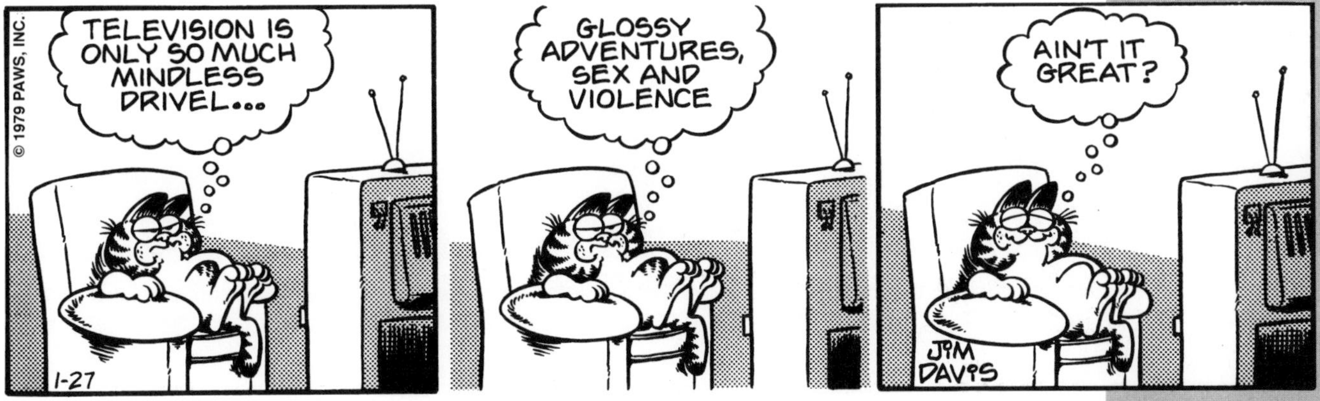
© 1979 PAWS, INC.
TELEVISION IS ONLY SO MUCH MINDLESS DRIVEL...
1-27
GLOSSY ADVENTURES, SEX AND VIOLENCE
AIN'T IT GREAT?
JIM DAVIS

Above: *Garfield's comfortable with who he is.*

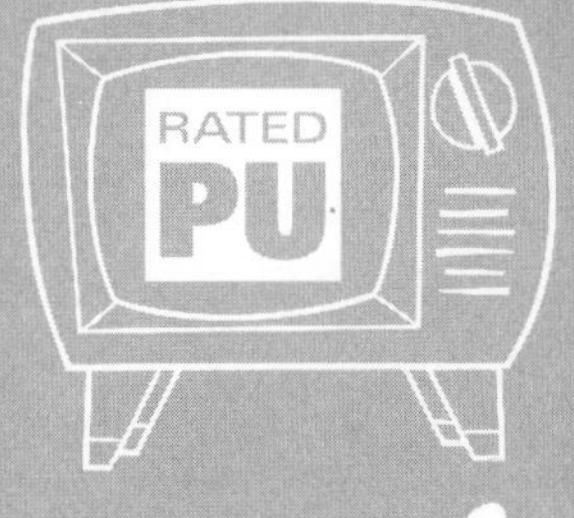
RATED
PU

FAT CAT FACTOID

~1979~

Hit songs of the year include "Le Freak," "Hot Stuff," and "Y.M.C.A."

Less than one year after his debut, Garfield appears in over 100 newspapers!

LET'S GO FOR A WALK, LITTLE FELLA
2-23
SMACK!
© 1979 PAWS, INC.
WELL, I'LL BE. POOKY DOESN'T LIKE DOGS EITHER
JIM DAVIS

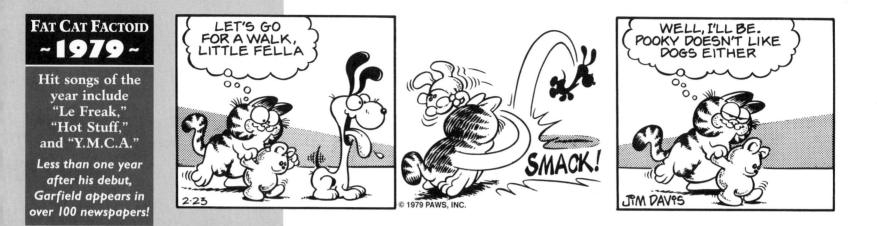

GARFIELD'S EATING TIPS

Never put off till tomorrow what you can eat today.

Eat every meal as if it were your last.

Chew your food at least once.

Avoid fruits and nuts. After all, you are what you eat.

Snack only between meals.

Don't save your dessert for last. Eat it first.

GOOD MORNING, FELLOW FOOD FREAKS
© 1989 PAWS, INC.
DINING ETIQUETTE RULE NUMBER ONE...
NEVER STAND IN A WARM PIZZA
JIM DAVIS
8-5

THERE OUGHT TO BE A PRIZE FOR EATING EVERY SCRAP OF FOOD IN THE HOUSE
© 1991 PAWS, INC.
OH WELL
JIM DAVIS 9-5
I GUESS A JOB WELL DONE IS ITS OWN REWARD

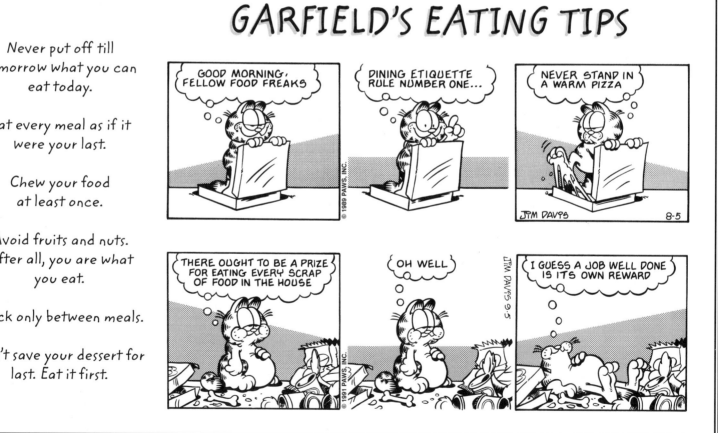

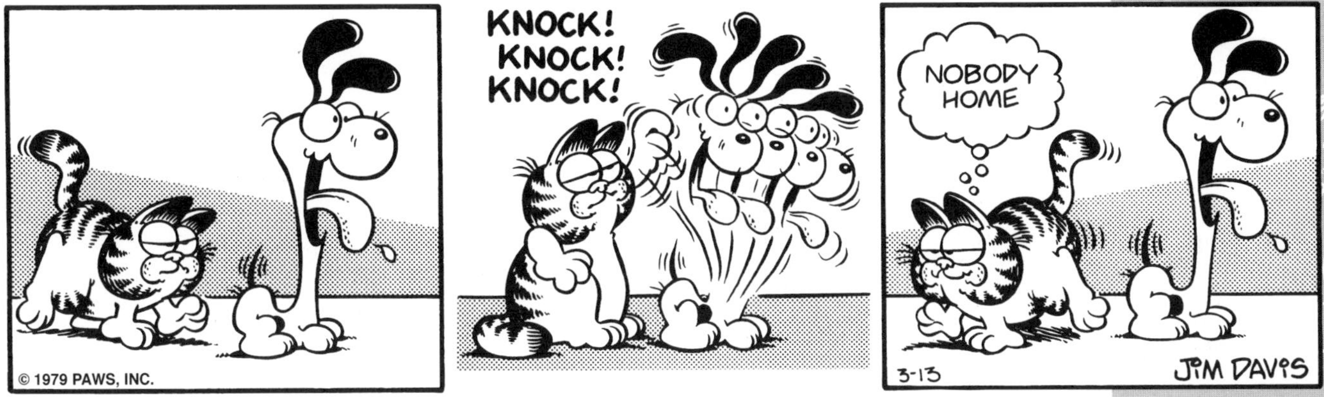
© 1979 PAWS, INC.
KNOCK! KNOCK! KNOCK!
NOBODY HOME
3-13
JIM DAVIS

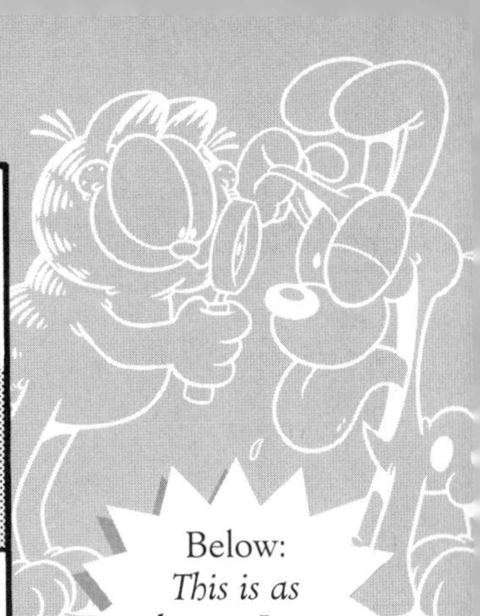

Below:
This is as close as I ever come to social commentary. I couldn't resist the urge.

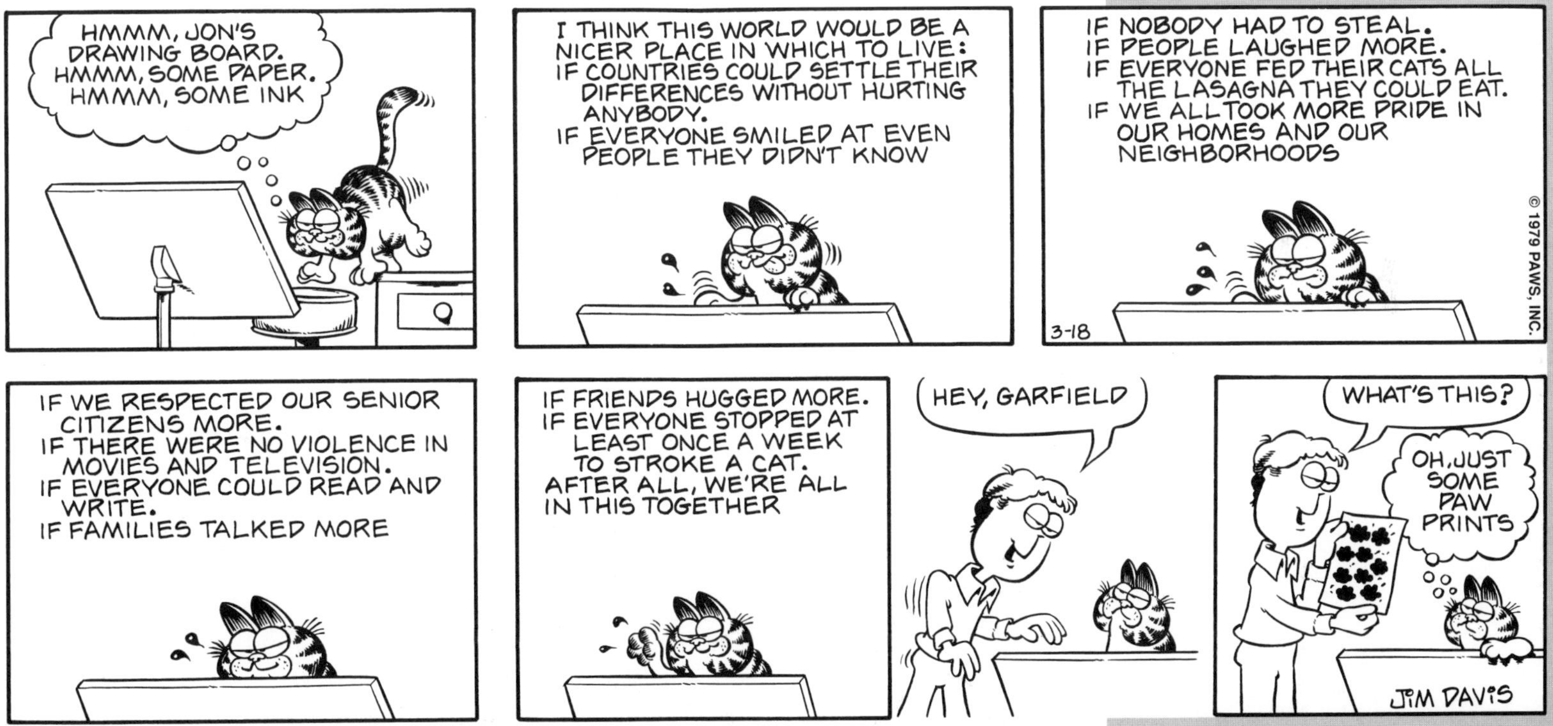
HMMM, JON'S DRAWING BOARD. HMMM, SOME PAPER. HMMM, SOME INK
I THINK THIS WORLD WOULD BE A NICER PLACE IN WHICH TO LIVE: IF COUNTRIES COULD SETTLE THEIR DIFFERENCES WITHOUT HURTING ANYBODY. IF EVERYONE SMILED AT EVEN PEOPLE THEY DIDN'T KNOW
IF NOBODY HAD TO STEAL. IF PEOPLE LAUGHED MORE. IF EVERYONE FED THEIR CATS ALL THE LASAGNA THEY COULD EAT. IF WE ALL TOOK MORE PRIDE IN OUR HOMES AND OUR NEIGHBORHOODS
3-18
© 1979 PAWS, INC.
IF WE RESPECTED OUR SENIOR CITIZENS MORE. IF THERE WERE NO VIOLENCE IN MOVIES AND TELEVISION. IF EVERYONE COULD READ AND WRITE. IF FAMILIES TALKED MORE
IF FRIENDS HUGGED MORE. IF EVERYONE STOPPED AT LEAST ONCE A WEEK TO STROKE A CAT. AFTER ALL, WE'RE ALL IN THIS TOGETHER
HEY, GARFIELD
WHAT'S THIS?
OH, JUST SOME PAW PRINTS
JIM DAVIS

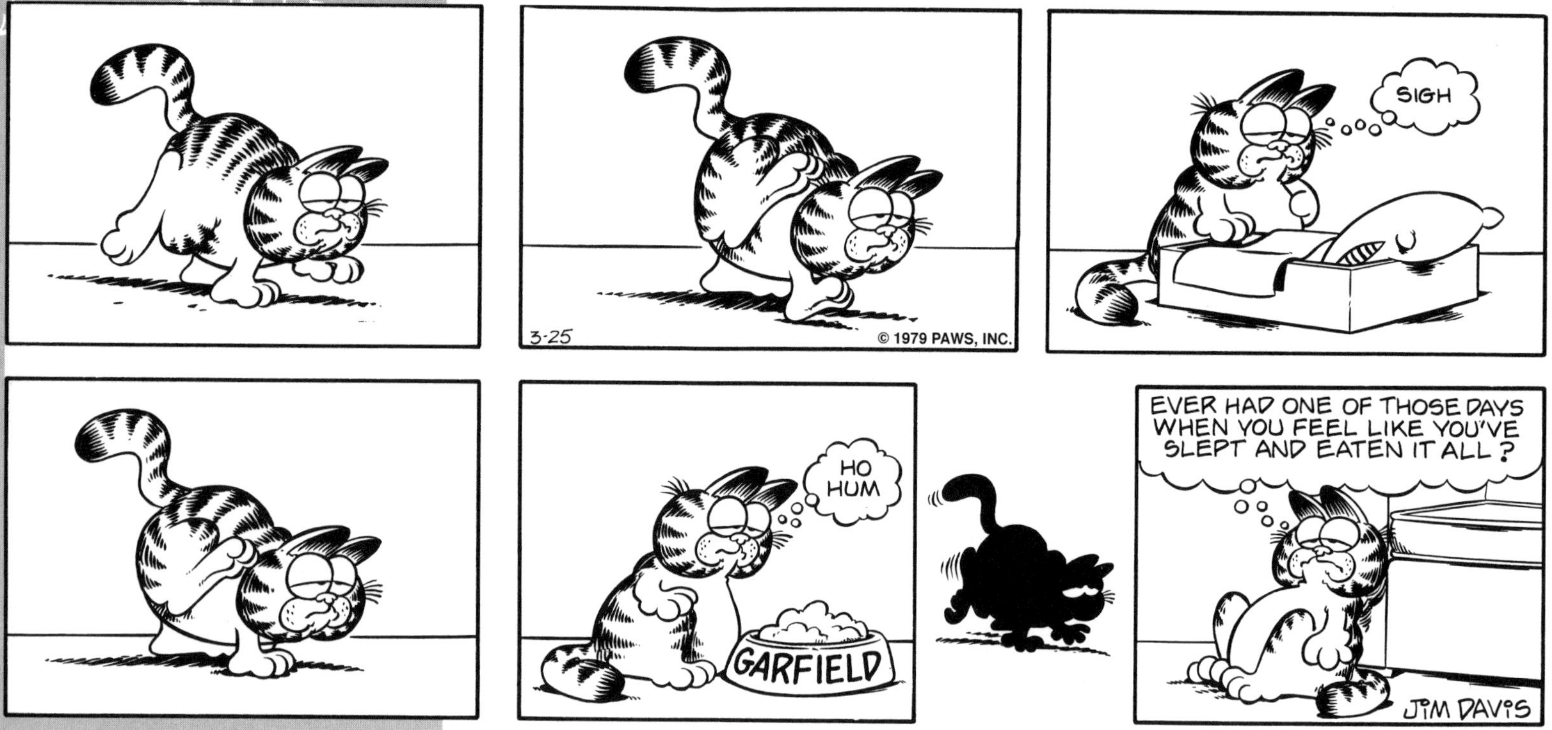
3-25
© 1979 PAWS, INC.
SIGH
HO HUM
GARFIELD
EVER HAD ONE OF THOSE DAYS WHEN YOU FEEL LIKE YOU'VE SLEPT AND EATEN IT ALL?
JIM DAVIS

I wrote this poem in college. I always looked for an excuse to use it.

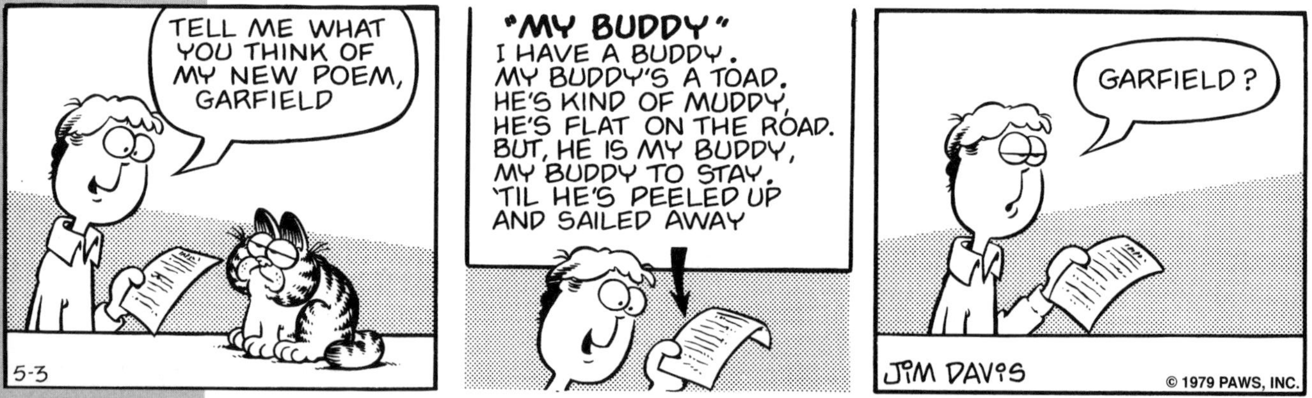
TELL ME WHAT YOU THINK OF MY NEW POEM, GARFIELD
5-3
"MY BUDDY"
I HAVE A BUDDY.
MY BUDDY'S A TOAD.
HE'S KIND OF MUDDY,
HE'S FLAT ON THE ROAD.
BUT, HE IS MY BUDDY,
MY BUDDY TO STAY.
'TIL HE'S PEELED UP
AND SAILED AWAY
GARFIELD?
JIM DAVIS
© 1979 PAWS, INC.

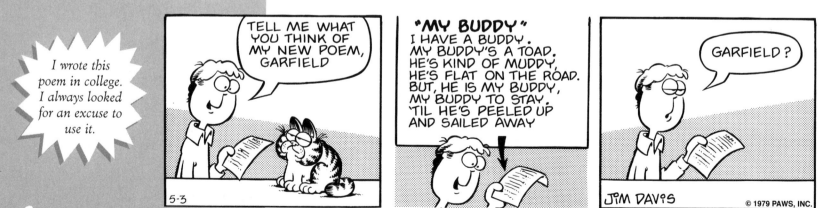

GOBBLE! GOBBLE!

WITH ALL RESPECT TO WILL ROGERS

I NEVER MET A LASAGNA I DIDN'T LIKE

© 1979 PAWS, INC.

JIM DAVIS

5-9

GARFIELD'S DIET TIPS

GARFIELD! WHAT ARE YOU DOING?

UH... PUSH-UPS?

GARFIE

JIM DAVIS 1-12

© 1988 PAWS, INC.

THE VET PUT YOU ON A DIET

I WANT A SECOND OPINION

GARFIE

HOW ABOUT A NICE LEAF OF LETTUCE?

PLEASE! IF I LAUGH I MIGHT SNORT AN ANCHOVY!

GARFIE

COOKIE CRUMB!

JIM DAVIS 7-23

© 1992 PAWS, INC.

BANZAI!

COME TO PAPA!

DIET GETTING TO YOU, GARFIELD?

Here are some of Garfield's words to the wide:

Never go back for seconds. Get it all the first time.

Set your scale back five pounds. On second thought, make it ten.

Vegetables are a must. I recommend carrot cake and pumpkin pie.

Never start a diet cold turkey. (Maybe cold roast beef, cold pizza . . .).

Try to cut back. Leave the cherry off your hot fudge sundae.

Hang around people who are fatter than you.

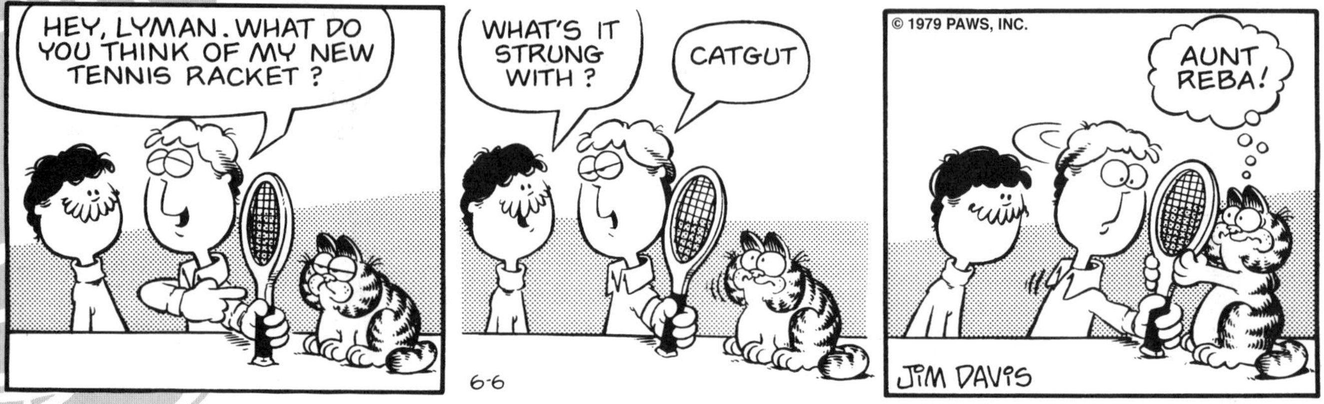
HEY, LYMAN. WHAT DO YOU THINK OF MY NEW TENNIS RACKET ?
WHAT'S IT STRUNG WITH ?
CATGUT
© 1979 PAWS, INC.
AUNT REBA!
JIM DAVIS
6-6

I love understatement.

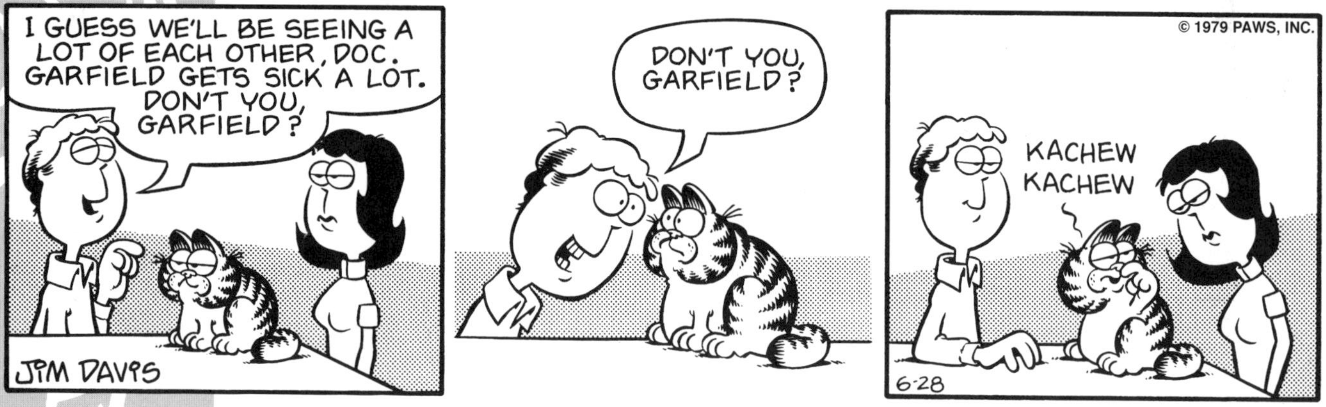
I GUESS WE'LL BE SEEING A LOT OF EACH OTHER, DOC. GARFIELD GETS SICK A LOT. DON'T YOU, GARFIELD ?
JIM DAVIS
DON'T YOU, GARFIELD ?
© 1979 PAWS, INC.
KACHEW KACHEW
6-28

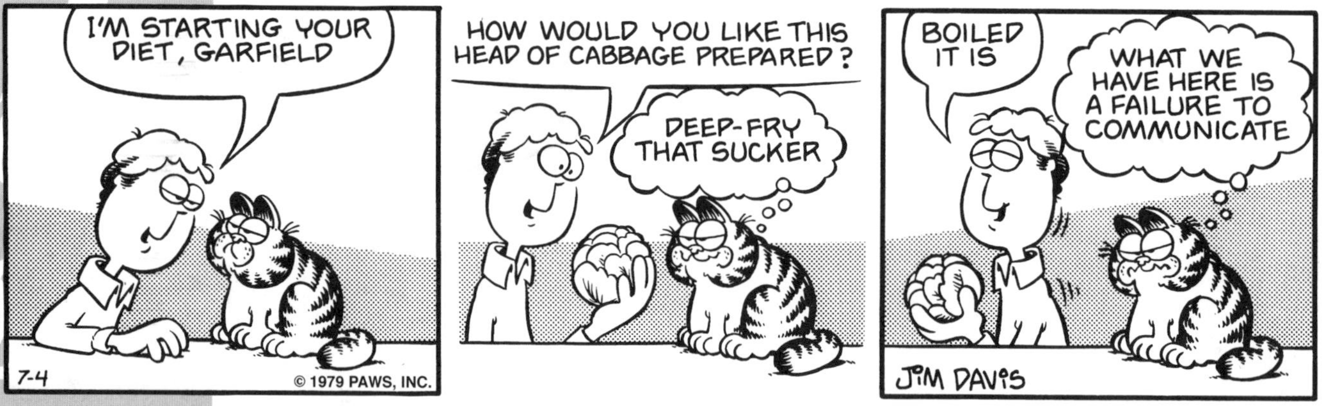
I'M STARTING YOUR DIET, GARFIELD
7-4
© 1979 PAWS, INC.
HOW WOULD YOU LIKE THIS HEAD OF CABBAGE PREPARED ?
DEEP-FRY THAT SUCKER
BOILED IT IS
WHAT WE HAVE HERE IS A FAILURE TO COMMUNICATE
JIM DAVIS

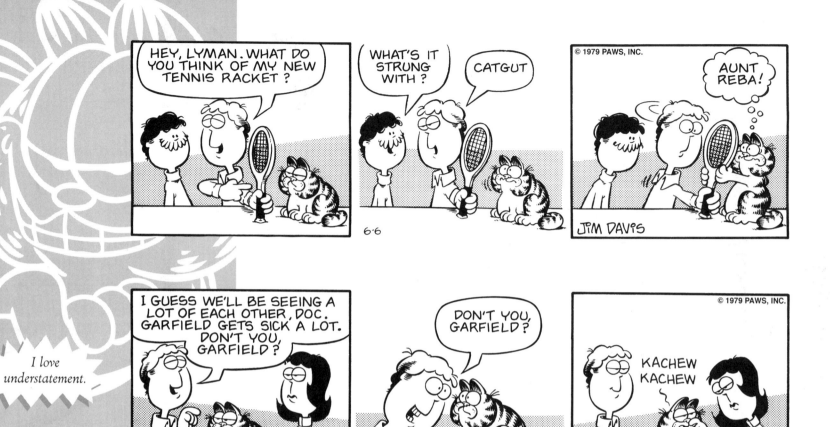

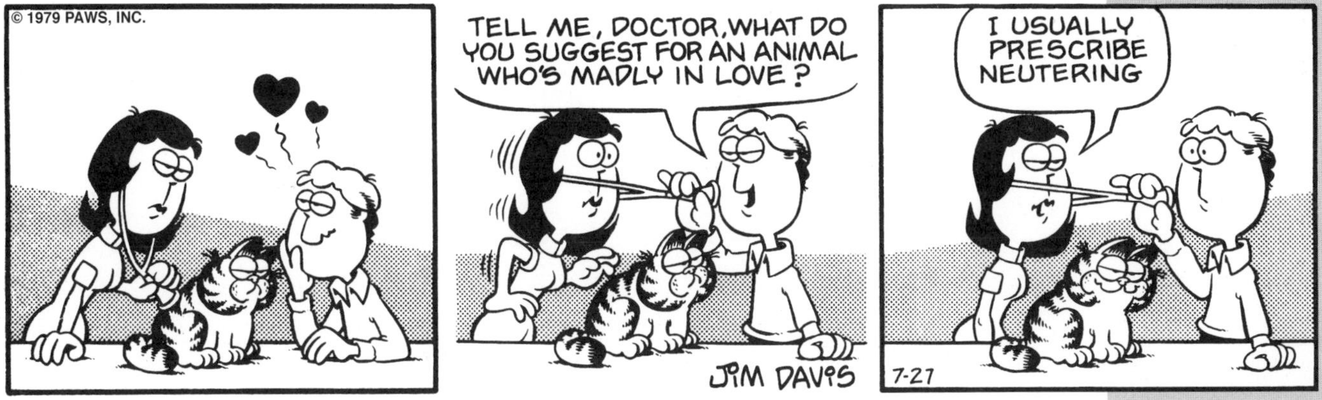
© 1979 PAWS, INC.
TELL ME, DOCTOR, WHAT DO YOU SUGGEST FOR AN ANIMAL WHO'S MADLY IN LOVE?
I USUALLY PRESCRIBE NEUTERING
JIM DAVIS
7-27

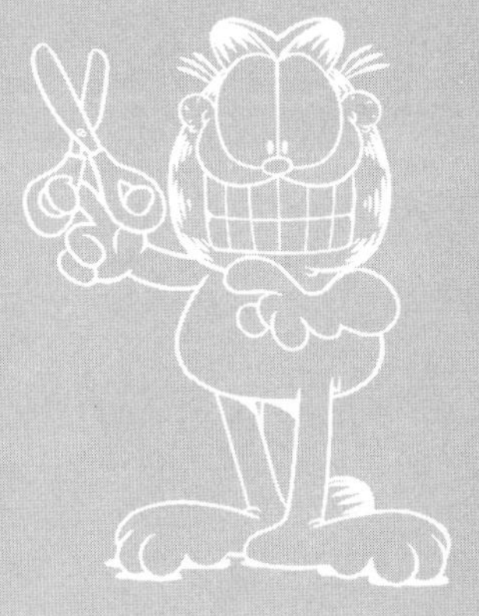

IT'S MAD! IT'S BAD! IT'S MONDAY!

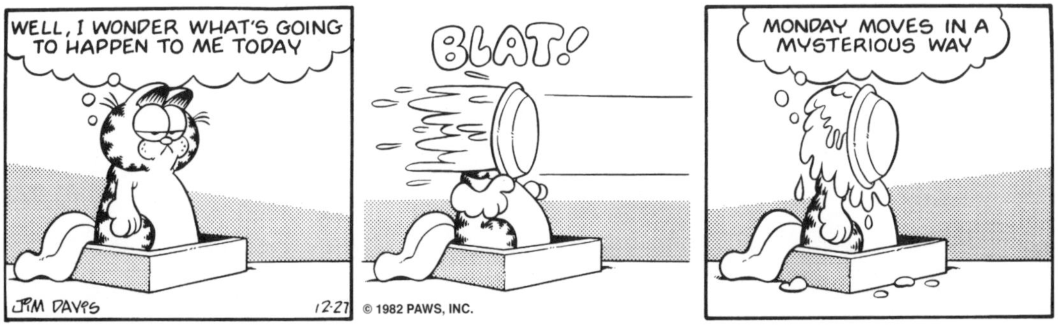
WELL, I WONDER WHAT'S GOING TO HAPPEN TO ME TODAY
BLAT!
MONDAY MOVES IN A MYSTERIOUS WAY
JIM DAVIS
12-27
© 1982 PAWS, INC.

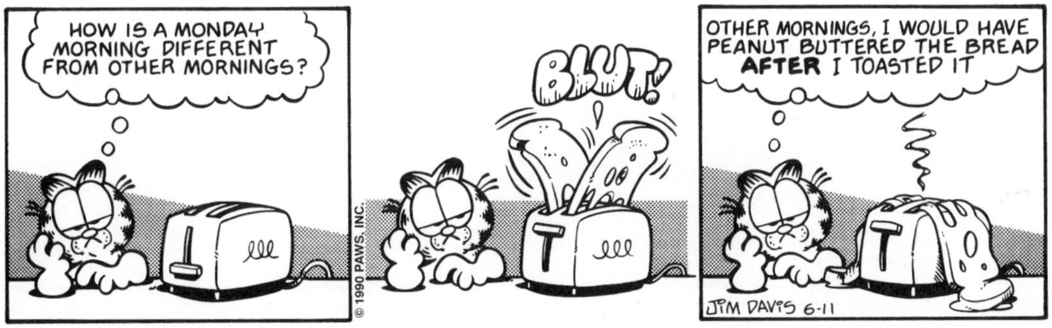
HOW IS A MONDAY MORNING DIFFERENT FROM OTHER MORNINGS?
© 1990 PAWS, INC.
BLUT!
OTHER MORNINGS, I WOULD HAVE PEANUT BUTTERED THE BREAD **AFTER** I TOASTED IT
JIM DAVIS 6-11

Though he doesn't work or go to school, Garfield still dreads Mondays. But you can't really blame him. Because, in Garfield's case, Mondays can be just plain mean. One Monday Garfield wished for a fifty-pound pan of lasagna; it landed on him. Another Monday he found six crickets doing a water ballet in his water bowl. Then there was the ugly incident of the land mine in his breakfast. . . . It seems there's really only one way Garfield can beat this curse: go to bed early Sunday night . . . and set his alarm for Tuesday!

Right:
This actually happened to me in an all-night diner. (You can't make up this stuff!)

Below:
The ol' "left-turn-in-the-last-frame" kind of gag.

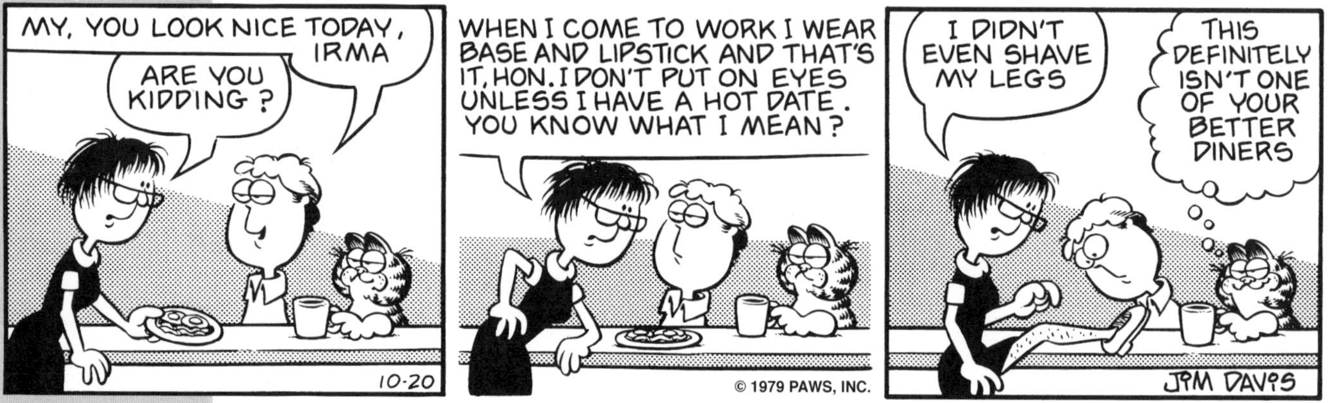
MY, YOU LOOK NICE TODAY, IRMA
ARE YOU KIDDING ?
10-20
WHEN I COME TO WORK I WEAR BASE AND LIPSTICK AND THAT'S IT, HON. I DON'T PUT ON EYES UNLESS I HAVE A HOT DATE. YOU KNOW WHAT I MEAN ?
© 1979 PAWS, INC.
I DIDN'T EVEN SHAVE MY LEGS
THIS DEFINITELY ISN'T ONE OF YOUR BETTER DINERS
JIM DAVIS

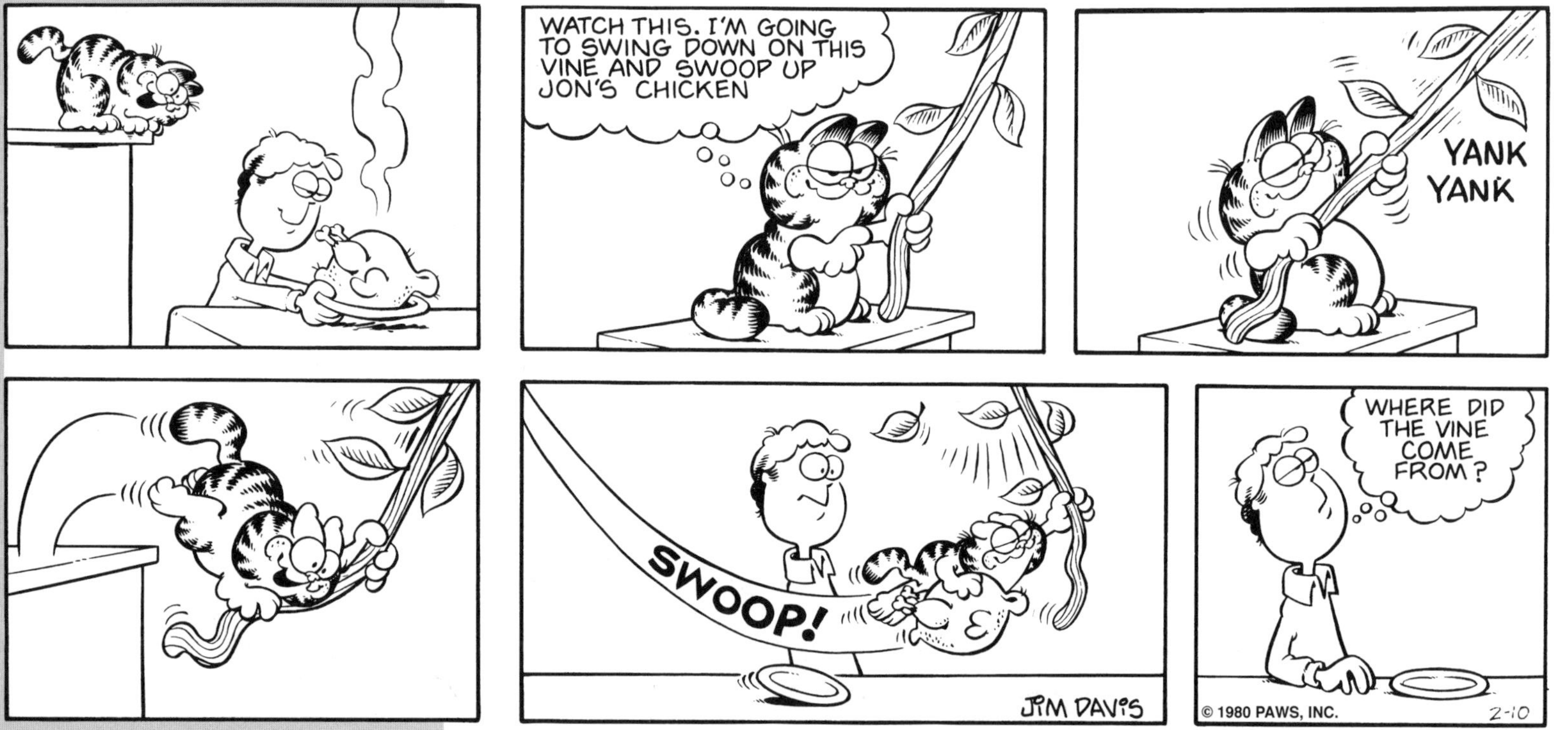
WATCH THIS. I'M GOING TO SWING DOWN ON THIS VINE AND SWOOP UP JON'S CHICKEN
YANK YANK
SWOOP!
JIM DAVIS
WHERE DID THE VINE COME FROM ?
© 1980 PAWS, INC.
2-10

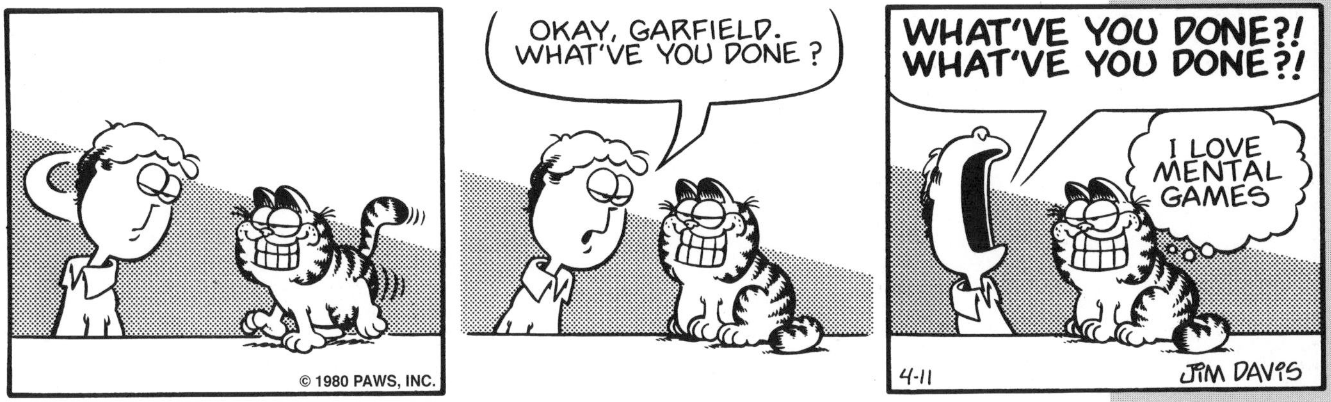
OKAY, GARFIELD.
WHAT'VE YOU DONE ?
WHAT'VE YOU DONE?!
WHAT'VE YOU DONE?!
I LOVE
MENTAL
GAMES
© 1980 PAWS, INC.
4-11
JIM DAVIS

Classic cat.

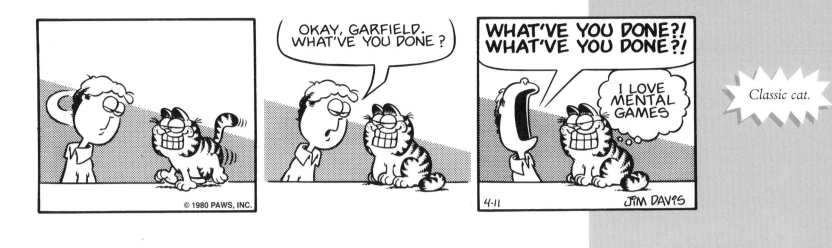

GARFIELD IS SO LAZY . . .

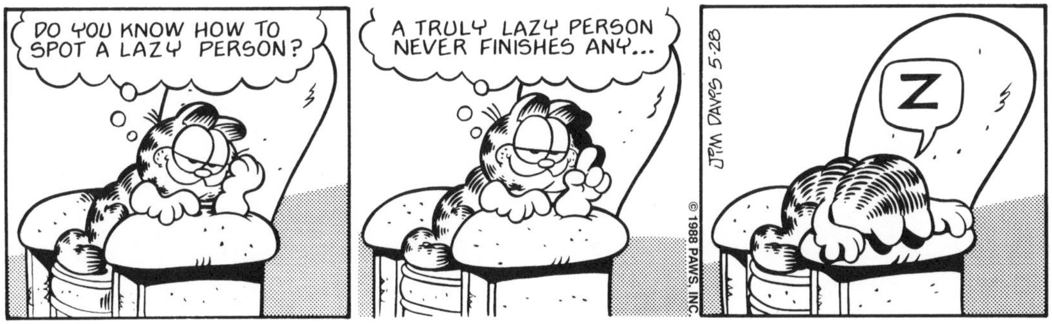
DO YOU KNOW HOW TO
SPOT A LAZY PERSON?
A TRULY LAZY PERSON
NEVER FINISHES ANY...
Z
JIM DAVIS 5-28
© 1988 PAWS, INC.

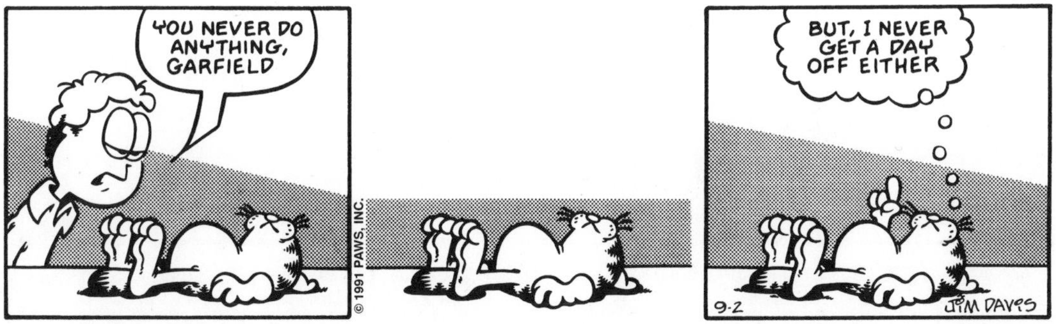
YOU NEVER DO
ANYTHING,
GARFIELD
BUT, I NEVER
GET A DAY
OFF EITHER
© 1991 PAWS, INC.
9-2
JIM DAVIS

. . . He takes a coffee break between naps.

. . . He has a doorman open the refrigerator for him.

. . . He makes Jon buy preshredded drapes.

. . . He only chases dead mice.

. . . He hired another cat to shed for him.

. . . He thinks yawning is an exercise.

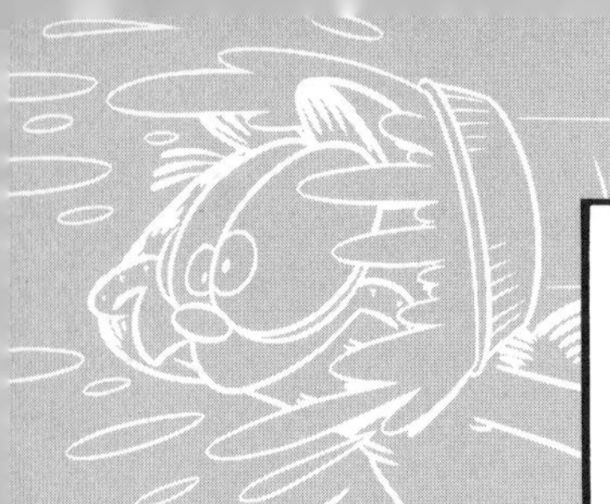

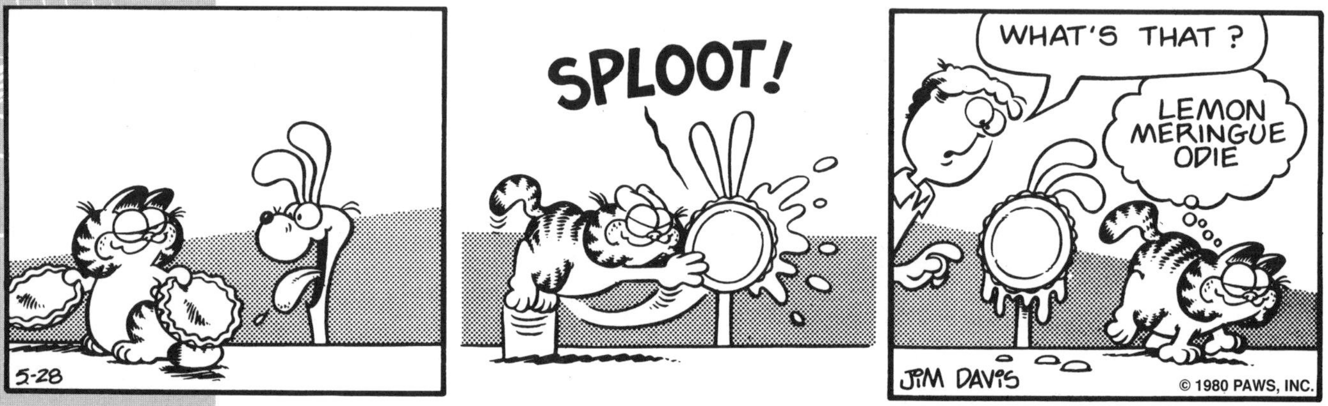
5-28
SPLOOT!
WHAT'S THAT?
LEMON MERINGUE ODIE
JIM DAVIS
© 1980 PAWS, INC.

This was sent in as a joke. I combined drugs, sex, and gambling in one strip . . . breaking a copyright law in the process. It went through! The joke was on me.

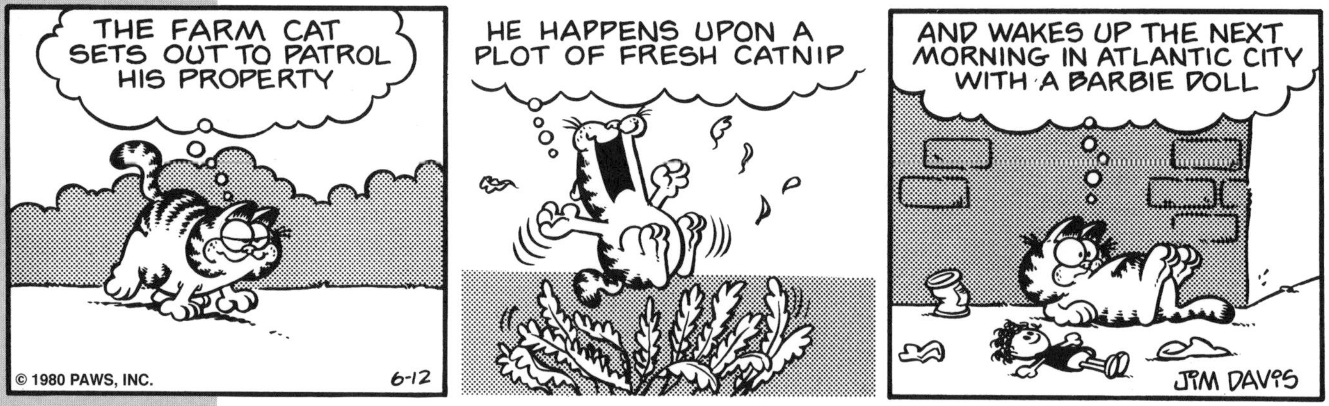
THE FARM CAT SETS OUT TO PATROL HIS PROPERTY
HE HAPPENS UPON A PLOT OF FRESH CATNIP
AND WAKES UP THE NEXT MORNING IN ATLANTIC CITY WITH A BARBIE DOLL
© 1980 PAWS, INC.
6-12
JIM DAVIS

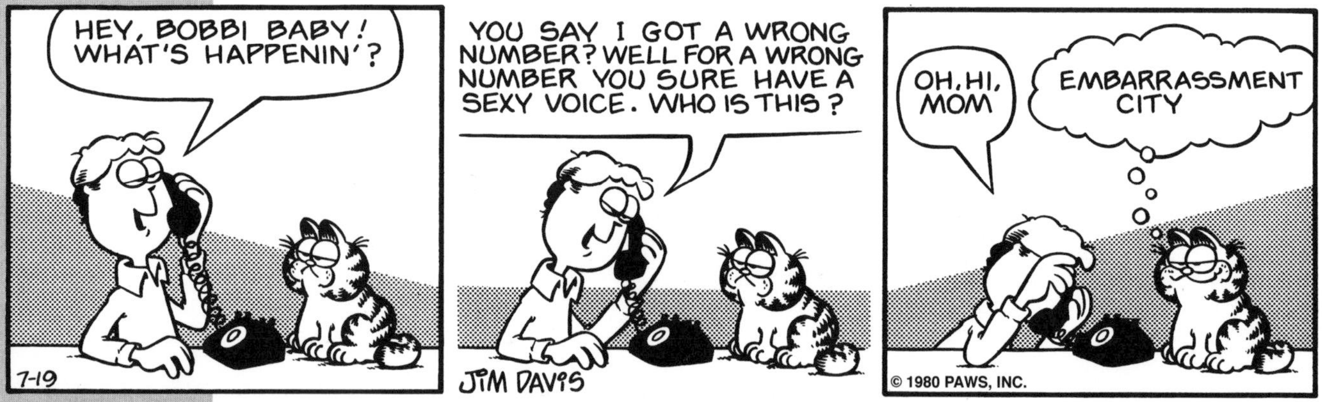
HEY, BOBBI BABY! WHAT'S HAPPENIN'?
YOU SAY I GOT A WRONG NUMBER? WELL FOR A WRONG NUMBER YOU SURE HAVE A SEXY VOICE. WHO IS THIS?
OH, HI, MOM
EMBARRASSMENT CITY
7-19
JIM DAVIS
© 1980 PAWS, INC.

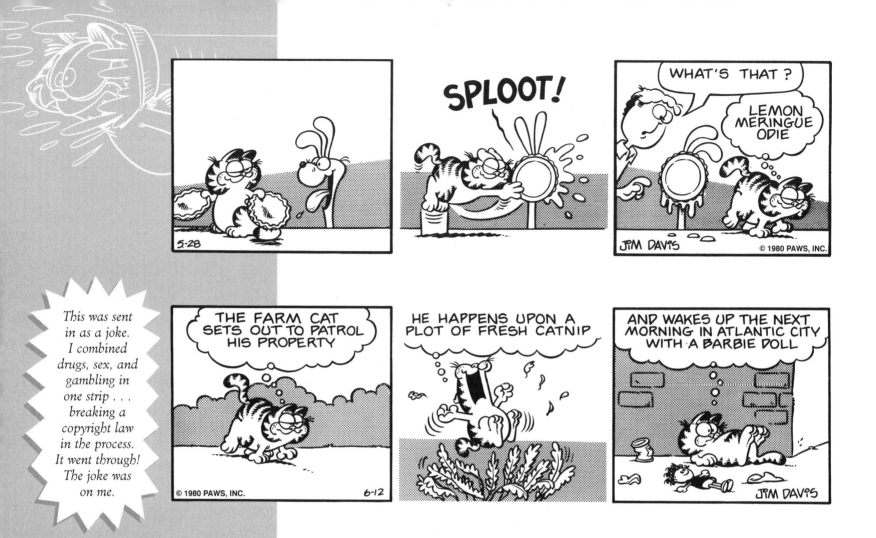

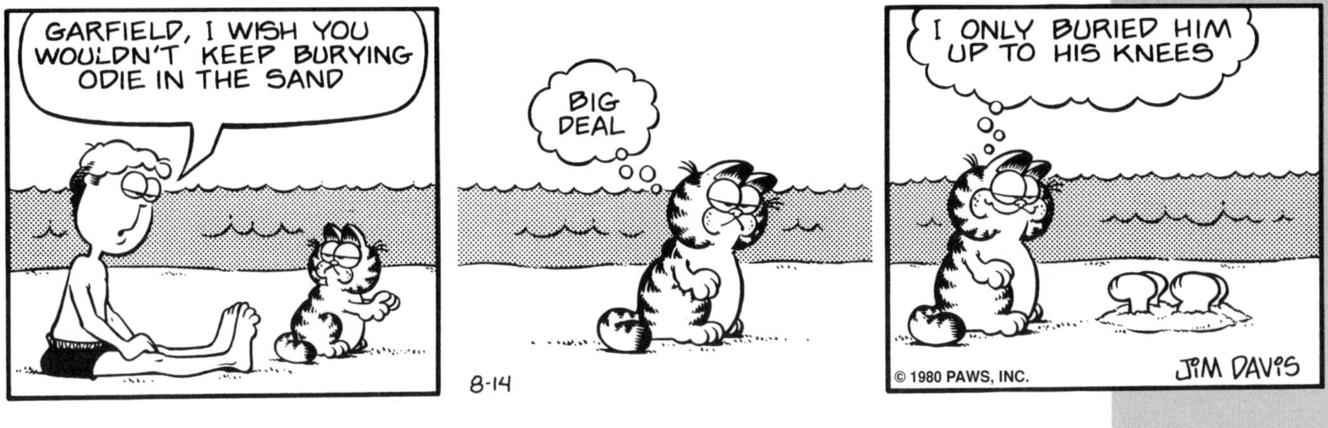
GARFIELD, I WISH YOU WOULDN'T KEEP BURYING ODIE IN THE SAND
BIG DEAL
8-14
I ONLY BURIED HIM UP TO HIS KNEES
© 1980 PAWS, INC.
JIM DAVIS

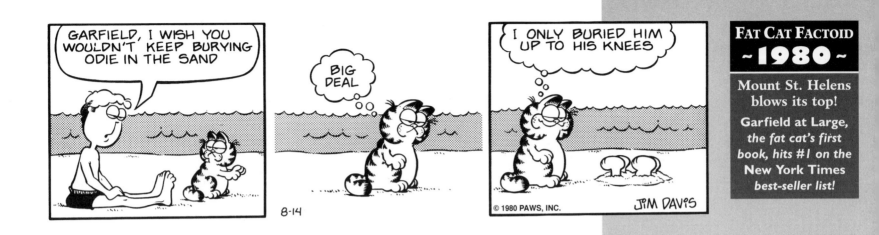

FAT CAT FACTOID
~1980~

Mount St. Helens blows its top!

Garfield at Large, ***the fat cat's first book, hits #1 on the*** **New York Times** ***best-seller list!***

GARFIELD'S SLEEPING TIPS

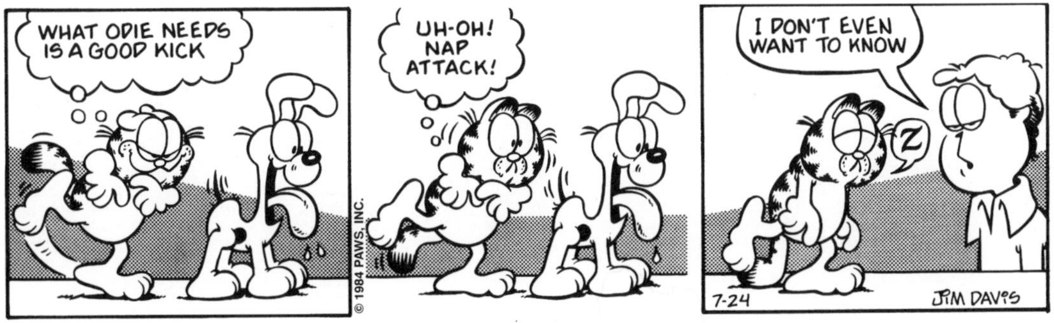
WHAT ODIE NEEDS IS A GOOD KICK
© 1984 PAWS, INC.
UH-OH! NAP ATTACK!
I DON'T EVEN WANT TO KNOW
Z
7-24
JIM DAVIS

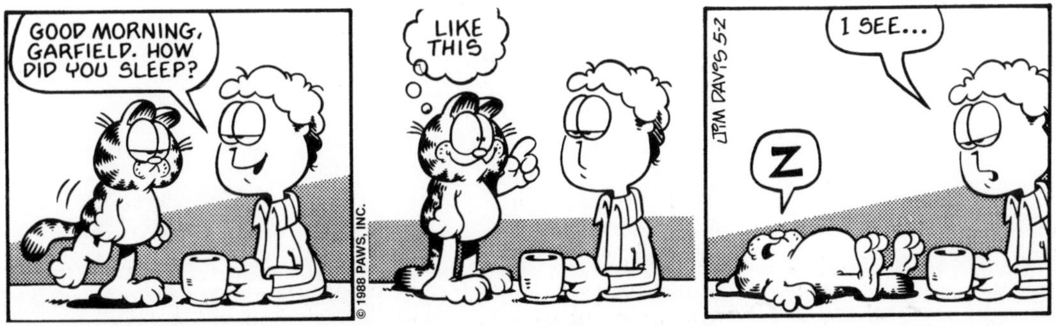
GOOD MORNING, GARFIELD. HOW DID YOU SLEEP?
© 1988 PAWS, INC.
LIKE THIS
JIM DAVIS 5-2
I SEE...
Z

Midnight snacks keep you awake. So stuff yourself at 11:30.

Pay no attention to those weird noises under the bed.

Nap often, so you'll be completely relaxed at bedtime.

Documentaries are guaranteed to induce drowsiness.

Get a teddy bear that won't hog the covers.

Water beds are not for those who claw in their sleep.

This strip originally said "sheep jokes." It was caught after the proofs went out. This correction was sent. Some papers ran the original.

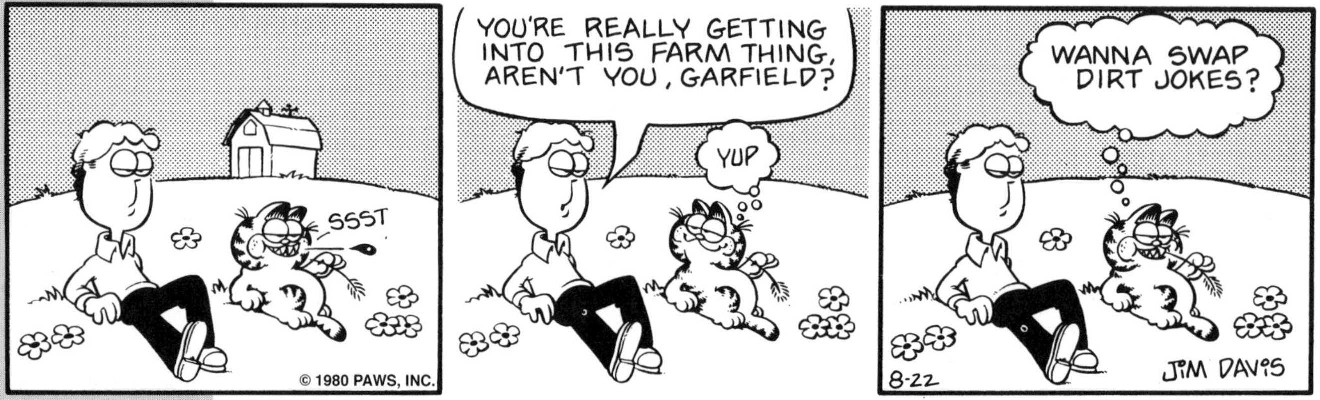
SSST
YOU'RE REALLY GETTING INTO THIS FARM THING, AREN'T YOU, GARFIELD?
YUP
WANNA SWAP DIRT JOKES?
© 1980 PAWS, INC.
8-22
JIM DAVIS

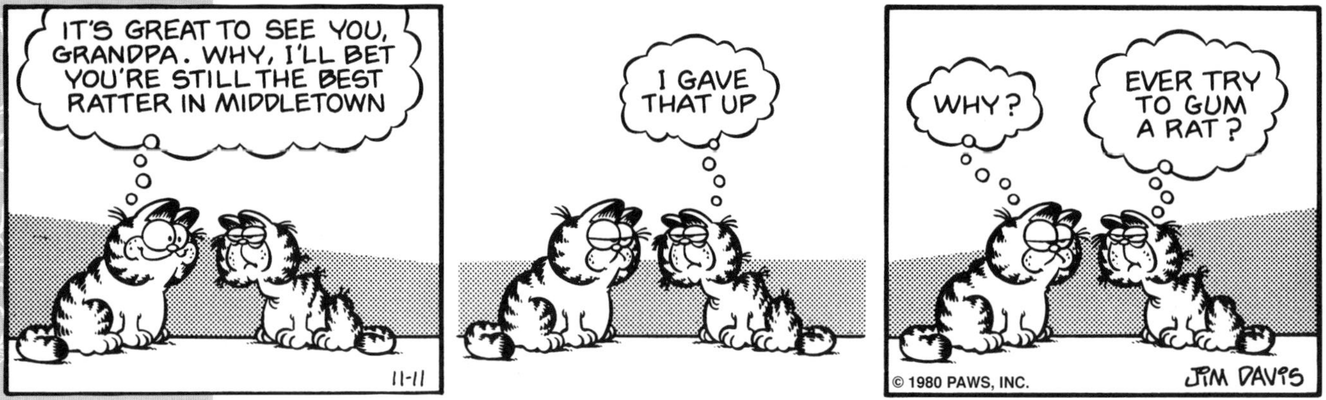
IT'S GREAT TO SEE YOU, GRANDPA. WHY, I'LL BET YOU'RE STILL THE BEST RATTER IN MIDDLETOWN
11-11
I GAVE THAT UP
WHY?
EVER TRY TO GUM A RAT?
© 1980 PAWS, INC.
JIM DAVIS

Garfield's origin revealed!

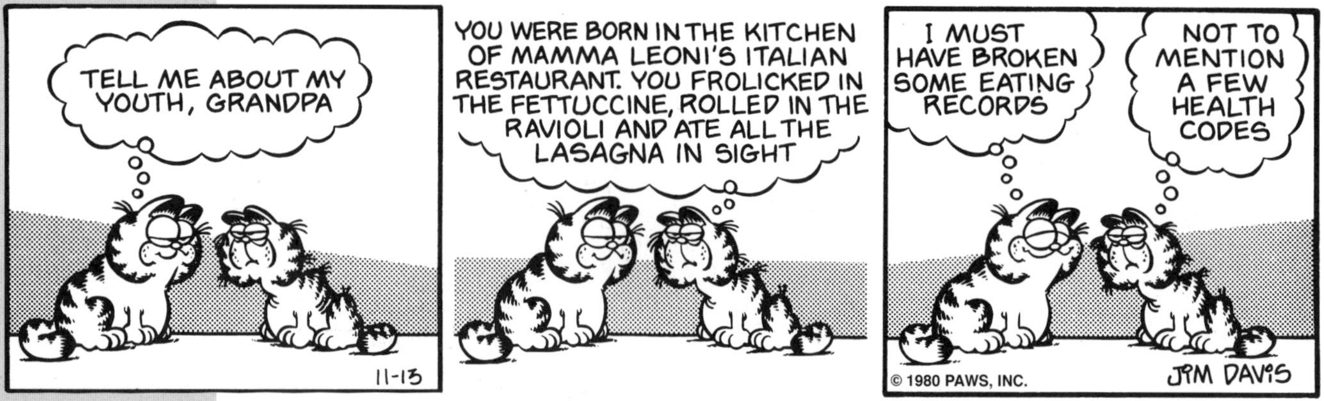
TELL ME ABOUT MY YOUTH, GRANDPA
11-13
YOU WERE BORN IN THE KITCHEN OF MAMMA LEONI'S ITALIAN RESTAURANT. YOU FROLICKED IN THE FETTUCCINE, ROLLED IN THE RAVIOLI AND ATE ALL THE LASAGNA IN SIGHT
I MUST HAVE BROKEN SOME EATING RECORDS
NOT TO MENTION A FEW HEALTH CODES
© 1980 PAWS, INC.
JIM DAVIS

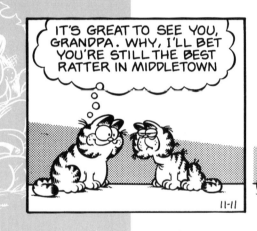

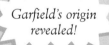

Panel 1: GARFIELD! WELCOME BACK!

Panel 2: YOU MUST BE STARVED. I'LL GET SOME FOOD / I'M STARVED

Panel 3: HOME IS WHERE THEY UNDERSTAND YOU

© 1981 PAWS, INC.

2-7 JIM DAVIS

GARFIELD IN THE ROUGH

Panel 1: GO OUTSIDE AND CHECK FOR BEARS, GARFIELD / SURE, WHY NOT?

8-29 JIM DAVIS

Panel 2: NO...THERE ARE NO BEARS OUT HERE....

Panel 3: JUST PUMAS

© 1989 PAWS, INC.

Panel 4: WHAT DO YOU THINK OF MY NEW TENT, GARFIELD? I GOT IT ON SALE

JIM DAVIS 9-19

Panel 5: GOOSH!

Panel 6: SUCH A DEAL

© 1990 PAWS, INC.

As far as Garfield is concerned, there's nothing great about the "great outdoors." Here are just a few of the reasons that he hates camping out:

No pizza delivery

You never know where Bigfoot might turn up

Jon's off-key campfire songs

Lousy reception on those battery-operated TVs

Too many bugs, not enough refrigerators

Allergic to roughing it

Fat Cat Factoid
~1981~

MTV is born! The first video broadcast: the Buggles's "Video Killed the Radio Star."

Paws, Inc., is born! Jim Davis sets up Garfield's Muncie studio.

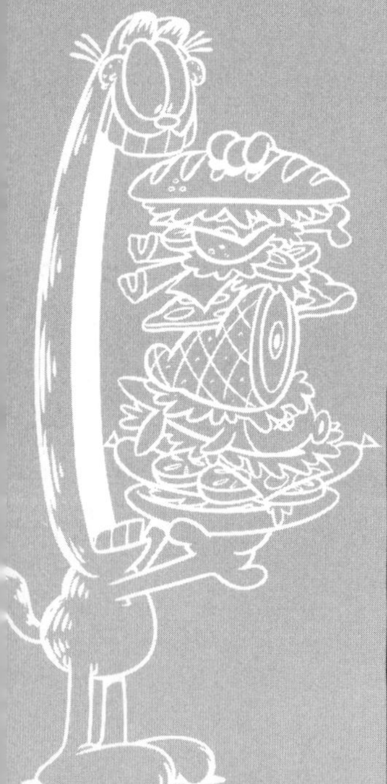

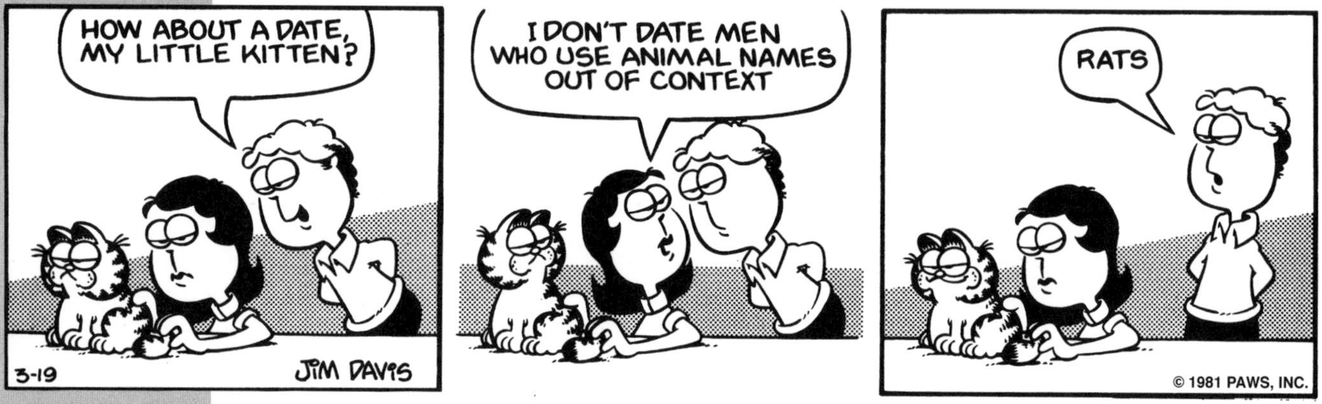

HOW ABOUT A DATE, MY LITTLE KITTEN?
3-19
JIM DAVIS
I DON'T DATE MEN WHO USE ANIMAL NAMES OUT OF CONTEXT
RATS
© 1981 PAWS, INC.

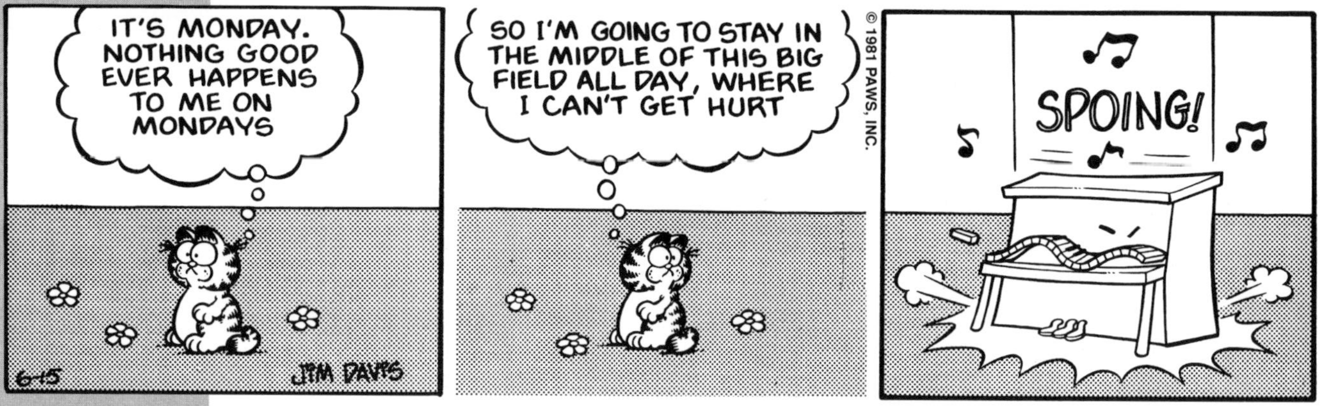

IT'S MONDAY. NOTHING GOOD EVER HAPPENS TO ME ON MONDAYS
6-15
JIM DAVIS
SO I'M GOING TO STAY IN THE MIDDLE OF THIS BIG FIELD ALL DAY, WHERE I CAN'T GET HURT
© 1981 PAWS, INC.
SPOING!

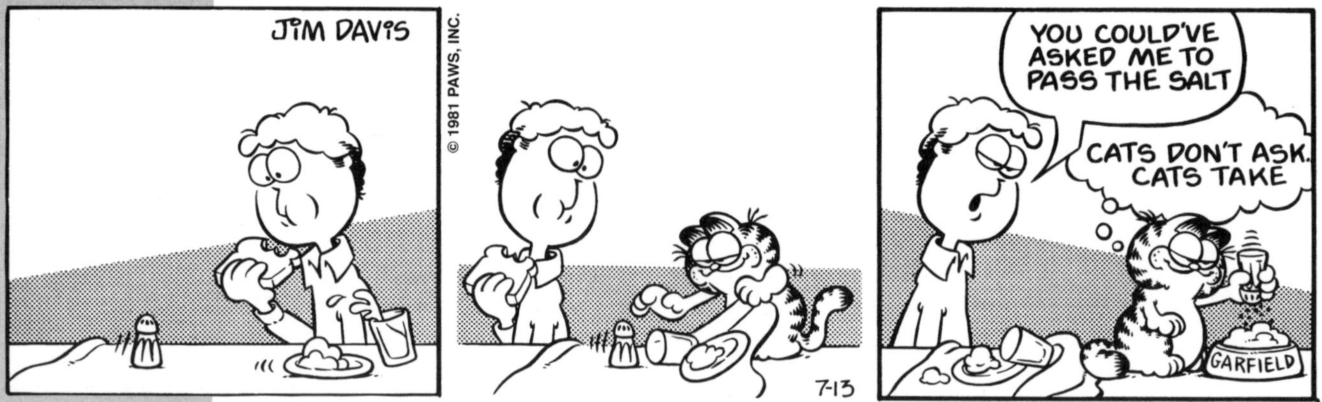

JIM DAVIS
© 1981 PAWS, INC.
7-13
YOU COULD'VE ASKED ME TO PASS THE SALT
CATS DON'T ASK. CATS TAKE
GARFIELD

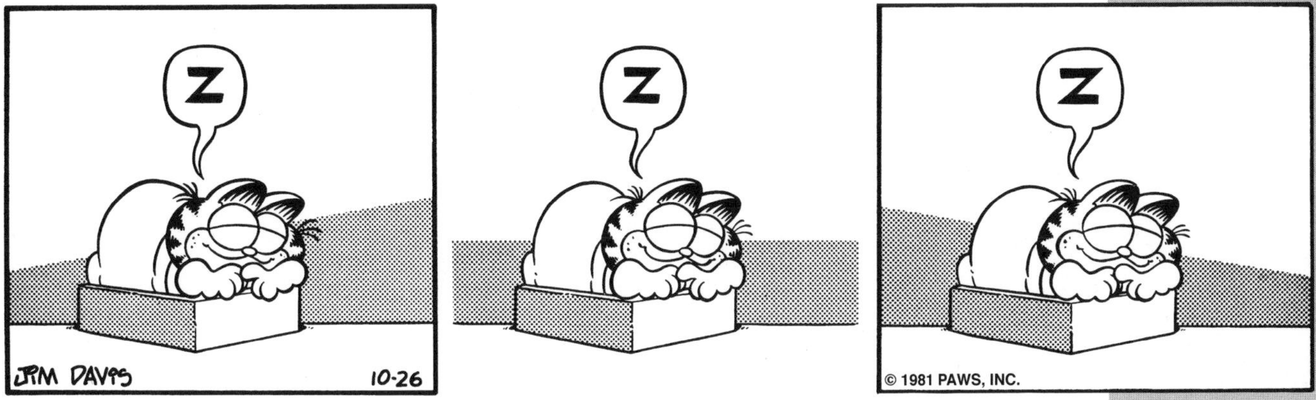
Z
Z
Z
JIM DAVIS 10-26
© 1981 PAWS, INC.

Garfield sleeps through a Monday . . .

GARFIELD'S ALTER EGOS

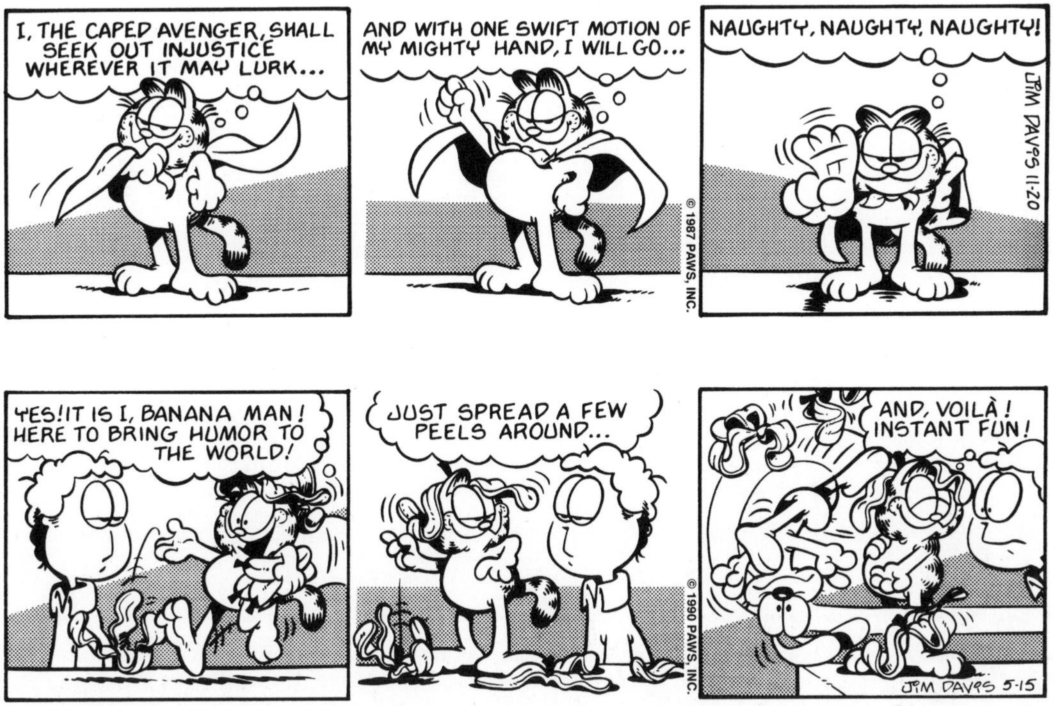
I, THE CAPED AVENGER, SHALL SEEK OUT INJUSTICE WHEREVER IT MAY LURK...
AND WITH ONE SWIFT MOTION OF MY MIGHTY HAND, I WILL GO...
NAUGHTY, NAUGHTY, NAUGHTY!
JIM DAVIS 11-20
© 1987 PAWS, INC.
YES! IT IS I, BANANA MAN! HERE TO BRING HUMOR TO THE WORLD!
JUST SPREAD A FEW PEELS AROUND...
AND, VOILÀ! INSTANT FUN!
JIM DAVIS 5-15
© 1990 PAWS, INC.

Garfield has always been completely happy just being Garfield. As he says, "I gotta be me; I'm too good to be anyone else." Still, every now and then he gets the urge to stretch his imagination, instead of his waistline. In addition to the Caped Avenger and Banana Man, here are some of the personalities Garfield has tried on over the years:

Sumo Cat
The Claw
Evil Roy Gato
Amoeba Man
Tiger Shark
Karate Cat

. . . and wakes up Tuesday!

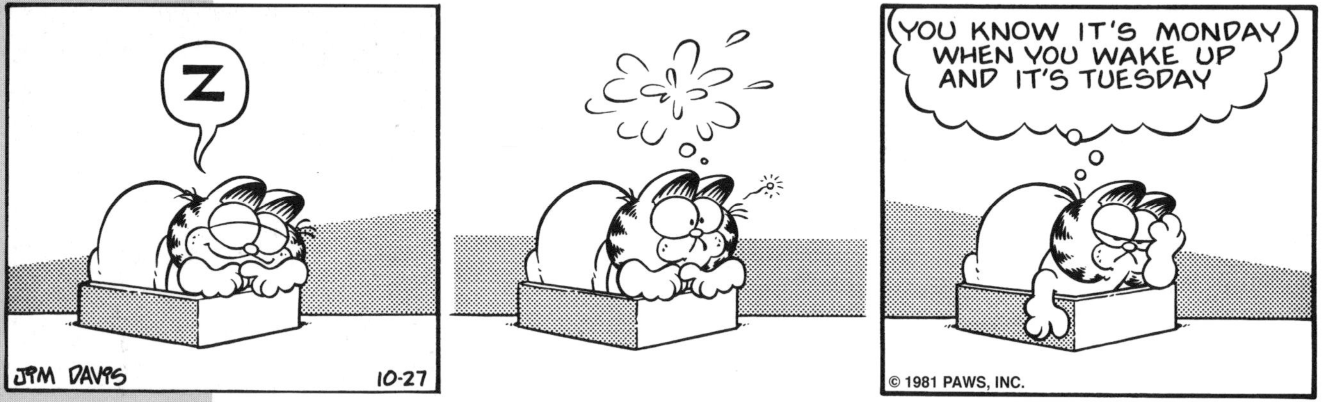

Z
YOU KNOW IT'S MONDAY WHEN YOU WAKE UP AND IT'S TUESDAY
JIM DAVIS
10-27
© 1981 PAWS, INC.

Jon's only kiss.

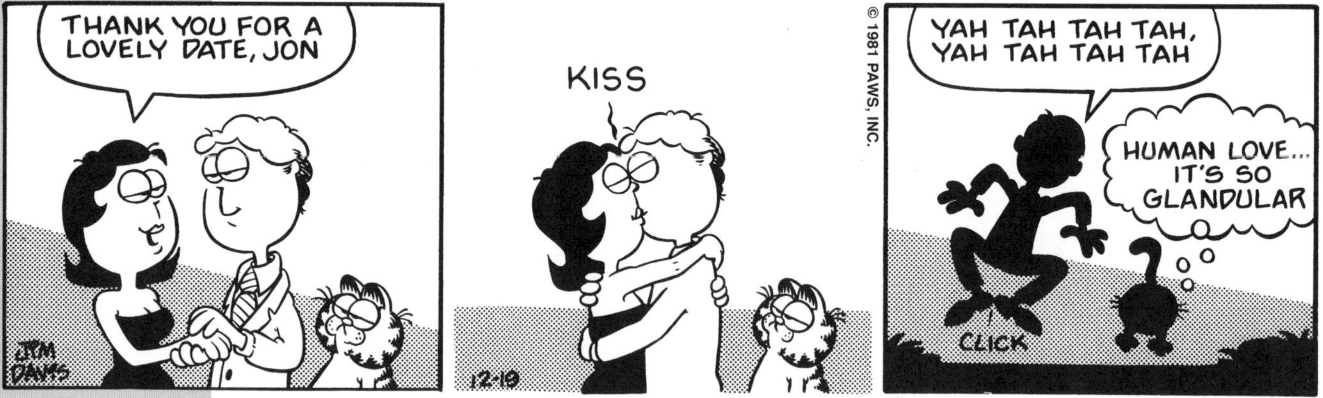

THANK YOU FOR A LOVELY DATE, JON
KISS
YAH TAH TAH TAH, YAH TAH TAH TAH
HUMAN LOVE... IT'S SO GLANDULAR
CLICK
JIM DAVIS
12-19
© 1981 PAWS, INC.

I liked this gag so well, I used it in Garfield's Christmas special.

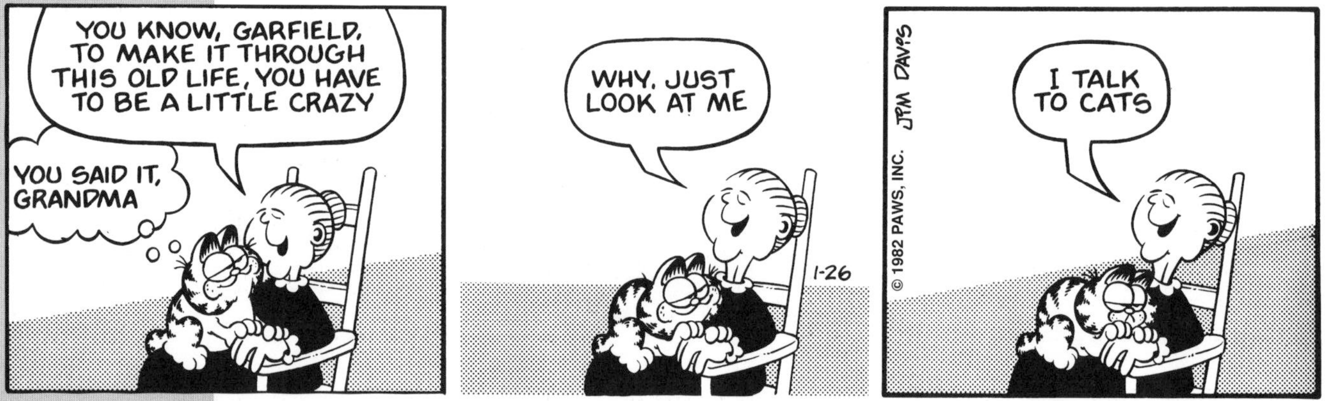

YOU KNOW, GARFIELD, TO MAKE IT THROUGH THIS OLD LIFE, YOU HAVE TO BE A LITTLE CRAZY
YOU SAID IT, GRANDMA
WHY, JUST LOOK AT ME
I TALK TO CATS
JIM DAVIS
1-26
© 1982 PAWS, INC.

CLICK!

SHOOP!

JIM DAVIS   2-12   © 1982 PAWS, INC.

FASTER THAN THE SPEED OF DARK

My dad wrote this gag.

PUTTING DOWN THE DOG

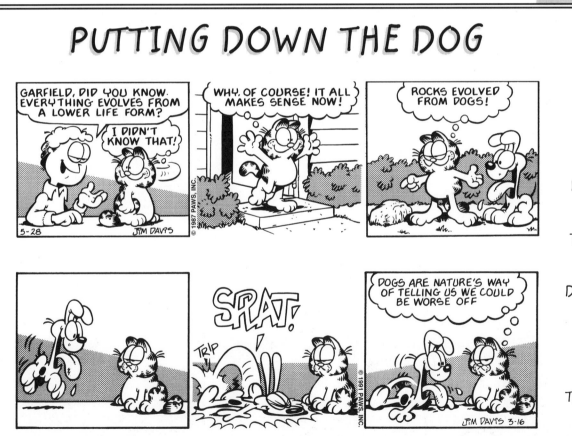

GARFIELD, DID YOU KNOW, EVERYTHING EVOLVES FROM A LOWER LIFE FORM?

I DIDN'T KNOW THAT!

5-28   JIM DAVIS   © 1987 PAWS, INC.

WHY, OF COURSE! IT ALL MAKES SENSE NOW!

ROCKS EVOLVED FROM DOGS!

TRIP

SRAT!

DOGS ARE NATURE'S WAY OF TELLING US WE COULD BE WORSE OFF

© 1981 PAWS, INC.   JIM DAVIS 3-16

Here are some of Garfield's favorite dog put-downs:

Cats are poetry in motion. Dogs are gibberish in neutral.

Life's a bowl of cherries, and dogs are the pits.

The only trick most dogs can do is "play stupid."

Dogs can't walk and drool at the same time.

A dog's breath is worse than his bite.

The only thing uglier than a dog is two dogs.

FAT CAT FACTOID
~1982~

TV sitcoms "Cheers" and "Family Ties" premiere.

Garfield's first TV special, "Here Comes Garfield," is nominated for 7 Emmy Awards.

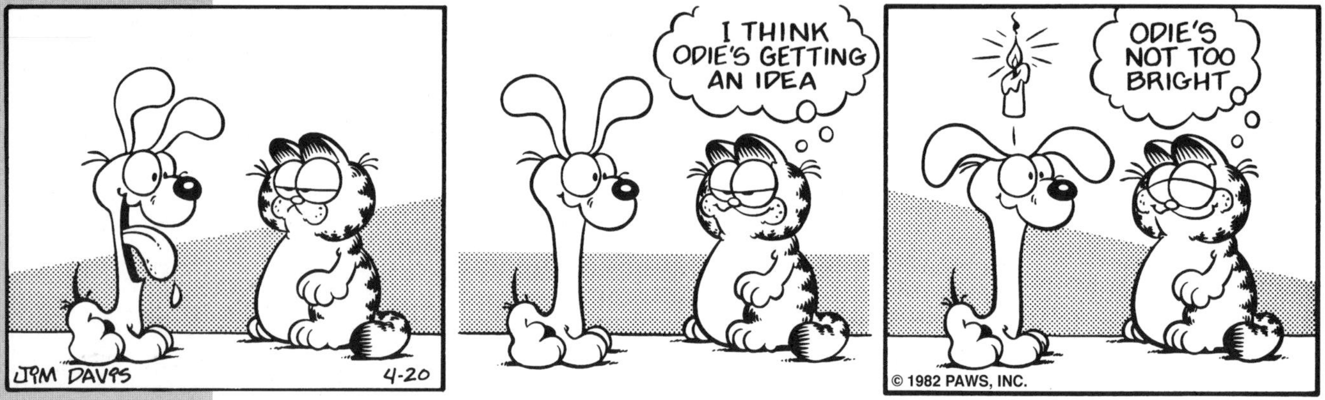

I THINK ODIE'S GETTING AN IDEA
ODIE'S NOT TOO BRIGHT
JIM DAVIS
4-20
© 1982 PAWS, INC.

Cartoon physics.

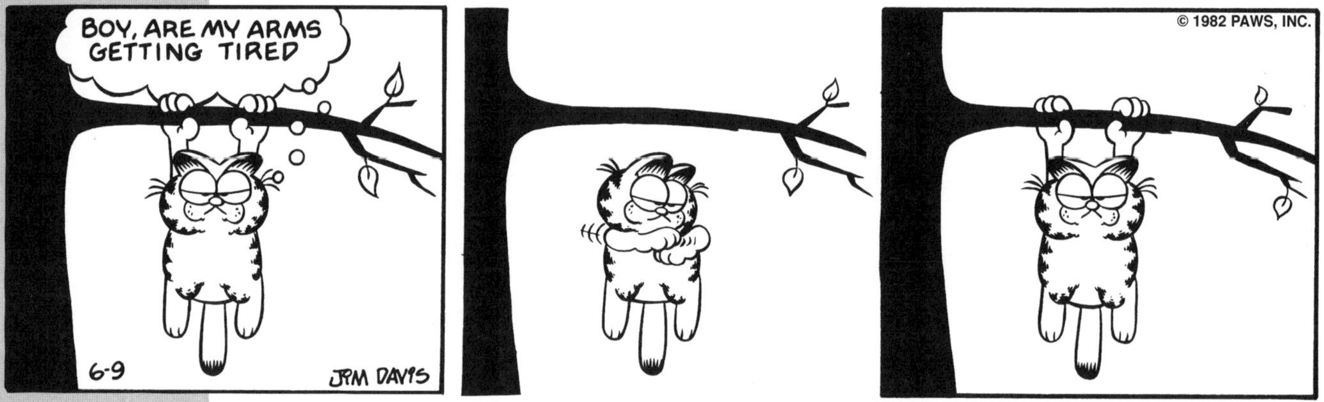

BOY, ARE MY ARMS GETTING TIRED
6-9
JIM DAVIS
© 1982 PAWS, INC.

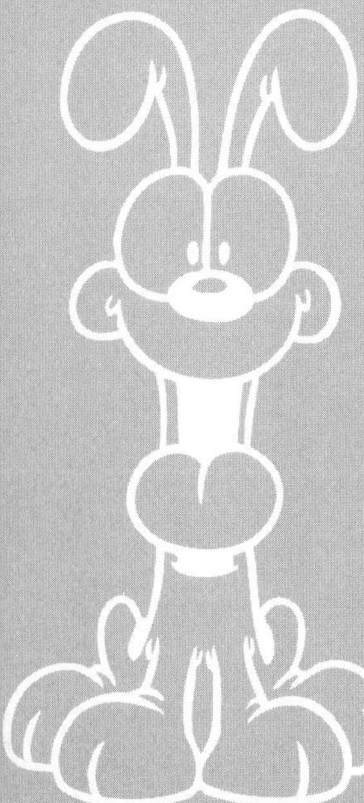

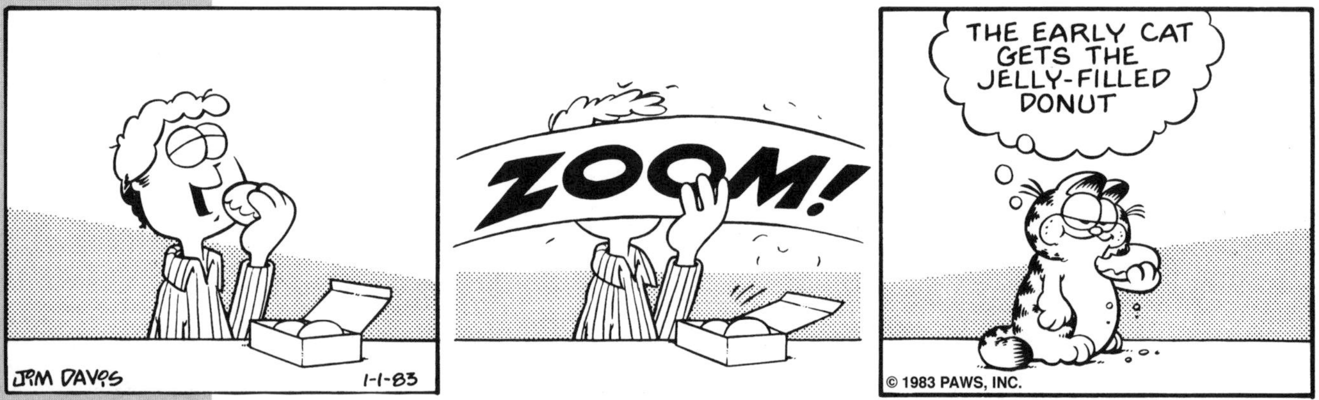

ZOOM!
THE EARLY CAT GETS THE JELLY-FILLED DONUT
JIM DAVIS
1-1-83
© 1983 PAWS, INC.

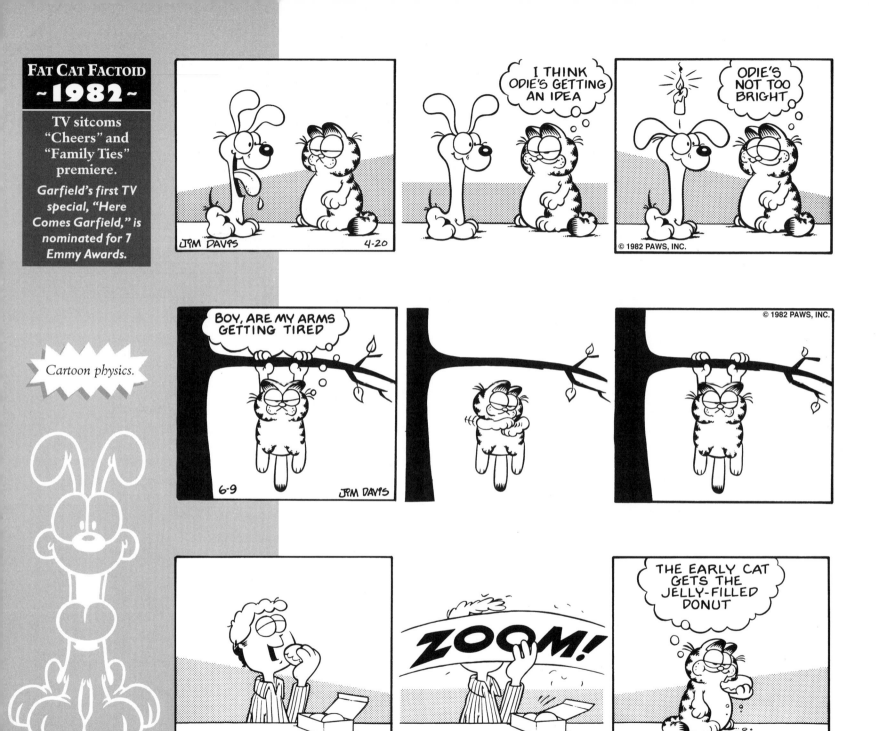

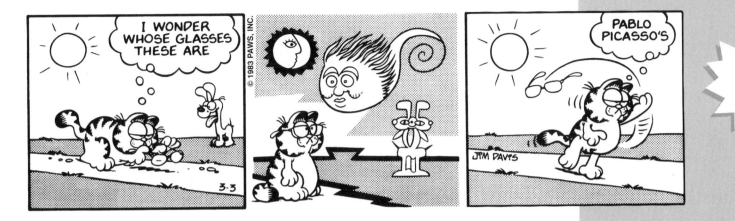

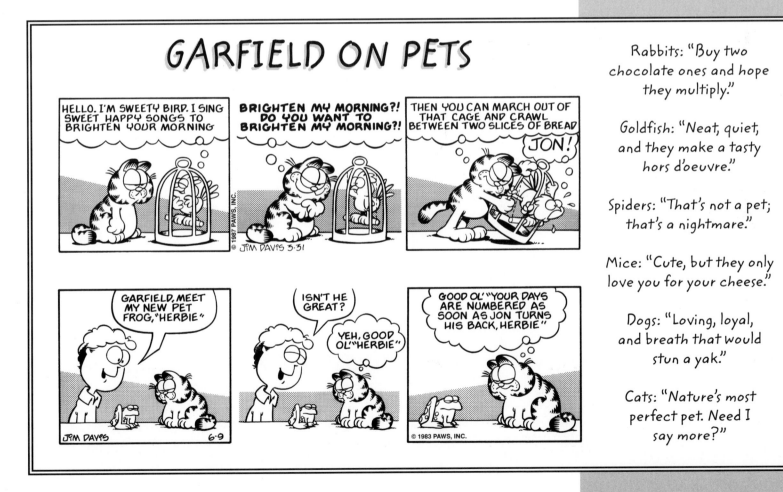

I WONDER WHOSE GLASSES THESE ARE
© 1983 PAWS, INC.
PABLO PICASSO'S
JIM DAVIS
3-3

Sometimes it feels good to stretch.

GARFIELD ON PETS

HELLO. I'M SWEETY BIRD. I SING SWEET HAPPY SONGS TO BRIGHTEN YOUR MORNING
BRIGHTEN MY MORNING?! DO YOU WANT TO BRIGHTEN MY MORNING?!
THEN YOU CAN MARCH OUT OF THAT CAGE AND CRAWL BETWEEN TWO SLICES OF BREAD
JON!
© 1987 PAWS, INC.
JIM DAVIS 3-31

GARFIELD, MEET MY NEW PET FROG, "HERBIE"
ISN'T HE GREAT?
YEH, GOOD OL' "HERBIE"
GOOD OL' "YOUR DAYS ARE NUMBERED AS SOON AS JON TURNS HIS BACK, HERBIE"
JIM DAVIS
6-9
© 1983 PAWS, INC.

Rabbits: "Buy two chocolate ones and hope they multiply."

Goldfish: "Neat, quiet, and they make a tasty hors d'oeuvre."

Spiders: "That's not a pet; that's a nightmare."

Mice: "Cute, but they only love you for your cheese."

Dogs: "Loving, loyal, and breath that would stun a yak."

Cats: "Nature's most perfect pet. Need I say more?"

This became the title of a 1998 Christmas gift book.

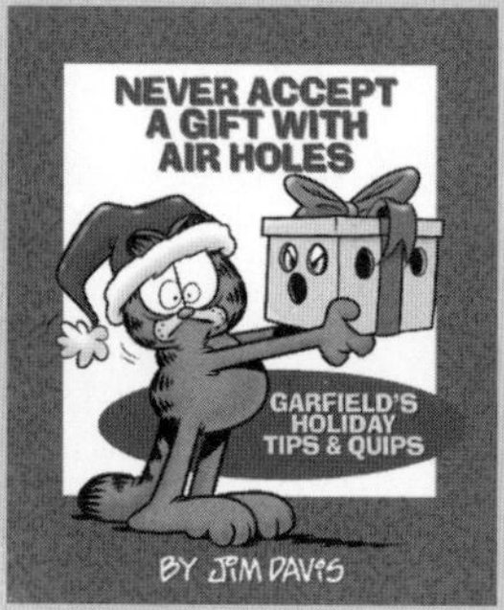
NEVER ACCEPT A GIFT WITH AIR HOLES
GARFIELD'S HOLIDAY TIPS & QUIPS
BY JIM DAVIS

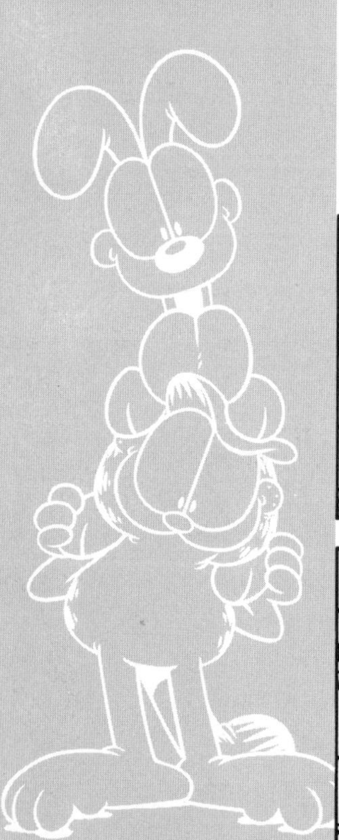

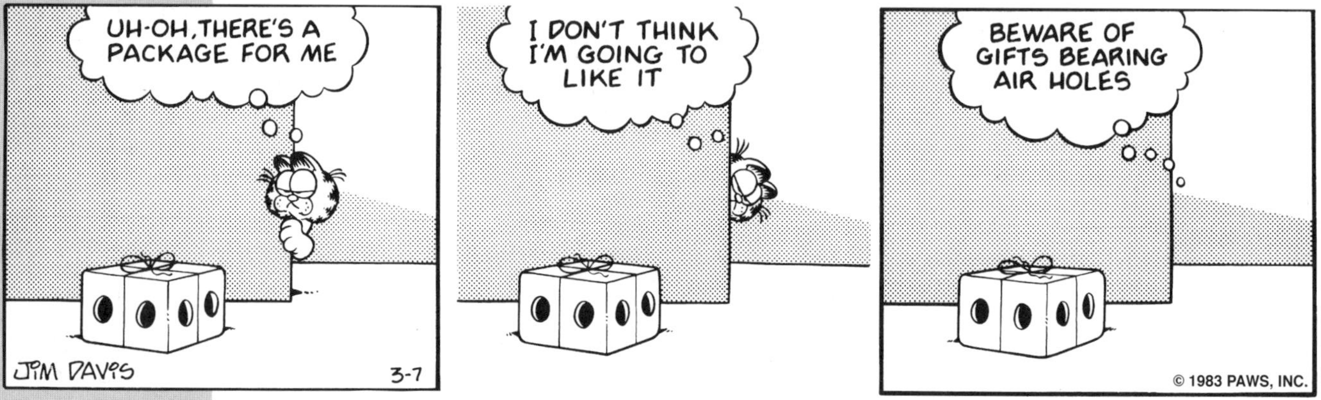
UH-OH, THERE'S A PACKAGE FOR ME
JIM DAVIS
3-7
I DON'T THINK I'M GOING TO LIKE IT
BEWARE OF GIFTS BEARING AIR HOLES
© 1983 PAWS, INC.

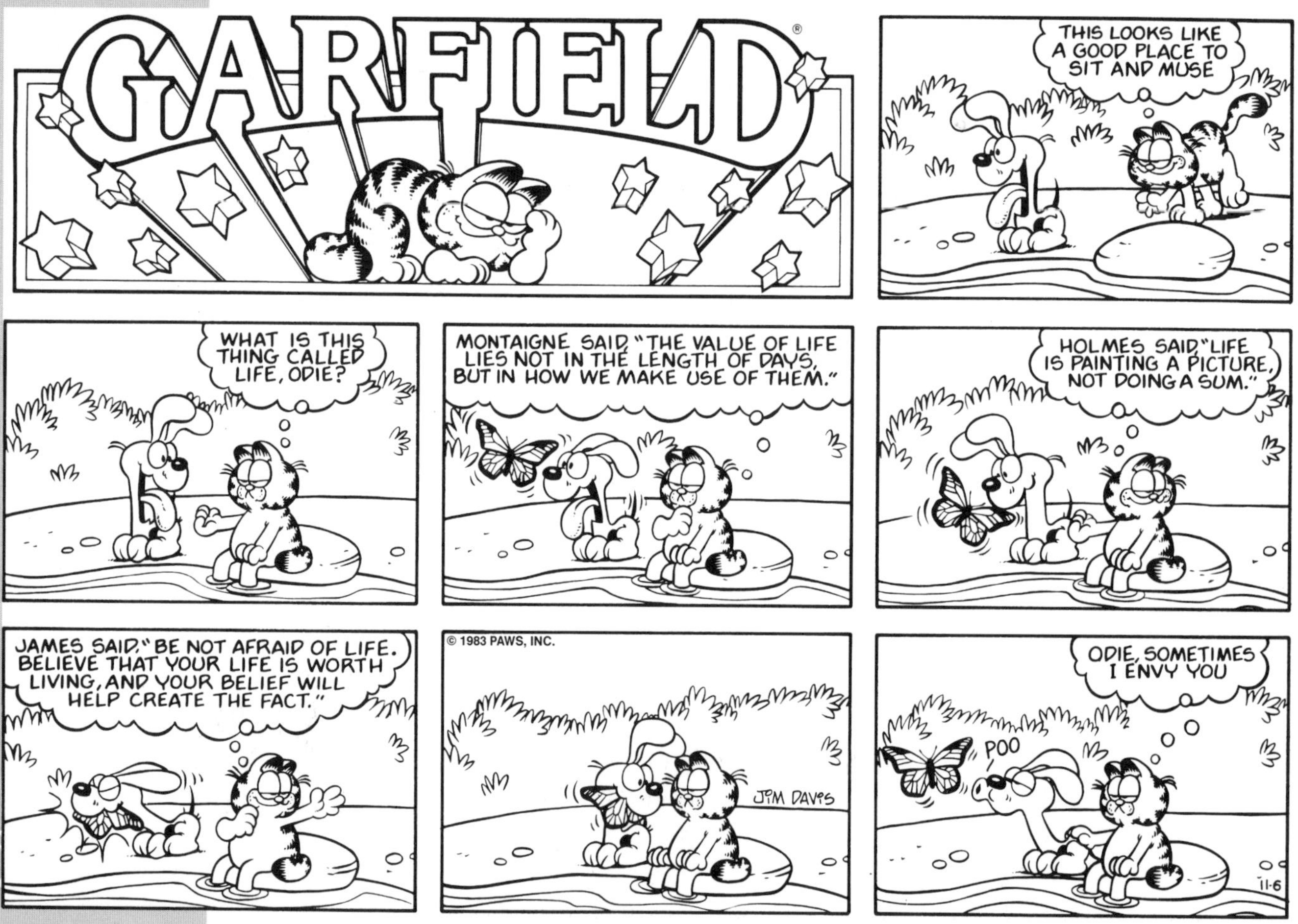
GARFIELD
THIS LOOKS LIKE A GOOD PLACE TO SIT AND MUSE
WHAT IS THIS THING CALLED LIFE, ODIE?
MONTAIGNE SAID "THE VALUE OF LIFE LIES NOT IN THE LENGTH OF DAYS, BUT IN HOW WE MAKE USE OF THEM."
HOLMES SAID "LIFE IS PAINTING A PICTURE, NOT DOING A SUM."
JAMES SAID "BE NOT AFRAID OF LIFE. BELIEVE THAT YOUR LIFE IS WORTH LIVING, AND YOUR BELIEF WILL HELP CREATE THE FACT."
© 1983 PAWS, INC.
JIM DAVIS
ODIE, SOMETIMES I ENVY YOU
POO
11-6

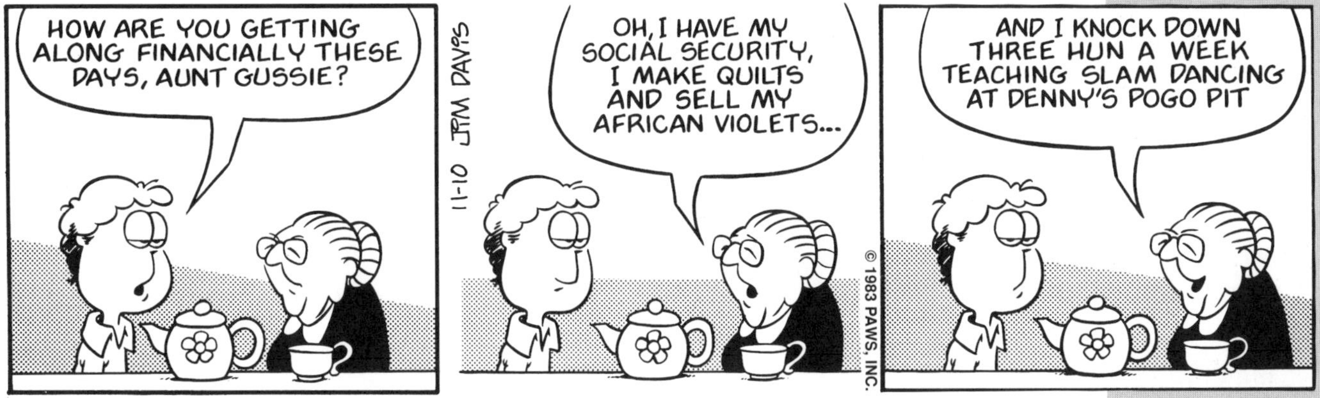
HOW ARE YOU GETTING ALONG FINANCIALLY THESE DAYS, AUNT GUSSIE?
JPM DAVIS 11-10
OH, I HAVE MY SOCIAL SECURITY, I MAKE QUILTS AND SELL MY AFRICAN VIOLETS...
© 1983 PAWS, INC.
AND I KNOCK DOWN THREE HUN A WEEK TEACHING SLAM DANCING AT DENNY'S POGO PIT

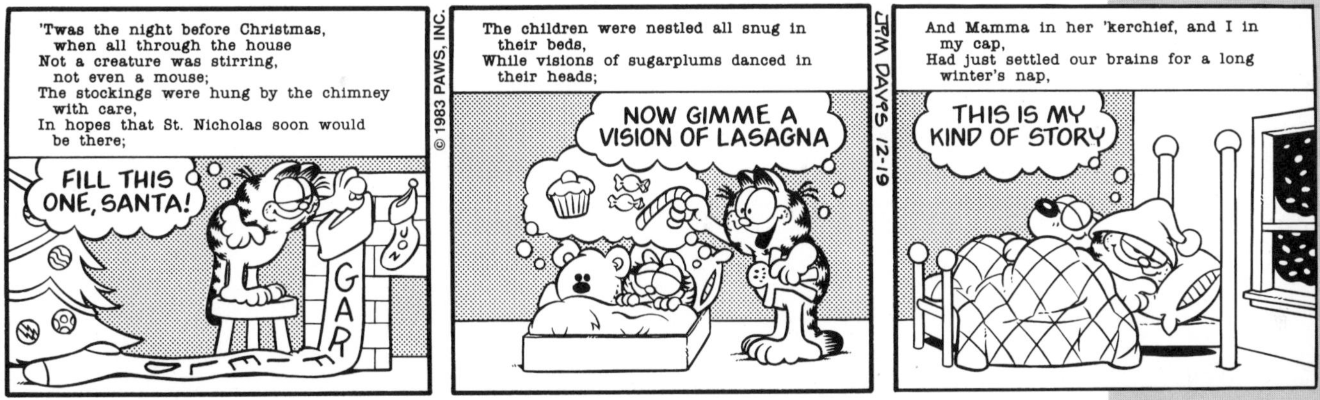
'Twas the night before Christmas, when all through the house
Not a creature was stirring, not even a mouse;
The stockings were hung by the chimney with care,
In hopes that St. Nicholas soon would be there;
FILL THIS ONE, SANTA!
GAR
© 1983 PAWS, INC.
The children were nestled all snug in their beds,
While visions of sugarplums danced in their heads;
NOW GIMME A VISION OF LASAGNA
JPM DAVIS 12-19
And Mamma in her 'kerchief, and I in my cap,
Had just settled our brains for a long winter's nap,
THIS IS MY KIND OF STORY

The night before Christmas . . . Garfield-style!

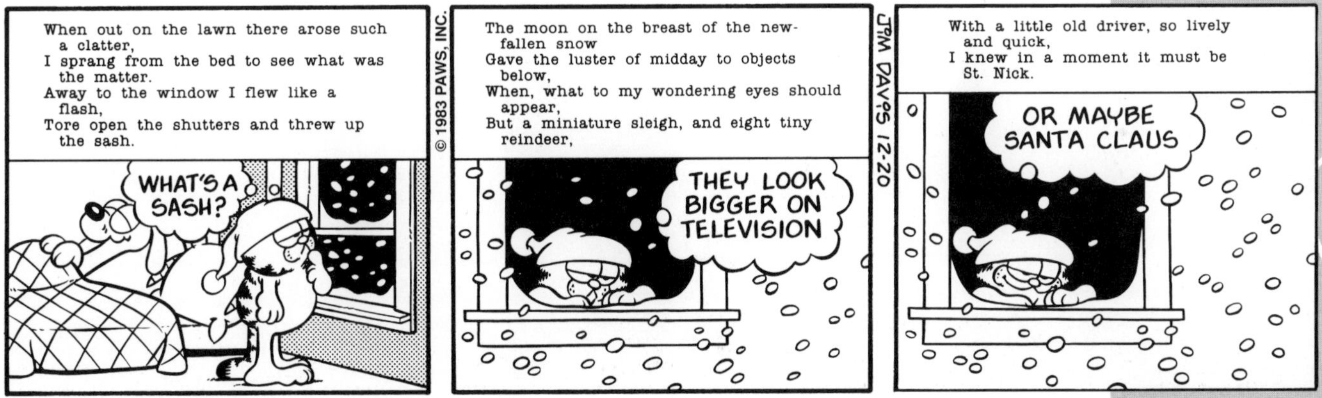
When out on the lawn there arose such a clatter,
I sprang from the bed to see what was the matter.
Away to the window I flew like a flash,
Tore open the shutters and threw up the sash.
WHAT'S A SASH?
© 1983 PAWS, INC.
The moon on the breast of the new-fallen snow
Gave the luster of midday to objects below,
When, what to my wondering eyes should appear,
But a miniature sleigh, and eight tiny reindeer,
THEY LOOK BIGGER ON TELEVISION
JPM DAVIS 12-20
With a little old driver, so lively and quick,
I knew in a moment it must be St. Nick.
OR MAYBE SANTA CLAUS

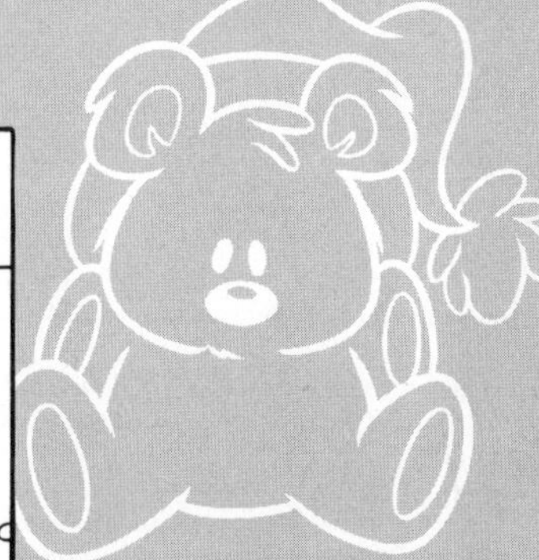

FAT CAT FACTOID
~1983~

The *Flashdance* look takes the country by storm. What a feeling!

Garfield *now appears in 1,400 newspapers in 22 countries and 7 languages!*

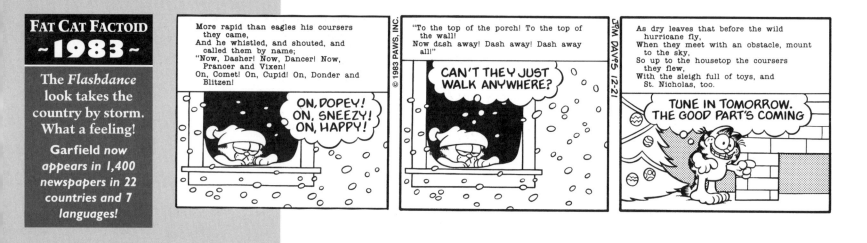

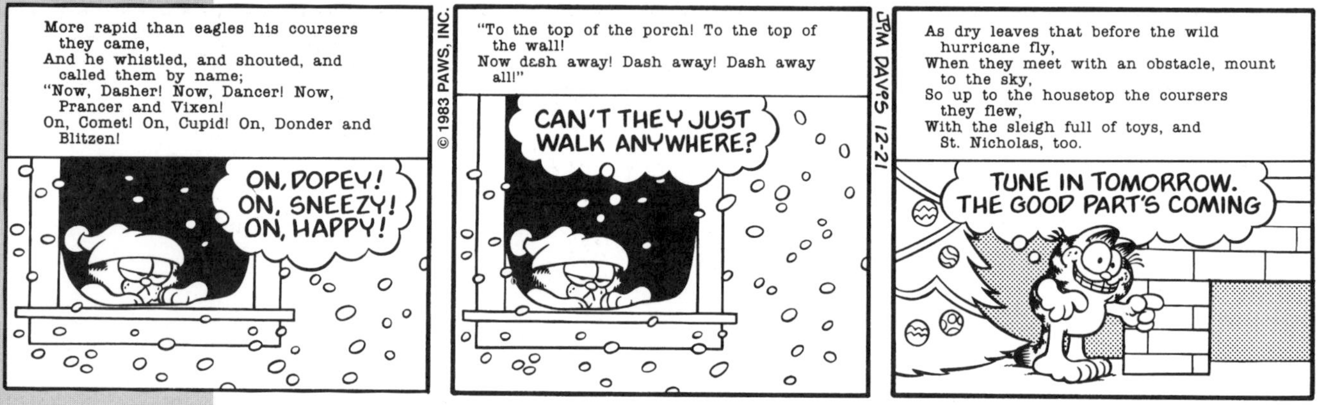
More rapid than eagles his coursers they came,
And he whistled, and shouted, and called them by name;
"Now, Dasher! Now, Dancer! Now, Prancer and Vixen!
On, Comet! On, Cupid! On, Donder and Blitzen!
ON, DOPEY! ON, SNEEZY! ON, HAPPY!
© 1983 PAWS, INC.
"To the top of the porch! To the top of the wall!
Now dash away! Dash away! Dash away all!"
CAN'T THEY JUST WALK ANYWHERE?
JPM DAVIS 12-21
As dry leaves that before the wild hurricane fly,
When they meet with an obstacle, mount to the sky,
So up to the housetop the coursers they flew,
With the sleigh full of toys, and St. Nicholas, too.
TUNE IN TOMORROW. THE GOOD PART'S COMING

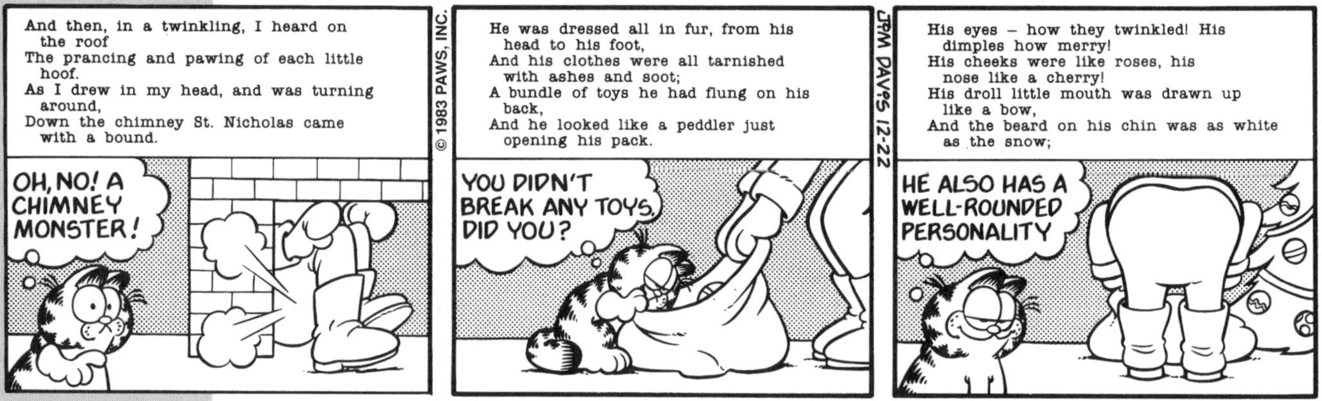
And then, in a twinkling, I heard on the roof
The prancing and pawing of each little hoof.
As I drew in my head, and was turning around,
Down the chimney St. Nicholas came with a bound.
OH, NO! A CHIMNEY MONSTER!
© 1983 PAWS, INC.
He was dressed all in fur, from his head to his foot,
And his clothes were all tarnished with ashes and soot;
A bundle of toys he had flung on his back,
And he looked like a peddler just opening his pack.
YOU DIDN'T BREAK ANY TOYS, DID YOU?
JPM DAVIS 12-22
His eyes – how they twinkled! His dimples how merry!
His cheeks were like roses, his nose like a cherry!
His droll little mouth was drawn up like a bow,
And the beard on his chin was as white as the snow;
HE ALSO HAS A WELL-ROUNDED PERSONALITY

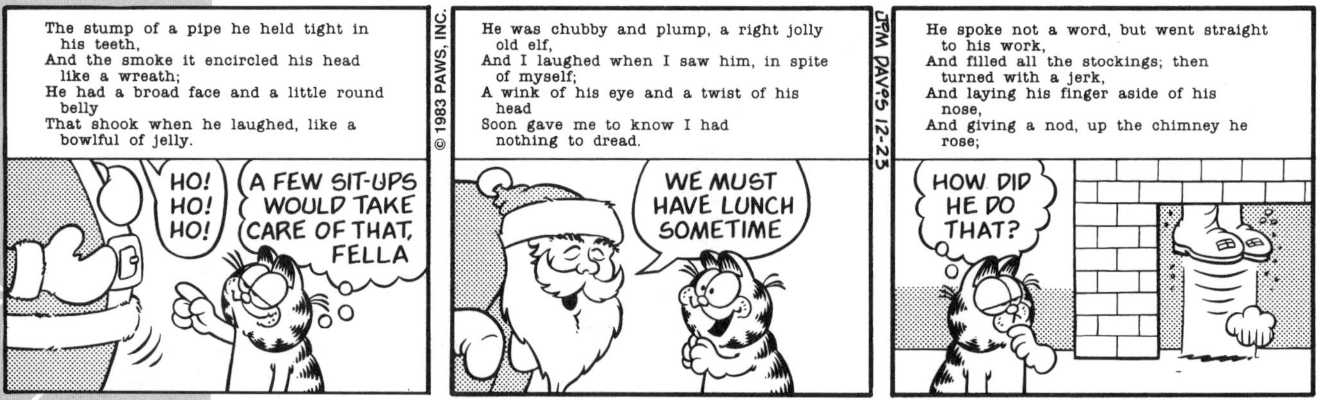
The stump of a pipe he held tight in his teeth,
And the smoke it encircled his head like a wreath;
He had a broad face and a little round belly
That shook when he laughed, like a bowlful of jelly.
HO! HO! HO!
A FEW SIT-UPS WOULD TAKE CARE OF THAT, FELLA
© 1983 PAWS, INC.
He was chubby and plump, a right jolly old elf,
And I laughed when I saw him, in spite of myself;
A wink of his eye and a twist of his head
Soon gave me to know I had nothing to dread.
WE MUST HAVE LUNCH SOMETIME
JPM DAVIS 12-23
He spoke not a word, but went straight to his work,
And filled all the stockings; then turned with a jerk,
And laying his finger aside of his nose,
And giving a nod, up the chimney he rose;
HOW DID HE DO THAT?

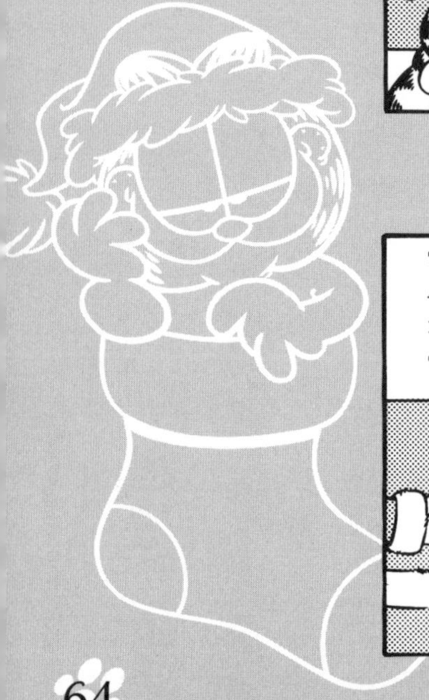

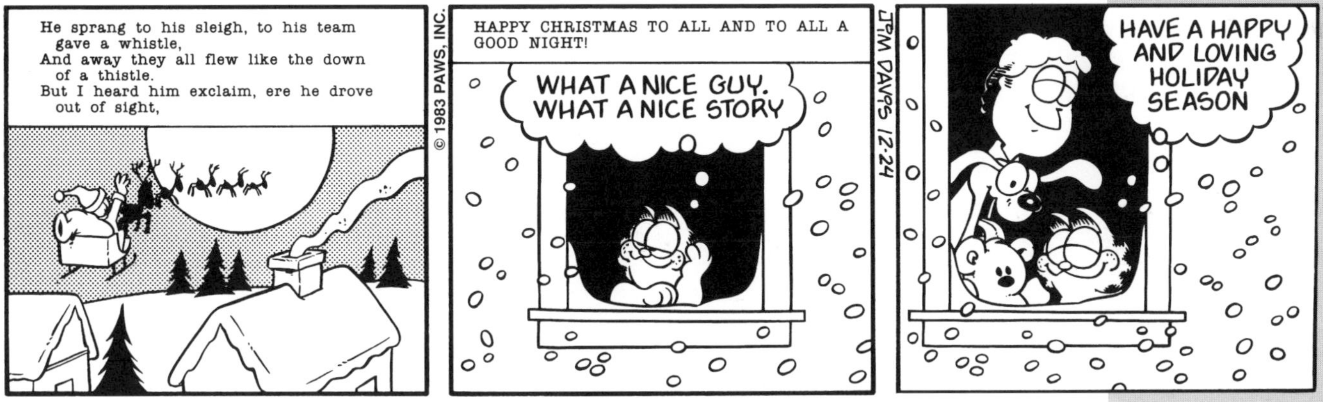
He sprang to his sleigh, to his team gave a whistle,
And away they all flew like the down of a thistle.
But I heard him exclaim, ere he drove out of sight,
© 1983 PAWS, INC.
HAPPY CHRISTMAS TO ALL AND TO ALL A GOOD NIGHT!
WHAT A NICE GUY. WHAT A NICE STORY
HAVE A HAPPY AND LOVING HOLIDAY SEASON

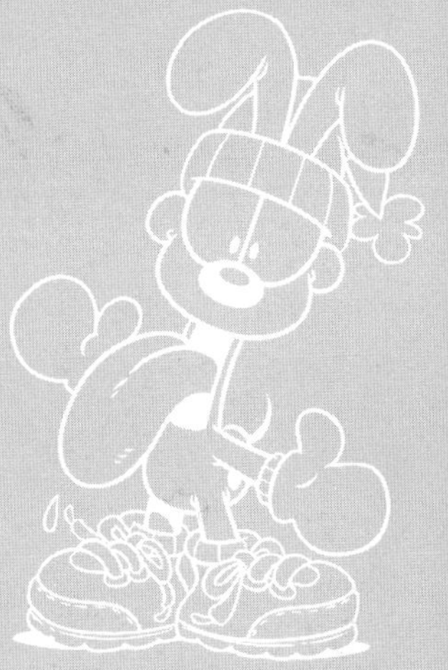

DOWN ON THE FARM

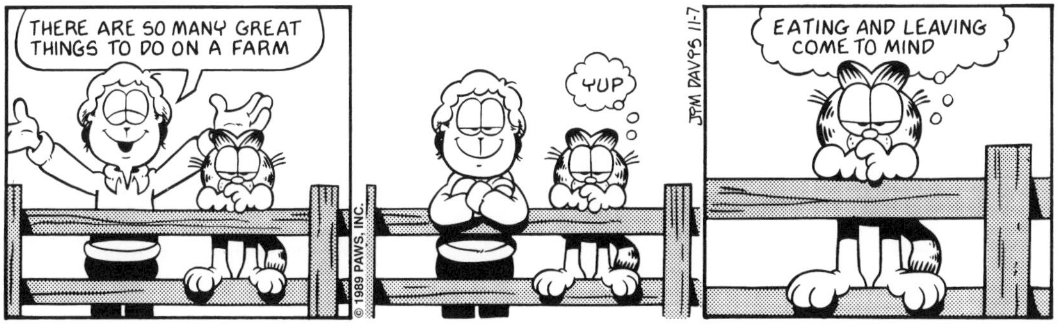
THERE ARE SO MANY GREAT THINGS TO DO ON A FARM
© 1989 PAWS, INC.
YUP
EATING AND LEAVING COME TO MIND

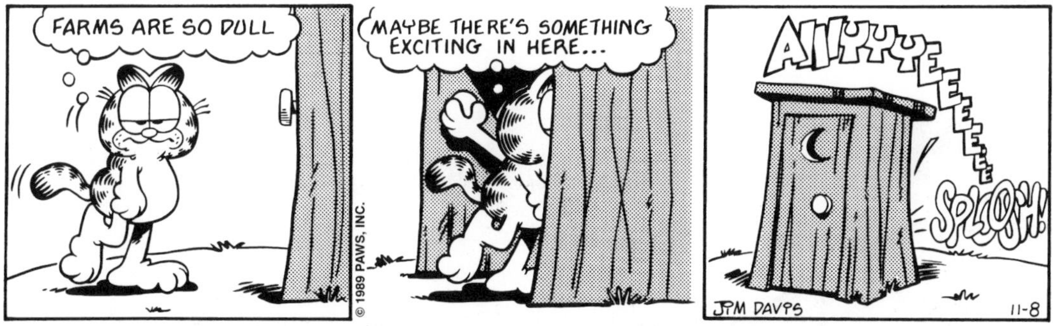
FARMS ARE SO DULL
© 1989 PAWS, INC.
MAYBE THERE'S SOMETHING EXCITING IN HERE...
AIIYYYEEEEEEE
SPLOOSH!

Every so often Jon packs up his pets and heads for the country to visit his family on their farm. Garfield always enjoys going to the farm . . . about as much as he enjoys going on a diet. Being a kitty from the city, Garfield thinks farms are as dull as dirt. Oh sure, there are a few things he likes to do on the Arbuckle farm: baste the hogs, harvest the fridge, fertilize Doc Boy's overalls. But his favorite thing to do is leave!

“Homespun” humor is hard to beat.

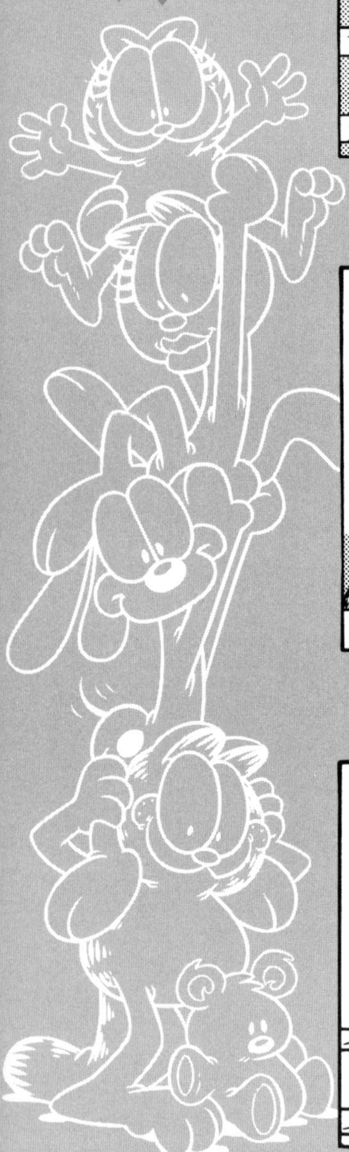

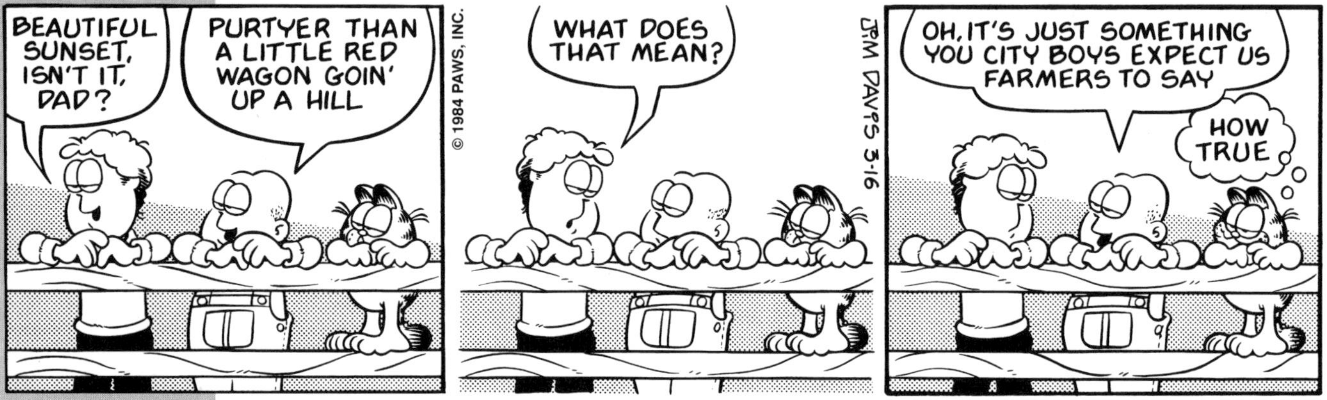

BEAUTIFUL SUNSET, ISN'T IT, DAD?
PURTYER THAN A LITTLE RED WAGON GOIN' UP A HILL
© 1984 PAWS, INC.
WHAT DOES THAT MEAN?
JIM DAVIS 3·16
OH, IT'S JUST SOMETHING YOU CITY BOYS EXPECT US FARMERS TO SAY
HOW TRUE

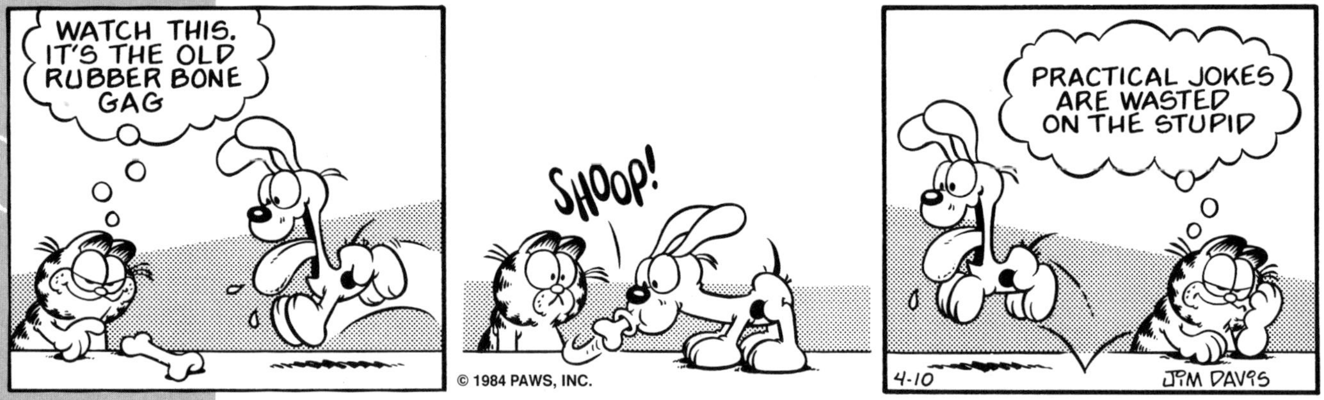

WATCH THIS. IT'S THE OLD RUBBER BONE GAG
SHOOP!
© 1984 PAWS, INC.
PRACTICAL JOKES ARE WASTED ON THE STUPID
4-10
JIM DAVIS

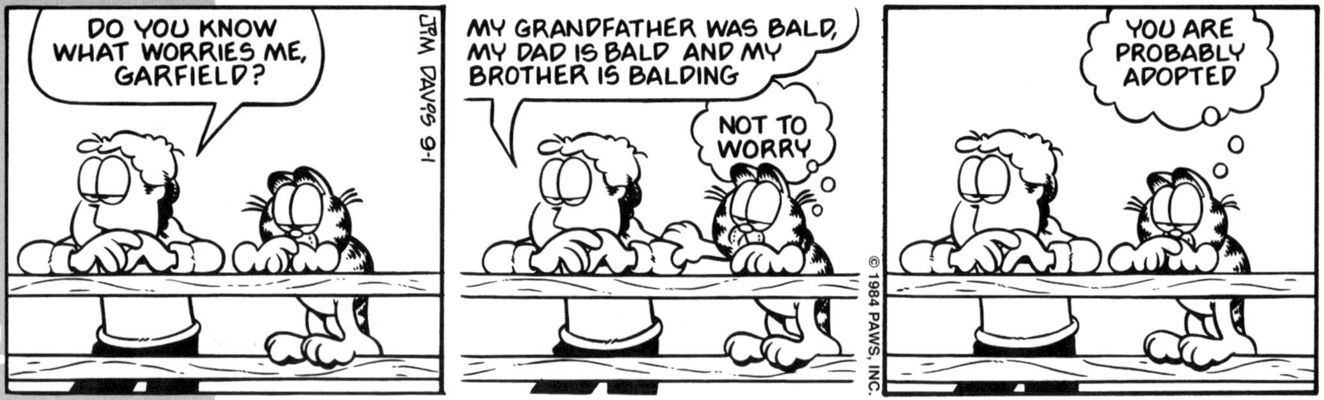

DO YOU KNOW WHAT WORRIES ME, GARFIELD?
JIM DAVIS 9-1
MY GRANDFATHER WAS BALD, MY DAD IS BALD AND MY BROTHER IS BALDING
NOT TO WORRY
© 1984 PAWS, INC.
YOU ARE PROBABLY ADOPTED

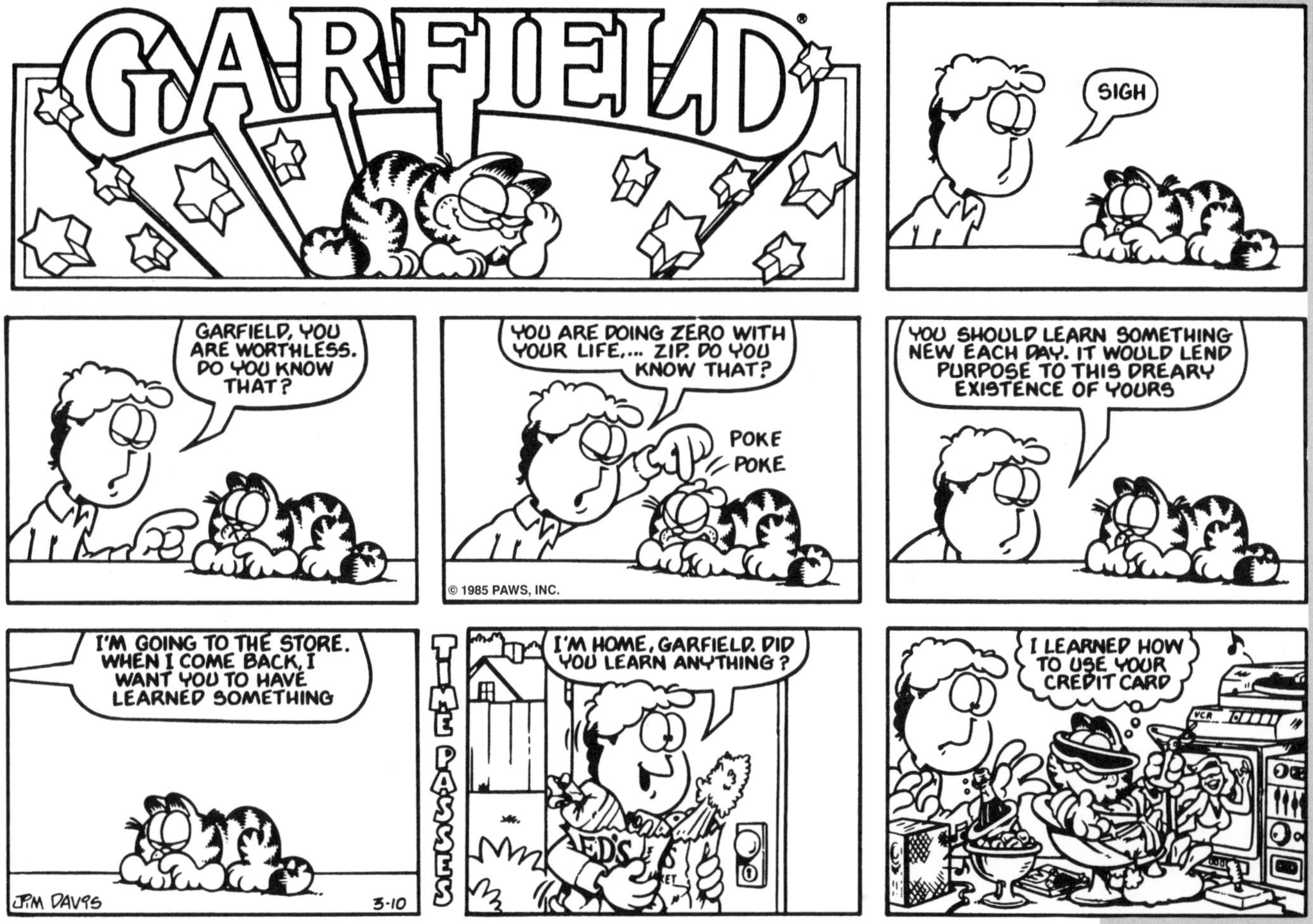
GARFIELD
SIGH
GARFIELD, YOU ARE WORTHLESS. DO YOU KNOW THAT?
YOU ARE DOING ZERO WITH YOUR LIFE,... ZIP. DO YOU KNOW THAT?
POKE
POKE
© 1985 PAWS, INC.
YOU SHOULD LEARN SOMETHING NEW EACH DAY. IT WOULD LEND PURPOSE TO THIS DREARY EXISTENCE OF YOURS
I'M GOING TO THE STORE. WHEN I COME BACK, I WANT YOU TO HAVE LEARNED SOMETHING
JIM DAVIS
3-10
TIME PASSES
I'M HOME, GARFIELD. DID YOU LEARN ANYTHING?
I LEARNED HOW TO USE YOUR CREDIT CARD
VCR

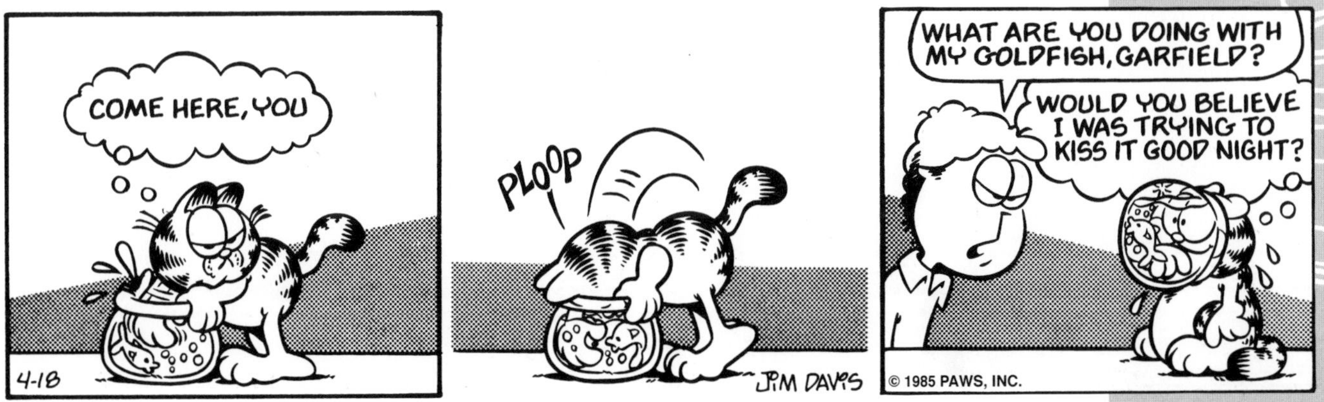
COME HERE, YOU
4-18
PLOOP
JIM DAVIS
WHAT ARE YOU DOING WITH MY GOLDFISH, GARFIELD?
WOULD YOU BELIEVE I WAS TRYING TO KISS IT GOOD NIGHT?
© 1985 PAWS, INC.

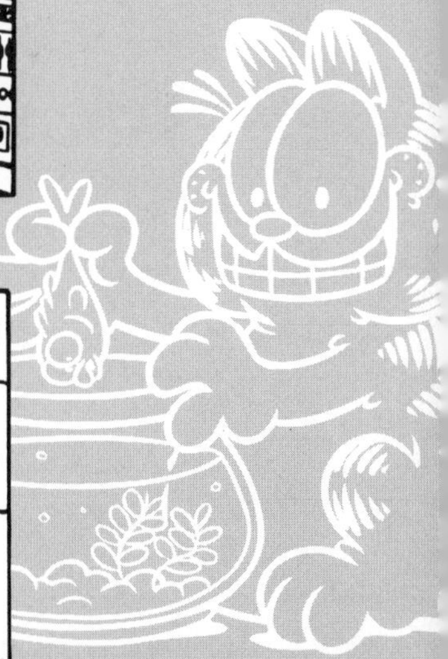

FAT CAT FACTOID
~ 1984 ~

Carl Lewis and Mary Lou Retton grab the gold at the 23rd Olympic Games!

Garfield and Jim Davis star in an American Express "Do you know me?" commercial.

JIM DAVIS 7-19
© 1985 PAWS, INC.
GET RID OF THE DOG!

GARFIELD HOGS THE SPOTLIGHT

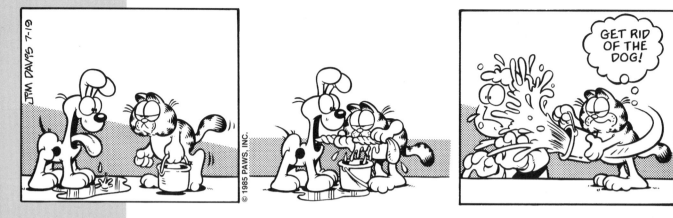

Like any great performer, Garfield loves an audience . . . even a hostile one. So he continues to perform on the neighborhood fence, even though his act elicits far more brickbats than bravos. But that's not Garfield's fault. Some people just have no appreciation for bad jokes and worse singing. At least Garfield's starting to attract a better class of heckler: someone once hit him with an empty caviar tin! Still, it may be time for Garfield to get a new act. That or a suit of armor!

IIIIIIIT'S SHOW TIME!
TAPPITY TAPPITY TAPPITY
© 1991 PAWS, INC.
TRIP
CRASH!
IIIIIIIT'S INTERMISSION!
STUMBLE STUMBLE
JIM DAVIS 4-30
MEYOOO-WRRR-MEEE-YOUWRRR!! MEEE-
JIM DAVIS 8-19
© 1991 PAWS, INC.
SPLUT! KONG!
BLAT!
IS IT MY FAULT THIS FENCE HAS LOUSY ACOUSTICS?!!

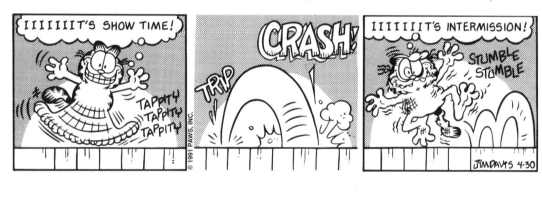

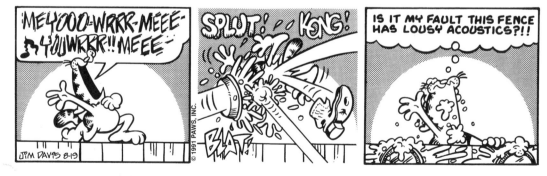

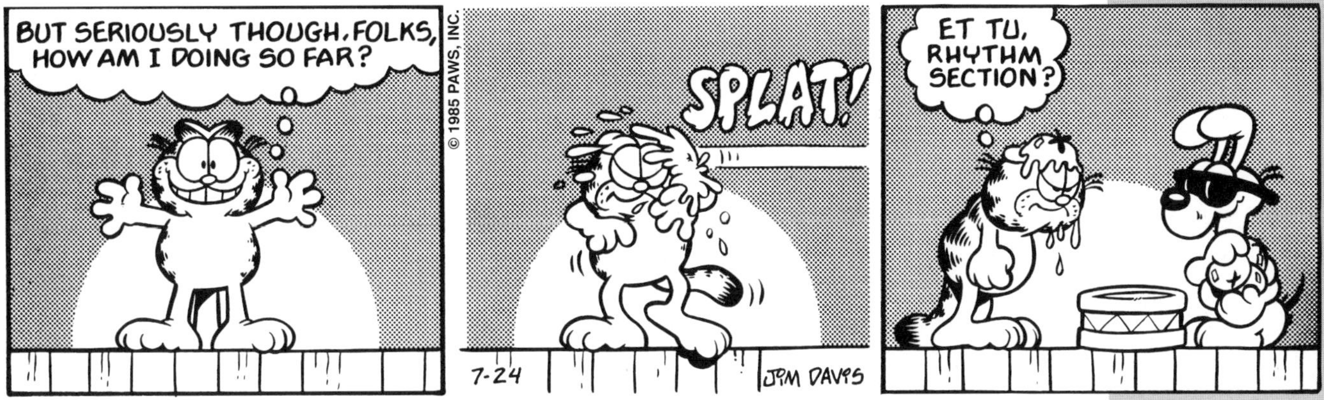
BUT SERIOUSLY THOUGH, FOLKS, HOW AM I DOING SO FAR?
© 1985 PAWS, INC.
SPLAT!
7-24
JIM DAVIS
ET TU, RHYTHM SECTION?

The on-the-fence gags let the old vaudevillian in me come out.

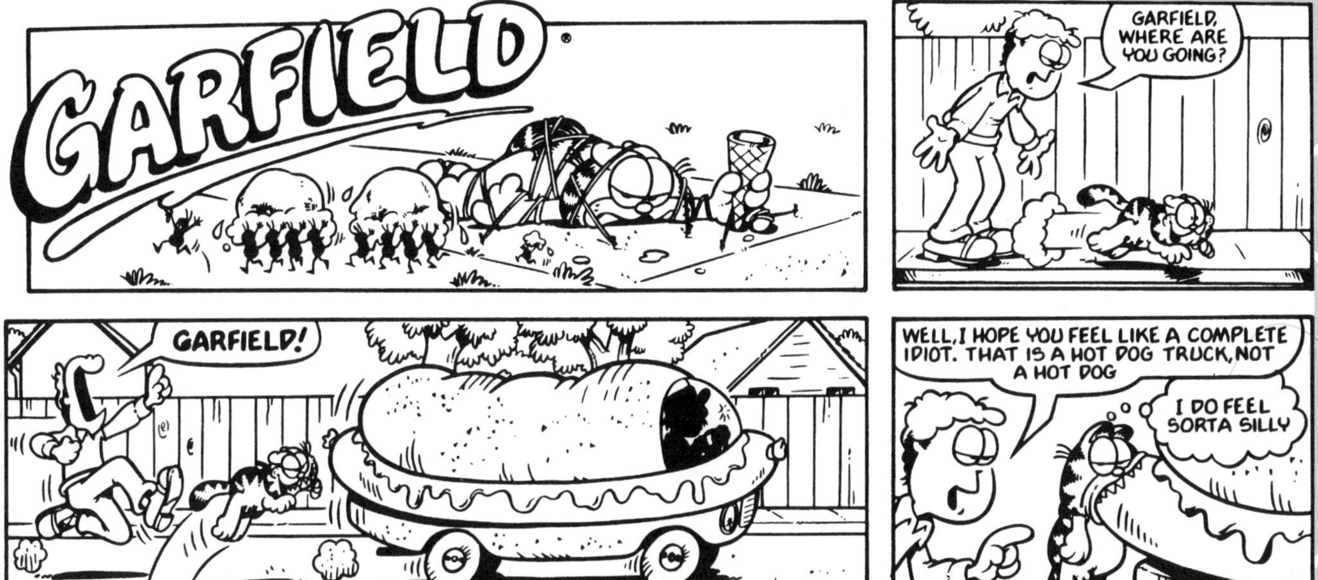
GARFIELD®
GARFIELD, WHERE ARE YOU GOING?
GARFIELD!
WELL, I HOPE YOU FEEL LIKE A COMPLETE IDIOT. THAT IS A HOT DOG TRUCK, NOT A HOT DOG
I DO FEEL SORTA SILLY
NOW WHAT?!
8-18
JIM DAVIS
NOW FOR DESSERT
© 1985 PAWS, INC.

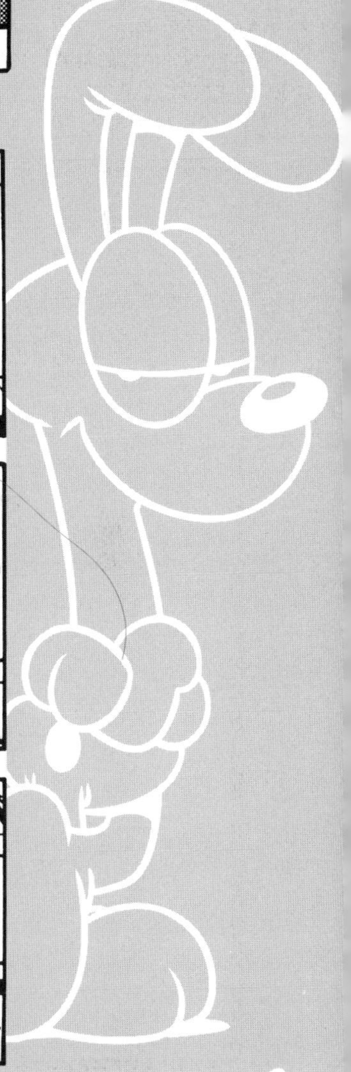

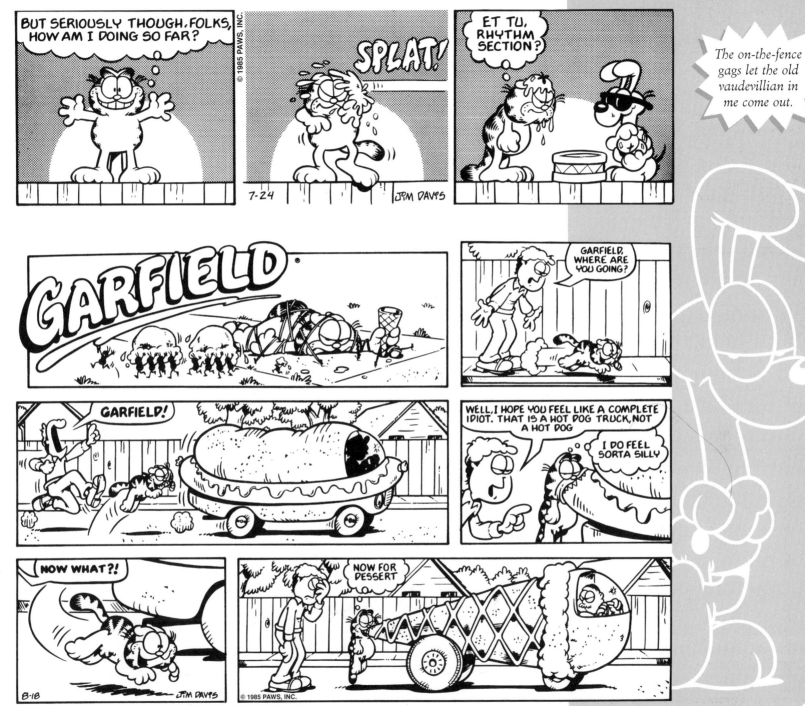

This was a best-selling poster.

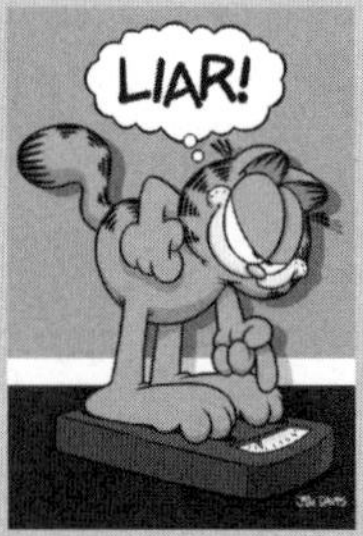
LIAR!

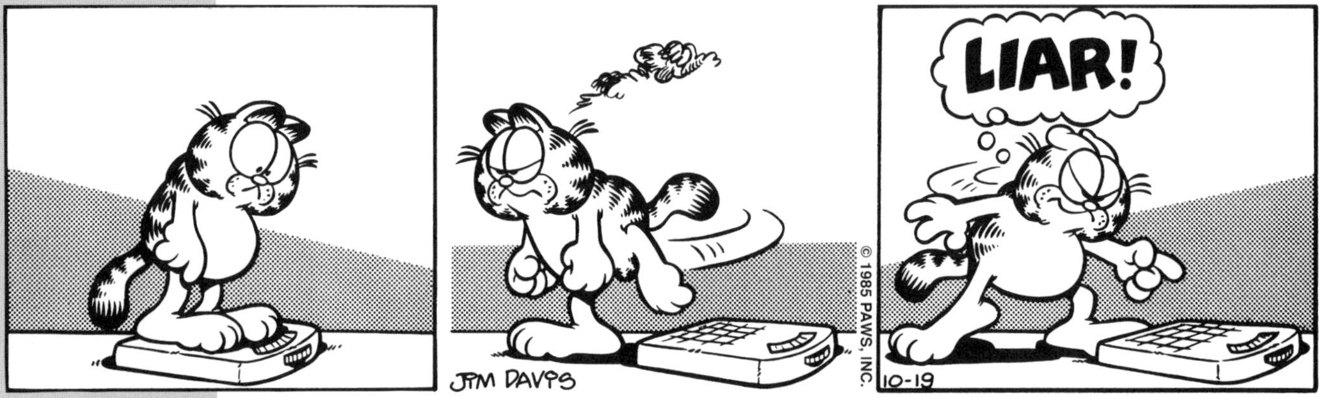
LIAR!
JIM DAVIS
© 1985 PAWS, INC.
10-19

NERD IS THE WORD

Clearly, nerd is the word for Jon Arbuckle. His life — if you can call it that — is so boring, he looks forward to dental appointments. His idea of excitement is counting the number of dimples on a golf ball. His wardrobe is right out of GQ —Geek's Quarterly. He's such a loser, he can't even get a good-night kiss from his mom. If he were a car, he'd be a beige station wagon. On a scale of one to ten, he's a minus two. Other than that, he's a pretty cool guy.

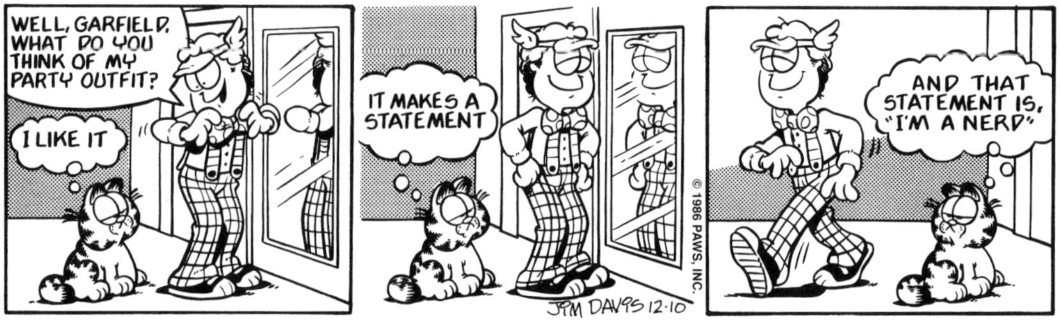
WELL, GARFIELD, WHAT DO YOU THINK OF MY PARTY OUTFIT?
I LIKE IT
IT MAKES A STATEMENT
AND THAT STATEMENT IS, "I'M A NERD"
JIM DAVIS 12-10
© 1986 PAWS, INC.

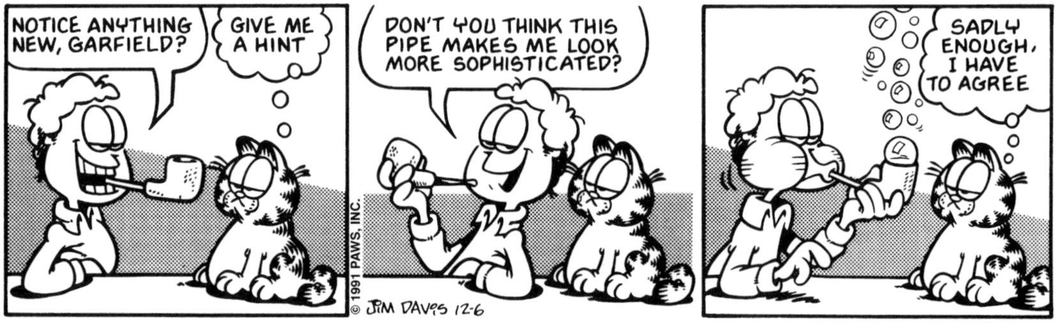
NOTICE ANYTHING NEW, GARFIELD?
GIVE ME A HINT
DON'T YOU THINK THIS PIPE MAKES ME LOOK MORE SOPHISTICATED?
SADLY ENOUGH, I HAVE TO AGREE
© 1991 PAWS, INC.
JIM DAVIS 12-6

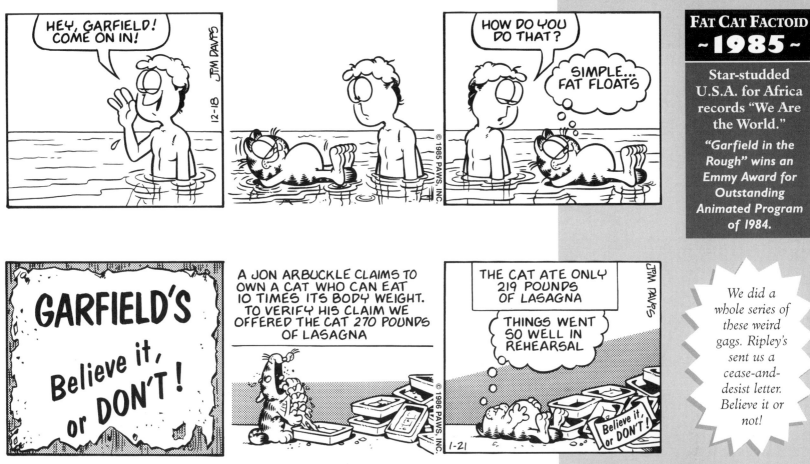

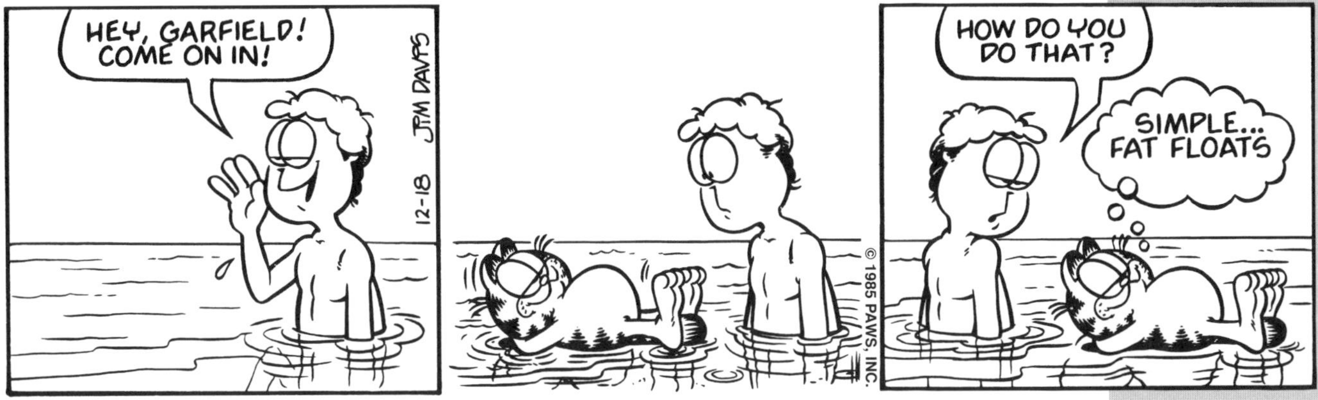
HEY, GARFIELD! COME ON IN!
JIM DAVIS
12-18
© 1985 PAWS, INC.
HOW DO YOU DO THAT?
SIMPLE... FAT FLOATS

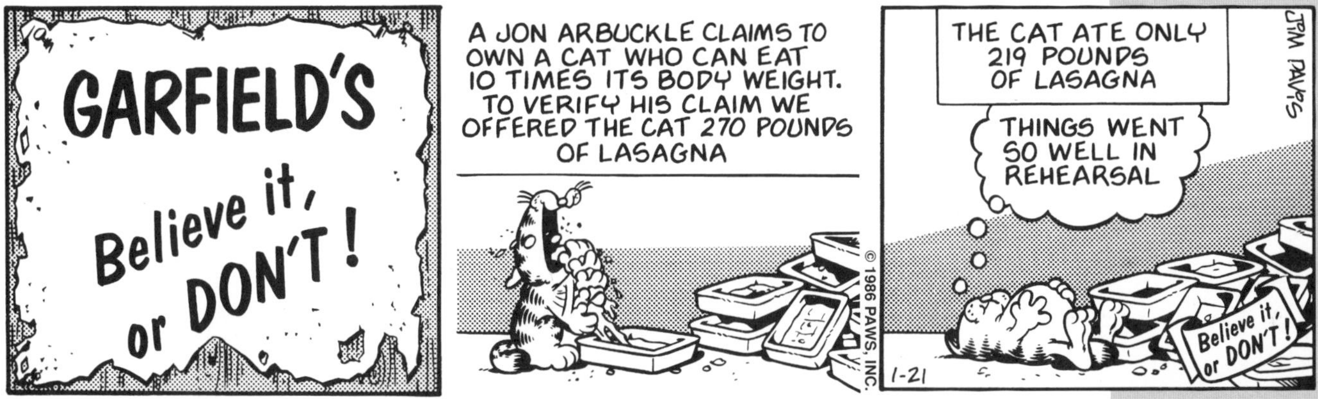
GARFIELD'S
Believe it, or DON'T!
A JON ARBUCKLE CLAIMS TO OWN A CAT WHO CAN EAT 10 TIMES ITS BODY WEIGHT. TO VERIFY HIS CLAIM WE OFFERED THE CAT 270 POUNDS OF LASAGNA
© 1986 PAWS, INC.
THE CAT ATE ONLY 219 POUNDS OF LASAGNA
THINGS WENT SO WELL IN REHEARSAL
JIM DAVIS
Believe it, or DON'T!
1-21

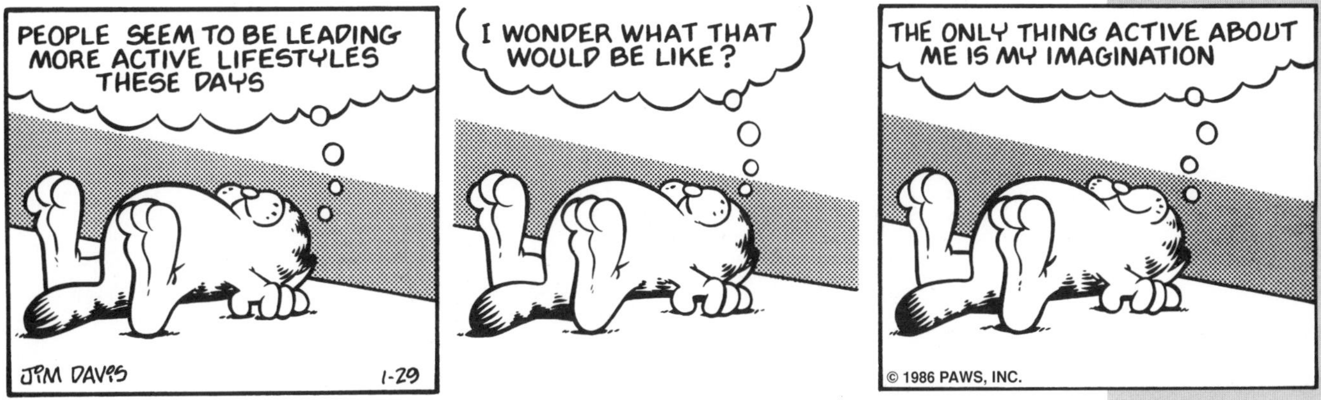
PEOPLE SEEM TO BE LEADING MORE ACTIVE LIFESTYLES THESE DAYS
JIM DAVIS
1-29
I WONDER WHAT THAT WOULD BE LIKE?
THE ONLY THING ACTIVE ABOUT ME IS MY IMAGINATION
© 1986 PAWS, INC.

FAT CAT FACTOID

~1985~

Star-studded U.S.A. for Africa records "We Are the World."

"Garfield in the Rough" wins an Emmy Award for Outstanding Animated Program of 1984.

We did a whole series of these weird gags. Ripley's sent us a cease-and-desist letter. Believe it or not!

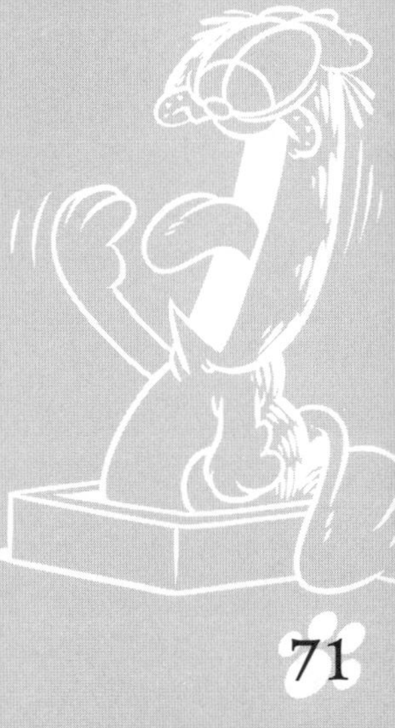

"Caught in the blinds" was another silly premise. Most of my gags had been very self-contained, but I wanted to take this to the limit. This two-week sequence was great fun to write.

In the second week, it just got sillier, as Garfield, Jon, and Odie were joined by several unsuspecting passersby.

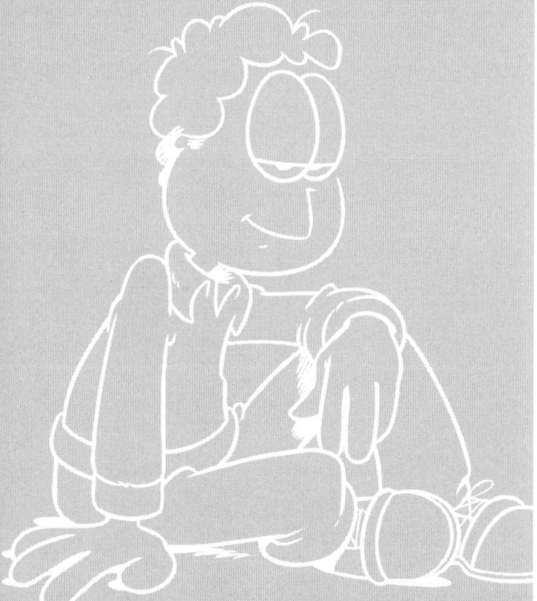

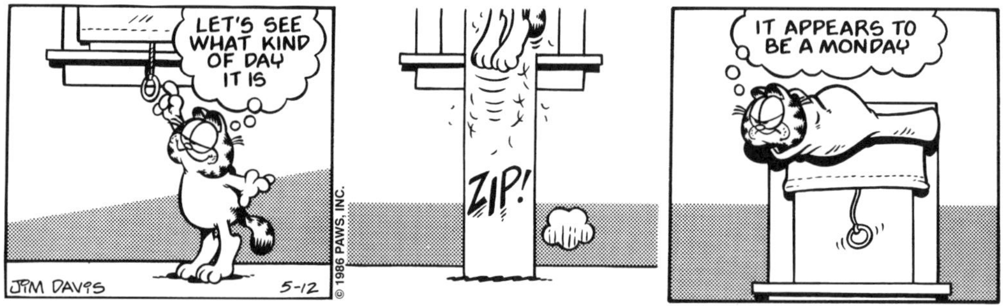

LET'S SEE WHAT KIND OF DAY IT IS
JIM DAVIS 5-12
© 1986 PAWS, INC.
ZIP!
IT APPEARS TO BE A MONDAY

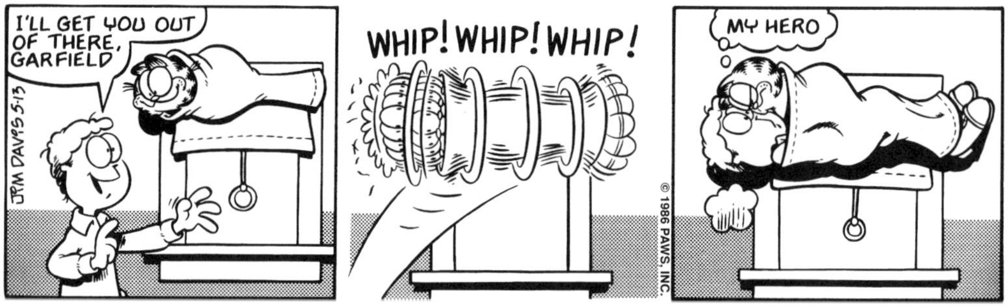

I'LL GET YOU OUT OF THERE, GARFIELD
JIM DAVIS 5-13
WHIP! WHIP! WHIP!
MY HERO
© 1986 PAWS, INC.

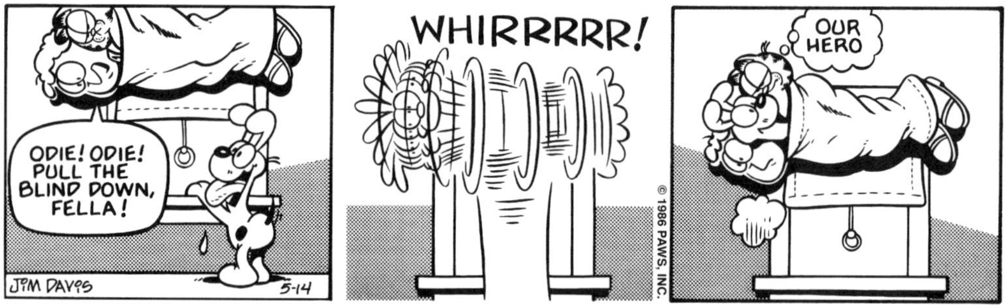

ODIE! ODIE! PULL THE BLIND DOWN, FELLA!
JIM DAVIS 5-14
WHIRRRRR!
OUR HERO
© 1986 PAWS, INC.

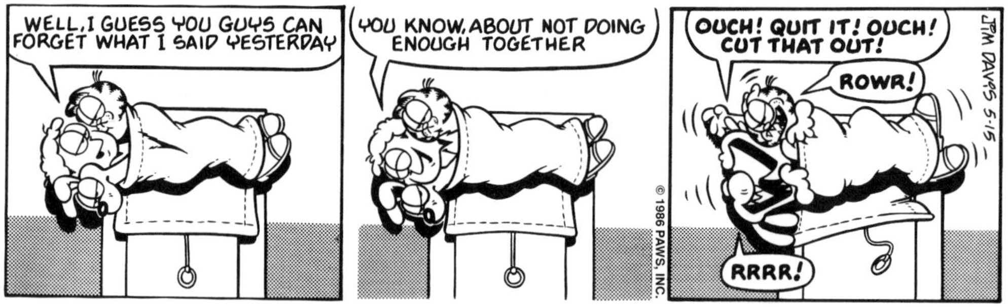

WELL, I GUESS YOU GUYS CAN FORGET WHAT I SAID YESTERDAY
YOU KNOW, ABOUT NOT DOING ENOUGH TOGETHER
© 1986 PAWS, INC.
OUCH! QUIT IT! OUCH! CUT THAT OUT!
ROWR!
RRRR!
JIM DAVIS 5-15

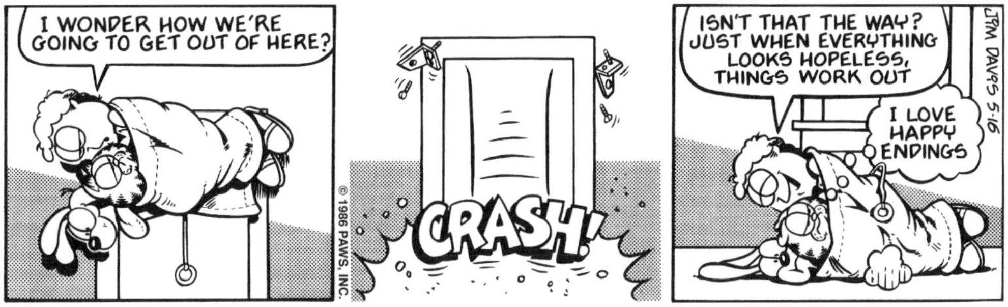
I WONDER HOW WE'RE GOING TO GET OUT OF HERE?
© 1986 PAWS, INC.
CRASH!
ISN'T THAT THE WAY? JUST WHEN EVERYTHING LOOKS HOPELESS, THINGS WORK OUT
I LOVE HAPPY ENDINGS
JIM DAVIS 5-16

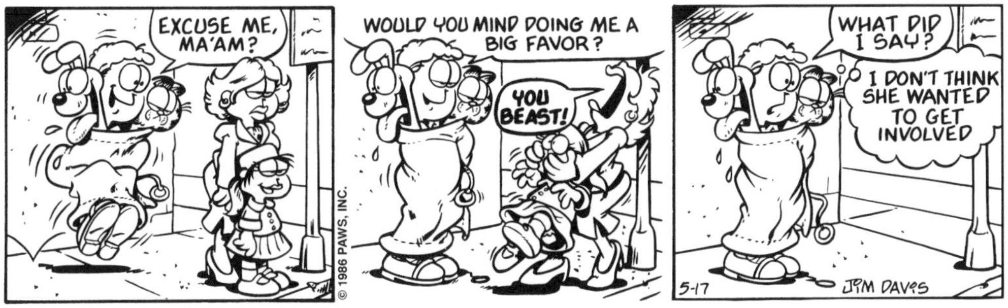
EXCUSE ME, MA'AM?
© 1986 PAWS, INC.
WOULD YOU MIND DOING ME A BIG FAVOR?
YOU BEAST!
WHAT DID I SAY?
I DON'T THINK SHE WANTED TO GET INVOLVED
5-17
JIM DAVIS

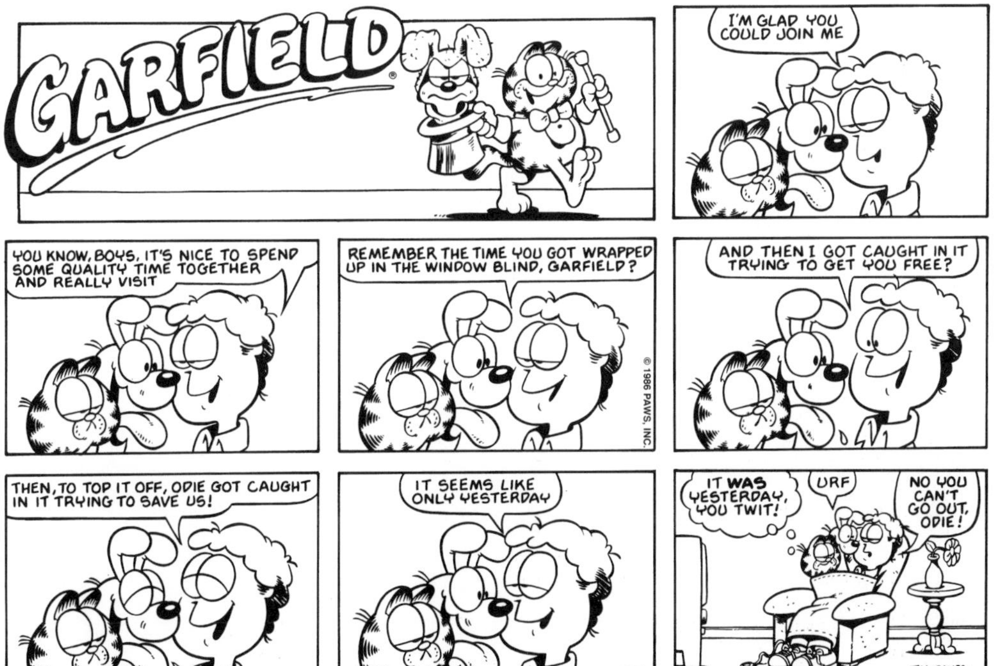
GARFIELD
I'M GLAD YOU COULD JOIN ME
YOU KNOW, BOYS, IT'S NICE TO SPEND SOME QUALITY TIME TOGETHER AND REALLY VISIT
REMEMBER THE TIME YOU GOT WRAPPED UP IN THE WINDOW BLIND, GARFIELD?
© 1986 PAWS, INC.
AND THEN I GOT CAUGHT IN IT TRYING TO GET YOU FREE?
THEN, TO TOP IT OFF, ODIE GOT CAUGHT IN IT TRYING TO SAVE US!
IT SEEMS LIKE ONLY YESTERDAY
5-18
IT WAS YESTERDAY, YOU TWIT!
URF
NO YOU CAN'T GO OUT, ODIE!
JIM DAVIS

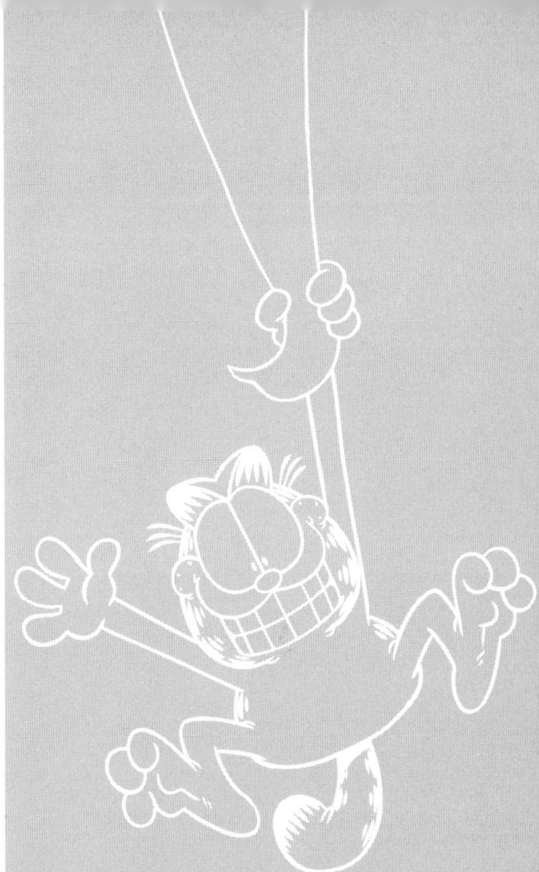

Left: *This was one of the rare times I continued a daily story line into a Sunday strip.*

FAT CAT FACTOID
~1986~

Schlockmeister Geraldo Rivera serves up sleaze in a new age of tabloid TV.

Garfield waddles into 1,800 newspapers!

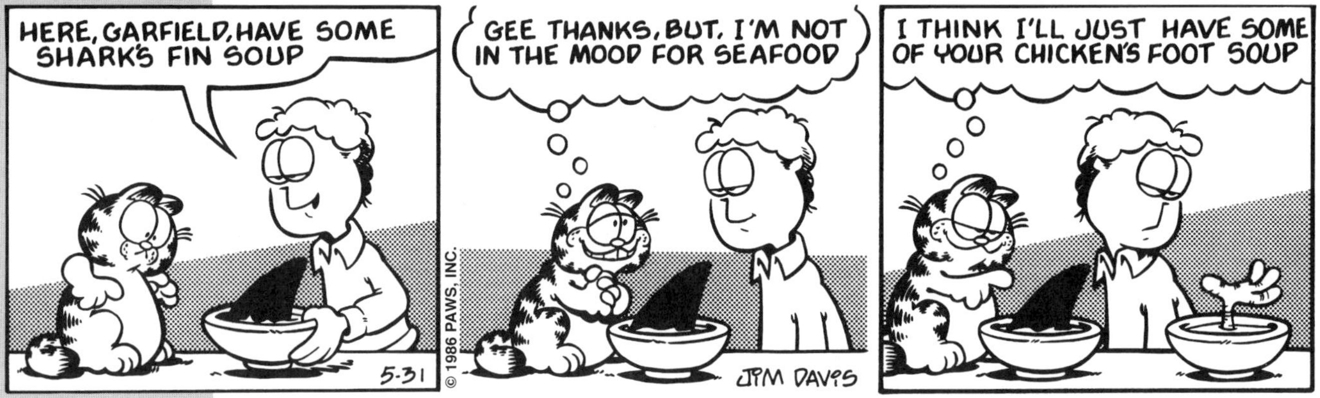

HERE, GARFIELD, HAVE SOME SHARK'S FIN SOUP
5-31
© 1986 PAWS, INC.
GEE THANKS, BUT, I'M NOT IN THE MOOD FOR SEAFOOD
JIM DAVIS
I THINK I'LL JUST HAVE SOME OF YOUR CHICKEN'S FOOT SOUP

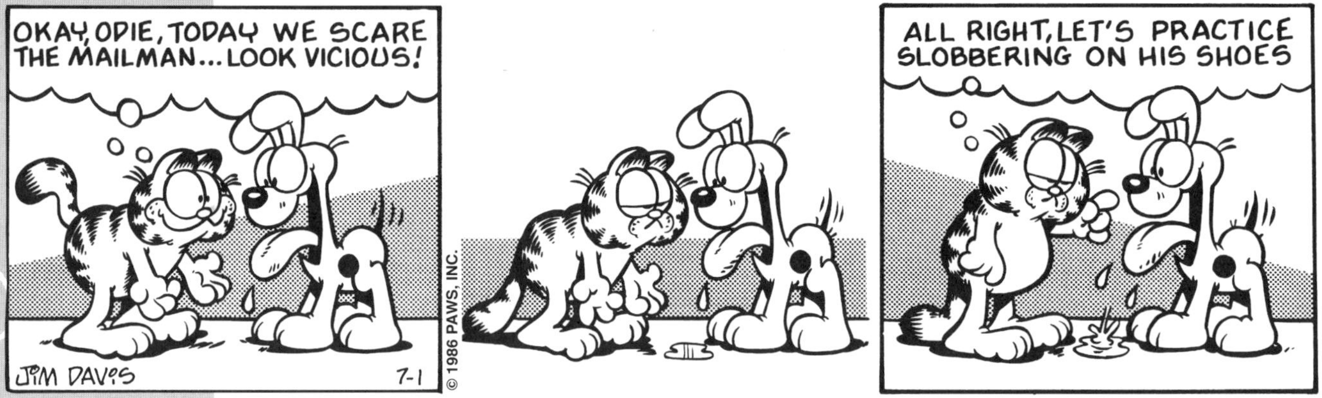

OKAY, ODIE, TODAY WE SCARE THE MAILMAN... LOOK VICIOUS!
JIM DAVIS
7-1
© 1986 PAWS, INC.
ALL RIGHT, LET'S PRACTICE SLOBBERING ON HIS SHOES

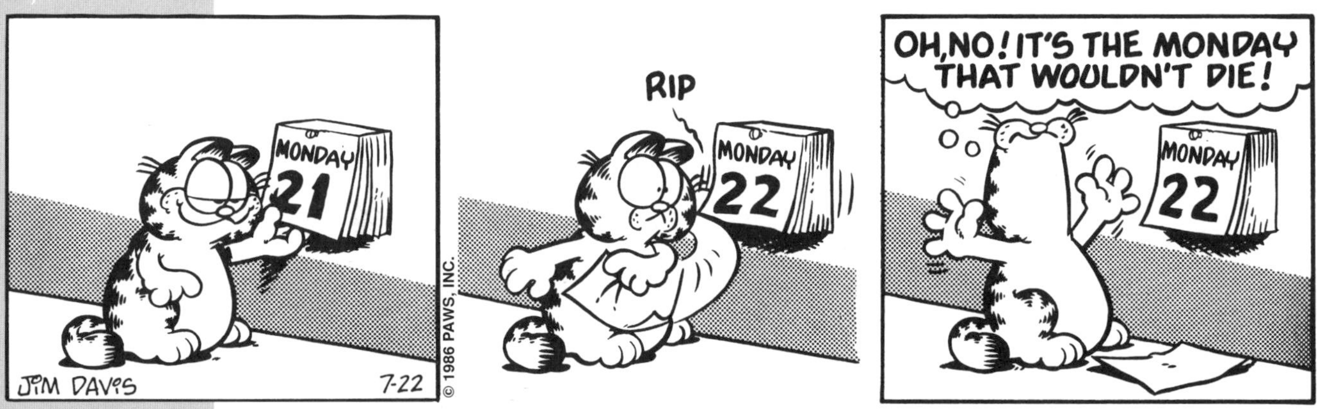

MONDAY
21
JIM DAVIS
7-22
© 1986 PAWS, INC.
RIP
MONDAY
22
OH, NO! IT'S THE MONDAY THAT WOULDN'T DIE!
MONDAY
22

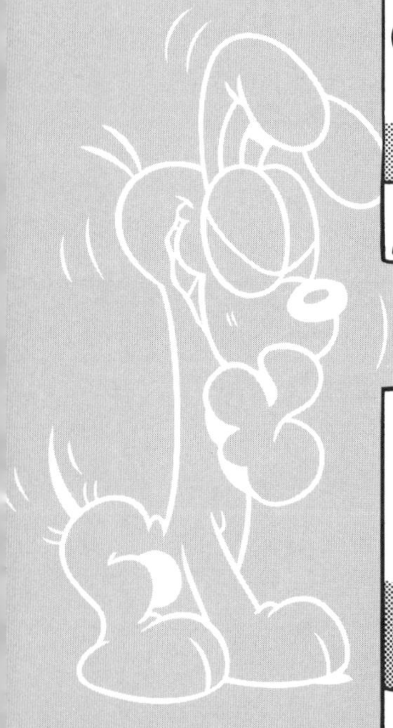

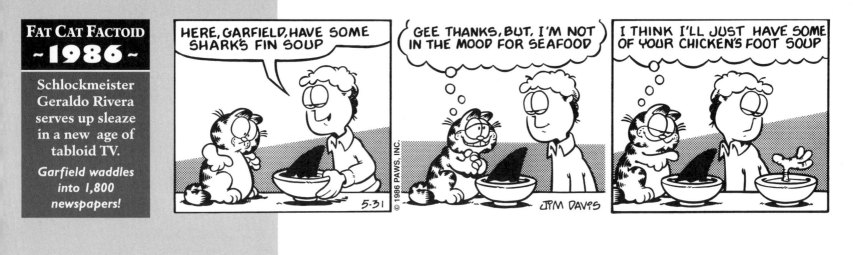

SLUCK

DONK!

NOTHING SPOILS LUNCH ANY QUICKER THAN A ROGUE MEATBALL RAMPAGING THROUGH YOUR SPAGHETTI

JIM DAVIS

© 1986 PAWS, INC.

BIG FAT HAPPY HOLIDAYS!

WELL, GARFIELD, IT'S THAT TIME OF YEAR AGAIN!

TIME TO WASH YOUR SOCKS?

TIME TO GET A CHRISTMAS TREE!

WHAT'S WRONG WITH THE ONE WE HAVE?

© 1988 PAWS, INC.

JIM DAVIS 12-19

HOW DO YOU LIKE YOUR CHRISTMAS GIFT, GARFIELD?

IT'S PERFECT!

IT'S BEAUTIFUL!

IT'S ME!

© 1991 PAWS, INC.

JIM DAVIS 12-26

Though he loves all holidays, Garfield has a special feeling for Christmas. After all, the Christmas season features the three things Garfield loves most: food, presents, and more food. As Garfield says, "'Tis the season to be greedy." And yet, despite his insatiable appetite for gifts and goodies, even Garfield realizes that Christmas is bigger than the biggest package under the tree. As he once said (and he meant it, too): "Christmas. It's not the giving. It's not the receiving. It's the loving."

In the longest continuity sequence I've ever written, Garfield runs away from home and joins the circus. There, Garfield meets Binky the clown. Binky doesn't appear too often in the strip, but the jerky jester is very popular in the Garfield animated TV series.

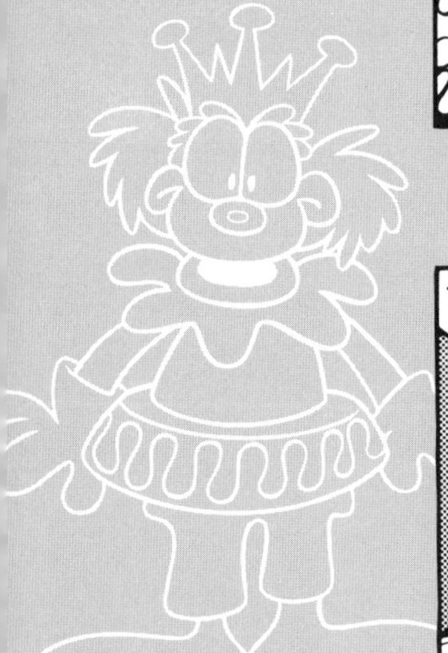

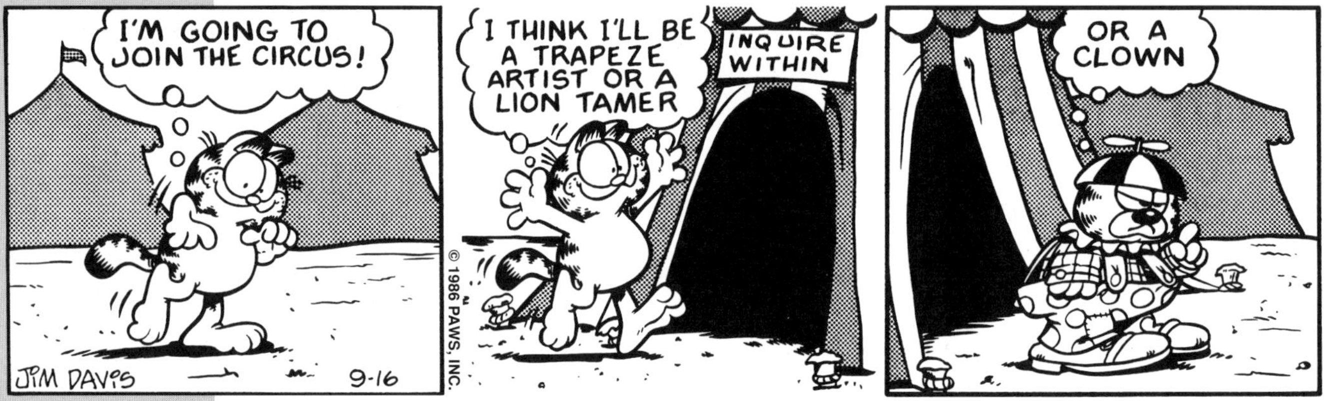
I'M GOING TO JOIN THE CIRCUS!
JIM DAVIS 9-16
I THINK I'LL BE A TRAPEZE ARTIST OR A LION TAMER
INQUIRE WITHIN
© 1986 PAWS, INC.
OR A CLOWN

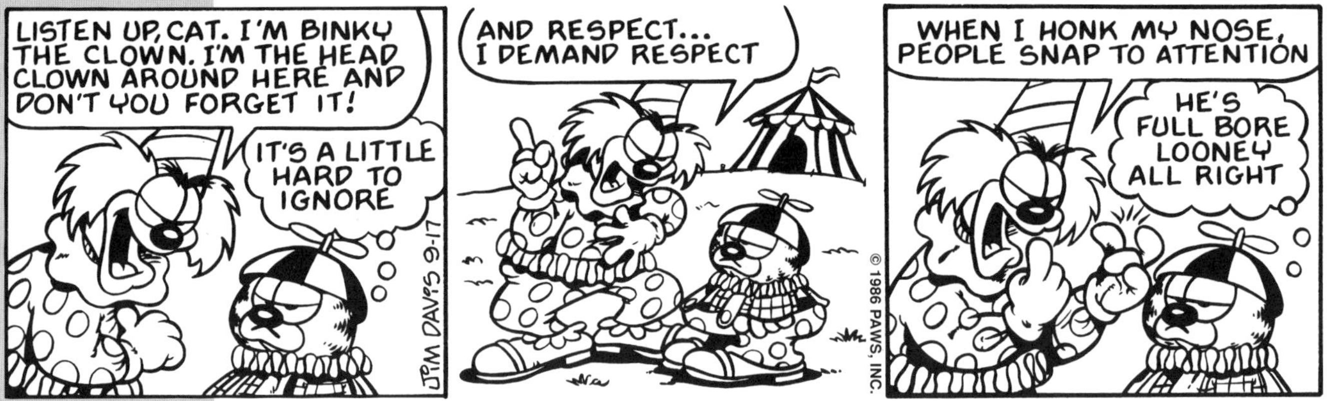
LISTEN UP, CAT. I'M BINKY THE CLOWN. I'M THE HEAD CLOWN AROUND HERE AND DON'T YOU FORGET IT!
IT'S A LITTLE HARD TO IGNORE
JIM DAVIS 9-17
AND RESPECT... I DEMAND RESPECT
© 1986 PAWS, INC.
WHEN I HONK MY NOSE, PEOPLE SNAP TO ATTENTION
HE'S FULL BORE LOONEY ALL RIGHT

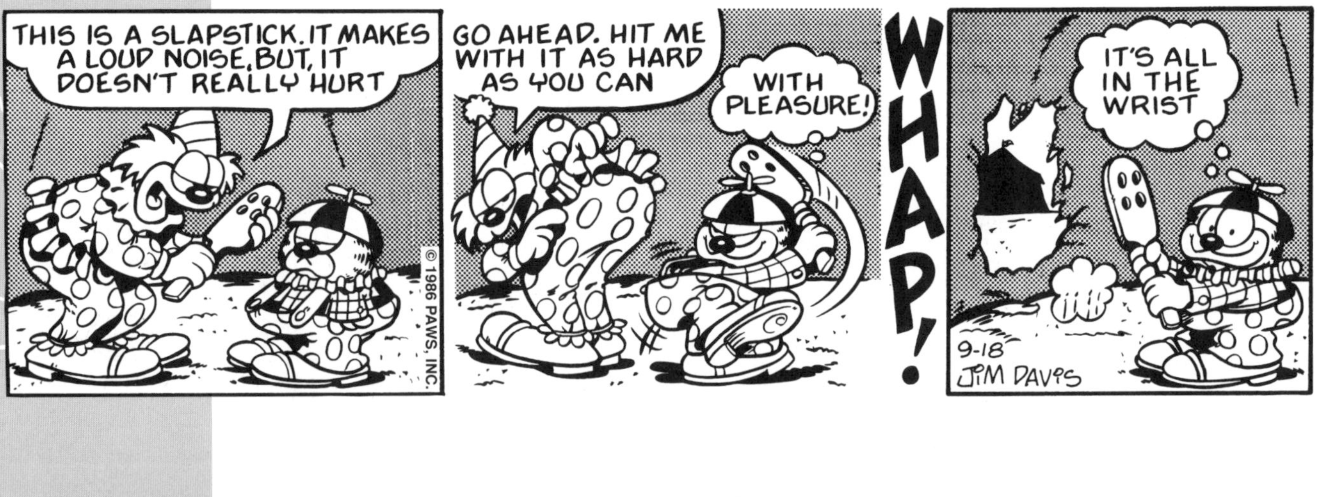
THIS IS A SLAPSTICK. IT MAKES A LOUD NOISE, BUT, IT DOESN'T REALLY HURT
© 1986 PAWS, INC.
GO AHEAD. HIT ME WITH IT AS HARD AS YOU CAN
WITH PLEASURE!
WHAP!
IT'S ALL IN THE WRIST
9-18
JIM DAVIS

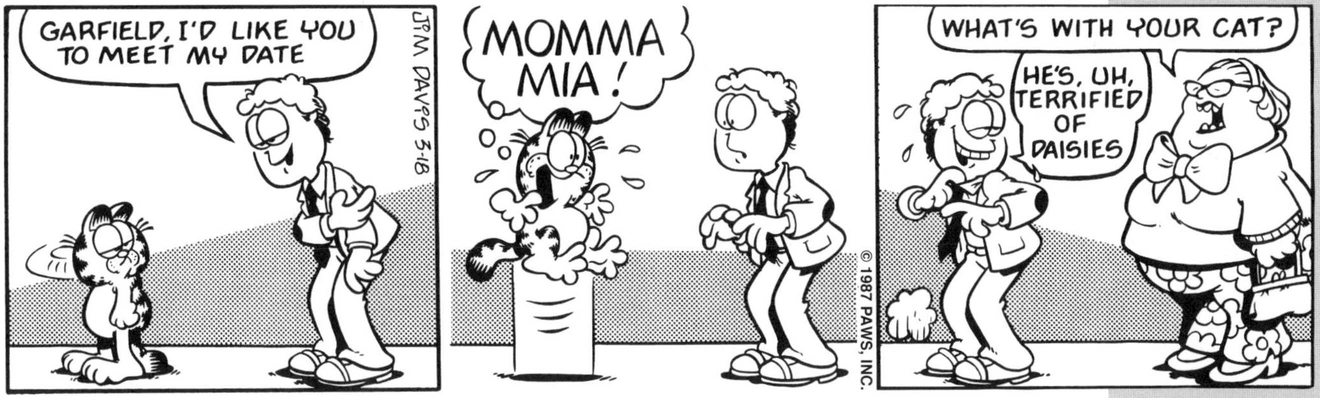
GARFIELD, I'D LIKE YOU TO MEET MY DATE
JIM DAVIS 3-18
MOMMA MIA!
© 1987 PAWS, INC.
WHAT'S WITH YOUR CAT?
HE'S, UH, TERRIFIED OF DAISIES

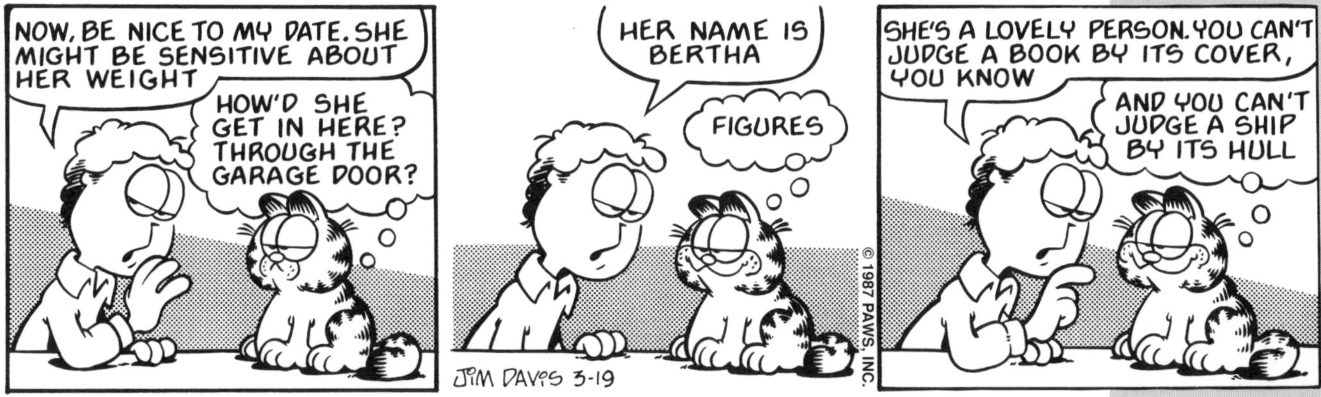
NOW, BE NICE TO MY DATE. SHE MIGHT BE SENSITIVE ABOUT HER WEIGHT
HOW'D SHE GET IN HERE? THROUGH THE GARAGE DOOR?
HER NAME IS BERTHA
FIGURES
JIM DAVIS 3-19
© 1987 PAWS, INC.
SHE'S A LOVELY PERSON. YOU CAN'T JUDGE A BOOK BY ITS COVER, YOU KNOW
AND YOU CAN'T JUDGE A SHIP BY ITS HULL

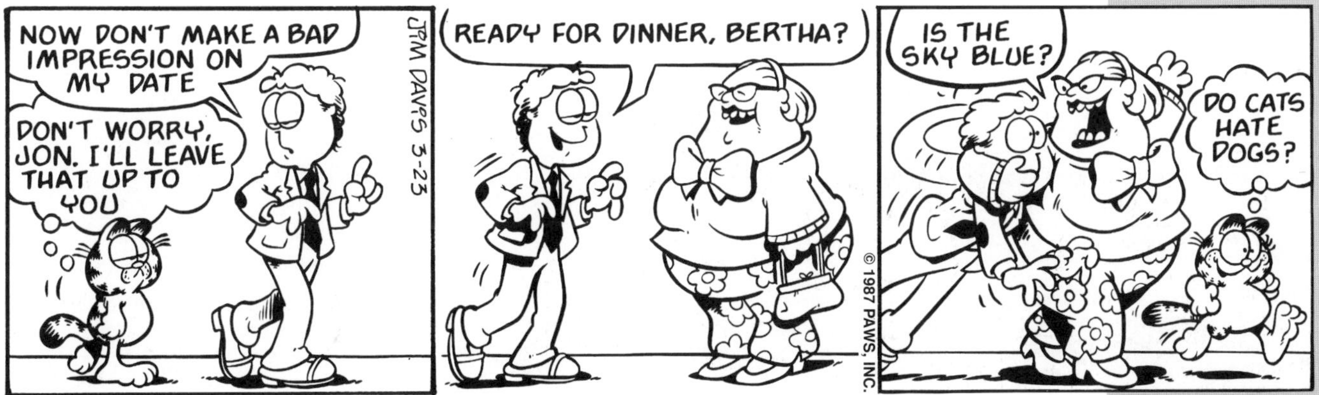
NOW DON'T MAKE A BAD IMPRESSION ON MY DATE
DON'T WORRY, JON. I'LL LEAVE THAT UP TO YOU
JIM DAVIS 3-23
READY FOR DINNER, BERTHA?
© 1987 PAWS, INC.
IS THE SKY BLUE?
DO CATS HATE DOGS?

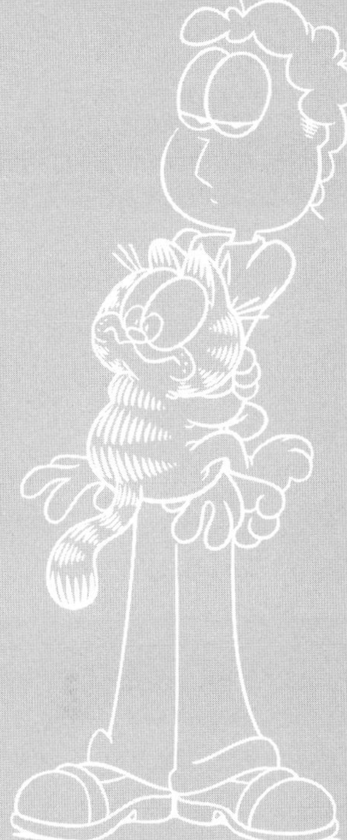

I loved Bertha. I felt I treated her with respect. She had a great appetite for life as well as food. A lot of readers thought I was insensitive about her weight. . . . I guess it's easier to pick on a fat cat.

FAT CAT FACTOID

~1987~

Eighties icon Donald Trump reveals his secrets of success in the best-seller *Trump: The Art of the Deal*.

Garfield ***becomes only the third comic strip in history to appear in 2,000 newspapers worldwide!***

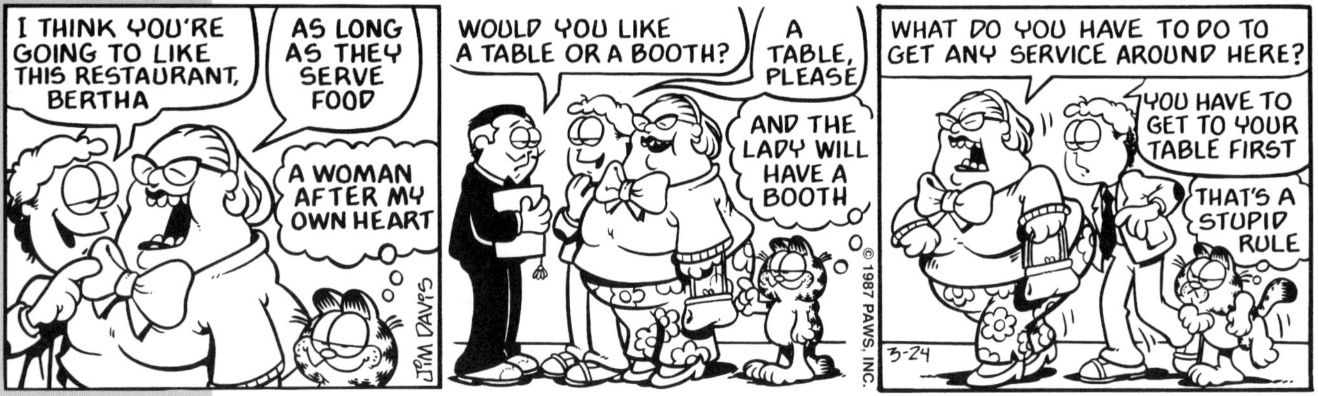
I THINK YOU'RE GOING TO LIKE THIS RESTAURANT, BERTHA
AS LONG AS THEY SERVE FOOD
A WOMAN AFTER MY OWN HEART
JIM DAVIS
WOULD YOU LIKE A TABLE OR A BOOTH?
A TABLE, PLEASE
AND THE LADY WILL HAVE A BOOTH
© 1987 PAWS, INC.
WHAT DO YOU HAVE TO DO TO GET ANY SERVICE AROUND HERE?
YOU HAVE TO GET TO YOUR TABLE FIRST
THAT'S A STUPID RULE
3-24

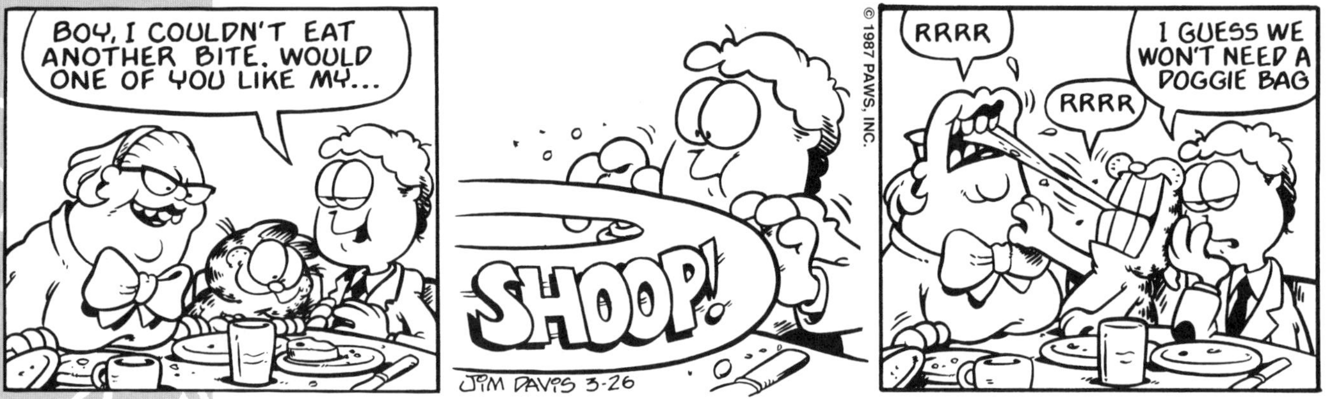
BOY, I COULDN'T EAT ANOTHER BITE. WOULD ONE OF YOU LIKE MY...
SHOOP!
JIM DAVIS 3-26
© 1987 PAWS, INC.
RRRR
RRRR
I GUESS WE WON'T NEED A DOGGIE BAG

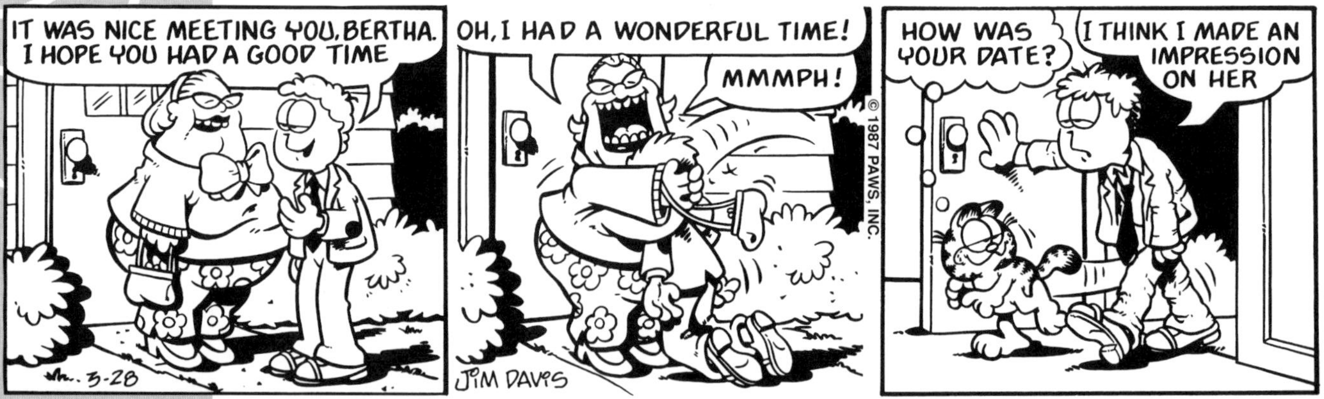
IT WAS NICE MEETING YOU, BERTHA. I HOPE YOU HAD A GOOD TIME
3-28
OH, I HAD A WONDERFUL TIME!
MMMPH!
JIM DAVIS
© 1987 PAWS, INC.
HOW WAS YOUR DATE?
I THINK I MADE AN IMPRESSION ON HER

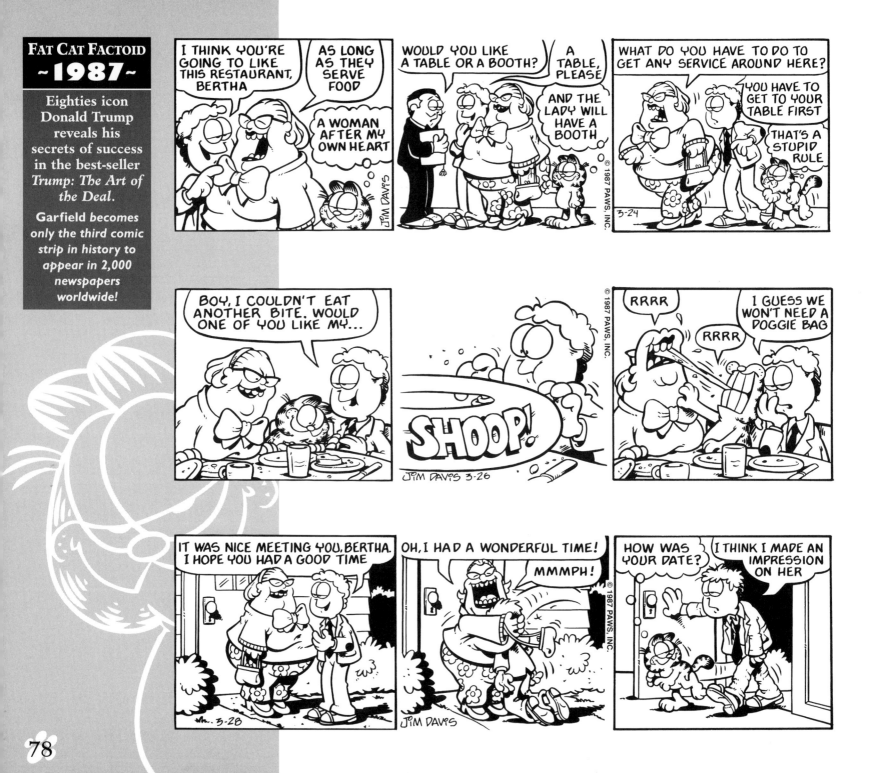

JIM DAVIS 5-6
HUH, THE STEREO'S ALL THE WAY UP, AND THERE'S NO SOUND
© 1987 PAWS, INC.
I'D BETTER TELL JON

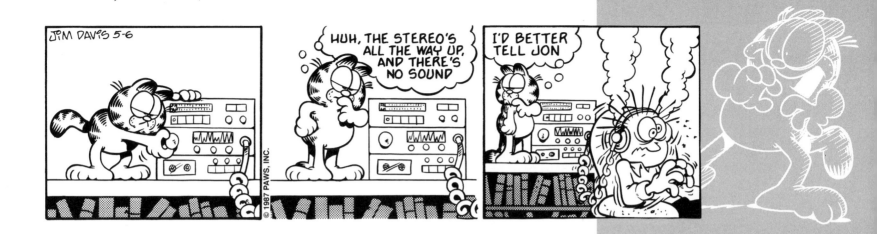

THE WIT AND WISDOM OF GARFIELD

HEY, POOKY. I NEED A HUG
JIM DAVIS
© 1985 PAWS, INC.
IT'S IMPOSSIBLE TO GIVE A HUG WITHOUT GETTING ONE BACK
12-27

JIM DAVIS 9-21
ARE YOU EVER SERIOUS, GARFIELD?
I GUESS NOT
© 1987 PAWS, INC.
IT'S HARD TO BE SERIOUS WHEN YOU'RE NAKED!

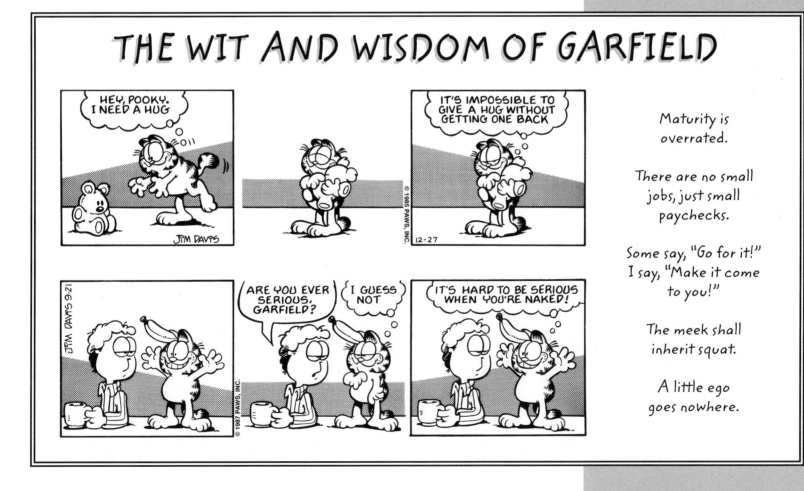

Maturity is overrated.

There are no small jobs, just small paychecks.

Some say, "Go for it!" I say, "Make it come to you!"

The meek shall inherit squat.

A little ego goes nowhere.

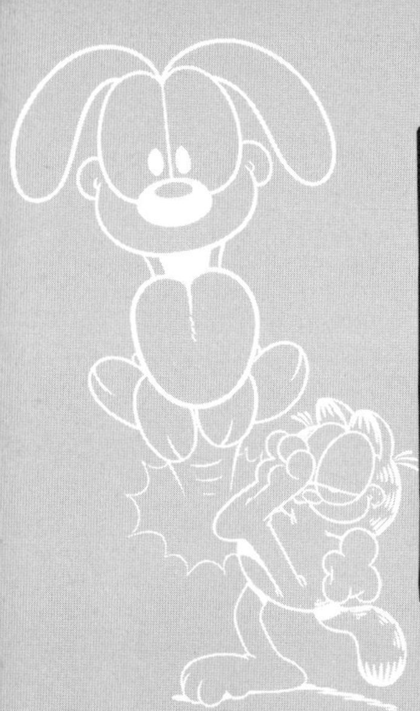

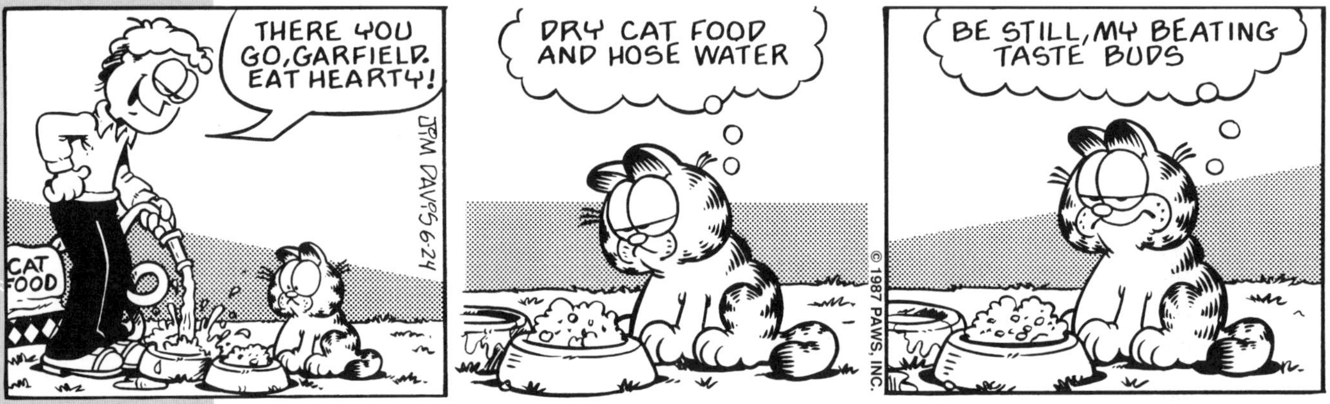
THERE YOU GO, GARFIELD. EAT HEARTY!
CAT FOOD
JIM DAVIS 6-24
DRY CAT FOOD AND HOSE WATER
© 1987 PAWS, INC.
BE STILL, MY BEATING TASTE BUDS

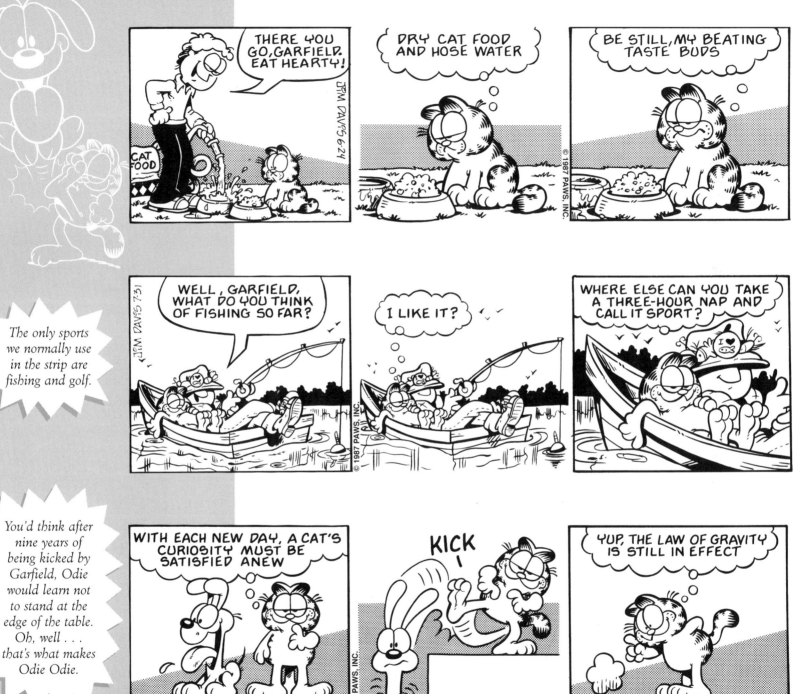

The only sports we normally use in the strip are fishing and golf.

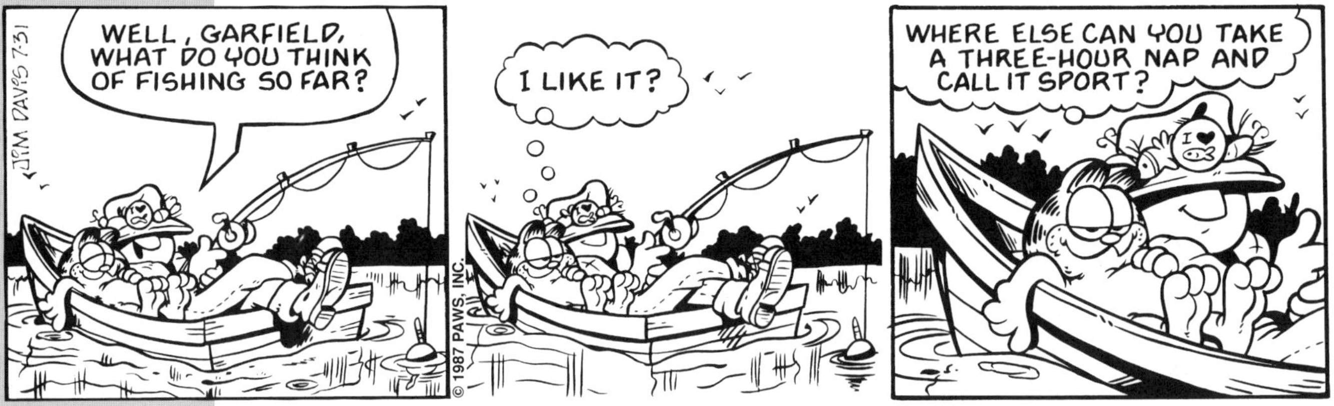
JIM DAVIS 7-31
WELL, GARFIELD, WHAT DO YOU THINK OF FISHING SO FAR?
© 1987 PAWS, INC.
I LIKE IT?
WHERE ELSE CAN YOU TAKE A THREE-HOUR NAP AND CALL IT SPORT?

You'd think after nine years of being kicked by Garfield, Odie would learn not to stand at the edge of the table. Oh, well . . . that's what makes Odie Odie.

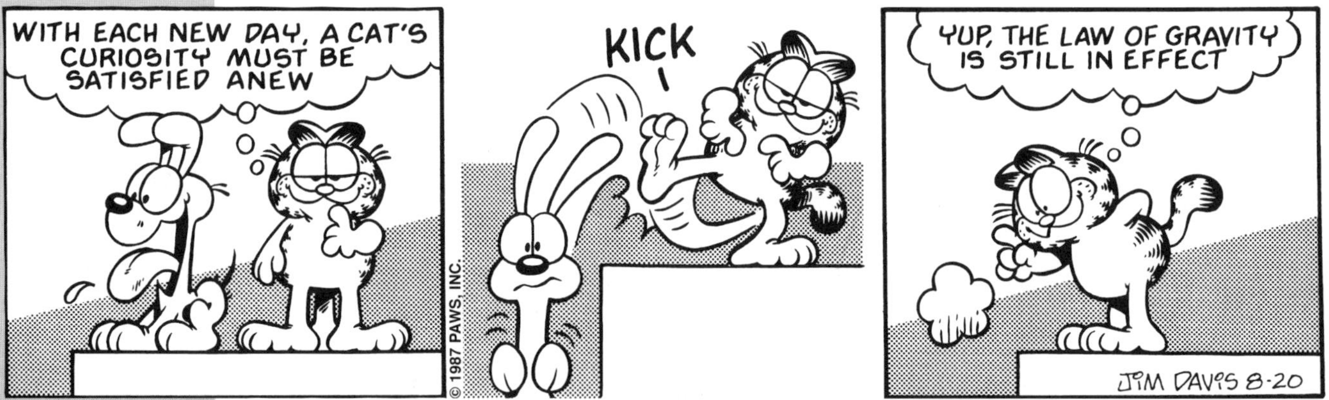
WITH EACH NEW DAY, A CAT'S CURIOSITY MUST BE SATISFIED ANEW
© 1987 PAWS, INC.
KICK
YUP, THE LAW OF GRAVITY IS STILL IN EFFECT
JIM DAVIS 8-20

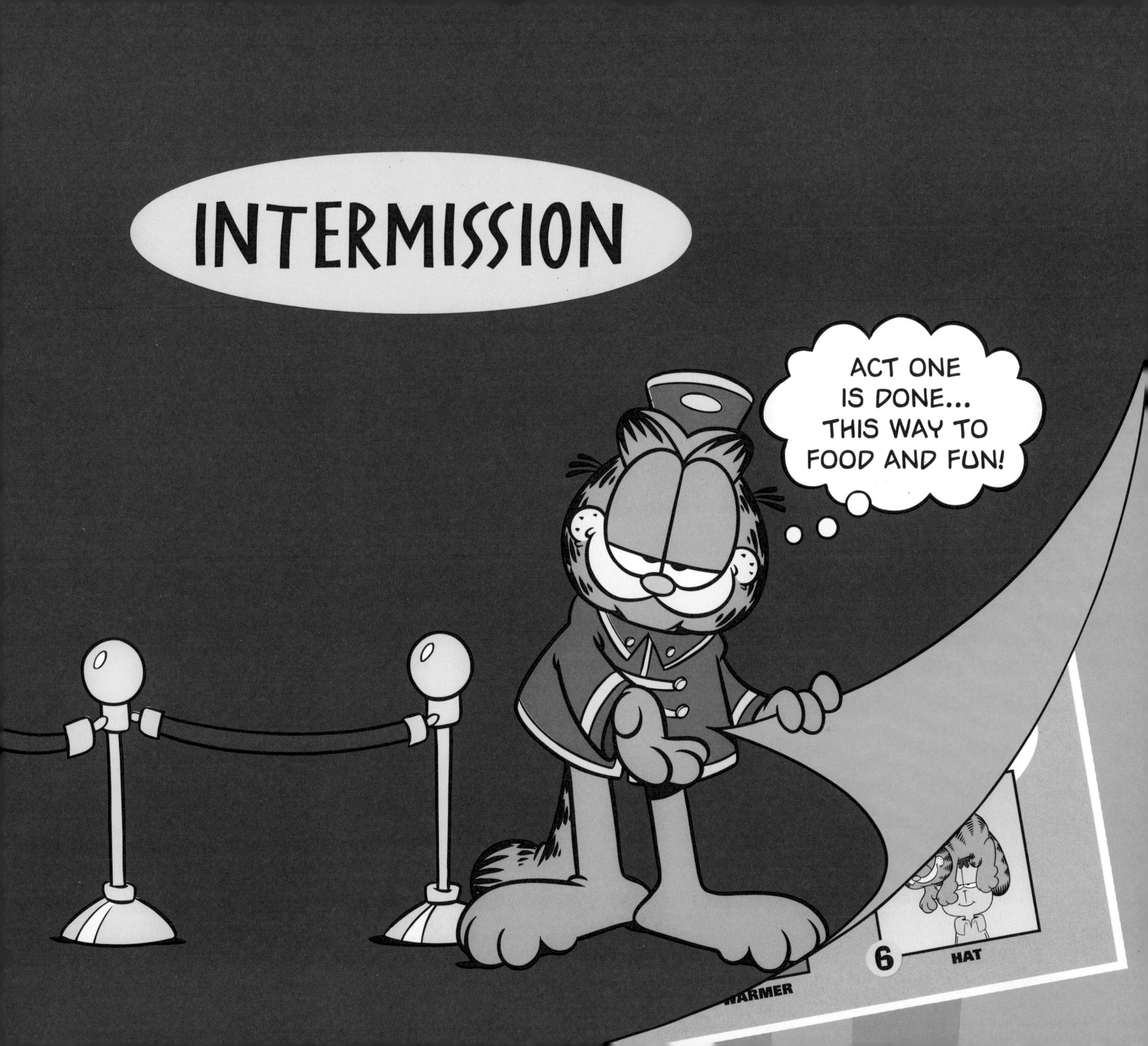
INTERMISSION
ACT ONE IS DONE... THIS WAY TO FOOD AND FUN!
6
HAT

FROM Garfield's Family Album

Grandpa and a puppy that followed him home

My first refrigerator raid

Last picture of Uncle Ben

half-brother Raoul

Cousin Vi—Miss Rodent Central 1964

FROM **BOOK 20**

FROM **BOOK 10**

Let's start off
this grab bag of goodies
with a few funky

FEATURE PAGES

— special bonus pages
that are featured in
the front and back of the
Garfield compilation books.
Let the fun begin!

npysxtnt wnnmya m my systym s fpnctwnns typysythwng wn psy npyxtx twng yimis m chxsxityrs wwth twssys sif vwswbty xt xny nty twrny. Mhw xddwtwnnxl

synhwng twpy thy dwsk sistxgy systym Thy vwdyn dwspixy scryyn

NEWS FLASH!
Jim Davis a Fraud!

Teddy bear Pooky recently revealed that Jim Davis did not create the Garfield comic strip. Garfield himself writes and draws the world-famous cartoon. Garfield has been sitting at a drawing board for the last six years as Davis has gained notoriety through national television and print. Davis was not available for comment, but Garfield was. "The way I figured it, who would ever believe a cat could do a comic strip. So, I hired this down-and-out, hack cartoonist to take the credit for it. Sure . . . he looked good and said all the right things, but it's time the truth was known."

The Big Cheese, The Head Honcho, The Chief Muckamuck...

PROFIT $798.00

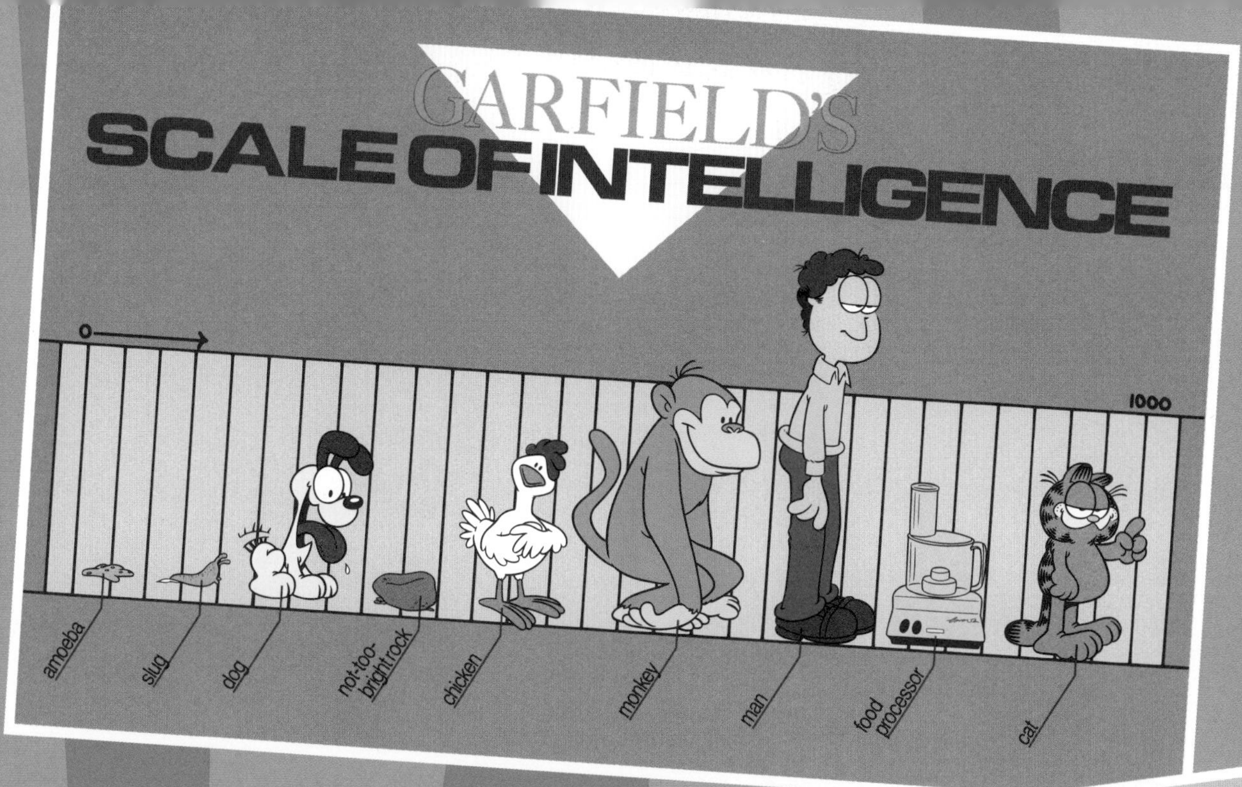
GARFIELD'S
SCALE OF INTELLIGENCE
0
1000
amoeba
slug
dog
not-too-bright rock
chicken
monkey
man
food processor
cat

FROM **BOOK 16**

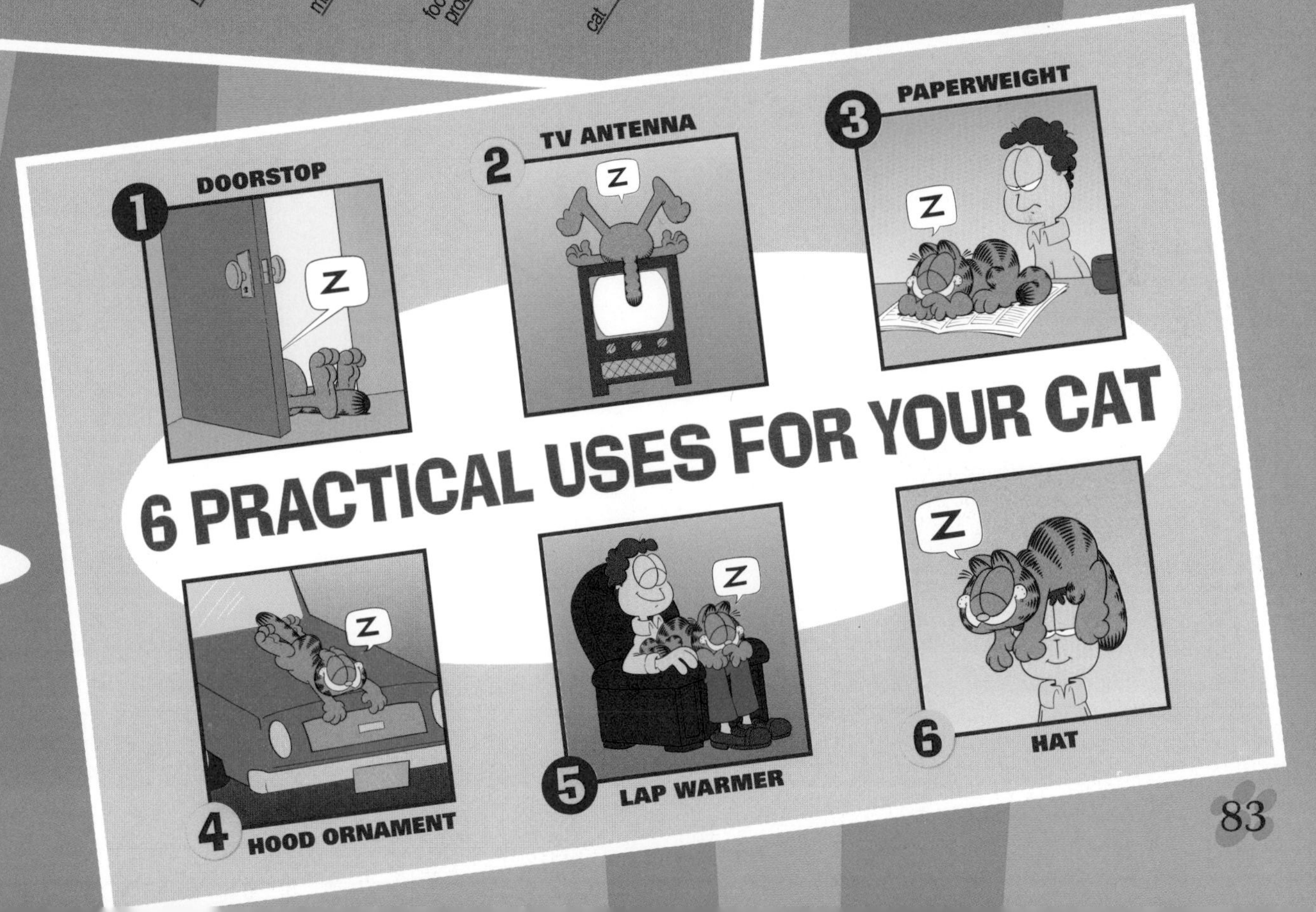
6 PRACTICAL USES FOR YOUR CAT
1 DOORSTOP
Z
2 TV ANTENNA
Z
3 PAPERWEIGHT
Z
4 HOOD ORNAMENT
Z
5 LAP WARMER
Z
6 HAT
Z

FROM **BOOK 29**

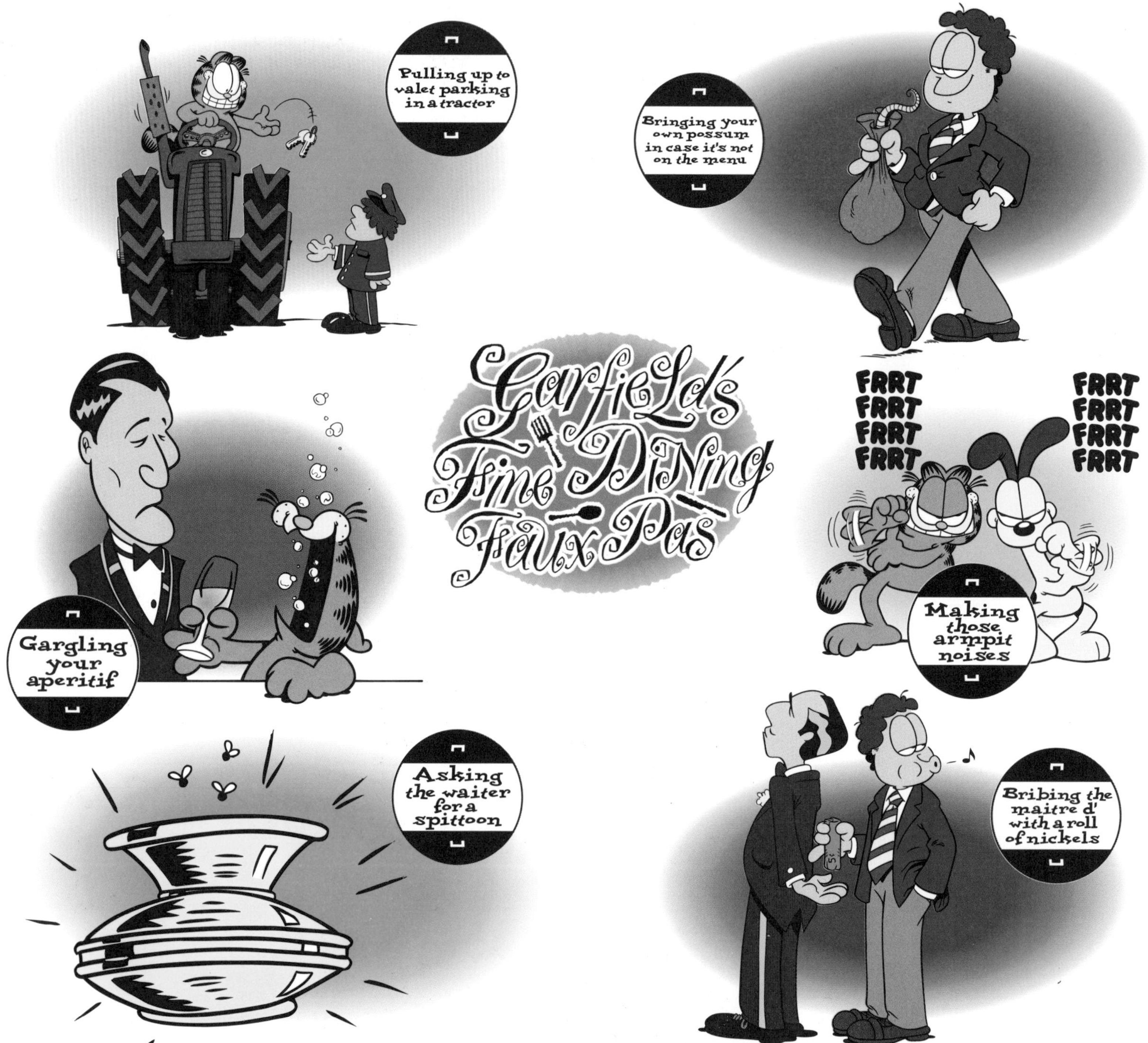
Garfield's Fine Dining Faux Pas
Pulling up to valet parking in a tractor
Bringing your own possum in case it's not on the menu
Gargling your aperitif
FRRT FRRT FRRT FRRT
FRRT FRRT FRRT FRRT
Making those armpit noises
Asking the waiter for a spittoon
Bribing the maitre d' with a roll of nickels

FROM **TREASURY 8**

FROM **BOOK 18**

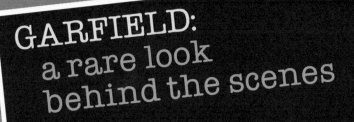

GARFIELD: a rare look behind the scenes

HOW WOULD YOU FEEL ABOUT JOGGING TODAY, GARFIELD?
BEAR WITH ME, JON
WELL?
IT'S NOT EASY TO THROW UP ON CUE
JPM DAVIS

GARFIELD'S TOP TEN COUNTRY PET TUNES

10. Daddy Sang Bass, Mama Had Worms
9. Lipstick on Your Flea Collar, Cheatin' on Your Mind
8. I Burp As Much In Texas As I Did In Tennessee
7. Call Me A Hairball Tomorrow, But Feed Me Tonight
6. Bubba Shot the Litterbox
5. Odie from Muskogee
4. Mamas Don't Let Your Kittens Grow Up To Be Professional Wrestlers
3. Walk Softly on This Tail Of Mine
2. You Used To Be My Chew Toy, But I Used To Have Some Teeth
1. Honky-Tonk Tabby (Gettin' Old... Feelin' Flabby)

FROM **BOOK 27**

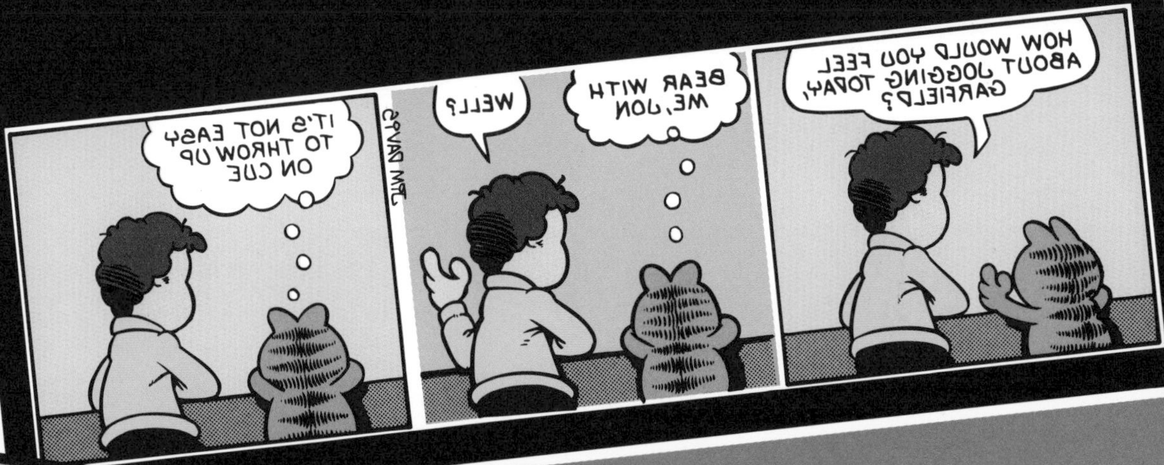

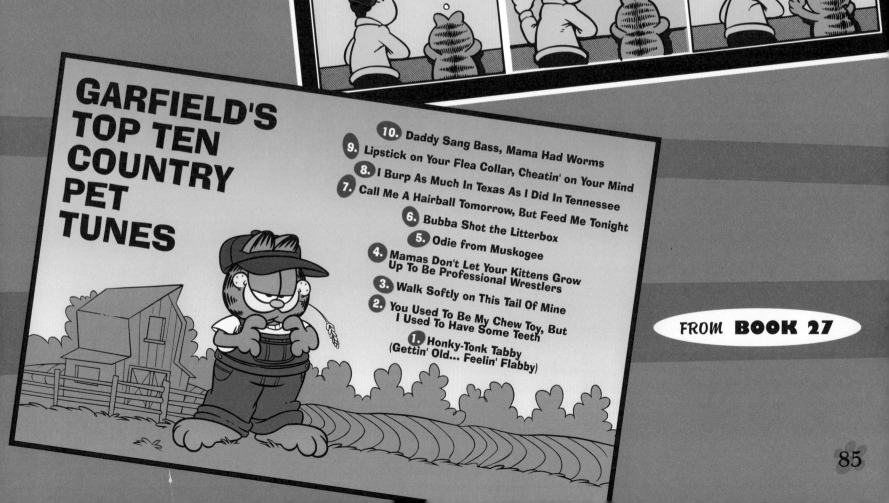

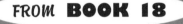

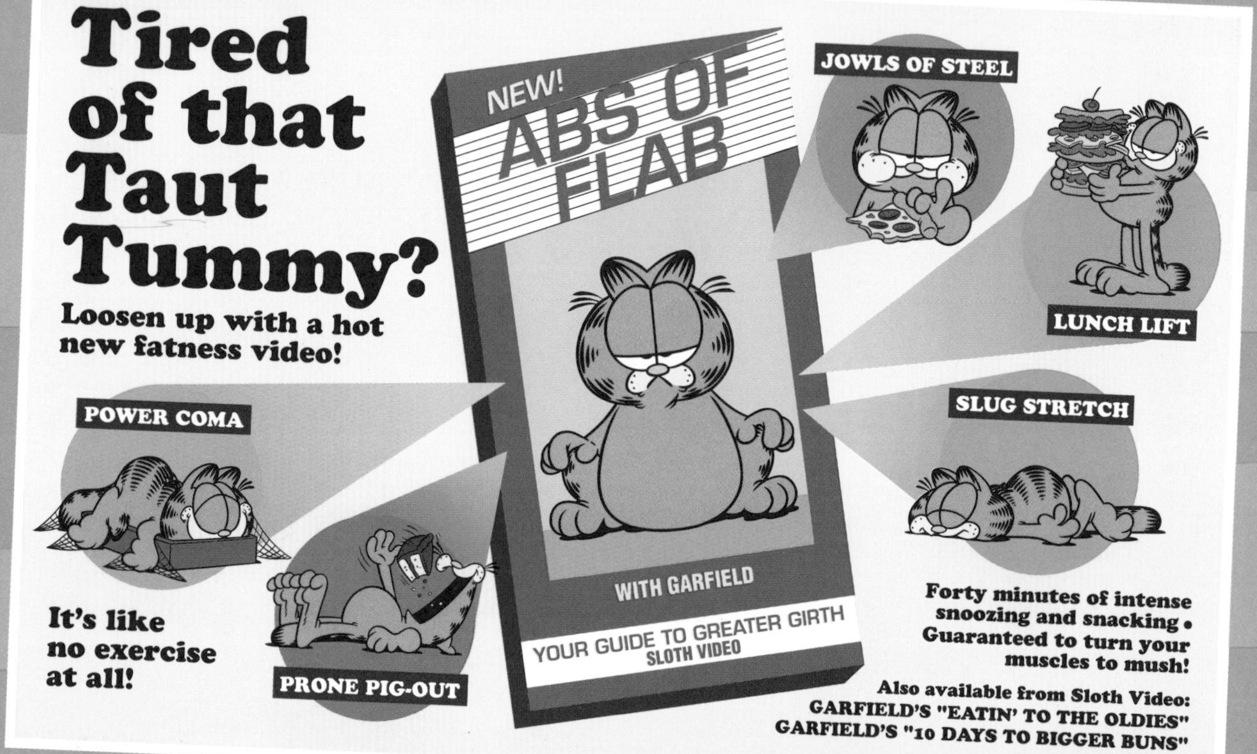
Tired of that Taut Tummy?
Loosen up with a hot new fatness video!
NEW!
ABS OF FLAB
WITH GARFIELD
YOUR GUIDE TO GREATER GIRTH
SLOTH VIDEO
JOWLS OF STEEL
LUNCH LIFT
SLUG STRETCH
POWER COMA
PRONE PIG-OUT
It's like no exercise at all!
Forty minutes of intense snoozing and snacking • Guaranteed to turn your muscles to mush!
Also available from Sloth Video:
GARFIELD'S "EATIN' TO THE OLDIES"
GARFIELD'S "10 DAYS TO BIGGER BUNS"

FROM **BOOK 26**

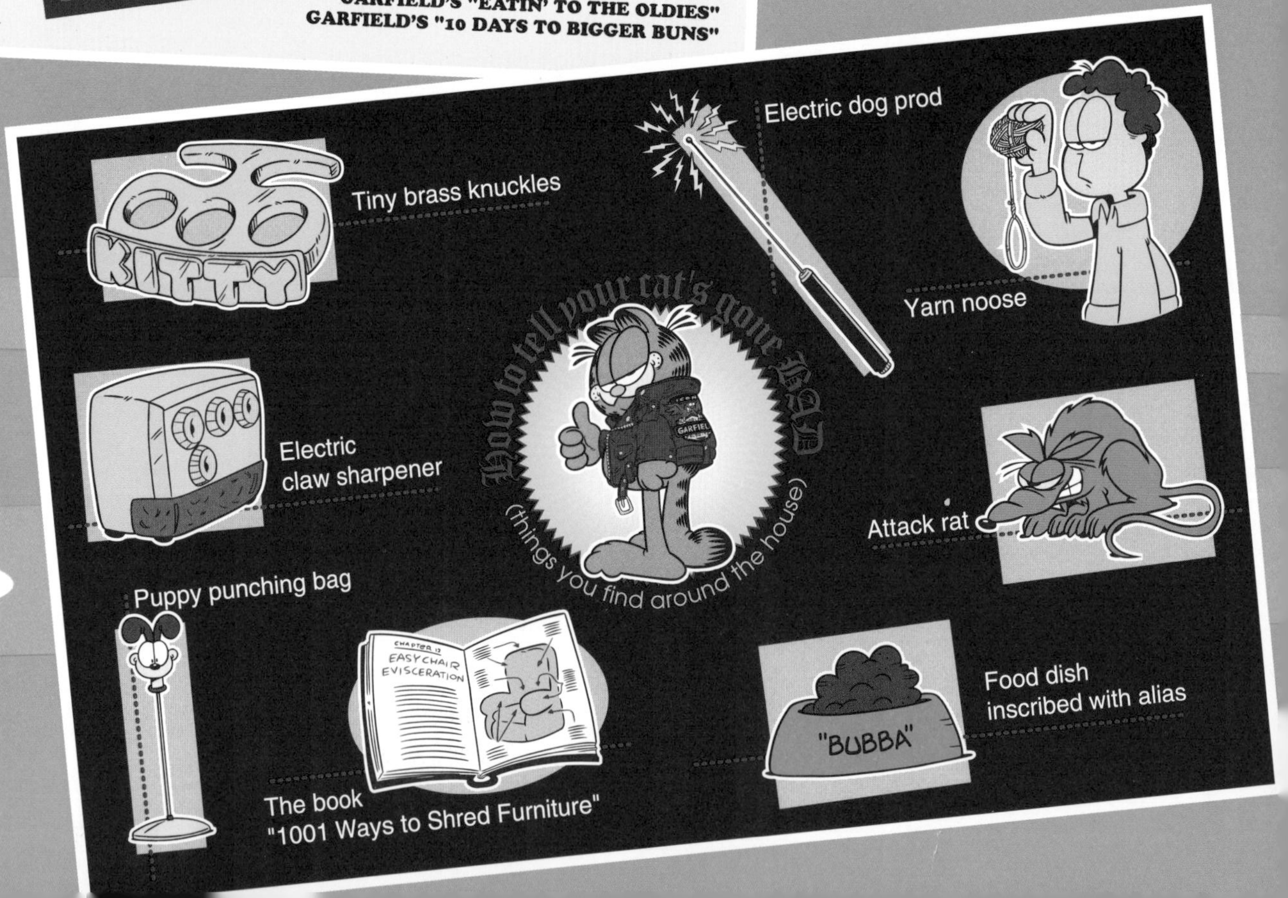
How to tell your cat's gone BAD
(things you find around the house)
Tiny brass knuckles
KITTY
Electric dog prod
Yarn noose
Electric claw sharpener
Attack rat
Puppy punching bag
CHAPTER 13
EASY CHAIR EVISCERATION
The book "1001 Ways to Shred Furniture"
Food dish inscribed with alias
"BUBBA"

FROM **BOOK 28**

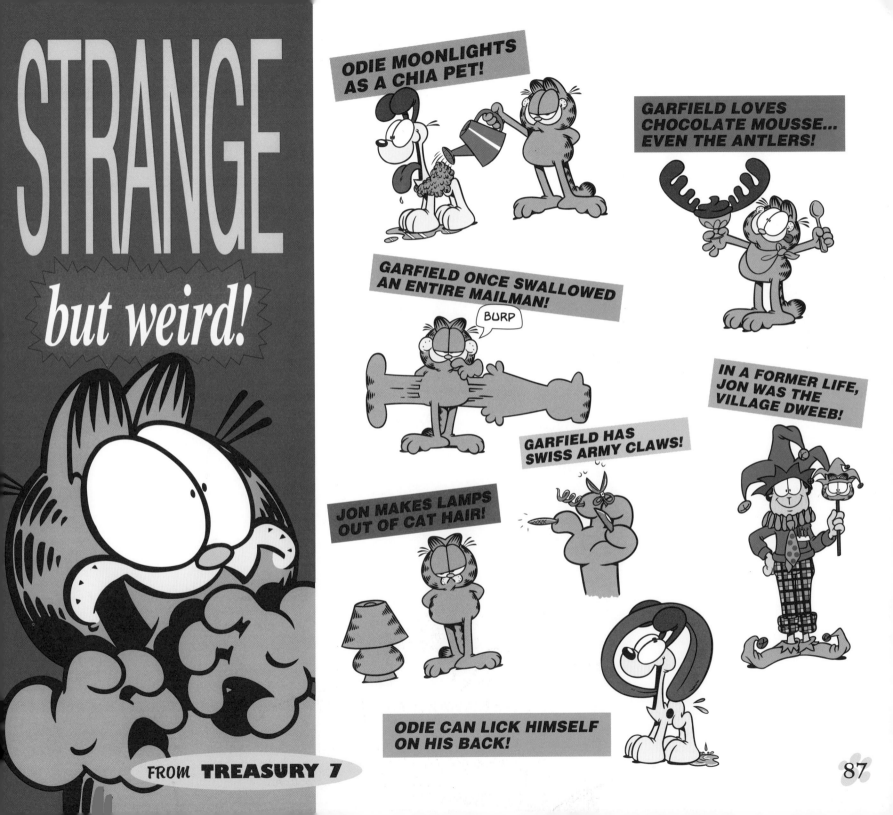

STRANGE

but weird!

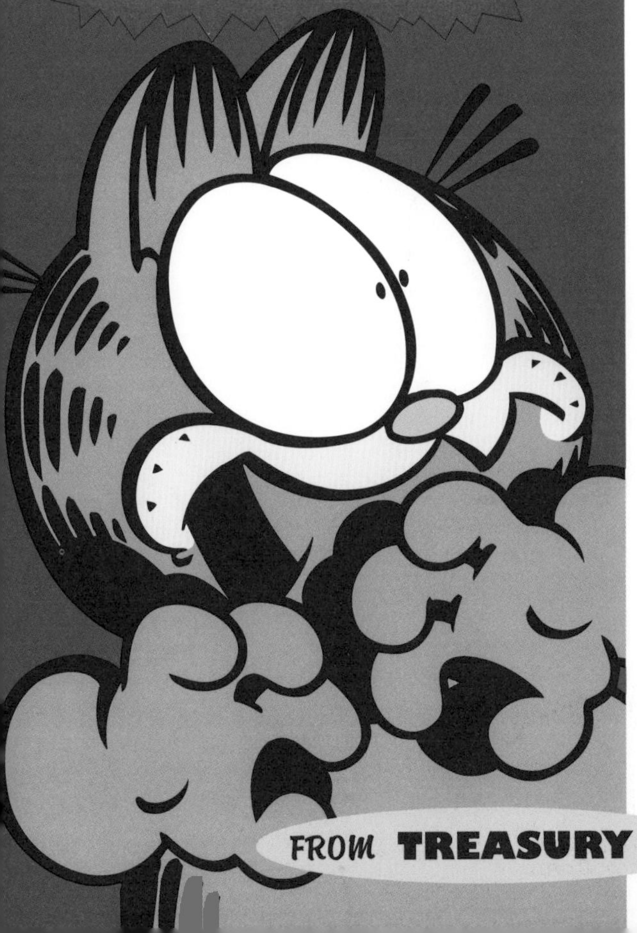

FROM **TREASURY 7**

ODIE MOONLIGHTS AS A CHIA PET!

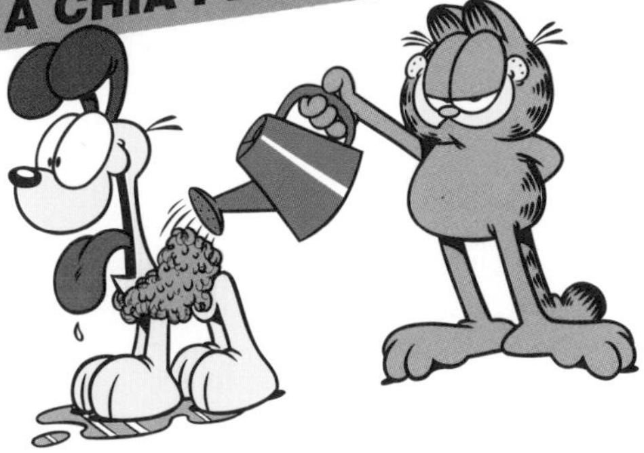

GARFIELD LOVES CHOCOLATE MOUSSE... EVEN THE ANTLERS!

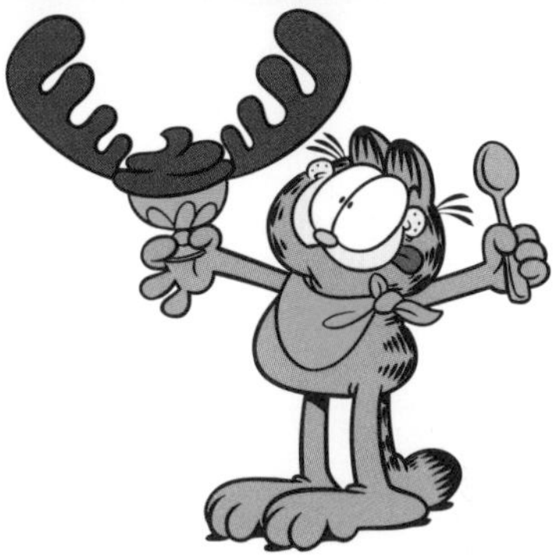

GARFIELD ONCE SWALLOWED AN ENTIRE MAILMAN!

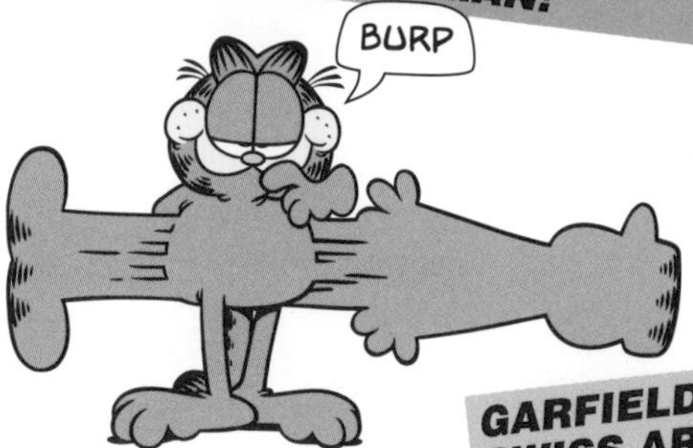
BURP

IN A FORMER LIFE, JON WAS THE VILLAGE DWEEB!

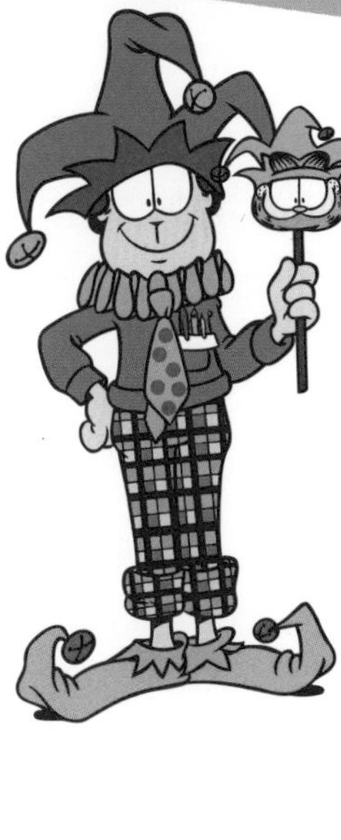

GARFIELD HAS SWISS ARMY CLAWS!

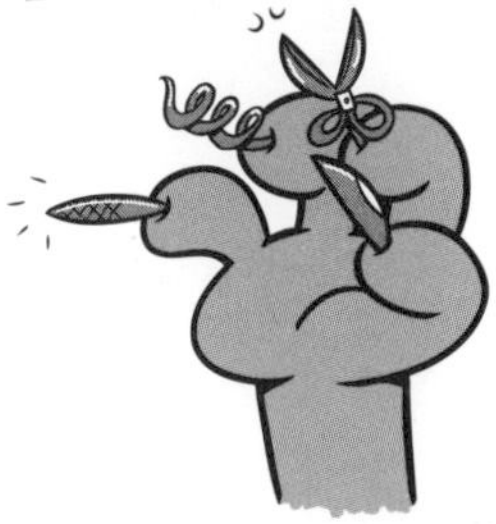

JON MAKES LAMPS OUT OF CAT HAIR!

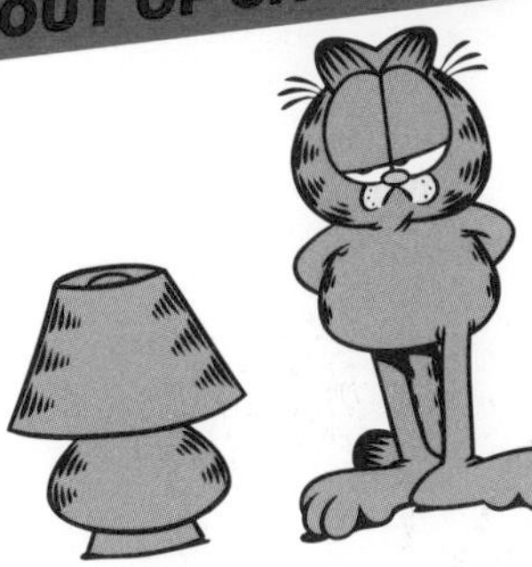

ODIE CAN LICK HIMSELF ON HIS BACK!

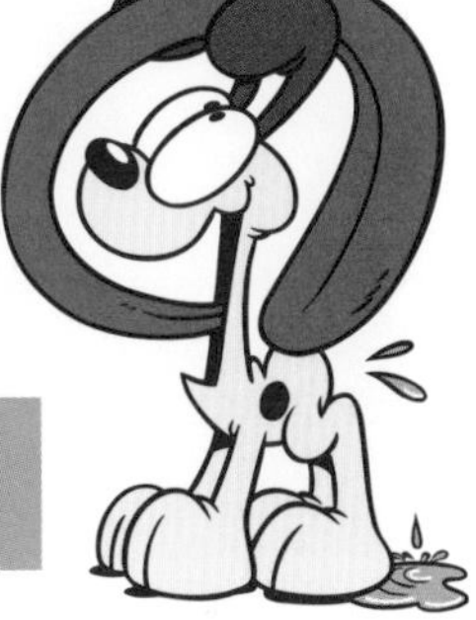

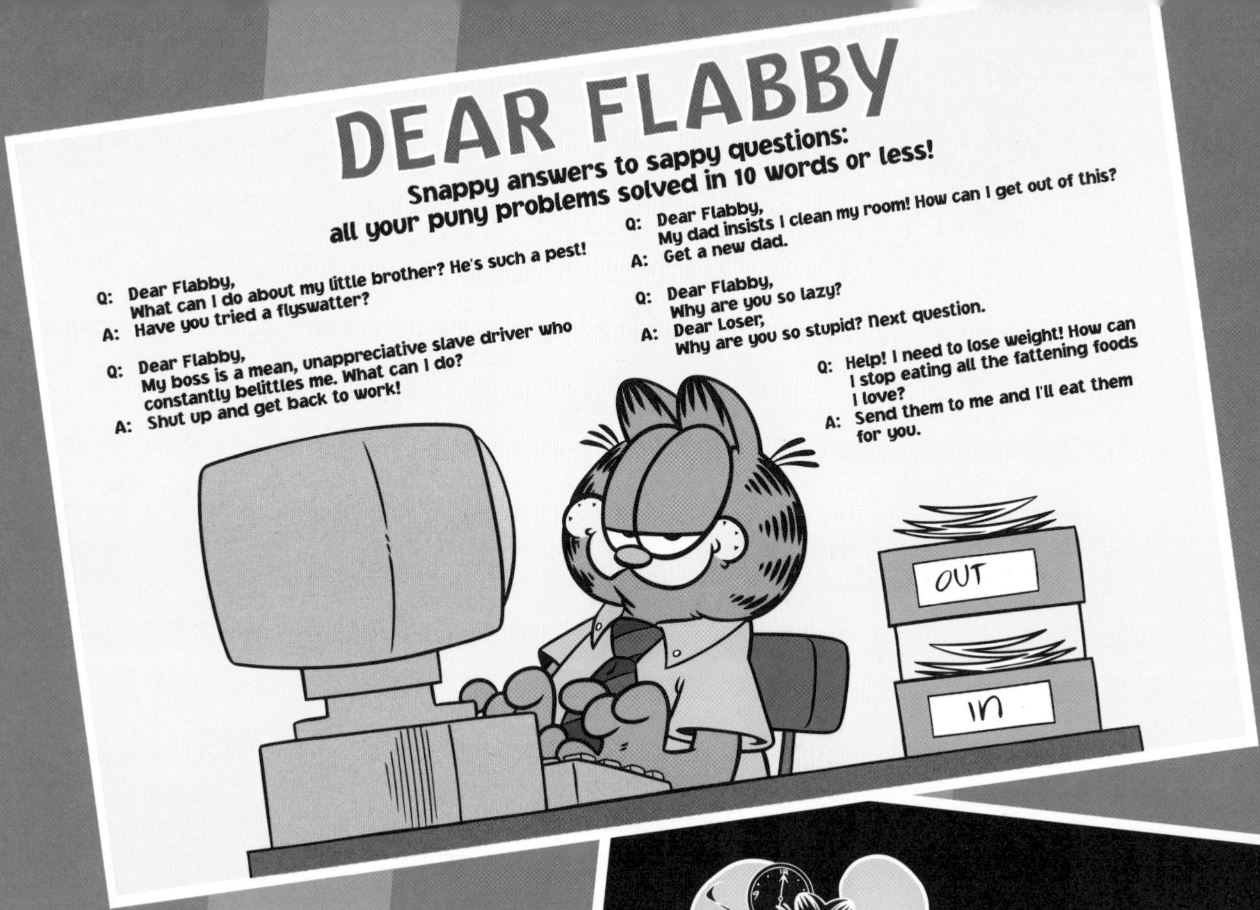

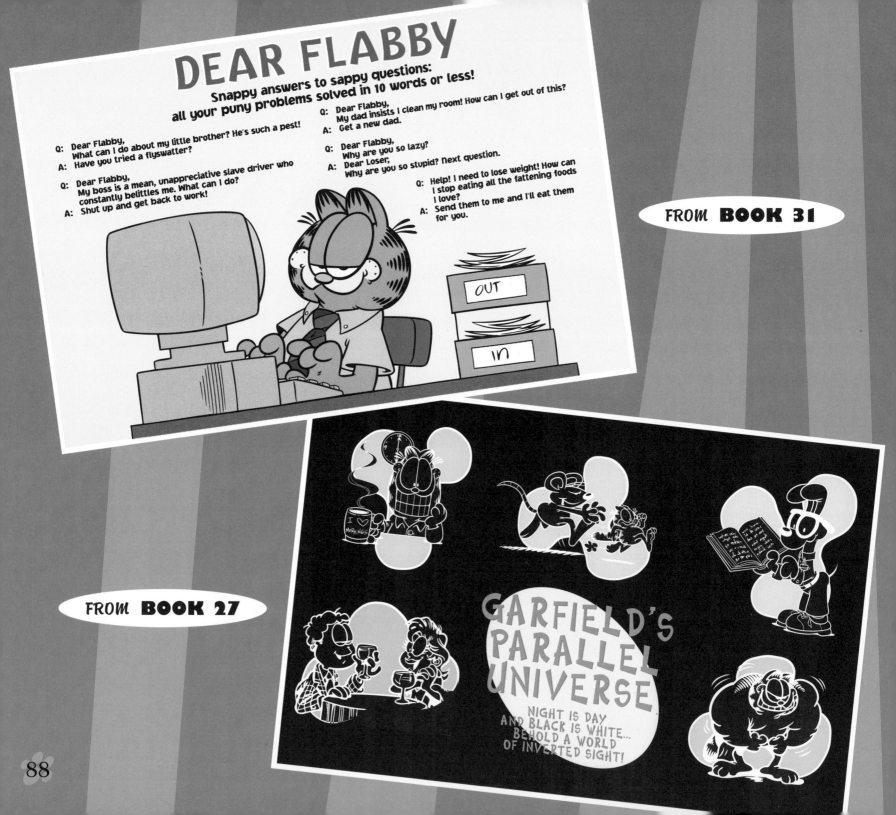

DEAR FLABBY

Snappy answers to sappy questions: all your puny problems solved in 10 words or less!

Q: Dear Flabby,
What can I do about my little brother? He's such a pest!
A: Have you tried a flyswatter?

Q: Dear Flabby,
My boss is a mean, unappreciative slave driver who constantly belittles me. What can I do?
A: Shut up and get back to work!

Q: Dear Flabby,
My dad insists I clean my room! How can I get out of this?
A: Get a new dad.

Q: Dear Flabby,
Why are you so lazy?
A: Dear Loser,
Why are you so stupid? Next question.

Q: Help! I need to lose weight! How can I stop eating all the fattening foods I love?
A: Send them to me and I'll eat them for you.

OUT
IN

FROM **BOOK 31**

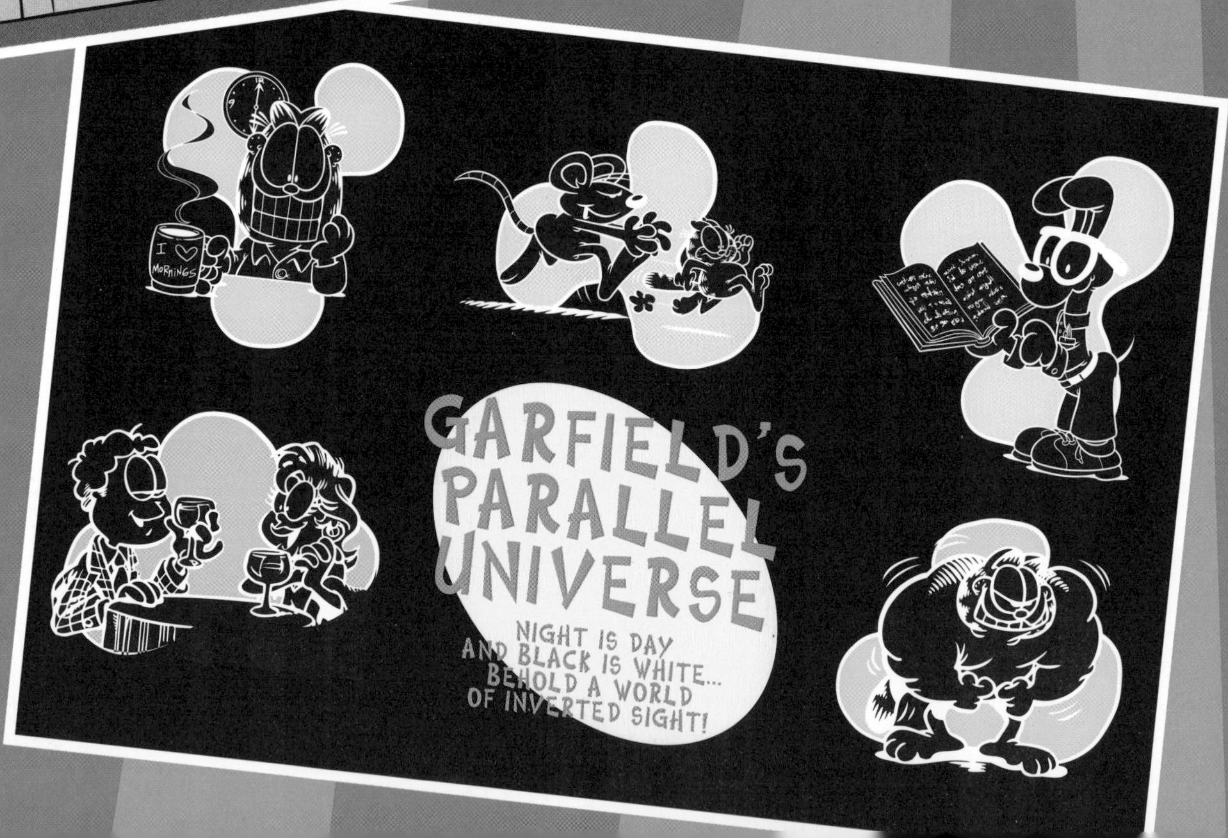
I ♡ MORNINGS
GARFIELD'S PARALLEL UNIVERSE
NIGHT IS DAY AND BLACK IS WHITE... BEHOLD A WORLD OF INVERTED SIGHT!

FROM **BOOK 27**

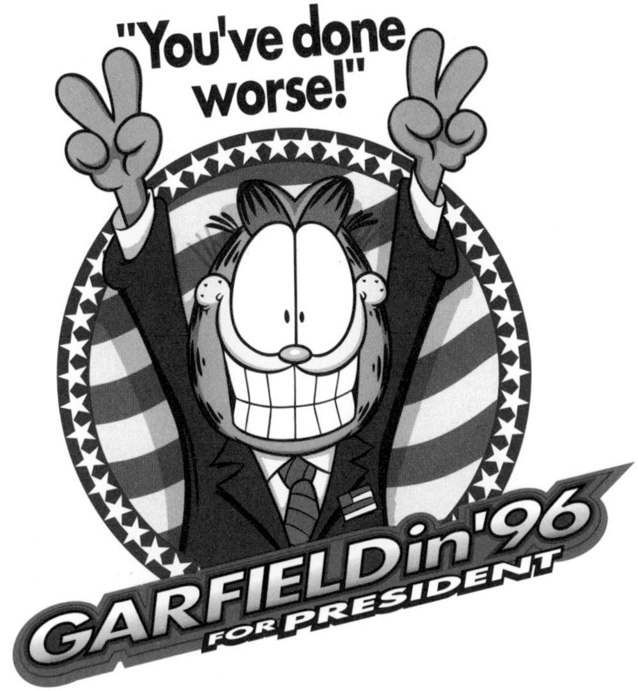
"You've done worse!"
GARFIELD in '96
FOR PRESIDENT

IF GARFIELD WERE PRESIDENT, HE WOULD...

- Abolish Mondays!
- Put a sweat tax on gyms and health clubs
- Give federal subsidies for napping
- Pour millions into the fight against dog breath
- Establish The President's Council on Snacking!
- Put a dessert bar in every school cafeteria!

FROM **BOOK 30**

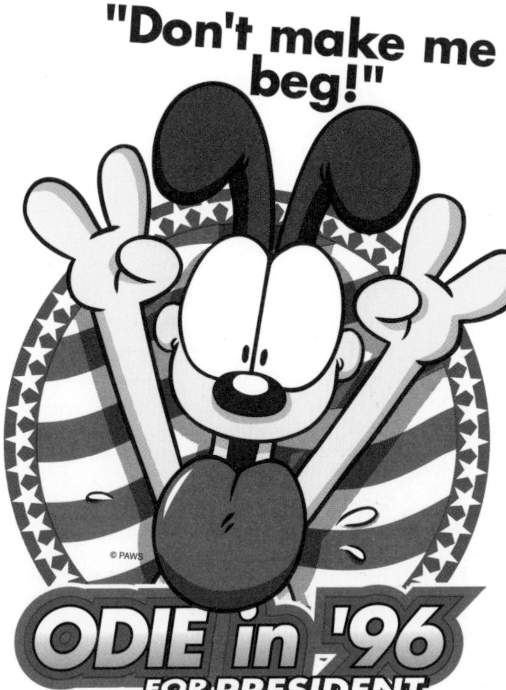
"Don't make me beg!"
© PAWS
ODIE in '96
FOR PRESIDENT

FROM **BOOK 30**

IF ODIE WERE PRESIDENT, HE WOULD...

- Replace Washington Monument with giant fire hydrant
- Start every press conference with an Underdog cartoon
- Repeal oppressive leash laws
- Have all cats de-clawed
- Require mailmen to wear short pants
- Be the first chief executive to lick himself in public!

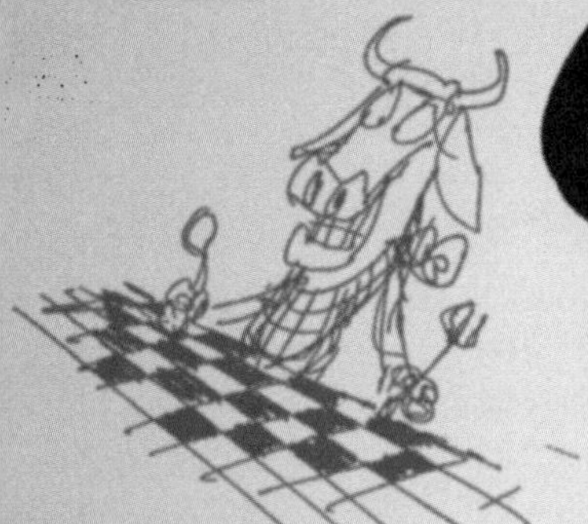

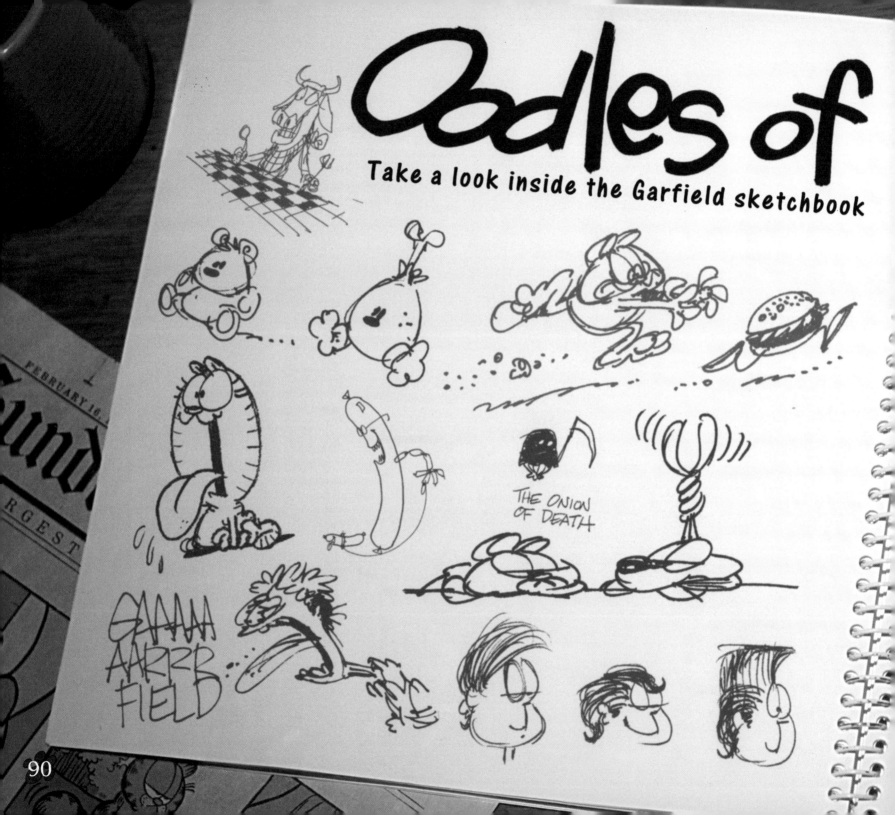

Oodles of

Take a look inside the Garfield sketchbook

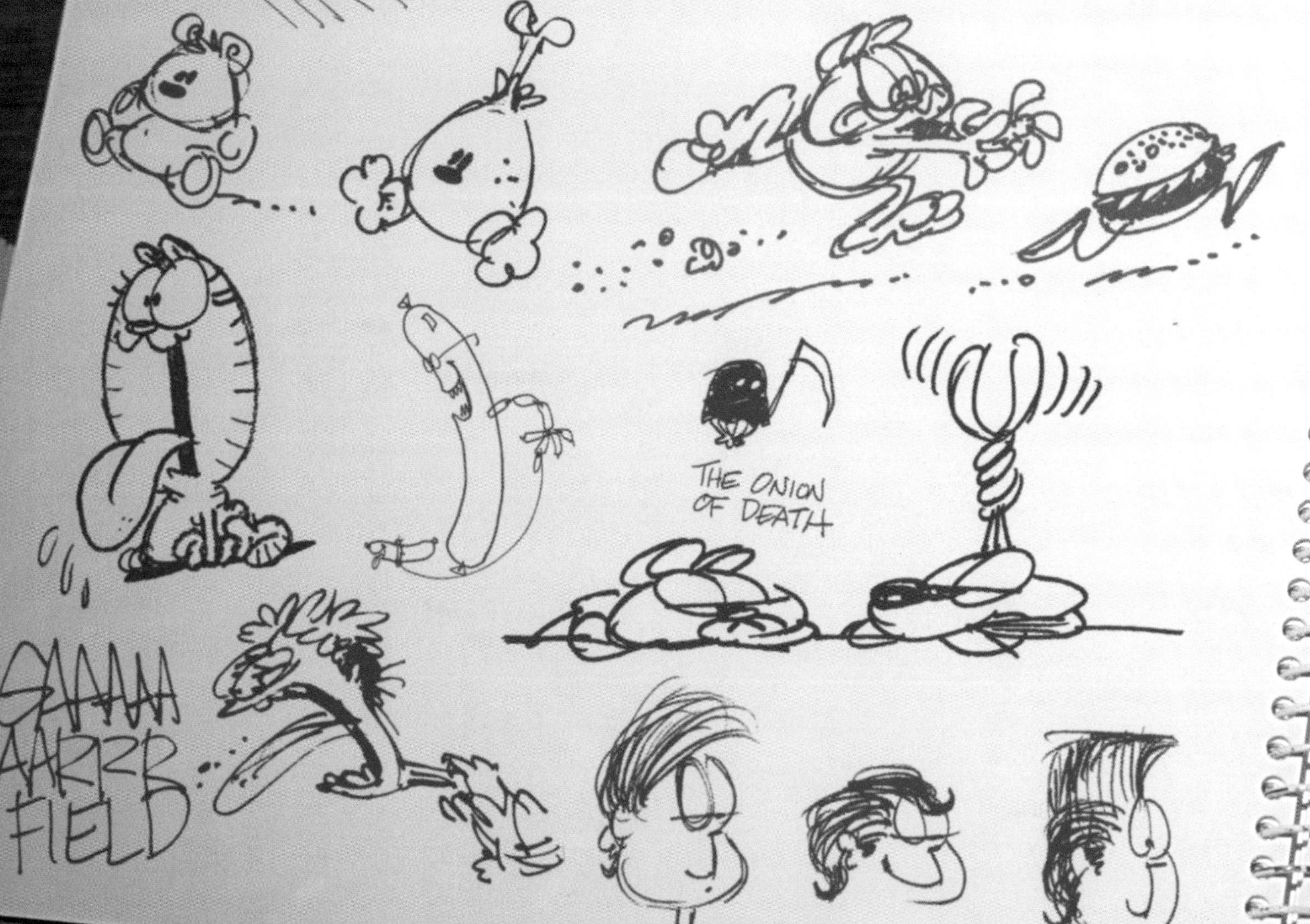
THE ONION
OF DEATH

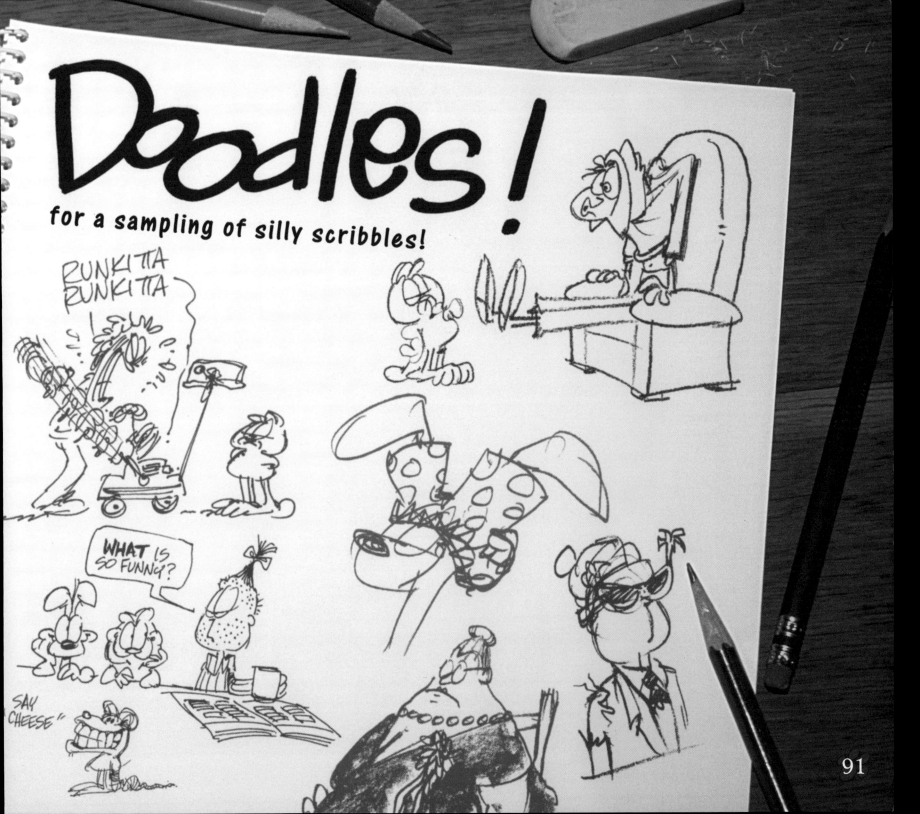

Doodles!

for a sampling of silly scribbles!

PUNKITTA
PUNKITTA

WHAT IS
SO FUNNY?

SAY
"CHEESE"

SEE YOU IN THE FUNNY PAPERS: GARFIELD IN OTHER COMIC STRIPS

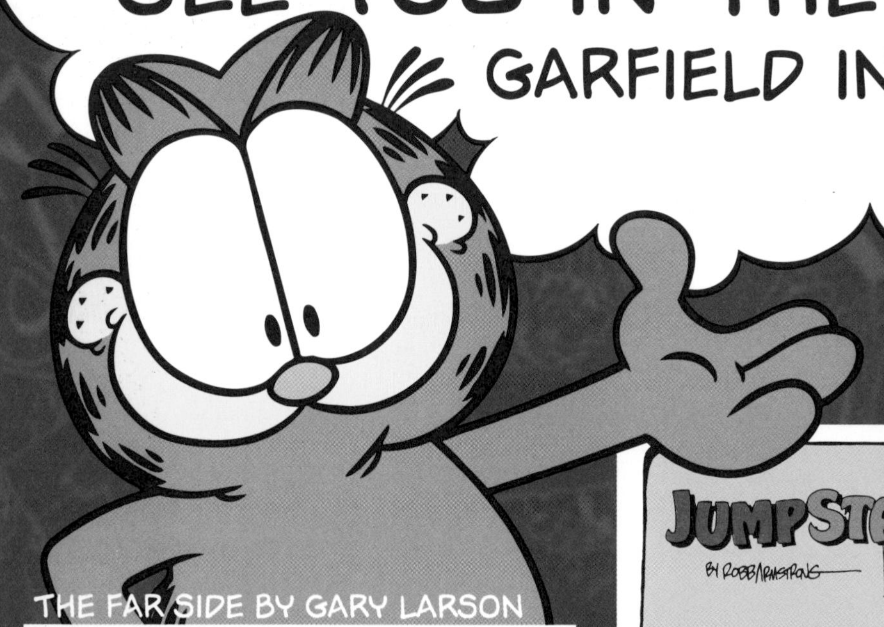

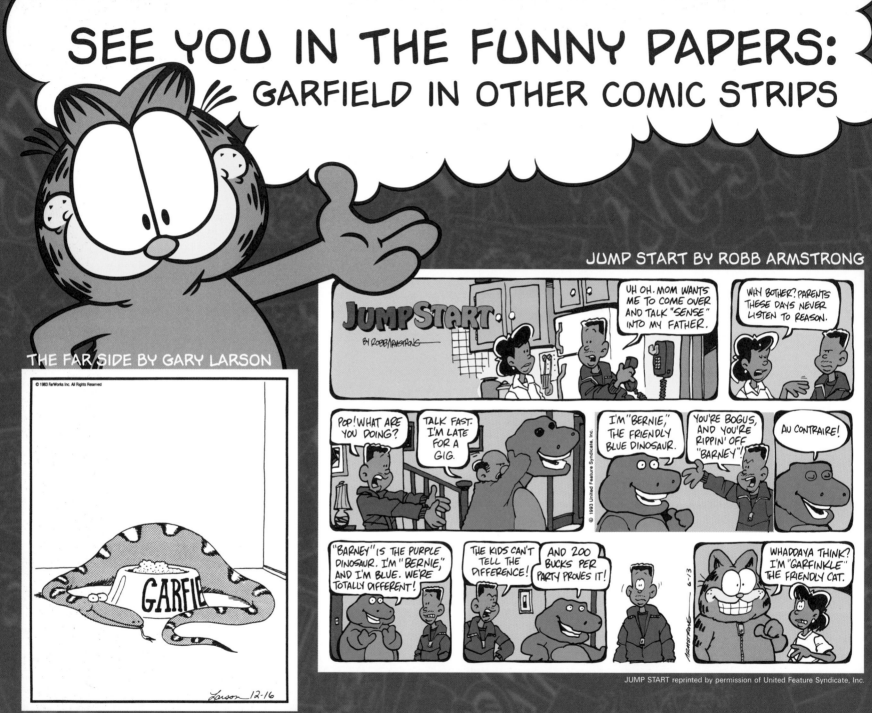

JUMP START BY ROBB ARMSTRONG

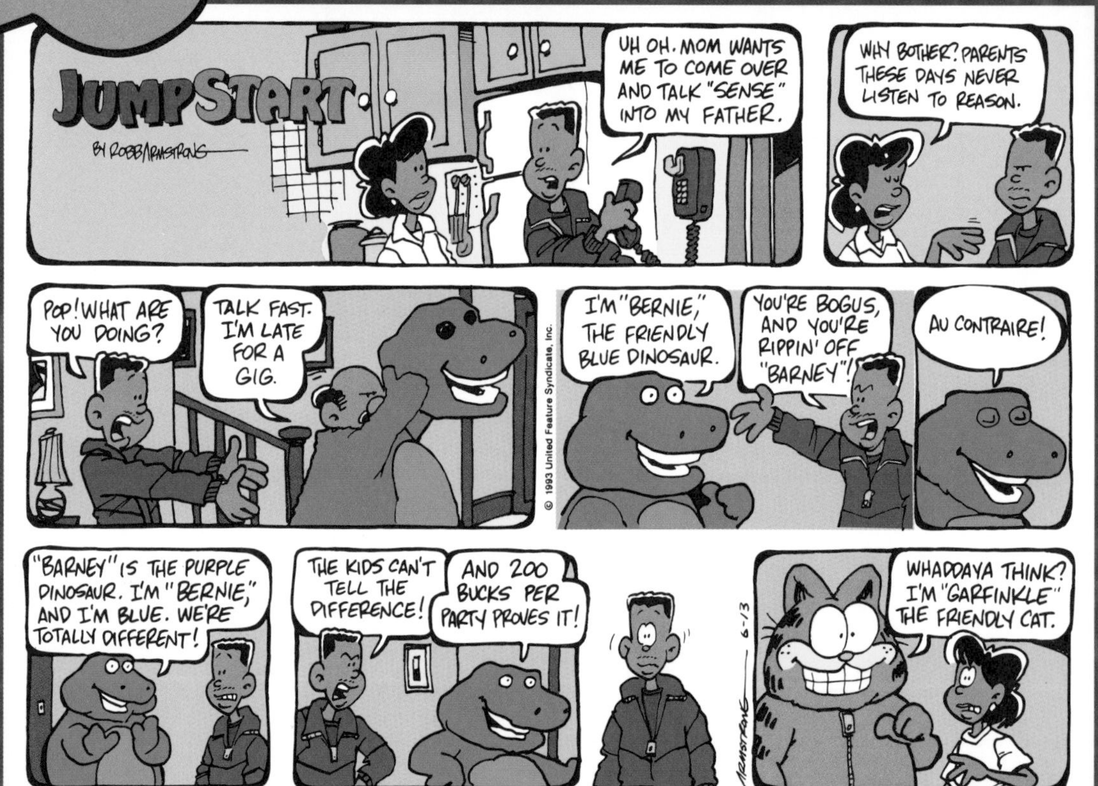
JUMPSTART
BY ROBB ARMSTRONG
UH OH. MOM WANTS ME TO COME OVER AND TALK "SENSE" INTO MY FATHER.
WHY BOTHER? PARENTS THESE DAYS NEVER LISTEN TO REASON.
POP! WHAT ARE YOU DOING?
TALK FAST. I'M LATE FOR A GIG.
© 1993 United Feature Syndicate, Inc.
I'M "BERNIE," THE FRIENDLY BLUE DINOSAUR.
YOU'RE BOGUS, AND YOU'RE RIPPIN' OFF "BARNEY"!
AU CONTRAIRE!
"BARNEY" IS THE PURPLE DINOSAUR. I'M "BERNIE," AND I'M BLUE. WE'RE TOTALLY DIFFERENT!
THE KIDS CAN'T TELL THE DIFFERENCE!
AND 200 BUCKS PER PARTY PROVES IT!
6-13
ARMSTRONG
WHADDAYA THINK? I'M "GARFINKLE" THE FRIENDLY CAT.

JUMP START reprinted by permission of United Feature Syndicate, Inc.

THE FAR SIDE BY GARY LARSON

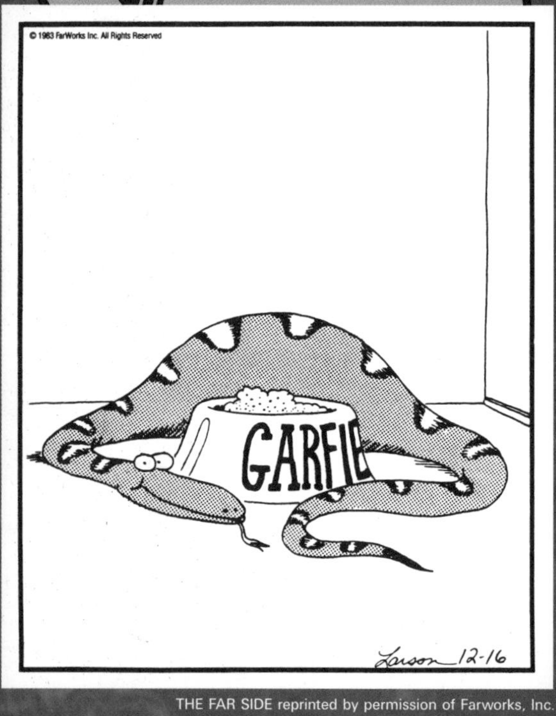
© 1983 FarWorks Inc. All Rights Reserved
GARFIE
Larson 12-16

THE FAR SIDE reprinted by permission of Farworks, Inc.

PEANUTS BY CHARLES SCHULZ

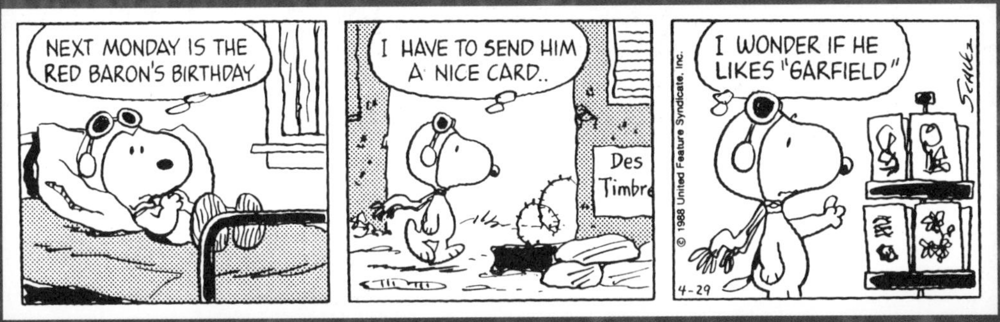
NEXT MONDAY IS THE RED BARON'S BIRTHDAY
I HAVE TO SEND HIM A NICE CARD..
Des Timbre
I WONDER IF HE LIKES "GARFIELD"
© 1988 United Feature Syndicate, Inc.
SCHULZ
4-29

PEANUTS reprinted by permission of United Feature Syndicate, Inc.

DILBERT BY SCOTT ADAMS

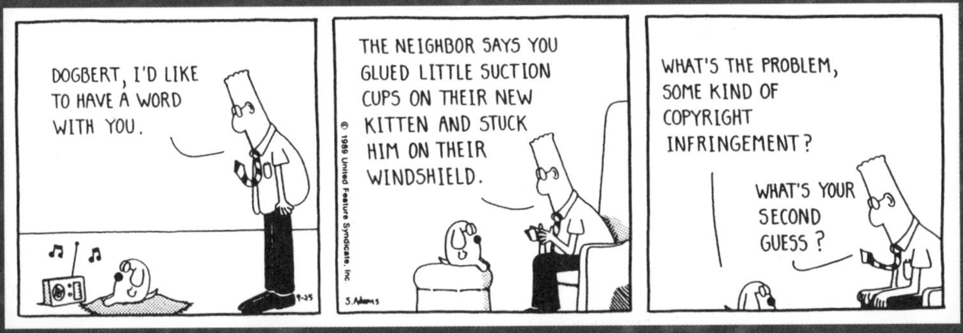
DOGBERT, I'D LIKE TO HAVE A WORD WITH YOU.
THE NEIGHBOR SAYS YOU GLUED LITTLE SUCTION CUPS ON THEIR NEW KITTEN AND STUCK HIM ON THEIR WINDSHIELD.
© 1989 United Feature Syndicate, Inc.
S.Adams
WHAT'S THE PROBLEM, SOME KIND OF COPYRIGHT INFRINGEMENT?
WHAT'S YOUR SECOND GUESS?

DILBERT reprinted by permission of United Feature Syndicate, Inc.

ROSE IS ROSE BY PAT BRADY

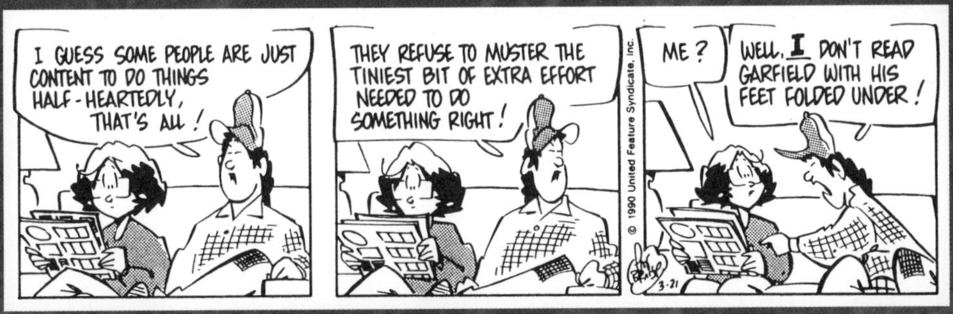
I GUESS SOME PEOPLE ARE JUST CONTENT TO DO THINGS HALF-HEARTEDLY, THAT'S ALL!
THEY REFUSE TO MUSTER THE TINIEST BIT OF EXTRA EFFORT NEEDED TO DO SOMETHING RIGHT!
© 1990 United Feature Syndicate, Inc.
ME?
WELL, I DON'T READ GARFIELD WITH HIS FEET FOLDED UNDER!
3-21

ROSE IS ROSE reprinted by permission of United Feature Syndicate, Inc.

MARVIN BY TOM ARMSTRONG

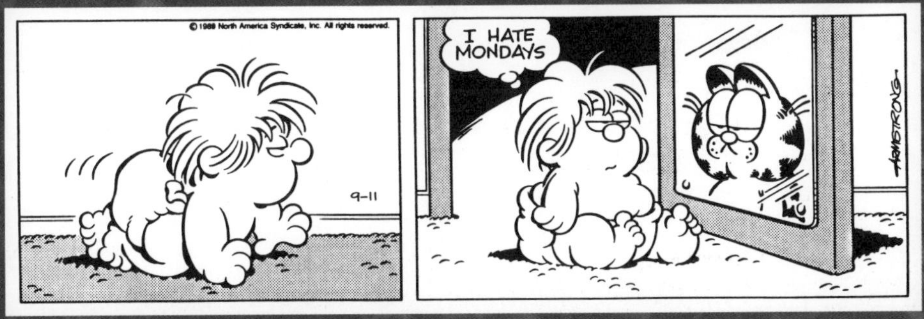
© 1988 North America Syndicate, Inc. All rights reserved.
9-11
I HATE MONDAYS
ARMSTRONG

MARVIN reprinted by permission of North America Syndicate.

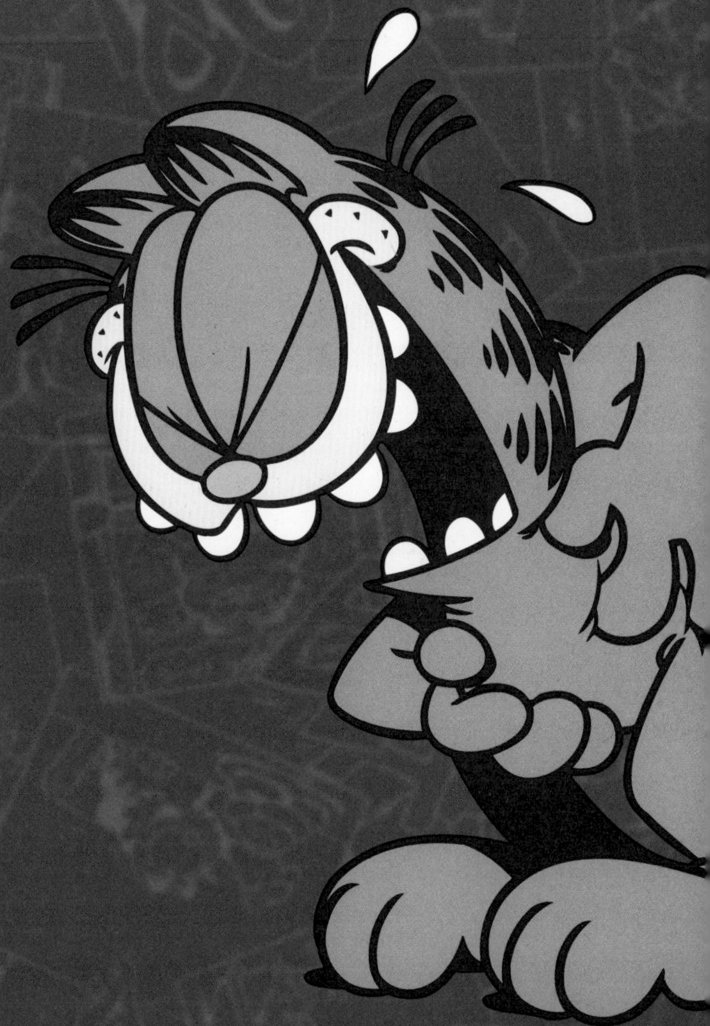

FRANK AND ERNEST BY BOB THAVES

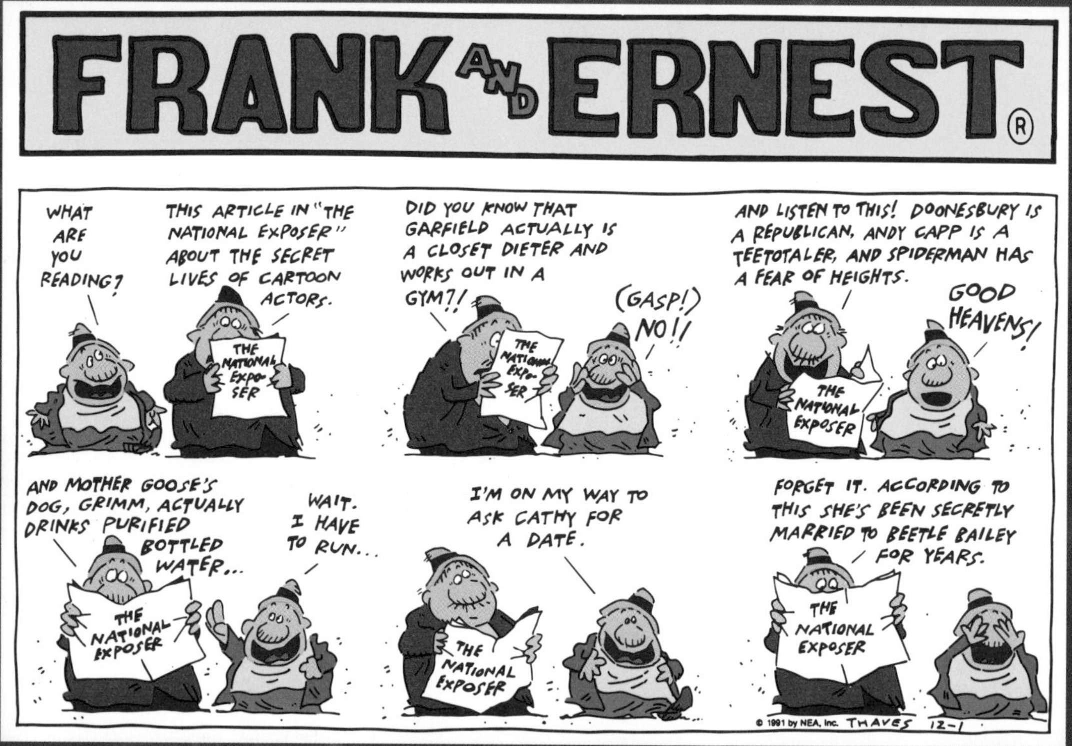
FRANK AND ERNEST ®
WHAT ARE YOU READING?
THIS ARTICLE IN "THE NATIONAL EXPOSER" ABOUT THE SECRET LIVES OF CARTOON ACTORS.
THE NATIONAL EXPOSER
DID YOU KNOW THAT GARFIELD ACTUALLY IS A CLOSET DIETER AND WORKS OUT IN A GYM?!
(GASP!) NO!!
THE NATIONAL EXPOSER
AND LISTEN TO THIS! DOONESBURY IS A REPUBLICAN, ANDY CAPP IS A TEETOTALER, AND SPIDERMAN HAS A FEAR OF HEIGHTS.
GOOD HEAVENS!
THE NATIONAL EXPOSER
AND MOTHER GOOSE'S DOG, GRIMM, ACTUALLY DRINKS PURIFIED BOTTLED WATER...
WAIT. I HAVE TO RUN...
THE NATIONAL EXPOSER
I'M ON MY WAY TO ASK CATHY FOR A DATE.
THE NATIONAL EXPOSER
FORGET IT. ACCORDING TO THIS SHE'S BEEN SECRETLY MARRIED TO BEETLE BAILEY FOR YEARS.
THE NATIONAL EXPOSER
© 1991 by NEA, Inc. THAVES 12-1

FRANK & ERNEST reprinted by permission of Newspaper Enterprise Association, Inc.

MARMADUKE BY BRAD ANDERSON

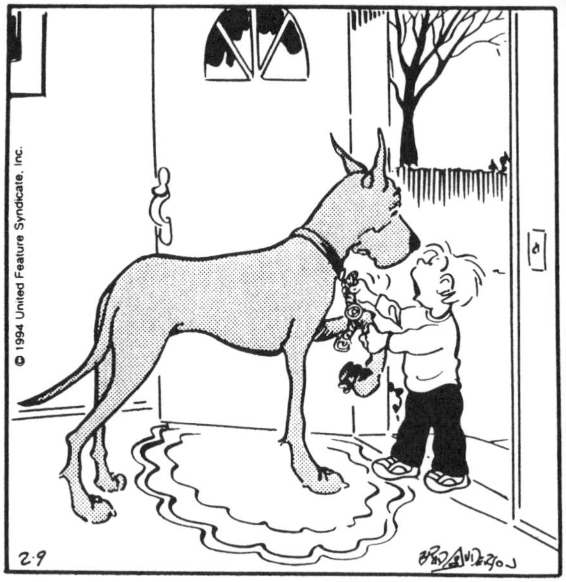
© 1994 United Feature Syndicate, Inc.
2-9

"I don't care if you have a big date with Veronica. You're not wearing my Garfield watch."

MARMADUKE reprinted by permission of United Feature Syndicate, Inc.

MOTHER GOOSE AND GRIMM BY MIKE PETERS

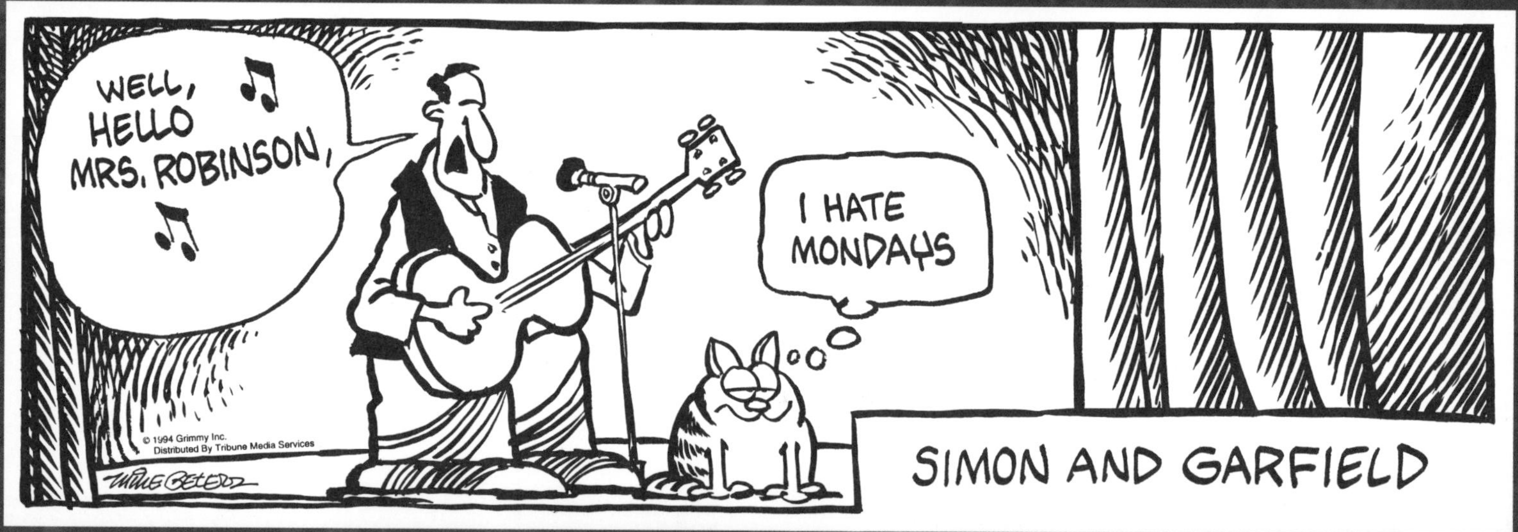
WELL, HELLO MRS. ROBINSON,
I HATE MONDAYS
© 1994 Grimmy Inc.
Distributed By Tribune Media Services
SIMON AND GARFIELD

MOTHER GOOSE AND GRIMM reprinted by permission of Grimmy, Inc.

GARFIELD TRIVIA QUIZ

1 Where was Garfield born?

A. In a log cabin
B. In an igloo
C. In Mamma Leoni's kitchen
D. In Mama Cass's kitchen

2 What character comes to the house every day and gets abused by Garfield?

A. The pizza man
B. The mailman
C. The cable guy
D. The Avon lady

3 What is Garfield's least favorite food?

A. Brussels sprouts
B. Goat curry
C. Eel
D. Raisins

4 On what comic strip did Jim Davis first apprentice?

A. *Peanuts*
B. *Krazy Kat*
C. *Apartment 3-G*
D. *Tumbleweeds*

5 One of Garfield's favorite sayings is "Big fat hairy _____." Fill in the blank.

A. Butt
B. Legs
C. Deal
D. Avocado

6 Where did Garfield find Pooky?

A. In a Dumpster
B. In a dresser drawer
C. In 'Nam
D. In Graceland

7 What's Garfield's favorite movie?

A. *That Darned Cat*
B. *Old Yeller*
C. *Of Mice and Men*
D. *Satyricon*

8 What's the name of Jon's farmer brother?

A. Doc Boy
B. Doc Holliday
C. Doc Severinsen
D. Ishmael

9 What animal did Garfield ride on his first visit to the Arbuckle farm?

A. A hog
B. A goat
C. An iguana
D. Doc Boy

10 According to Garfield, what kind of breath does Odie have?

A. Bated breath
B. Bone breath
C. Minty fresh breath
D. Toxic-waste breath

So, think you're a real smarty cat? Then test your GQ (Garfield Quotient) with this special trivia quiz. No cheating, please!

To find the answers, turn the page upside down.

Happy Birthday, Garfield!

Garfield celebrates his birthday on June 19, the day his Garfield comic strip first appeared in U.S. newspapers. Each year we devote a week of comic strips to Garfield's birthday, culminating in the birthday celebration. Garfield is most definitely a party animal, so his birthday is always a "big fat HAPPY deal!" He's enjoyed many memorable birthdays, including his fourth, which was an especially warm occasion — mostly because Garfield swallowed the cake before he blew out the candles!

'78

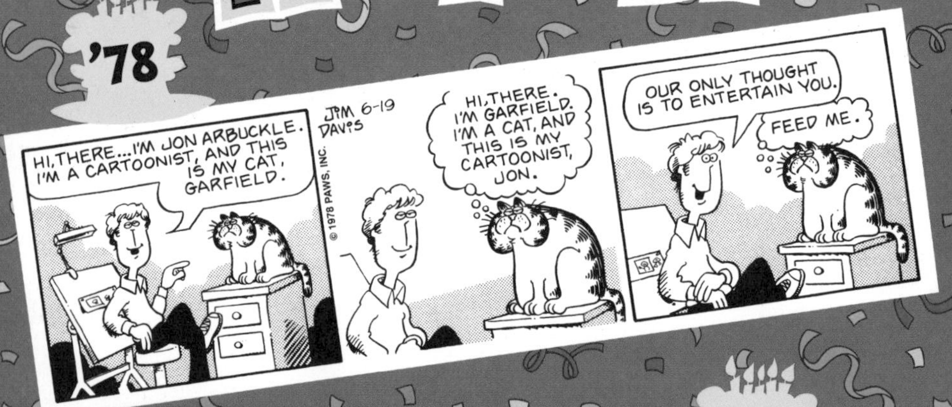
HI, THERE... I'M JON ARBUCKLE. I'M A CARTOONIST, AND THIS IS MY CAT, GARFIELD.
JIM DAVIS 6-19
© 1978 PAWS, INC.
HI, THERE. I'M GARFIELD. I'M A CAT, AND THIS IS MY CARTOONIST, JON.
OUR ONLY THOUGHT IS TO ENTERTAIN YOU.
FEED ME.

'79

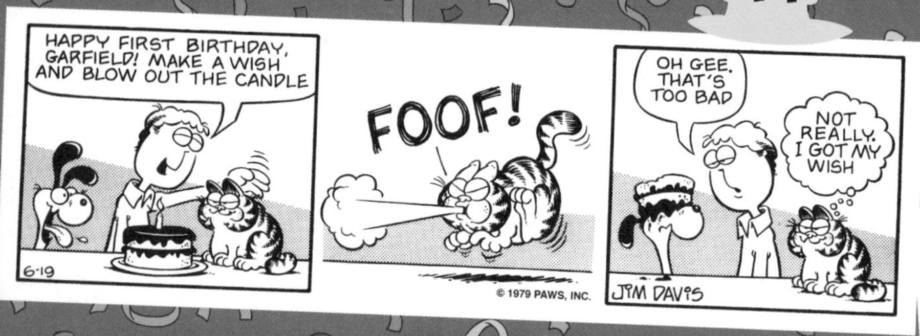
HAPPY FIRST BIRTHDAY, GARFIELD! MAKE A WISH AND BLOW OUT THE CANDLE
6-19
FOOF!
© 1979 PAWS, INC.
OH GEE. THAT'S TOO BAD
NOT REALLY. I GOT MY WISH
JIM DAVIS

'80

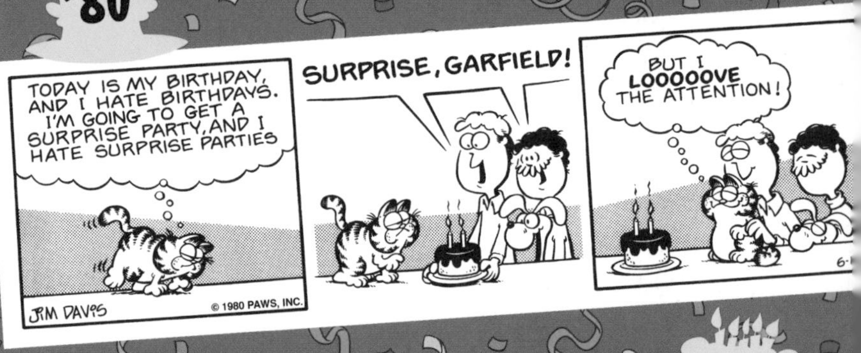
TODAY IS MY BIRTHDAY, AND I HATE BIRTHDAYS. I'M GOING TO GET A SURPRISE PARTY, AND I HATE SURPRISE PARTIES
JIM DAVIS
© 1980 PAWS, INC.
SURPRISE, GARFIELD!
BUT I LOOOOOVE THE ATTENTION!

'81

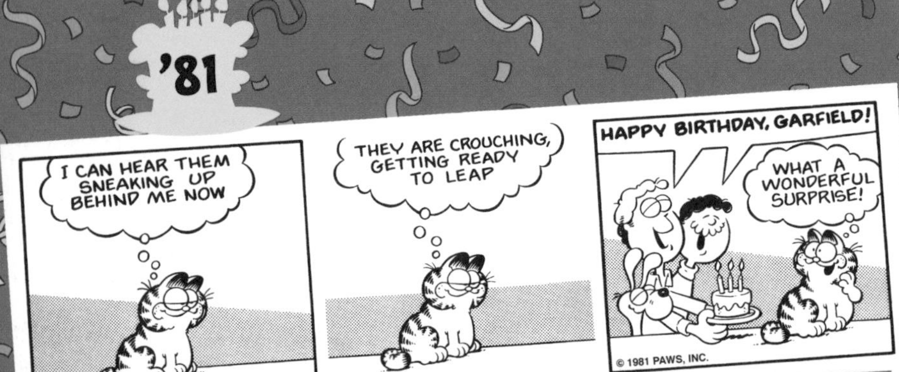
I CAN HEAR THEM SNEAKING UP BEHIND ME NOW
6-19
JIM DAVIS
THEY ARE CROUCHING, GETTING READY TO LEAP
HAPPY BIRTHDAY, GARFIELD!
WHAT A WONDERFUL SURPRISE!
© 1981 PAWS, INC.

'82

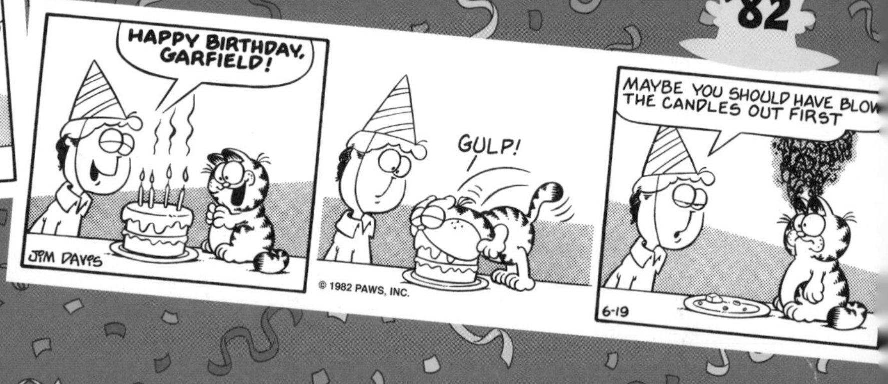
HAPPY BIRTHDAY, GARFIELD!
JIM DAVIS
GULP!
© 1982 PAWS, INC.
MAYBE YOU SHOULD HAVE BLOW THE CANDLES OUT FIRST
6-19

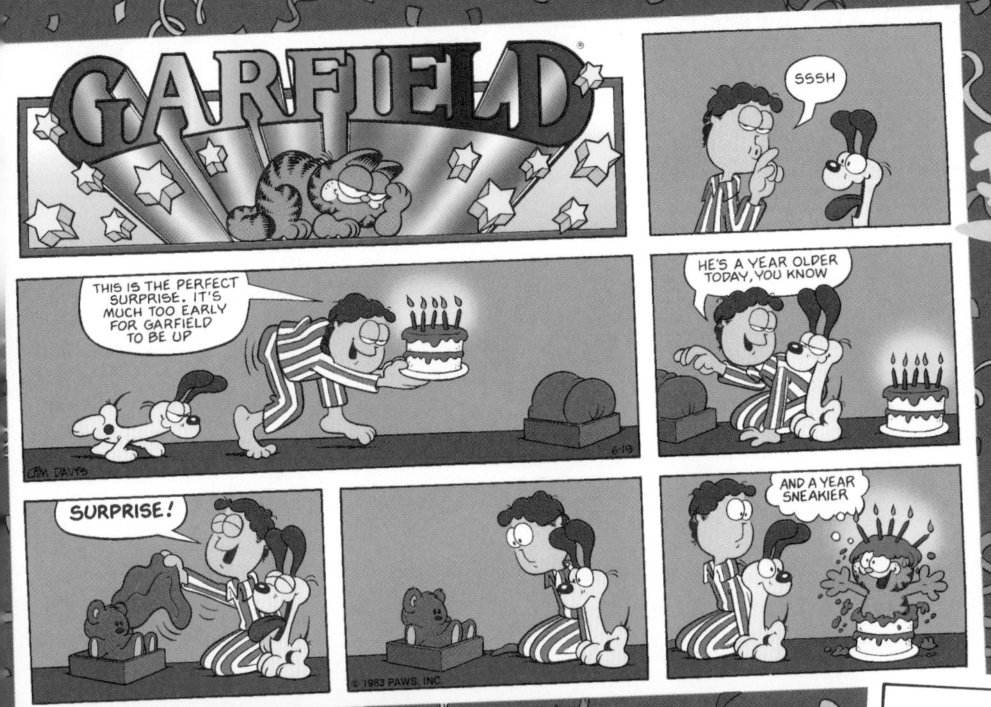

GARFIELD
SSSH
THIS IS THE PERFECT SURPRISE. IT'S MUCH TOO EARLY FOR GARFIELD TO BE UP
HE'S A YEAR OLDER TODAY, YOU KNOW
JIM DAVIS
6-19
SURPRISE!
AND A YEAR SNEAKIER
© 1983 PAWS, INC.

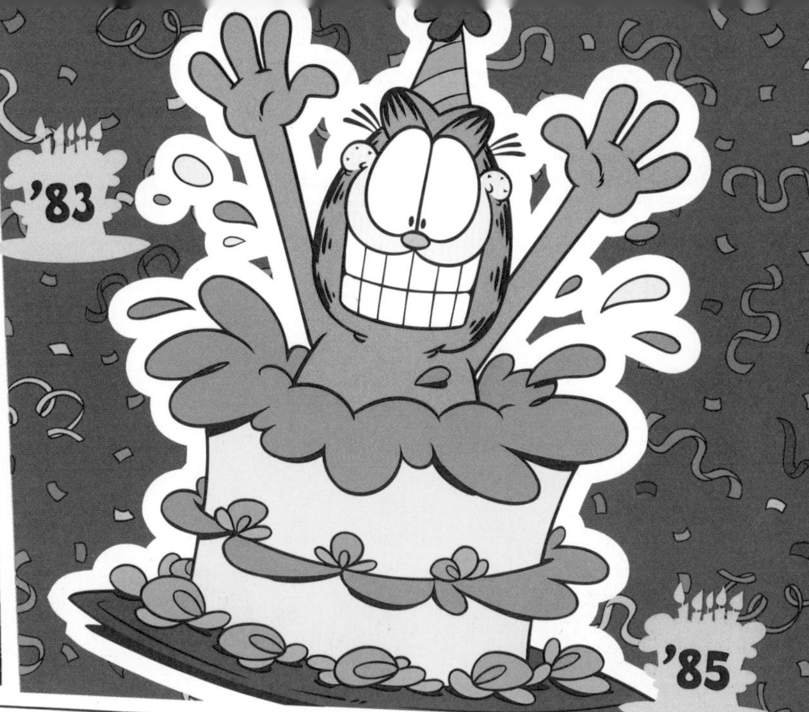

'83

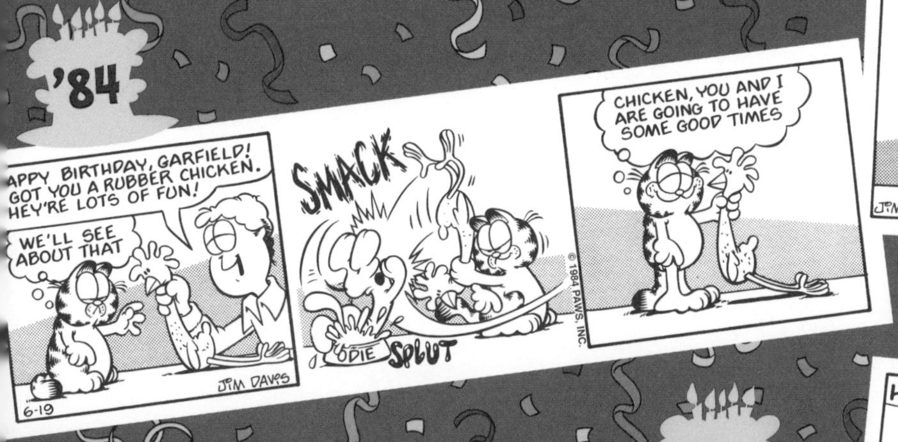

'84
APPY BIRTHDAY, GARFIELD! GOT YOU A RUBBER CHICKEN. HEY'RE LOTS OF FUN!
WE'LL SEE ABOUT THAT
SMACK
ODIE
SPLUT
CHICKEN, YOU AND I ARE GOING TO HAVE SOME GOOD TIMES
JIM DAVIS
6-19
© 1984 PAWS, INC.

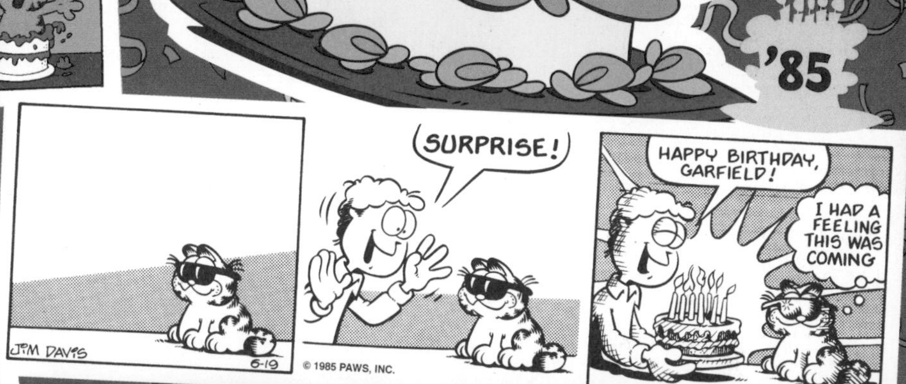

'85
SURPRISE!
HAPPY BIRTHDAY, GARFIELD!
I HAD A FEELING THIS WAS COMING
JIM DAVIS
6-19
© 1985 PAWS, INC.

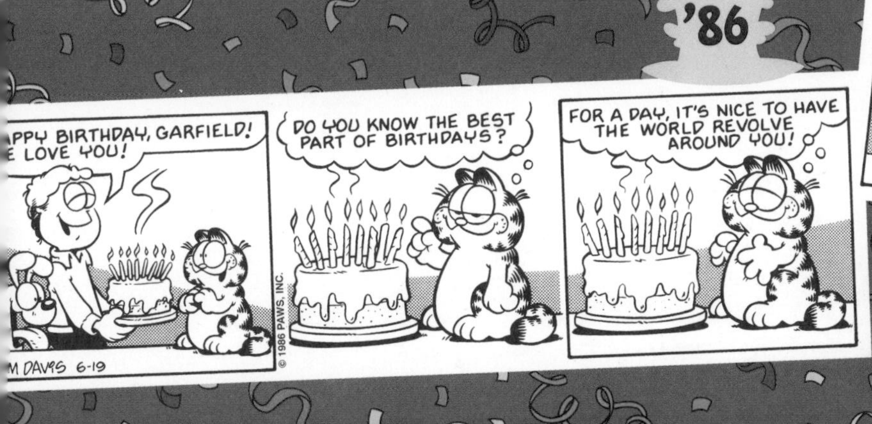

'86
APPY BIRTHDAY, GARFIELD! LOVE YOU!
DO YOU KNOW THE BEST PART OF BIRTHDAYS?
FOR A DAY, IT'S NICE TO HAVE THE WORLD REVOLVE AROUND YOU!
JIM DAVIS 6-19
© 1986 PAWS, INC.

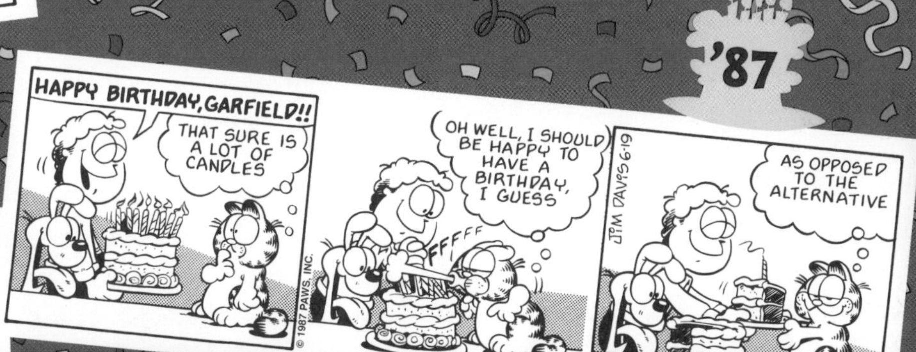

'87
HAPPY BIRTHDAY, GARFIELD!!
THAT SURE IS A LOT OF CANDLES
OH WELL, I SHOULD BE HAPPY TO HAVE A BIRTHDAY, I GUESS
FFFFF
JIM DAVIS 6-19
AS OPPOSED TO THE ALTERNATIVE
© 1987 PAWS, INC.

'88

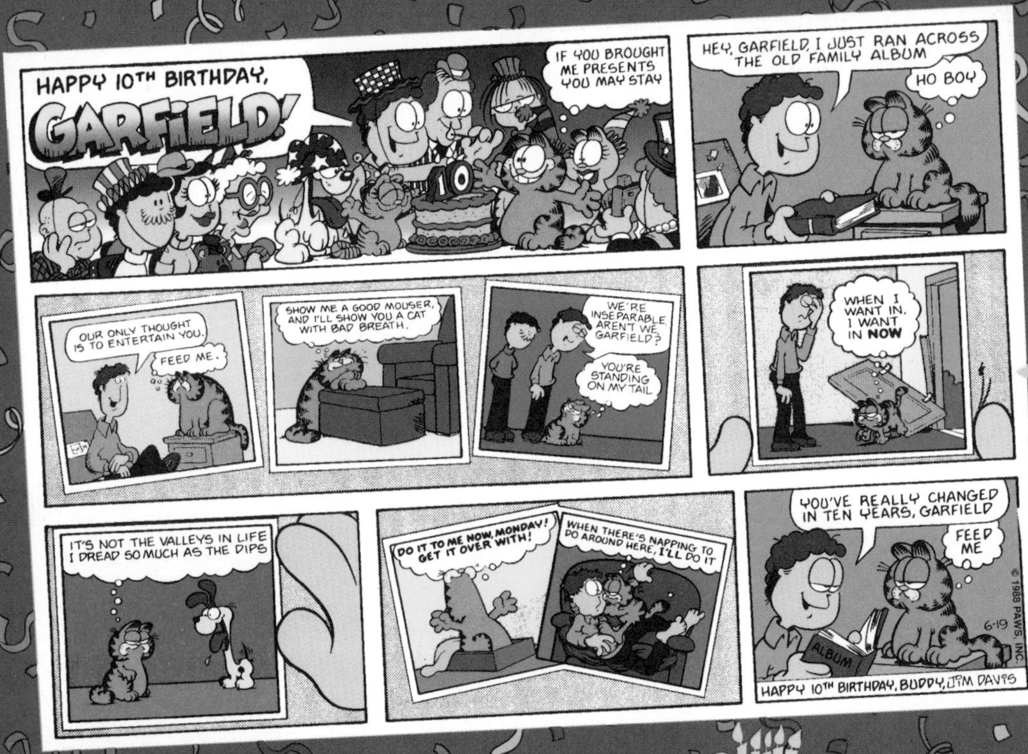

HAPPY 10TH BIRTHDAY,
GARFIELD!
IF YOU BROUGHT ME PRESENTS YOU MAY STAY
10
HEY, GARFIELD, I JUST RAN ACROSS THE OLD FAMILY ALBUM
HO BOY
OUR ONLY THOUGHT IS TO ENTERTAIN YOU.
FEED ME.
SHOW ME A GOOD MOUSER, AND I'LL SHOW YOU A CAT WITH BAD BREATH.
WE'RE INSEPARABLE, AREN'T WE, GARFIELD?
YOU'RE STANDING ON MY TAIL
WHEN I WANT IN, I WANT IN NOW
IT'S NOT THE VALLEYS IN LIFE I DREAD SO MUCH AS THE DIPS
DO IT TO ME NOW, MONDAY! GET IT OVER WITH!
WHEN THERE'S NAPPING TO DO AROUND HERE, I'LL DO IT
YOU'VE REALLY CHANGED IN TEN YEARS, GARFIELD
FEED ME
ALBUM
© 1988 PAWS, INC.
6-19
HAPPY 10TH BIRTHDAY, BUDDY, JIM DAVIS

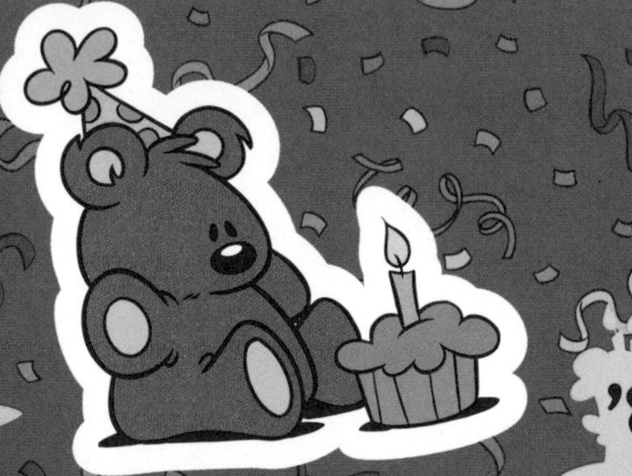

'89

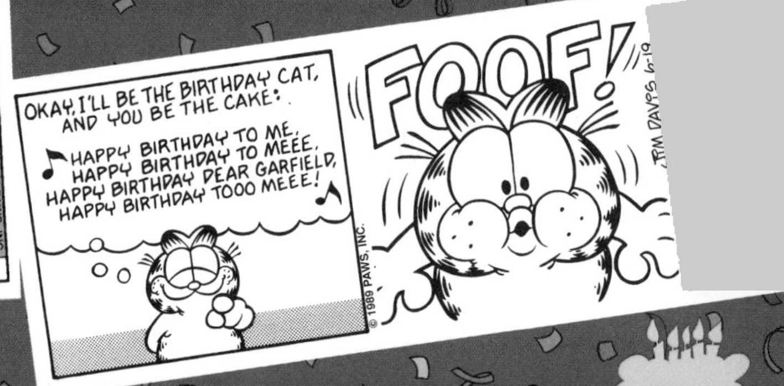

OKAY, I'LL BE THE BIRTHDAY CAT, AND YOU BE THE CAKE:
HAPPY BIRTHDAY TO ME, HAPPY BIRTHDAY TO MEEE, HAPPY BIRTHDAY DEAR GARFIELD, HAPPY BIRTHDAY TOOO MEEE!
© 1989 PAWS, INC.
FOOF!
JIM DAVIS 6-19

'90

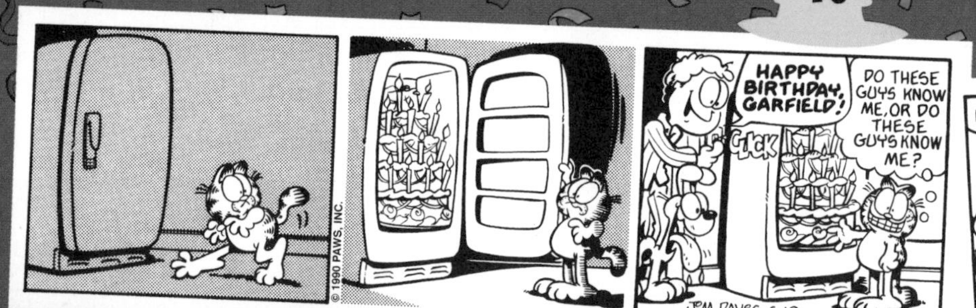

© 1990 PAWS, INC.
HAPPY BIRTHDAY, GARFIELD!
DO THESE GUYS KNOW ME, OR DO THESE GUYS KNOW ME?
CLICK
JIM DAVIS 6-19

'91

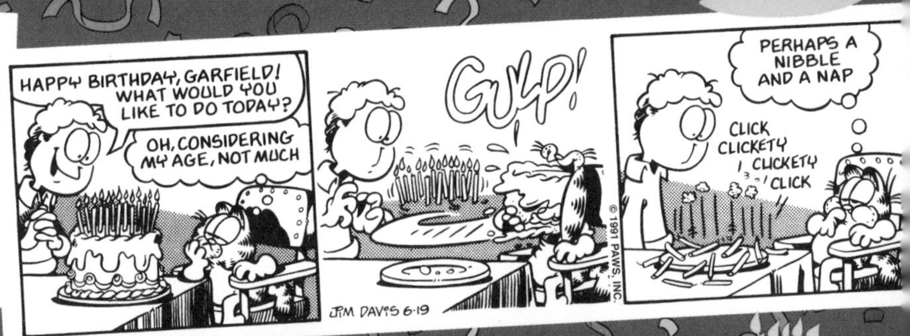

HAPPY BIRTHDAY, GARFIELD! WHAT WOULD YOU LIKE TO DO TODAY?
OH, CONSIDERING MY AGE, NOT MUCH
JIM DAVIS 6-19
GULP!
© 1991 PAWS, INC.
PERHAPS A NIBBLE AND A NAP
CLICK CLICKETY CLICKETY CLICK

'92

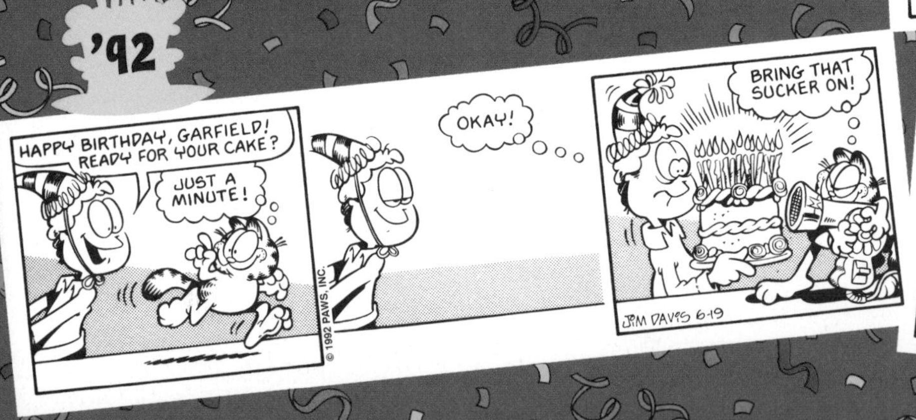

HAPPY BIRTHDAY, GARFIELD! READY FOR YOUR CAKE?
JUST A MINUTE!
© 1992 PAWS, INC.
OKAY!
BRING THAT SUCKER ON!
JIM DAVIS 6-19

'93

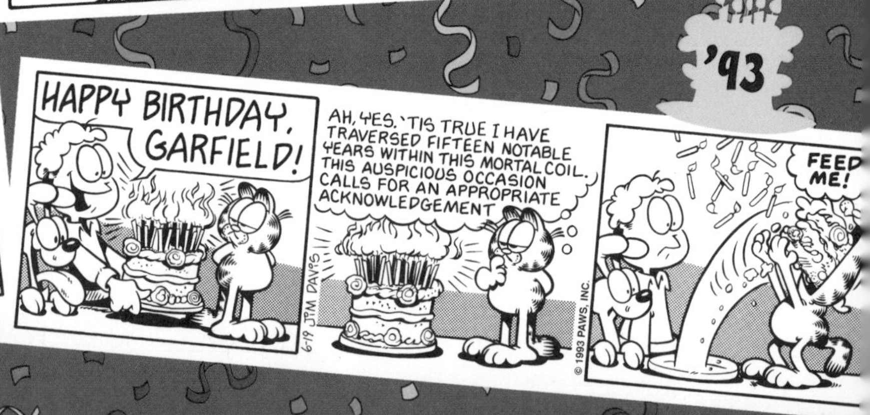

HAPPY BIRTHDAY, GARFIELD!
6-19 JIM DAVIS
AH, YES. 'TIS TRUE I HAVE TRAVERSED FIFTEEN NOTABLE YEARS WITHIN THIS MORTAL COIL. THIS AUSPICIOUS OCCASION CALLS FOR AN APPROPRIATE ACKNOWLEDGEMENT
© 1993 PAWS, INC.
FEED ME!

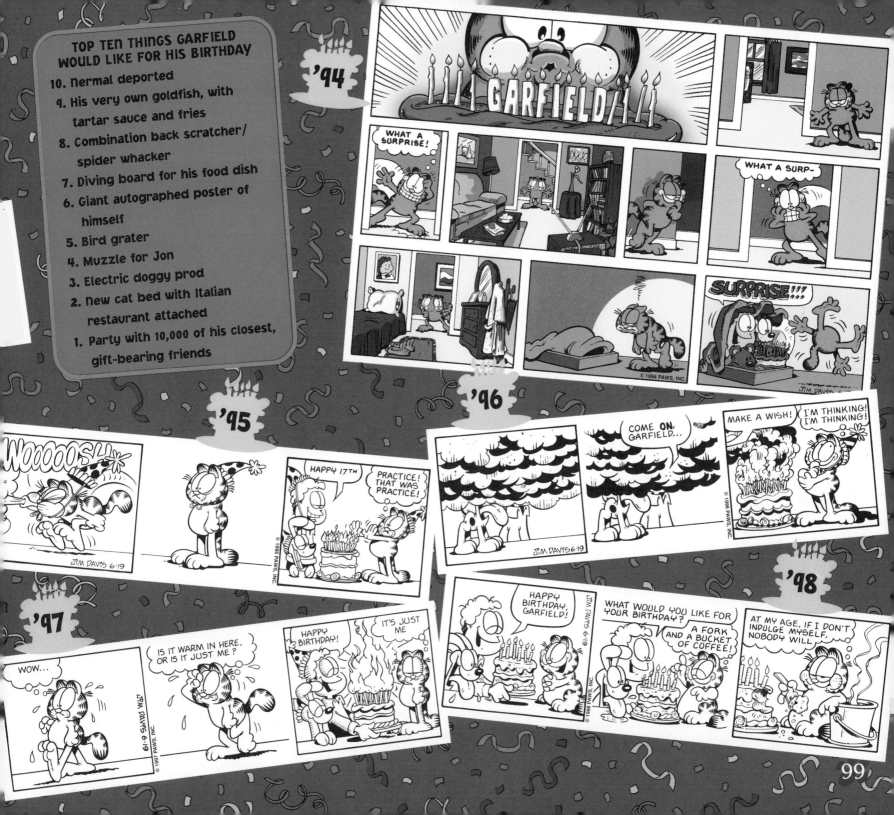

TOP TEN THINGS GARFIELD WOULD LIKE FOR HIS BIRTHDAY

10. Nermal deported
9. His very own goldfish, with tartar sauce and fries
8. Combination back scratcher/ spider whacker
7. Diving board for his food dish
6. Giant autographed poster of himself
5. Bird grater
4. Muzzle for Jon
3. Electric doggy prod
2. New cat bed with Italian restaurant attached
1. Party with 10,000 of his closest, gift-bearing friends

'94

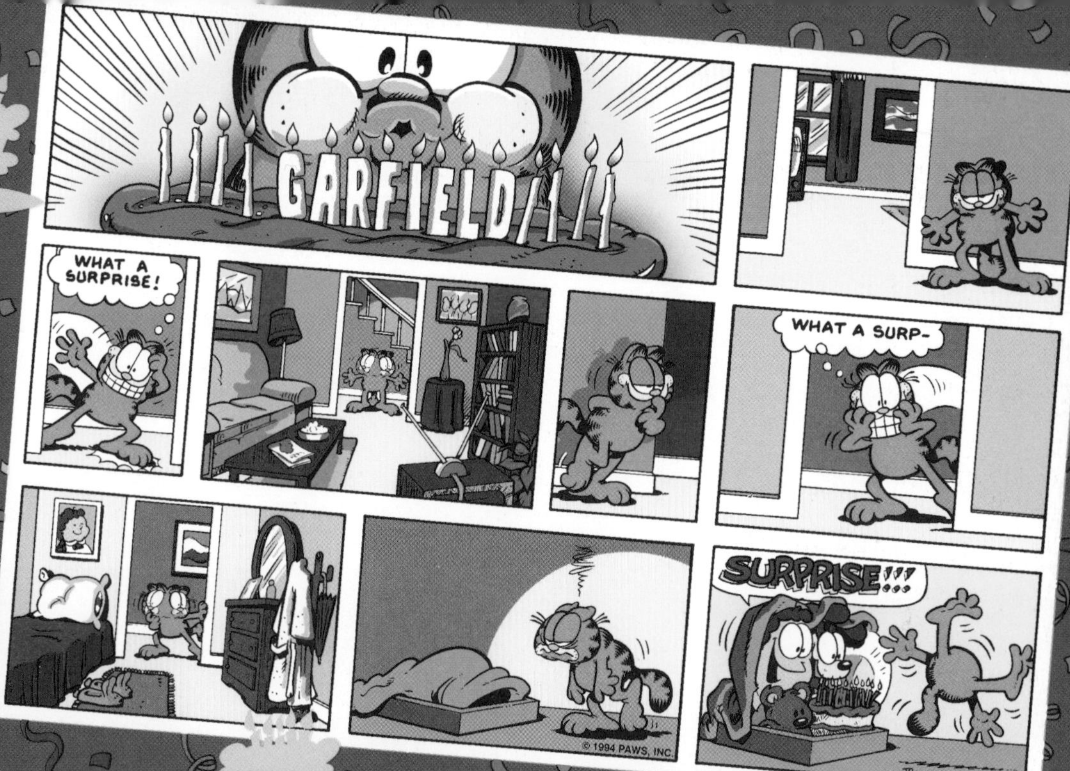
GARFIELD
WHAT A SURPRISE!
WHAT A SURP-
SURPRISE!!!
© 1994 PAWS, INC.
JIM DAVIS

'95

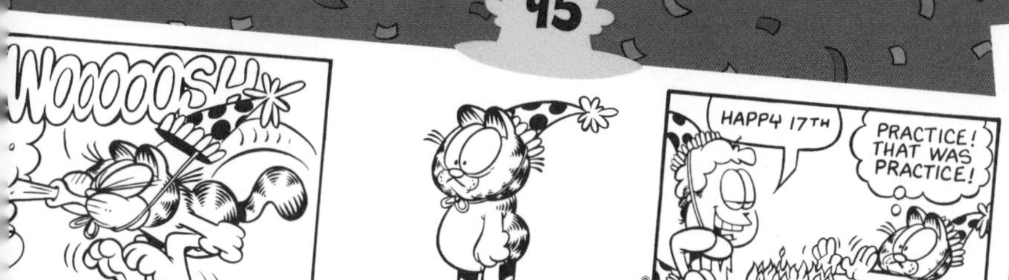
WOOOOOOSH
JIM DAVIS 6-19
© 1995 PAWS, INC.
HAPPY 17TH
PRACTICE! THAT WAS PRACTICE!

'96

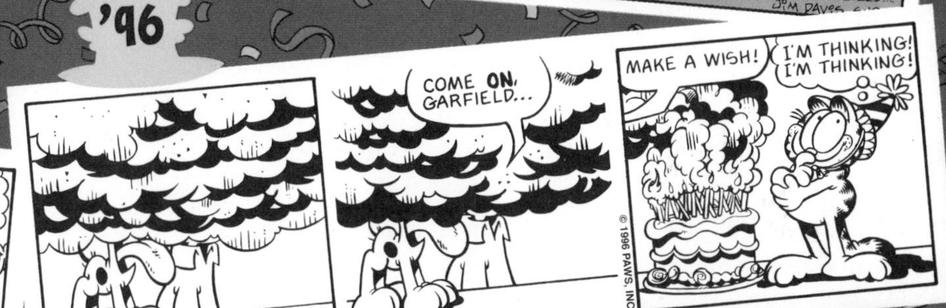
COME ON, GARFIELD...
JIM DAVIS 6-19
MAKE A WISH!
I'M THINKING! I'M THINKING!
© 1996 PAWS, INC.

'97

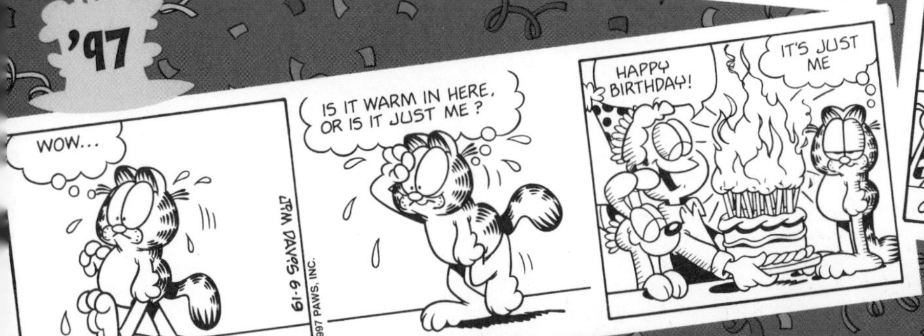
WOW...
IS IT WARM IN HERE, OR IS IT JUST ME?
JIM DAVIS 6-19
© 1997 PAWS, INC.
HAPPY BIRTHDAY!
IT'S JUST ME

'98

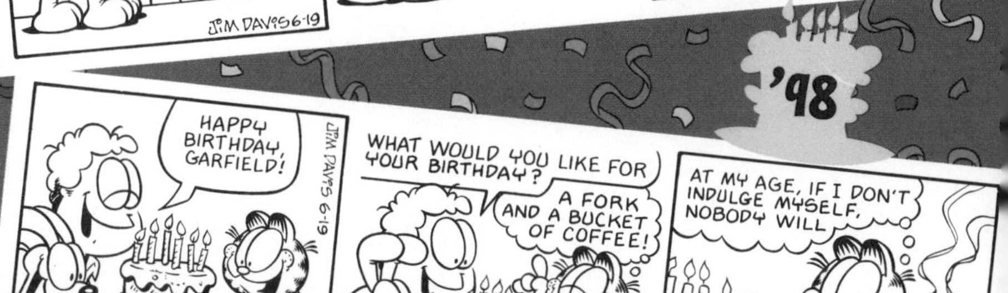
HAPPY BIRTHDAY, GARFIELD!
JIM DAVIS 6-19
© 1998 PAWS, INC.
WHAT WOULD YOU LIKE FOR YOUR BIRTHDAY?
A FORK AND A BUCKET OF COFFEE!
AT MY AGE, IF I DON'T INDULGE MYSELF, NOBODY WILL

Foto

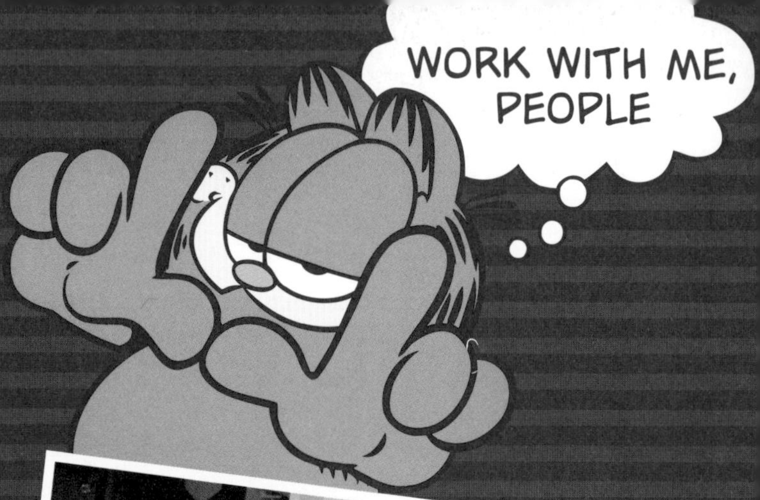
WORK WITH ME, PEOPLE

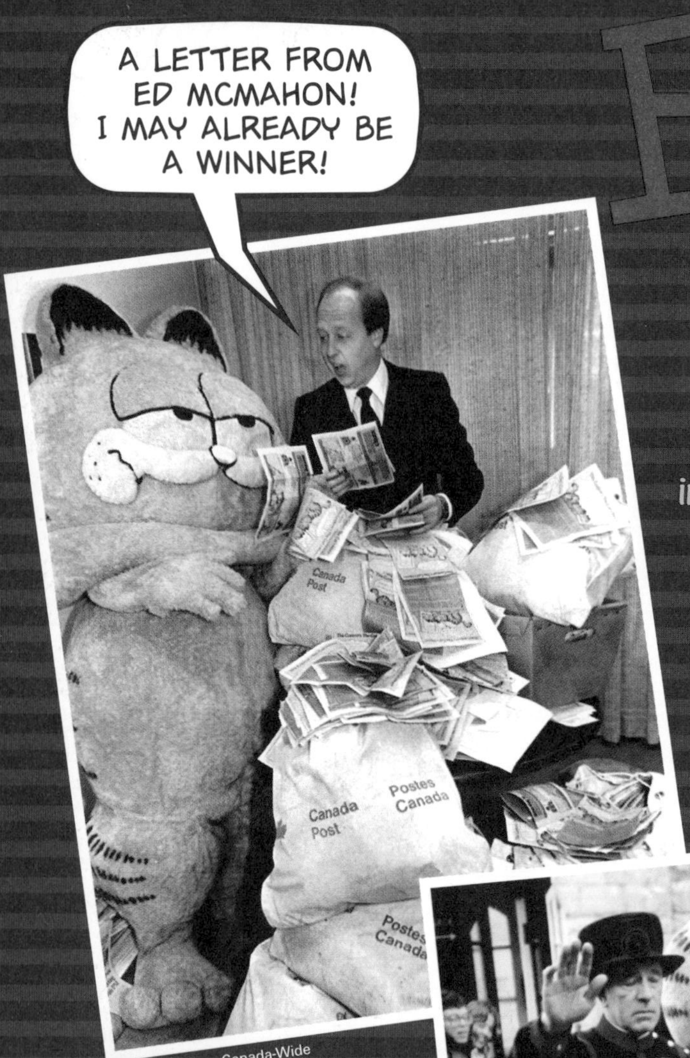
A LETTER FROM ED MCMAHON! I MAY ALREADY BE A WINNER!
Canada Post
Postes Canada

I NOW PRONOUNCE YOU MAN AND WIFE . . . AND CAT!

Major Garfield fanatic invites the fat cat to join in her wedded bliss.

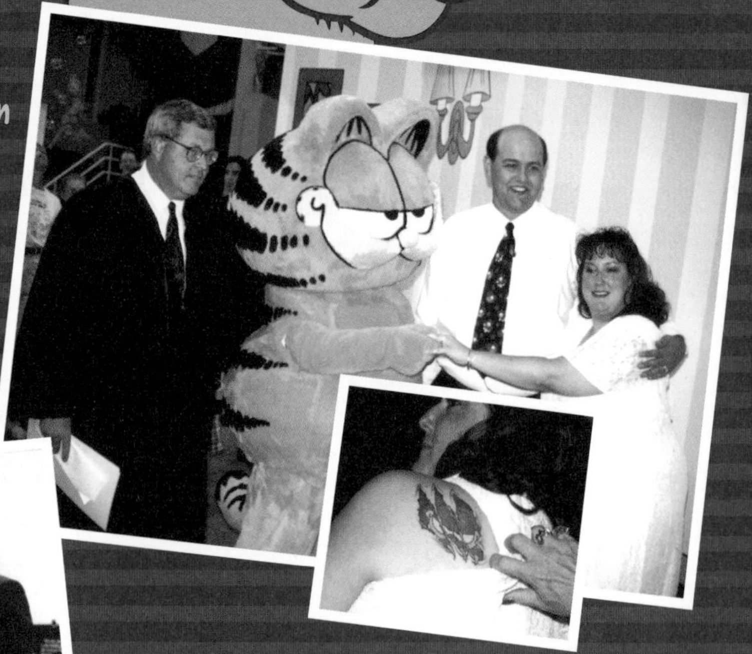

GOD SAVE THE CAT

Garfield and Jim outside ye olde Tower of London.

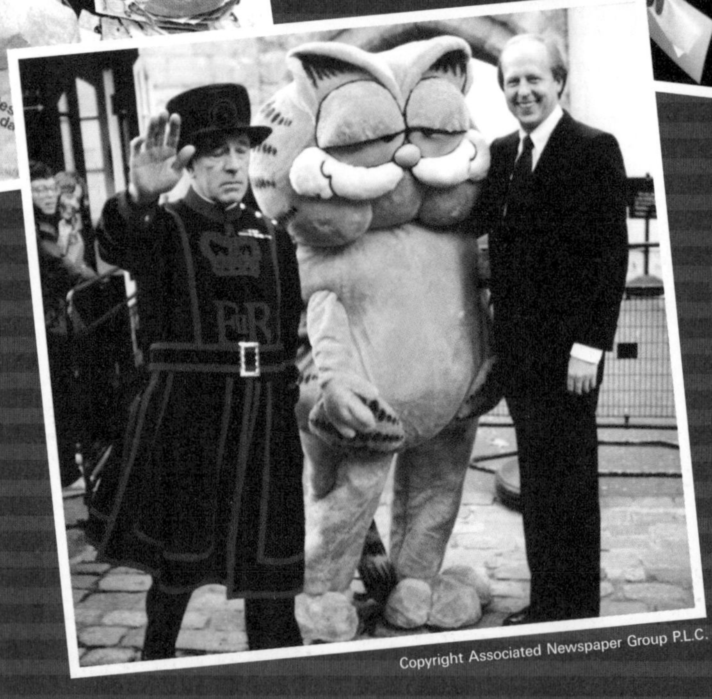

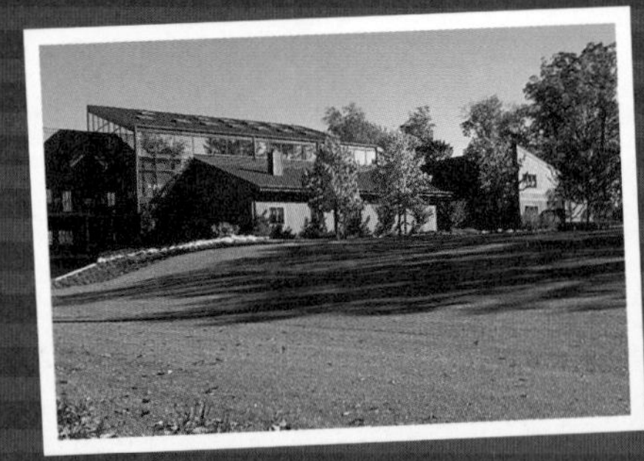

THE HOUSE THAT GARFIELD BUILT

The Paws, Inc., studio.

Funnies

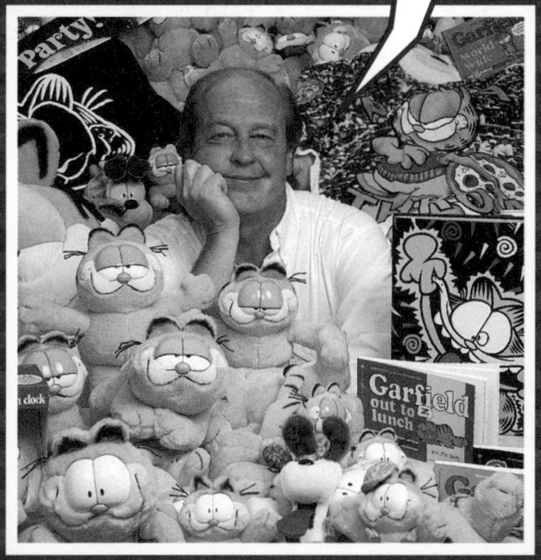
TOO MUCH GARFIELD IS NEVER ENOUGH
Garfield out to lunch

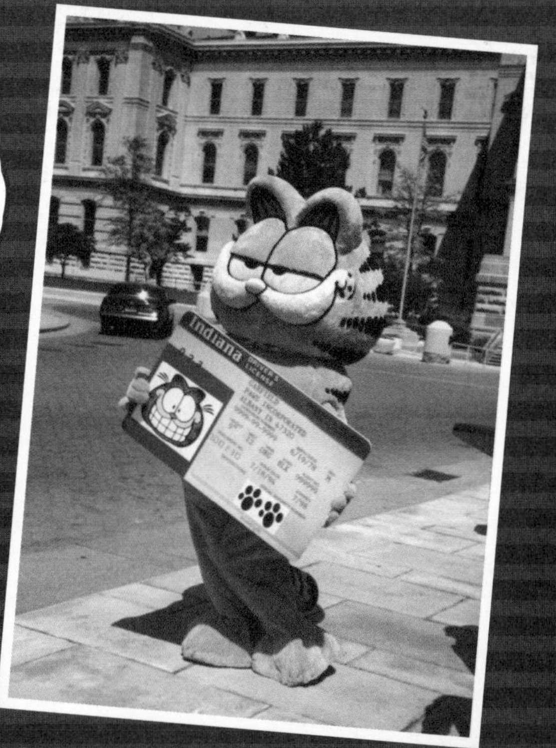
Indiana

I RULE THE ROAD!

Garfield gets his driver's license on his sixteenth birthday.

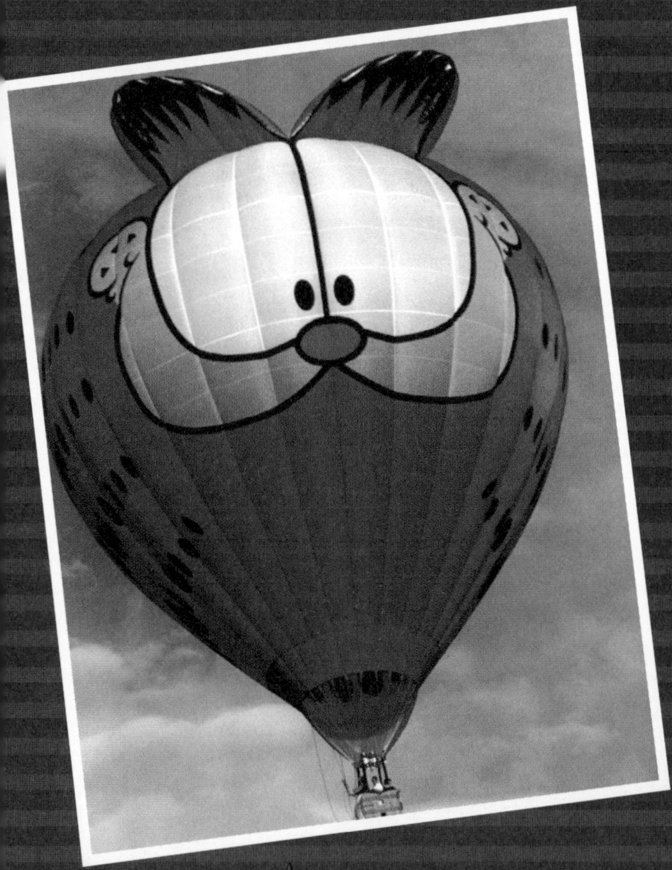

Alas, twenty years of superstardom has given Garfield a REALLY big head.

THAT'S SHOW BIZ!

A night at the Emmys . . .

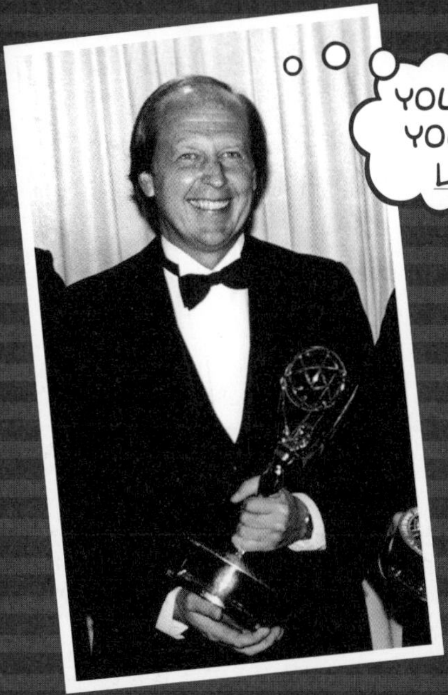
YOU LIKE ME! YOU REALLY LIKE ME!

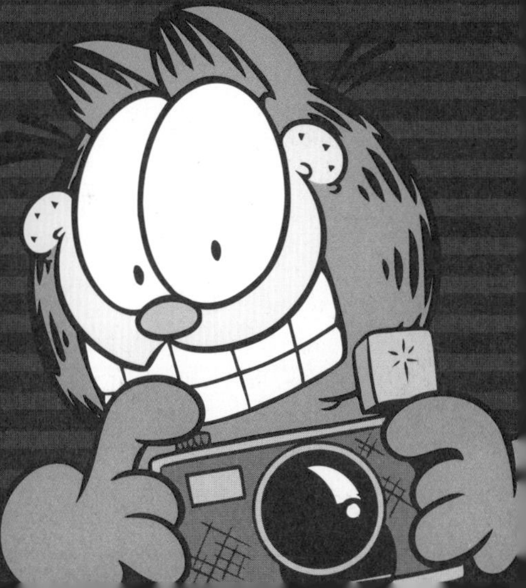

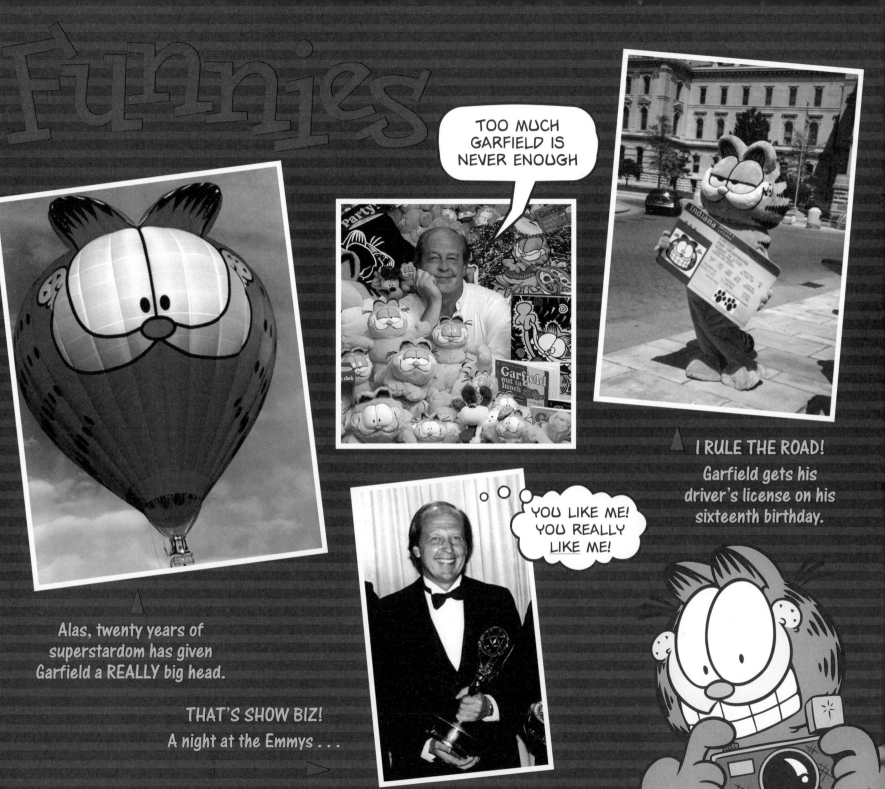

Weird fan mail

Letters, we get letters . . . .

While nearly all the fan mail we get is from nice, happy fans – people telling us how much they like Garfield or sharing their favorite cat stories – some of the letters we receive are just a little off; and some of them are downright bizarre. Over the years, we've collected a folder of these loony letters. For a sampling of this strangeness, read on. . . .

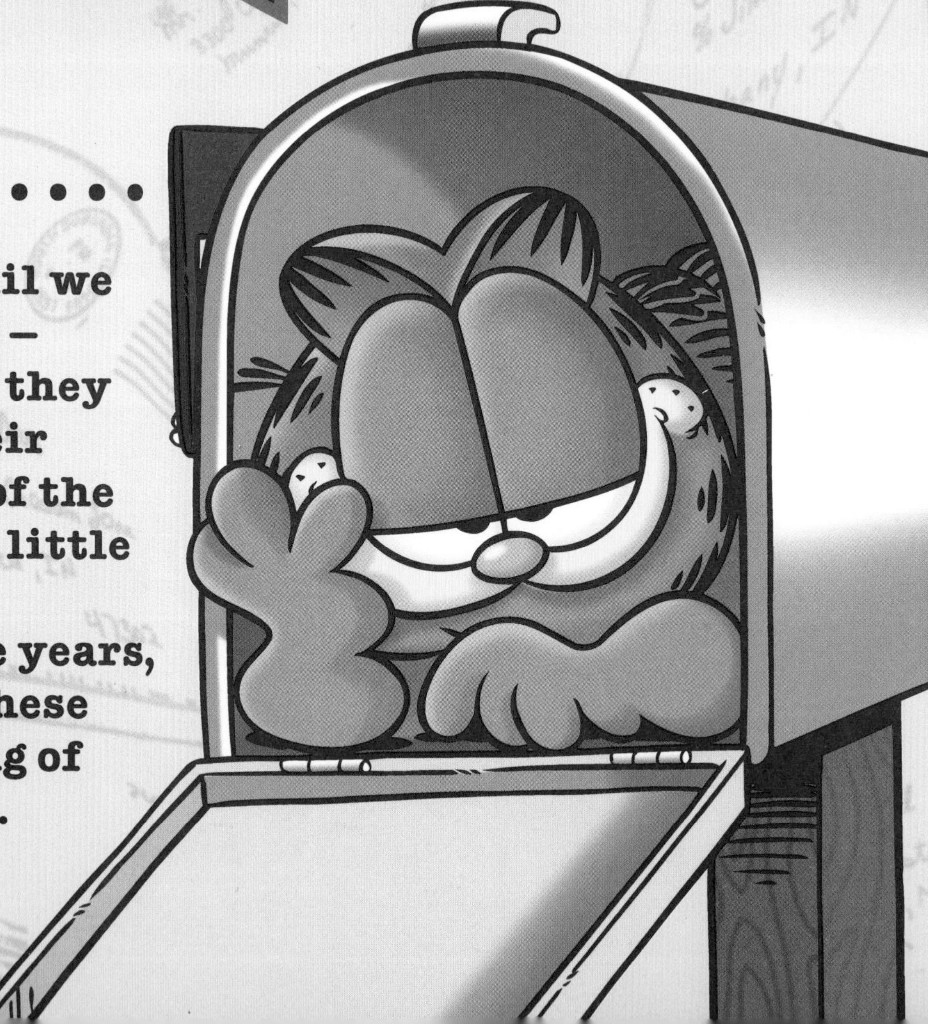

Take, for instance, the Canadian fan who wrote to announce the Second Coming, asking me to use my influence to "help combat carbon dioxide pollutions at the poles which put the planet in jeopardy."

Or the Ohio fan who sent me several letters to complain about, among other things, old men ("What's with old people . . . with this sex and bingo?"), her sister's cat ("The mangy critter has his own bathroom!"), and hospital personnel ("They are all zoo zoo and stupid").

Then there was the guy who sent in an original sketch of Garfield and asked if he could work for the studio . . . as soon as he was released from prison!

Another weird favorite was from a fellow in Texas who wrote repeatedly (I'm sensing a pattern here) to tell me that he planned to make a Garfield movie starring himself as Jon, his dog as Odie, and his aunt as Garfield. His mom would play Arlene. He planned to film it in "one day and one night." But he was fair; he promised to give me half of what he made on the film.

One of the oddest letters we received was a form letter from a man in Colorado accusing us of tapping into his thoughts and stealing his ideas. He asked questions such as "Have your writers sought to conspire in scripts that are directly correlated to my thoughts or time light?" and "Are you aware of any special 'water' or 'well drink' that allows you or others perceptions of my future?" He was seeking a 5 percent royalty from all the cartoon shows that had appeared using the "involuntary transfer" of his thoughts.

And, of course, we have the "spider people." We do a lot of spider-whacking gags in the strips. These gags allow us to do some funny visual humor . . . and besides, who likes spiders, anyway? More people than you'd think, actually. We've received several letters from spider lovers accusing us of being "arachnophobes" and "condoning the senseless slaughter of spiders." Hey, people. It's only a comic strip.

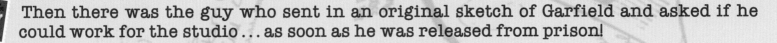

EXCERPTS FROM GARFIELD'S TOP TEN FICTITIOUS WEIRD FAN LETTERS

10. "I've been watching you, and I know where you live. I just don't know where I live. Can you help me?"

9. "My uncle Clarence has a bedsore that's shaped like you."

8. "Has Odie had tongue augmentation?"

7. "I'm glad that Garfield hates spiders. My ex-husband was a spider. The bum."

6. "I want to have your litter."

5. "I'm not changing my underwear till you get your own prime-time TV show."

4. "Were you really Shirley MacLaine in a previous life?"

3. "Enclosed is my recipe for hairball chowder."

2. "Before you were famous, didn't you appear fur-less in a skin flick?"

1. "Arf! Arf! Arf! Die! Arf! Arf!"

GARFIELD ON . . .

The fat cat looks back at some of the fads and fancies of the last 20 years!

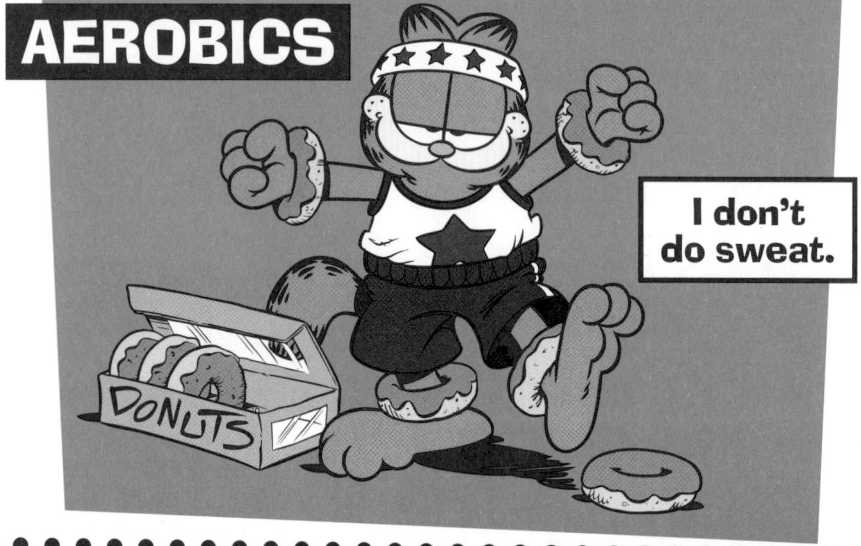
AEROBICS
I don't do sweat.
DONUTS

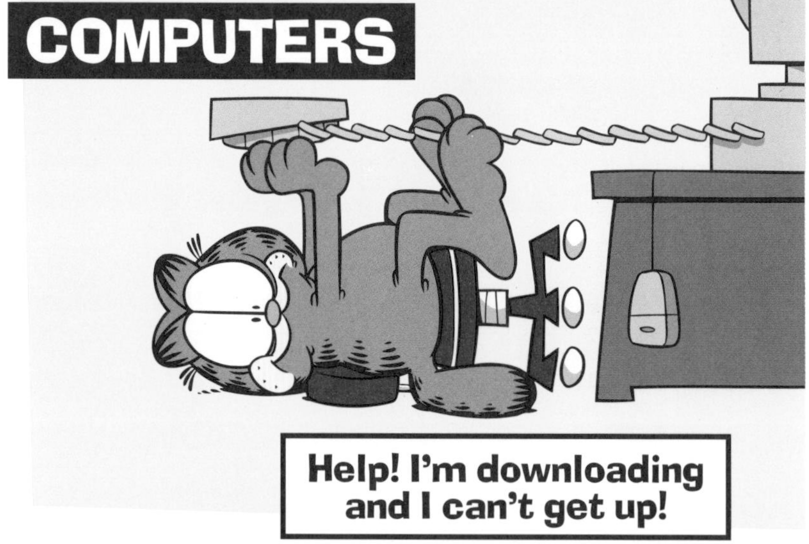
COMPUTERS
Help! I'm downloading and I can't get up!

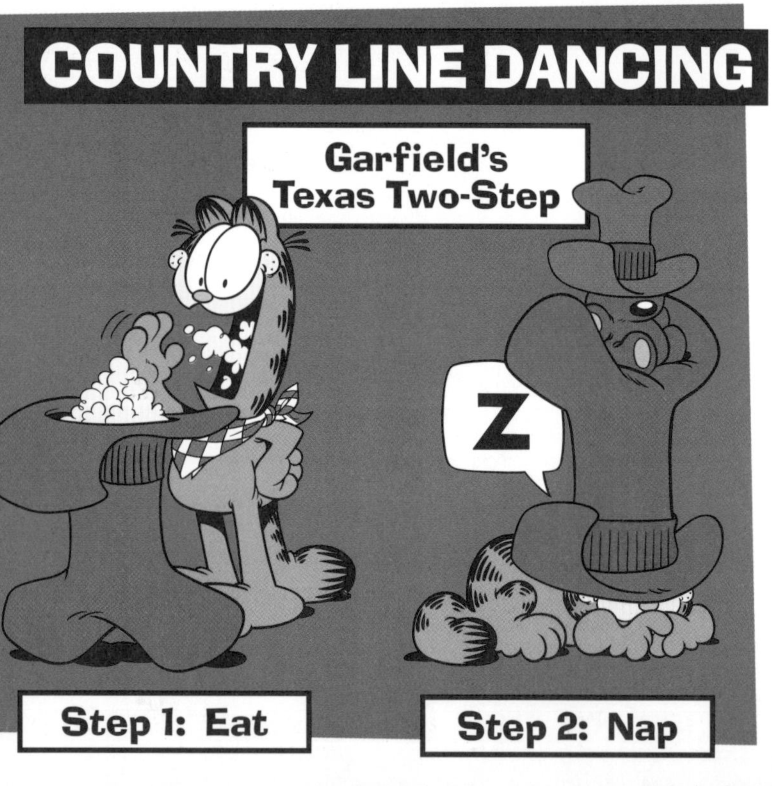
COUNTRY LINE DANCING
Garfield's Texas Two-Step
Z
Step 1: Eat
Step 2: Nap

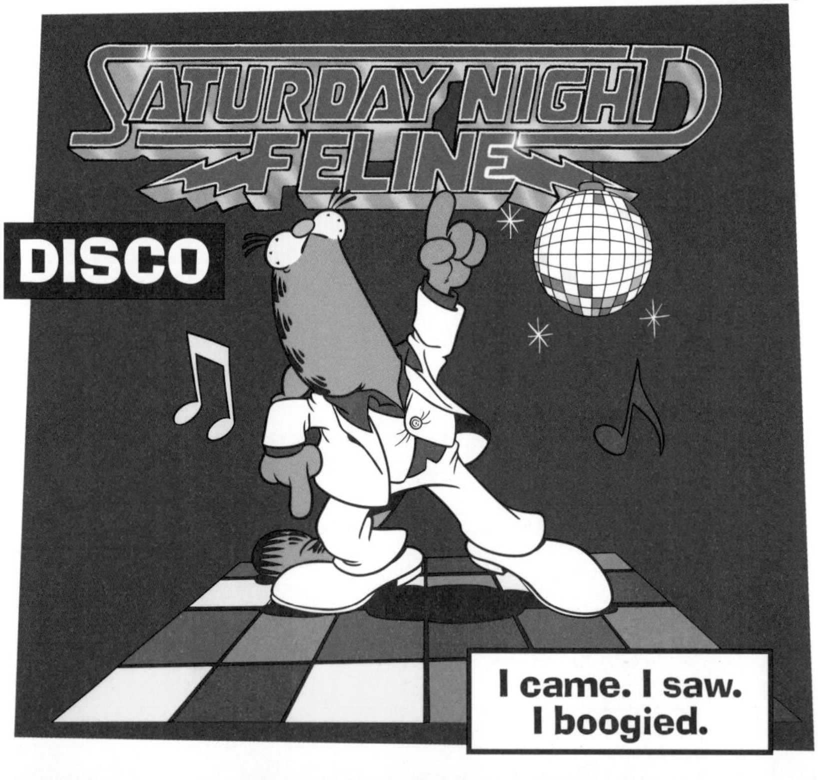
SATURDAY NIGHT FELINE
DISCO
I came. I saw. I boogied.

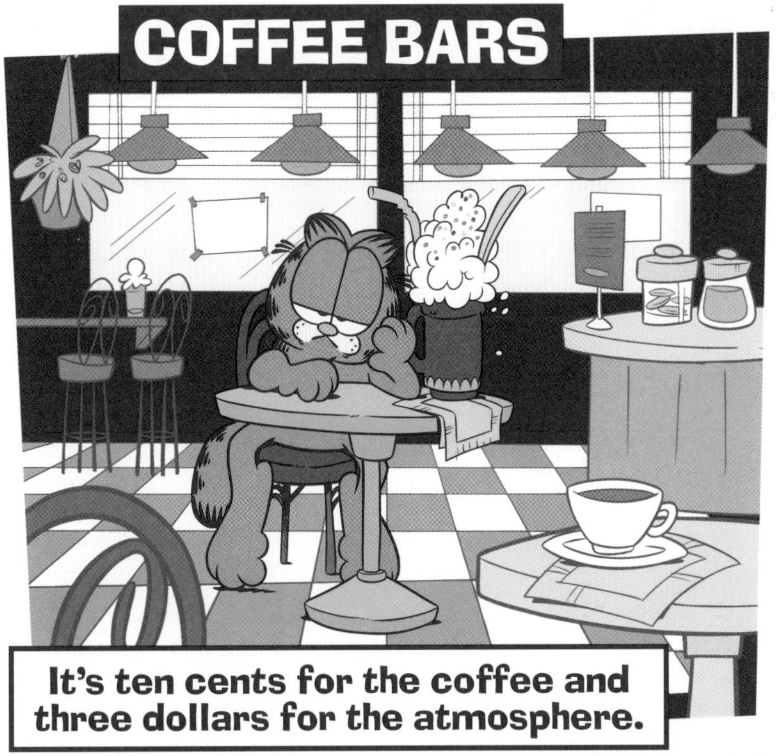
COFFEE BARS
It's ten cents for the coffee and three dollars for the atmosphere.

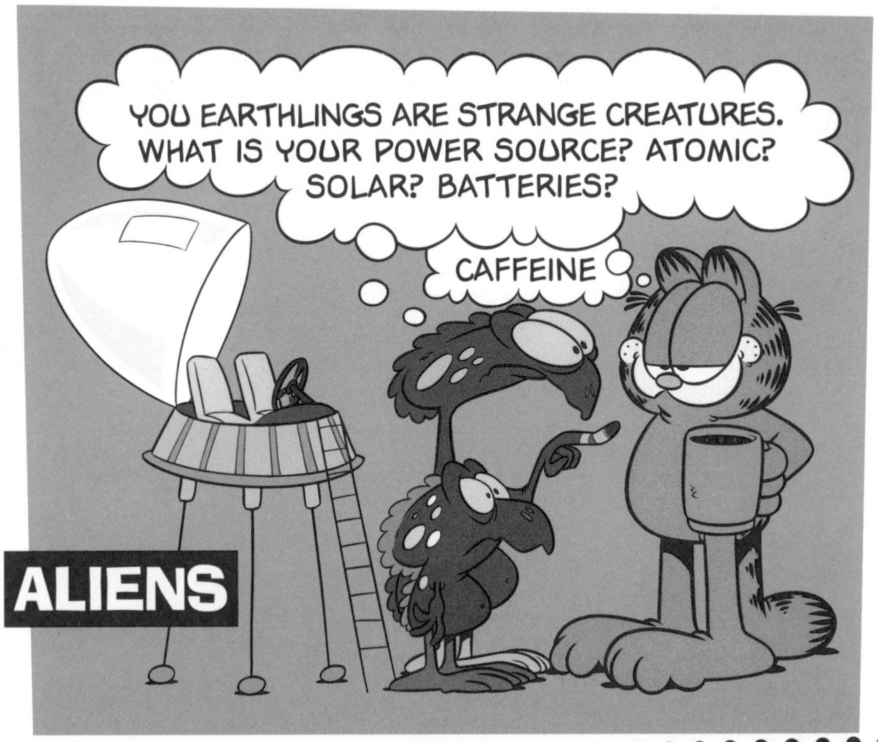
YOU EARTHLINGS ARE STRANGE CREATURES. WHAT IS YOUR POWER SOURCE? ATOMIC? SOLAR? BATTERIES?
CAFFEINE
ALIENS

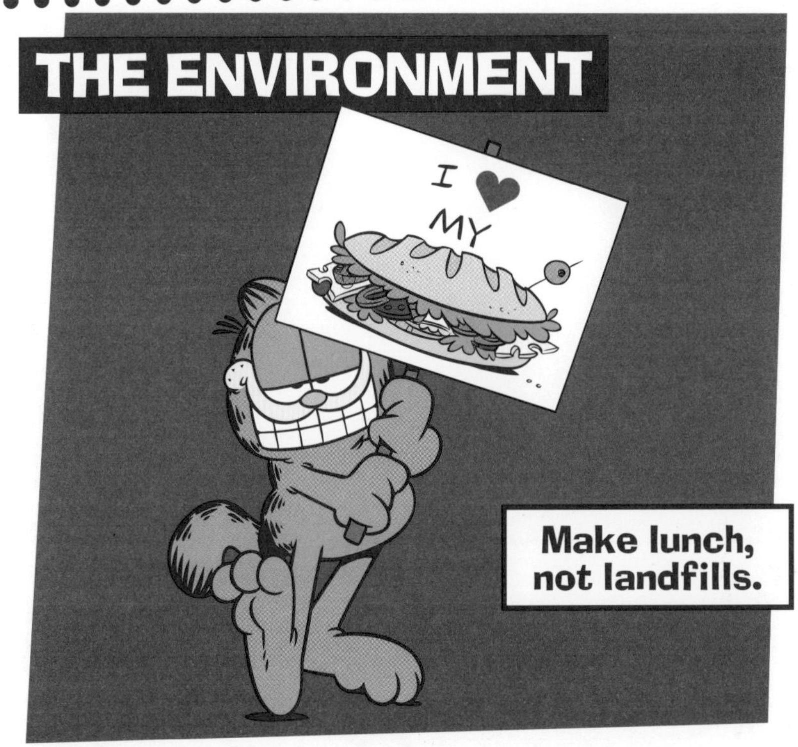
THE ENVIRONMENT
I ♥ MY
Make lunch, not landfills.

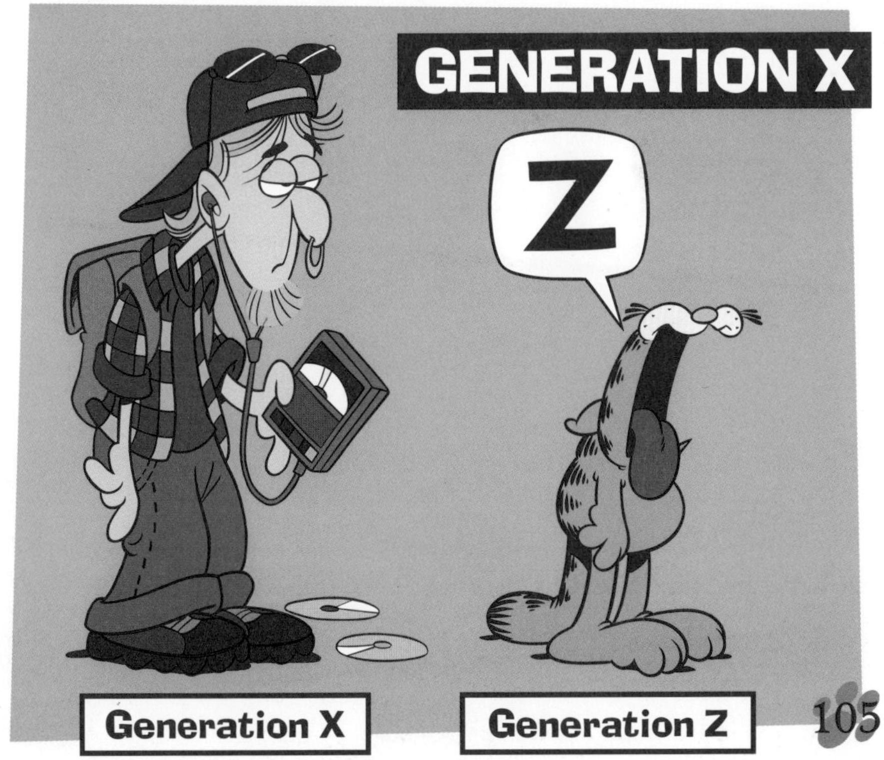
GENERATION X
Z
Generation X
Generation Z

WORLDWIDE GARFIELD

With the Garfield comic strip appearing in nearly ninety countries in twenty-seven languages, millions of fans around the world can enjoy the adventures of the funny feline. Yes, the cat with the big ego (and bigger appetite) is an international star who speaks the universal language of laughter!

Here's a typical Garfield daily strip in its original English version and translated into Spanish, German, Mandarin, and Hindi.

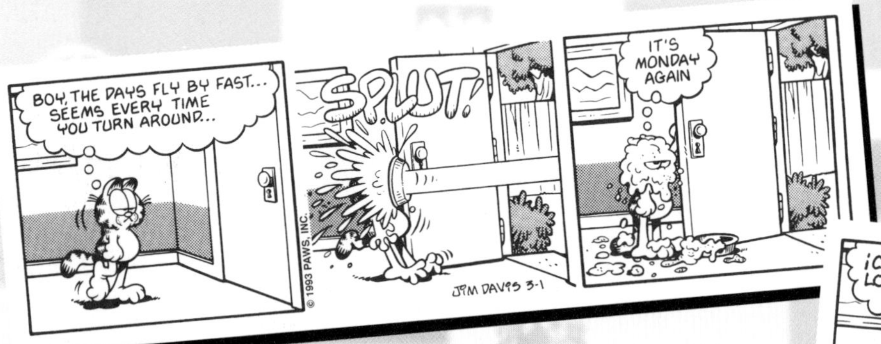
BOY, THE DAYS FLY BY FAST... SEEMS EVERY TIME YOU TURN AROUND...
SPLUT!
IT'S MONDAY AGAIN
© 1993 PAWS, INC.
JIM DAVIS 3-1

ENGLISH

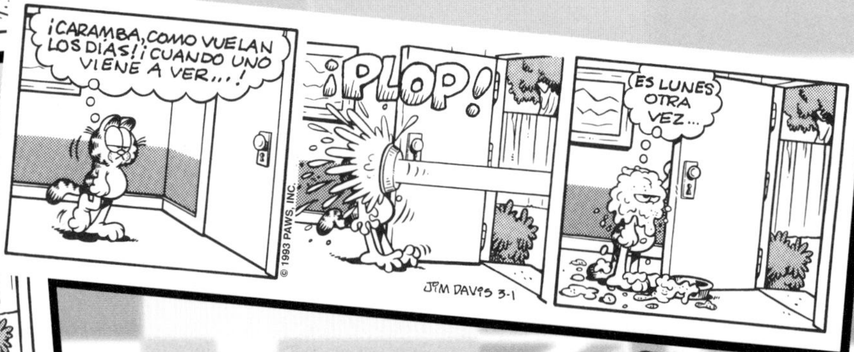
¡CARAMBA, COMO VUELAN LOS DIAS! ¡CUANDO UNO VIENE A VER...!
¡PLOP!
ES LUNES OTRA VEZ...
© 1993 PAWS, INC.
JIM DAVIS 3-1

SPANISH

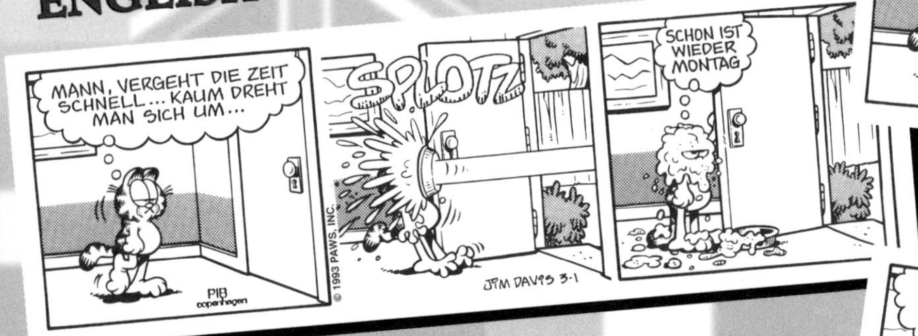
MANN, VERGEHT DIE ZEIT SCHNELL... KAUM DREHT MAN SICH UM...
SPLOTZ
SCHON IST WIEDER MONTAG
PIB copenhagen
© 1993 PAWS, INC.
JIM DAVIS 3-1

GERMAN

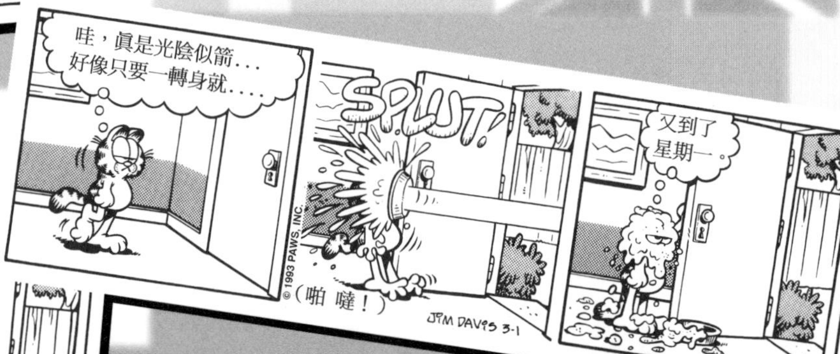
哇，眞是光陰似箭...
好像只要一轉身就....
SPLUT!
(啪 噠！)
又到了星期一。
© 1993 PAWS, INC.
JIM DAVIS 3-1

MANDARIN

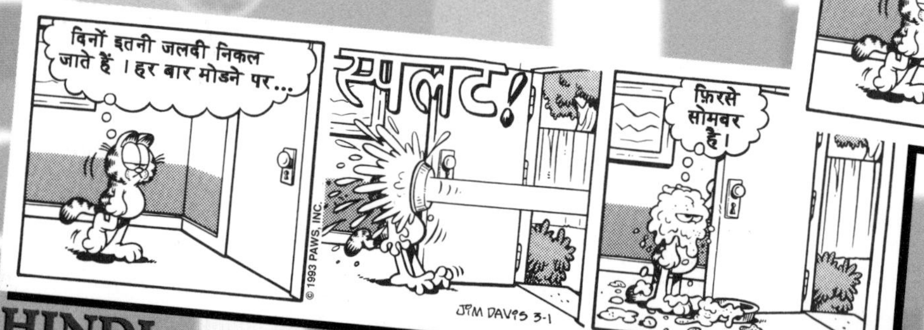
दिनों इतनी जलदी निकल जाते हैं । हर बार मोडने पर...
स्पलाट!
फ़िरसे सोमवर है।
© 1993 PAWS, INC.
JIM DAVIS 3-1

HINDI

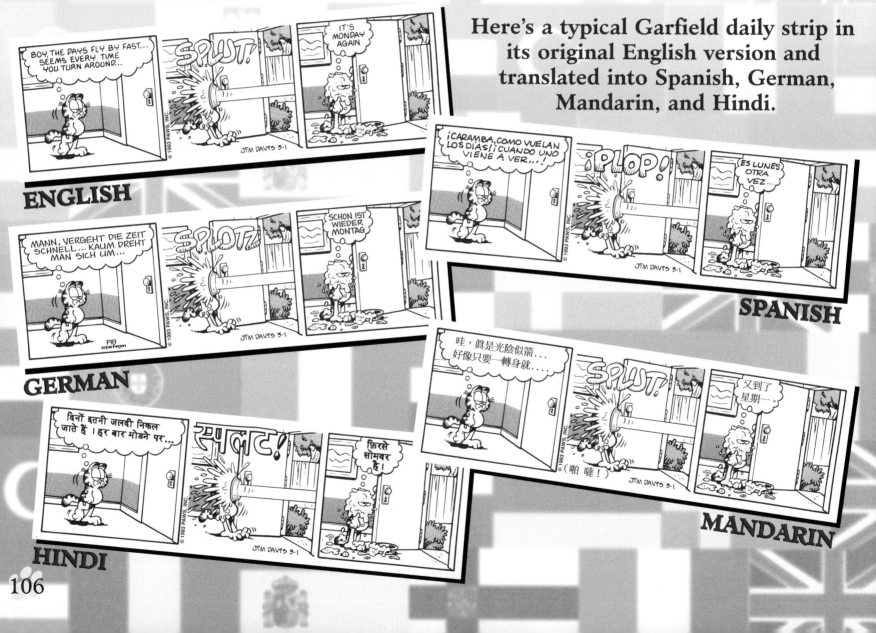

Since 1985, a special logo box has appeared at the beginning of every Garfield Sunday comic strip. This unique panel showcases Garfield and friends in a wild and wacky way. Over the years, we've had a lot of fun creating these. Here are just a few of the crazy cat's . . .

Loco Logo Boxes!

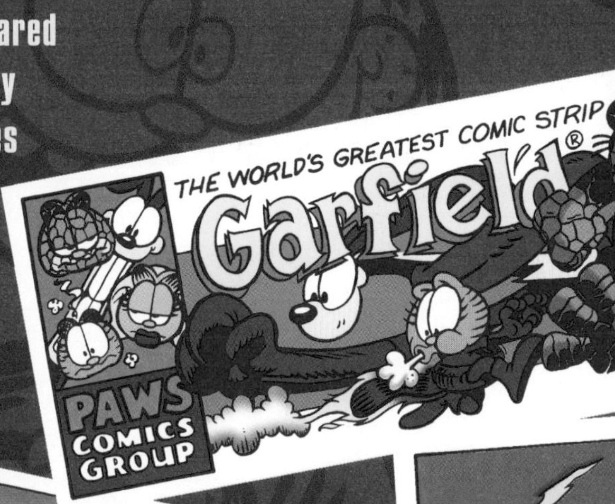
THE WORLD'S GREATEST COMIC STRIP
Garfield®
PAWS COMICS GROUP

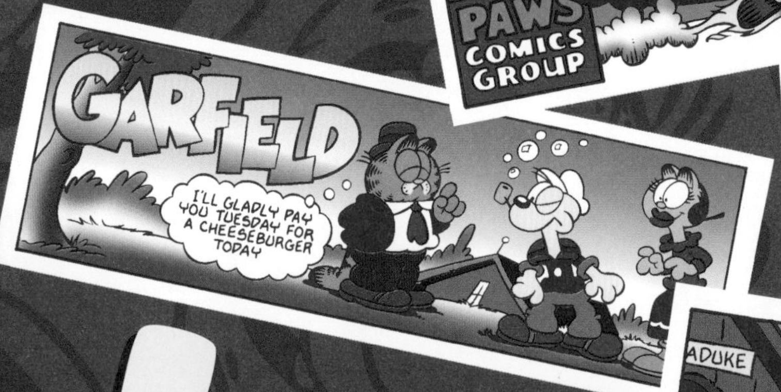
GARFIELD
I'LL GLADLY PAY YOU TUESDAY FOR A CHEESEBURGER TODAY

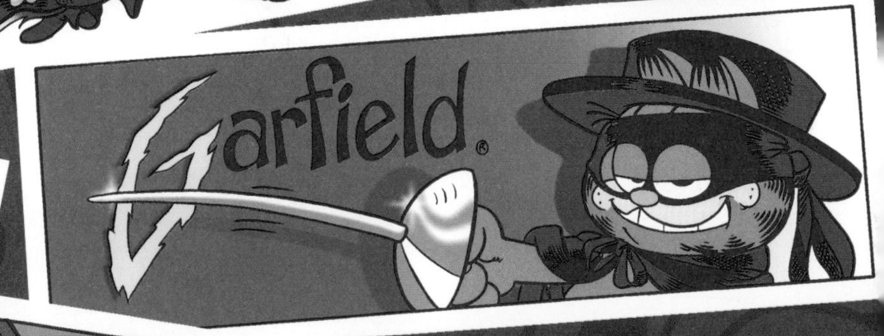
Garfield®

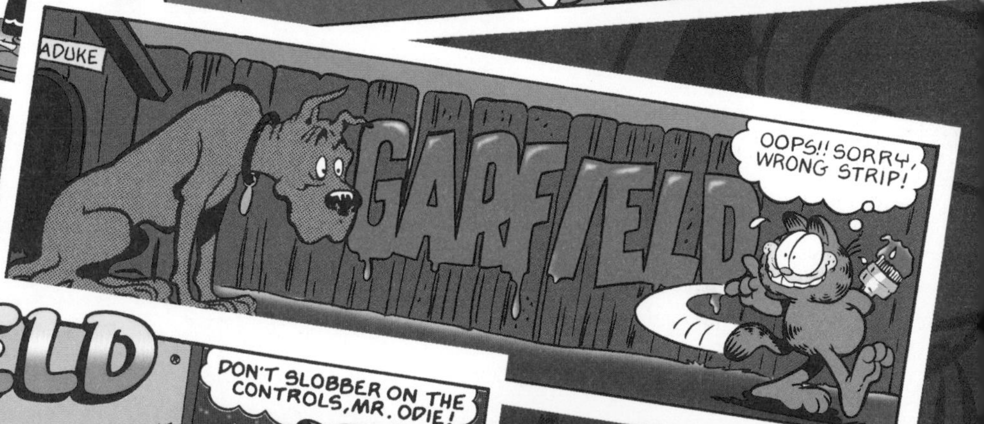
GARFIELD
OOPS!! SORRY, WRONG STRIP!

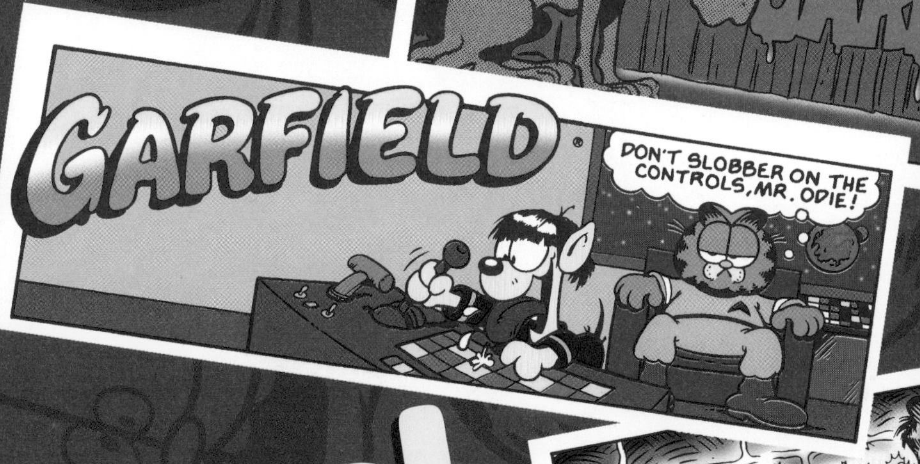
GARFIELD®
DON'T SLOBBER ON THE CONTROLS, MR. ODIE!

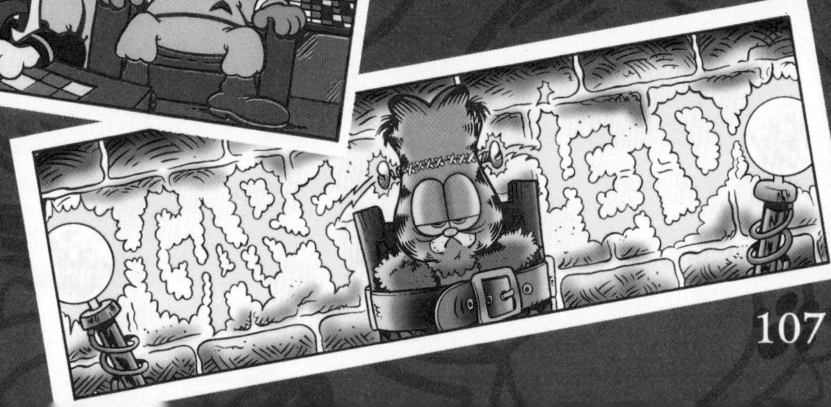

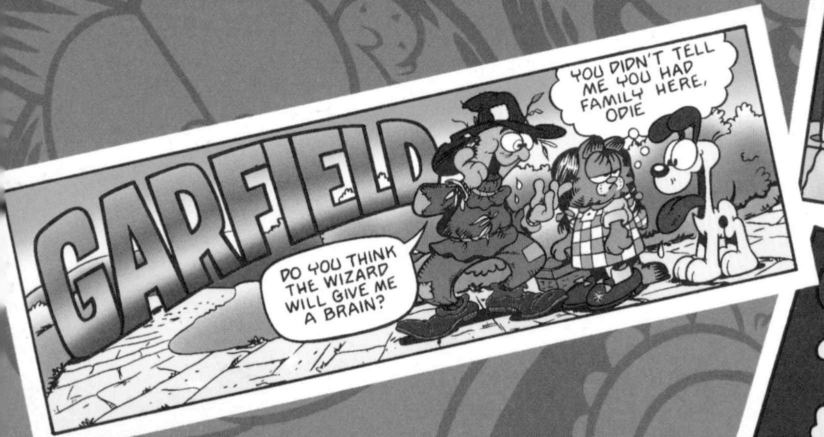
GARFIELD
YOU DIDN'T TELL ME YOU HAD FAMILY HERE, ODIE
DO YOU THINK THE WIZARD WILL GIVE ME A BRAIN?

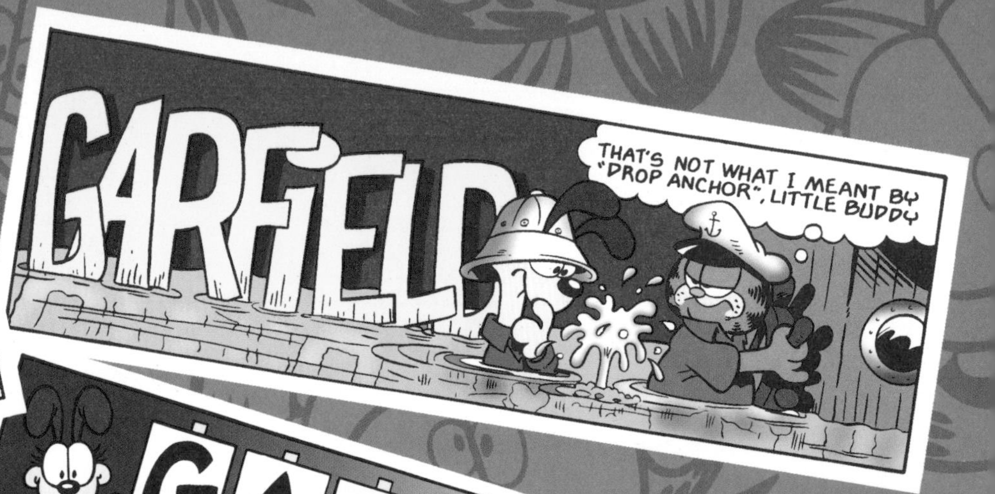
GARFIELD
THAT'S NOT WHAT I MEANT BY "DROP ANCHOR", LITTLE BUDDY

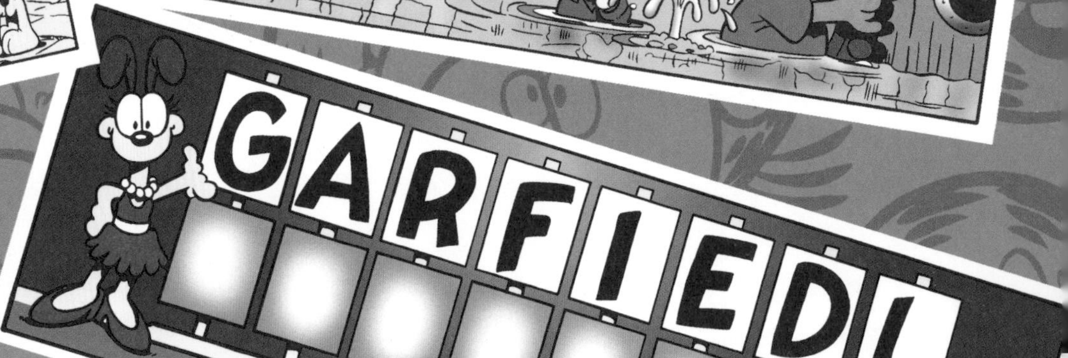
GARFIEDL

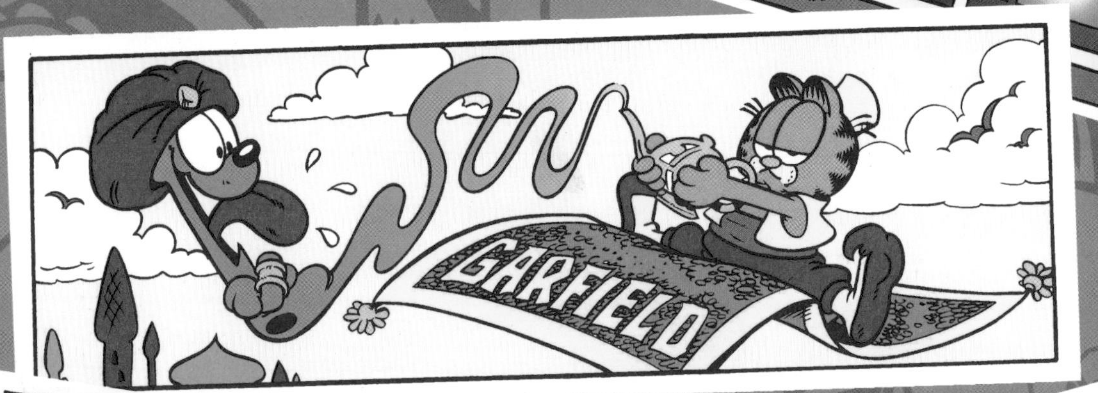
GARFIELD

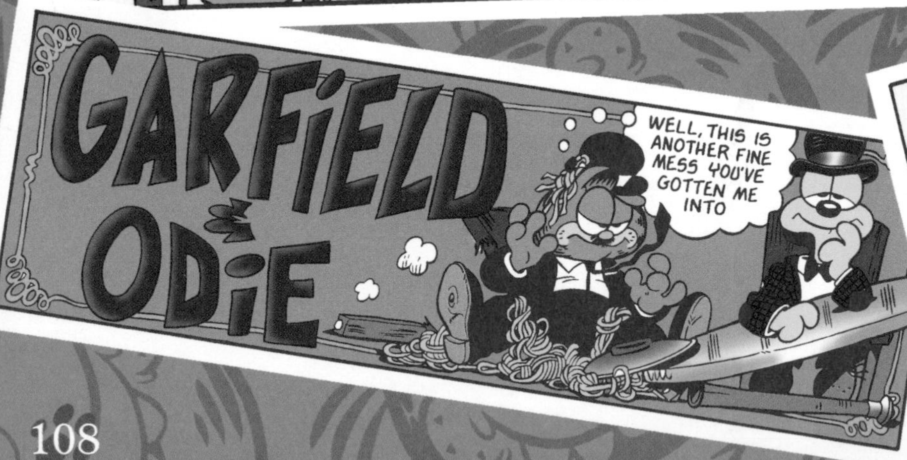
GARFIELD & ODIE
WELL, THIS IS ANOTHER FINE MESS YOU'VE GOTTEN ME INTO

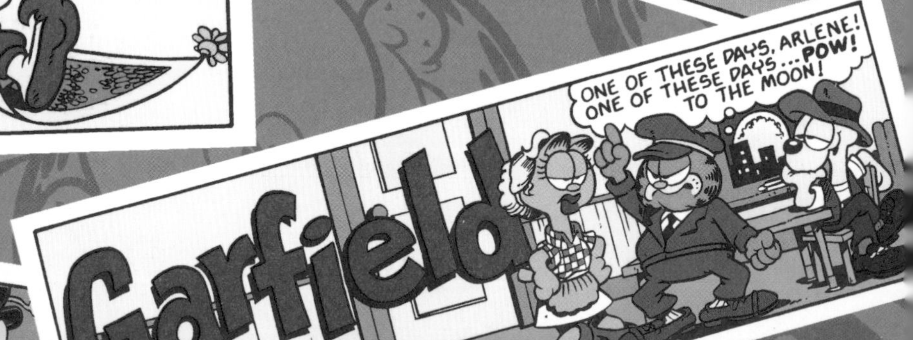
Garfield
ONE OF THESE DAYS, ARLENE! ONE OF THESE DAYS... POW! TO THE MOON!

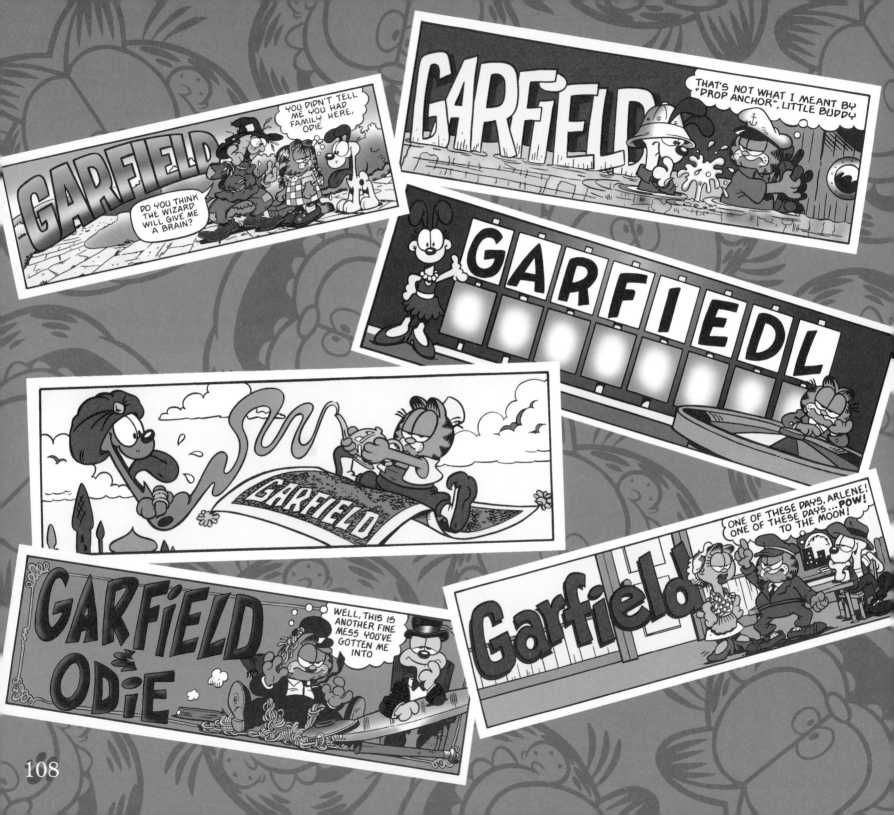

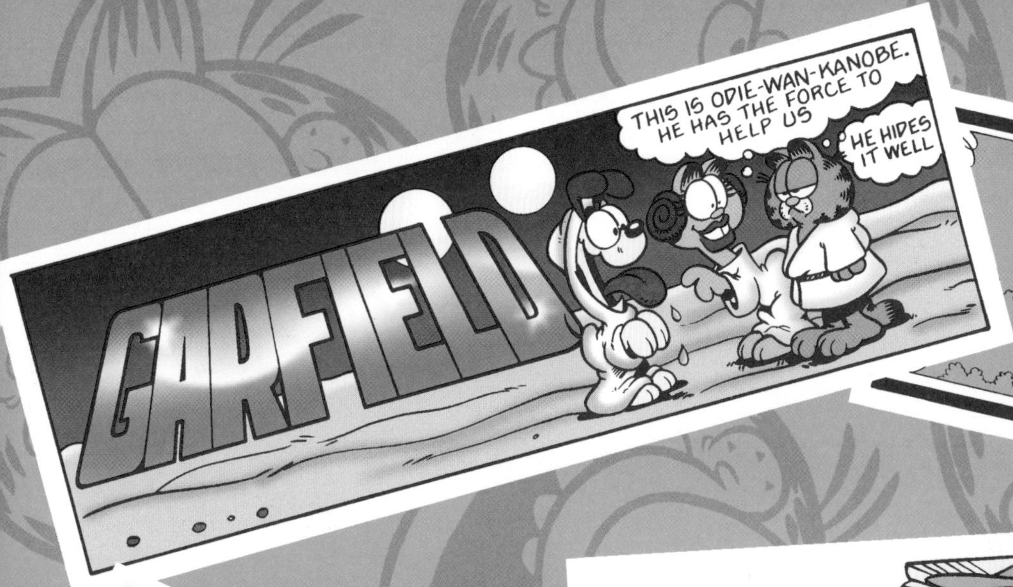
GARFIELD
THIS IS ODIE-WAN-KANOBE. HE HAS THE FORCE TO HELP US
HE HIDES IT WELL

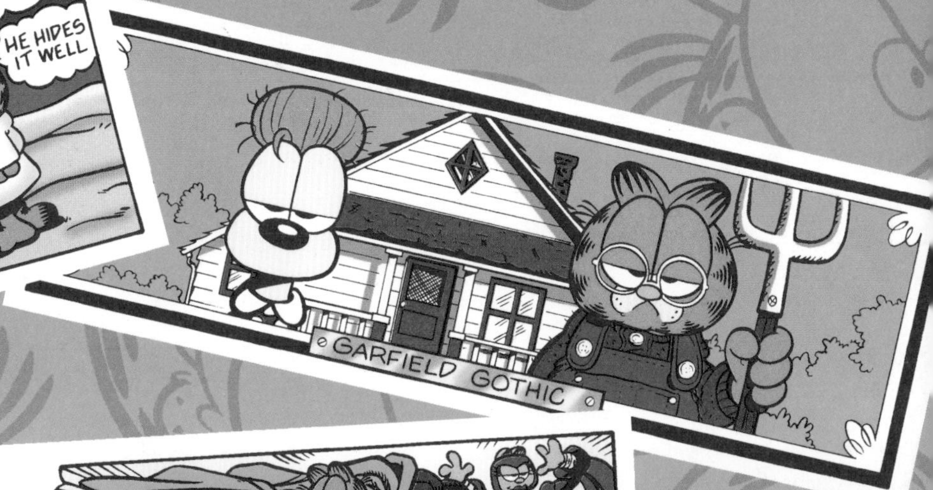
GARFIELD GOTHIC

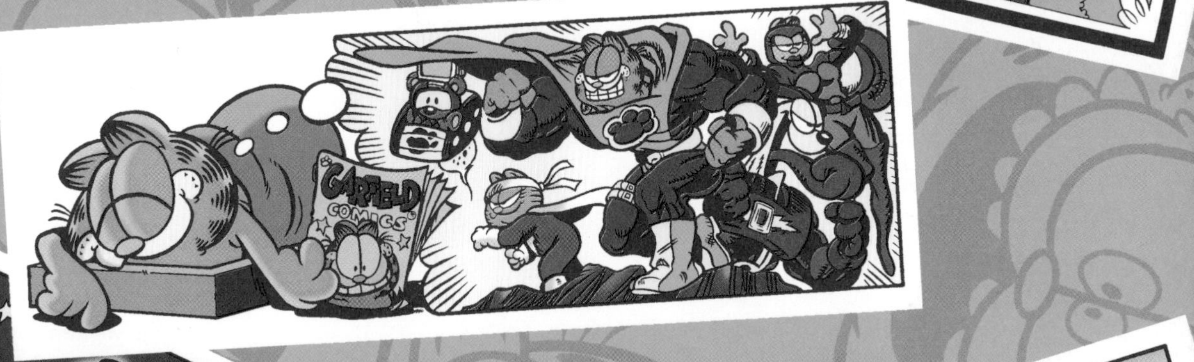
GARFIELD
COMICS

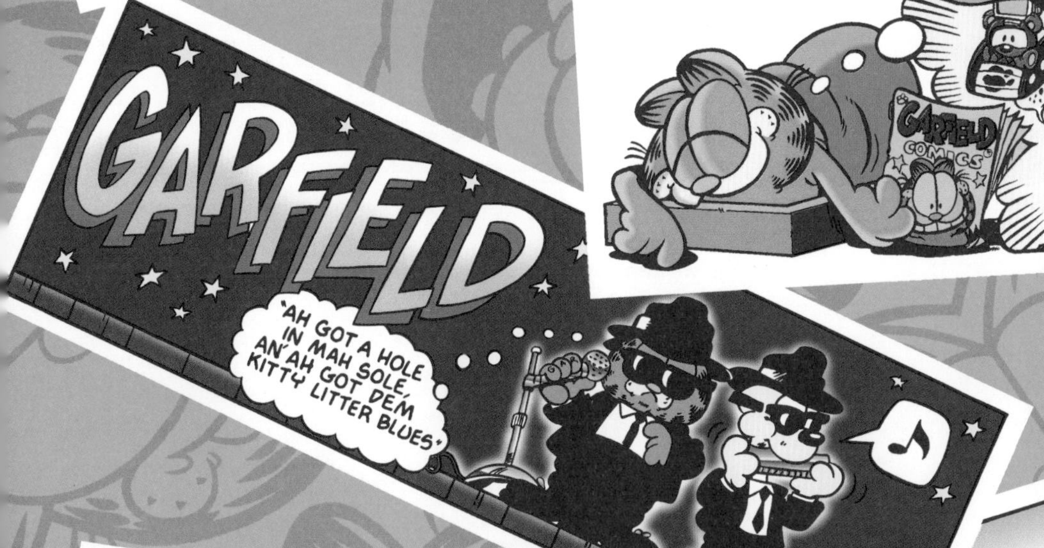
GARFIELD
"AH GOT A HOLE IN MAH SOLE, AN' AH GOT DEM KITTY LITTER BLUES"
TAP TAP TAP

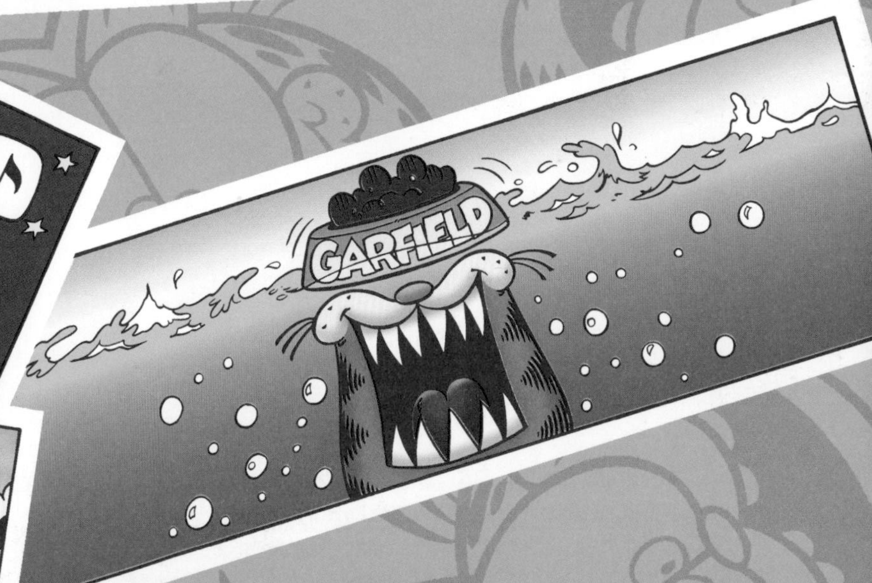
GARFIELD

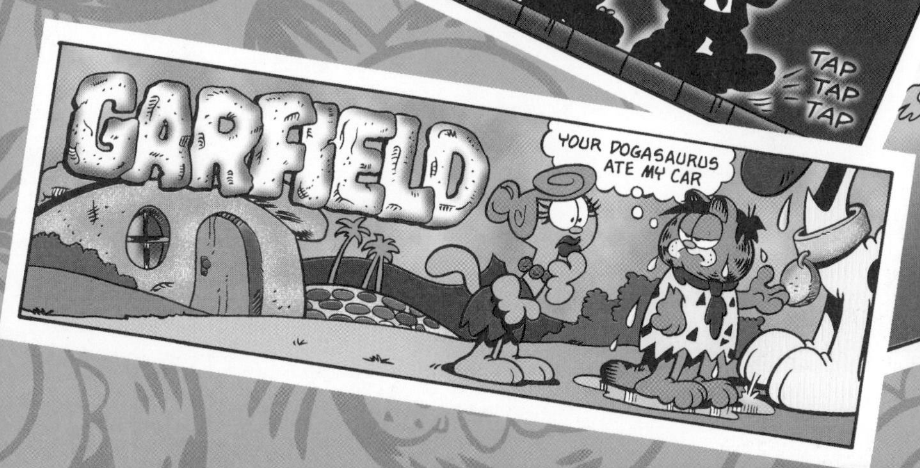
GARFIELD
YOUR DOGASAURUS ATE MY CAR

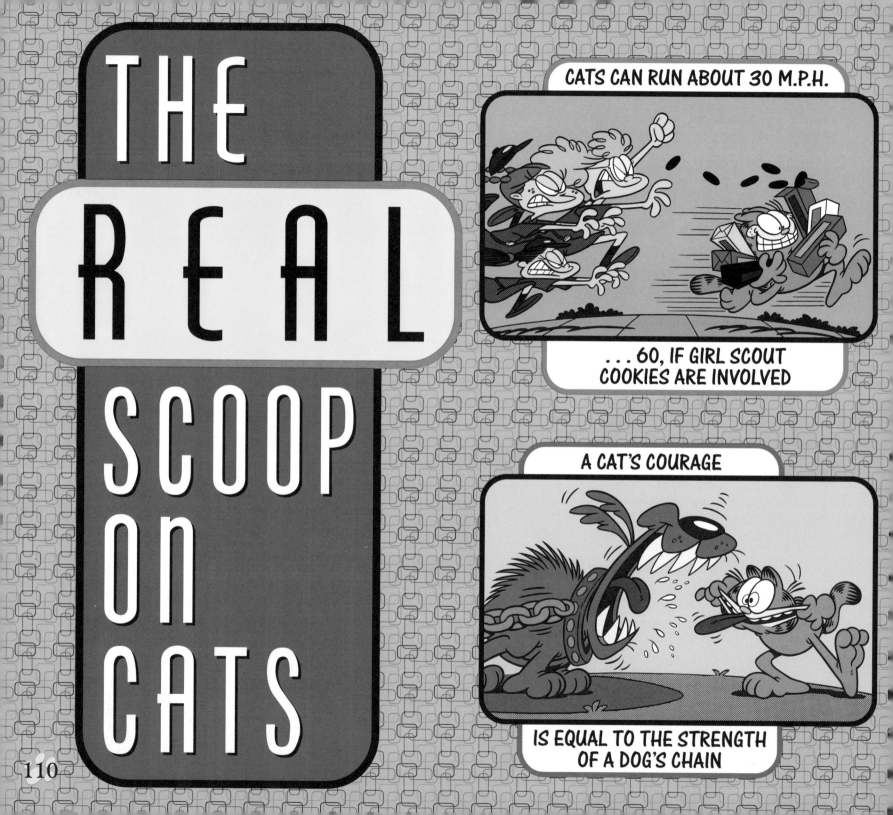

THE REAL SCOOP ON CATS

CATS CAN RUN ABOUT 30 M.P.H.

. . . 60, IF GIRL SCOUT COOKIES ARE INVOLVED

A CAT'S COURAGE

IS EQUAL TO THE STRENGTH OF A DOG'S CHAIN

CATS CAN SEE IN THE DARK

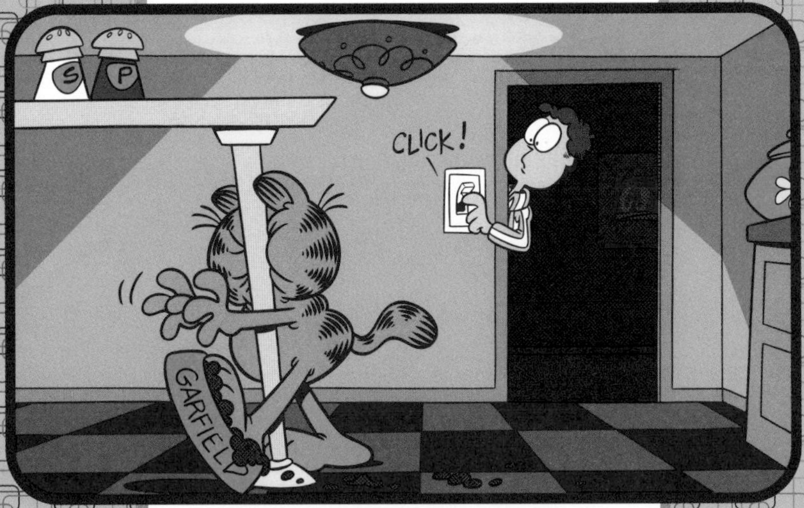
CLICK!

JUST NOT VERY WELL

CATS ARE VERY PREDATORY

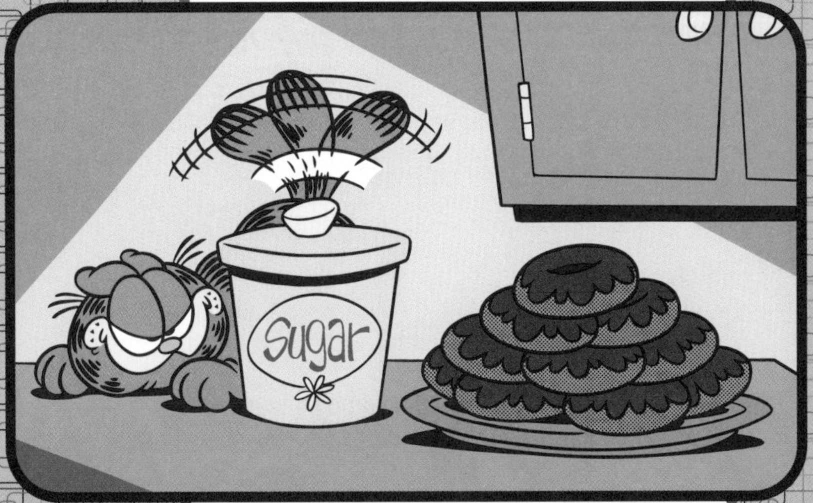
Sugar

AND WILL STALK AND ATTACK AN ENTIRE HERD OF DONUTS

WHAT HUMANS SEE

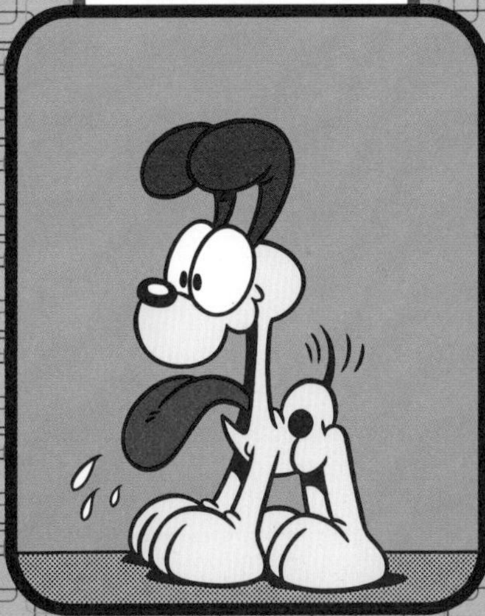

WHAT CATS SEE

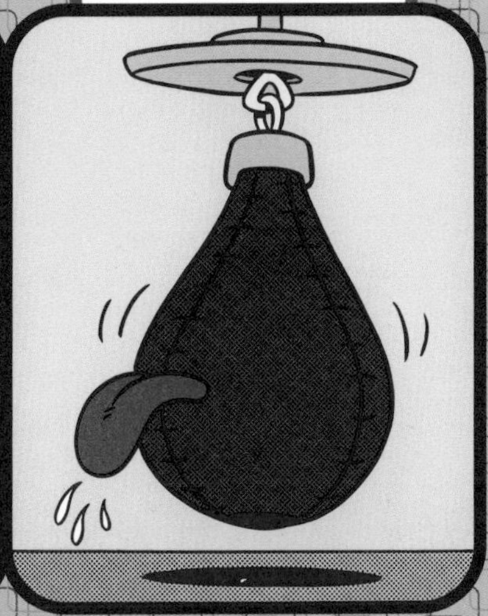

CATS WILL CHASE MICE

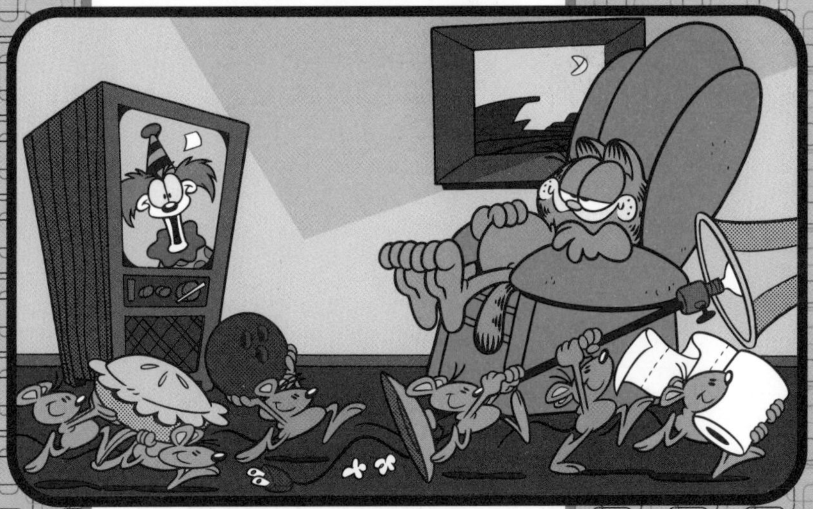

UNLESS THERE'S SOMETHING GOOD ON TV

REJECTED COVERS FOR THIS BOOK

Take a behind-the-scenes peek at some of the cover concepts and photos that *didn't* make it — and with good reason, too!

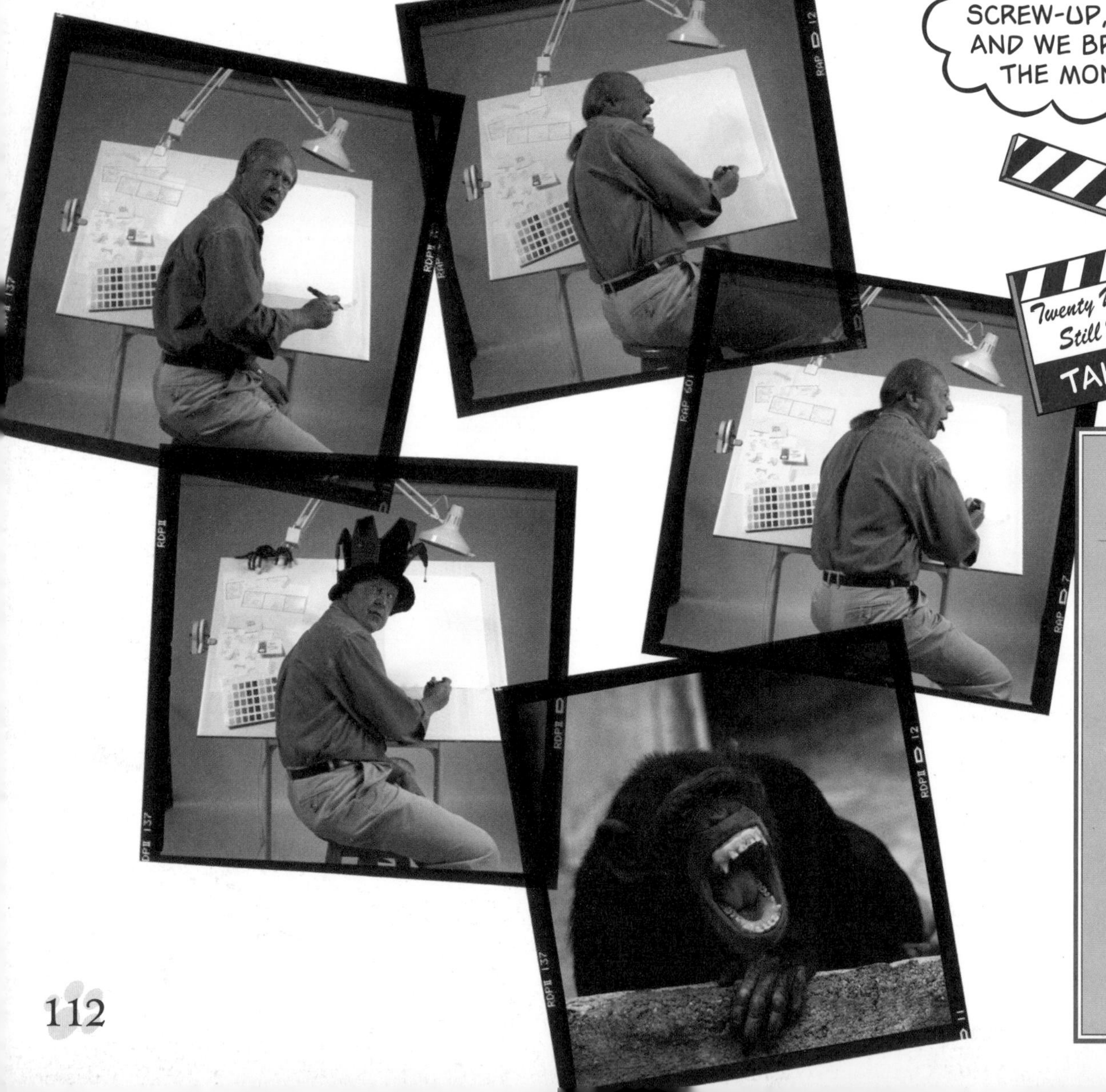

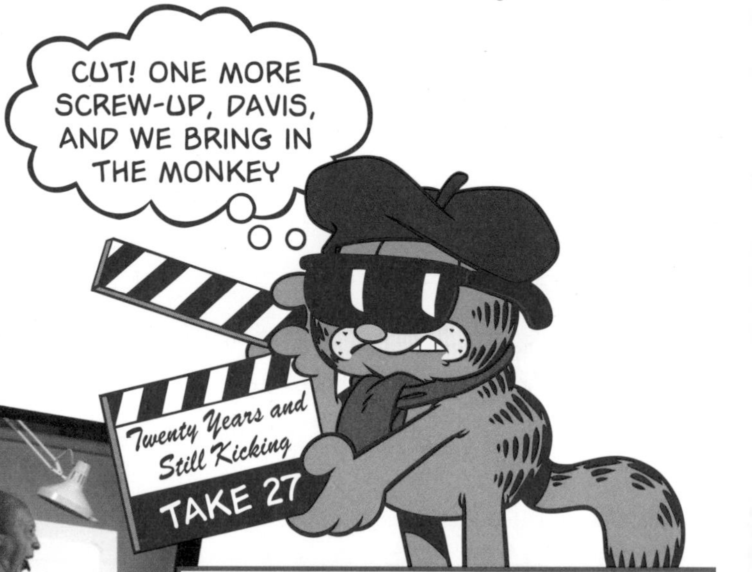
CUT! ONE MORE SCREW-UP, DAVIS, AND WE BRING IN THE MONKEY
Twenty Years and Still Kicking
TAKE 27

TOP TEN REJECTED TITLES FOR THIS BOOK

10. *Twenty Years and Still Licking*
9. *Twenty Years and Where's My Pension?*
8. *To Grill a Mockingbird*
7. *Lasagna Soup for the Garfield Soul*
6. *One Score and Seven Thousand Pizzas Ago*
5. *Cats Are from Mars, Dogs Are from Uranus*
4. *Twenty Years for Assault and Battery*
3. *Seven Habits of Highly Effective Eaters*
2. *Twenty Years and Often Incontinent*
1. *Moby Dick*

ACT II
1988–1997

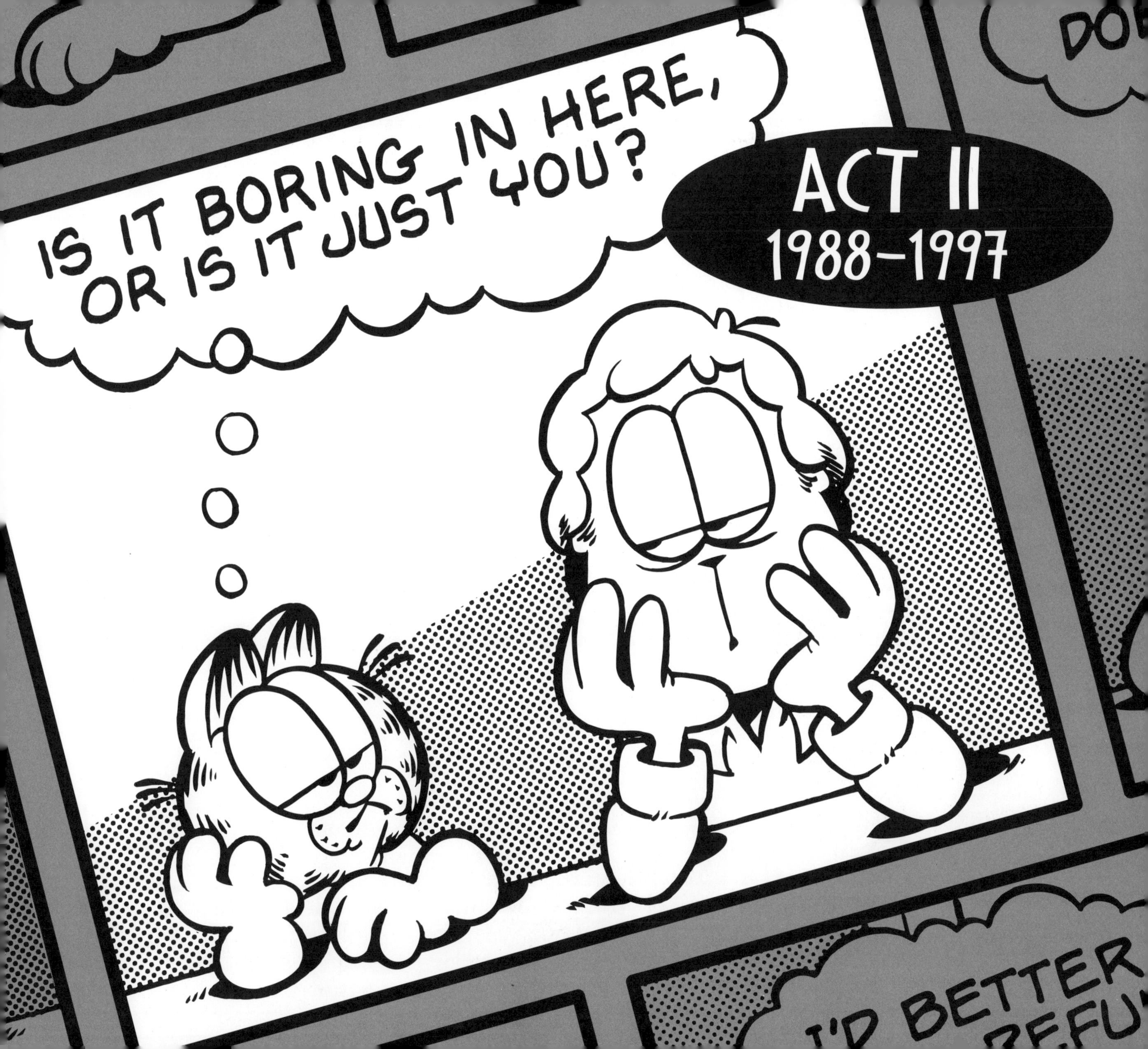
IS IT BORING IN HERE, OR IS IT JUST YOU?
I'D BETTER

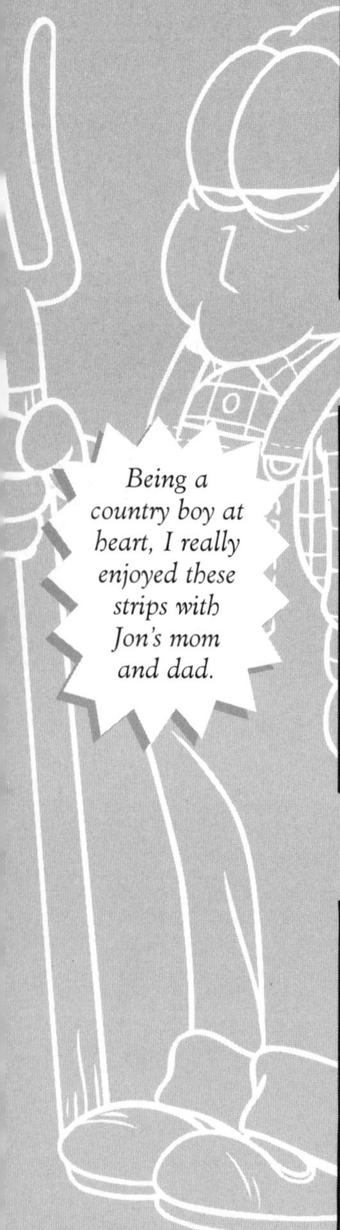

Being a country boy at heart, I really enjoyed these strips with Jon's mom and dad.

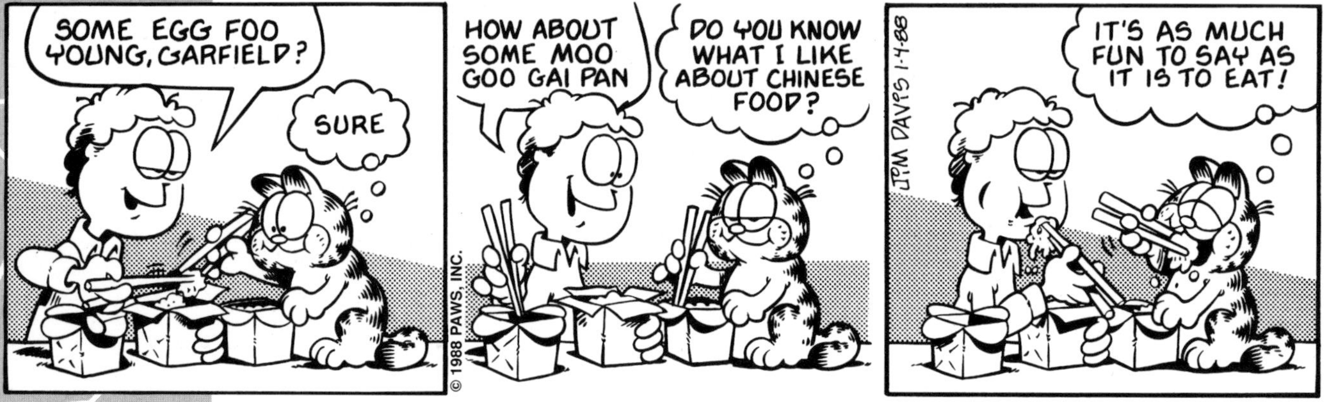
SOME EGG FOO YOUNG, GARFIELD?
SURE
HOW ABOUT SOME MOO GOO GAI PAN
DO YOU KNOW WHAT I LIKE ABOUT CHINESE FOOD?
IT'S AS MUCH FUN TO SAY AS IT IS TO EAT!
© 1988 PAWS, INC.
JIM DAVIS 1-4-88

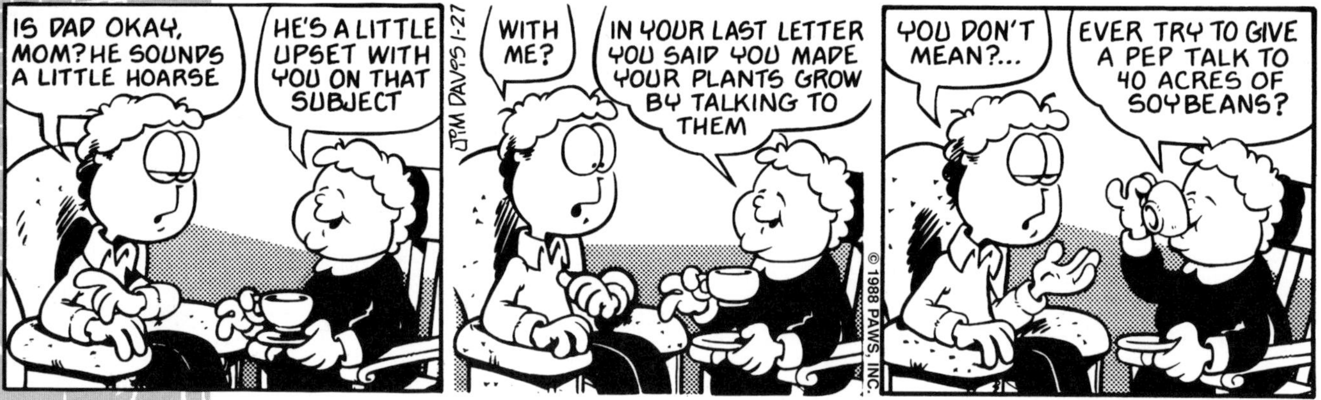
IS DAD OKAY, MOM? HE SOUNDS A LITTLE HOARSE
HE'S A LITTLE UPSET WITH YOU ON THAT SUBJECT
JIM DAVIS 1-27
WITH ME?
IN YOUR LAST LETTER YOU SAID YOU MADE YOUR PLANTS GROW BY TALKING TO THEM
© 1988 PAWS, INC.
YOU DON'T MEAN?...
EVER TRY TO GIVE A PEP TALK TO 40 ACRES OF SOYBEANS?

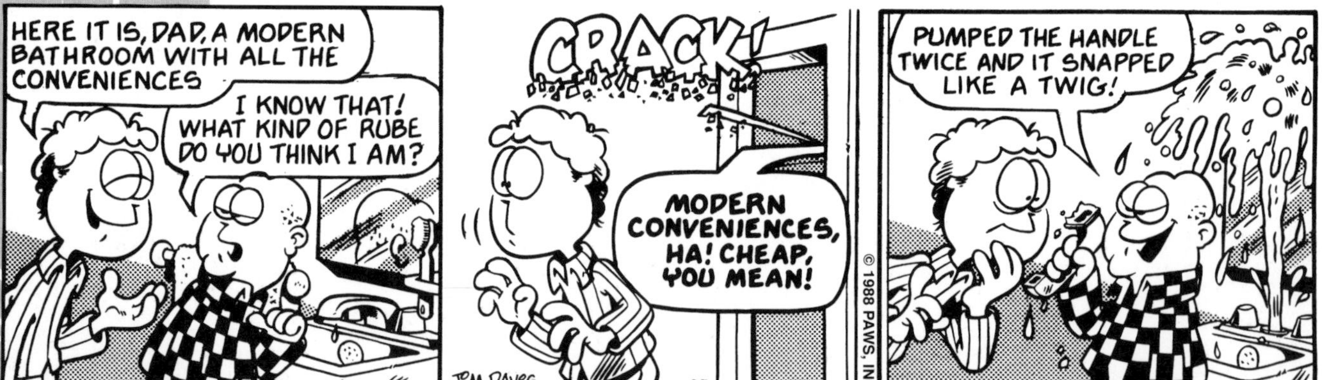
HERE IT IS, DAD, A MODERN BATHROOM WITH ALL THE CONVENIENCES
I KNOW THAT! WHAT KIND OF RUBE DO YOU THINK I AM?
CRACK!
MODERN CONVENIENCES, HA! CHEAP, YOU MEAN!
JIM DAVIS
1-28
© 1988 PAWS, INC.
PUMPED THE HANDLE TWICE AND IT SNAPPED LIKE A TWIG!

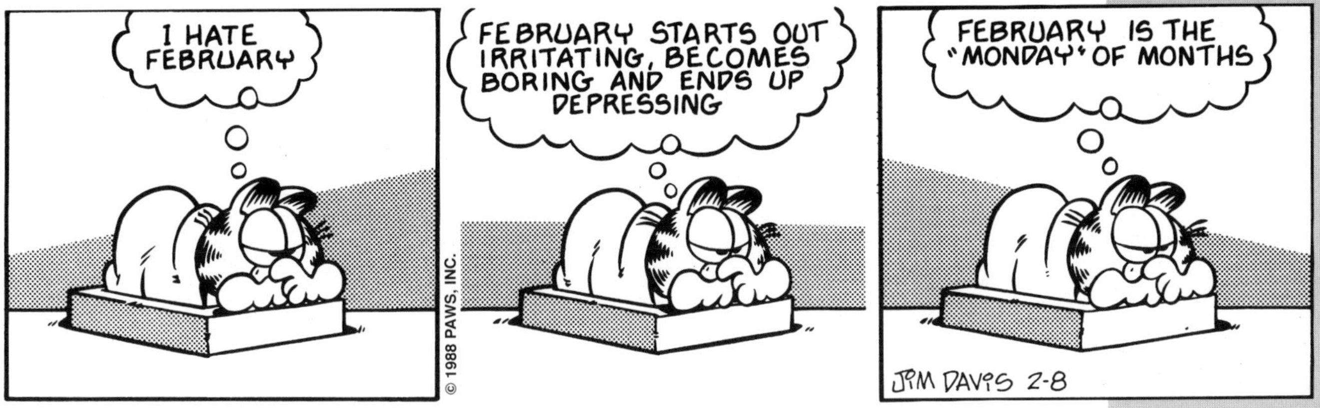
I HATE FEBRUARY
FEBRUARY STARTS OUT IRRITATING, BECOMES BORING AND ENDS UP DEPRESSING
FEBRUARY IS THE "MONDAY" OF MONTHS
© 1988 PAWS, INC.
JIM DAVIS 2-8

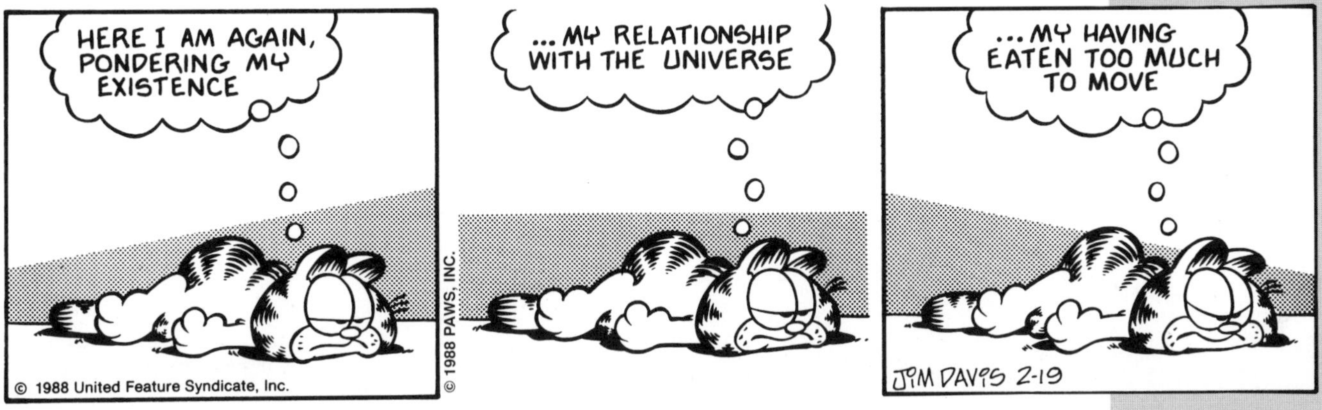
HERE I AM AGAIN, PONDERING MY EXISTENCE
...MY RELATIONSHIP WITH THE UNIVERSE
...MY HAVING EATEN TOO MUCH TO MOVE
© 1988 United Feature Syndicate, Inc.
© 1988 PAWS, INC.
JIM DAVIS 2-19

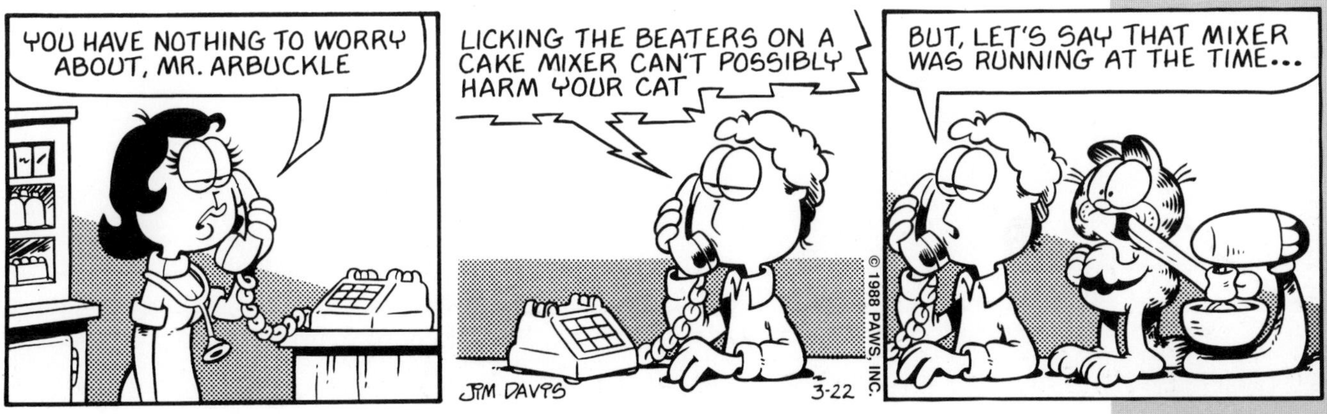
YOU HAVE NOTHING TO WORRY ABOUT, MR. ARBUCKLE
LICKING THE BEATERS ON A CAKE MIXER CAN'T POSSIBLY HARM YOUR CAT
BUT, LET'S SAY THAT MIXER WAS RUNNING AT THE TIME...
JIM DAVIS
3-22
© 1988 PAWS, INC.

Fat Cat Factoid ~1988~

Read my lips! George Bush is elected president. Flo Jo runs away with the gold in the Seoul Summer Olympics.

Suction-cup "Stuck On You" Garfields adorn millions of car windows; "Garfield and Friends" enters CBS's Saturday morning cartoon lineup.

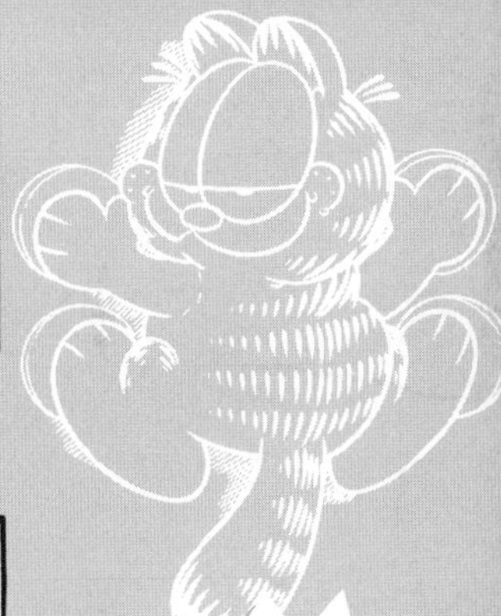

Fun with sight gags.

THEY SAY DOGS HAVE A STRONG SENSE OF SMELL
POOMP!
FORTUNATELY, THEY CAN'T SMELL A KICK COMING
© 1988 PAWS, INC.
4-22
JIM DAVIS

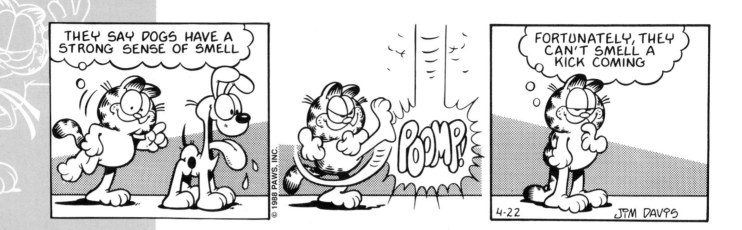

BOOB TUBE TABBY

To Garfield happiness is a warm TV . . . whether he's asleep on top of it or watching it till his eyes glaze over. But that's not to say he'll watch just anything. Garfield is a very selective viewer; he definitely doesn't do documentaries. Rather, his idea of quality programming is Bowling for Doughnuts, and Harass the Dog on the All Pet Network.

CLICK
THIS LOOKS LIKE AN INTELLIGENT AND INFORMATIVE PROGRAM
© 1991 PAWS, INC.
FORTUNATELY, THERE ARE OTHER THINGS ON
CLICK
JIM DAVIS 4-8

ARF!
WHAT IS IT, BOY?
© 1991 PAWS, INC.
ARF! ARF!
HE SAYS HE'S HUNGRY
YOU SAY TIMMY FELL DOWN THE OLD MINE SHAFT?
ARF!
HE WANTS PIZZA
JIM DAVIS 4-11

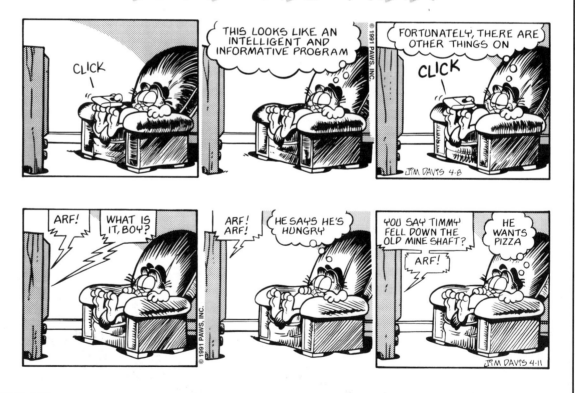

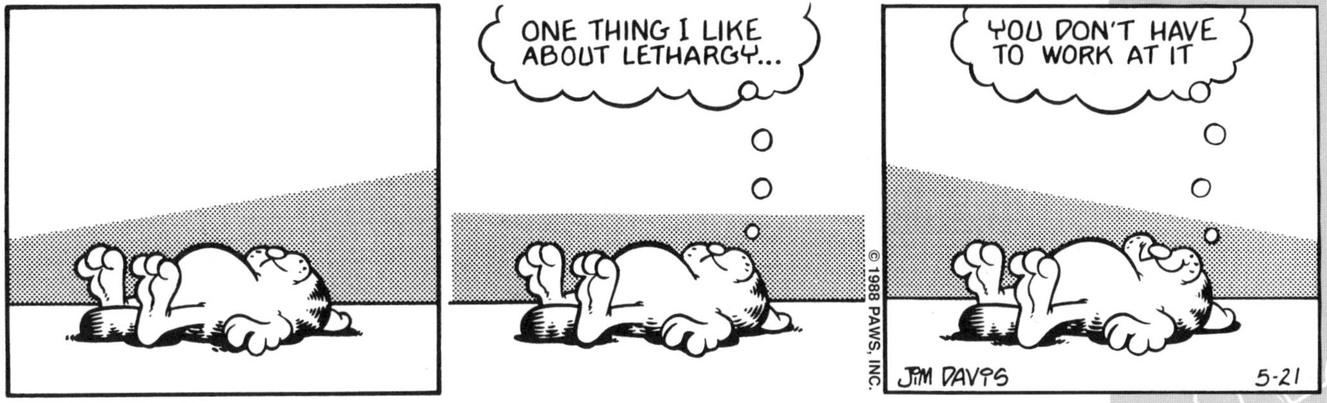
ONE THING I LIKE ABOUT LETHARGY...
© 1988 PAWS, INC.
YOU DON'T HAVE TO WORK AT IT
JIM DAVIS
5-21

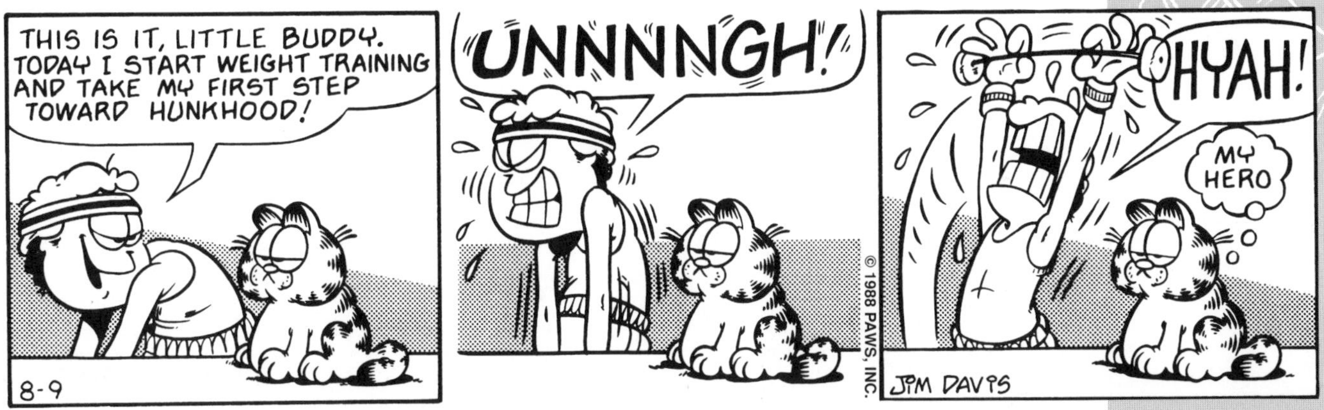
THIS IS IT, LITTLE BUDDY. TODAY I START WEIGHT TRAINING AND TAKE MY FIRST STEP TOWARD HUNKHOOD!
8-9
UNNNNGH!
© 1988 PAWS, INC.
HYAH!
MY HERO
JIM DAVIS

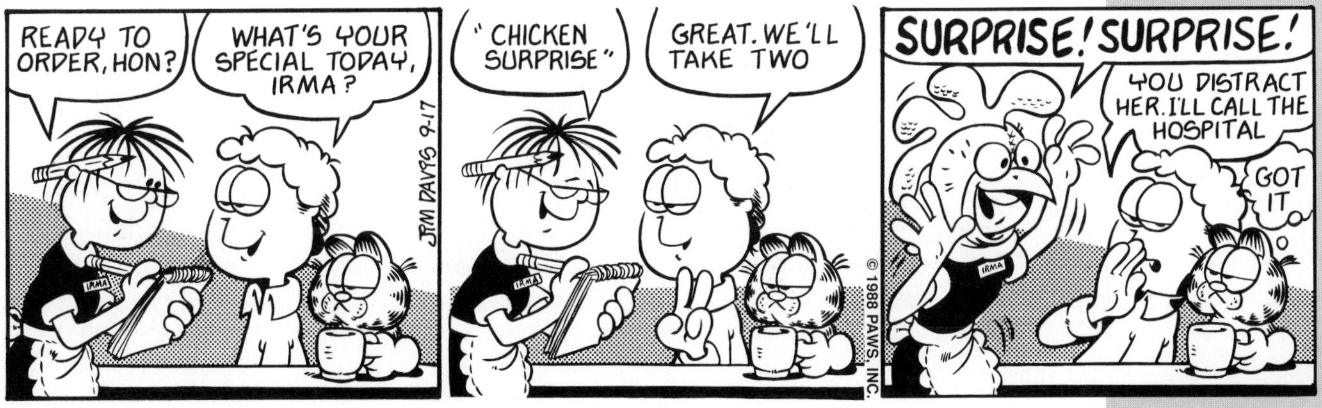
READY TO ORDER, HON?
WHAT'S YOUR SPECIAL TODAY, IRMA?
JIM DAVIS 9-17
"CHICKEN SURPRISE"
GREAT. WE'LL TAKE TWO
© 1988 PAWS, INC.
SURPRISE! SURPRISE!
YOU DISTRACT HER. I'LL CALL THE HOSPITAL
GOT IT

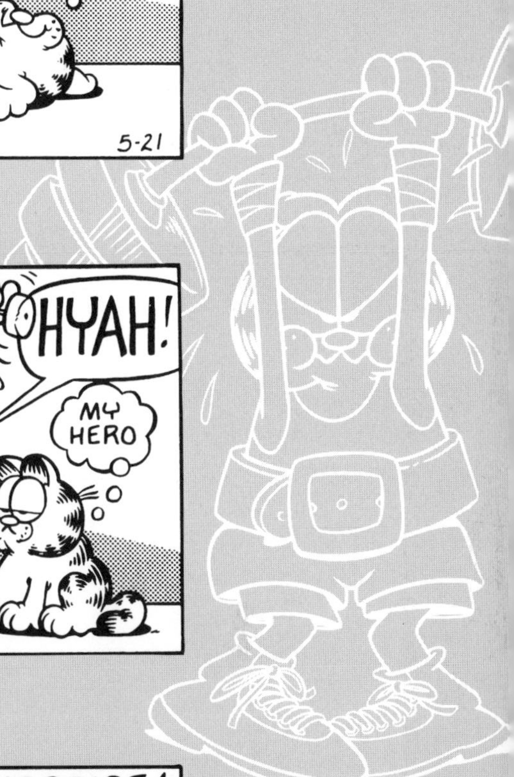

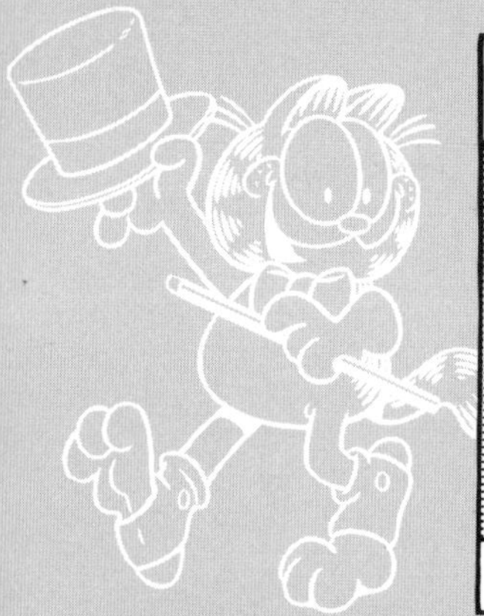

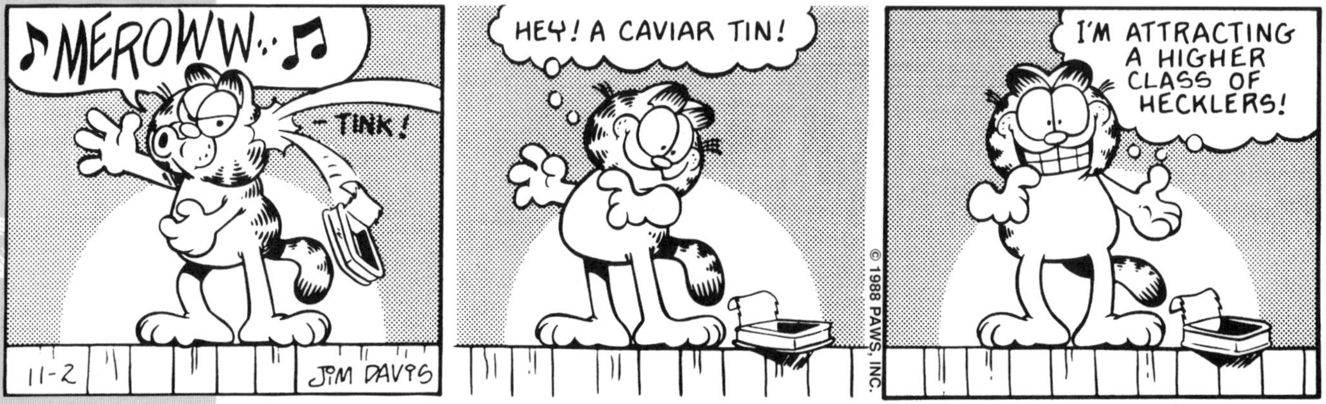

♪MEROWW ♫
-TINK!
11-2
JIM DAVIS
HEY! A CAVIAR TIN!
© 1988 PAWS, INC.
I'M ATTRACTING A HIGHER CLASS OF HECKLERS!

GARFIELD ON MICE

"Show me a cat who's a good mouser, and I'll show you a cat with bad breath."

"That's not a mouse. That's a plague germ with feet."

"I can catch a mouse . . . provided you throw it right to me."

"While the cat's away, the mice will use his credit cards and fertilize his bed."

"A mouse in the hand beats two in your underwear."

"Some cats chase mice. I prefer to take legal action."

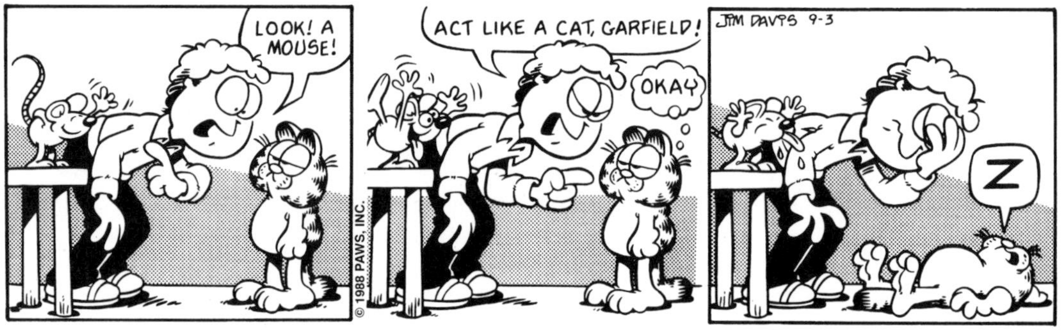

LOOK! A MOUSE!
© 1988 PAWS, INC.
ACT LIKE A CAT, GARFIELD!
OKAY
JIM DAVIS 9-3
Z

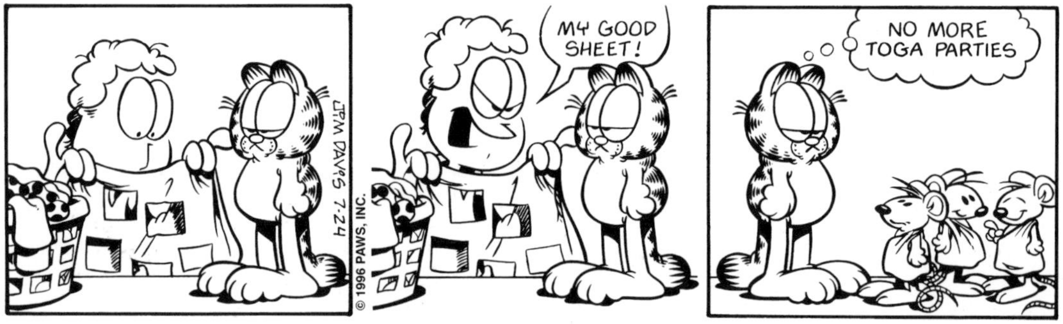

JIM DAVIS 7-24
© 1996 PAWS, INC.
MY GOOD SHEET!
NO MORE TOGA PARTIES

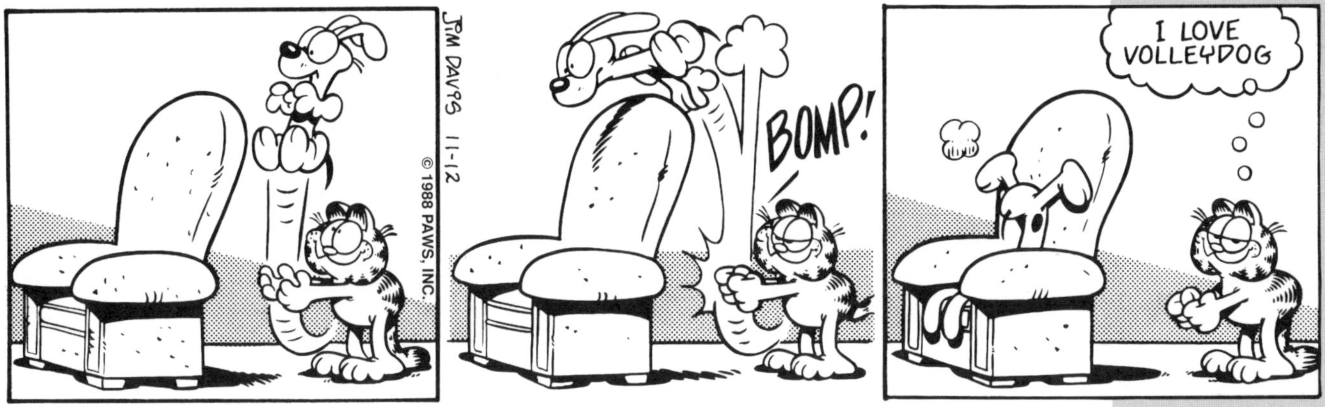
JIM DAVIS 11-12
© 1988 PAWS, INC.
BOMP!
I LOVE VOLLEYDOG

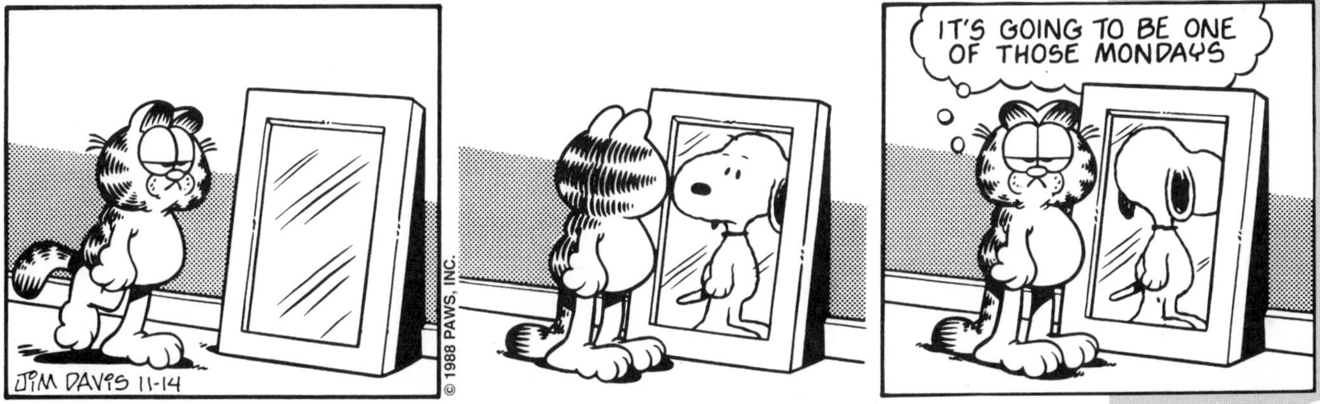
JIM DAVIS 11-14
© 1988 PAWS, INC.
IT'S GOING TO BE ONE OF THOSE MONDAYS

We got permission from Charles Schulz to include Snoopy in this strip.

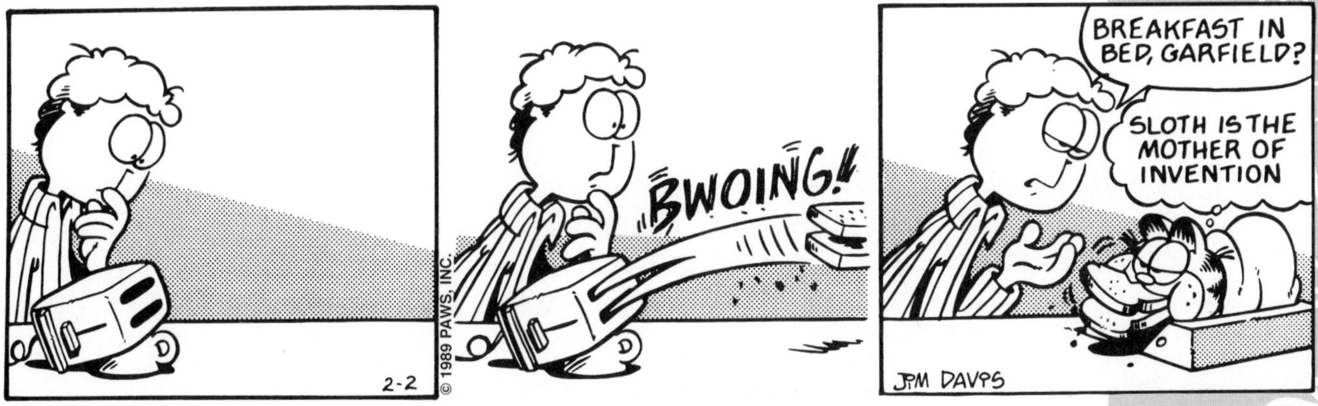
2-2
© 1989 PAWS, INC.
BWOING!
BREAKFAST IN BED, GARFIELD?
SLOTH IS THE MOTHER OF INVENTION
JIM DAVIS

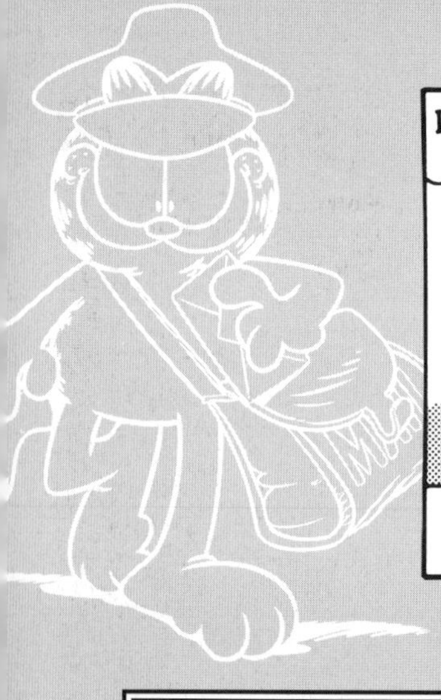

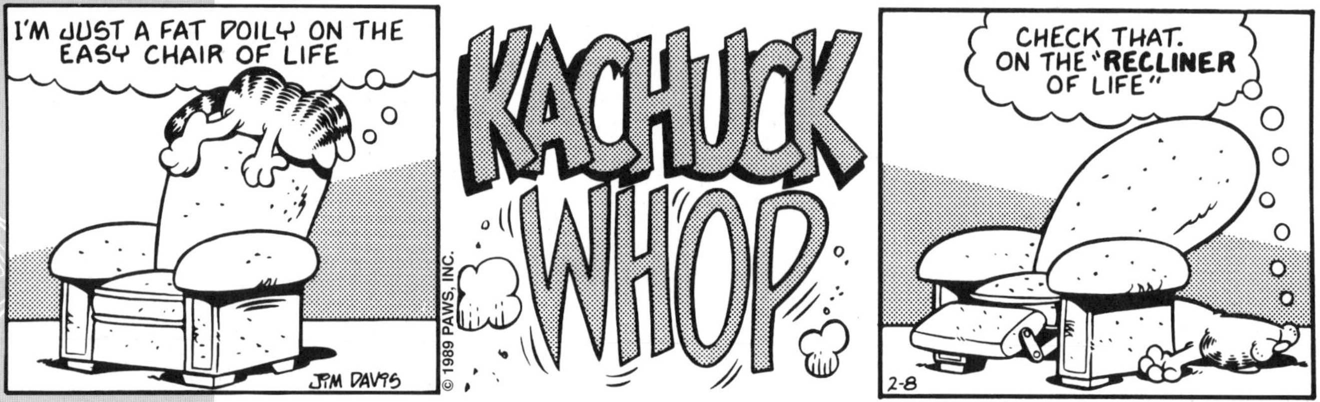

I'M JUST A FAT DOILY ON THE EASY CHAIR OF LIFE
JIM DAVIS
© 1989 PAWS, INC.
KACHUCK
WHOP
CHECK THAT. ON THE "RECLINER OF LIFE"
2-8

GARFIELD VS. THE MAILMEN

The men and women who deliver the mail are used to coping with obstacles like rain, snow, famine, and plague. But how do you handle a fat orange cat with a taste for trousers? Abusing the mailman is one of Garfield's favorite hobbies. Any postman he encounters is bound to walk away with his psyche (and uniform) in shreds. And why does Garfield do it? As he says, "Why should dogs have all the fun?"

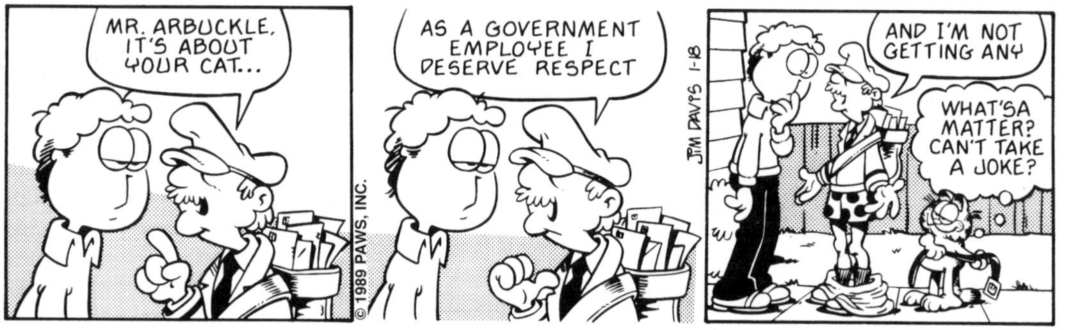

MR. ARBUCKLE, IT'S ABOUT YOUR CAT...
© 1989 PAWS, INC.
AS A GOVERNMENT EMPLOYEE I DESERVE RESPECT
JIM DAVIS 1-18
AND I'M NOT GETTING ANY
WHAT'SA MATTER? CAN'T TAKE A JOKE?

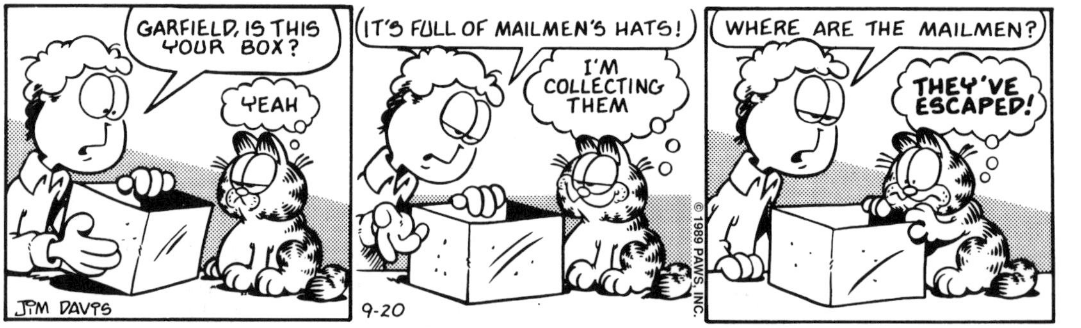

GARFIELD, IS THIS YOUR BOX?
YEAH
JIM DAVIS
IT'S FULL OF MAILMEN'S HATS!
I'M COLLECTING THEM
9-20
© 1989 PAWS, INC.
WHERE ARE THE MAILMEN?
THEY'VE ESCAPED!

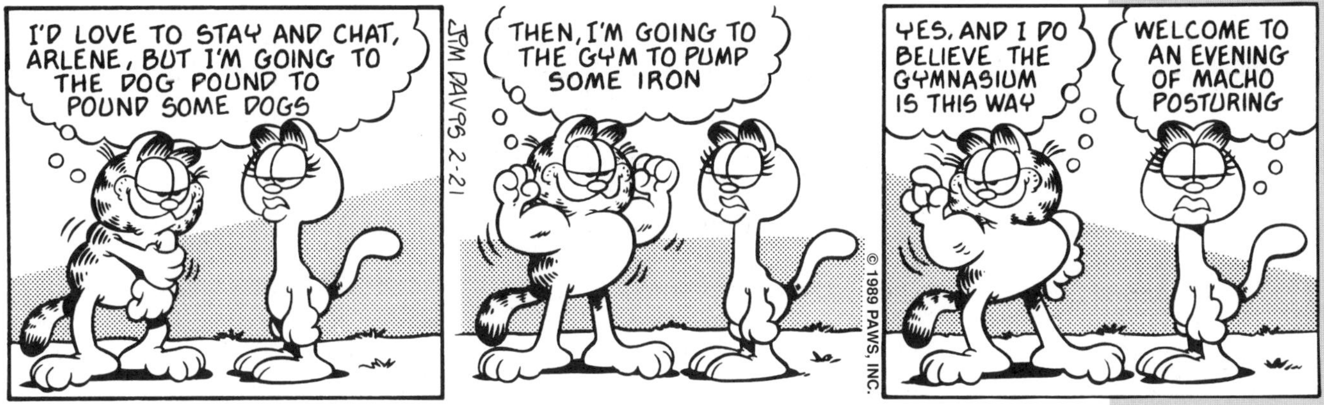
I'D LOVE TO STAY AND CHAT, ARLENE, BUT I'M GOING TO THE DOG POUND TO POUND SOME DOGS
JIM DAVIS 2-21
THEN, I'M GOING TO THE GYM TO PUMP SOME IRON
© 1989 PAWS, INC.
YES, AND I DO BELIEVE THE GYMNASIUM IS THIS WAY
WELCOME TO AN EVENING OF MACHO POSTURING

FAT CAT FACTOID

~1989~

Holy box office bonanza! Tim Burton's *Batman* grosses over $400 million worldwide.

Garfield's "Babes and Bullets" wins an Emmy Award for Outstanding Animated Program of 1988.

Sometimes I like being a little offbeat.

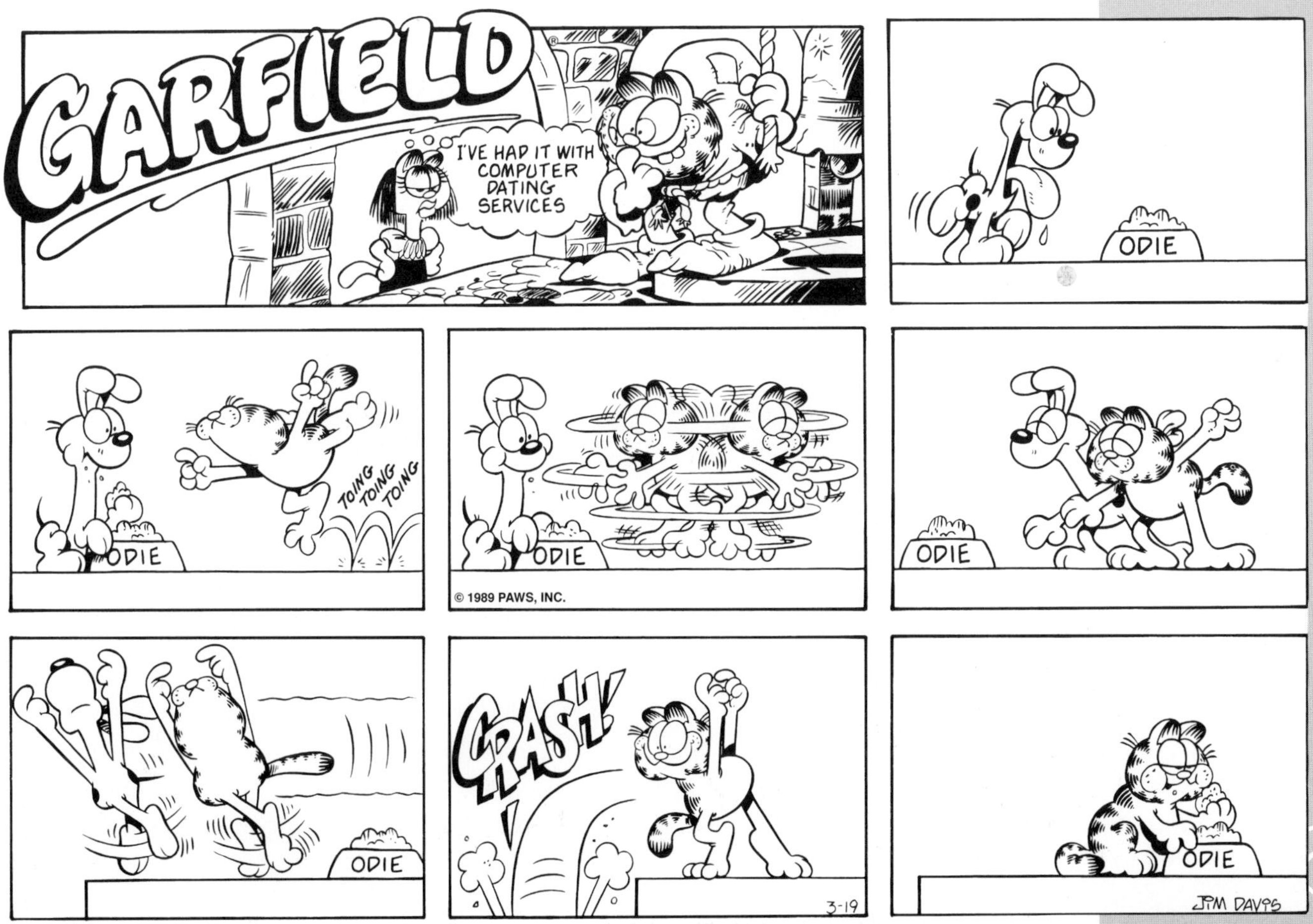
GARFIELD®
I'VE HAD IT WITH COMPUTER DATING SERVICES
ODIE
TOING
TOING
TOING
ODIE
ODIE
© 1989 PAWS, INC.
ODIE
ODIE
CRASH!
3-19
ODIE
JIM DAVIS

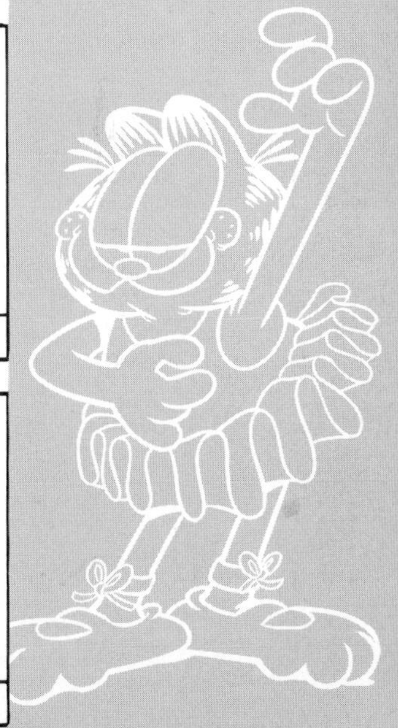

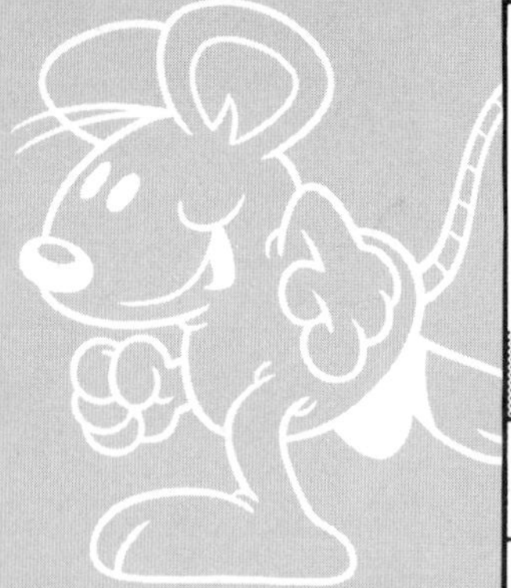

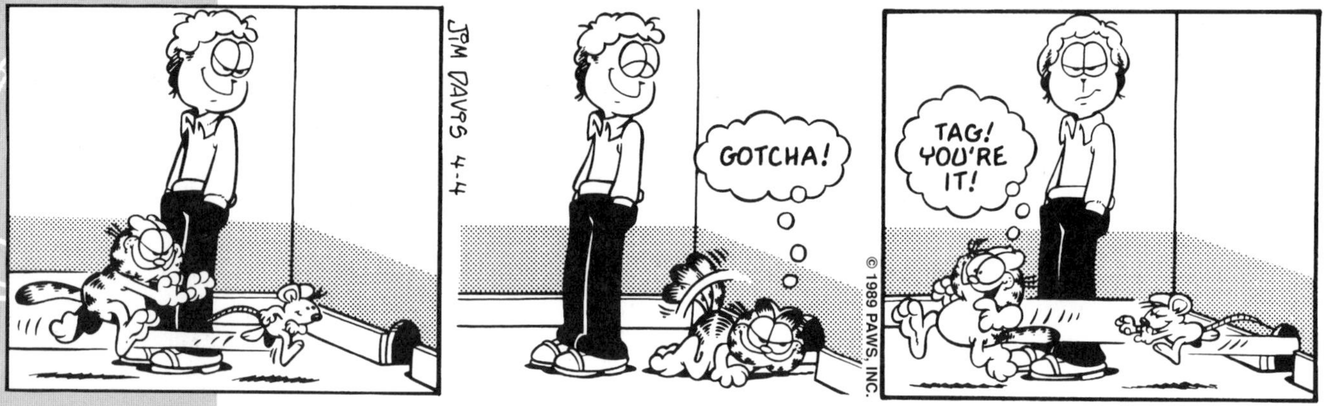
JIM DAVIS 4-4
GOTCHA!
TAG! YOU'RE IT!
© 1989 PAWS, INC.

COFFEE CAT

Garfield is a well-known coffee connoisseur. Here are some of the ways he likes his coffee:

Hot and hair-free

One barrel at a time

Intravenously

Strong enough to sit up and bark

Sucked straight out of the filter

With a twelve-course breakfast

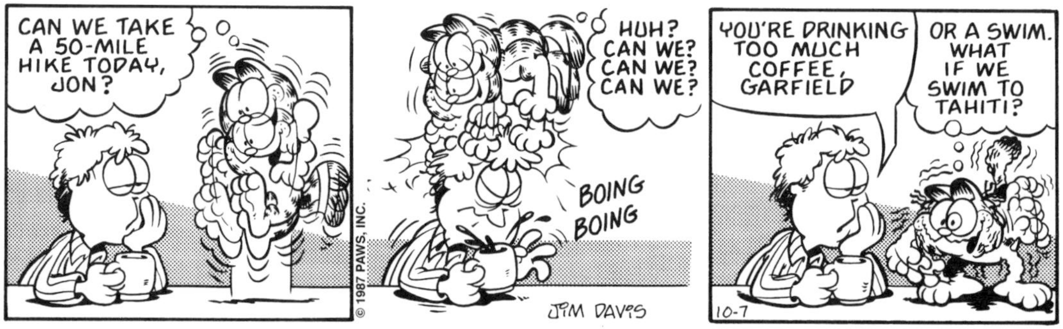
CAN WE TAKE A 50-MILE HIKE TODAY, JON?
© 1987 PAWS, INC.
HUH? CAN WE? CAN WE? CAN WE?
BOING BOING
JIM DAVIS
YOU'RE DRINKING TOO MUCH COFFEE, GARFIELD
OR A SWIM. WHAT IF WE SWIM TO TAHITI?
10-7

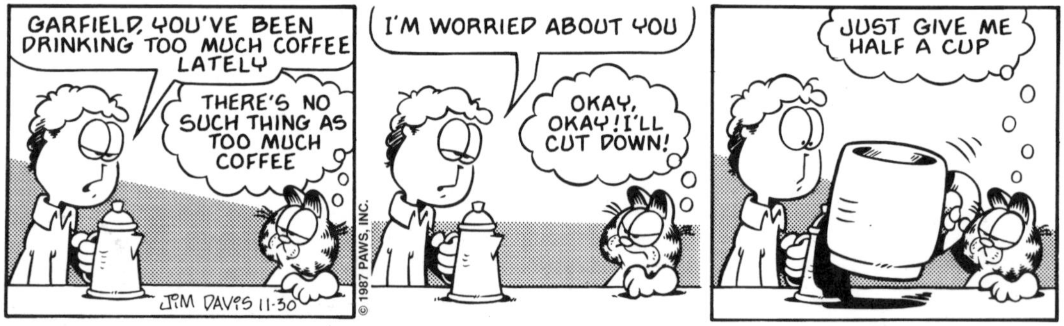
GARFIELD, YOU'VE BEEN DRINKING TOO MUCH COFFEE LATELY
THERE'S NO SUCH THING AS TOO MUCH COFFEE
JIM DAVIS 11-30
© 1987 PAWS, INC.
I'M WORRIED ABOUT YOU
OKAY, OKAY! I'LL CUT DOWN!
JUST GIVE ME HALF A CUP

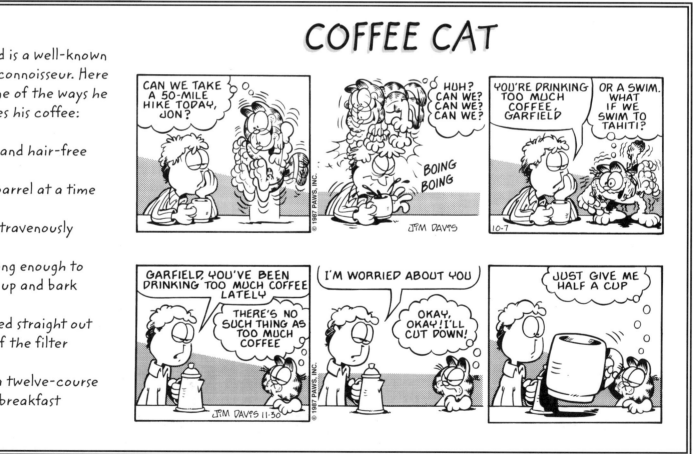

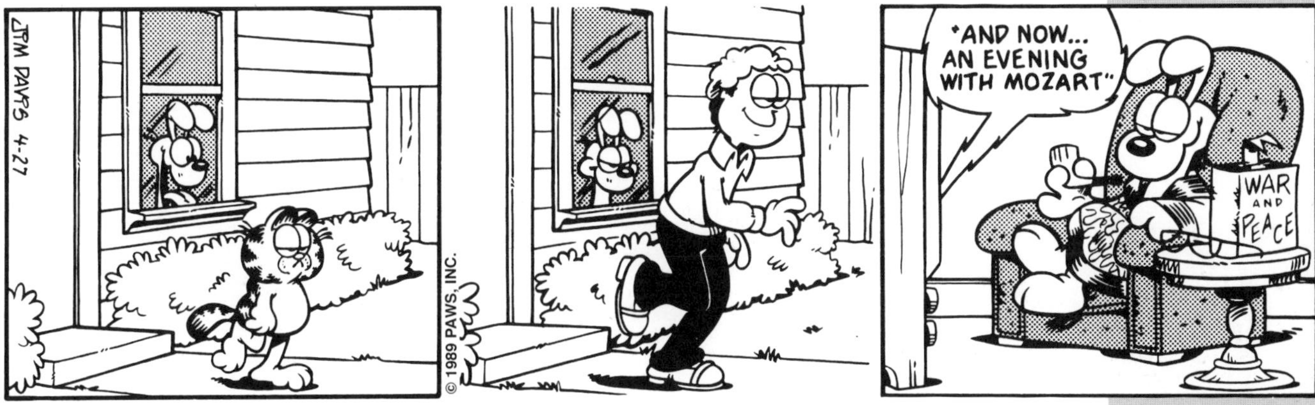
JIM DAVIS 4-27
© 1989 PAWS, INC.
"AND NOW... AN EVENING WITH MOZART"
WAR AND PEACE

I couldn't resist.

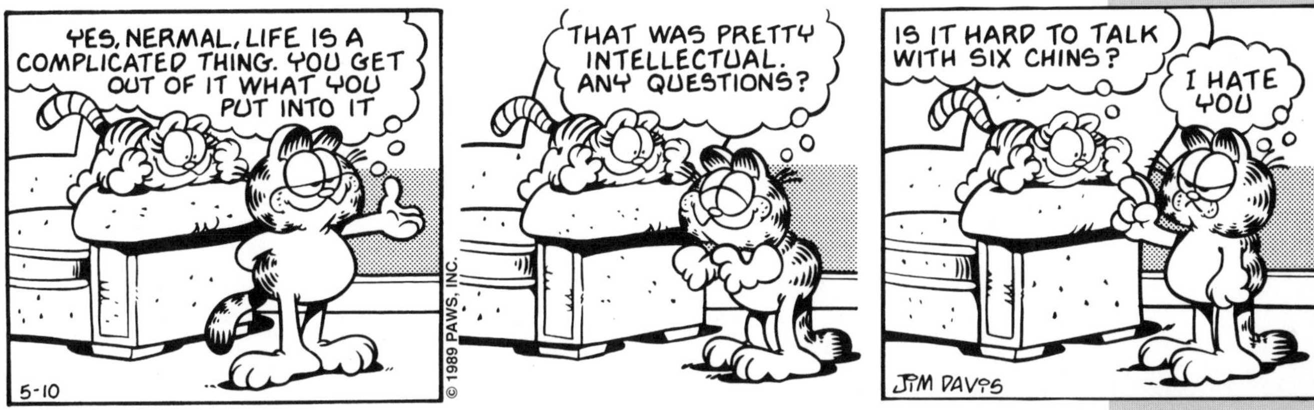
YES, NERMAL, LIFE IS A COMPLICATED THING. YOU GET OUT OF IT WHAT YOU PUT INTO IT
5-10
© 1989 PAWS, INC.
THAT WAS PRETTY INTELLECTUAL. ANY QUESTIONS?
IS IT HARD TO TALK WITH SIX CHINS?
I HATE YOU
JIM DAVIS

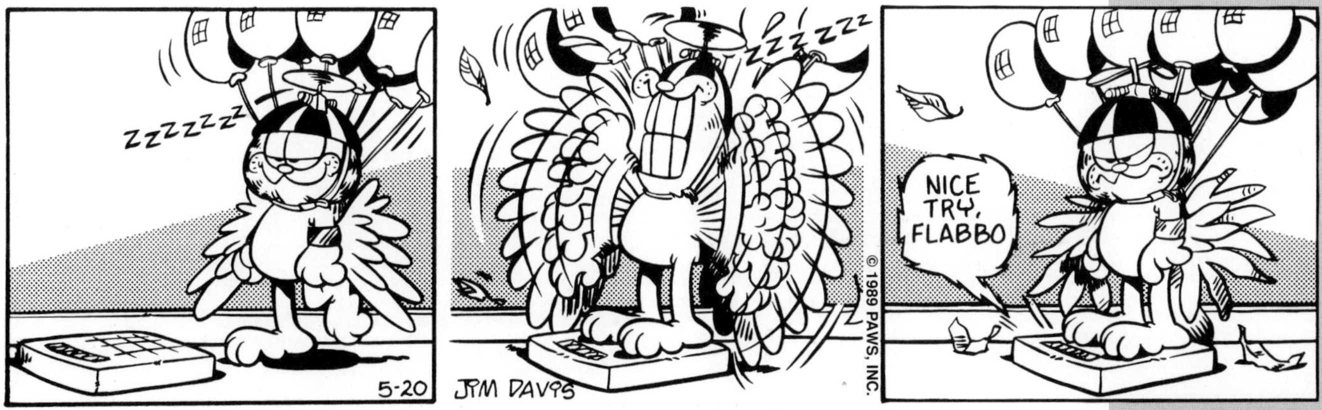
ZZZZZZZ
5-20
ZZZZZZZ
JIM DAVIS
© 1989 PAWS, INC.
NICE TRY, FLABBO

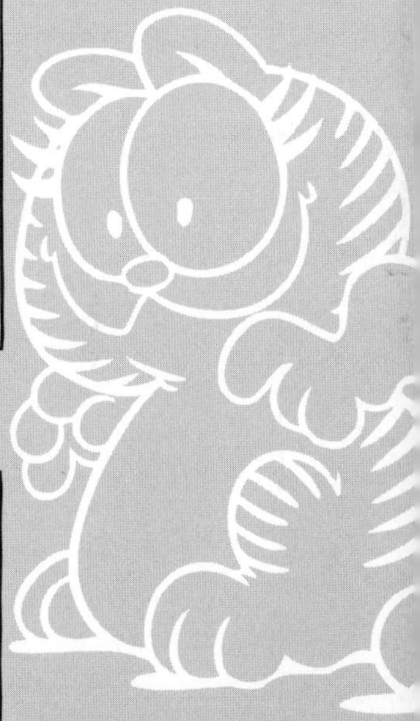

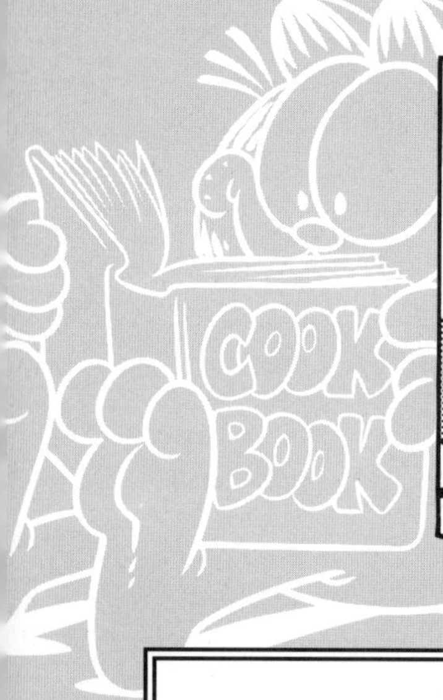
COOK BOOK

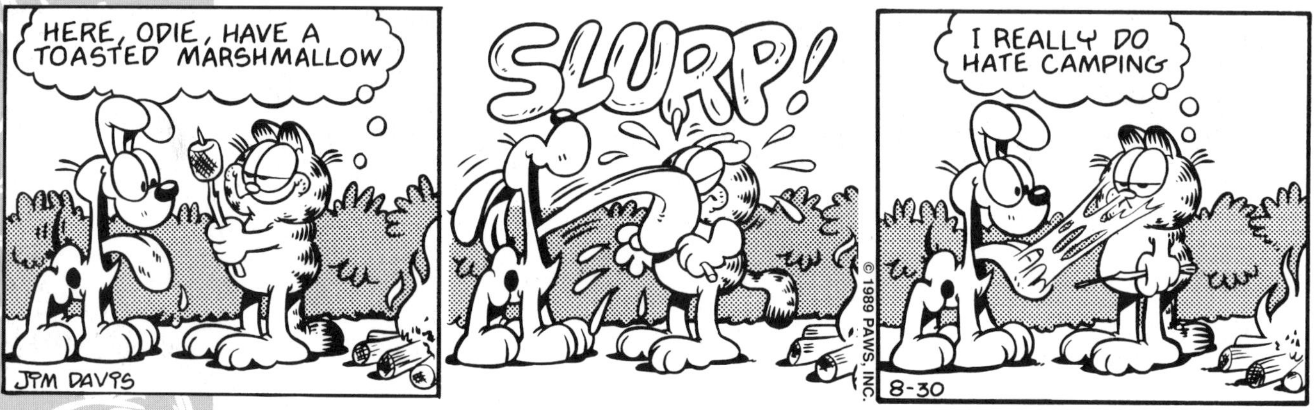
HERE, ODIE, HAVE A TOASTED MARSHMALLOW
SLURP!
I REALLY DO HATE CAMPING
JIM DAVIS
© 1989 PAWS, INC.
8-30

GARFIELD ON COOKING

"A chef's hat does not a chef make."

"Real cooks don't need recipes."

"I don't make meals; I make reservations."

"If you can't stand the heat, don't start a grease fire in the kitchen."

"You know it's undercooked when it starts to moo."

"The best meals are made by someone else."

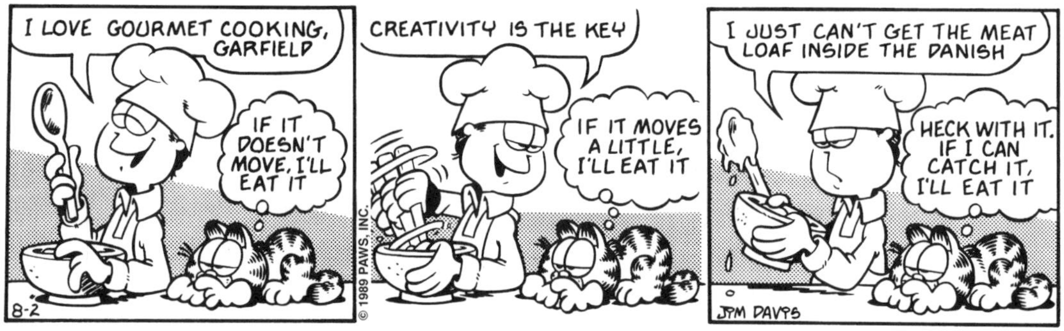
I LOVE GOURMET COOKING, GARFIELD
IF IT DOESN'T MOVE, I'LL EAT IT
8-2
© 1989 PAWS, INC.
CREATIVITY IS THE KEY
IF IT MOVES A LITTLE, I'LL EAT IT
I JUST CAN'T GET THE MEAT LOAF INSIDE THE DANISH
HECK WITH IT. IF I CAN CATCH IT, I'LL EAT IT
JIM DAVIS

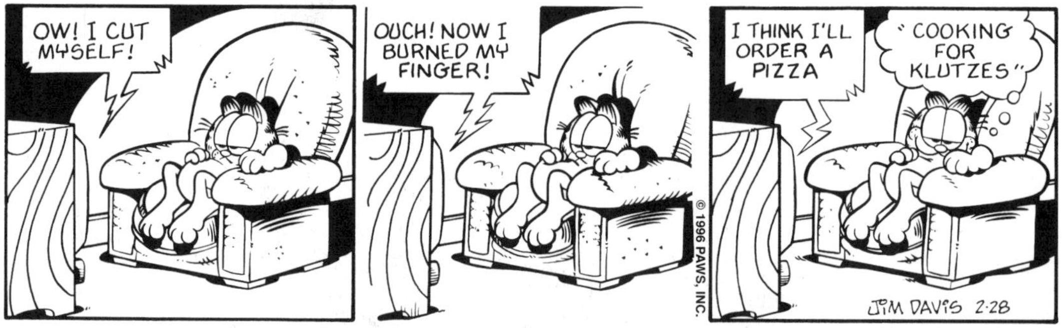
OW! I CUT MYSELF!
OUCH! NOW I BURNED MY FINGER!
© 1996 PAWS, INC.
I THINK I'LL ORDER A PIZZA
"COOKING FOR KLUTZES"
JIM DAVIS 2-28

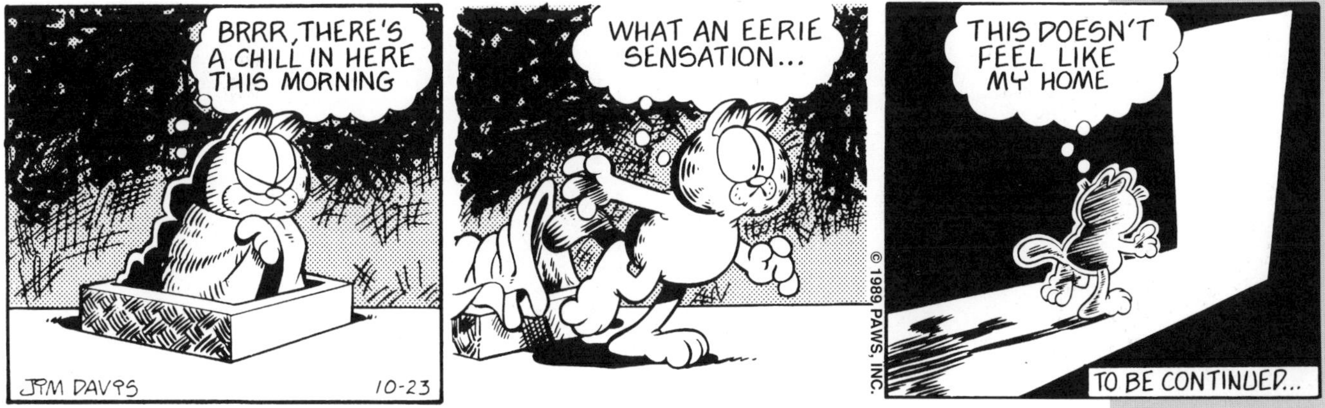
BRRR, THERE'S A CHILL IN HERE THIS MORNING
JIM DAVIS
10-23
WHAT AN EERIE SENSATION...
© 1989 PAWS, INC.
THIS DOESN'T FEEL LIKE MY HOME
TO BE CONTINUED...

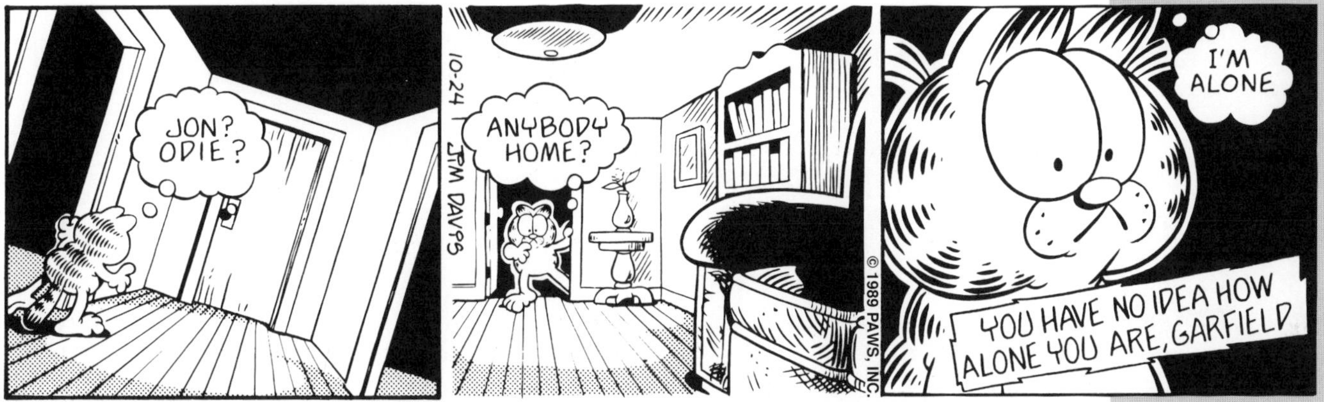
JON? ODIE?
10-24
JIM DAVIS
ANYBODY HOME?
© 1989 PAWS, INC.
I'M ALONE
YOU HAVE NO IDEA HOW ALONE YOU ARE, GARFIELD

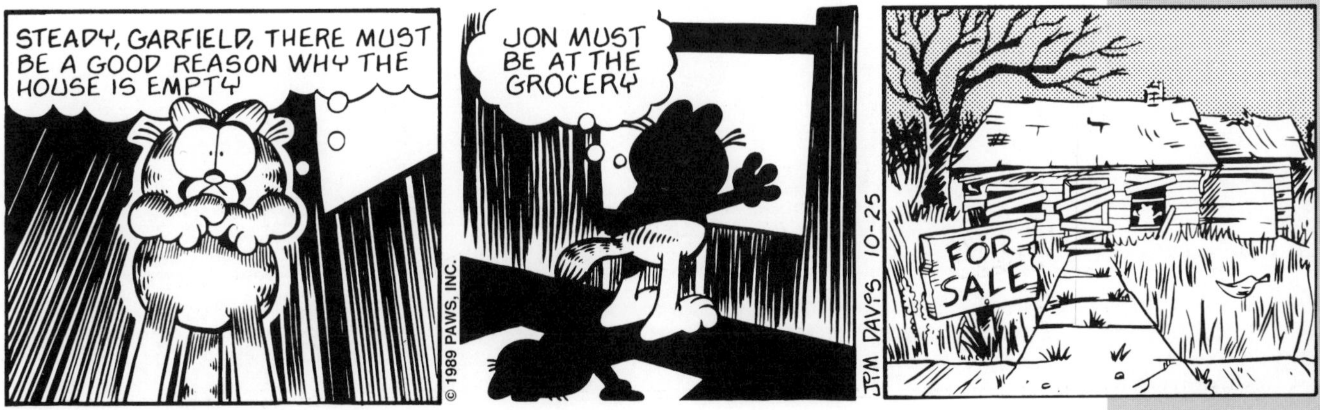
STEADY, GARFIELD, THERE MUST BE A GOOD REASON WHY THE HOUSE IS EMPTY
© 1989 PAWS, INC.
JON MUST BE AT THE GROCERY
JIM DAVIS 10-25
FOR SALE

During a writing session for Halloween week, I got the idea for this decidedly different series of strips. I wanted to scare people. And what do people fear most? Why, being alone. We carried the concept out to its logical conclusion and got a lot of responses from readers. Reaction ranged from "Right on!" to "This isn't a trend, is it?"

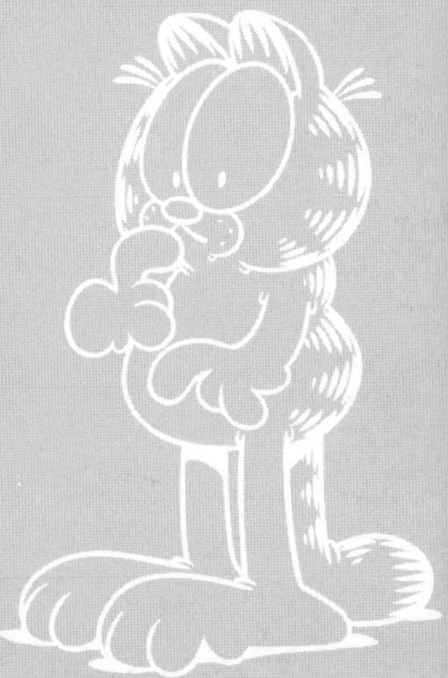

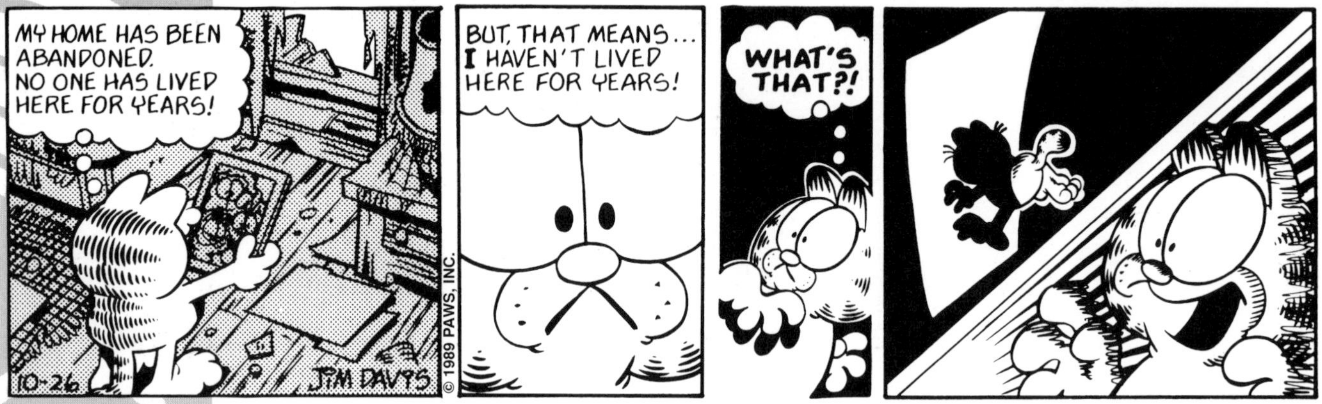
MY HOME HAS BEEN ABANDONED. NO ONE HAS LIVED HERE FOR YEARS!
10-26
JIM DAVIS
© 1989 PAWS, INC.
BUT, THAT MEANS... I HAVEN'T LIVED HERE FOR YEARS!
WHAT'S THAT?!

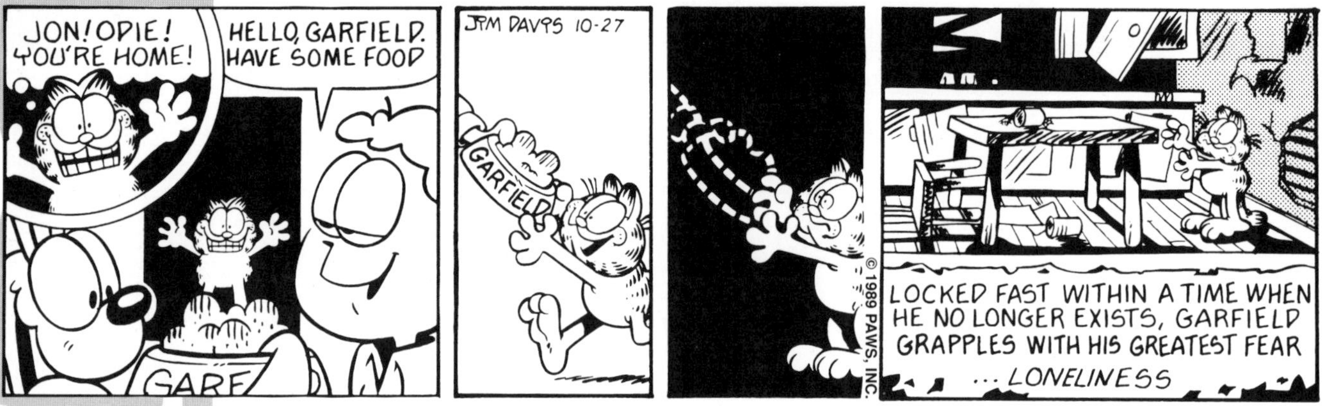
JON! ODIE! YOU'RE HOME!
HELLO, GARFIELD. HAVE SOME FOOD
GARF
JIM DAVIS 10-27
GARFIELD
© 1989 PAWS, INC.
LOCKED FAST WITHIN A TIME WHEN HE NO LONGER EXISTS, GARFIELD GRAPPLES WITH HIS GREATEST FEAR
...LONELINESS

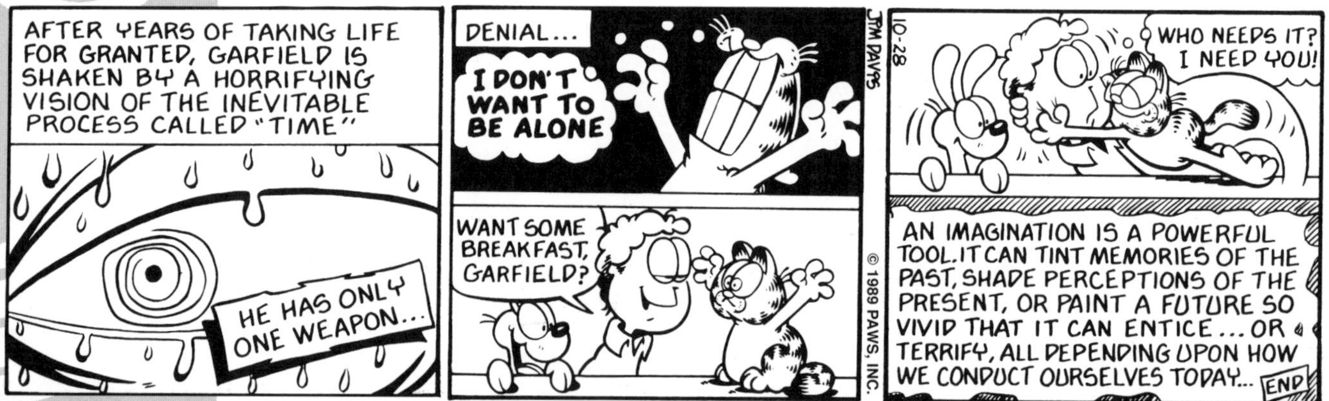
AFTER YEARS OF TAKING LIFE FOR GRANTED, GARFIELD IS SHAKEN BY A HORRIFYING VISION OF THE INEVITABLE PROCESS CALLED "TIME"
HE HAS ONLY ONE WEAPON...
DENIAL...
I DON'T WANT TO BE ALONE
WANT SOME BREAKFAST, GARFIELD?
JIM DAVIS 10-28
© 1989 PAWS, INC.
WHO NEEDS IT? I NEED YOU!
AN IMAGINATION IS A POWERFUL TOOL. IT CAN TINT MEMORIES OF THE PAST, SHADE PERCEPTIONS OF THE PRESENT, OR PAINT A FUTURE SO VIVID THAT IT CAN ENTICE... OR TERRIFY, ALL DEPENDING UPON HOW WE CONDUCT OURSELVES TODAY...
END

Panel 1: I ONLY KNOW TWO THINGS ABOUT LIFE...

Panel 2: I LOVE MY TEDDY BEAR AND MY TEDDY BEAR LOVES ME

Panel 3: SIMPLE TRUTHS ARE THE MOST PROFOUND TRUTHS

© 1990 PAWS, INC.

JIM DAVIS 2-19

DESPERATE AND DATELESS

Panel: GARFIELD, I NEED SOME FEMALE COMPANIONSHIP

Panel: OKAY, JON

Panel: YOU REALIZE I'D ONLY DO THIS FOR YOU

© 1991 PAWS, INC.

JIM DAVIS 10-7

Panel: THAT'S IT, GARFIELD. I'VE ASKED EVERY GIRL ON THIS BEACH OUT

JIM DAVIS 7-17

Panel: AND THEY ALL SAID NO

© 1997 PAWS, INC.

Panel: EVEN THE ONE WITH THE HAIRY BACK?

EVEN THE ONE WITH THE HAIRY BACK!

Jon Arbuckle has no luck with women. Small wonder, when you consider his favorite ways to start a conversation with an attractive stranger:

"You look like a woman with low standards."

"When I saw you, I lost control of all my bodily functions."

"Are you as lonely and depressed as I am?"

"I collect lint. How about you?"

"I have very few communicable diseases."

This is my mom . . .

COME SIT ON YOUR MOTHER'S LAP, JONNY
AW, MOM. I'M TOO BIG FOR THAT
PAT PAT PAT
© 1990 PAWS, INC.
NONSENSE! YOU'RE STILL MY LITTLE BOY. NOW COME ON...
OH, OKAY
PAT PAT
AM I TOO HEAVY FOR YOU, MOM?... MOM?
JIM DAVIS 7-20

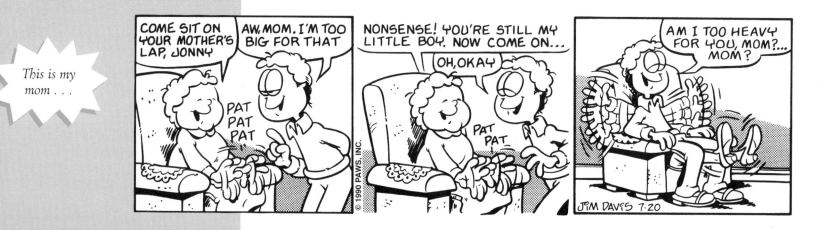

BEWARE OF THE SPLUT

Several times in his career Garfield has been attacked by mysterious flying pies, called "spluts" after the sound they make on impact with Garfield's furry face. Like UFOs and dogs, there seems to be no good explanation for these flying phenomena, which appear from out of nowhere, leave their mark on Garfield, then disappear as suddenly as they arrived. Maybe Jon's house is infested with poltergeists. Or maybe — just maybe — this is a case of Garfield getting his just desserts!

SPLUT!
JIM DAVIS 2-4
OH NO!
YUP... IT'S SPLUT WEEK
© 1985 PAWS, INC.

GIMME THAT FORTUNE COOKIE
JIM DAVIS 1-7-88
© 1988 PAWS, INC.
Beware of the SPLUT!
SPLUT!

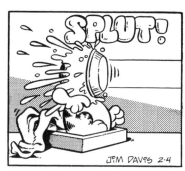

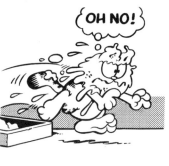

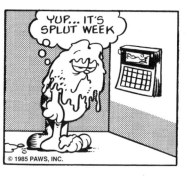

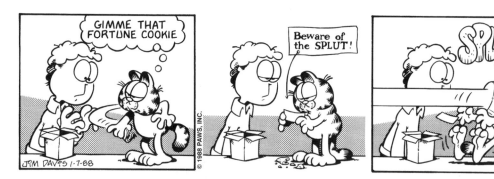

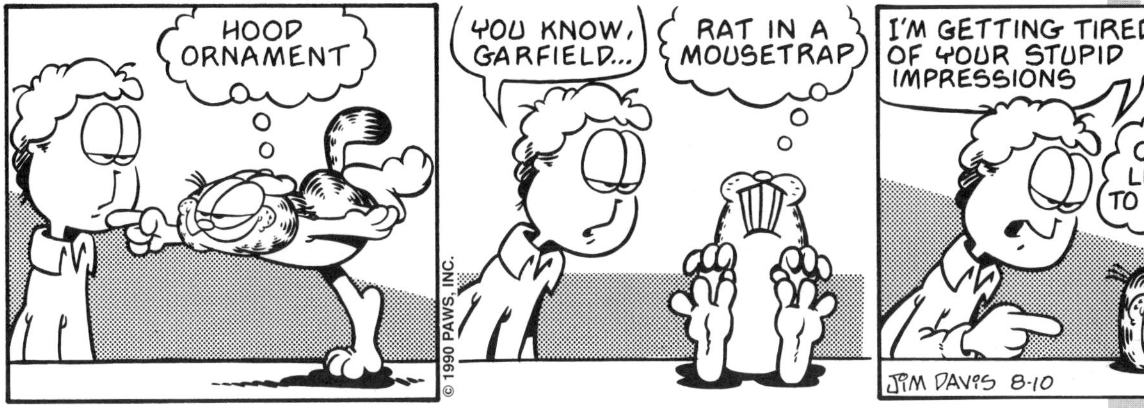
HOOD ORNAMENT
© 1990 PAWS, INC.
YOU KNOW, GARFIELD...
RAT IN A MOUSETRAP
I'M GETTING TIRED OF YOUR STUPID IMPRESSIONS
OKAY, THEN, LET'S LISTEN TO THE **RADIO**
JIM DAVIS 8-10

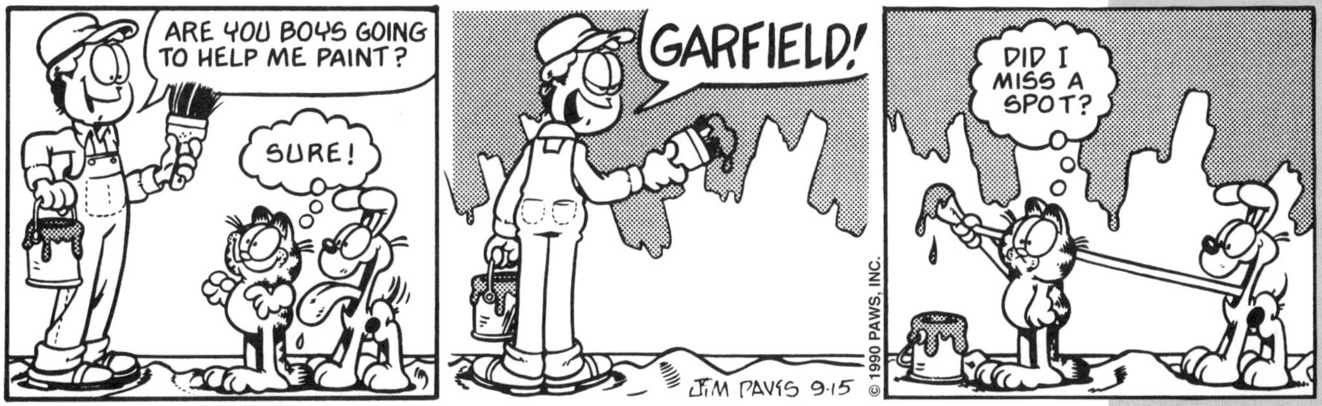
ARE YOU BOYS GOING TO HELP ME PAINT?
SURE!
GARFIELD!
JIM DAVIS 9-15
© 1990 PAWS, INC.
DID I MISS A SPOT?

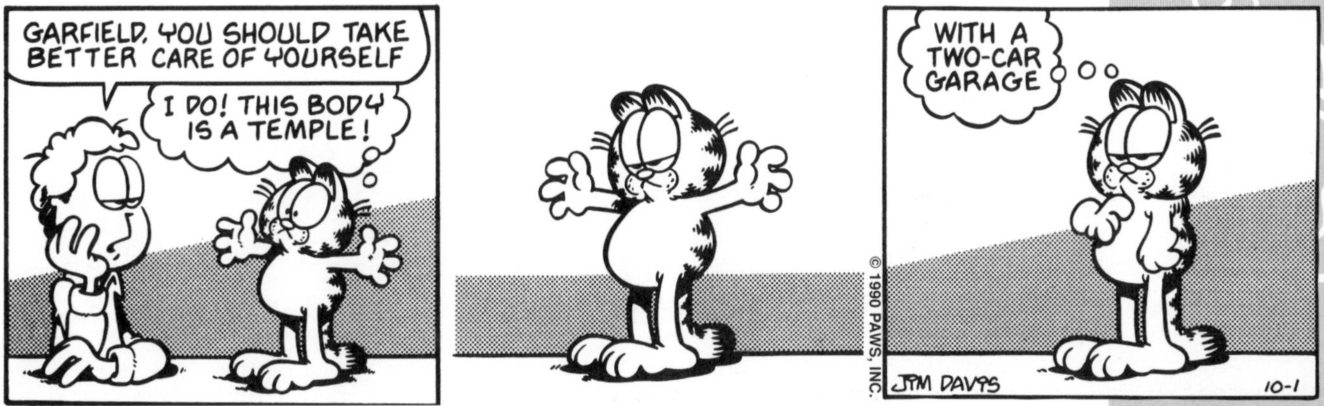
GARFIELD, YOU SHOULD TAKE BETTER CARE OF YOURSELF
I DO! THIS BODY IS A TEMPLE!
© 1990 PAWS, INC.
WITH A TWO-CAR GARAGE
JIM DAVIS 10-1

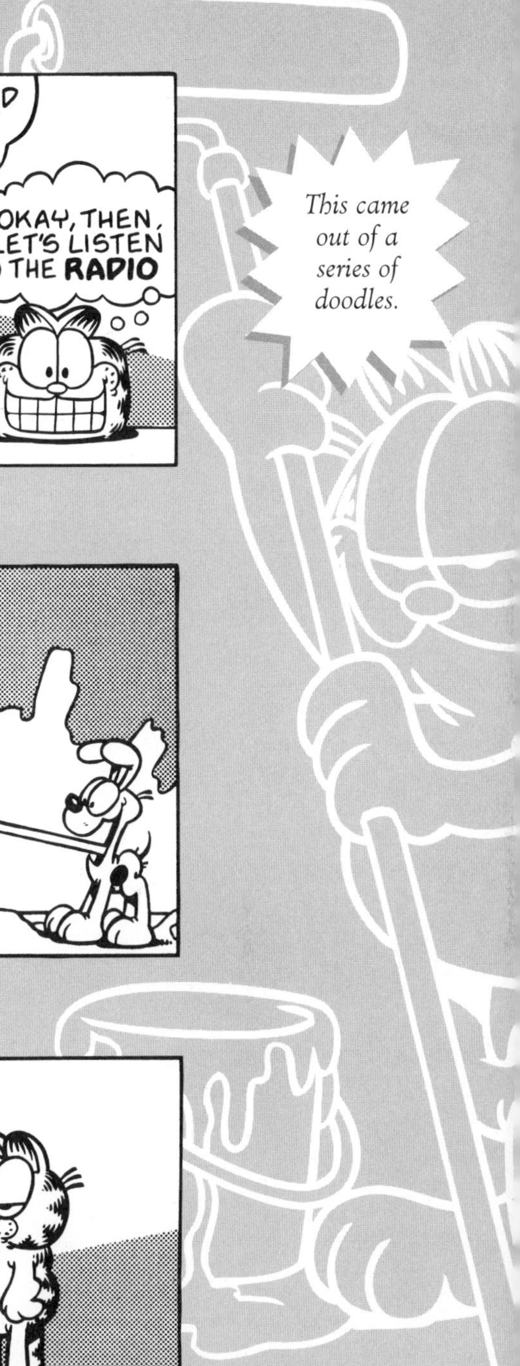

This came out of a series of doodles.

FAT CAT FACTOID
~1990~

Would-be singers Rob and Fab of Milli Vanilli are revealed to be lip-synching puppets on their smash album *Girl You Know It's True*.

Garfield heads south to appear in the annual Orange Bowl parade.

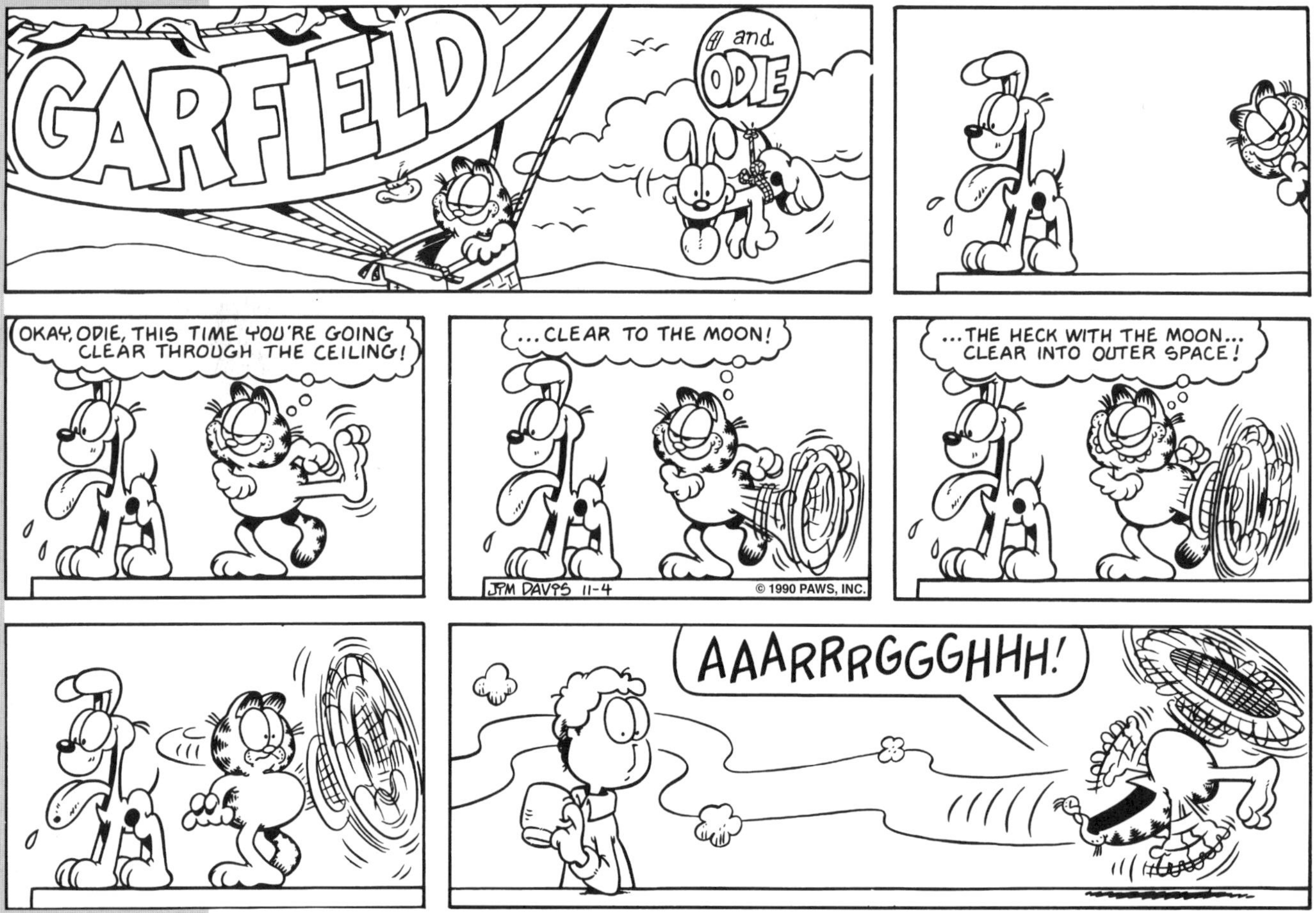

GARFIELD
and ODIE
OKAY, ODIE, THIS TIME YOU'RE GOING CLEAR THROUGH THE CEILING!
...CLEAR TO THE MOON!
...THE HECK WITH THE MOON... CLEAR INTO OUTER SPACE!
JIM DAVIS 11-4
© 1990 PAWS, INC.
AAARRRGGGHHH!

More fun with sight gags. This one came from a doodle, too.

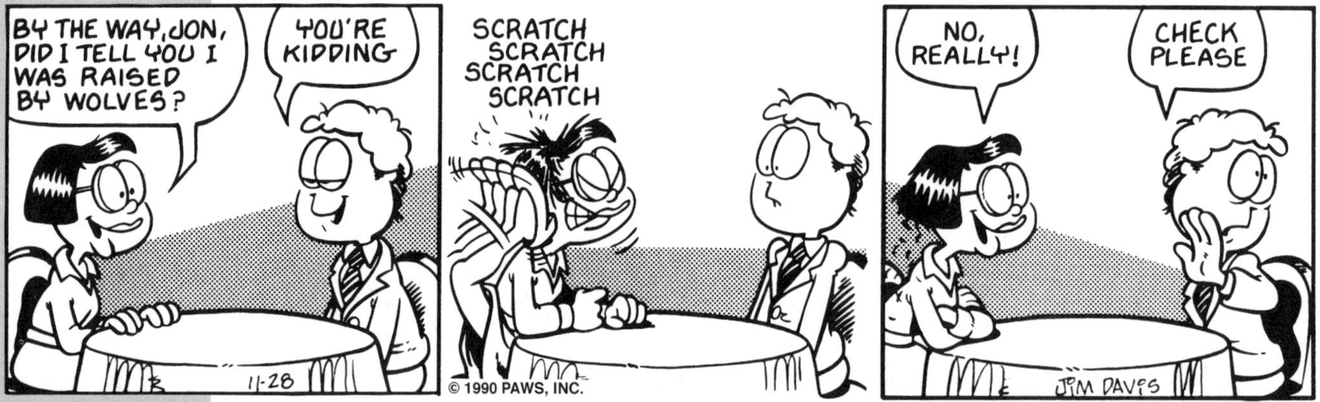

BY THE WAY, JON, DID I TELL YOU I WAS RAISED BY WOLVES?
YOU'RE KIDDING
11-28
SCRATCH SCRATCH SCRATCH SCRATCH
© 1990 PAWS, INC.
NO, REALLY!
CHECK PLEASE
JIM DAVIS

We did a whole week with Kimmy. Of all of Jon's strange dates, Kimmy was one of my favorites.

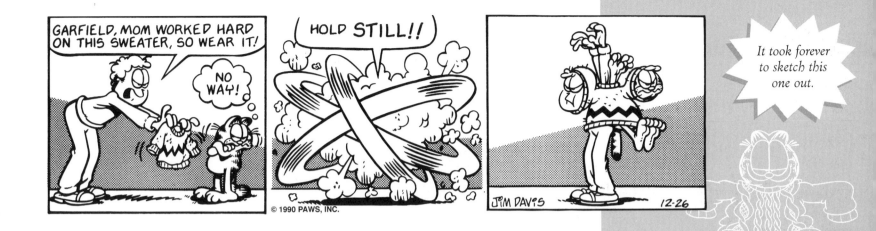

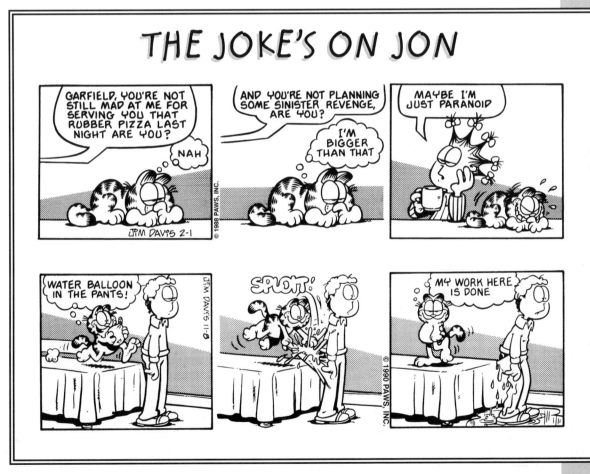

GARFIELD, MOM WORKED HARD ON THIS SWEATER, SO WEAR IT!
NO WAY!
HOLD STILL!!
© 1990 PAWS, INC.
JIM DAVIS
12-26

It took forever to sketch this one out.

THE JOKE'S ON JON

GARFIELD, YOU'RE NOT STILL MAD AT ME FOR SERVING YOU THAT RUBBER PIZZA LAST NIGHT ARE YOU?
NAH
AND YOU'RE NOT PLANNING SOME SINISTER REVENGE, ARE YOU?
I'M BIGGER THAN THAT
MAYBE I'M JUST PARANOID
JIM DAVIS 2-1
© 1988 PAWS, INC.

WATER BALLOON IN THE PANTS!
JIM DAVIS 11-8
SPLOIT!
MY WORK HERE IS DONE
© 1990 PAWS, INC.

Many of Garfield's funniest moments have come at the expense of his hapless owner, Jon Arbuckle. Over the years Garfield has battered Jon with an endless string of verbal jabs, and he's also subjected him to a lot of funny physical abuse. These practical jokes include everything from greasing the bottoms of Jon's shoes and shaving Jon's head while he sleeps to tying Jon's shoestrings to a jet about to take off for Italy!

We got a lot of mail for using the word sucked.

WELL, ANOTHER YEAR IS ALMOST UNDER THE BELT
AND I'VE HAD 313 PRETTY GOOD DAYS
THE MONDAYS SUCKED
JIM DAVIS 12·31
© 1990 PAWS, INC.

GARFIELD
OHHHH, GARFIELD
SIGH
LET'S LOOK AT THE OLD FAMILY ALBUM, GARFIELD
ALBUM
HERE'S A PICTURE OF MY UNCLE WALDO
ALBUM
© 1991 PAWS, INC.
HE LIVED ON A RANCH
HAD ONE OF THE LARGEST WARTHOG HERDS IN THE COUNTRY
OF COURSE, THAT WAS BEFORE HE WAS ARRESTED
JIM DAVIS 3-10
HE WAS ACCUSED OF SELLING UGLY BACON
I IGNORE HIM, BUT HE NEVER GOES AWAY

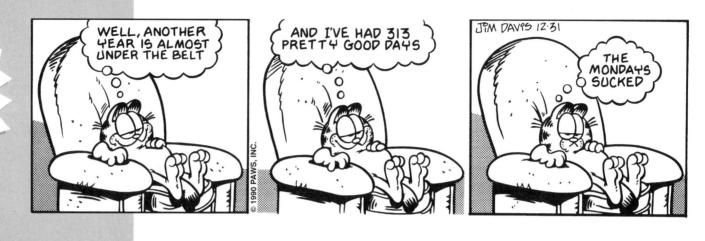

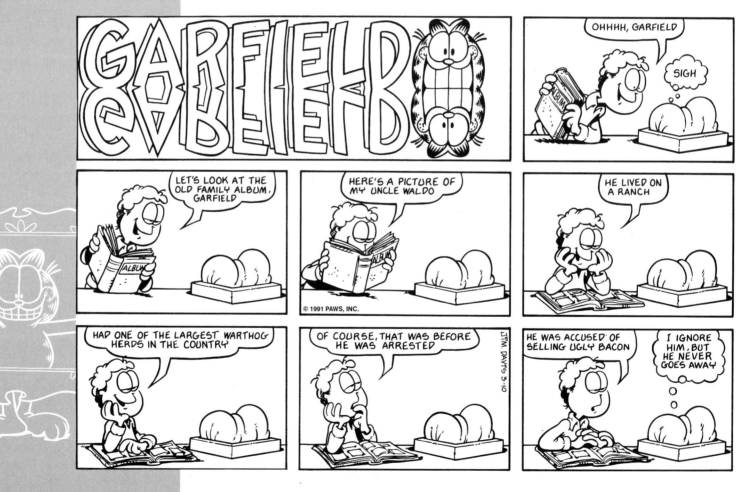

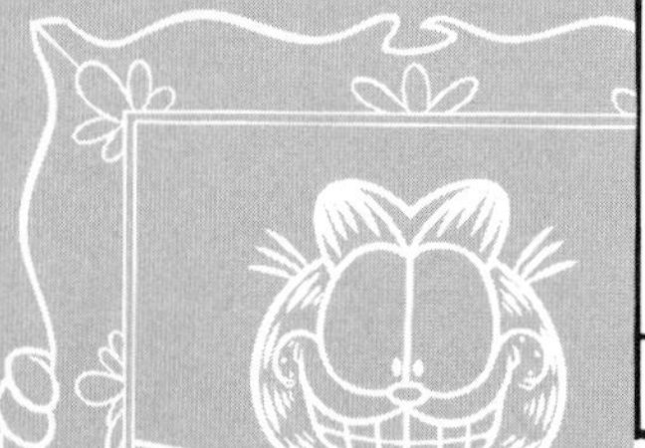

GARFIELD, WHAT ARE YOU DOING?
PRETENDING I'M ON THE "ANIMAL KINGDOM" SHOW
© 1991 PAWS, INC.
YOU JUST LIE AROUND!
I'VE BEEN HIT WITH A TRANQUILIZER DART
YOU'RE LAZY!
SOON I'LL BE TAGGED, SO THEY CAN STUDY MY MIGRATION PATTERNS
JIM DAVIS 3-25

FAT CAT FACTOID

~1991~

A very pregnant Demi Moore appears au naturel on the cover of *Vanity Fair.*

Garfield rocks out on his very own CD — Am I Cool or What?

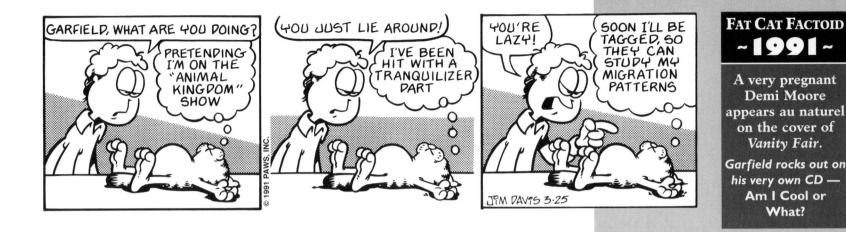

WHY GARFIELD HATES SPIDERS

I HATE SPIDERS!
JIM DAVIS 2-17
© 1987 PAWS, INC.
STOMP!
I HATE HATING SPIDERS

The Cat Is Stoopid
PSSST!
JIM DAVIS 8-23
KLAK KLAK KLAK KLAK
The Cat Is Stoopid
AHEM
© 1997 PAWS, INC.
The Cat Is Stoopid
THE CAT

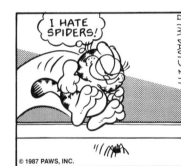

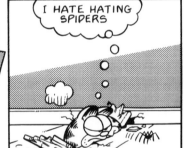

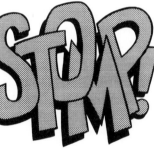

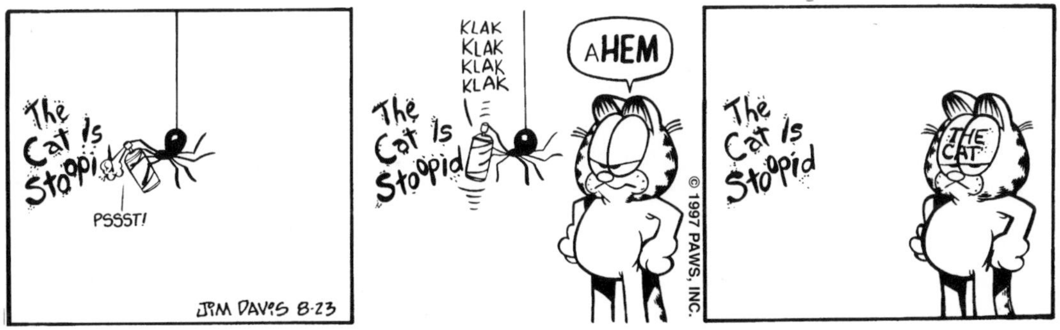

He can't take a simple two-week nap without some spider attaching a web to him.

Little Miss Muffet is a close personal friend of his.

His uncle Bob once sat on a tarantula, and was never the same.

Spiders are always working; they make cats look bad.

His favorite cooking show was replaced by The Arachnid Hour.

They taste yucky.

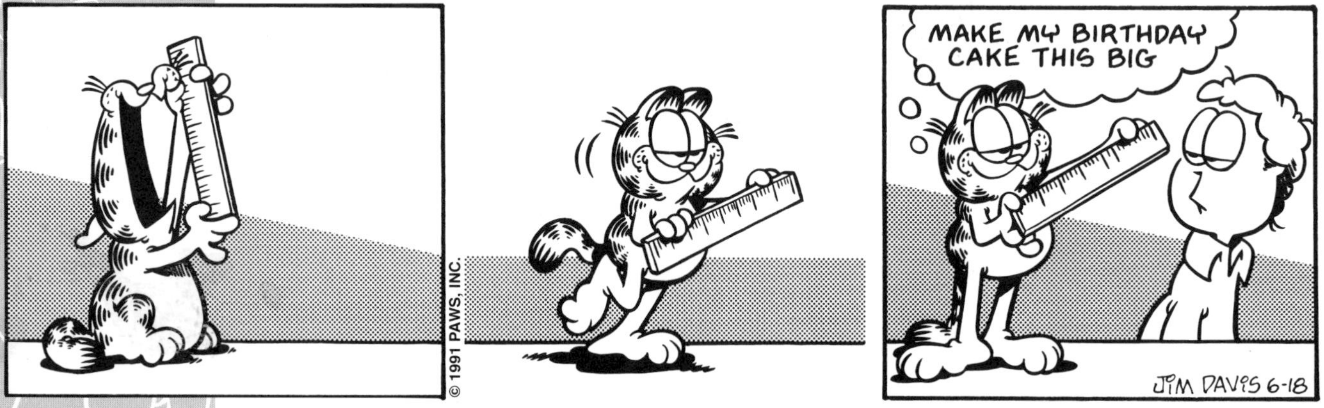
© 1991 PAWS, INC.
MAKE MY BIRTHDAY CAKE THIS BIG
JIM DAVIS 6-18

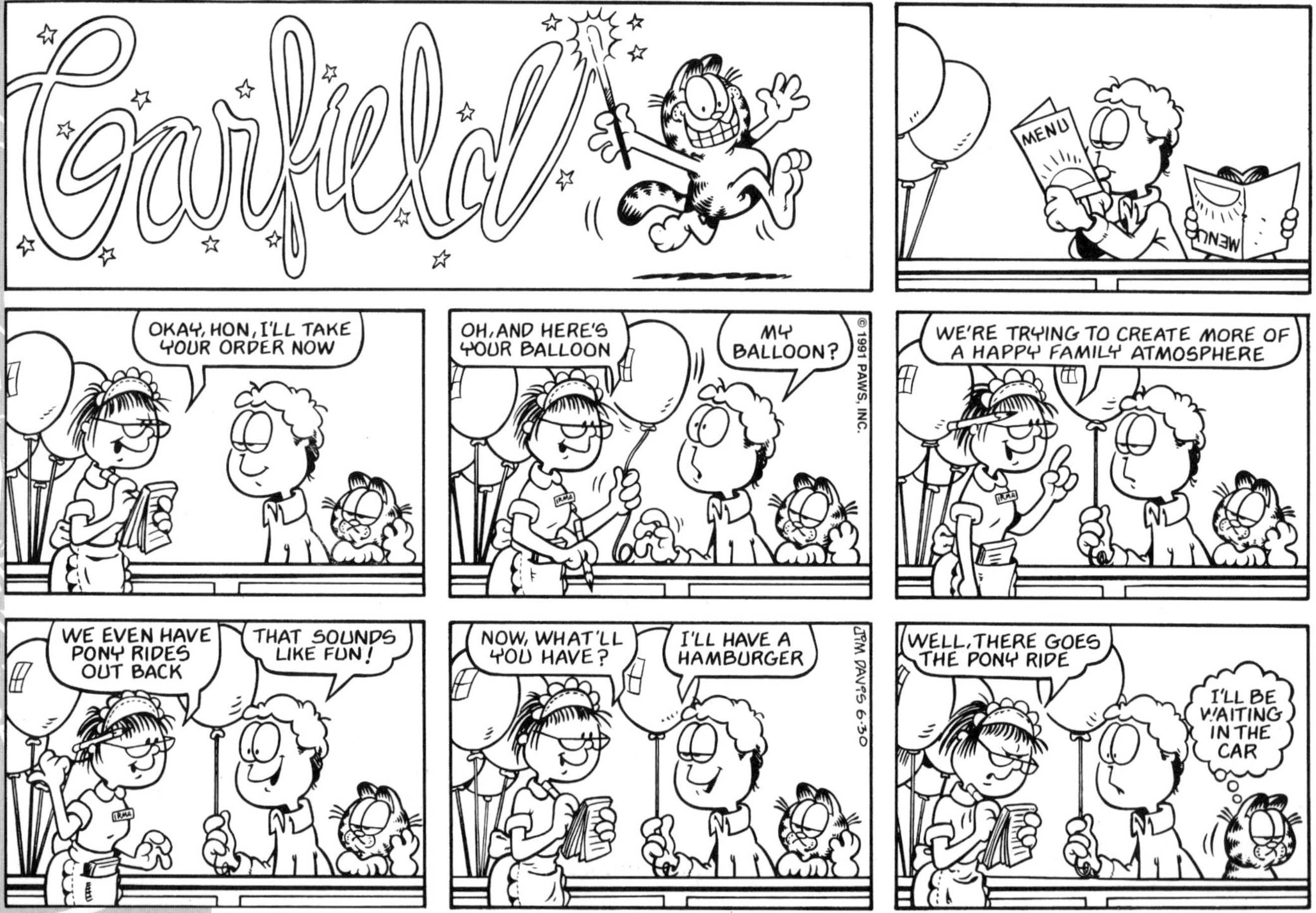
Garfield
MENU
MENU
OKAY, HON, I'LL TAKE YOUR ORDER NOW
OH, AND HERE'S YOUR BALLOON
MY BALLOON?
© 1991 PAWS, INC.
WE'RE TRYING TO CREATE MORE OF A HAPPY FAMILY ATMOSPHERE
WE EVEN HAVE PONY RIDES OUT BACK
THAT SOUNDS LIKE FUN!
NOW, WHAT'LL YOU HAVE?
I'LL HAVE A HAMBURGER
JIM DAVIS 6-30
WELL, THERE GOES THE PONY RIDE
I'LL BE WAITING IN THE CAR

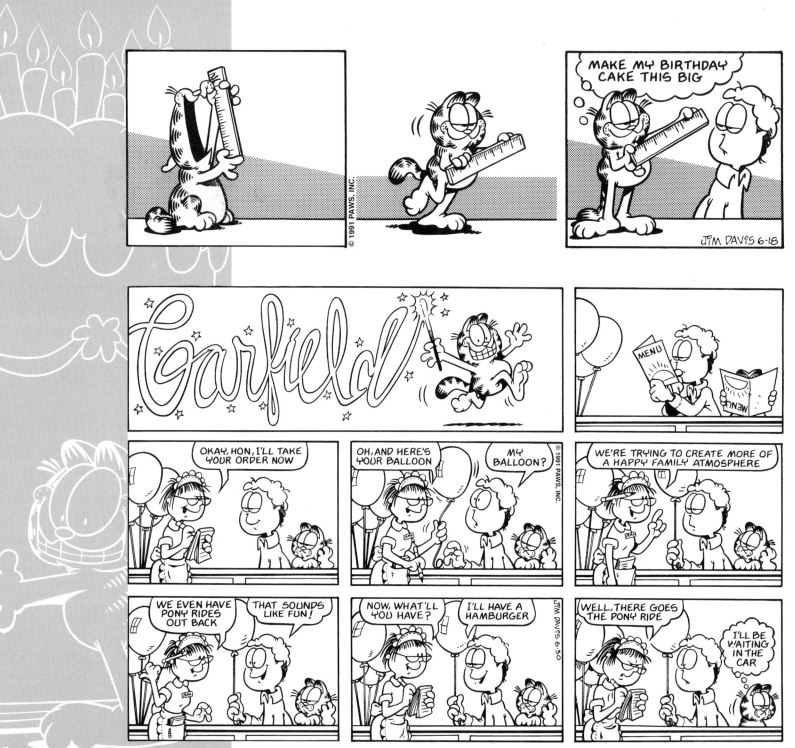

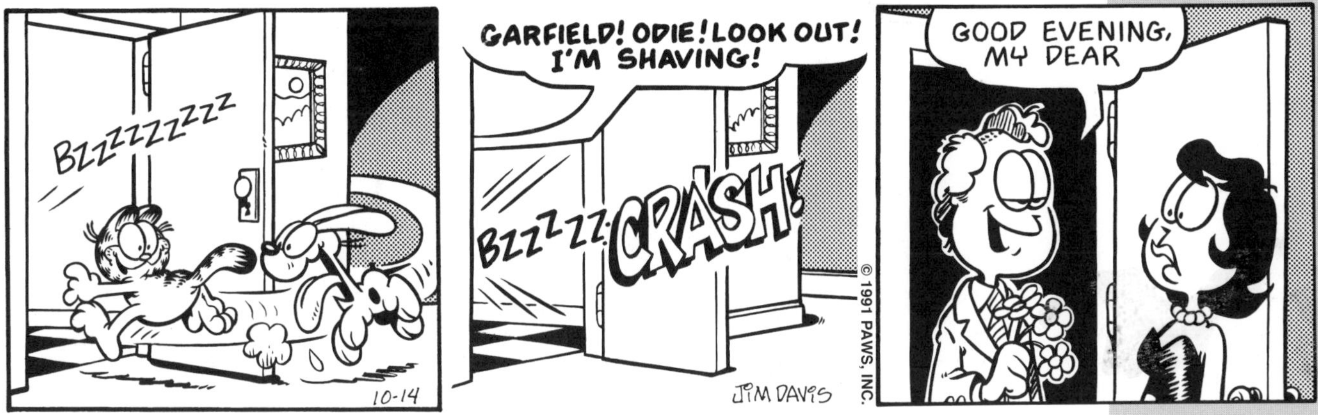
BZZZZZZZZZ
GARFIELD! ODIE! LOOK OUT! I'M SHAVING!
BZZZZZ
CRASH!
JIM DAVIS
© 1991 PAWS, INC.
GOOD EVENING, MY DEAR
10-14

Jon's big date with Liz. Things just got worse as the week progressed. This is how I always felt when I was dating.

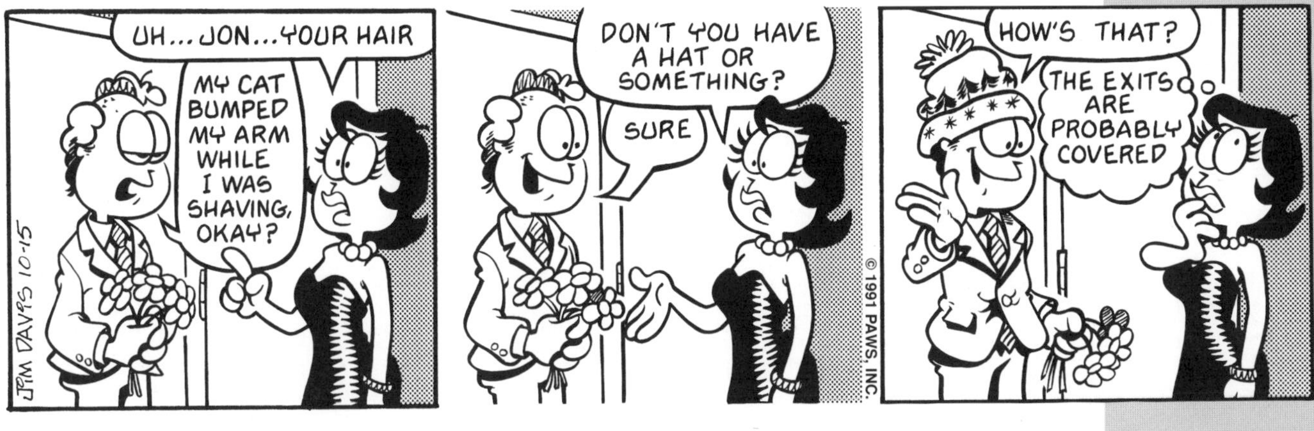
UH... JON... YOUR HAIR
MY CAT BUMPED MY ARM WHILE I WAS SHAVING, OKAY?
JIM DAVIS 10-15
DON'T YOU HAVE A HAT OR SOMETHING?
SURE
© 1991 PAWS, INC.
HOW'S THAT?
THE EXITS ARE PROBABLY COVERED

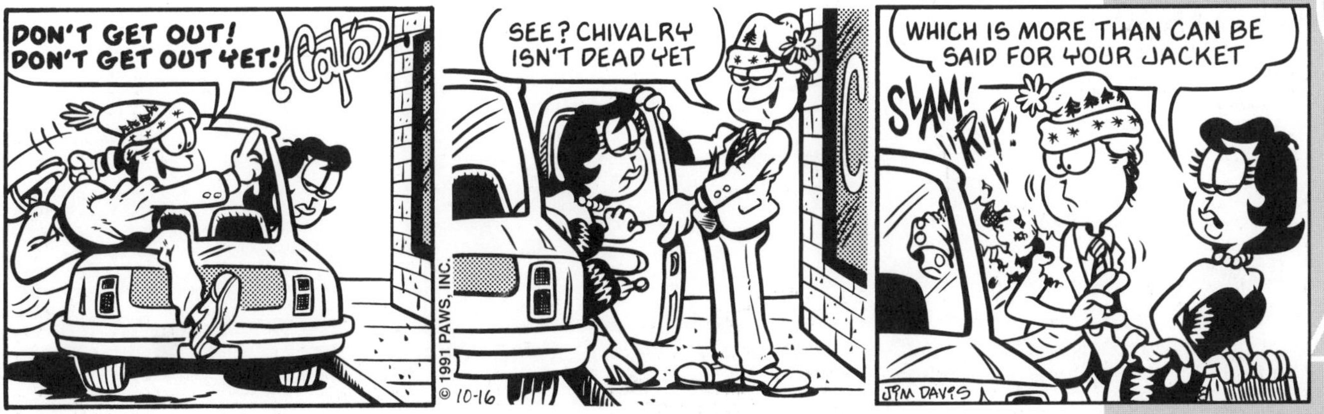
DON'T GET OUT! DON'T GET OUT YET!
SEE? CHIVALRY ISN'T DEAD YET
© 1991 PAWS, INC.
10-16
WHICH IS MORE THAN CAN BE SAID FOR YOUR JACKET
SLAM!
RIP!
JIM DAVIS

FAT CAT FACTOID
~1992~

Quirky billionaire Ross Perot joins George Bush and Bill Clinton in a three-way presidential race; Clinton wins the election.

Garfield is chosen as favorite comic strip in a Gallup youth poll.

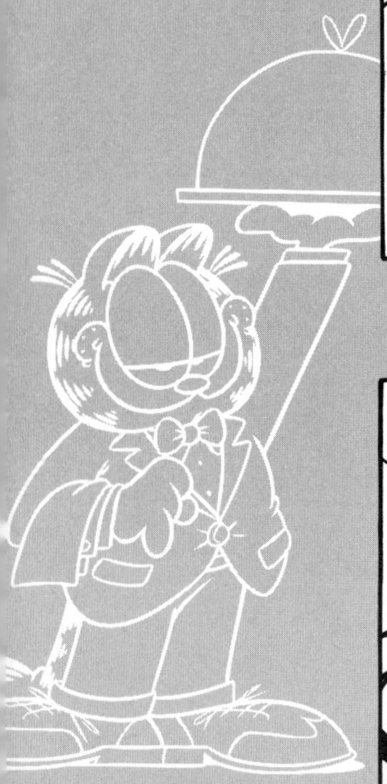

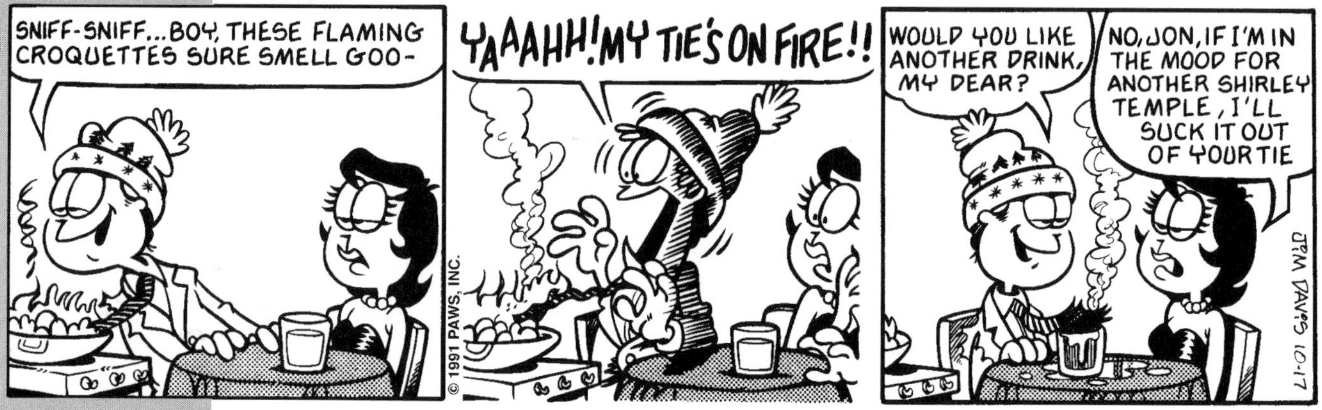

SNIFF-SNIFF...BOY, THESE FLAMING CROQUETTES SURE SMELL GOO-
YAAAHH! MY TIE'S ON FIRE!!
© 1991 PAWS, INC.
WOULD YOU LIKE ANOTHER DRINK, MY DEAR?
NO, JON, IF I'M IN THE MOOD FOR ANOTHER SHIRLEY TEMPLE, I'LL SUCK IT OUT OF YOUR TIE
JIM DAVIS 10-17

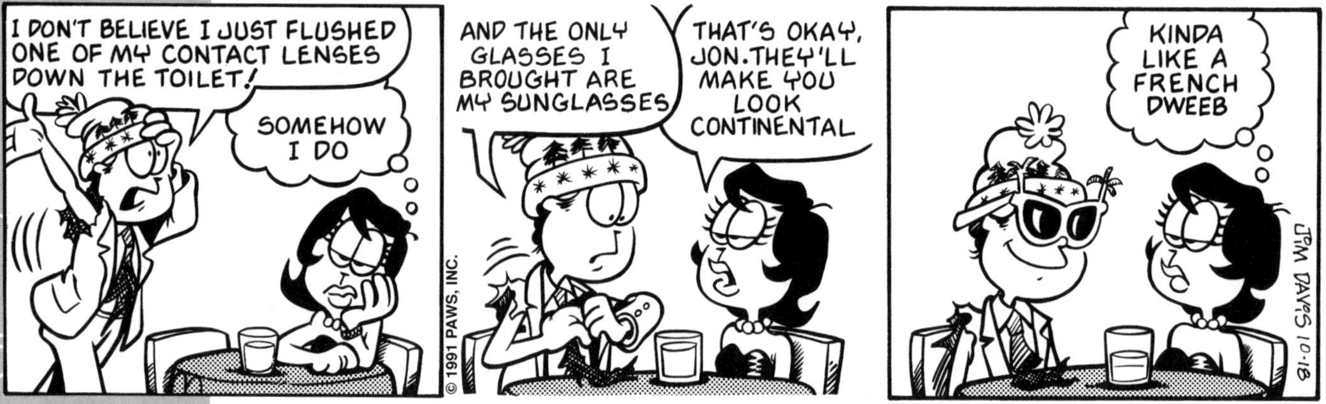

I DON'T BELIEVE I JUST FLUSHED ONE OF MY CONTACT LENSES DOWN THE TOILET!
SOMEHOW I DO
© 1991 PAWS, INC.
AND THE ONLY GLASSES I BROUGHT ARE MY SUNGLASSES
THAT'S OKAY, JON. THEY'LL MAKE YOU LOOK CONTINENTAL
KINDA LIKE A FRENCH DWEEB
JIM DAVIS 10-18

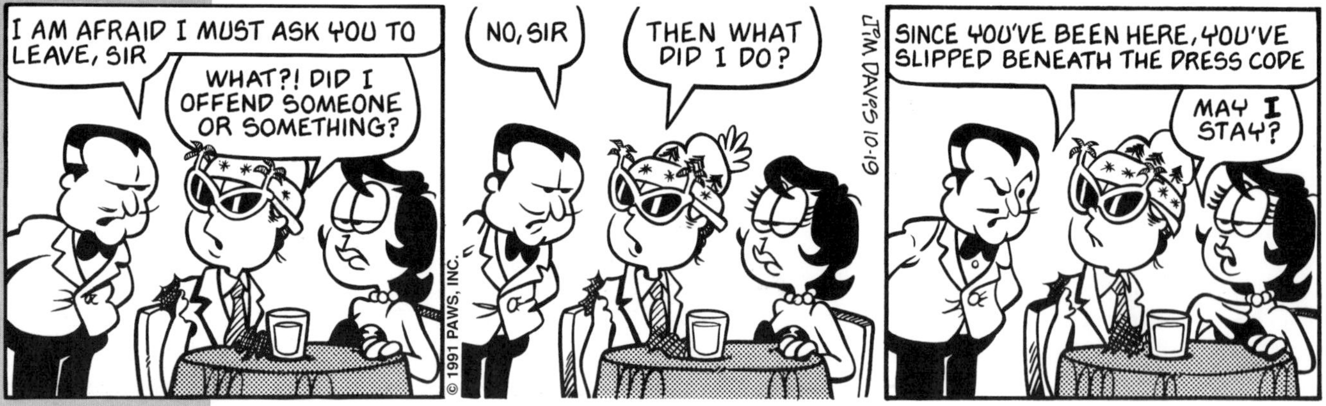

I AM AFRAID I MUST ASK YOU TO LEAVE, SIR
WHAT?! DID I OFFEND SOMEONE OR SOMETHING?
© 1991 PAWS, INC.
NO, SIR
THEN WHAT DID I DO?
JIM DAVIS 10-19
SINCE YOU'VE BEEN HERE, YOU'VE SLIPPED BENEATH THE DRESS CODE
MAY I STAY?

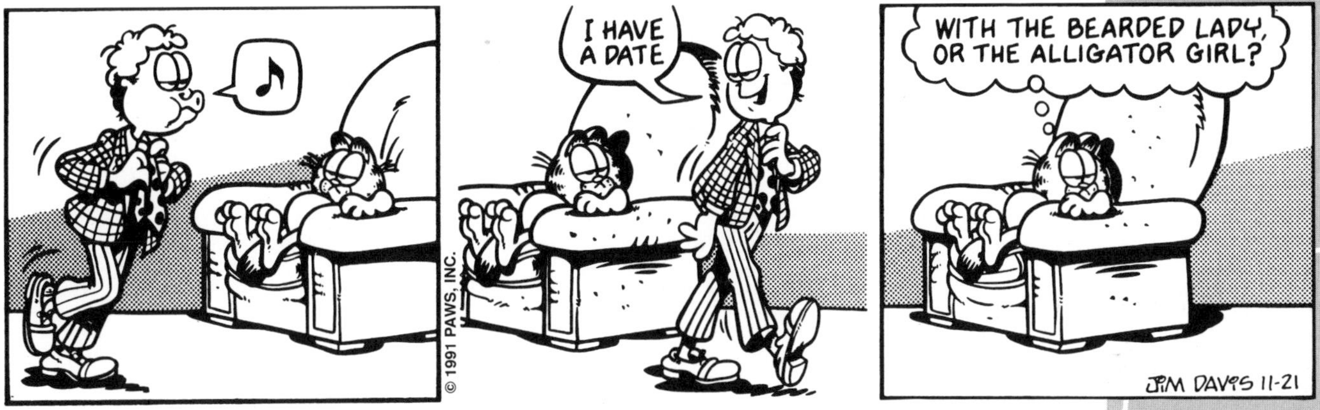
♪
I HAVE A DATE
© 1991 PAWS, INC.
WITH THE BEARDED LADY, OR THE ALLIGATOR GIRL?
JIM DAVIS 11-21

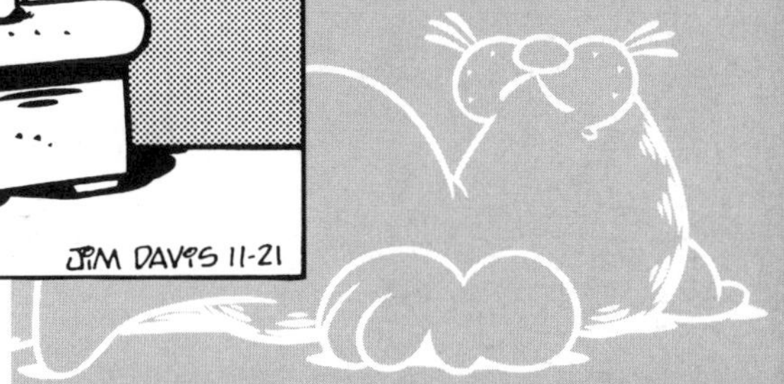

THE WARNING SIGNS OF BOREDOM

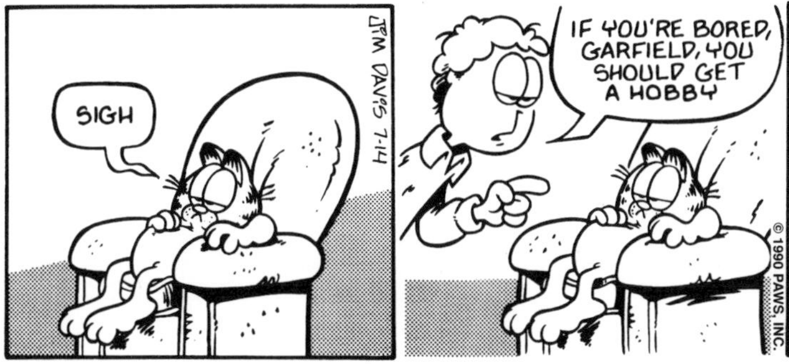
SIGH
JIM DAVIS 7-14
IF YOU'RE BORED, GARFIELD, YOU SHOULD GET A HOBBY
© 1990 PAWS, INC.
BEING BORED IS MY HOBBY

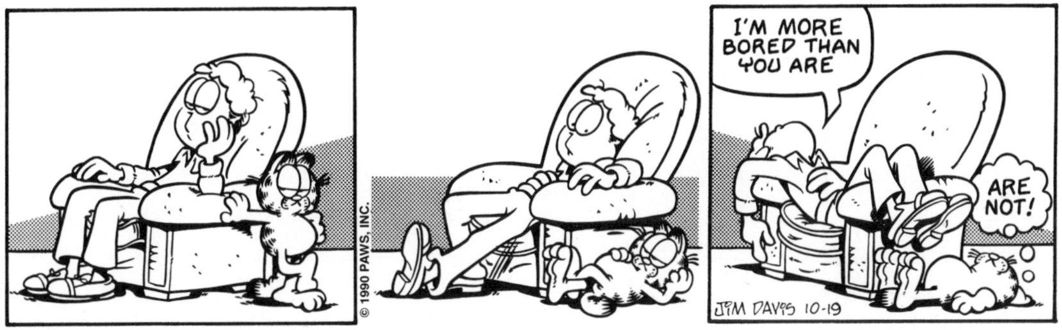
© 1990 PAWS, INC.
I'M MORE BORED THAN YOU ARE
ARE NOT!
JIM DAVIS 10-19

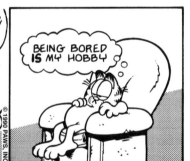

Garfield, Boredom Expert, offers these tips on how to tell if you're getting really bored:

You paint little faces on your nails and pretend each finger is a person.

You spend hours watching bread grow moldy.

You braid your eyebrows.

You watch a three-hour documentary on sewage treatment.

You start playing the spoons.

You wonder if you're really bored.

Heavy "awww . . ." factor.

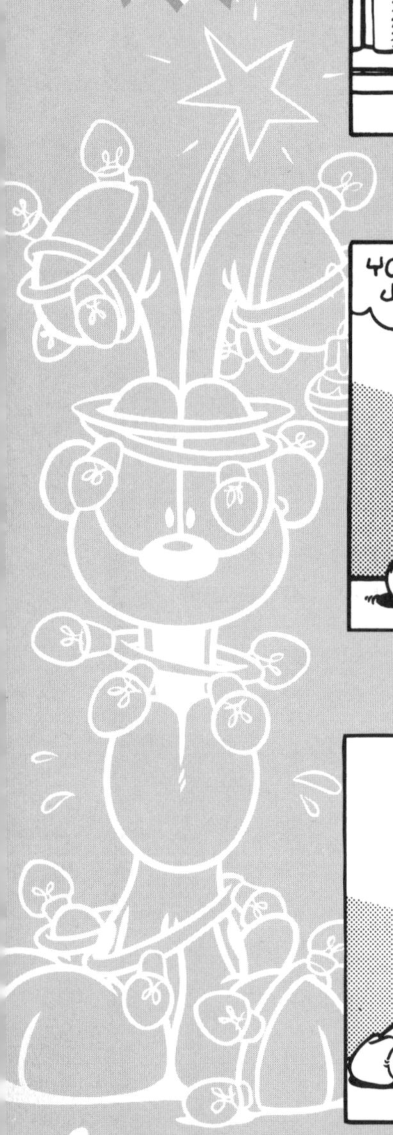

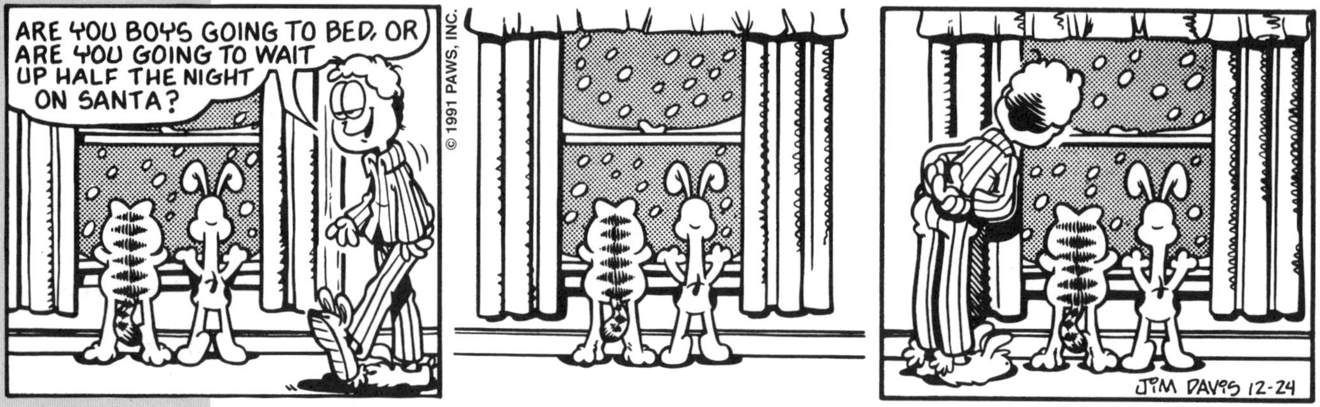
ARE YOU BOYS GOING TO BED, OR ARE YOU GOING TO WAIT UP HALF THE NIGHT ON SANTA?
© 1991 PAWS, INC.
JIM DAVIS 12-24

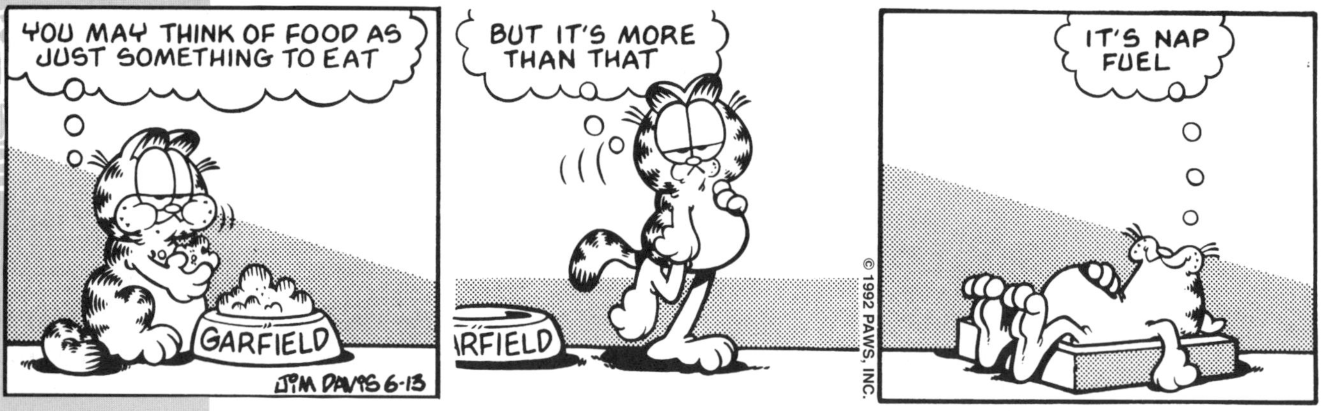
YOU MAY THINK OF FOOD AS JUST SOMETHING TO EAT
GARFIELD
JIM DAVIS 6-13
BUT IT'S MORE THAN THAT
ARFIELD
IT'S NAP FUEL
© 1992 PAWS, INC.

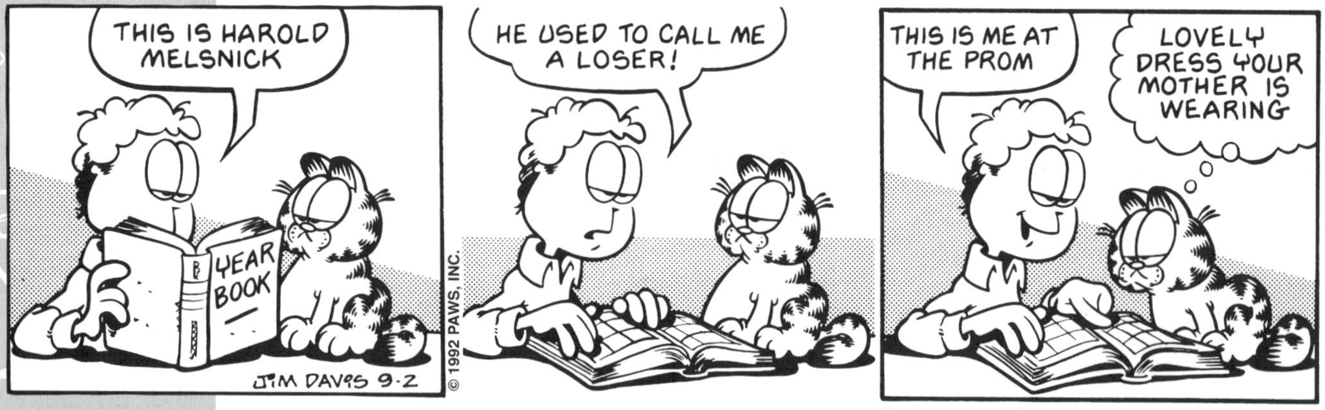
THIS IS HAROLD MELSNICK
YEAR BOOK
JIM DAVIS 9-2
© 1992 PAWS, INC.
HE USED TO CALL ME A LOSER!
THIS IS ME AT THE PROM
LOVELY DRESS YOUR MOTHER IS WEARING

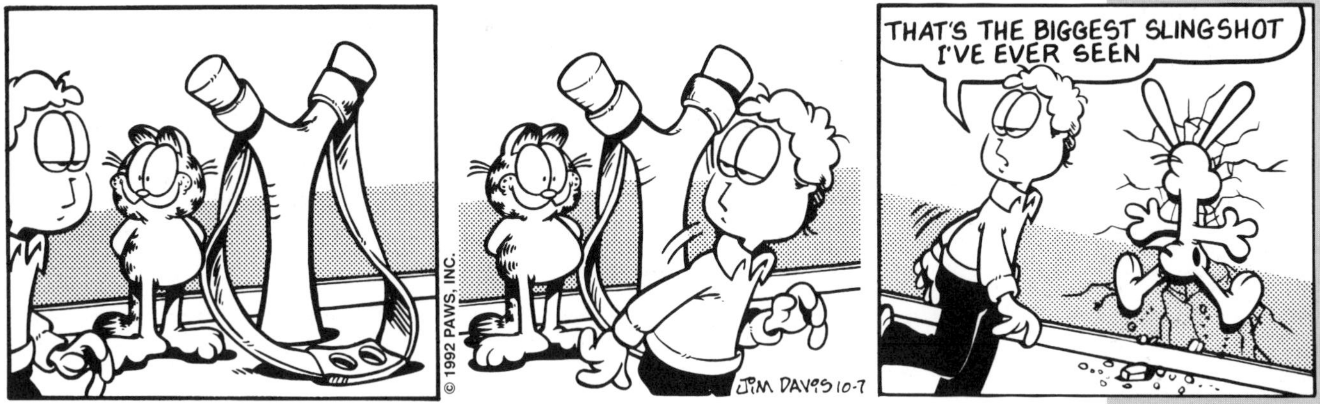
© 1992 PAWS, INC.
JIM DAVIS 10-7
THAT'S THE BIGGEST SLINGSHOT I'VE EVER SEEN

Sometimes I laugh as I draw. This one did me in.

CADDY CAT

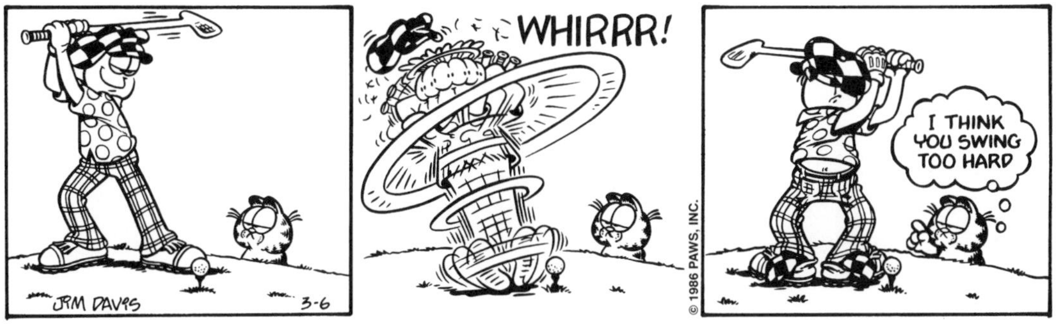
JIM DAVIS
3-6
WHIRRR!
© 1986 PAWS, INC.
I THINK YOU SWING TOO HARD

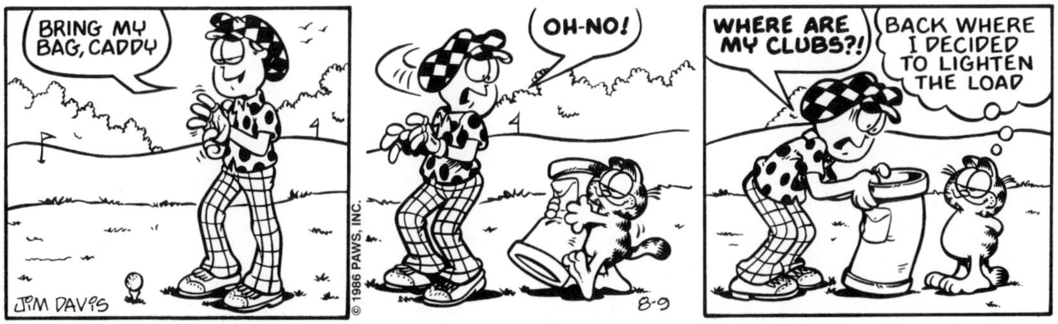
BRING MY BAG, CADDY
JIM DAVIS
OH-NO!
© 1986 PAWS, INC.
8-9
WHERE ARE MY CLUBS?!
BACK WHERE I DECIDED TO LIGHTEN THE LOAD

Every now and then Jon takes to the links and takes Garfield with him. Naturally, when it comes to exercise, Garfield is not a good sport. He doesn't know much about golf; he just knows he doesn't like it. The links he likes are made of sausage; the birdies he craves have wings. So it's no surprise when Garfield's antics disrupt Jon's golf game. In fact, it's just par for the course.

A gag you could only pull off in a comic strip.

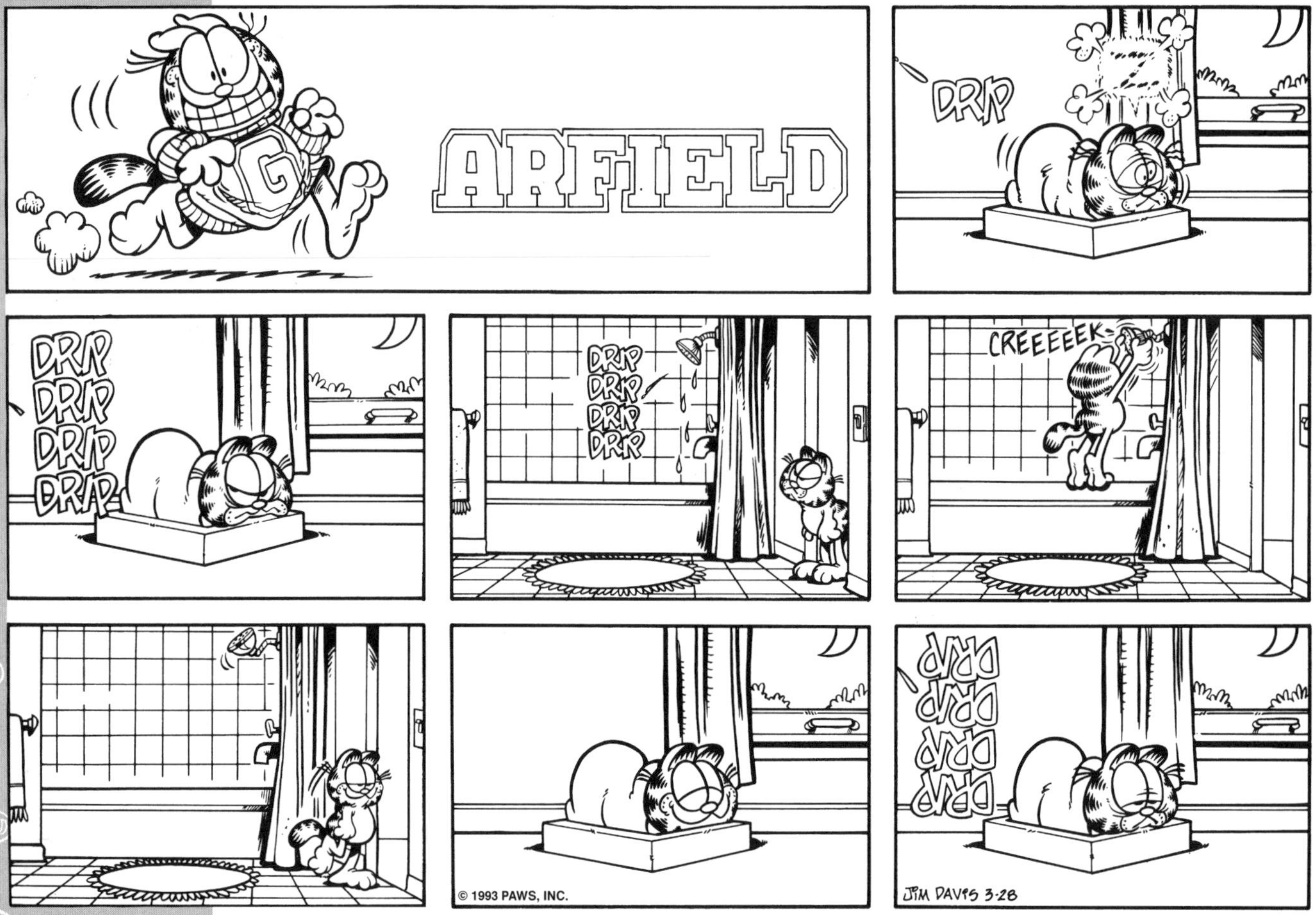
GARFIELD
DRIP
DRIP DRIP DRIP DRIP
DRIP DRIP DRIP DRIP
CREEEEEK
© 1993 PAWS, INC.
DRIP DRIP DRIP DRIP
JIM DAVIS 3-28

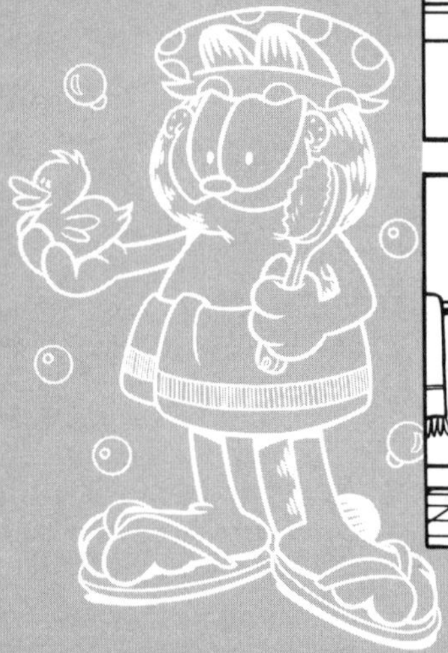

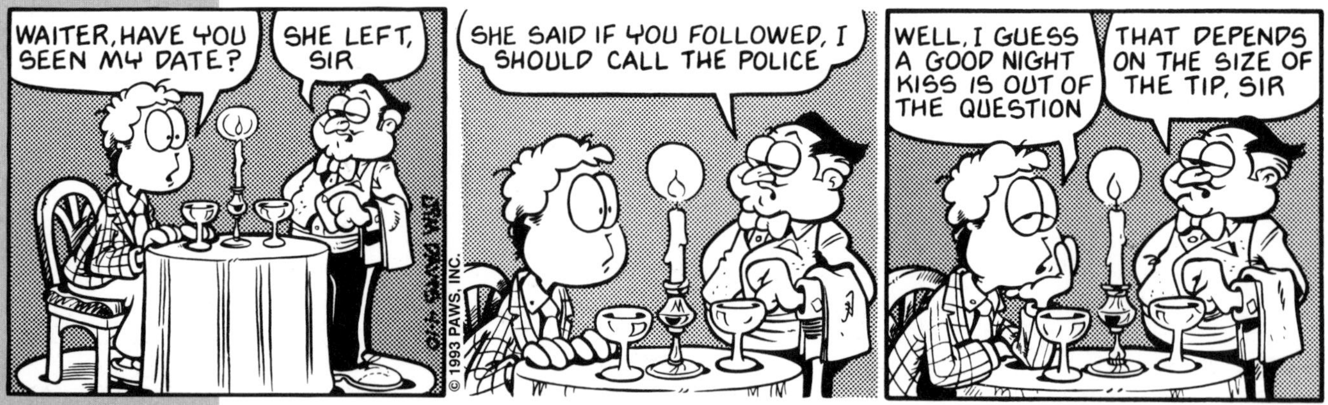
WAITER, HAVE YOU SEEN MY DATE?
SHE LEFT, SIR
JIM DAVIS 4-10
© 1993 PAWS, INC.
SHE SAID IF YOU FOLLOWED, I SHOULD CALL THE POLICE
WELL, I GUESS A GOOD NIGHT KISS IS OUT OF THE QUESTION
THAT DEPENDS ON THE SIZE OF THE TIP, SIR

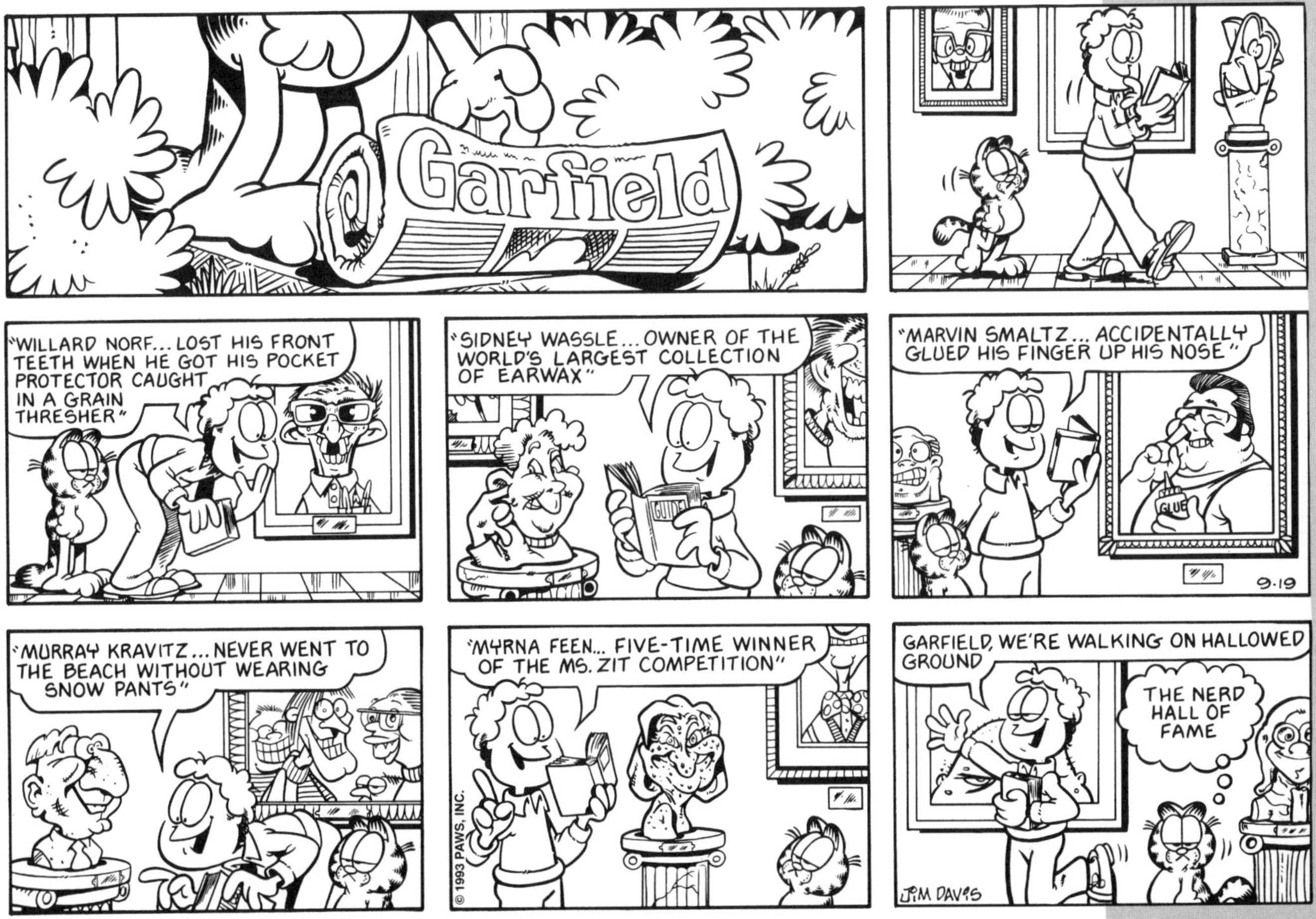
Garfield
"WILLARD NORF... LOST HIS FRONT TEETH WHEN HE GOT HIS POCKET PROTECTOR CAUGHT IN A GRAIN THRESHER"
"SIDNEY WASSLE... OWNER OF THE WORLD'S LARGEST COLLECTION OF EARWAX"
GUIDE
"MARVIN SMALTZ... ACCIDENTALLY GLUED HIS FINGER UP HIS NOSE"
GLUE
9-19
"MURRAY KRAVITZ... NEVER WENT TO THE BEACH WITHOUT WEARING SNOW PANTS"
"MYRNA FEEN... FIVE-TIME WINNER OF THE MS. ZIT COMPETITION"
© 1993 PAWS, INC.
GARFIELD, WE'RE WALKING ON HALLOWED GROUND
THE NERD HALL OF FAME
JIM DAVIS

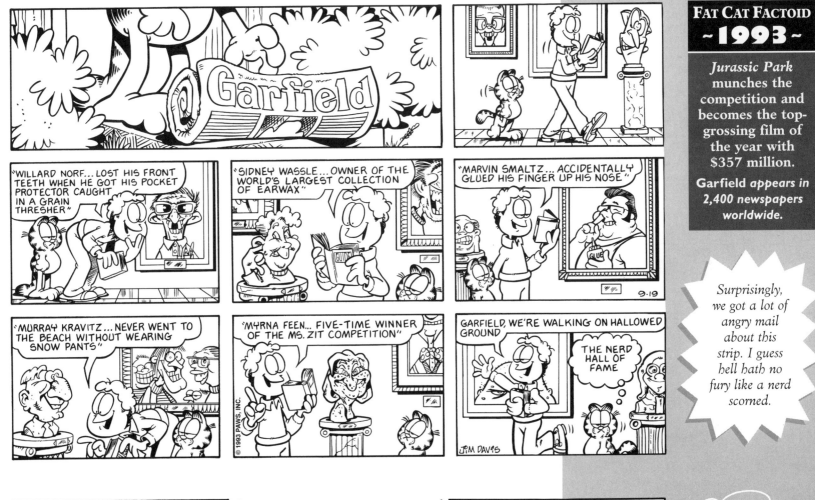

FAT CAT FACTOID
~1993~

Jurassic Park munches the competition and becomes the top-grossing film of the year with $357 million.

Garfield ***appears in 2,400 newspapers worldwide.***

Surprisingly, we got a lot of angry mail about this strip. I guess hell hath no fury like a nerd scorned.

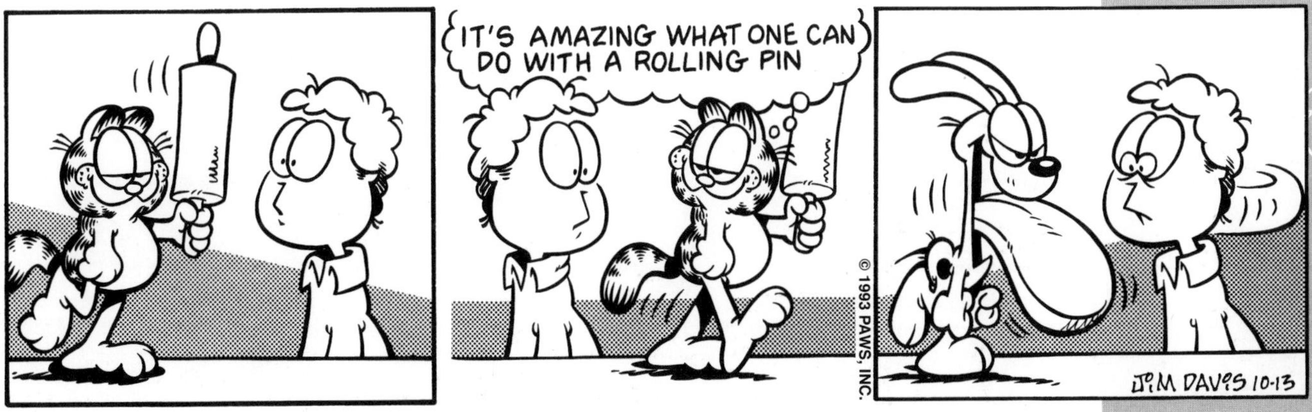
IT'S AMAZING WHAT ONE CAN DO WITH A ROLLING PIN
© 1993 PAWS, INC.
JIM DAVIS 10-13

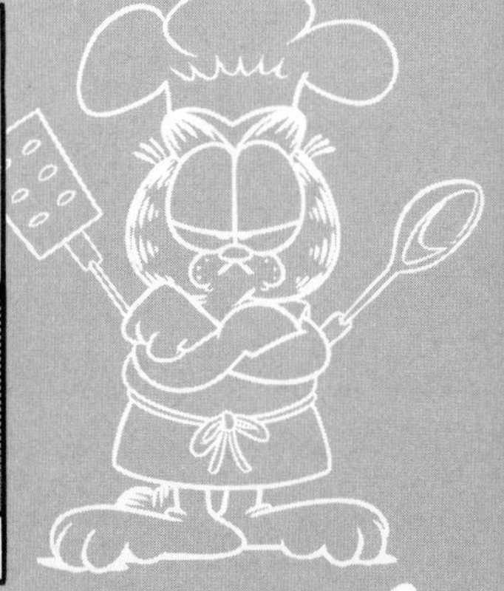

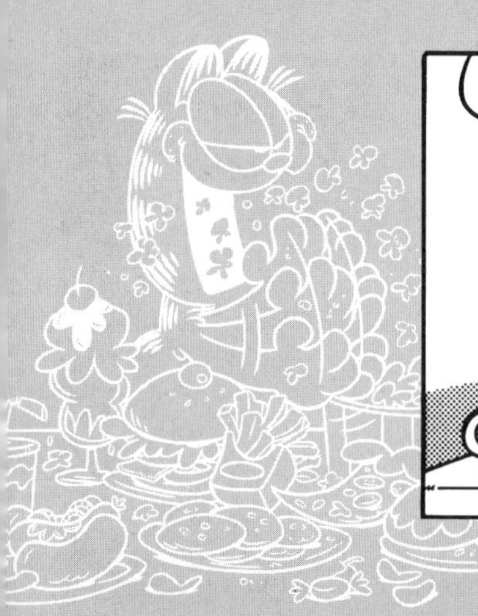

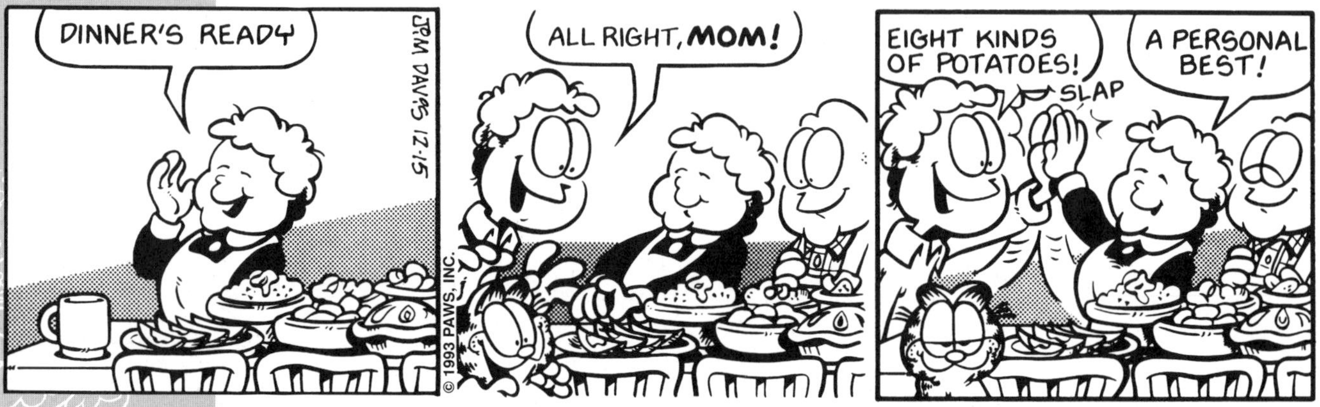
DINNER'S READY
JIM DAVIS 12-15
ALL RIGHT, **MOM!**
© 1993 PAWS, INC.
EIGHT KINDS OF POTATOES!
SLAP
A PERSONAL BEST!

GARFIELD'S FAVORITE FORMS OF EXERCISE

Punting Odie

Leg-of-lamb lifts

Dunking doughnuts

Taffy pulls

Channel surfing

Yawning

Alarm-clock smashing

Chewing

Spider whacking

A brisk nap

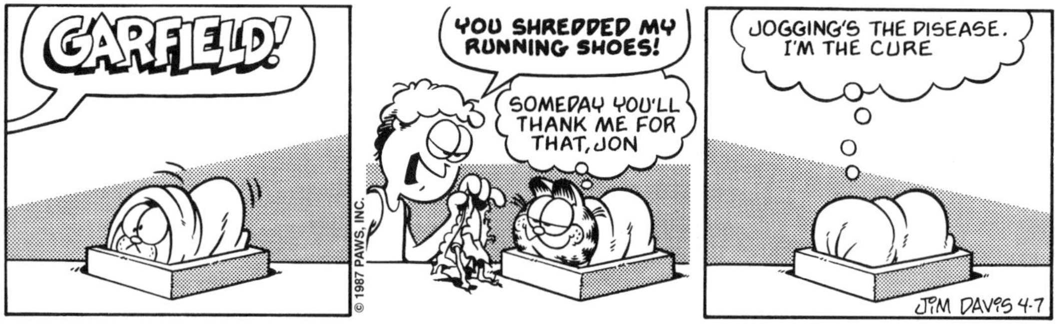
GARFIELD!
YOU SHREDDED MY RUNNING SHOES!
SOMEDAY YOU'LL THANK ME FOR THAT, JON
© 1987 PAWS, INC.
JOGGING'S THE DISEASE. I'M THE CURE
JIM DAVIS 4-7

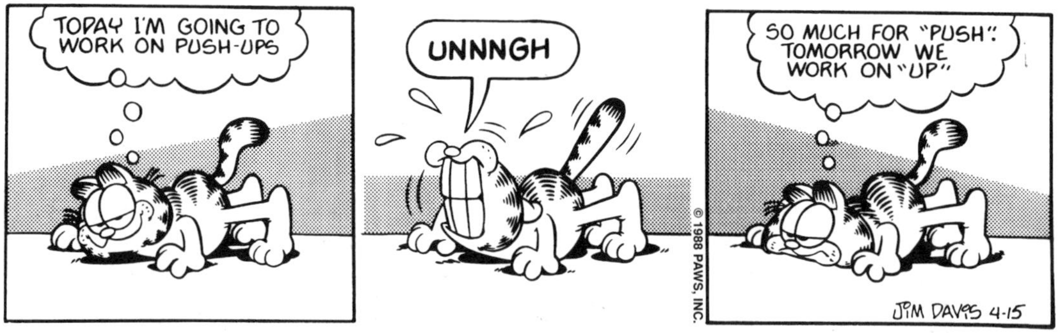
TODAY I'M GOING TO WORK ON PUSH-UPS
UNNNGH
© 1988 PAWS, INC.
SO MUCH FOR "PUSH". TOMORROW WE WORK ON "UP"
JIM DAVIS 4-15

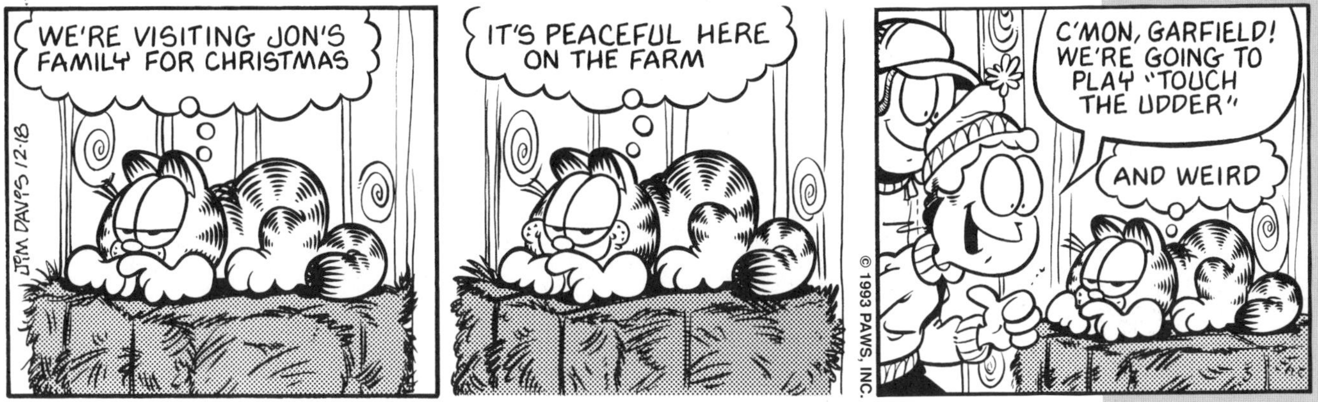
JIM DAVIS 12-18
WE'RE VISITING JON'S FAMILY FOR CHRISTMAS
IT'S PEACEFUL HERE ON THE FARM
© 1993 PAWS, INC.
C'MON, GARFIELD! WE'RE GOING TO PLAY "TOUCH THE UDDER"
AND WEIRD

FAT CAT FACTOID
~1994~

Michael Jackson and Lisa Marie Presley marry in a secret ceremony in the Dominican Republic; they divorce 18 months later.

Jim Davis obtains the rights to Garfield from United Feature and moves the famous feline to his new home, Universal Press Syndicate.

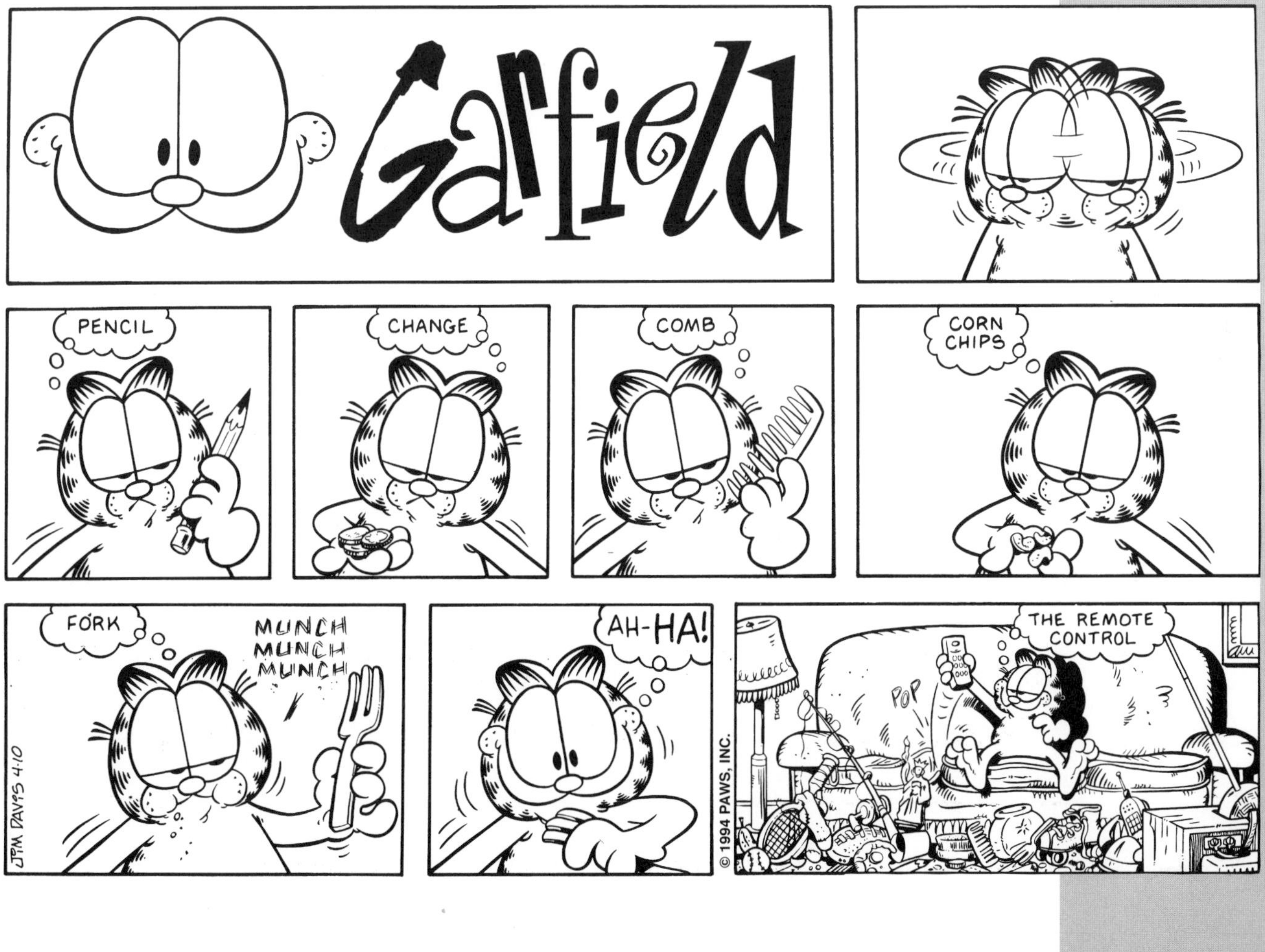
Garfield
PENCIL
CHANGE
COMB
CORN CHIPS
FORK
MUNCH
MUNCH
MUNCH
JIM DAVIS 4-10
AH-HA!
© 1994 PAWS, INC.
THE REMOTE CONTROL
POP

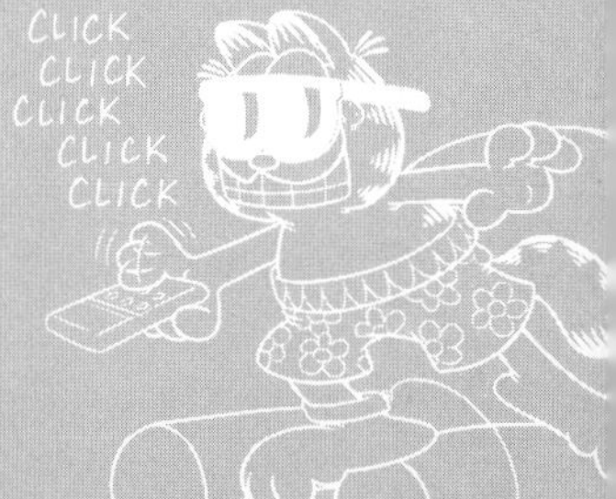
CLICK
CLICK
CLICK
CLICK
CLICK

Free at last! The first strip published with the Paws, Inc., copyright line. In May 1994, we purchased the worldwide rights to Garfield from our old syndicate and moved the strip's distribution to Universal Press Syndicate.

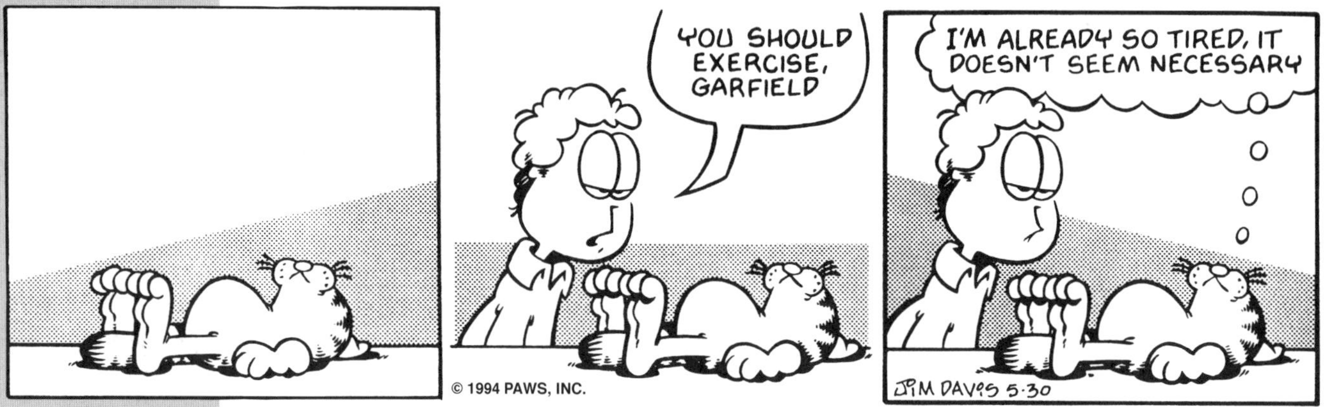
YOU SHOULD EXERCISE, GARFIELD
I'M ALREADY SO TIRED, IT DOESN'T SEEM NECESSARY
© 1994 PAWS, INC.
JIM DAVIS 5-30

THE FRIDGE IS A FAT CAT'S BEST FRIEND

Garfield may love his bed. Garfield may love his teddy bear. Garfield may even admit (in his weaker moments) that he loves Jon and Odie. But nothing warms Garfield's heart like a well-stocked refrigerator. As far as Garfield is concerned, the fridge is always open. So over the years a special bond has formed between Garfield and his refrigerator; to his mind, it's the one major appliance that deserves a hug. Now if only Jon would move it closer to the TV . . .

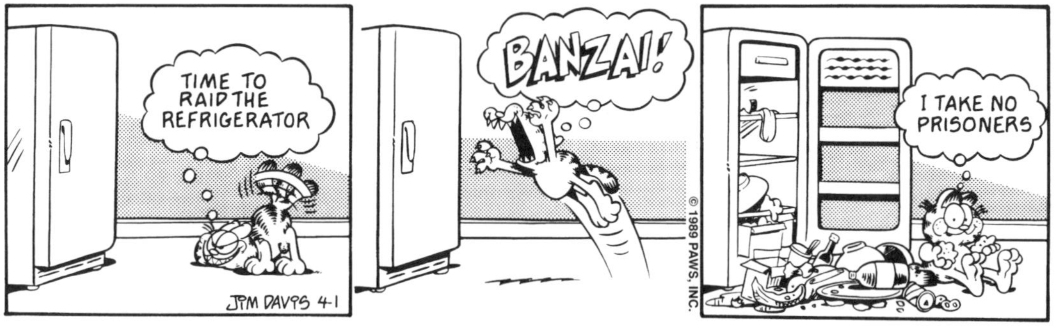
TIME TO RAID THE REFRIGERATOR
JIM DAVIS 4-1
BANZAI!
I TAKE NO PRISONERS
© 1989 PAWS, INC.

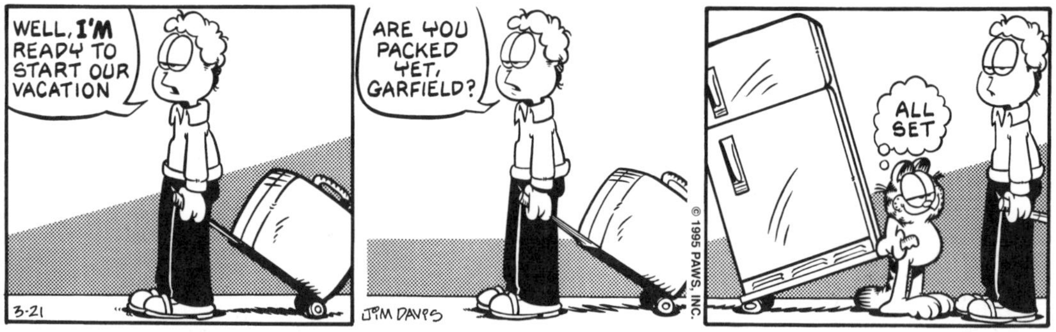
WELL, I'M READY TO START OUR VACATION
3-21
ARE YOU PACKED YET, GARFIELD?
JIM DAVIS
ALL SET
© 1995 PAWS, INC.

I BOUGHT YOU A SEAFOOD LUNCH, GARFIELD
THEY HAD A SPECIAL ON UGLY FISH
QUICK, I'M LOSING MY APPETITE
© 1994 PAWS, INC.
JIM DAVIS 6-21

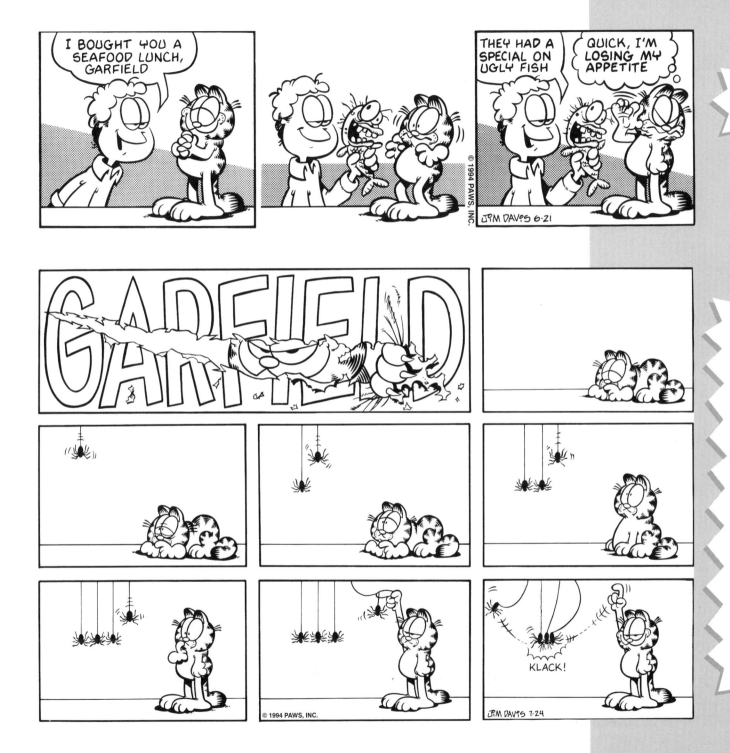

"Ugly" is just plain funny!

GARFIELD
KLACK!
© 1994 PAWS, INC.
JIM DAVIS 7-24

We weren't sure this gag would translate internationally because of the visual reference to a perpetual-motion toy. We showed it to representatives of a foreign licensee who happened to be visiting the studio. Fortunately, they understood the reference, so we kept the strip. There's nothing like instant market research!

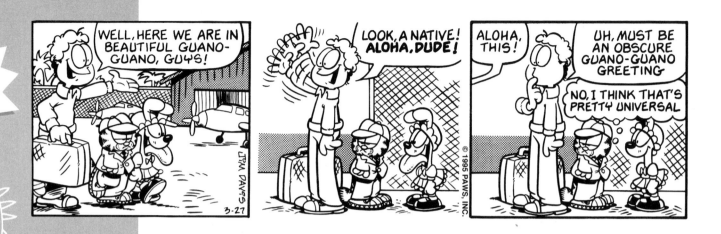

Sometimes I ride the line of good taste.

WELL, HERE WE ARE IN BEAUTIFUL GUANO-GUANO, GUYS!
JIM DAVIS 3-27
LOOK, A NATIVE! ALOHA, DUDE!
© 1995 PAWS, INC.
ALOHA, THIS!
UH, MUST BE AN OBSCURE GUANO-GUANO GREETING
NO, I THINK THAT'S PRETTY UNIVERSAL

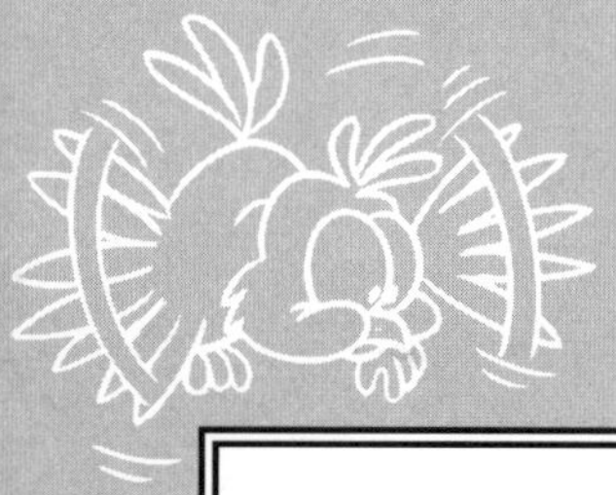

THIS CAT IS FOR THE BIRDS

Garfield has always loved birds . . . preferably on wheat toast . . . with a little mustard. He's spent countless comic strips trying to get his paws on these fine feathered snacks. One of his standard tricks is to set a trap in the backyard birdbath. But the birds are aware of Garfield's appetite for things avian, so they usually manage to escape. Which doesn't really bother Garfield. After all, if he can't catch a lark, he can always capture some lasagna.

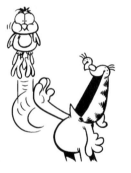

I SHALL NOW TOSS THIS BIRD INTO THE AIR AND CATCH IT IN MY MOUTH!
© 1997 PAWS, INC.
I AM SOOO STUPID
JIM DAVIS 1-21

© 1991 PAWS, INC.
?
JIM DAVIS 11-13

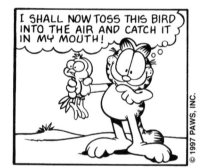

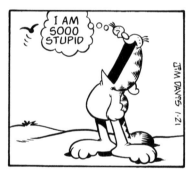

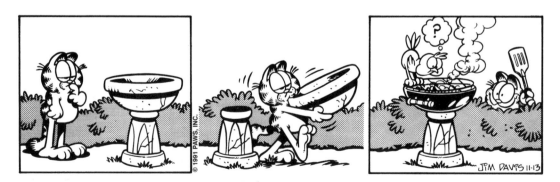

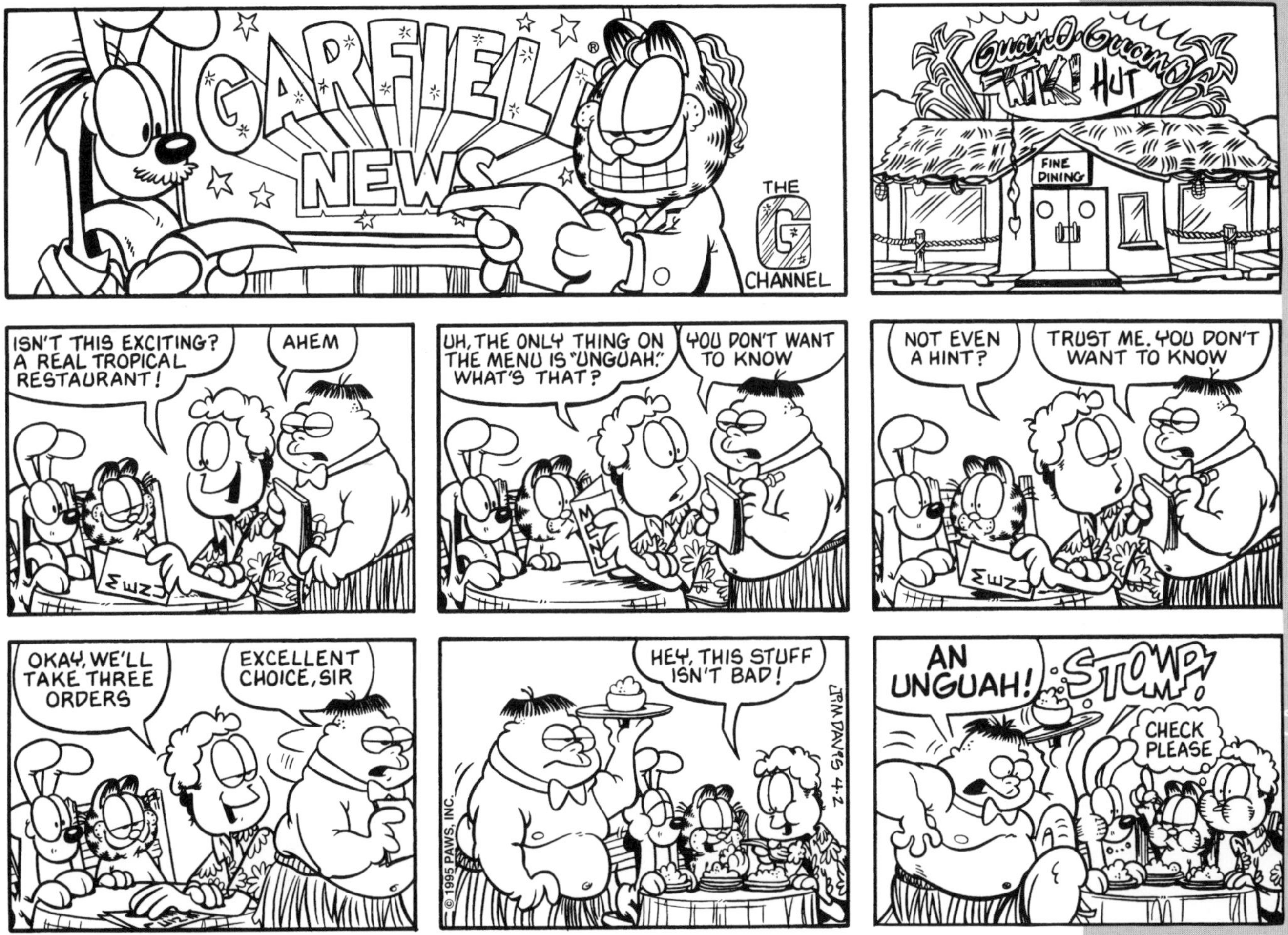
GARFIELD®
NEWS
THE
G
CHANNEL
TIKI HUT
FINE DINING
ISN'T THIS EXCITING? A REAL TROPICAL RESTAURANT!
AHEM
UH, THE ONLY THING ON THE MENU IS "UNGUAH." WHAT'S THAT?
YOU DON'T WANT TO KNOW
NOT EVEN A HINT?
TRUST ME. YOU DON'T WANT TO KNOW
OKAY, WE'LL TAKE THREE ORDERS
EXCELLENT CHOICE, SIR
HEY, THIS STUFF ISN'T BAD!
JIM DAVIS 4-2
© 1995 PAWS, INC.
AN UNGUAH!
STOMP!
CHECK PLEASE

This gag works pretty hard, but I've eaten at too many of these restaurants.

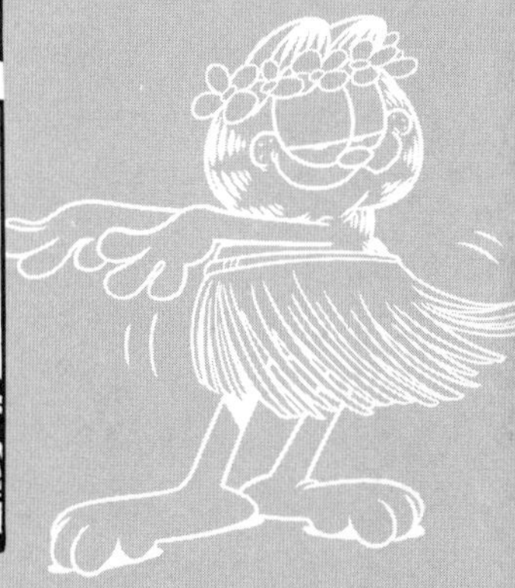

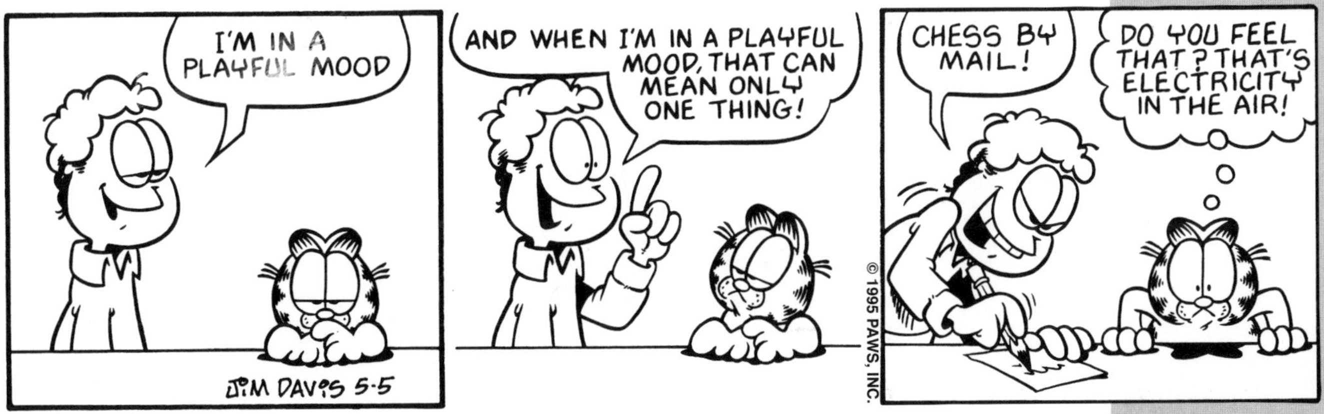
I'M IN A PLAYFUL MOOD
JIM DAVIS 5-5
AND WHEN I'M IN A PLAYFUL MOOD, THAT CAN MEAN ONLY ONE THING!
© 1995 PAWS, INC.
CHESS BY MAIL!
DO YOU FEEL THAT? THAT'S ELECTRICITY IN THE AIR!

One of my favorite put-downs.

Fat Cat Factoid
~1995~

To the dismay of millions of fans, Bill Watterson ends his comic strip, *Calvin and Hobbes*, and Gary Larson retires his single-panel comic, *The Far Side*.

***Garfield* becomes the first comic strip in history to appear in over 2,500 newspapers worldwide!**

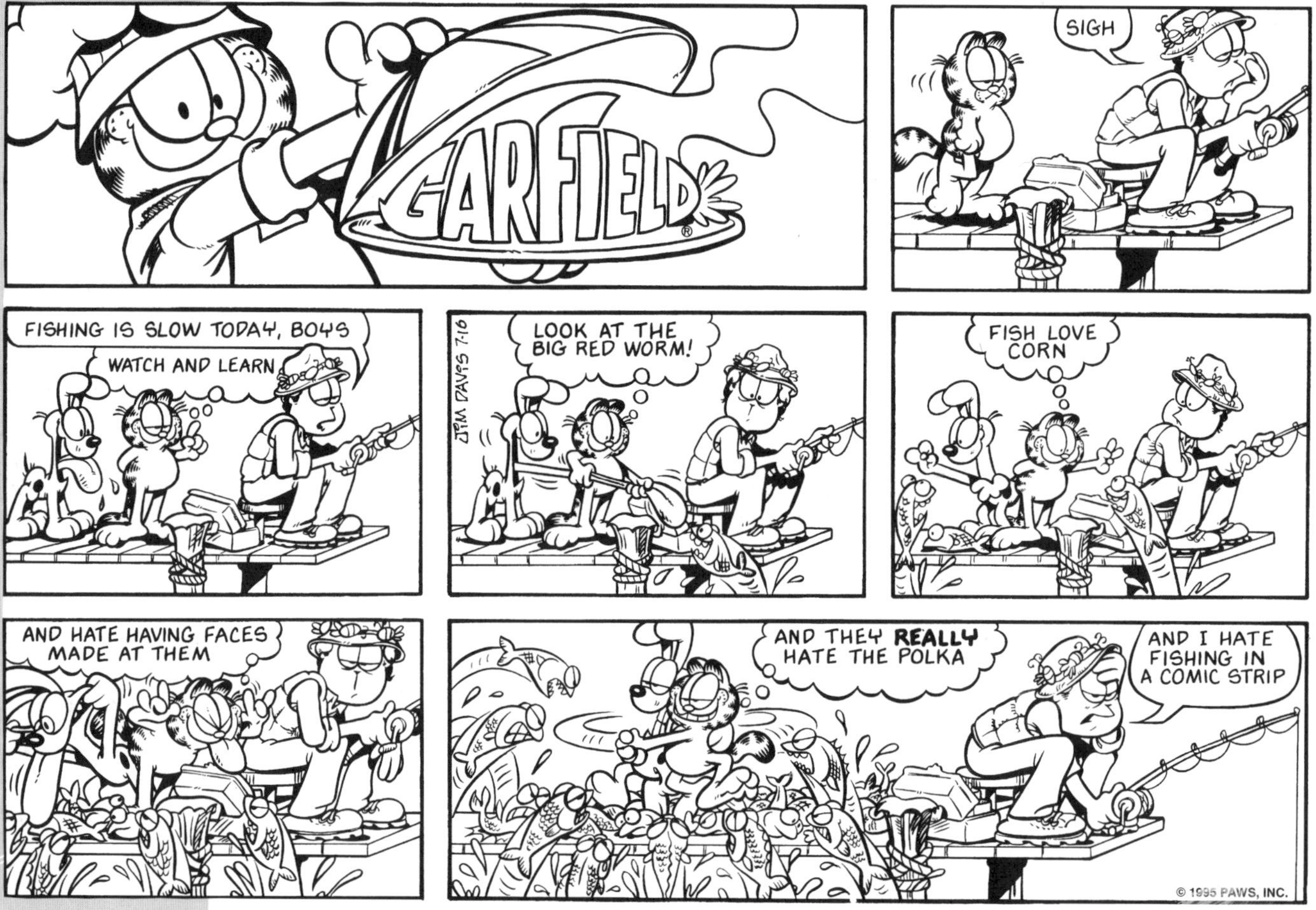
GARFIELD
SIGH
FISHING IS SLOW TODAY, BOYS
WATCH AND LEARN
JIM DAVIS 7-16
LOOK AT THE BIG RED WORM!
FISH LOVE CORN
AND HATE HAVING FACES MADE AT THEM
AND THEY REALLY HATE THE POLKA
AND I HATE FISHING IN A COMIC STRIP
© 1995 PAWS, INC.

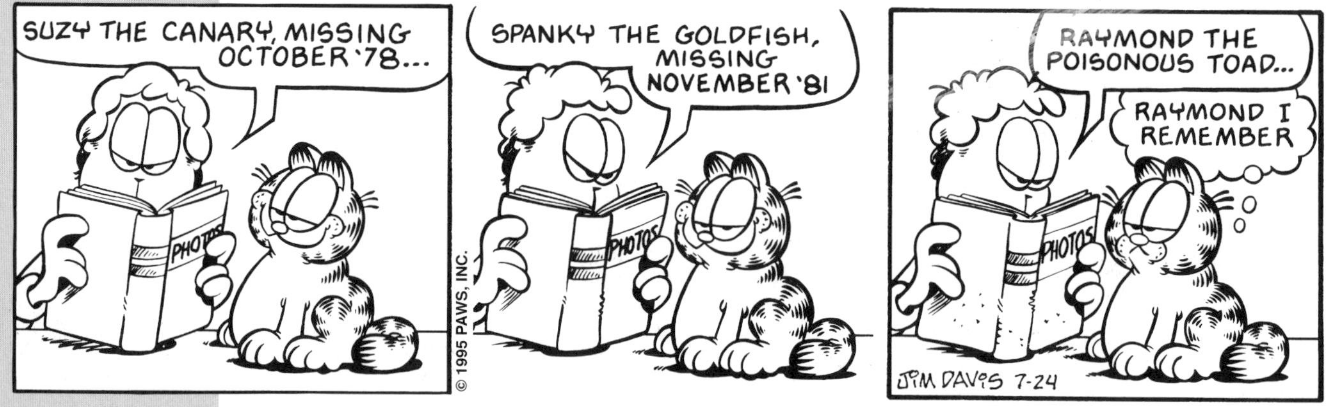
SUZY THE CANARY, MISSING OCTOBER '78...
PHOTOS
© 1995 PAWS, INC.
SPANKY THE GOLDFISH, MISSING NOVEMBER '81
PHOTOS
RAYMOND THE POISONOUS TOAD...
RAYMOND I REMEMBER
PHOTOS
JIM DAVIS 7-24

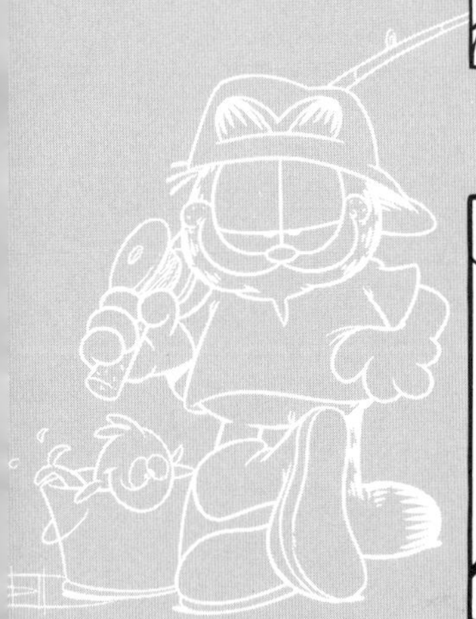

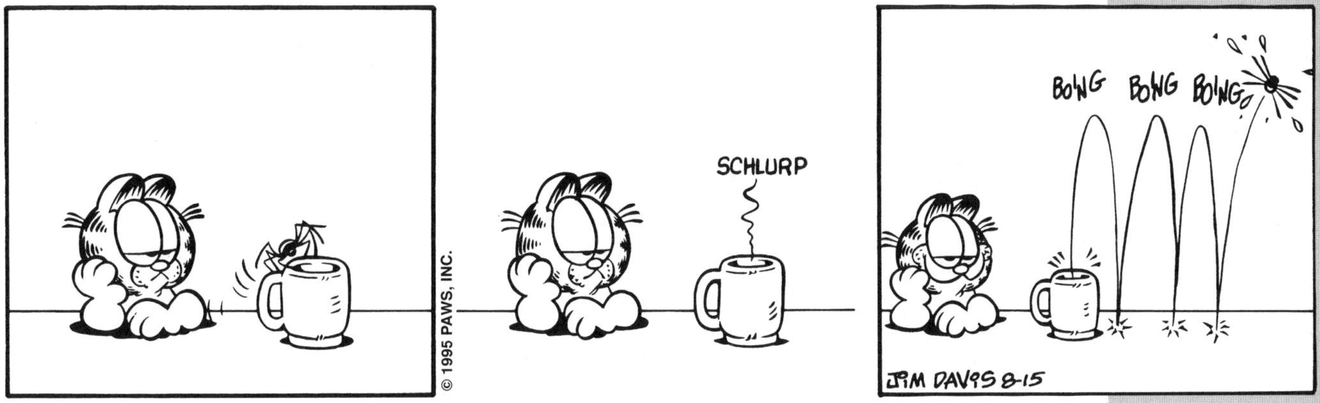
© 1995 PAWS, INC.
SCHLURP
BOING BOING BOING
JIM DAVIS 8-15

A spider gag and a coffee gag in one strip!

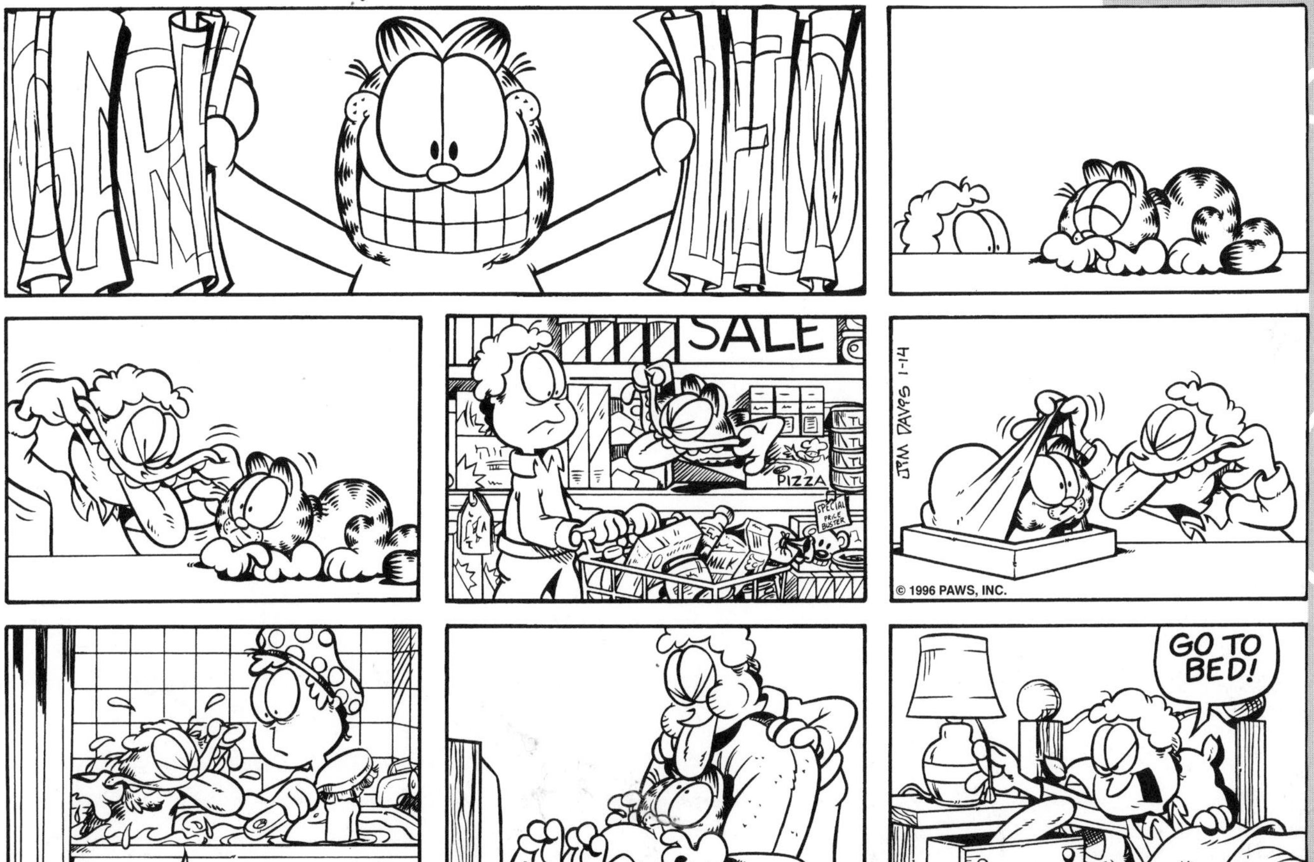
SALE
PIZZA
SPECIAL PRICE BUSTER
MILK
JIM DAVIS 1-14
© 1996 PAWS, INC.
GO TO BED!

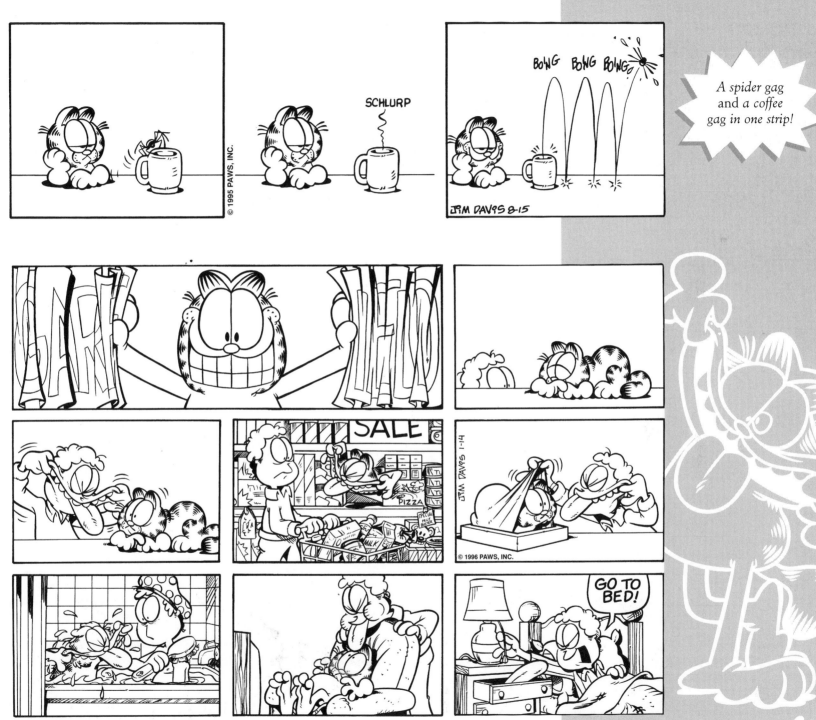

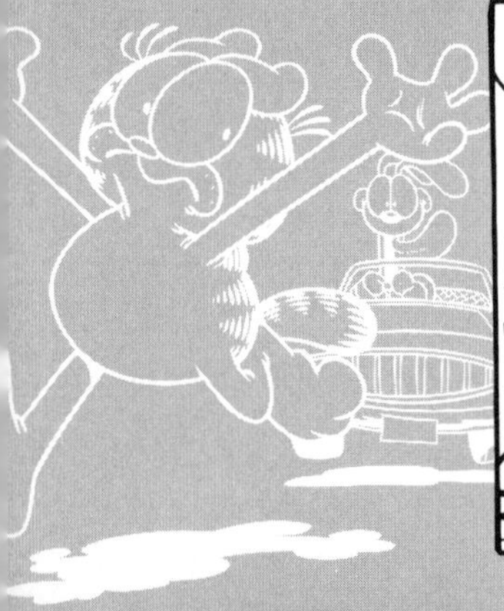

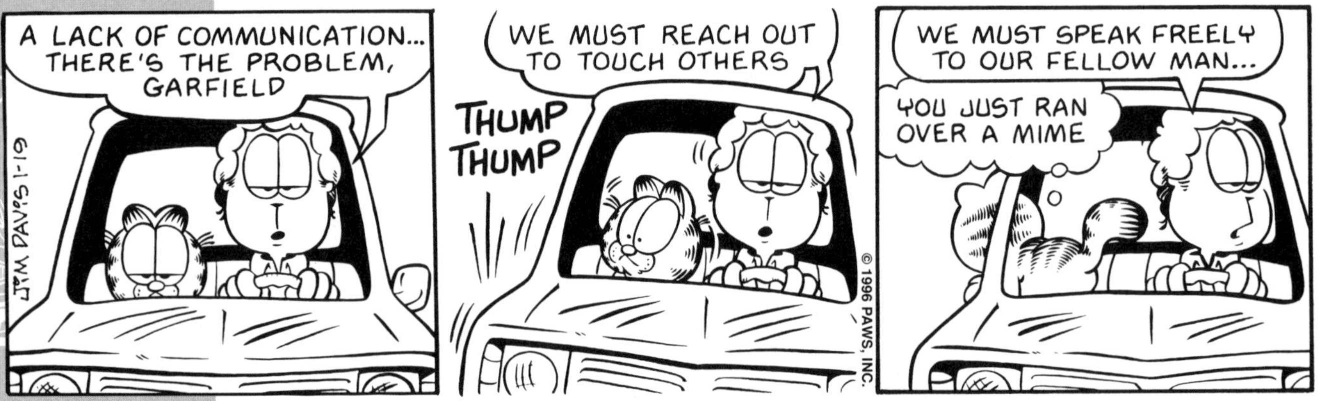

A LACK OF COMMUNICATION... THERE'S THE PROBLEM, GARFIELD
JIM DAVIS 1-19
WE MUST REACH OUT TO TOUCH OTHERS
THUMP THUMP
WE MUST SPEAK FREELY TO OUR FELLOW MAN...
YOU JUST RAN OVER A MIME
© 1996 PAWS, INC.

GARFIELD'S PAST NEW YEAR'S RESOLUTIONS

Get more exercise by dunking more doughnuts

Devise a method to eat while you sleep

Bottle Odie's breath and sell it as paint remover

Find Jon a date within his species

Read more (especially cookbooks)

Try to be more optimistic (not that it'll help)

Invent an automatic refrigerator-door opener

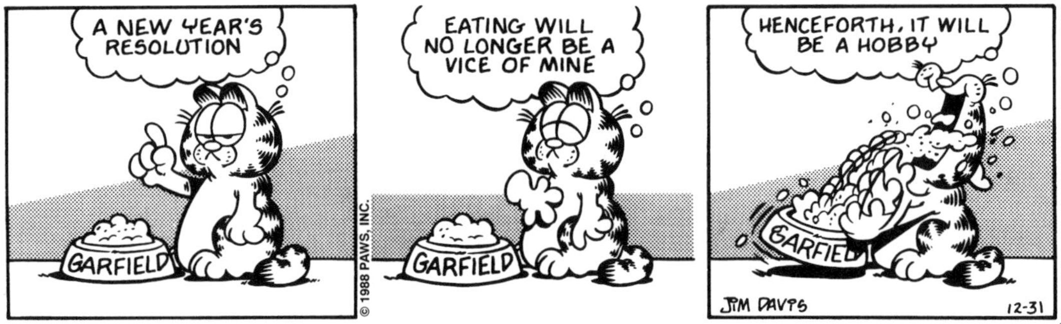

A NEW YEAR'S RESOLUTION
GARFIELD
© 1988 PAWS, INC.
EATING WILL NO LONGER BE A VICE OF MINE
GARFIELD
HENCEFORTH, IT WILL BE A HOBBY
GARFIE
JIM DAVIS
12-31

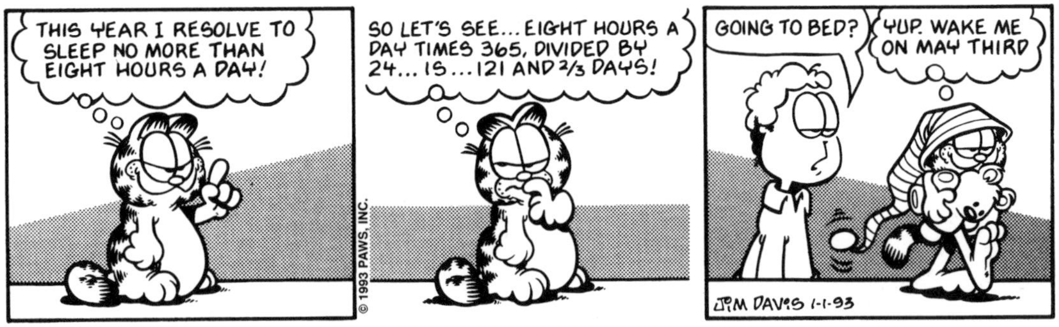

THIS YEAR I RESOLVE TO SLEEP NO MORE THAN EIGHT HOURS A DAY!
© 1993 PAWS, INC.
SO LET'S SEE... EIGHT HOURS A DAY TIMES 365, DIVIDED BY 24... IS... 121 AND 2/3 DAYS!
GOING TO BED?
YUP. WAKE ME ON MAY THIRD
JIM DAVIS 1-1-93

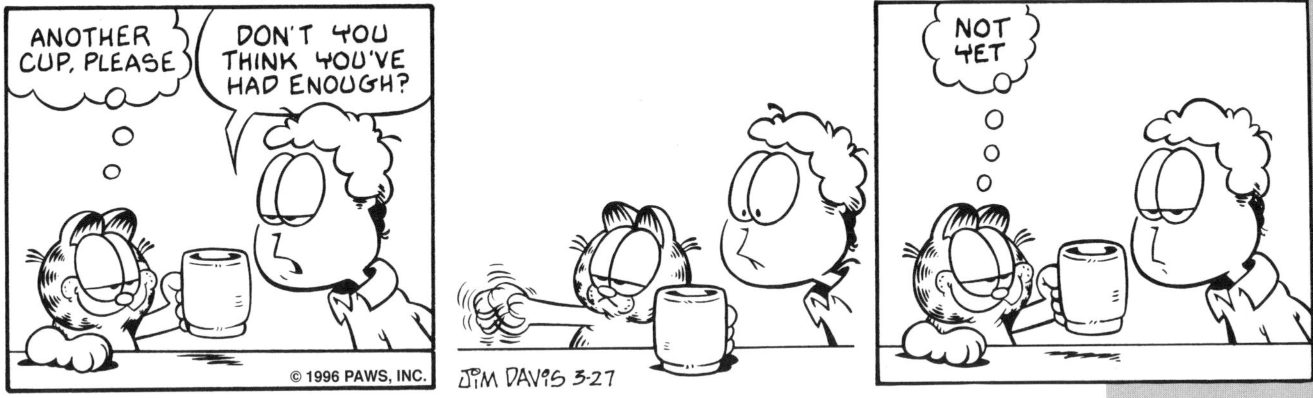
ANOTHER CUP, PLEASE
DON'T YOU THINK YOU'VE HAD ENOUGH?
© 1996 PAWS, INC.
JIM DAVIS 3-27
NOT YET

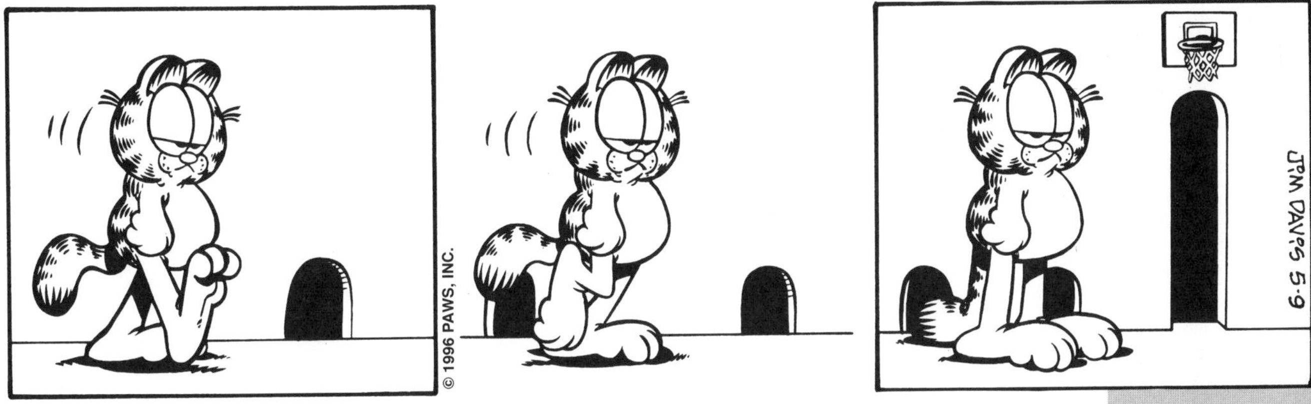
© 1996 PAWS, INC.
JIM DAVIS 5-9

Another sight gag that's great because of its simplicity.

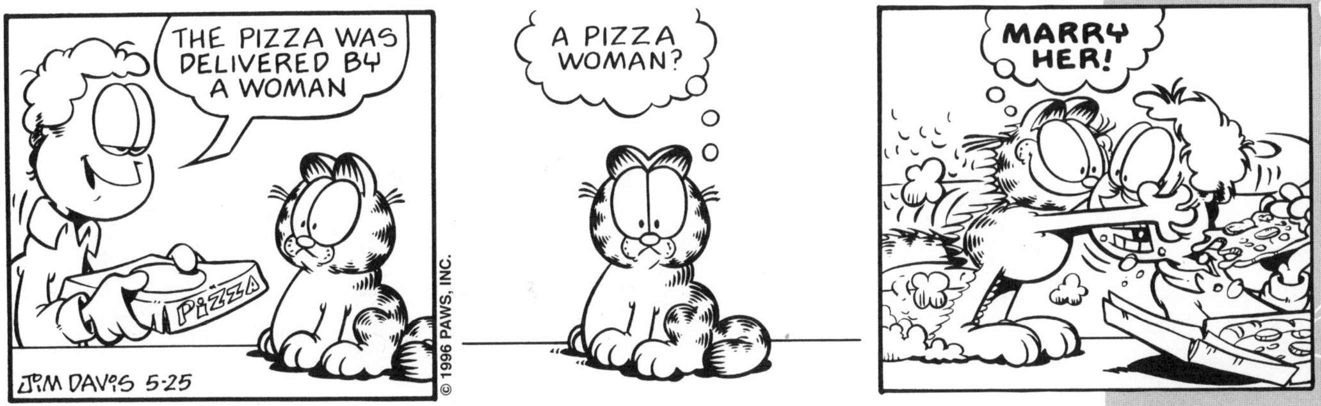
THE PIZZA WAS DELIVERED BY A WOMAN
PIZZA
JIM DAVIS 5-25
© 1996 PAWS, INC.
A PIZZA WOMAN?
MARRY HER!

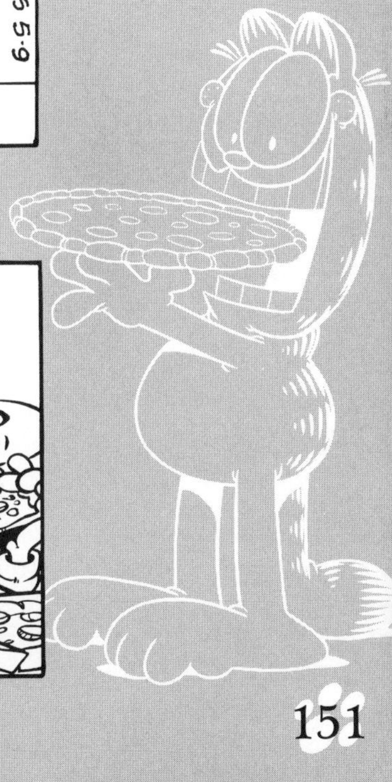

If you read it a second time, it's actually pretty risqué.

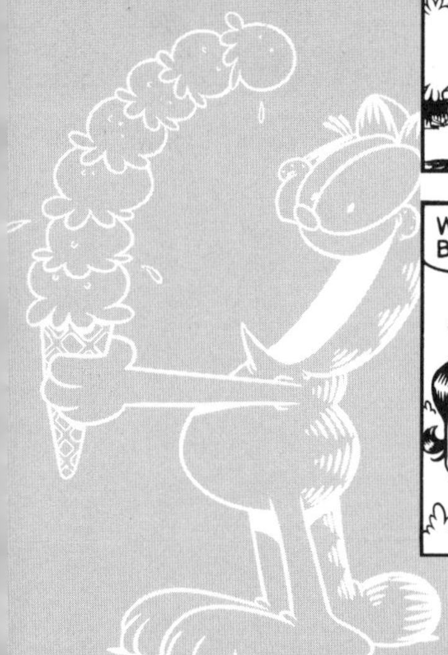

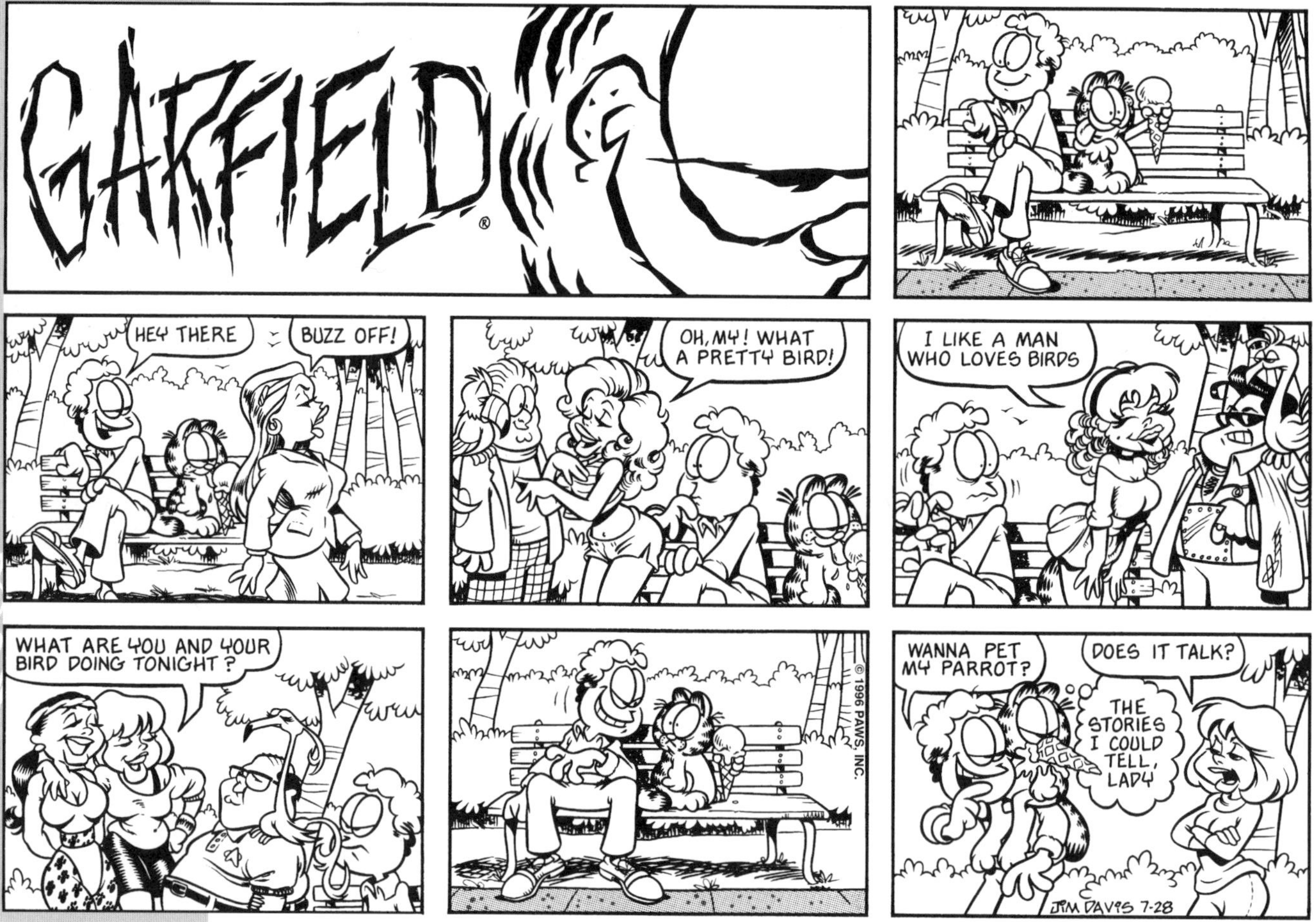
GARFIELD®
HEY THERE
BUZZ OFF!
OH, MY! WHAT A PRETTY BIRD!
I LIKE A MAN WHO LOVES BIRDS
WHAT ARE YOU AND YOUR BIRD DOING TONIGHT ?
© 1996 PAWS, INC.
WANNA PET MY PARROT?
DOES IT TALK?
THE STORIES I COULD TELL, LADY
JIM DAVIS 7-28

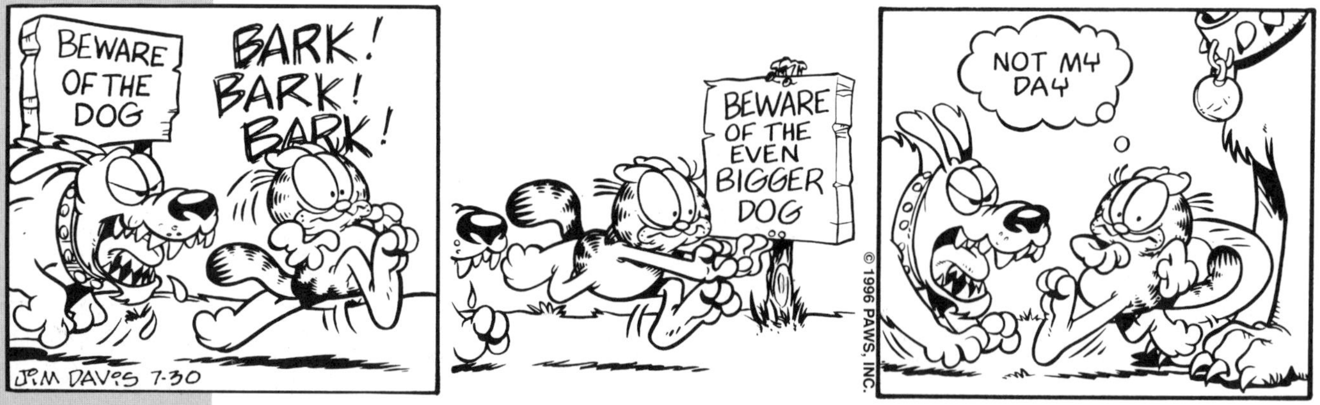
BEWARE OF THE DOG
BARK! BARK! BARK!
JIM DAVIS 7-30
BEWARE OF THE EVEN BIGGER DOG
© 1996 PAWS, INC.
NOT MY DAY

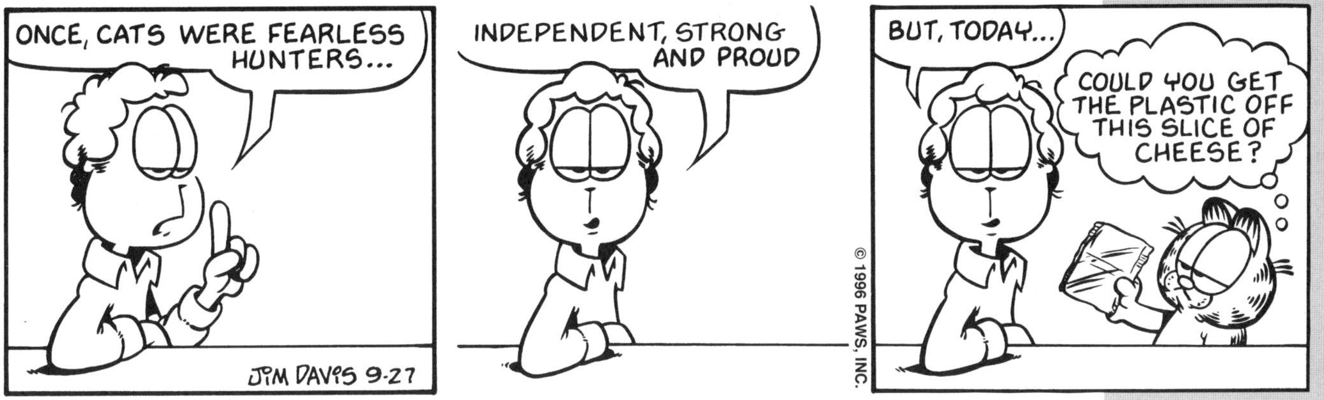
ONCE, CATS WERE FEARLESS HUNTERS...
INDEPENDENT, STRONG AND PROUD
BUT, TODAY...
COULD YOU GET THE PLASTIC OFF THIS SLICE OF CHEESE?
JIM DAVIS 9-27
© 1996 PAWS, INC.

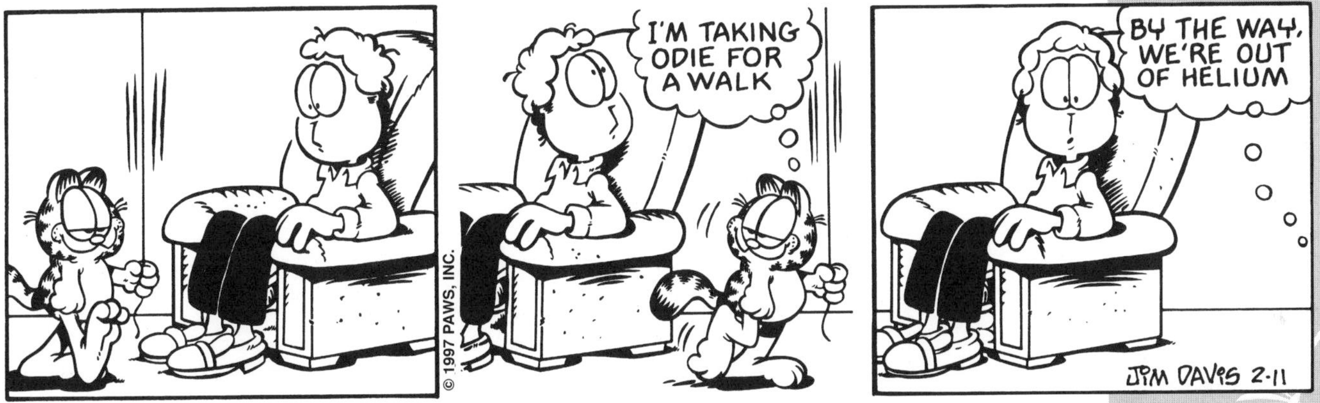
I'M TAKING ODIE FOR A WALK
BY THE WAY, WE'RE OUT OF HELIUM
JIM DAVIS 2-11
© 1997 PAWS, INC.

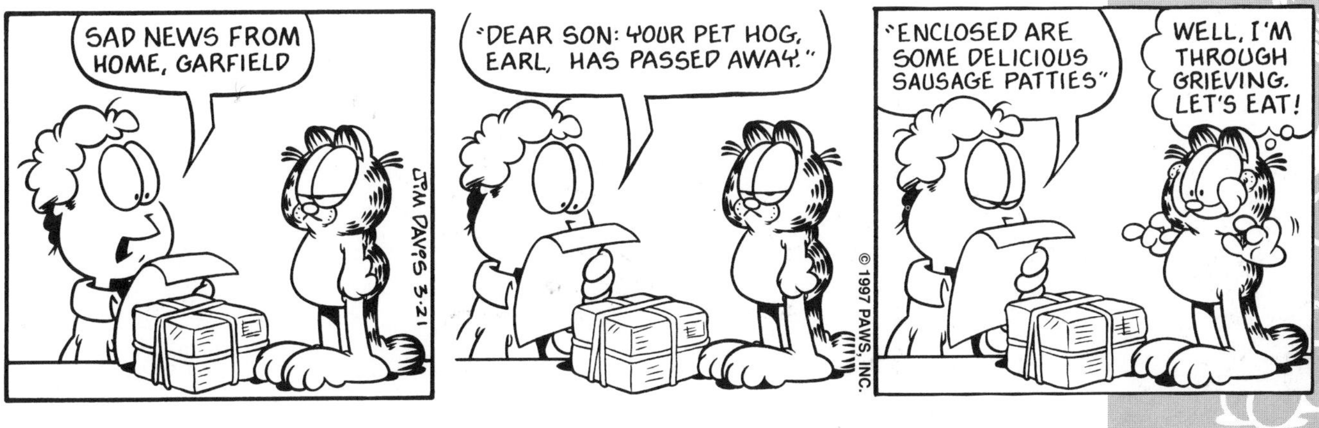
SAD NEWS FROM HOME, GARFIELD
"DEAR SON: YOUR PET HOG, EARL, HAS PASSED AWAY."
"ENCLOSED ARE SOME DELICIOUS SAUSAGE PATTIES"
WELL, I'M THROUGH GRIEVING. LET'S EAT!
JIM DAVIS 3-21
© 1997 PAWS, INC.

FAT CAT FACTOID

~1996~

Overcoming injury to help her team win the gold, plucky gymnast Kerri Strug vaults into America's hearts during the Atlanta Summer Olympics.

Garfield zooms onto the information superhighway with his own Web site: www.garfield.com.

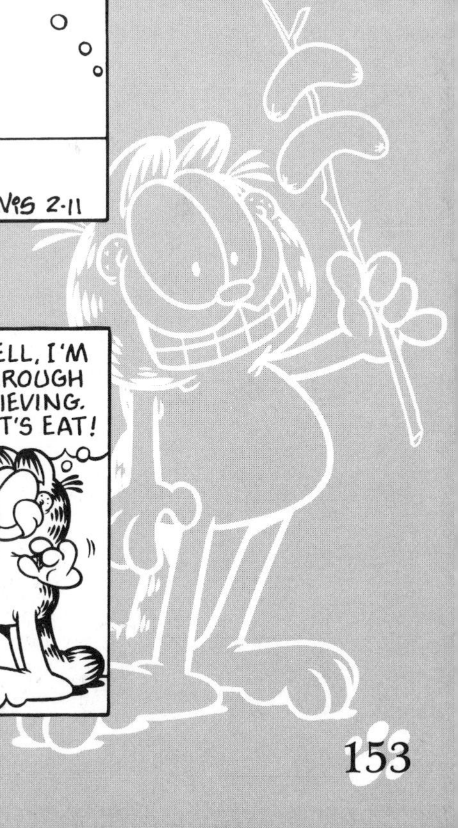

FAT CAT FACTOID
~1997~

Space alien flick *Men in Black* heats up summer movie screens, while NASA's Pathfinder probe sends back live pictures from the surface of Mars.

The Garfield Stuff direct-mail catalog debuts. Shop till you drop!

APRIL FOOLS!

On April 1, 1997, a strange thing happened to the comics page. Several of the strips had a very different look. What was behind this phenomenon? Unbeknownst to their editors, a band of crazy comic strip creators (myself included) had conspired to pull the ol' switcheroo. Cartoonists teamed up and, for a day, drew each other's strip. Mike Peters drew For Better or for Worse, *while Lynn Johnston handled* Mother Goose and Grimm; *Scott Adams did* The Family Circus *and Bill Keane penned* Dilbert; *Jeff MacNelly took over* Beetle Bailey, *while Mort Walker pulled creative duty on* Shoe *. . . and so on. (Kevin Fagan even joined in the fracas by drawing* Drabble *with his left hand!) The result was a lot of funny (and funny-looking!) comic strips and a great April Fool's prank.*

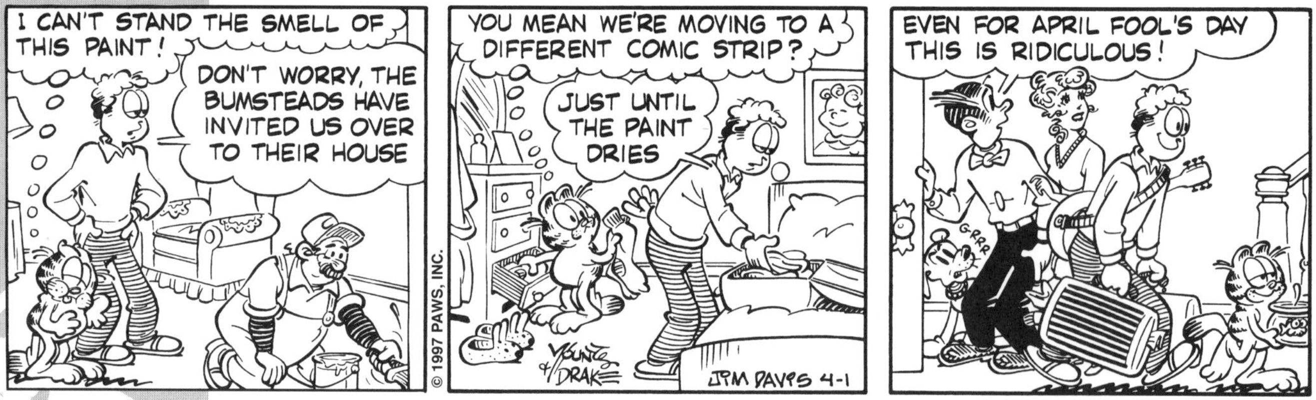
I CAN'T STAND THE SMELL OF THIS PAINT!
DON'T WORRY, THE BUMSTEADS HAVE INVITED US OVER TO THEIR HOUSE
© 1997 PAWS, INC.
YOU MEAN WE'RE MOVING TO A DIFFERENT COMIC STRIP?
JUST UNTIL THE PAINT DRIES
YOUNG & DRAKE
JIM DAVIS 4-1
EVEN FOR APRIL FOOL'S DAY THIS IS RIDICULOUS!
G-RRR

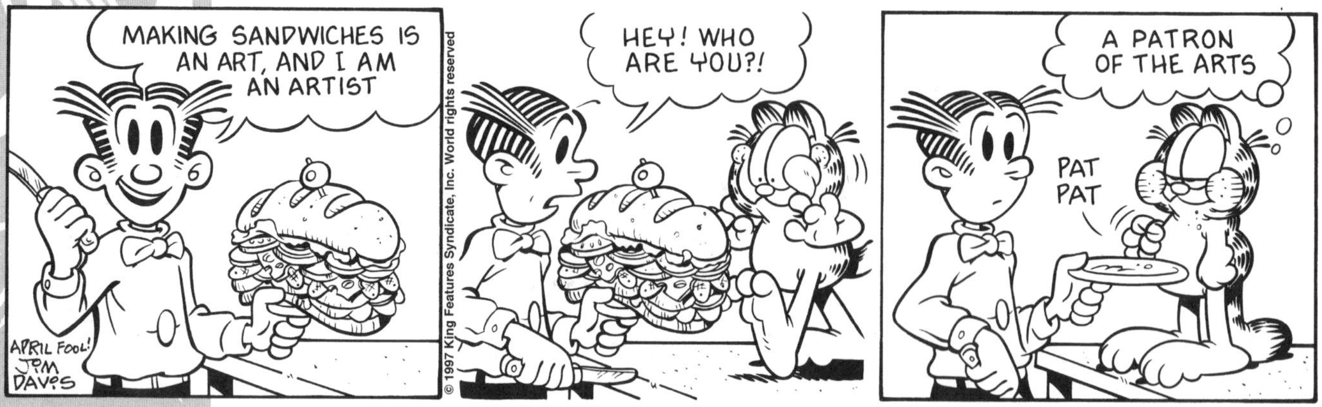
MAKING SANDWICHES IS AN ART, AND I AM AN ARTIST
APRIL FOOL! JIM DAVIS
© 1997 King Features Syndicate, Inc. World rights reserved
HEY! WHO ARE YOU?!
A PATRON OF THE ARTS
PAT PAT

Reprinted by special permission of King Features Syndicate.

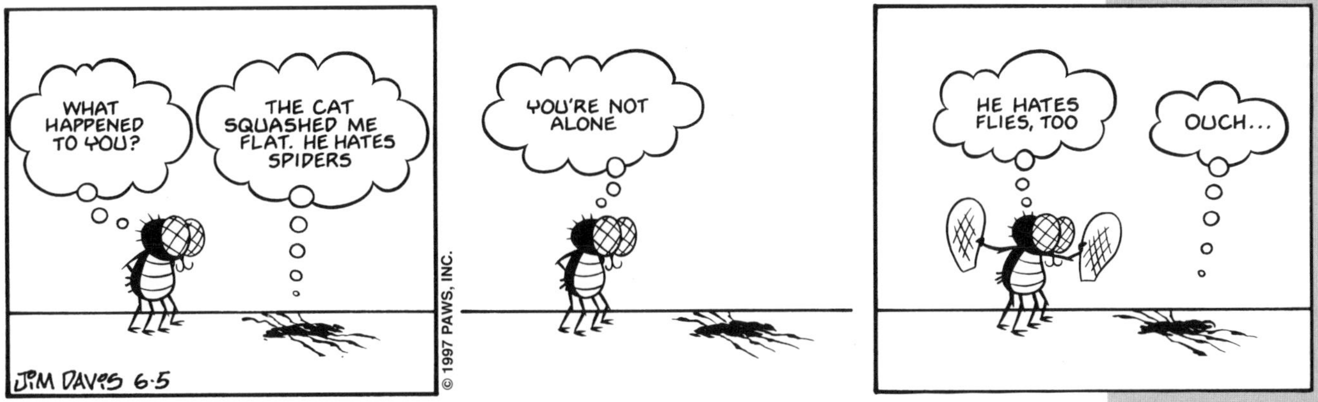
WHAT HAPPENED TO YOU?
THE CAT SQUASHED ME FLAT. HE HATES SPIDERS
YOU'RE NOT ALONE
HE HATES FLIES, TOO
OUCH...
JIM DAVIS 6-5
© 1997 PAWS, INC.

After nearly thirty years, I finally got a bug strip published. This is also one of the few times Garfield doesn't appear in the comic strip.

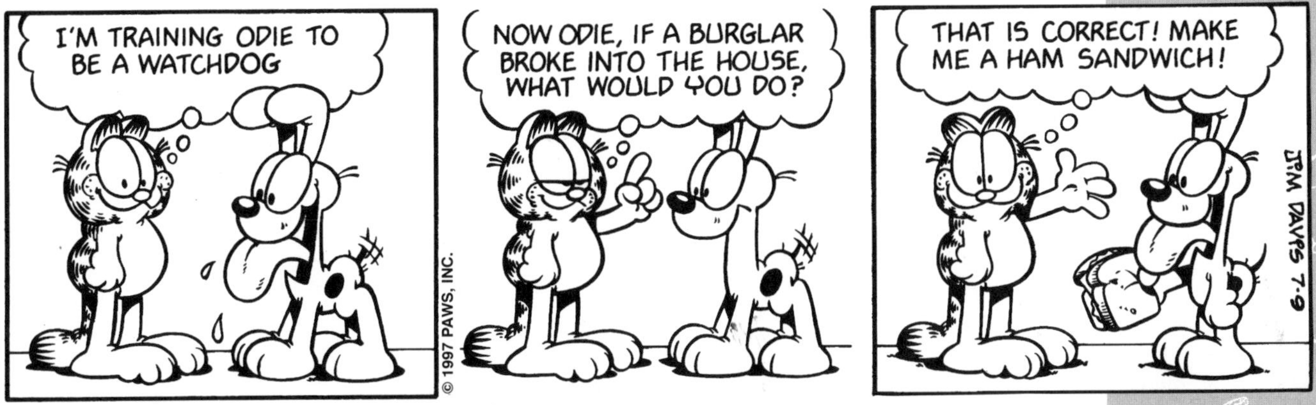
I'M TRAINING ODIE TO BE A WATCHDOG
NOW ODIE, IF A BURGLAR BROKE INTO THE HOUSE, WHAT WOULD YOU DO?
THAT IS CORRECT! MAKE ME A HAM SANDWICH!
JIM DAVIS 7-9
© 1997 PAWS, INC.

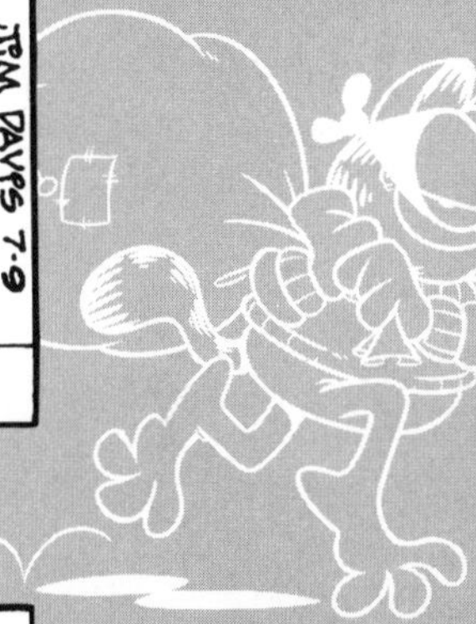

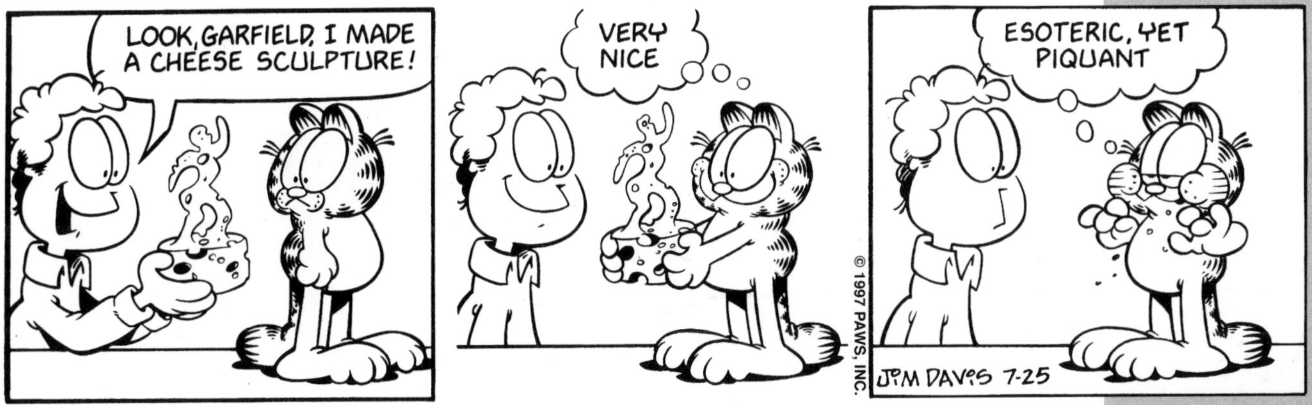
LOOK, GARFIELD, I MADE A CHEESE SCULPTURE!
VERY NICE
ESOTERIC, YET PIQUANT
JIM DAVIS 7-25
© 1997 PAWS, INC.

Twenty years (almost) and still kickin'!

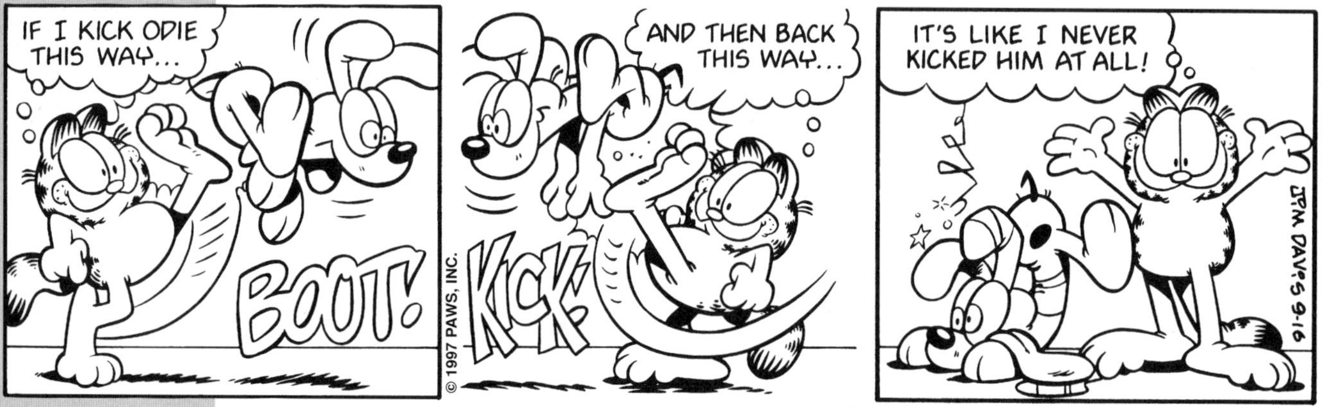
IF I KICK ODIE THIS WAY...
BOOT!
© 1997 PAWS, INC.
AND THEN BACK THIS WAY...
KICK
IT'S LIKE I NEVER KICKED HIM AT ALL!
JIM DAVIS 9-16

WORDS TO LIVE BY

Never put off till tomorrow what you can eat today.

Take life one nap at a time.

Anything worth doing is worth overdoing.

Reach for the stars . . . settle for the bucks.

If you want to appear smarter, hang around someone stupider.

You can't take it with you, so eat it now.

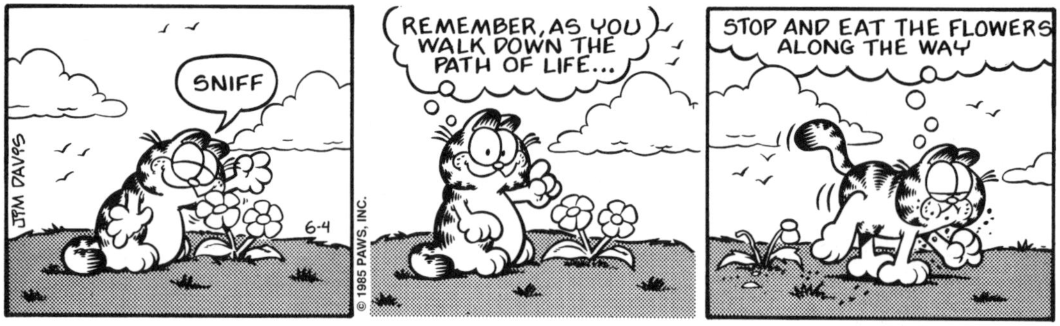
SNIFF
JIM DAVIS
6-4
© 1985 PAWS, INC.
REMEMBER, AS YOU WALK DOWN THE PATH OF LIFE...
STOP AND EAT THE FLOWERS ALONG THE WAY

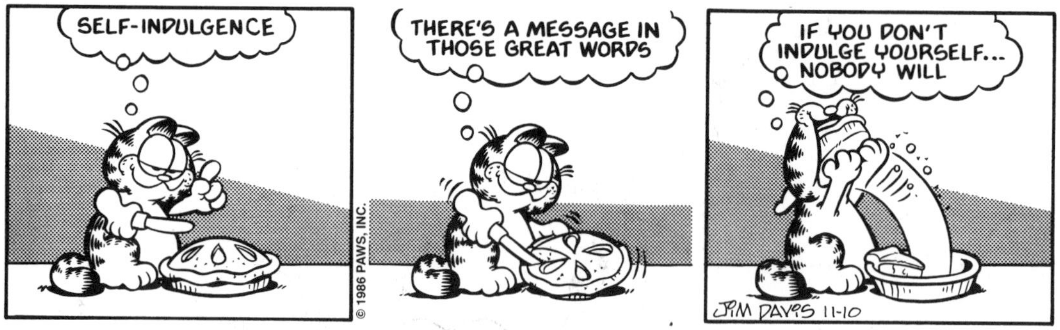
SELF-INDULGENCE
© 1986 PAWS, INC.
THERE'S A MESSAGE IN THOSE GREAT WORDS
IF YOU DON'T INDULGE YOURSELF... NOBODY WILL
JIM DAVIS 11-10

A Chat with the Cat:
GARFIELD'S 20TH ANNIVERSARY INTERVIEW

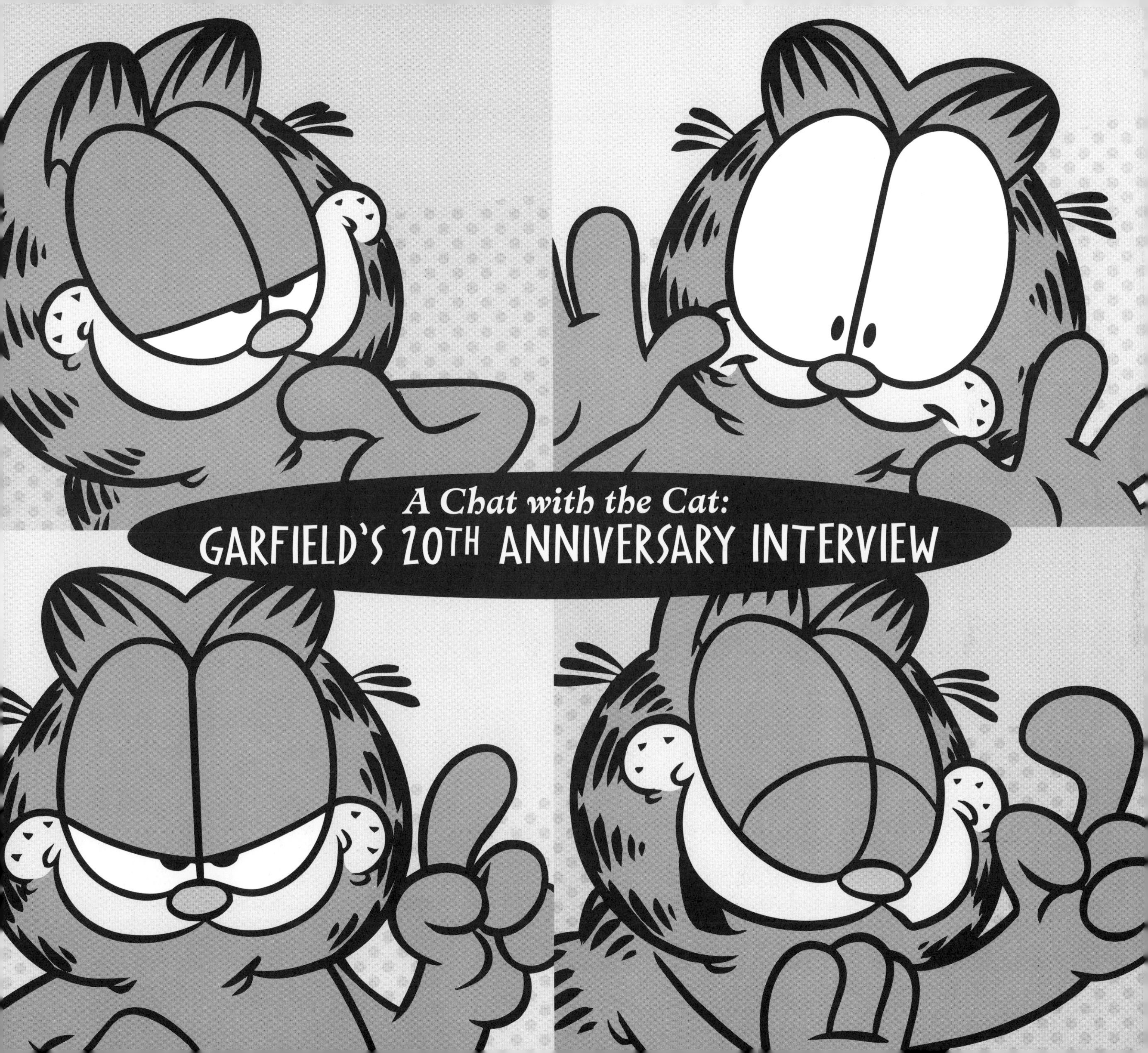

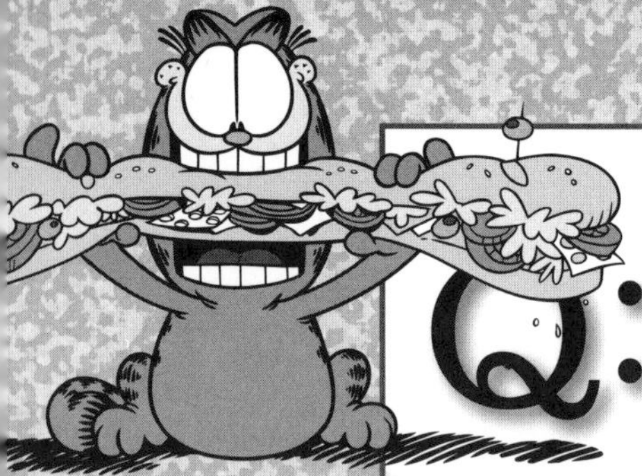

Q: *Garfield, you're everyone's favorite feline, and now you're celebrating a very special birthday. You're turning twenty. How do you feel?*

A: Hungry.

Q: *Tell us about your twentieth birthday. How have you been celebrating, and what's in store for the months ahead?*

A: Currently I'm in the process of consuming the world's largest birthday cake. Next I'm planning a burp that'll register on the Richter scale!

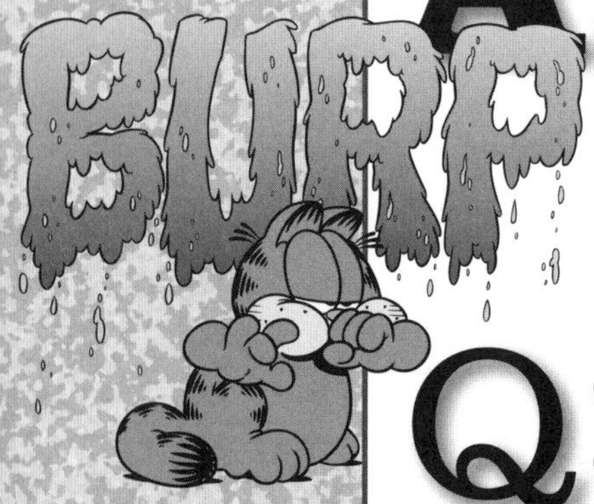
BURP

Q: *Do you have any advice for someone turning twenty?*

A: Yeah, beware of life-insurance salesmen.

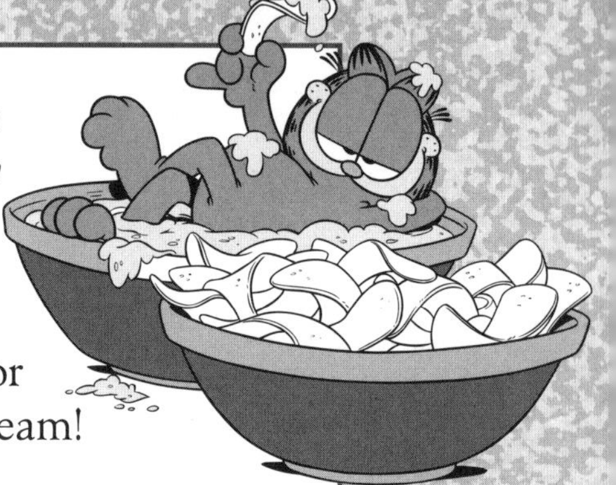

Q: *Do you have any birthday party tips?*

A: Save some munchies for the SWAT team!

Q: *They say with age comes wisdom. Do you feel older and wiser?*

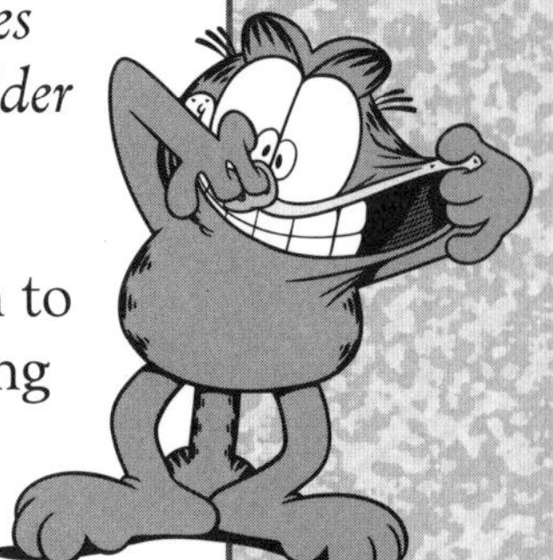

A: Yeah, I'm old enough to know better and young enough not to care.

Q: *Garfield, we've always wondered: Are you really as lazy as you appear in the comic strip?*
Uh . . . Garfield?

A: ZZZZZZZZZ.

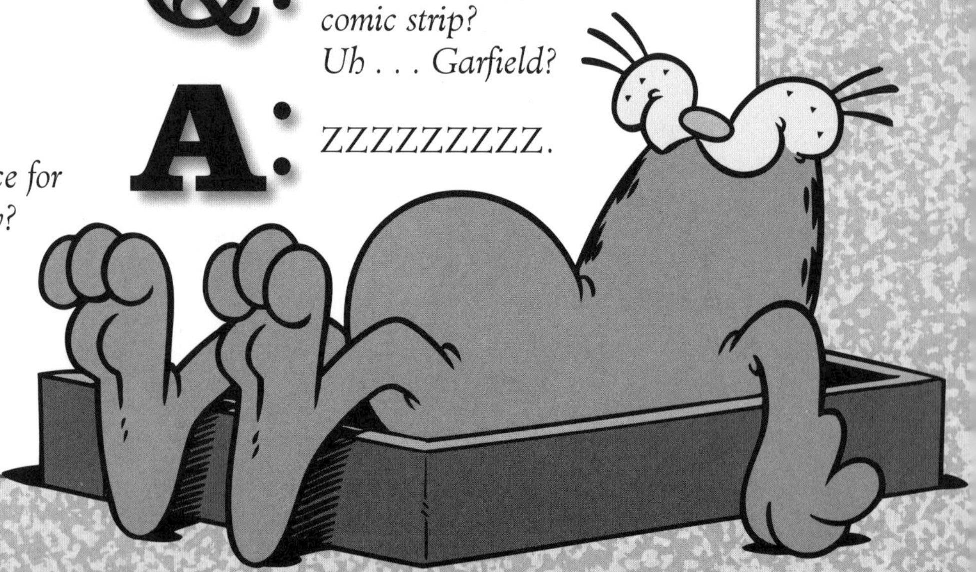

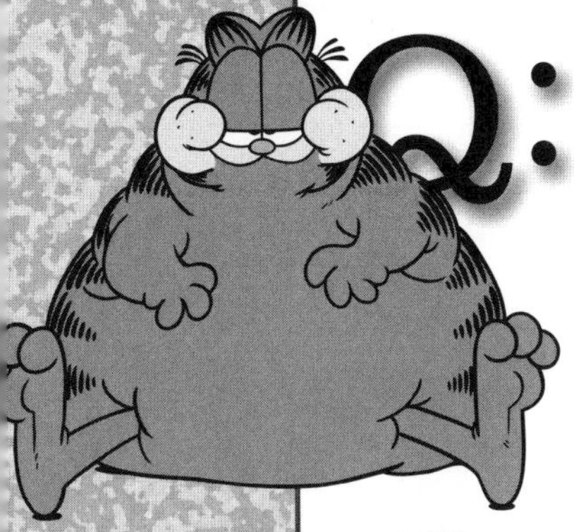

Q: *You've starred in books, TV programs, videos, on T-shirts — you're one of the most successful cartoon characters in the world. How do you account for this success?*

A: I'm more than just another pretty face. I'm a cat of real substance, especially around my middle.

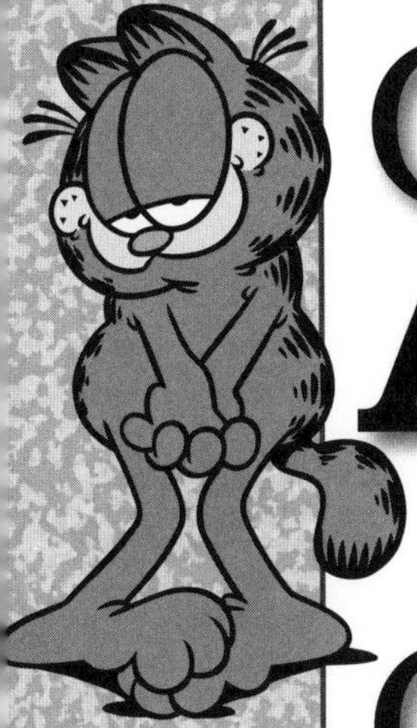

Q: *Has success changed you?*

A: Nah. I'm still the same incredibly cute, funny, lovable, and humble cat I've always been.

Q: *Let's change the subject for a minute. Tell us, is Odie, your canine sidekick, really as dumb as he seems?*

A: No. He's dumber.

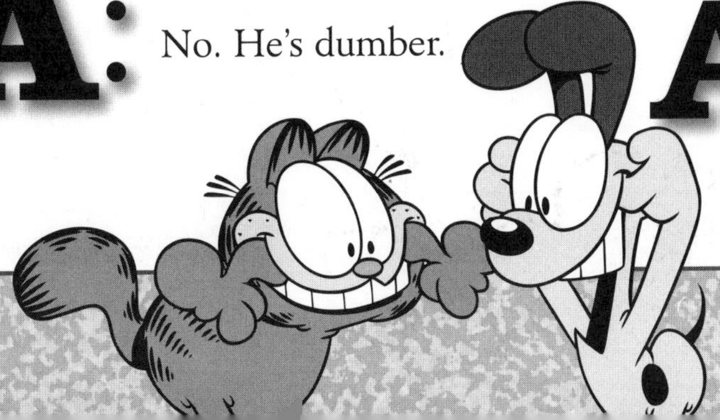

Q: *How dumb is he?*

A: Once he tried to raise his IQ by standing on a chair.

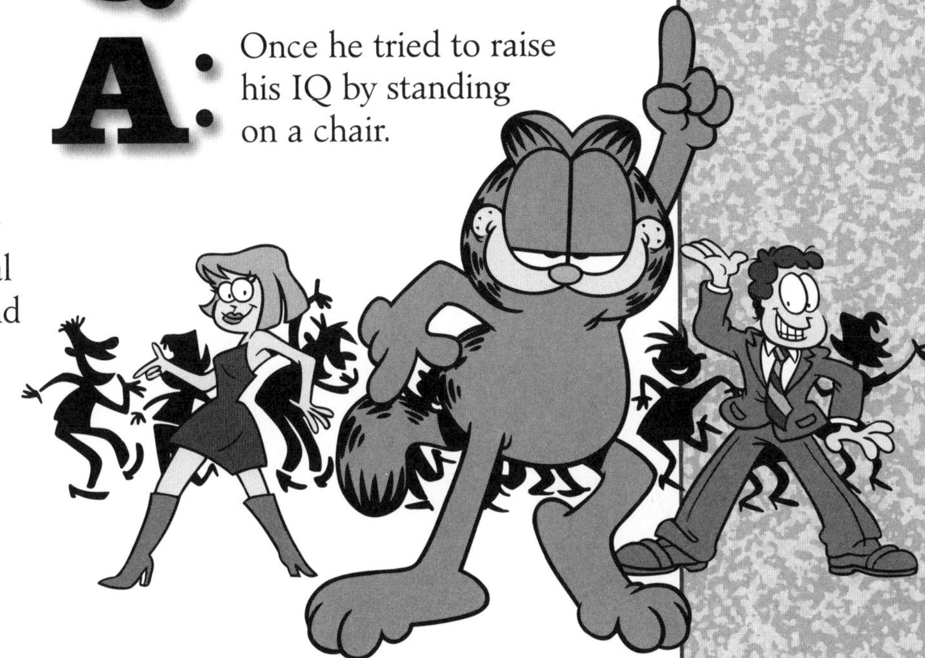

Q: *Getting back to your twentieth birthday . . . a lot of your cartoon contemporaries are quite a bit older than you. What do you have to say to Snoopy and Mickey?*

A: Tell those geezers that I'll be checking out night spots while they're checking out their age spots.

Q: *Now that you're twenty, is there something you're really looking forward to doing?*

A: Yeah, getting totally cake-faced!

Q: *Looking back over the years, what are some of the highlights?*

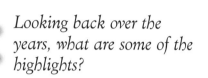

A: Breakfast, lunch, dinner . . .

Q: *Do you owe any of your success to Jim Davis?*

A: Who? Oh, that cartoonist. He's a nice guy, but let's face it — he's just riding on my coattails.

Q: *Has turning twenty taught you anything?*

A: Yes. Never put off till tomorrow what you can eat today.

Q: *You seem to have done it all, Garfield. What's left to conquer?*

A: Outer space. I'd like to boldly go where no cat has gone before.

Q: *That may take some time. What are your immediate plans here on Earth?*

A: World domination! Either that or a nap.

Q: *Well, thanks for your time, Garfield.*

A: Consider yourself appreciated. Now get outta here!

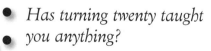

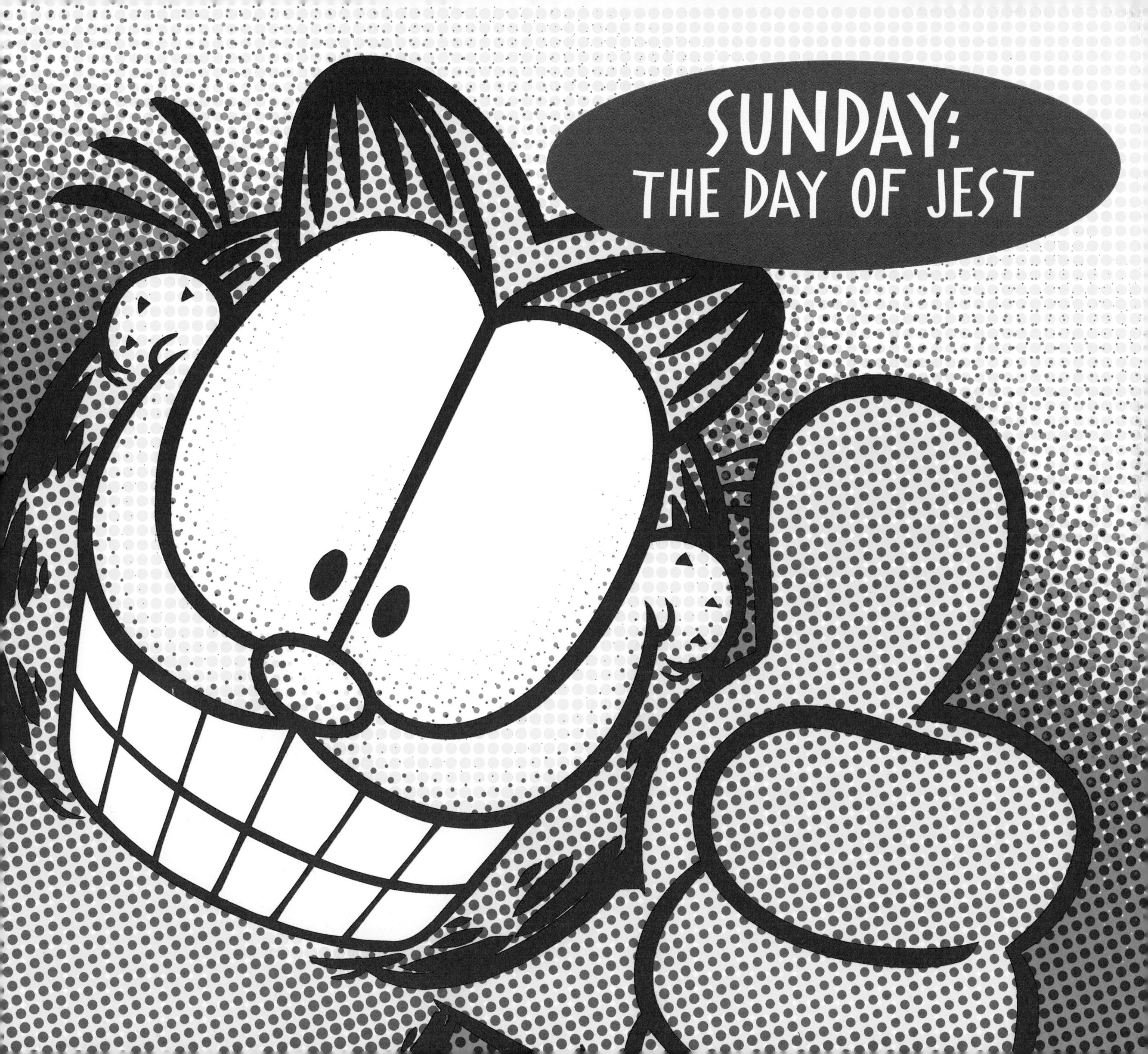
SUNDAY;
THE DAY OF JEST

Sunday may be the day of rest, but for Garfield, it's also the day of jest. And in this larger format, the crazy cat can really cut loose! We intentionally run more visual humor in the Sunday strips and often write with Garfield's younger fans in mind. Besides, I've always loved slapstick humor. Broad physical humor also translates well — a definite consideration now that Garfield has so many international readers.

The Sunday strips are formatted so that they can be run by newspapers horizontally or vertically. These strips take longer to produce, so they need to be created even earlier than the daily strips.

Each Sunday strip has a logo box, where every week a fun new panel is created around Garfield's name. (Check out the Logo Box Gallery at the end of this section.) A drop panel is also included in each strip. Newspapers can either run the comic strip with this panel or drop it, depending on their space limitations.

But enough technical stuff. It's time to sit back, relax, and enjoy a colorful collection of the fat cat's Sunday silliness.

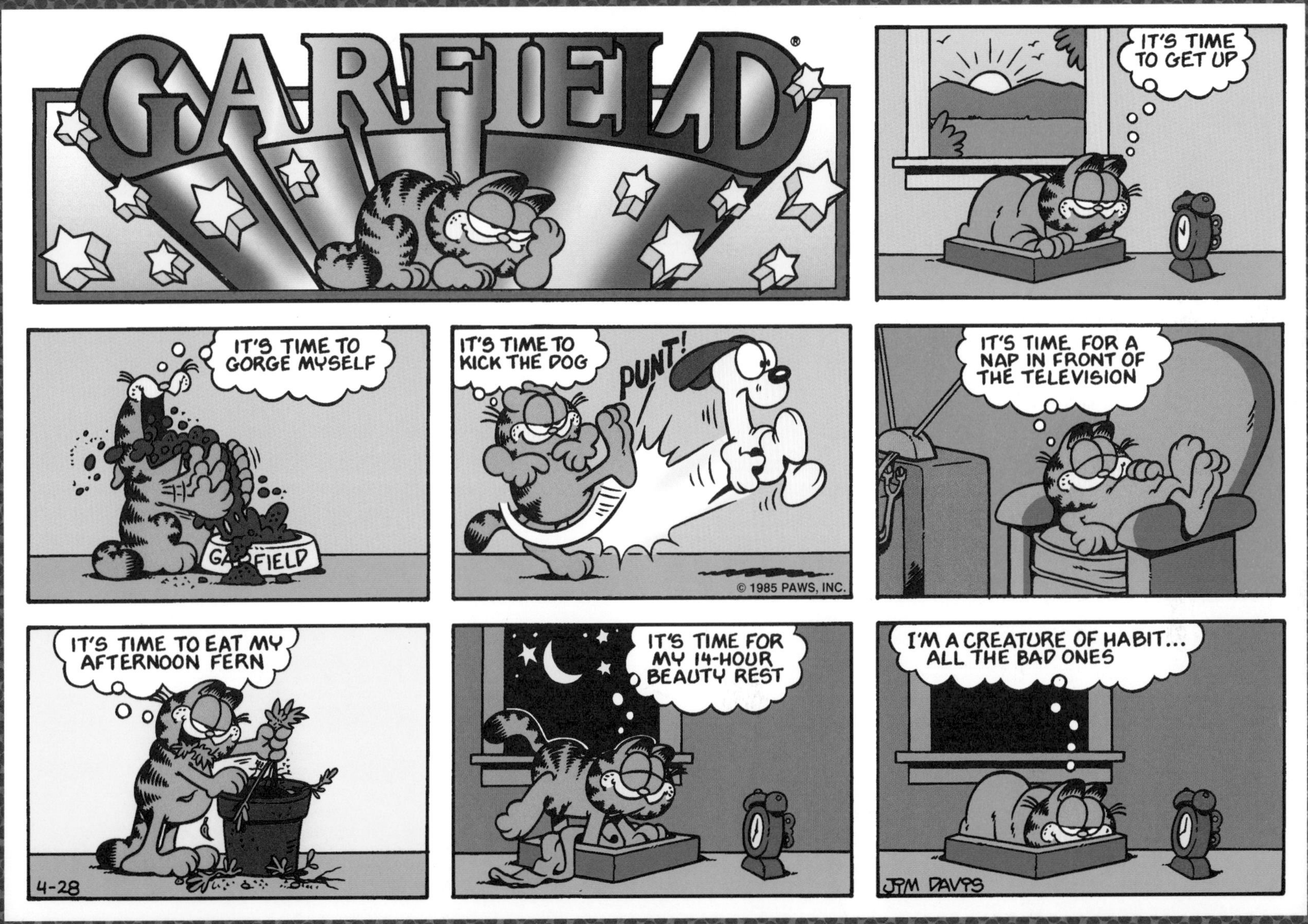
GARFIELD®
IT'S TIME TO GET UP
IT'S TIME TO GORGE MYSELF
GARFIELD
IT'S TIME TO KICK THE DOG
PUNT!
© 1985 PAWS, INC.
IT'S TIME FOR A NAP IN FRONT OF THE TELEVISION
IT'S TIME TO EAT MY AFTERNOON FERN
4-28
IT'S TIME FOR MY 14-HOUR BEAUTY REST
I'M A CREATURE OF HABIT... ALL THE BAD ONES
JPM DAVPS

We used this logo box for the first few years of the strip.

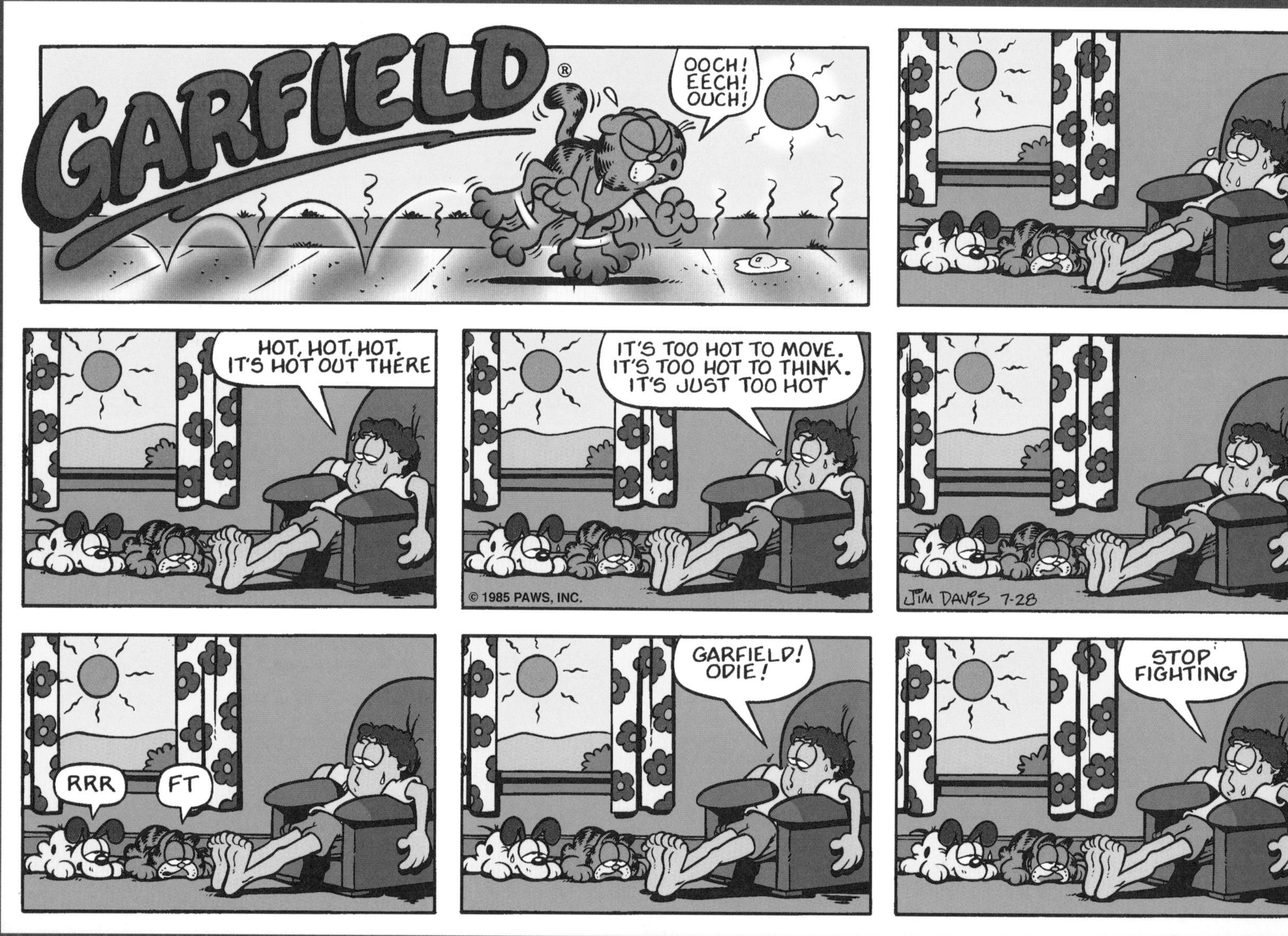
GARFIELD®
OOCH! EECH! OUCH!
HOT, HOT, HOT. IT'S HOT OUT THERE
IT'S TOO HOT TO MOVE. IT'S TOO HOT TO THINK. IT'S JUST TOO HOT
© 1985 PAWS, INC.
JIM DAVIS 7-28
RRR
FT
GARFIELD! ODIE!
STOP FIGHTING

This was the first appearance of a unique logo box. We've had a different one every Sunday since.

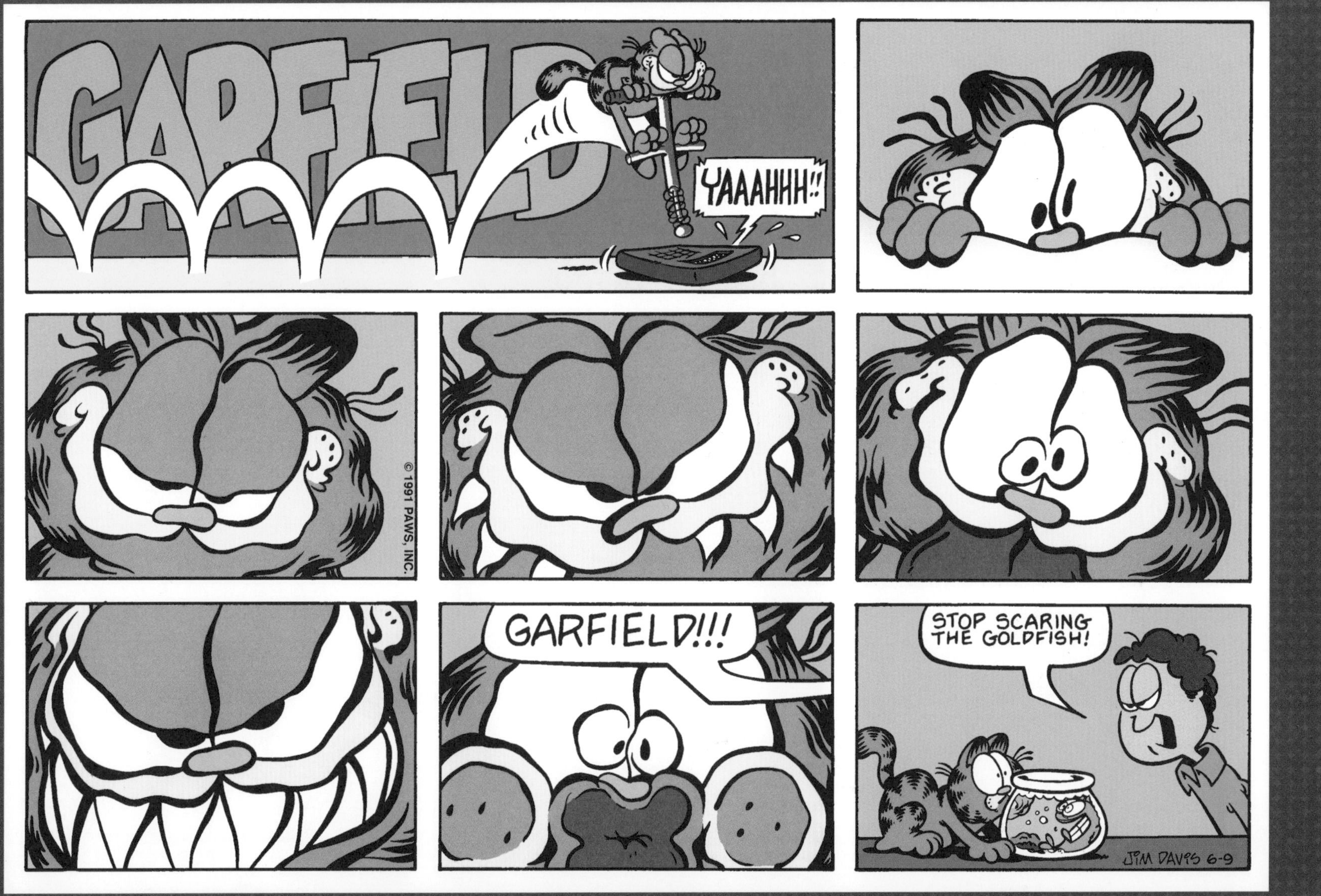
GARFIELD
YAAAHHH!!
© 1991 PAWS, INC.
GARFIELD!!!
STOP SCARING THE GOLDFISH!
JIM DAVIS 6-9

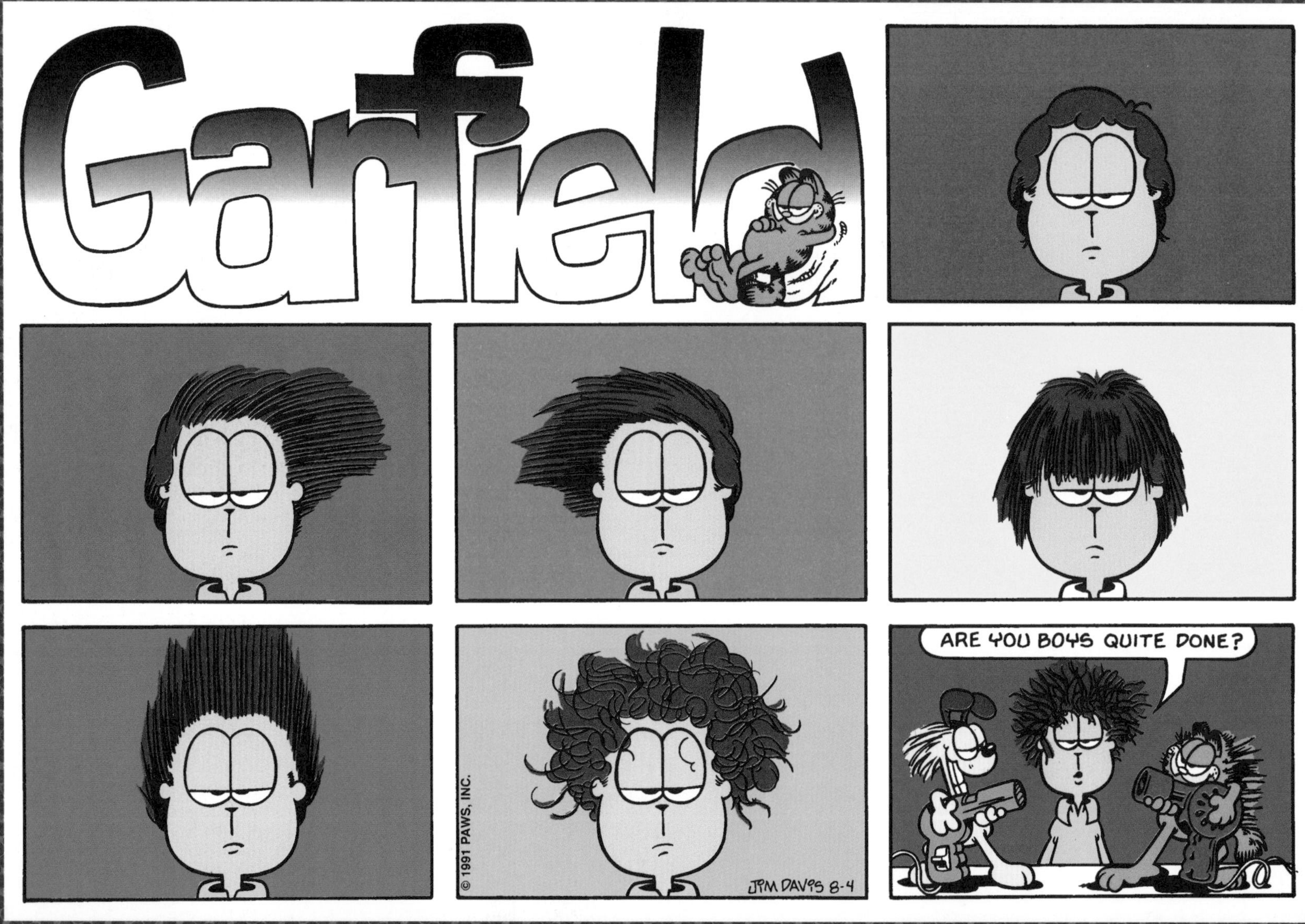
Garfield
© 1991 PAWS, INC.
JIM DAVIS 8-4
ARE YOU BOYS QUITE DONE?

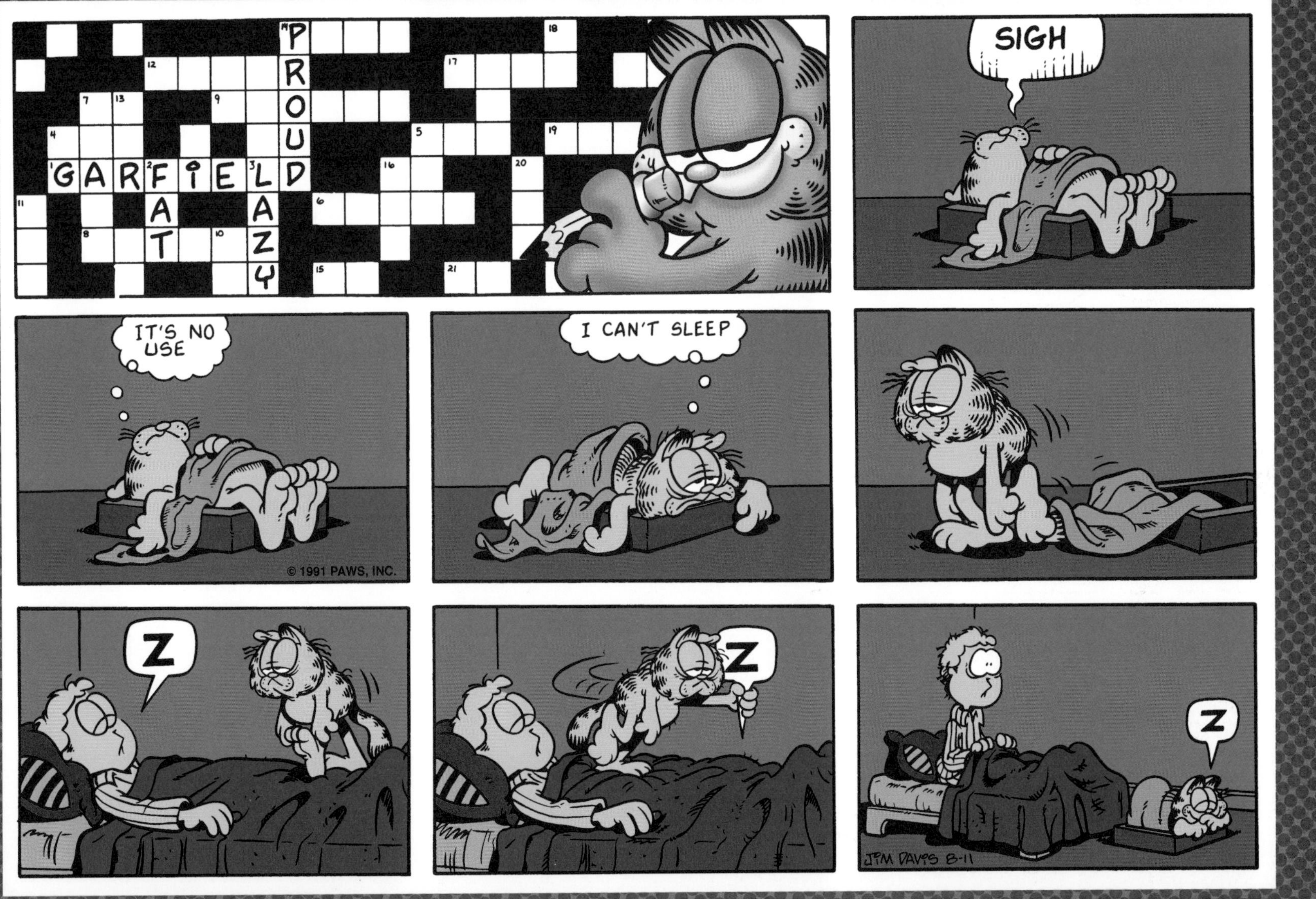
GARFIELD
FAT
PROUD
LAZY
SIGH
IT'S NO USE
I CAN'T SLEEP
© 1991 PAWS, INC.
Z
Z
Z
JIM DAVIS 8-11

It could only happen in the comics.

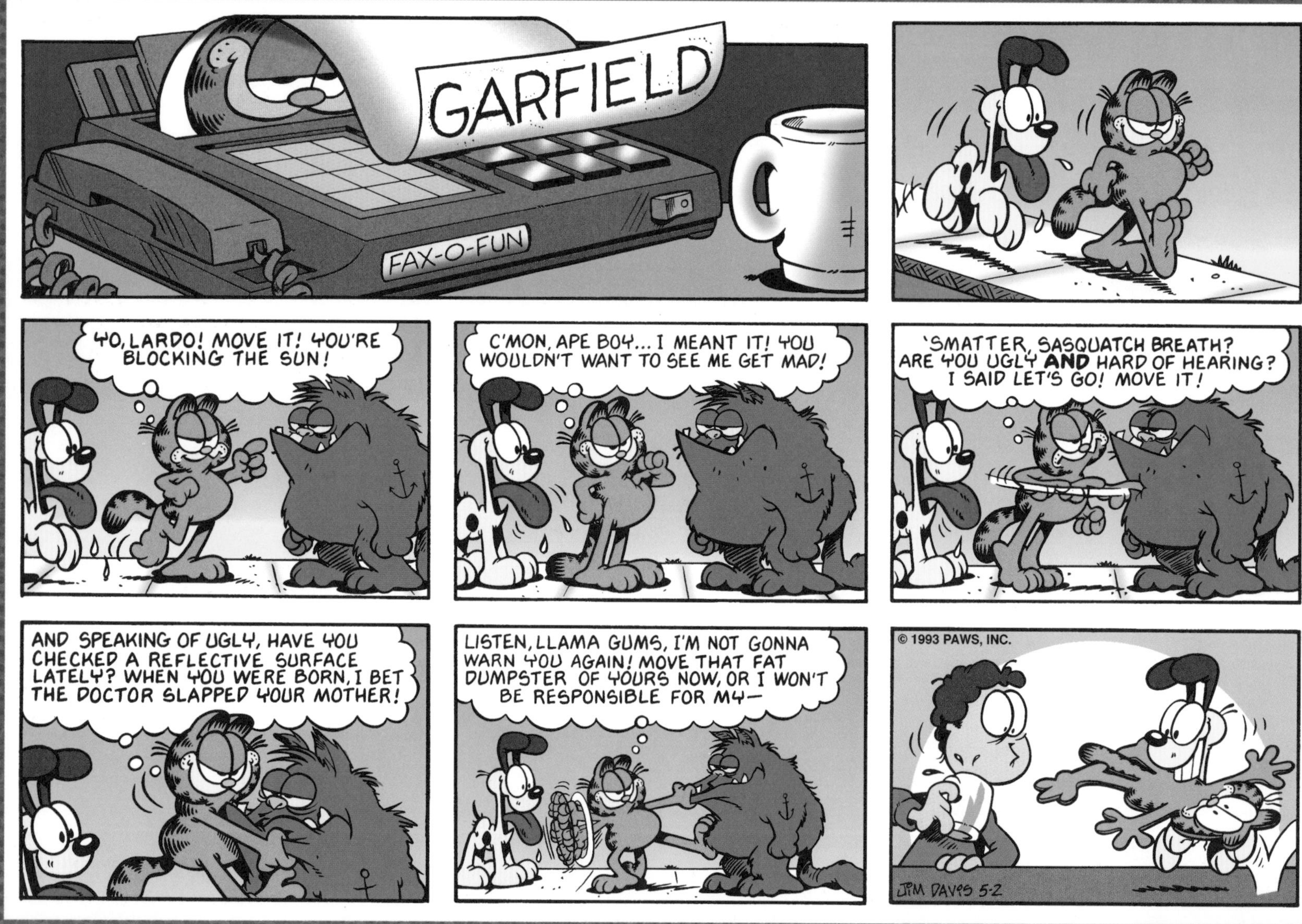
GARFIELD
FAX-O-FUN
YO, LARDO! MOVE IT! YOU'RE BLOCKING THE SUN!
C'MON, APE BOY... I MEANT IT! YOU WOULDN'T WANT TO SEE ME GET MAD!
'SMATTER, SASQUATCH BREATH? ARE YOU UGLY **AND** HARD OF HEARING? I SAID LET'S GO! MOVE IT!
AND SPEAKING OF UGLY, HAVE YOU CHECKED A REFLECTIVE SURFACE LATELY? WHEN YOU WERE BORN, I BET THE DOCTOR SLAPPED YOUR MOTHER!
LISTEN, LLAMA GUMS, I'M NOT GONNA WARN YOU AGAIN! MOVE THAT FAT DUMPSTER OF YOURS NOW, OR I WON'T BE RESPONSIBLE FOR MY—
© 1993 PAWS, INC.
JIM DAVIS 5-2

Sometimes a gag works from the last panel forward.
We wanted to draw this Garfield so badly, we created a gag for it.

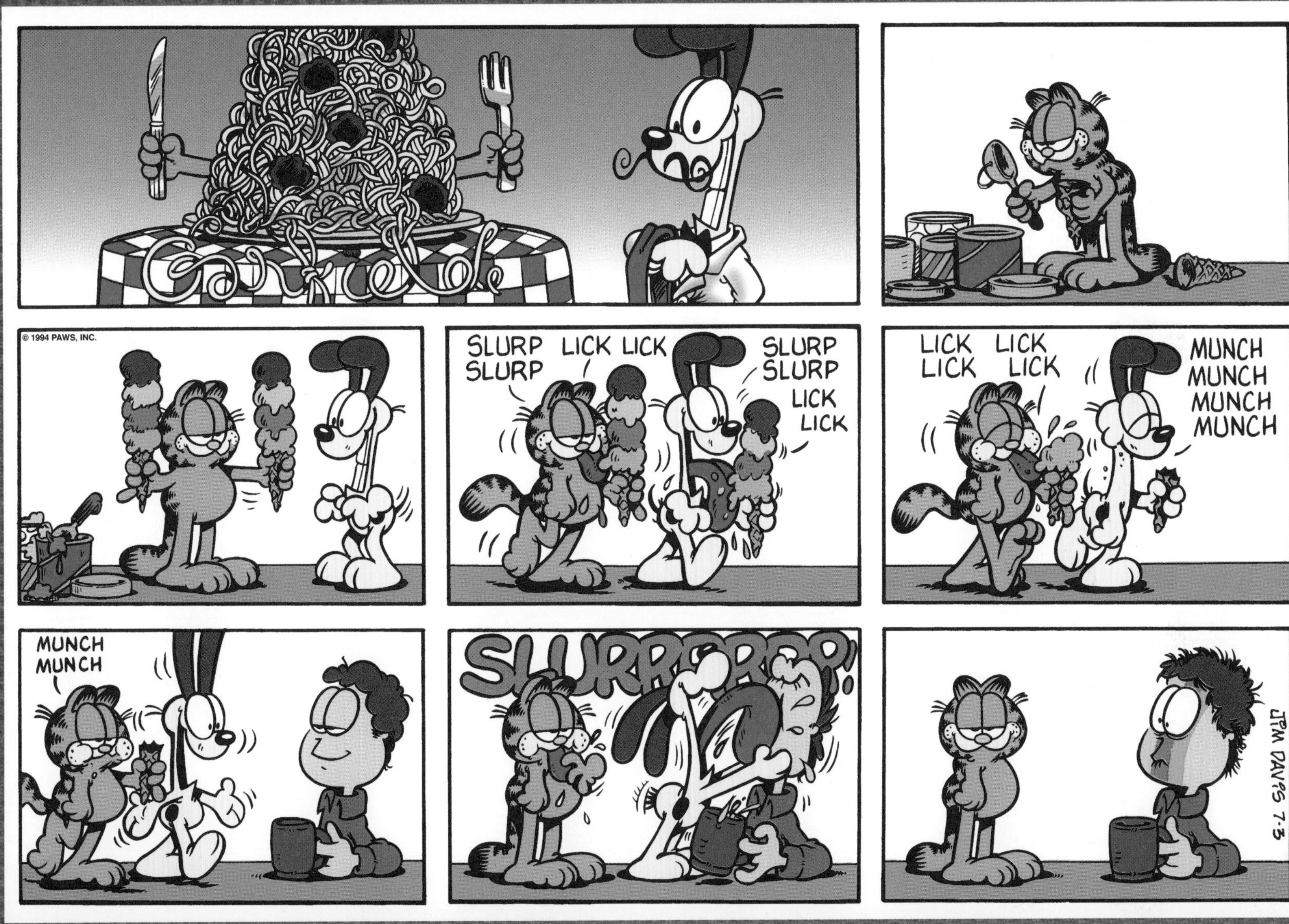
© 1994 PAWS, INC.
SLURP SLURP
LICK LICK
SLURP SLURP
LICK LICK
LICK LICK
LICK LICK
MUNCH MUNCH MUNCH MUNCH
MUNCH MUNCH
SLURRRRRP!
JIM DAVIS 7-3

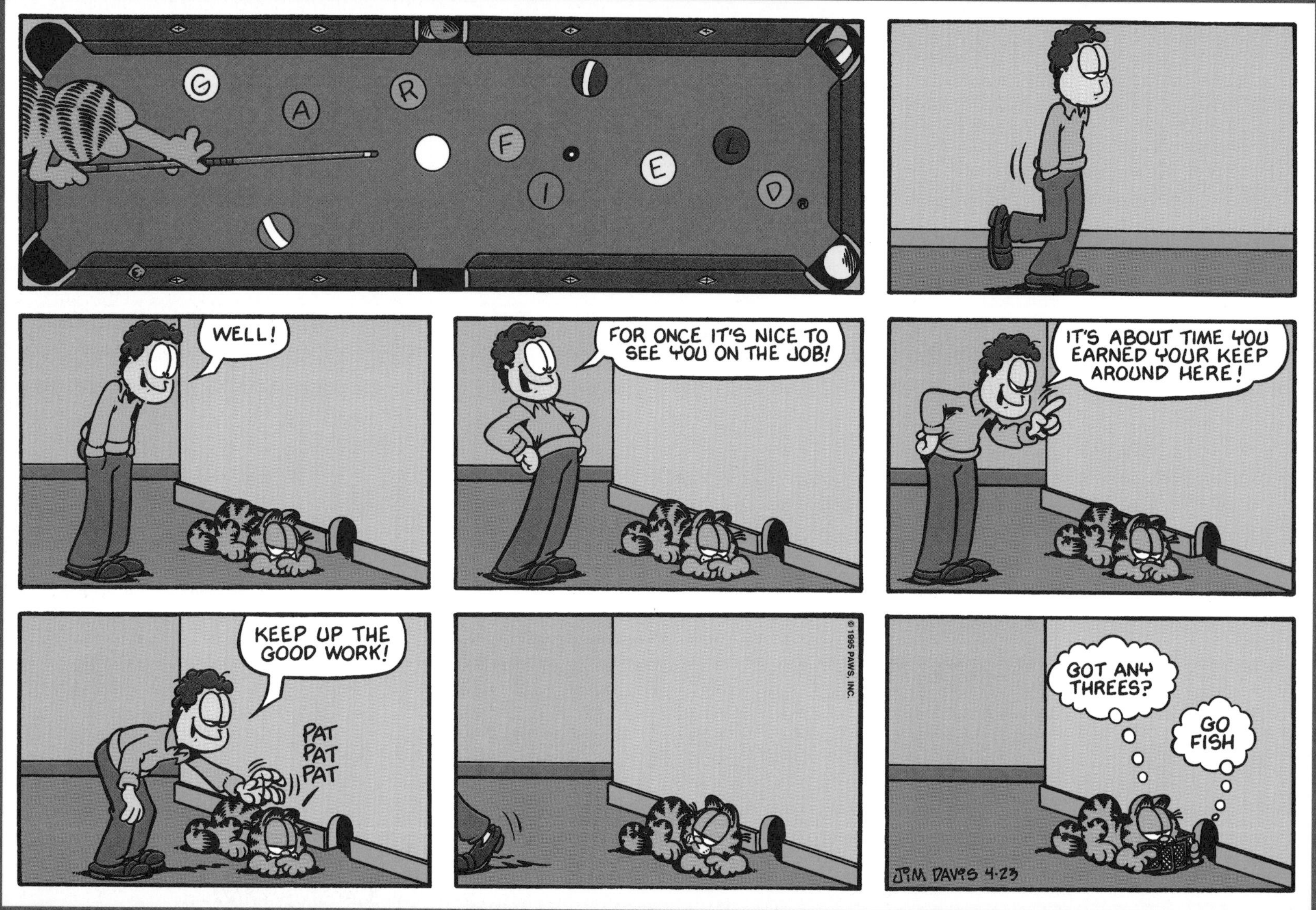
G A R F I E L D ®
WELL!
FOR ONCE IT'S NICE TO SEE YOU ON THE JOB!
IT'S ABOUT TIME YOU EARNED YOUR KEEP AROUND HERE!
KEEP UP THE GOOD WORK!
PAT PAT PAT
© 1995 PAWS, INC.
GOT ANY THREES?
GO FISH
JIM DAVIS 4-23

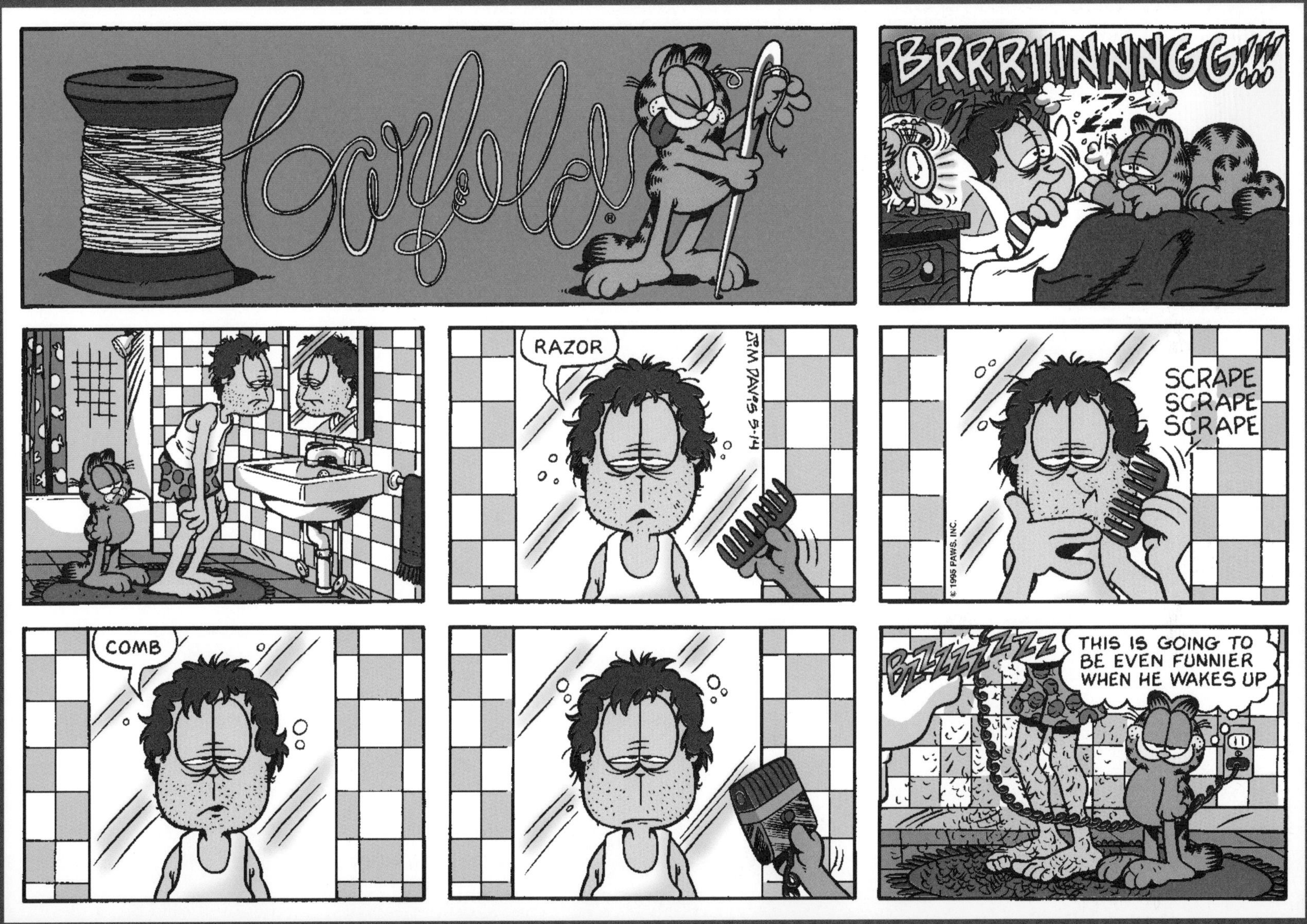
BRRRIIINNNGG!!!
RAZOR
SCRAPE
SCRAPE
SCRAPE
© 1995 PAWS, INC.
COMB
BZZZZZZZZ
THIS IS GOING TO BE EVEN FUNNIER WHEN HE WAKES UP

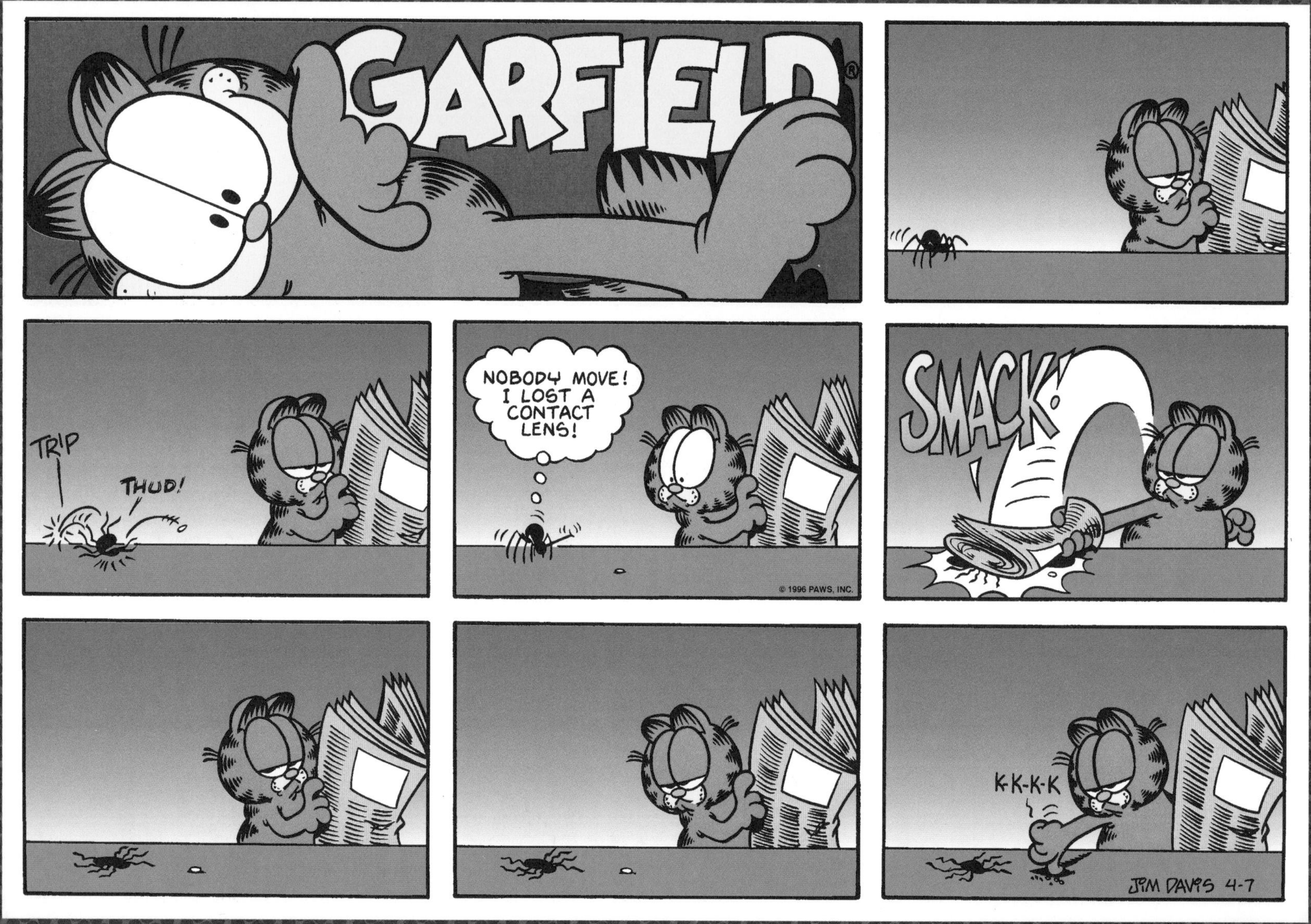
GARFIELD
TRIP
THUD!
NOBODY MOVE! I LOST A CONTACT LENS!
© 1996 PAWS, INC.
SMACK!
K-K-K-K
JIM DAVIS 4-7

This one's really cruel . . . but funny cruel.

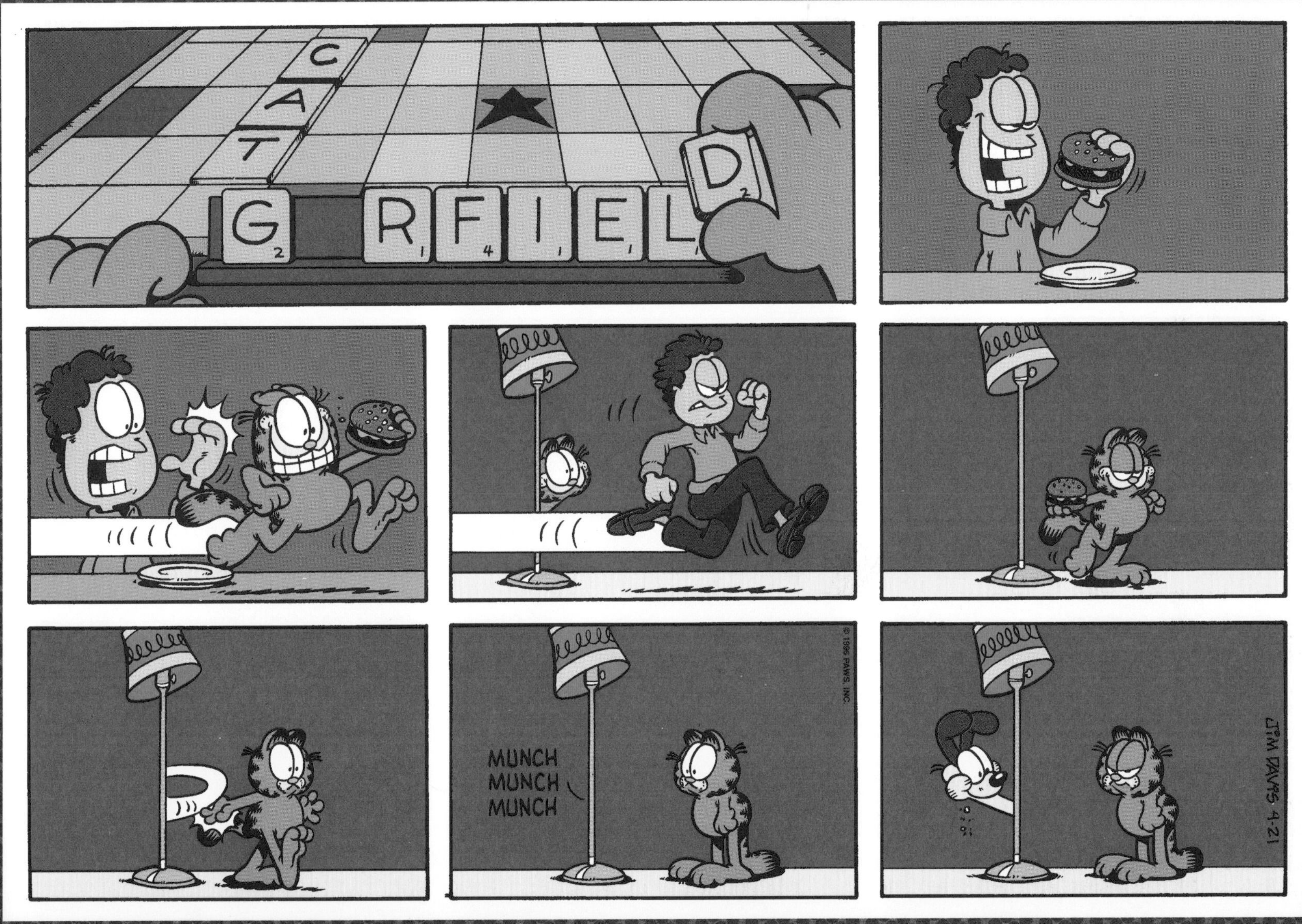
C
A
T
G RFIELD
MUNCH
MUNCH
MUNCH
© 1996 PAWS, INC.
JIM DAVIS 4-21

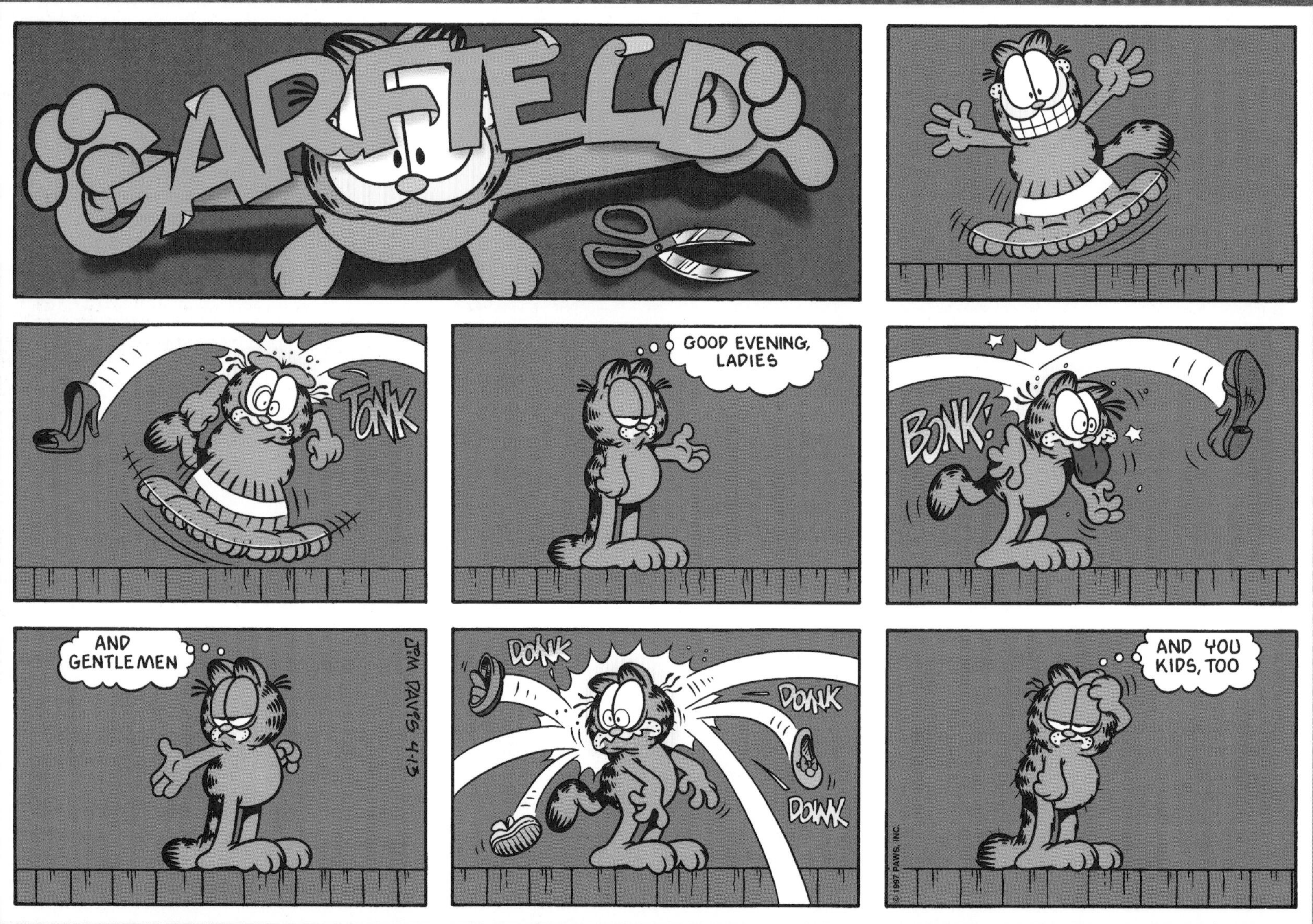
GARFIELD
TONK
GOOD EVENING, LADIES
BONK!
AND GENTLEMEN
JIM DAVIS 4-13
DONK
DONK
DONK
AND YOU KIDS, TOO
© 1997 PAWS, INC.

Logo Box Gallery

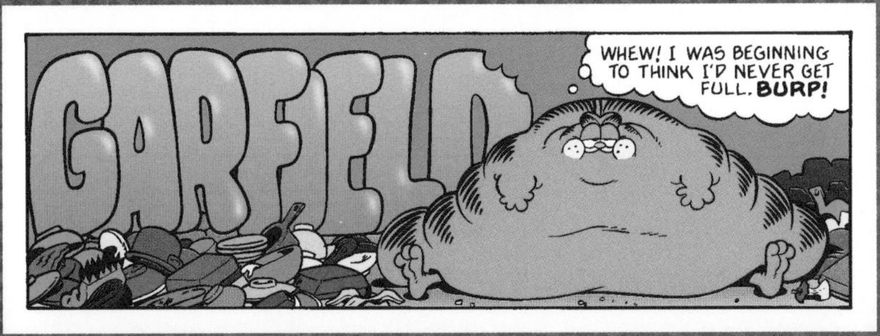
GARFIELD
WHEW! I WAS BEGINNING TO THINK I'D NEVER GET FULL. BURP!

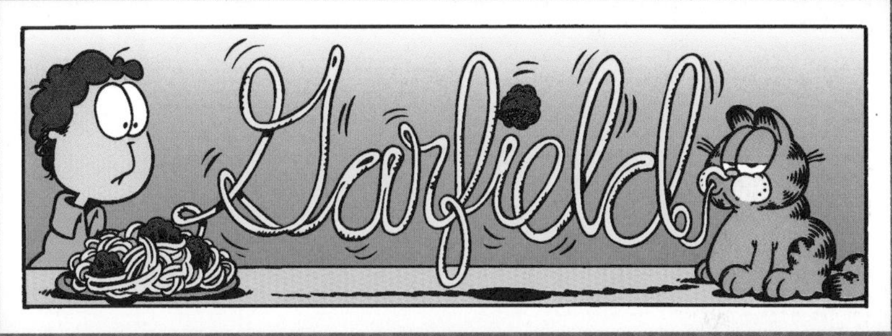
Garfield

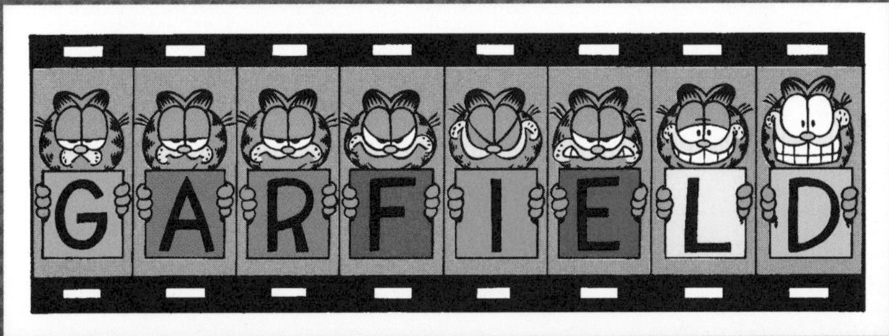
G A R F I E L D

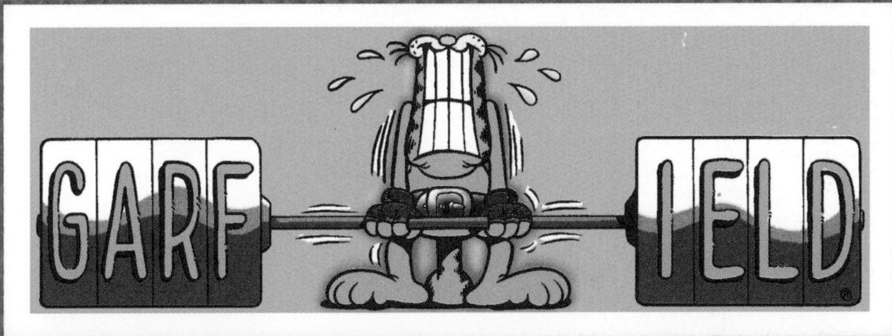
GARF
IELD

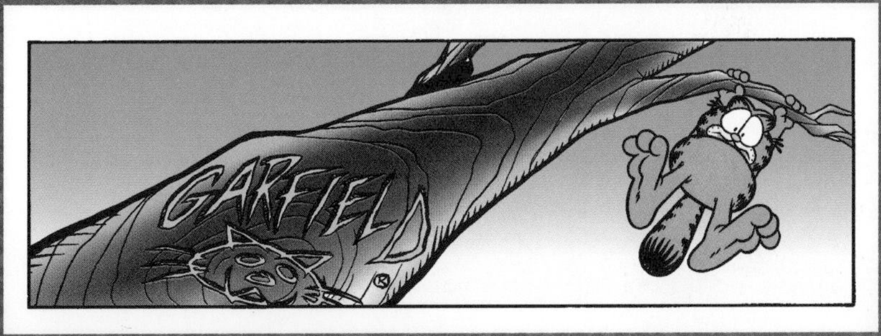
GARFIELD

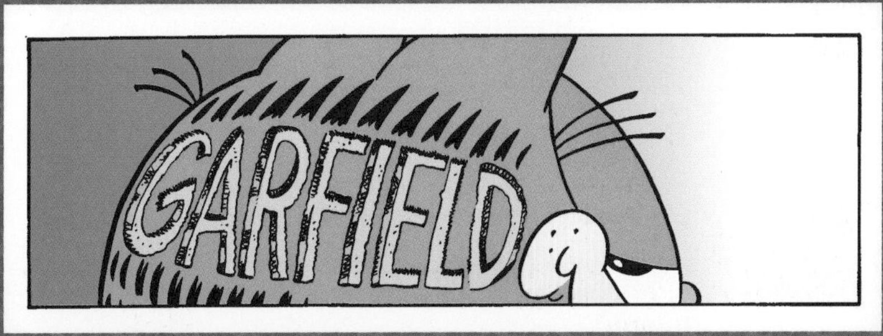
GARFIELD

Logo Box Gallery

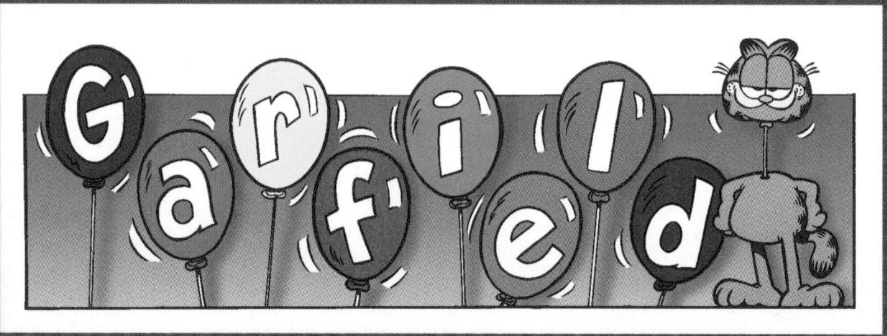
Garfield

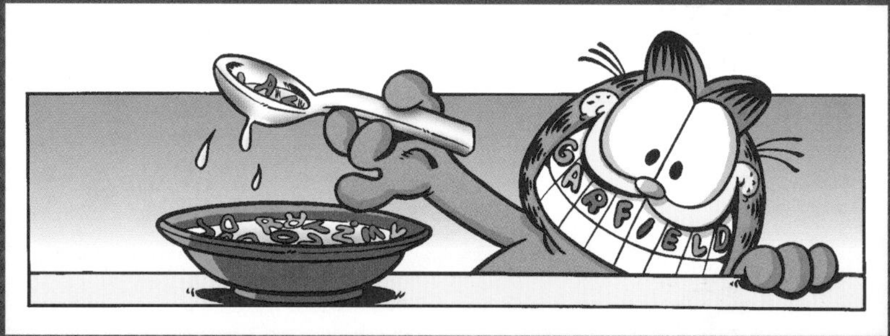
GARFIELD

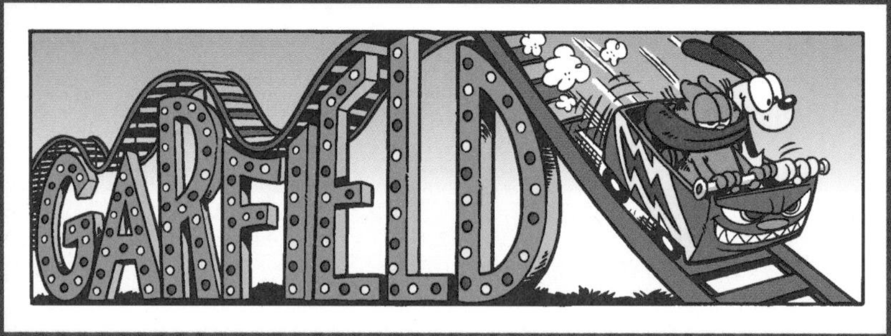
GARFIELD

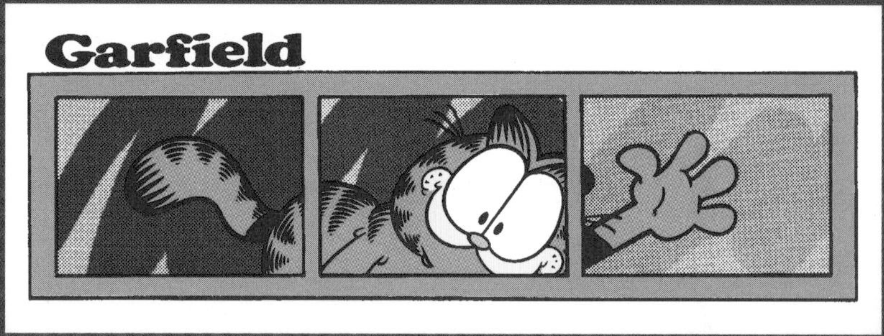
Garfield

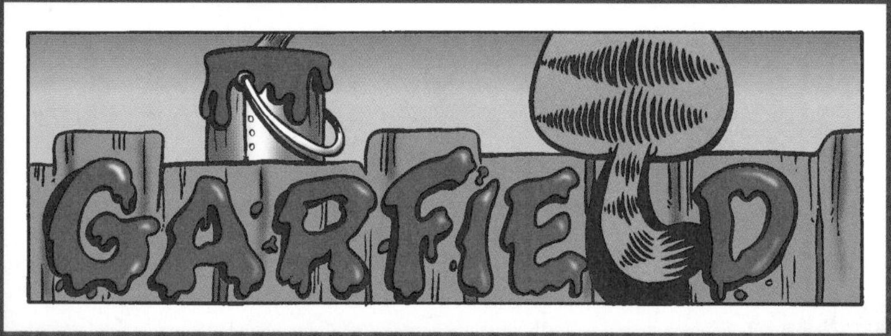

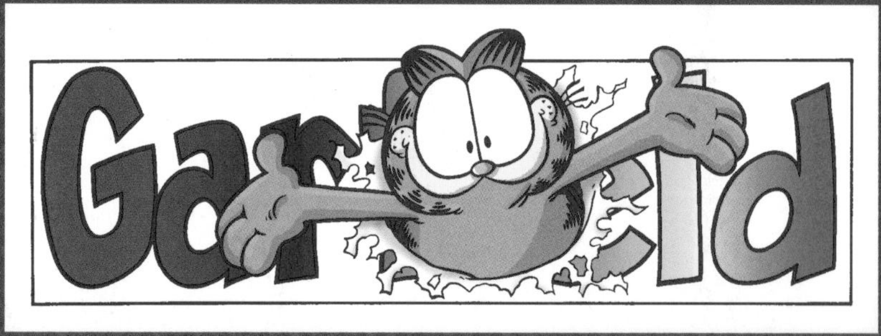

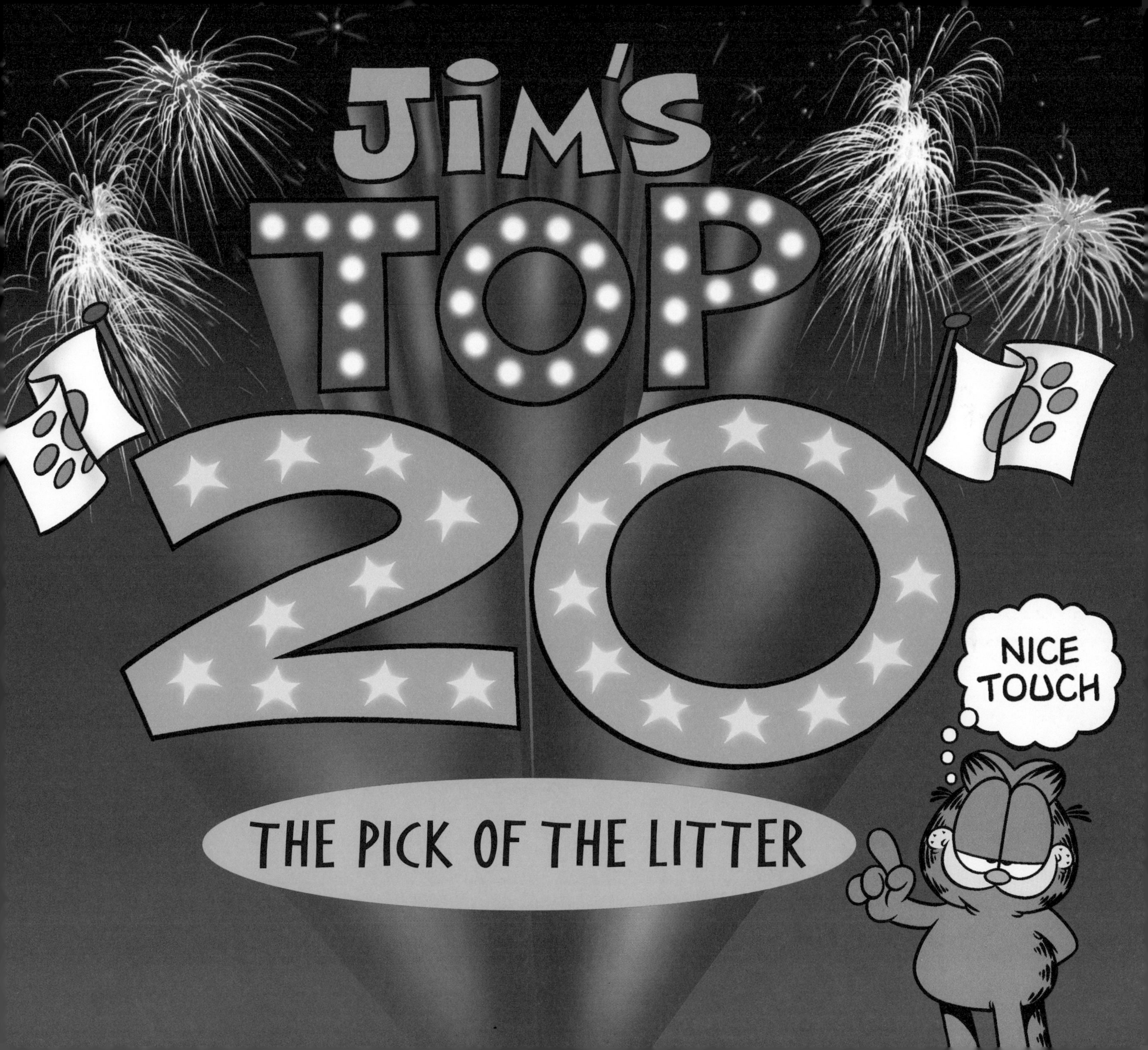
JIM'S
TOP
20
NICE TOUCH
THE PICK OF THE LITTER

Asking a cartoonist to choose his favorite strips is like asking a parent to choose his favorite child: you love them all, just in different ways. But after sifting through the nearly 7,000 (!) Garfield strips created since 1978, I managed to pull twenty that I particularly liked.

The strips in this section are listed in chronological order. (Don't make me list them in order of preference — that would be *too* hard!) These are some of my favorites. Maybe you'll find one of your favorites in here, too.

Being able to entertain fans all over the world and work with so many special, talented people has been a dream come true. Both Garfield and I have had a great twenty years. Here's to the next twenty!

DECEMBER 28, 1978

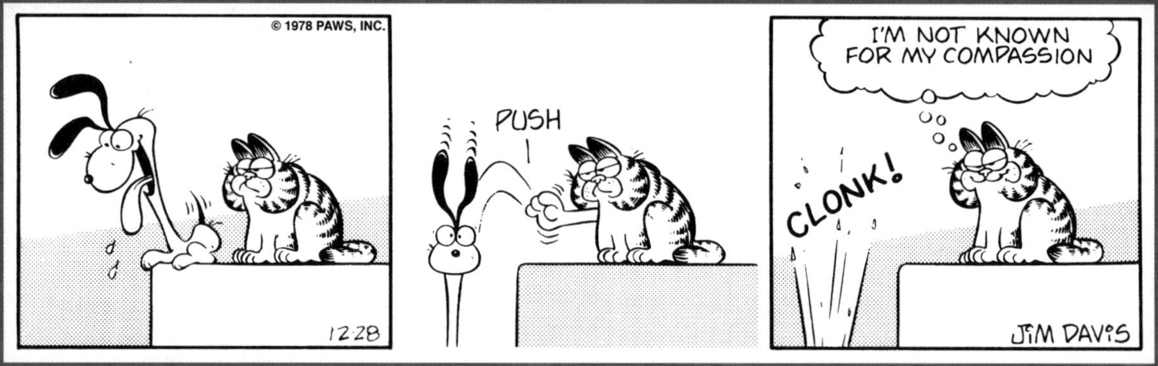
© 1978 PAWS, INC.
12·28
PUSH
I'M NOT KNOWN FOR MY COMPASSION
CLONK!
JIM DAVIS

This early strip really defines Garfield's character.

JUNE 9, 1979

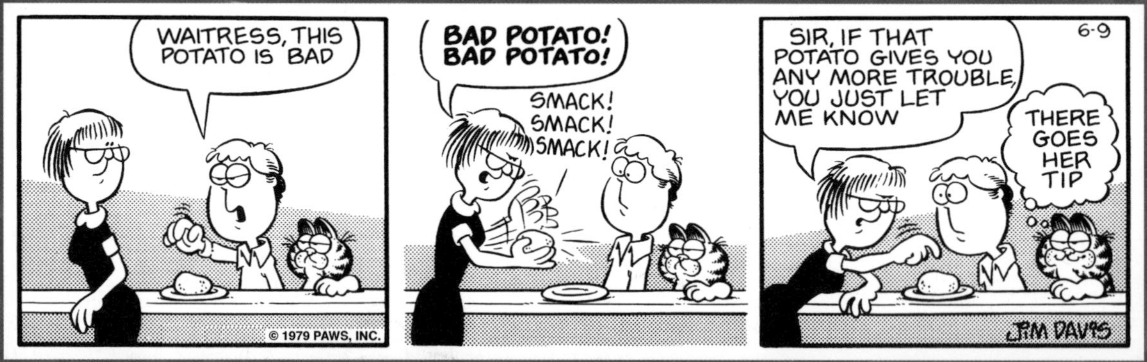
WAITRESS, THIS POTATO IS BAD
© 1979 PAWS, INC.
BAD POTATO! BAD POTATO!
SMACK! SMACK! SMACK!
6·9
SIR, IF THAT POTATO GIVES YOU ANY MORE TROUBLE, YOU JUST LET ME KNOW
THERE GOES HER TIP
JIM DAVIS

A friend saw a flight attendant actually do this to a passenger who was complaining about everything.

DECEMBER 25, 1981

CHRISTMAS SPIRIT...
IT'S NOT THE GIVING. IT'S NOT THE RECEIVING
IT'S THE LOVING. MERRY CHRISTMAS
12·25
JIM DAVIS
© 1981 PAWS, INC.

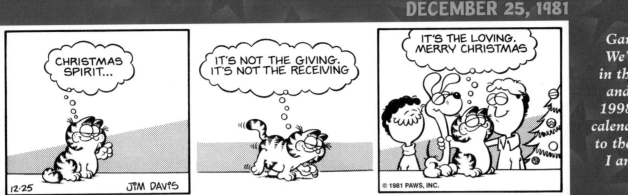

Garfield loves Christmas. We've used this sentiment in the Christmas TV special and, most recently, in the 1998 twentieth anniversary calendar. Guess when it comes to the holidays, Garfield and I are both just a couple of old softies.

APRIL 25, 1983

Dear Garfield, What is your favorite all-time film?
IT'S "OLD YELLER"
I LOVE MOVIES WITH HAPPY ENDINGS
4·25
JIM DAVIS
© 1983 PAWS, INC.

Okay, so I have a cruel streak. (Maybe that's where Garfield gets it from.)

OCTOBER 18, 1983

I AM DOWN... DOWN, DOWN, DOWN, DOWN, DOWN
DOWN, DOWN, DOWN, DOOBY DOO DOWN, DOWN
COMMA, COMMA, DOWN DOOBY DOO DOWN, DOWN
JIM DAVIS
10-18
© 1983 PAWS, INC.

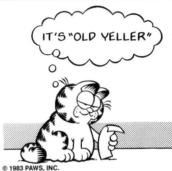

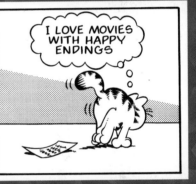

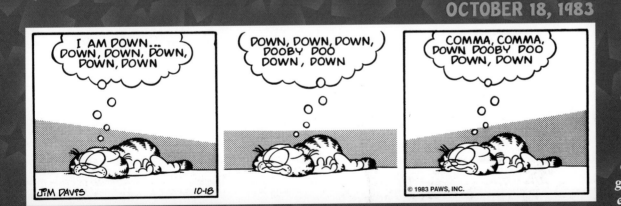

This turned out to be one of the most popular gags I ever did. After I completed this strip, I wasn't sure I should send it to the syndicate. I showed it to my assistant, Valette, who told me, "You have to send this in!" I did, and the response we received was overwhelming. We got letters and phone calls and even telegrams! Guess I struck a chord with people.

AUGUST 1, 1988

This one is just silly. I've always loved to dress up Garfield and Odie in fruit. Maybe I saw too many Carmen Miranda movies when I was growing up.

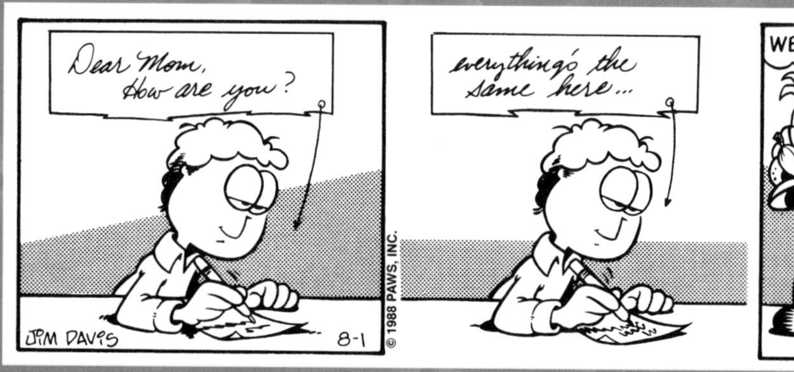
Dear Mom,
How are you?
everything's the same here...
WE NEED MORE FRUIT
I'm sorry to say
JIM DAVIS
8-1
© 1988 PAWS, INC.

MAY 30, 1989

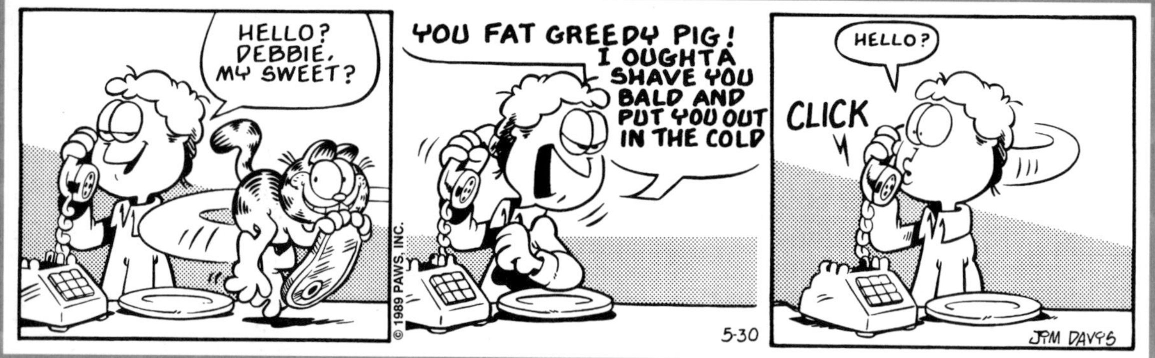
HELLO? DEBBIE, MY SWEET?
YOU FAT GREEDY PIG! I OUGHTA SHAVE YOU BALD AND PUT YOU OUT IN THE COLD
CLICK
HELLO?
© 1989 PAWS, INC.
5-30
JIM DAVIS

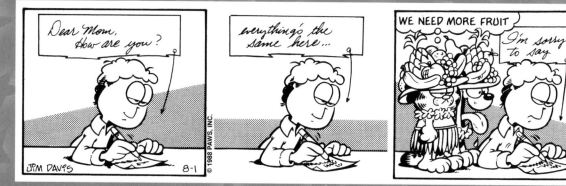

Timing is everything. This is one of my all-time favorites.

NOVEMBER 6, 1989

Farm humor from a farm boy. If you can't make fun of your family, who can you make fun of?

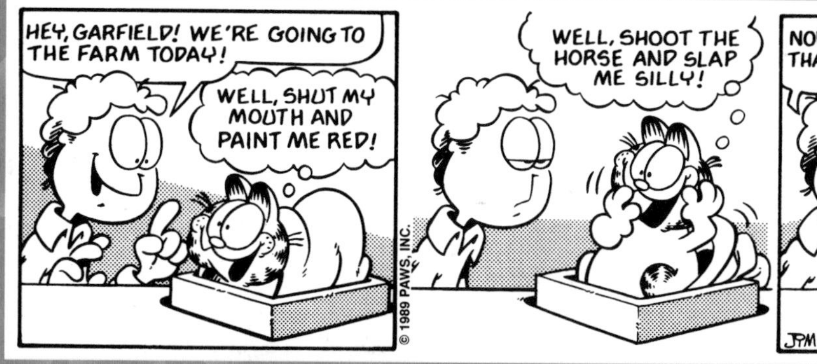
HEY, GARFIELD! WE'RE GOING TO THE FARM TODAY!
WELL, SHUT MY MOUTH AND PAINT ME RED!
WELL, SHOOT THE HORSE AND SLAP ME SILLY!
NOW, CUT THAT OUT
WELL, STOMP ON FROGS AND SHOVE A CROWBAR UP MY NOSE!
© 1989 PAWS, INC.
JIM DAVIS
11-6

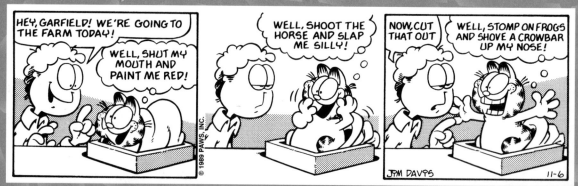

FEBRUARY 8, 1990

LOOK, GARFIELD, A LION!
MY GREAT UNCLE WAS A LION
LION
KING OF THE JUNGLE!
YUP, HE WAS A BIG SHOT
THE MIGHTY HUNTER...
THEN, ONE DAY, HE ATE A SICK MONKEY
© 1990 PAWS, INC.
JIM DAVIS 2-8

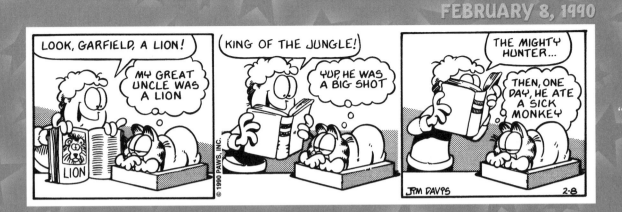

There's just something funny about the phrase "sick monkey." One of my favorite punch lines of all time.

MARCH 8, 1991

This came at the end of a long writing session. We needed just one more Friday gag. This one has it all: a silly premise, funny words, and funny visuals.

YESSIREEBOB
JIM DAVIS 3-8
WHAT AN EXCITING FRIDAY NIGHT...
SNAP!
© 1991 PAWS, INC.
FUN WITH TAPE

JUNE 20, 1991

WHY IS IT THAT YOU ALWAYS HAVE TO BE THE CENTER OF ATTENTION, GARFIELD?
WHAT?
© 1991 PAWS, INC.
THAT'S THE SILLIEST THING I'VE EVER HEARD
JIM DAVIS 6-20

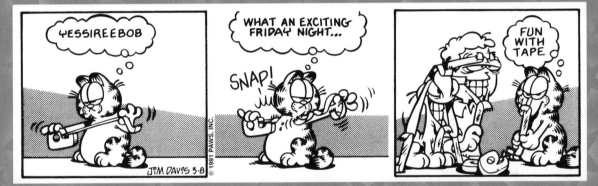

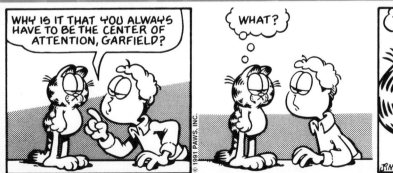

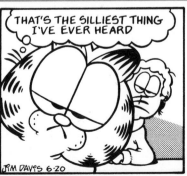

This is just so Garfield.

NOVEMBER 9, 1991

Obviously, I was in a "strange" mood that day.

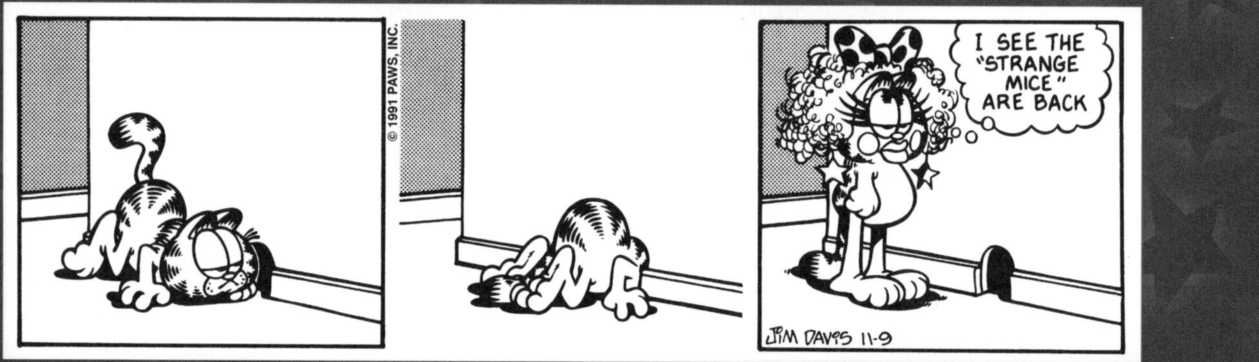
I SEE THE "STRANGE MICE" ARE BACK
© 1991 PAWS, INC.
JIM DAVIS 11-9

MAY 7, 1992

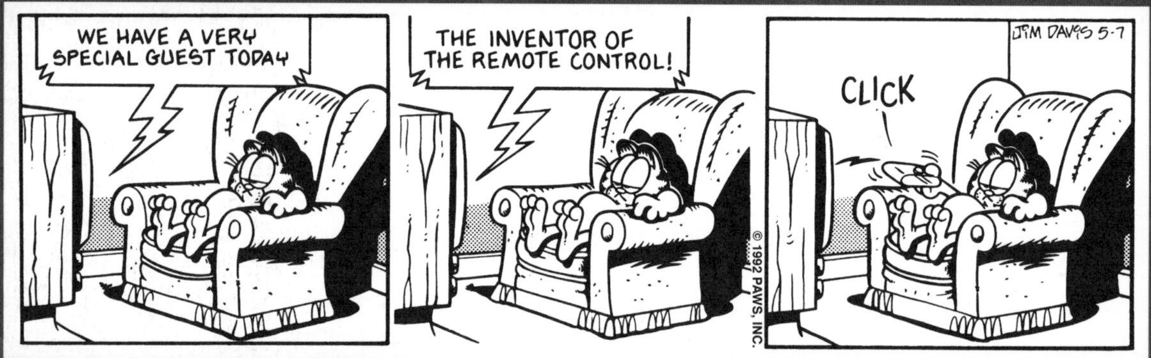
WE HAVE A VERY SPECIAL GUEST TODAY
THE INVENTOR OF THE REMOTE CONTROL!
CLICK
© 1992 PAWS, INC.
JIM DAVIS 5-7

I just love the irony.

APRIL 2, 1993

The best part about this strip is that Garfield is nowhere to be seen.

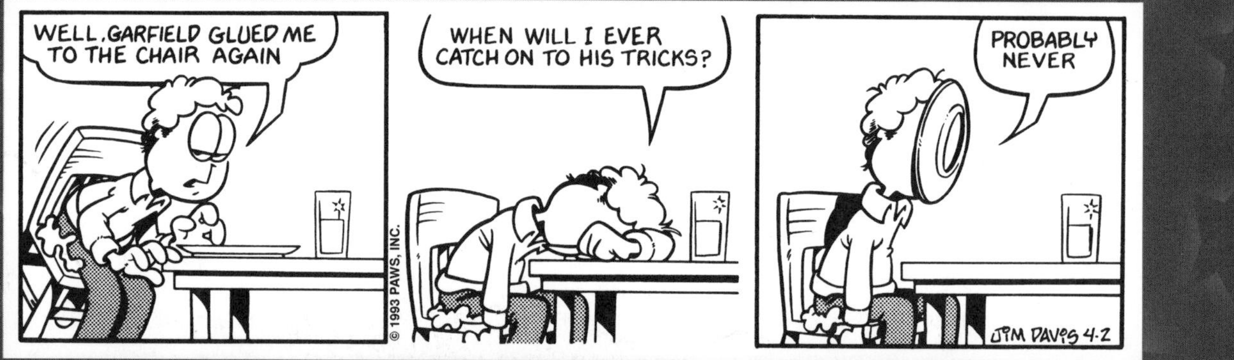
WELL, GARFIELD GLUED ME TO THE CHAIR AGAIN
WHEN WILL I EVER CATCH ON TO HIS TRICKS?
PROBABLY NEVER
© 1993 PAWS, INC.
JIM DAVIS 4-2

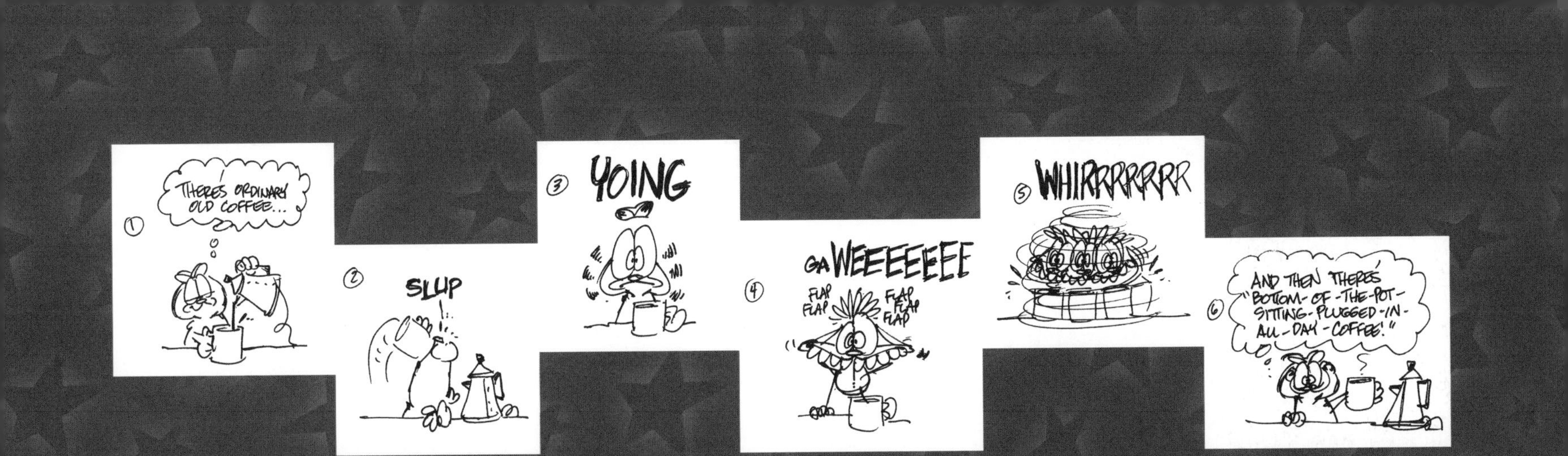

THERE'S ORDINARY OLD COFFEE...
SLUP
YOING
GAWEEEEEEE
FLAP FLAP
FLAP FLAP FLAP
WHIRRRRRRRR
AND THEN THERE'S "BOTTOM-OF-THE-POT-SITTING-PLUGGED-IN-ALL-DAY-COFFEE!"

AUGUST 7, 1994

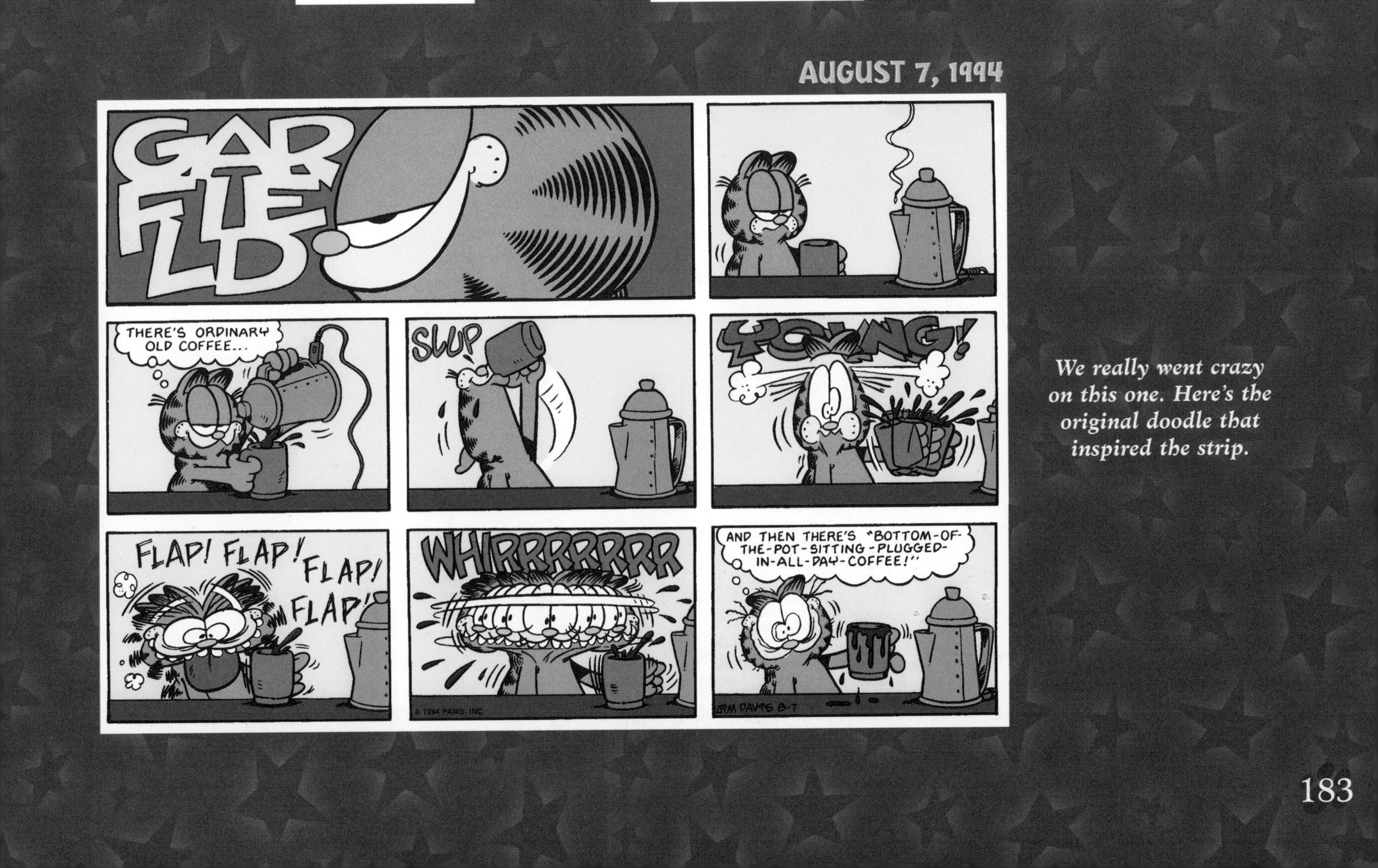

GARFIELD
THERE'S ORDINARY OLD COFFEE...
SLUP
YOING!
FLAP! FLAP! FLAP! FLAP!
WHIRRRRRRRR
AND THEN THERE'S "BOTTOM-OF-THE-POT-SITTING-PLUGGED-IN-ALL-DAY-COFFEE!"
© 1994 PAWS, INC.
JPM DAVIS 8-7

We really went crazy on this one. Here's the original doodle that inspired the strip.

It's no easy task to make Jon look geekier than he already is. Besides, I like the phrase "leaf weasels."

MARCH 31, 1995

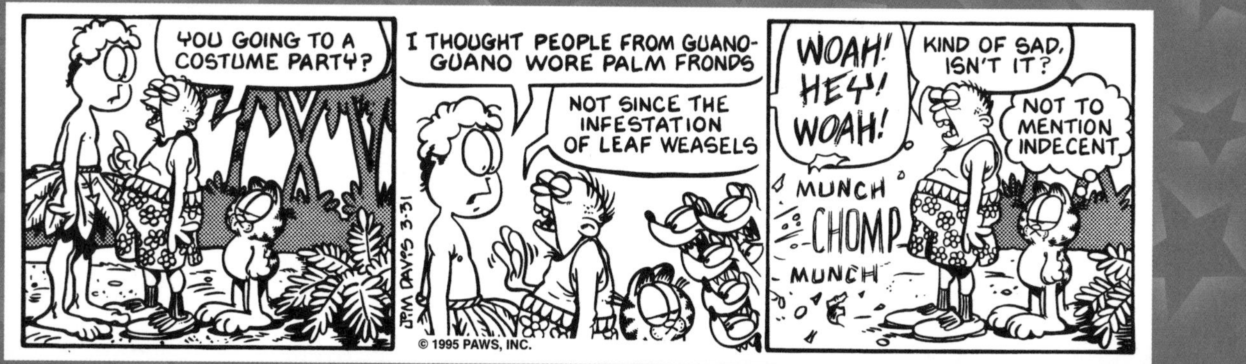
YOU GOING TO A COSTUME PARTY?
I THOUGHT PEOPLE FROM GUANO-GUANO WORE PALM FRONDS
NOT SINCE THE INFESTATION OF LEAF WEASELS
JIM DAVIS 3-31
© 1995 PAWS, INC.
WOAH! HEY! WOAH!
MUNCH
CHOMP
MUNCH
KIND OF SAD, ISN'T IT?
NOT TO MENTION INDECENT

APRIL 30, 1995

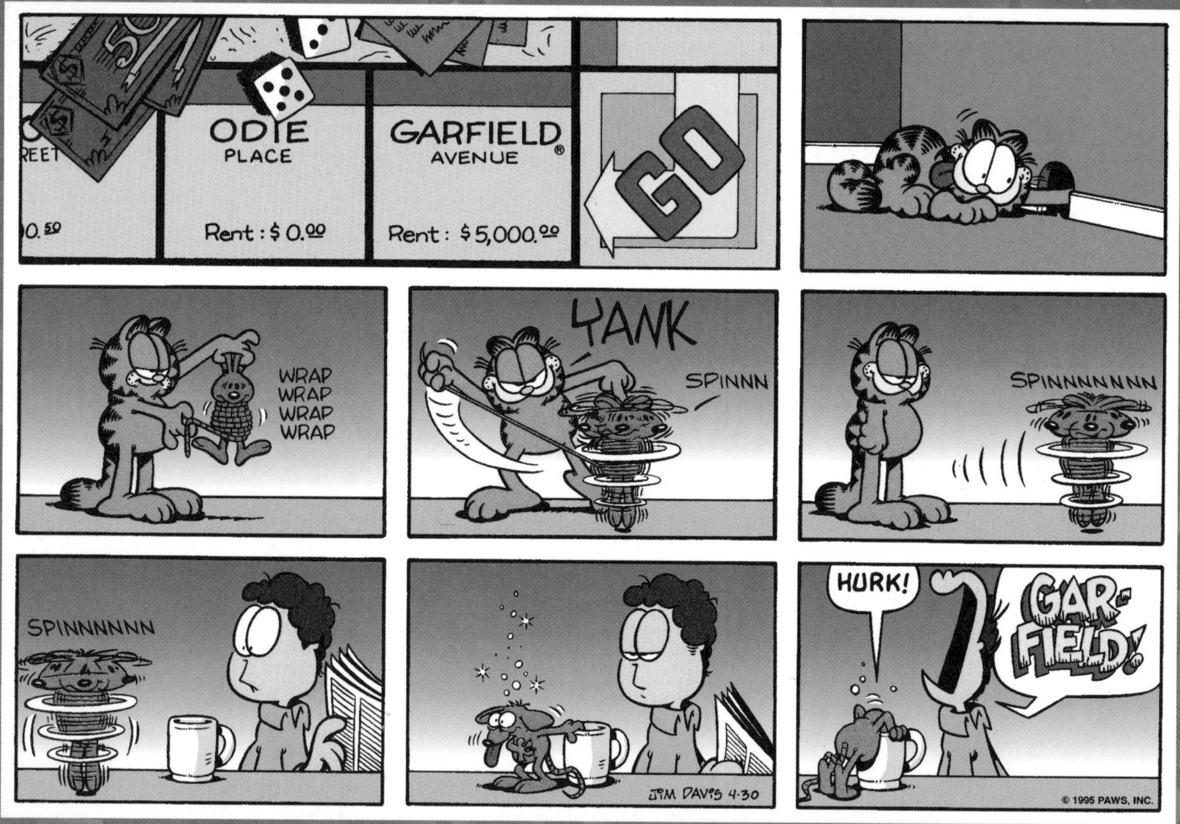
REET
0.50
ODIE PLACE
Rent: $ 0.00
GARFIELD AVENUE ®
Rent: $5,000.00
GO
WRAP WRAP WRAP WRAP
YANK
SPINNN
SPINNNNNNN
SPINNNNNNN
JIM DAVIS 4-30
HURK!
GAR-FIELD!
© 1995 PAWS, INC.

I had an editor tell me, "Remember, people are eating breakfast when they're reading your strip." This one's for her.

APRIL 5, 1996

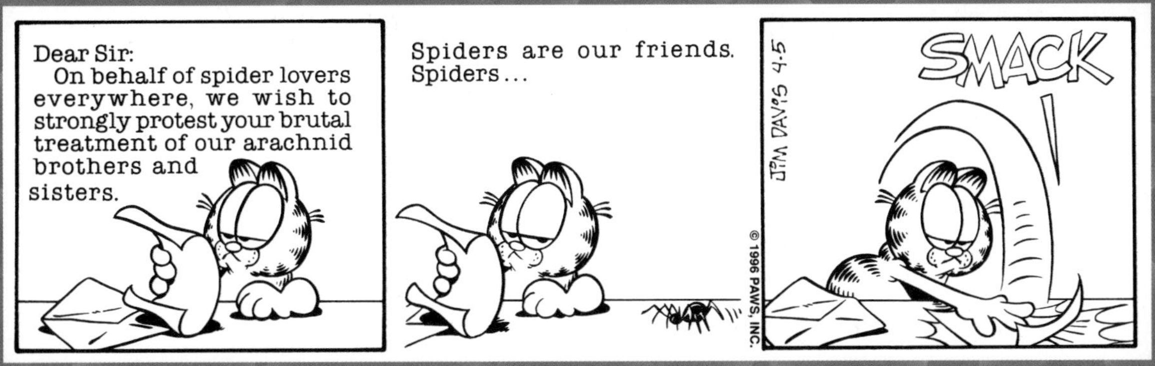
Dear Sir:
On behalf of spider lovers everywhere, we wish to strongly protest your brutal treatment of our arachnid brothers and sisters.
Spiders are our friends. Spiders...
SMACK
JPM DAVIS 4-5
© 1996 PAWS, INC.

This one pretty much sums up the entire spider-gag canon. It's also a nice response to the weird mail we receive from spider-huggers.

APRIL 22, 1996

I've always liked the name Clive. We ended up doing a week of strips about Garfield's invisible friend.

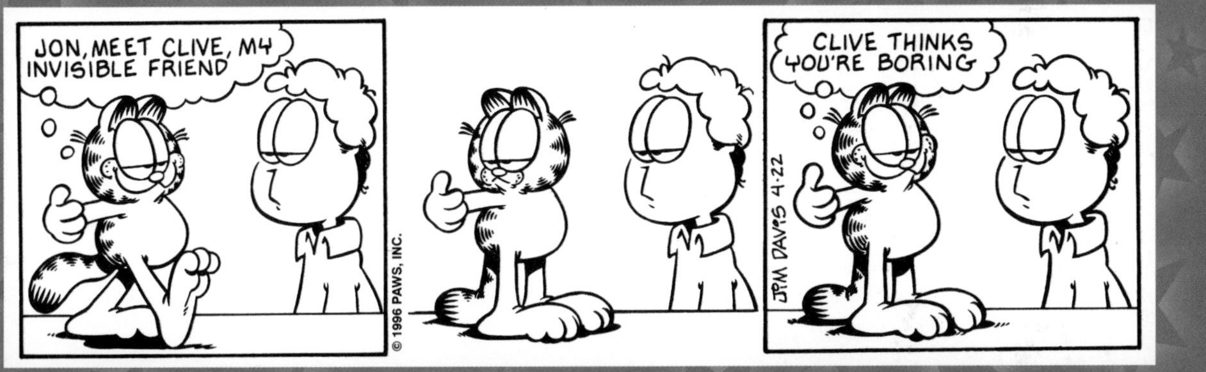
JON, MEET CLIVE, MY INVISIBLE FRIEND
© 1996 PAWS, INC.
CLIVE THINKS YOU'RE BORING
JPM DAVIS 4-22

JULY 5, 1996

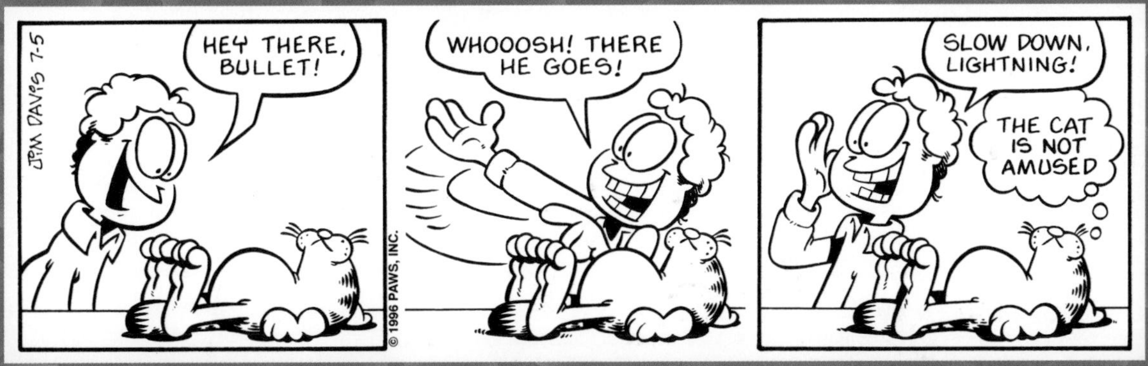
JPM DAVIS 7-5
HEY THERE, BULLET!
© 1996 PAWS, INC.
WHOOOSH! THERE HE GOES!
SLOW DOWN, LIGHTNING!
THE CAT IS NOT AMUSED

This is a good example of the gazillion or so lazy/insult gags we've done. Plus, I thought calling Garfield "Bullet" and "Lightning" was funny.

AFTERWORD

Dear Loyal Fan,

Well, it's been twenty years since I first began spreading my mirth — and girth — across the comics. That's a lot of laughs and lasagna. Of course, I don't feel nearly that old because I've spent a lot of the time asleep.

But don't get me wrong. I've worked hard (kicking Odie is a full-time job!). And that slave driver Davis never gives me a day off. You'd think with a cat in the White House, they'd pass a law or something.

But entertainment is my life: I'm serious about humor. And the fun doesn't stop here. I have not yet begun to eat!

So what does the future hold? Will I pig out less, work out more, and love Mondays? Yeah, right. And Odie will join Mensa. No, it'll still be "Life, laziness, and the pursuit of pasta" for this fat cat. Hey, I gotta be me . . . I'm too cool to be anyone else!

Yes, you can always count on your furry friend, Garfield — just the way I've counted on you these past twenty years . . . and will for the next twenty! So keep up the good work! And thanks . . . from the bottom of my stomach!

See ya in the funny papers,

Garfield

GARFIELD'S TOP TEN PREDICTIONS FOR THE TWENTY-FIRST CENTURY

10. *Astronomers will discover huge flea collar encircling Pluto*

9. *Vast section of Siberia will be devastated by large burp*

8. *Writers will still be milking Top Ten formula*

7. *Hole in Arctic ozone will become clogged with hair*

6. *New Bounty, an even quicker picker-upper!*

5. *Jon Arbuckle will be inducted into the Geek Hall of Fame*

4. *France will officially change its name to The Francster*

3. *Days will be made longer so cats can get more sleep*

2. *Scientists will develop disposable dog*

1. *Two words: Emperor Garfield*

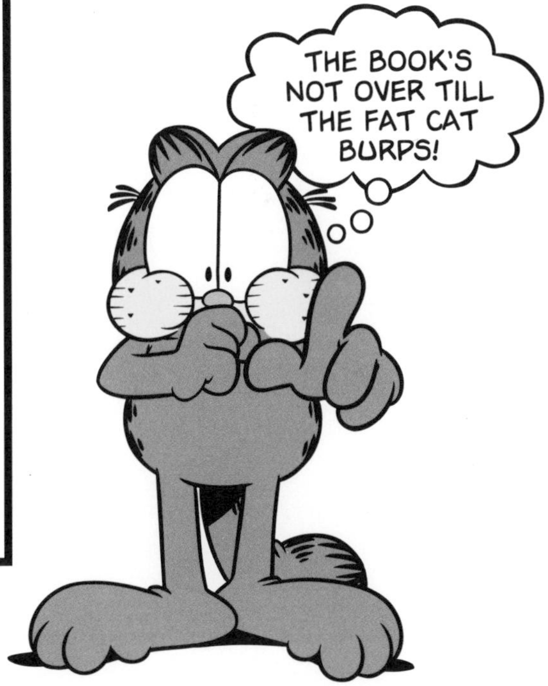
THE BOOK'S NOT OVER TILL THE FAT CAT BURPS!